st magnus festival
a celebration

st magnus festival
a celebration

compiled and edited by **Pamela Beasant**

THE ORCADIAN

Printed and published by

The Orcadian Limited,

Hell's Half Acre, Hatston,

Kirkwall, Orkney, KW15 1DW.

Tel 01856 879000

Fax 01856 879001

www.orcadian.co.uk

Designed by Iain Ashman

Published 2002

ISBN 1 902957 17 2

contents

editor's note

An enormous number of people have given their time selflessly and shared their memories of the festival, either in spoken or written form, to whom I am very grateful. Some have gone beyond this, and have been indispensable. To Judy Arnold, Glenys Hughes, Archie and Elizabeth Bevan, George Rendall and Peter Maxwell Davies, I would like to extend a huge, but forever inadequate, thank you.

My grateful thanks also go to James Miller, Ian Croy and the staff of *The Orcadian*, Phil Astley (Orkney Archives), Eileen Sabiston (for typing the chronology), Angela Henderson (for translating Thomas Schulz's article), Gunnie Moberg, Alistair Peebles, Ken Amer, Toots Cromarty and all those who have spent a great deal of time sorting through masses of photographs and other documents. My thanks, too, to the Photograph Archive of the Orkney Library for permission to print from the Phoenix Photos Collection.

For permission to quote from previously published material, graciously given, I am indebted to Keith Bruce at *The Herald*; Moira Stevenson of *The Scotsman* Publications; Denby Richards at *Musical Opinion*; Carlos Alba, deputy editor of *The Sunday Times Scotland*; John Murray (Publishers) Ltd; Boosey & Hawkes; Archie Bevan, Stewart Conn, Brian McCabe, James MacMillan, Michael Tumelty, John Warnaby, Conrad Wilson, Paul Driver, Kenneth Walton, Roderic Dunnett, Morag MacInnes, Tom Morton, Cathy Graham, John Constable and Seamus Heaney.

There are a large number of contributors to this book, and an even larger number of people who have been involved in the festival, but time and space did not allow me to contact them. Some will no doubt breathe a sigh of relief, but to those who would like to have been in the book and are not, I apologise. Of necessity, the book gives a representational cross-section of events, opinions and experiences, and all omissions are regretted. I would like to pay tribute to all those who have worked so hard for the festival over the last twenty five years. The numbers are staggering, and the commitment and talent of everybody involved. It has been an enlightening experience to glimpse the full extent of the amazing festival 'machine', and to be given the chance to put some of those experiences and events together in this book, which can only reflect a small part of the whole.

Pamela Beasant
Editor

Text note   Most of the material in this book is original, specially written by the contributors, or taken from taped interviews. (Spoken contributions are all headed 'in conversation'.)

All material quoted from other sources - books, newspapers or magazines - is printed in italic type, to differentiate it from original text.

preface

by Sir Peter Maxwell Davies

I first came to Orkney in the summer of 1970, like any other visitor, to see the prehistoric remains and St Magnus Cathedral. One day, in the Stromness bookshop, I chanced upon a copy of *An Orkney Tapestry* by George Mackay Brown, and was so entranced by this that I sat up in my room at the Kirkwall Hotel all night, unable to stop reading. The next day I visited Hoy, where fate decreed I should meet George himself, who was spending a few days in Rackwick with the Bevan family. We spent a most convivial day, the drizzle made irrelevant by good food and wine, and it was George who suggested that I should spend time in that very house, the Muckle House, to write music - it belongs to Dr Johnstone, who was then the Stromness GP. He was indeed quite happy for me to borrow it, which I did for the first time in November of that year, to produce the music for Ken Russell's film *The Devils*. It was also George who pointed out an abandoned house at the top of

the cliff, without door, windows or roof, and with sixty years of sheep-muck inside: it was this house which, restored three years later by David Nelson, with help from the Bevans, became my home for the next quarter of a century.

The extraordinary land and seascape had an immediate effect on my work: in 1971 I returned north to arrange the score for another Ken Russell film, *The Boy Friend*, and had to interrupt work on this, inspired to write a setting of a poem from *An Orkney Tapestry* for my group, The Fires of London. Orkney had started to work its magic, and I felt both my work and my own self reaching for a new, still centre, to do with a sense of place and of calm, engendered by living and working in Rackwick, Hoy. (I should point out that the restored house there consists of two very small rooms, and had for years no electricity, that the nearest access point by car was a twenty minute hike away, so that all provisions had to be carried steeply uphill on one's back, and that water came from a spring behind the house.)

George Mackay Brown continued to be a good friend and a positive influence on my work - not only did I set many of his poems and make dramatic musical works out of his stories, but his use of the simplest English language possible to express complex emotions and situations became a most stimulating example in my own creation.

In the mid seventies I had the idea of returning some of the good Orkney had done for me, not only in terms of musical inspiration, but equally by so many people here making me welcome with uncalled-for kindness, by establishing a music festival. Judy Arnold, my manager, did sterling work on this, both in the earliest, formative stages, and ever since. Norman Mitchell, then organist at the cathedral and music teacher at Kirkwall Grammar School, joined me as co-director, and the first St Magnus Festival was launched in midsummer, 1977. The whole thing was plotted in the Bevans' Stromness kitchen, and made possible by the vision and generosity of Robert Ponsonby at the BBC.

I had received a BBC commission for the Queen's silver jubilee that year, which became *The Martyrdom of St Magnus*, the opera with which we, The Fires of London, opened the first festival. I remember conducting from a position in the cathedral just by the pillar in which rests St Magnus' split skull - this made me much more nervous than the presence of an audience and the BBC microphones.

We determined at the outset that the festival should be one which takes the local community as its core, bringing the best available in the professional music world to Orkney, and showing Orkney's cultural heritage and contemporary talent to best advantage, both for its own enjoyment, and that of visitors - and not only in music, but in all the arts. An essential part of ensuring local involvement and a constructive community spirit was to involve Orcadians in all aspects of organisation, and I made a point of writing numerous works for performance at the festival by the community - particularly the schoolchildren. Where composers from outside were commissioned, it was policy to enmesh them as often and as much as possible in community educational work, related to their new work.

I do not wish to give the impression that all was plain sailing. There was opposition a-plenty from various influential people here - this was only to be expected, and firmly ignored. I decided to remain director for just ten years, to give the festival enough opportunity to establish itself - if it took root, I would hand over to someone else, and if not, well, tough! - I would have learned a lot in the effort.

By the festival's nature, and that of the islands where it takes place, I do not see it expanding much in length - it always seems to gain from its intimacy and from its concentration into just a few days. I trust it will go from strength to strength, in steadier and safer hands than mine, and never losing its original vision of community involvement at the highest artistic level.

Peter Maxwell Davies
Sanday, Orkney
December, 2001

a meeting

The characteristically distilled language of George Mackay Brown's *An Orkney Tapestry* had already caught the imagination of Peter Maxwell Davies when he visited Hoy for the first time in July, 1970. There, through a fortuitous meeting with the book's author, and the Bevans from Stromness, (Archie Bevan was an English teacher and later deputy rector at Stromness Academy), the young composer was introduced to the place which would become home, and the people who would be among his closest friends on Orkney. The meeting not only paved the way for that move, and the festival, but for the many compositions based on George Mackay Brown's writing - all of which would come later.

After five miles the road ends abruptly at a glint of sea and the farm of Glen. The dark hills are still all round, but they hold in their scarred hands a green valley. This is Rackwick. The bowl is tilted seawards - its lip is a curving bay, half huge round sea-sculptured boulders, half sand. Out in the bay, like guardians, stand two huge cliffs, The Sneuk and The Too.

A burn, having gathered its waters from the surrounding hills, fed with small tinkling tributaries, moves slowly though the valley; it deepens into a reflective pool; then rushes foaming at the sea over a ravelment of round boulders. After a heavy rainfall the stepping-stones are awash.

The poignant thing about this beautiful valley ('the bay of wreckage') is that, apart from Glen, farmed by Jack Rendall, it has been utterly abandoned. The floor of its valley and its fertile western slope are littered with half-ruined crofts - the windows blind, the roofs fallen in, the hearth-stones forever black.

(George Mackay Brown, *An Orkney Tapestry*, 1969)

Archie Bevan festival vice-president (in conversation)

Elizabeth, George and I, and our family, were on holiday in Rackwick, at Dr Johnstone's cottage, Mucklehoose, which is down reasonably close to the shore - a wee, slate-roofed building. We were expecting Elizabeth's brother and his family to come over that particular Sunday, (in those days it was the *Watchful* that used to ply between Stromness and Lyness), and we took the car down to Lyness, to see if they were there, but they weren't. Kulgin Duval, however, a dealer in rare books and manuscripts, was coming over to meet George, and he was coming ashore talking to a couple of strangers from the boat. 'May I introduce you to Peter Maxwell Davies, composer?' he said. I hadn't heard of Peter Maxwell Davies, composer!

This was the summer of 1970 - and Max was visiting with his manager, James Murdoch, from Australia. They were on a day-trip to Hoy, and had hired Isaac Moar to take them around. They indicated - or rather, Kulgin indicated - that Max would like to meet George, because he'd just been reading his book, *An Orkney Tapestry*. I invited him to visit Rackwick, meet George and have some food with us. So that was the arrangement, and in due course, Isaac drove them into the valley at lunch time and they came up to Mucklehoose. It was a day of mist and haar - not a very pleasant day - but warm enough, because we did sit outside for most of the time. (We have a photograph of it, in which you can see this flashing-eyed, dark-haired, intense young composer, who would have been in his mid-thirties at that time.)

He struck up an immediate rapport with George - they got on famously and it all seemed to go swimmingly. There was a big pot of curry on, and lots of homemade wine to slosh back. Then it transpired that Max was not only up on holiday in Orkney, he was quite interested in finding a place - a retreat - to move into. I think Dorset was becoming a bit noisy, with aircraft and so on, and his cottage there had had a damaging fire. He was on the look out for somewhere really remote, where he could get away from it all. We took him down to the beach, to the sands at Burnmouth, thinking that this was a remote enough place, but agreed that it was right on the track that brought visitors to the beach, so it wasn't going to be as quiet as all that. Anyway - we had no doubt that the place was making a big impression on Max. Bunertoon was out of the calculation at that time - after all, it was just a little roofless shell of a place, perched up on the cliffs. I can remember him standing among the rocks there, the sea crashing around him; there was a tremendous electricity about his gaze, and his engagement with the place was very obvious.

They went away - and for us it was just an interesting interlude. A few months later, George had a letter from Max, explaining that he had a film score to write. He had been very impressed by Mucklehoose, and asked George if he might contact Dr Johnstone to see if he could make use of the place for some weeks in January. Derek Johnstone agreed and Max duly turned up. That's when he made his score for *The Devils*. He was with another young

previous page: **Peter Maxwell Davies and George Mackay Brown, July, 1970, at Mucklehoose, Rackwick; their first meeting.**

composer, Geoffrey King. The two of them went over, on a terrible day - it was very wild indeed. Ginger Brown, the ferry man, was in a bad mood. The weather was so awful that it was going to be pretty dicey at the pier at Moaness, and the infernal people who wanted to get across were late. (They were having an extra dram with George, I think, before departing.) So, the first encounter with Ginger was not a happy one.

It became much better. Ginger became very close, latterly, to Max, and engaged in what he was doing. He was always very obliging in trying to ferry him, because there was no regular service at that time in the winter. Anyway, that first day, they made it to the pier at Moaness. The abiding memory of that event is that their supplies were scattered around the pier, with a string of sausages wrapped around a bollard, threatening to take off through Scapa Flow! It was quite a stormy baptism.

They duly became established in Mucklehoose. Geoffrey King left after a few days and Max simply went at it. That was his first real encounter with the place, and it impressed him greatly. At Easter, by which time he had another musical commission, this time for Ken Russell's film, *The Boy Friend*, he came back again and wrote not only the film score but also his first Orkney piece, *From Stone to Thorn*, which was a spiky, taxing little piece, for anybody who wasn't acquainted with The Fires of London, and Max's avant garde tendencies. (By that stage, we were diligently coming to terms with his music!)

It was now 1971. In July, there was word from Max again, that he'd like to come up and do a bit of house-hunting. By that time he had stayed with us (when he came back from *The Boy Friend* visit), which established communications between us. And so he came back, and we took Max and George to Rousay and spent a glorious day there. The Stromness Boys' Brigade was camped there at the time, so we were able to borrow transport and go round the island. We looked at one or two cottages that were available, but I could see that he wasn't just over the moon about them. I think Rackwick was exercising its pull.

We arrived back home in the evening and were sitting down for supper when Max said, 'I would like to go back to Rackwick, just to see if there are any possibilities'. We went back the next morning, and he looked round a few places before we went up the hill to Bunertoon. He stood on top of all that sheep muck, grinned and said, 'This is where I want to be'. We blinked in surprise. 'Folk will reckon I'm mad' he said. 'I am - but I'll do it.' And do it he did.

He didn't take any action right away. The tenant of Rackwick at that time was Jack Rendall. The place was let to him and he sub-let cottages to visitors such as Derek Johnstone. Somewhere in the winter of 1971, Max screwed up the courage to approach Jack about the let of Bunertoon. 'You're welcome to it,' said Jack, 'but it's going to be difficult to get it into shape.' There was another hiatus, of about a year, while Max measured up the place and decided what would be required in the way of timber, and roofing, and

Archie Bevan

Peter Maxwell Davies and Anne Bevan
in the ruins of Bunertoon, 1971.

I'd never heard of Max when he came here first. Archie and Elizabeth Bevan took him over here and he fell in love with Rackwick. Then he wanted the old cottage that was standing up there, just a shelter for the sheep. No one had lived in it from 1920 - and he thought this was the ideal spot. There were no roads to it, and you wouldn't be getting anyone driving up to the door. He asked if he could rent it - and I told him that nobody else would be wanting it!

Later, we saw Max nearly every day, as his mail was always left here. And he had no phone, so he had to come down and use the kiosk when he wanted to contact people.

He was very fit - he used to go for walks in the hills at all sorts of times of the day and night. When he had been writing half the night he would set off to St John's Head. He used to appear in the morning and say that he had just been to the Old Man of Hoy.
Jack Rendall (in conversation)

Max loved Orkney from the start. He felt that the whole environment gave him peace of mind and inspiration, which he probably felt had been lacking in his hectic life prior to his move there. And, out of this, he conceived the idea that it would be a good idea to have a festival.
Judy Arnold, manager,
Sir Peter Maxwell Davies

all the rest of it. The stuff duly arrived, but the question of how to get it to Bunertoon was certainly exercising us. Helicopter? But helicopters weren't thick on the ground in those days. Jack helped the matter along, however, by carting all the stuff up to Scar, which is about half a mile from Bunertoon itself, over pretty rough terrain - just a track, and a nasty little gully to negotiate as well. The Stromness Boys' Brigade was engaged, and, for a donation from Max, the lads did the necessary. We went over to help out as well. He had all his stuff stashed away in an outhouse, to give it protection against the weather, and that's where it was for several months until the rebuilding of Bunertoon commenced in 1973.

David Nelson was the main builder. (He was a teacher of technical and environmental studies who eventually became an educational psychologist. David was an incredibly well-versed guy - a walking encyclopaedia.) By the late summer of 1974, you could camp out in the place, which we'd been doing already. The box bed had been built, and then Max had his first stay. It was still very primitive - oil lamps, of course, and candles - all the fuel had to be gathered off the beach and carted in sacks.

Max got down to the business of living there. It was just what he wanted. Of course, the big problem arose when he had to get off the island in a hurry - maybe to go down and conduct a concert or go off on a lecture tour, or whatever it might be. Sometimes it was just impossible to get away - sometimes it was difficult just to get through from Rackwick to the pier at the other end of Hoy. Jack took him on his tractor on one occasion, but by the time they got through Ginger Brown had given up hope of them coming and had gone back. Max, I think, spent the night in the school hostel, wrapped up in a blanket. The next morning Ginger managed to bring him over. From the Orkney mainland he was to fly out, but the weather was deteriorating - hail and snow showers - and it was very doubtful whether the plane would get down. I borrowed Derek Johnstone's Land Rover to take Max from Stromness to the airport in Kirkwall, because the roads were pretty bad too. As we arrived, however, we heard the aeroplane clearly disappearing into the distance. It had overflown and decided against landing. Back we went, and the next day Max boarded the *St Ola*, and started the long, long trek south.

Peter Maxwell Davies outside a restored Bunertoon.

Orkney Photographic

setting up

Peter Maxwell Davies settled on Hoy, and Orkney influences were immediately apparent in his new work. When the BBC commissioned a piece to celebrate the Queen's silver jubilee in 1977, the decision to write a chamber opera based on George Mackay Brown's novel, *Magnus*, became the catalyst for the whole idea of the festival. With PMD's chamber ensemble, The Fires of London, it would be possible to mount a series of concerts around the new opera, *The Martyrdom of St Magnus*, in St Magnus Cathedral. Essentially, too, there were local people with both the talent and the will to mount additional concerts and events with performers from the community. From the outset, the proposed festival was going to involve local people on all levels, practical and artistic. It was to be a festival rooted in the community, while attracting a prestigious array of professionals to the islands.

Once the idea was in place, the practicalities had to be carried out. In Orkney, Norman Mitchell (cathedral organist and head of music at Kirkwall Grammar School) and Archie and Elizabeth Bevan were the early prime movers. There were difficulties locally, both financially and in the perception of Peter Maxwell Davies and the festival, which had to be confronted. Judy Arnold, Max's manager, and her husband, Michael, were vital at the London end. From the beginning, they planned, budgeted and negotiated with funding bodies, orchestras and celebrity performers, and ensured that high profile festival events would come to fruition. Without the imagination, commitment and sheer hard work of that core of people, the festival would simply not have happened.

Norman Mitchell festival co-founder and
co-artistic director, 1977-1979

I got so much out of the place, from friends like George and the Bevans - and Norman Mitchell of the cathedral - and friends on Hoy like Jack Rendall (and later his wife, Dorothy). It was very important to me that I should do something which returned that a little bit to Orkney. Benjamin Britten, of Aldeburgh, said: 'It will be very tough and you will be resented a lot' - and indeed that's just how it was. But you take no notice - you just can't.
Peter Maxwell Davies
(in conversation)

I first met Sir Peter Maxwell Davies in the early seventies. He had already made friends with Archie and Elizabeth Bevan and also with George Mackay Brown. The island of Hoy, Rackwick Bay and Bunertoon were to have a distinct influence upon both Max's life and his composition.

Early in 1973, the *Hymn to St Magnus* came to fruition and it was Max's great hope that this new work would be performed in St Magnus Cathedral in Kirkwall. At that time I was organist and master of music at the cathedral, having arrived in Orkney five years earlier. Each summer, I arranged a series of Thursday evening concerts in the cathedral, 'Music in St Magnus', and this enterprise drew soloists from near and far. In addition to providing a musical evening for the many visitors to Orkney, the concerts were also well attended by local people from all over the mainland. It was natural that Archie Bevan should bring Max and me together to explore the possibility of a performance of the new work in St Magnus.

The Fires of London, an extremely able group of musicians, appeared one day in spring 1973, with a full programme of Max's music, including his new work *Hymn to St Magnus*, to be performed to an audience drawn in the main from the local community. It was, perhaps, a new experience for the listeners insofar as the music was not what one could call conventional for 'untutored' ears. It must be said that all present marvelled at the complexity of the writing and the professional way in which it was played. Indeed the performance did provoke considerable discussion for many days afterwards! It would be unfair to expect a wholesale acclamation of the evening: this new style of writing (to Orkney) would take some time to be savoured and appreciated. The idiom was perhaps foreign, but, like all new things of quality and value, it would take further hearings to realise the depth of thought and musicianship which was used to produce this pioneering style of music. By this time Max's music had begun to make a huge impression on those nearest to it.

**Norman Mitchell
and Peter Maxwell Davies.**

Stephen Pruslin pianist and writer
co-founder of The Fires of London

Stephen Pruslin

Hearing Sir Peter's *Antarctic Symphony* broadcast live from the twenty-fifth St Magnus Festival carried my thoughts back beyond the first festival to what I consider its seven-year prehistory - a period that I experienced both as a participant and a witness. PMD's musical response to the frozen south recalled his very first descriptions of Orkney, which for me conjured up the brooding darkness of Sibelius's Fourth Symphony and the luminous white light of his Sixth, just as Ingmar Bergman's then recent films *Through a Glass Darkly* and *Winter Light* had also fuelled my image of a 'Farthest North' that acted as an 'Ultima Thule' of the mind.

Max suggested that I might enjoy reading George Mackay Brown's *An Orkney Tapestry*. Enhanced by the atmospheric drawings of Sylvia Wishart, this quickly became one of my essential books. Its language was like lace - it rendered audible the silence behind the words. I didn't yet realise how soon I would meet the author, let alone have the honour of counting him as a friend. But the wellsprings of Orkney poured from the pages of the *Tapestry* - this was a journey that had to be made.

The moment came when, after giving a concert in Edinburgh, PMD and I headed north. The night train to Inverness had no sleepers; the early one to Thurso, neither heating nor speed. At the last minute, we were denied the legendary view of Hoy's western cliffs - the train veered off to Wick, from where we flew to Kirkwall. Stormy seas were implied, but not yet endured (those were saved for the journey south). We made it, though, and Orkney proceeded to cast its spell. The air glistened with mysterious place-names: Yesnaby, Birsay - and the places were as magical as their names. Long-standing friendships were begun. The boundless hospitality of Archie and Elizabeth Bevan buffered the inclement weather, their daughter Anne became an instant soulmate, while George's courtliness and wicked humour were irresistible. He and I soon embarked on *jeux d'esprit* that always ended in peals of laughter - as George often quipped, 'When Quality meet, the compliments fly!'.

Even on that first visit, I noticed something directly relevant to the eventual founding of a festival - the Orcadian ability to look and to listen. I felt it when Jack Rendall, having arrived at Hoy pier in advance of Stevie Mowat's ferry, was quite content to observe the view without any need for conversation. I sensed it again when the Bevan family and friends listened with utmost concentration to an impromptu recital I gave on the upright piano at Hopedale after dinner. But there were two subsequent musical experiences that further crystallised the idea of Orkney as fertile ground for a festival. In 1972, Max and I devised a programme for The Fires of London called 'A Musical Tribute to Northern Britain', which included his newly composed *Hymn to St Magnus*, based on the original 12th-century hymn whose manuscript

The Fires of London was an ensemble of six musicians (flute, clarinet, violin, cello, keyboards and percussion) plus a soprano (Mary Thomas) which had been started in 1967 by Max and Harrison Birtwistle under the name of The Pierrot Players. A group of musicians, centred on the Royal Academy of Music in London, with Harry and Alan Hacker, the clarinettist, got together to form an ensemble which would concentrate on performing works by Harry and Max. They caused a considerable stir in the musical world, particularly with Max's *Eight Songs for a Mad King* and *Vesalii Icones*.

In 1971, Harrison Birtwistle decided to leave The Pierrot Players, wanting to concentrate more on larger-scale orchestral works, and the group was renamed The Fires of London by Stephen Pruslin, with Max as the artistic director. This coincided with Max deciding to move away from the south of England to Orkney.

Judy Arnold, manager,
Sir Peter Maxwell Davies

now resides in the library of Uppsala University in Sweden. The idea of performing the programme in St Magnus Cathedral felt inevitable, and a Scottish tour provided the opportunity to make it happen. The Orcadian audience listened to this beautiful but challenging work with a rapt attention comparable in our experience at the time only to Eastern Europe, where one had a sense of music being a matter of life and death. It was an unforgettable moment that still lingers in the memory.

The other musical event was a solo recital in Kirkwall that the Orkney Arts Society invited me to give in 1974. Shortly before, the Fires had done a tour of Sweden that included an important Orcadian pilgrimage: during a rare free moment in Uppsala, PMD and I went to the University Library, where we asked to see the manuscript of the Hymn to St Magnus. The librarian, looking puzzled, returned empty-handed. Grasping at straws, we suggested trying 'Nobilis, Humilis' (the first words of the hymn). This proved to be the key, and for the next half hour we took turns holding a thick volume at whose innermost core two pages of music were revealed. The impact of this experience was still vivid when I arrived in Orkney to do the recital. For several days, I took the bus from Stromness to Kirkwall, in order to coax a rather recalcitrant grand piano in the Infants' School into meeting at least some of the demands of Beethoven's Sonata, Opus 111. On Sunday, though, Archie Bevan offered to drive me in. As we entered Kirkwall, the fabled 'St Magnus effect' suddenly occurred - the sun hit the cathedral in a way that caused its rose-coloured sandstone to burst into flame. Was an invisible ley-line between Kirkwall and Uppsala activated that day - who can say that it wasn't?

But the recital again demonstrated the degree of concentration of which an Orcadian audience was capable, especially in the face of intermittent competition from Guy Fawkes which must have been as testing to them as it was for me. At this stage, having set a number of George Mackay Brown's poems to music, Max now conceived the idea of a chamber opera based on the author's recently published second novel, *Magnus*. Here the threads - what George would have called 'the warp and weft, the web and woof' - of a possible festival began to proliferate and entwine. The symbolically appropriate venue for the premiere of *The Martyrdom of St Magnus* seemed predestined. The opera itself could form the keystone of a balanced, concentrated programme of other events.

Of course, there was much more to it than that. Administrative and financial structures had to be put in place. Different constituencies of the community had to be brought together within an overall vision. What I am trying to indicate here, however, is the confluence of powerful artistic impulses that gave the festival its inner life. From the outset, it was clear that something specific and individual had occurred, which was worth carrying forward. Perhaps this had its roots in Orkney's unique Norse/Scottish culture, which suggested a pluralistic attitude that could nurture and cultivate valuable local traditions together with the importation of professional artistic events on to

Orcadian soil.

Certain aspects of my own youthful odyssey became increasingly linked to a set of wider, shared imperatives that eventually took on the force of inner necessity and led to the birth of the St Magnus Festival. One salutes the festival as it enters its second quarter-century, in the hope that it will find new ways of sustaining the unique and specific profile that has been the source of its survival, under the aegis of the invisible guiding presence whose name it honours.

Norman Mitchell

During those early years I kept abreast of Max's prowess as an international force in composition. It was indeed humbling to have a prestigious friend who enjoyed such huge success and acclaim outside his adopted homeland, who was simply 'Max' on his return. The idea of a festival of the arts was dear to his heart and Max desperately wanted to share his success and bring his music to Orkney as a way of thanking the many people who had welcomed him to these shores. The not too dissimilar association of Benjamin Britten with Aldeburgh may have been the springboard for Max's proposed festival. It is significant that the BBC had already commissioned Max to write an opera in recognition of Her Majesty the Queen's silver jubilee celebrations in June 1977. Perhaps this could form the centrepiece for the new festival?

Max and I discussed outline plans in some detail in 1975; the provision of funding for the venture was left in the hands of Judy Arnold, Max's highly capable business manager. For someone totally unknown in Orkney to negotiate with the local authorities and others for financial assistance was perhaps courting disaster, especially before ideas had fully emerged. Consequently, the plans for the festival fell at the first fence. Max was totally devastated, and we all shared in his disappointment. The rejection was sorer to bear insofar as Max passionately believed in what he wanted to give. Others, I knew, would give their eye teeth to have a composer of such distinction in their midst. History points so often to great composers who were rejected by those in high places around them. The festival, it seemed, was now dead and over. Max's dream had been tossed aside like some flotsam washed up by the sea.

About six months later I approached some friends of mine (and friends in business) to support the idea of a festival of the arts in Orkney. I knew roughly the funds required to mount the opera and it seemed a distinct possibility to realise the performance by spreading the costs over a wide spectrum of interested parties. Once the idea gained momentum and the finance was nearly in place for the production, I contacted Archie Bevan and Max with a view to restarting the planning process. A group of us met together to form a committee. Along with Archie, Max and myself, we were joined by Josh Gourlay the tourist officer, Jack Ridgway from British Airways, the cathedral's minister, the Rev Bill Cant, and Bobby Macrae, the Queen's Lord Lieutenant. A number of interested parties from the local community completed our committee. The festival's name was the first topic of discussion: St Magnus and his cathedral provided a clear focus and an obvious choice of title.

Meantime, the mounting sums associated with the production of an opera were to prove the greatest hurdle to negotiate. The original figure mentioned had failed to take into account the making of costumes, lighting, and many other expenses, which kept appearing like rabbits out of a hat. The BBC would meet the fees for the players and singers. Transport, however, had been a grey area, and it now looked as if the costs of conveying people from London would also land in the lap of the festival committee. It was soon evident that the money raised was insufficient to meet the increasing costs.

The Scottish Arts Council looked to be an obvious bedfellow, but unfortunately their association with Orkney was through the Orkney Arts Society. There was deep suspicion of this new composer to the islands and his music which people 'didn't understand'. In some ways, I was caught in the middle as the secretary of this august local arts organisation; but even my views for a festival were not shared by others on the committee. Without the support of the local society, the SAC wanted no involvement. There was also tremendous unrest from a core of people in Kirkwall who were deeply against the establishment of the festival. I bore the brunt of considerable ill-feeling from some whom I thought should have known better.

Frustrations were incalculable. I did question the credibility of the government-funded agency for the arts. They were content for us to take all the risks first time round and perhaps, if successful, consider a festival in the future. There was one hope left. Occidental, the oil conglomerate, was trying to establish itself as a credible neighbour in Orkney but they were newcomers too, and, although providing much-needed employment, they were often the subject of criticism by a watchful public. It was their wish (in association with the Orkney Arts Society) to purchase a new Steinway piano for Orkney in order to attract ensembles of prestige. The SAC had just announced a scheme to provide fifty per cent funding for such a purchase. Here, perhaps, was a way for Occidental to give something of lasting value to Orkney.

In the end, the purchase was made and the piano now graces Stromness Town Hall: the SAC paid their share of the piano, Occidental paid the whole account and the SAC contribution was gifted to the festival from the Arts Society. There were the inevitable lengthy meetings in Orkney and in Edinburgh but these are not recorded here.

Archie Bevan festival vice-president (in conversation)

The Orkney Arts Society's nose was put a bit out of joint by the festival - entirely understandably. I was fairly gung-ho about it at that time - everybody associated with it had to be enthusiastic otherwise it just wouldn't have happened at all. In fact, I recognised at the same time that the Arts Society had done a power of good for the musical life and the artistic life in the county, and it was quite understandable that they would be a bit put out by the festival coming in independently. A lot of that had to do with misunderstandings - it had got off on a bad footing. The festival should have had a close relationship with the Arts Society from the start, but it just didn't happen.

Max had been asked, by Conrad Wilson of *The Scotsman*, if the festival had the blessing of local folk. Max had said yes, which was printed in the article. The Arts Society said, 'You never asked us!'. You could say that things were going mildly pear-shaped. So we arranged a meeting of the Arts Society to hear from Max and let him explain his plans.

I acted as the go-between in this particular crisis. We met up at the old school staff-room, I remember, and the vibes were not very good! Max made his apologies and explained that it certainly wasn't his intention to ignore the people in the Arts Society who represented the musical public of Orkney, but that the article had jumped the gun. He then went on to outline his plans for the festival. At that point, Norman [who was secretary of the Arts Society at that time] came down heavily on Max's side. He said, 'I like it - I think it's great - we should be supporting it'. The Arts Society, when the time came, allocated a portion of that spare money that was swashing around, to the festival.

Norman Mitchell

We were more than halfway there. The original sum required was £1,500; now we were looking at a festival budget of £10,000 - £11,000. A paltry amount when compared with today's standards; but with that sum one could purchase a substantial house in Kirkwall in the mid-seventies. Translate this to the funds which must be invested annually on the festival and it can be seen that, financially, we were all walking on a tightrope. If the venture failed we would be liable for the shortfall. So, this was an act of faith and our eyes were never removed from our final objective. Josh Gourlay, the tourist officer, was successful in attracting the attention of the Highlands and Islands Development Board from the tourism angle and a further £2,000 came to our rescue.

The mould was set and thus there would be a press conference in London to give details of the festival to a wider public. This conference coincided with the first performance of Max's *A Mirror of Whitening Light* at the Queen Elizabeth Hall on the South Bank. Howie Firth, of BBC's new Radio Orkney, and I, travelled to London just in time to hear the first performance. The following day saw our meeting with the press which aroused considerable interest and we all looked forward to some coverage in the

I remember that I was travelling south on the plane, and Jack Ridgway was there at the BA desk and told me that he had some news for me. The original plans for a festival had looked too expensive for Orkney - 'But Norman Mitchell and Archie Bevan and I have been getting together,' he said, 'and we think that we can do something.'

And so it proved. That conversation with Jack would have been in early 1977, as I was travelling back and fore to Glasgow and London for training with the BBC before getting to work on the plans to open a new community radio station in Orkney. I can remember a talk by Peter Maxwell Davies in Kirkwall, on Beethoven and the process of transformation in his music, and I can remember travelling down to London with Norman to see Max and The Fires of London in the first performance of *A Mirror of Whitening Light*.
Howie Firth
senior producer,
BBC Radio Orkney 1977-87

columns of the prestigious broadsheets so that the news of the new festival could reach a wider public.

Judy and Michael Arnold

Judy Arnold   manager, Sir Peter Maxwell Davies

I started working with Max on 19 October 1975. I had two jobs; one of them was to be Max's manager and the other was to be the manager of The Fires of London. The idea that it would be a good idea to have a festival had been conceived by Max, and he began to think about the sort of festival it might be. Discussions had taken place with the Orkney Arts Society and preliminary budgets had even been made (although it would have been very difficult at that point to make any form of constant contact with Max, as he did not have a telephone).

Max had started to talk to me of his plans for a festival, and of writing *The Martyrdom of St Magnus*. The thought of both filled me with very considerable apprehension. The opera was to be the centrepiece of the new festival. All this was very clear in Max's mind, but the idea of writing an opera for The Fires of London would be a monumental undertaking. Whilst the Fires had toured the world with Max's music theatre works, an opera would be of a totally different scale and dimension, not to mention cost.

In January 1976 I went to Orkney for the first time, and saw Max's croft in Rackwick and met Archie and Elizabeth. It was at that point that the idea of my returning again quite shortly to try to have proper discussions was talked about. I knew that the Orkney Arts Society had been given a Steinway piano, which resided in Stromness. I remember sitting in St Magnus Cathedral and thinking to myself that somehow, together with the magnificence of the cathedral and the fact of having an excellent piano, the festival just might be possible. I think that without those two carrots it would have been difficult to lure world-class performers to Orkney.

It was also in January 1976 that I talked to Robert Ponsonby, who was the director of both BBC Radio 3 and of the Proms, and he said that he would like a commission from Max for the Queen's silver jubilee. I suggested to him that instead of an orchestral work for one of the BBC orchestras, which was (and still is) the way that the BBC commissions, he would give the commission for *The Martyrdom of St Magnus* to be performed by the Fires. This was a complete departure from the usual practice. I also asked Robert whether he thought that it would be possible to launch the opera at the proposed festival. He said that indeed this could happen, and that there would be a second performance at the Proms, to be held at the Round House - a venue which the BBC were using for several of their concerts at that time. So we knew that whatever happened Max would write the opera, and that it would be performed, if not in Orkney at the festival, then, as a fail-safe, at the Proms in the same year, which would be 1977.

In February 1976, I went with the Fires to Edinburgh for the premiere of a song-cycle called *The Blind Fiddler*, which was, again, a setting from George Mackay Brown's book, *A Spell for Green Corn*. This was for the ensemble, and, again, for Mary Thomas. Whilst I was in Edinburgh, I went to see Christie Duncan, who was in charge of music at the Scottish Arts Council, to propose to him, officially, the concept and idea of a festival in Orkney, kicking off with *The Martyrdom of St Magnus*. He was very enthusiastic about the idea, and told me that there must be 'official' enthusiasm and commitment from the local community. This meant the Orkney Islands Council putting in money, which, Christie said, the Scottish Arts Council would match pound for pound.

Thus, armed with the commission from the BBC, and Christie Duncan's firm nod, I then went to Orkney in April 1976, and stayed with the Bevans. Archie had given me the names of the people I should attempt to see. These included George Marwick, convener of Orkney Islands Council; several other council members; Col. Macrae, the Lord Lieutenant; George Marshall, education officer; Josh Gourlay of the tourist board; Jack Ridgway, British Airways - and Norman Mitchell from the Orkney Arts Society. I had given myself a week, hired a car and was able to get round to see everyone in that time and talk to them of Max's plans.

At the end of the week, a meeting took place, and Max was introduced to everyone. He explained his ideas and it was generally agreed that it would be an excellent idea to try to go ahead with the scheme. The question of finance came up, and it was asked who was going to raise the money. I, with some lofty wave of my hand, said that I would.

Following on from that, my husband, Michael, who did all the budgets for the Fires, made a budget based on the proposed new opera, and the additional one or two smaller concerts which were to form part of the weekend of the first festival for June 1977. Based on these budgets, applications were made both to the OIC and to the SAC. On top of that, I also went to meet Alistair Dunnett, who was the chairman of Occidental Oil. I met him in London, and he was extremely sympathetic and supportive of the whole venture, and I had high hopes that some funding would come through from that source.

The applications were all in place, and we waited for the responses. In October and November 1976, The Fires of London undertook an enormous tour of the United States and Canada lasting six weeks. It was while we were in Halifax, Nova Scotia, that the Bevans' letter arrived enclosing the cuttings from *The Orcadian* telling the sad tale that the applications for funds had been refused by the OIC. It appeared that the main reason for the refusal was that there were 'commercial connotations' attached to the festival, these being that the artists, namely the singers and the players, would receive fees for their performances. This was the part which hurt, and this was the part to which Max responded most fiercely.

"A recent minute of the policy and resources committee of Orkney Islands Council stated that 'although the council had agreed in principle with the proposed presentation of the production of Peter Maxwell Davies's 'The Martyrdom of St Magnus', the overall proposals for the festival had escalated far beyond the original concept first put to the council.

He (the convener, Mr George Marwick), felt that the council could not be satisfied as to the extent of the commercial element in the proposed festival and in view of all these aspects and the many financial difficulties already facing the council, he moved that no action be taken in support of the festival'."

The Orcadian
December 9, 1976

He resolved to write an open letter to *The Orcadian*, condemning the refusal of the OIC. We sat in my hotel bedroom where I had hired a typewriter, and Max dictated the letter to me. This went on well into the night, and then Max left, only to return again an hour or so later, knocking furiously on my door and coming in with 'another thing', which was also added to the letter. We polished it up the next morning, and I vividly remember posting it, thinking to myself, 'Well, that is the end of that'.

We continued our successful tour, and Max returned to Orkney. In the meantime, *The Orcadian* had printed his letter on its front page. This was the first time that many people in Orkney had been aware of Max's presence, and, when he returned, there was even a small piece in *The Orcadian* to say that he was back in Orkney. This was in December, 1976.

In January 1977, I received a phone call from Max with the words, 'How much did you say that festival would cost?'. I was quite cross. 'What festival?' I asked through clenched teeth. 'You know, the one we had wanted to do with *The Martyrdom*.' 'Why?' I asked. 'Because they are wanting to try to make it happen anyway,' replied Max. 'Well, it depends what you want to have in it.' 'The same as we had when we made the applications.' 'When is the meeting you are having?' 'Tomorrow.' 'Oh, and you want a budget by tomorrow?' 'Yes.'

Michael had to start all over again, but not in the same way as the previous applications. This was to be an overall budget for the whole festival. Max phoned to get the figures, which were £15,000. The meeting duly took place, and the following day Norman Mitchell phoned and said 'Well, Judy, that doesn't seem so bad'. 'What do you mean?' I asked, 'how on earth are we going to find £15,000?' 'Oh,' said Norman, 'Max told us last night that the sum involved would be £1,500.' Silence. I don't know how or why Max had got the wrong end of the stick. It was probably wishful thinking. But, whatever it was, it was, of course, wildly inaccurate to a degree of ten times. But it had made the Orkney Arts Society think that it might be possible to proceed.

Michael and I went to have a meeting with Robert Ponsonby to seek his advice and to see what might be done. Robert was overwhelmingly helpful in every respect. He already had a commitment to his commission of *The Martyrdom*, and he knew that monies had to be allocated to realise the commission in terms of provision of rehearsal rooms, instruments and payment to the singers and players. In fact, everything to do with the musical aspect of the opera. However, the visual aspects were missing; what is generally called 'the production'.

Max had worked with Murray Melvin, the actor, in connection with the music that he had written for Ken Russell's films, *The Boy Friend* and *The Devils*, both of which Murray had acted in. Murray had been directing some shows, and Max asked him if he would be willing to take on *The Martyrdom of St Magnus*, which he said he would. A budget had been made concerning the production, which had been added to the costs of the musical part of the opera.

What Robert Ponsonby now suggested was that the BBC would mount a performance in Orkney which would have an invited audience, which meant that no charge would be made for the tickets. This would enable the BBC to regard the performance as taking place in a studio, albeit one very far removed from London. Robert said that the BBC would undertake all the costs of providing the studios for rehearsals, the percussion instruments and keyboard instruments, payment of the musicians and singers for all their rehearsals and for the performance itself, and for the transportation of everything from London up to Orkney, including all the costumes and sets of the proposed production. This left the visual element of the production to be taken care of by the festival, which came to around £4,000. This was put to the committee and they decided that they would go along with it. Max had in any case been writing the opera (which he wrote very quickly).

The singers had already been selected and booked in the previous year (1976). There were four male singers and, as always, Mary Thomas. The four new people in the group included Michael Rippon, baritone, who was very soon to sing in Max's music theatre work *Eight Songs for a Mad King* with the Fires for the first time. This was a role which he subsequently performed on numerous occasions with the group, and also all over the world with many other ensembles. And the role of Magnus was to be performed by the young singer Neil Mackie, who had come with a very strong recommendation from Peter Pears.

For my part, I had to go about putting the whole project together, which was a very daunting prospect. I always say that in managing performing groups there are three aspects which are real killers on top of all the usual hassles. One of them is new music, another is touring, and the third is the dramatic element - opera, music theatre, dance or whatever. Each one causes so many intrinsic problems. In my case, as manager of the Fires, I had all three, altogether, all the time.

Things had been further complicated by the fact that the personnel of the Fires had undergone a very considerable change at the time of the North American tour. With the exception of Stephen Pruslin, all of the other five members of the group had decided to leave for various reasons. This had necessitated, over a period of several months, auditioning many players. David Campbell, the clarinettist, had already joined for the tour of North America.

I was constantly in touch with Murray Melvin, and Sue Plummer, the designer, and Claire Mitchell, who was making the costumes; and most particularly with Kris Misselbrook, who was to be the stage manager. Up until this point, there had been no professional stage manager or lighting person working with the Fires. The advent of Kris Misselbrook, to take over all of this, was nothing less than a godsend.

I had got everything arranged for the rehearsals for *The Martyrdom*,

Robert Ponsonby, 1996.

Kris Misselbrook

which would start almost immediately on our return. They were to take place in the BBC studios in Delaware Road, Maida Vale. All the additional percussion and keyboard instruments were to be provided from the BBC's store, which was in the same building. It was to Maida Vale that the five singers convened, together with Murray.

Sue Plummer and Claire Mitchell would arrive with this or that. It might be part of a costume, or a prop. Fittings were made with the singers in between rehearsals. It all looked very confusing. Things would appear, then disappear, presumably while they were altered or replaced. I found it all most disconcerting. I always vowed that whenever we had a theatrical work in the future, this business of costumes and sets would be done weeks in advance, so that we wouldn't have all this extra worry and undue excitement. But I never came anywhere near to that particular dream!

The singers had all learnt their parts wonderfully well, and were getting used to their costumes, and I was endeavouring to keep in touch with Norman Mitchell at the Orkney end. I had persuaded Max's publishers, Boosey & Hawkes, to give a press conference to launch the festival. They had never done such a thing before, and, to the best of my knowledge, they have never done it since.

There was a buffet party in London to which all the press came, and Max gave out the details of the festival. There wasn't much in it, of course, for obvious reasons. Max had asked the members of the Fires if they would agree to give an additional concert for free, and this they did. There was a similar agreement from the Edinburgh String Quartet, and Norman was to give a concert with his own pupils from Kirkwall Grammar School. There would also be some readings of George Mackay Brown's poems. (I remember that George wouldn't agree to do that himself as he was too shy.) The interest from the press was enormous.

Communication with Orkney was proving difficult, as Norman was fully occupied with his teaching at the school. My main worry on arrival was that we would not have a local person to help us set up. These days the festival has a superb crew, led by the Rushbrooks, who take care of absolutely everything to do with stage management and moving things in and out of places. But at that point we had Kris, together with Mark Pritchard, who was to do the lighting. We had to bring the lighting with us from London, in the van, along with everything else. We were also worried about what things would be like in Kirkwall. Would we be able to find refreshments? What would the weather be like? Would the cathedral authorities allow us the kind of access we needed?

Meanwhile, the rehearsals in London went well, and we finally gave a complete run-through to a small selected audience. The stage management then packed everything into the huge van, and set off for Orkney. We waited in London for a couple of days, to allow the van to get there. Our journey would be by train from London to Glasgow, and then by plane to Kirkwall.

I had the whole team with me. This was the first time, as manager, that I had had brass players with me - two trumpets and a horn. I was very frightened, as brass players had a fierce reputation and I didn't quite know what to expect. As it turned out they were wonderful, especially John Wallace, the first trumpet, who has continued to work with Max in one way or another from that day to this.

Robert Ponsonby former controller of music, BBC

I first met Max in January, 1972. I had just joined the BBC and it seemed important to introduce myself to a young composer of great promise and personality. He had a tiny London flat, very spartanly furnished; it appeared that he slept on a narrowish platform above the wardrobe. I liked him at once and was fascinated by the liveliness of his ideas. Later that year, I heard his music in Glasgow (*Antechrist, Hymnos* and *Vesalii Icones*), at the Edinburgh Festival (*Eight Songs for a Mad King*) and at Covent Garden, where his amazing *Taverner* was produced. It seemed obvious to me that the BBC should at some stage commission a large-scale work from him.

My predecessor at the BBC had commissioned some important works (including one by Max) but I was able to enlarge his programme and, for 1977, the Queen's silver jubilee year, I had funds for one or two substantial pieces. When I discovered that Max had in mind a chamber opera, on a text by Mackay Brown, for performance in St Magnus Cathedral, I knew that we had to commission it: the work would bring Orkney centre-stage and it was likely to be strikingly original.

There were of course obstacles, most of them financial, and I wrote to *The Orcadian* urging the local authorities to put some money into the presentation of Max's piece. Whether it had any effect I have no idea, but the first performance of *The Martyrdom of St Magnus* was eventually given in St Magnus Cathedral on 18 June 1977, and I was bitterly disappointed to be tied up in London and so to miss the work in its proper setting. The Round House, in London's Camden Town, where I heard it on 25 July as part of the Proms, was in stark and ugly contrast, but the music came over with impressive force and I was very proud of the commission.

I had first visited Orkney, with a section of the SNO, in 1967. I shall never forget the warbling of curlews as we waited for the BEA flight to take us back to Glasgow. My last visit was to the festival in 1996, when the Royal Philharmonic premiered Max's latest symphony. This time I came and went by sea. The curlews were still warbling. One day I took the boat to Hoy, walked past Max's croft and on towards the Old Man; it was a magical day. Indeed the whole visit was unforgettable and it was exhilarating to find the St Magnus Festival in gallant good health. If, inadvertently, I played any part in its success I am proud and more than content.

"Sir...I was very happy to hear of the proposal for an Orkney festival and the BBC was more than content that its commission was to be performed during the festival in Kirkwall cathedral. Now it seems that this won't happen because of a supposedly 'commercial' element in the proposal. With respect to those who take this view, Mr Maxwell Davies's group The Fires of London, is no more commercial than the Edinburgh Festival, or... for that matter - the BBC. It deserves, and receives, grants and guarantees from... organisations concerned with the encouragement of the arts.

Is it too late to hope that the policy and resources committee would reverse its decision...? I stress that the BBC has no financial interest: if not first performed in Orkney, 'The Martyrdom of St Magnus' would be given elsewhere - probably in London. I think this would be a pity. I hope music-lovers and others in Orkney might agree with me."

Robert Ponsonby, BBC
The Orcadian
December 9, 1976

"Sir, In 1937 we launched a pageant to celebrate the octocenteny of St Magnus Cathedral. I can remember the scepticism, derision and jeers which greeted the idea when we campaigned for support in the West Mainland... Everyone knows the outcome. The pageant was a triumphant success...Now exactly forty years later, we have another opportunity to celebrate - this time the silver jubilee of our reigning monarch - with music and drama. How better to mark the occasion than a performance of 'The Martyrdom of St Magnus'? A world premiere in Kirkwall! Whatever the cost, Orcadians must seize this opportunity which, if lost, we shall forever regret."

Marjorie Linklater
The Orcadian,
December 16, 1976

Hoy had become the home of a mysterious composer called Peter Maxwell Davies. Marjorie knew nothing about him, except that nobody could understand his music. That didn't matter. What she liked was that he was surprising, and he caused argument.

Once, when I had come to stay with her for a while in Orkney, she told me that this composer had proposed celebrating the Queen's silver jubilee with the performance of his opera, *The Martyrdom of St Magnus*, but that his offer had been turned down. It seemed rather a pity, but no doubt the council had its reasons.

A few days later she looked up from her *Orcadian* and said, 'he's right, you know'.

'Who is?'

'Look at this. A long letter from Peter Maxwell Davies. He says he suggested some sort of festival to the council - an opera, concerts and so on - and it's been refused. He sees no reason why there shouldn't be a festival and he's expressing his disappointment.'

'No wonder.'

Marjorie made a tut-tut noise.

'It would have been such fun,' she said. 'George's story turned into an opera. Musicians from all over the place zooming up to Orkney. Making it into another Aldeburgh...'

I said that Orkney now had the chance to do the same sort of thing. Marjorie's eyes flashed.

'We can't let the council go on turning it down,' she said. 'Quick - we must write to *The Orcadian*.'

Letters to *The Orcadian*, from the pen of Marjorie Linklater came about as frequently as seagulls to Stromness harbour. But this was one of the most serious she had yet written. Her letter, which was published a week later, was accompanied by others in the same vein. Whether this was one of the factors which caused the council to reverse its decision I do not know. But a festival committee was duly formed, its first meeting taking place in Kirkwall's Royal Hotel.

Marjorie Linklater, Stromness, 1982.

Judy Arnold

The Martyrdom of St Magnus

Against all the odds, the St Magnus Festival was becoming a reality. Musicians, singers, production crew, visitors and the national media, converged on Orkney for the premiere of *The Martyrdom of St Magnus*; nerves were raw and the anticipation was intense. Other events had been organised which, with *The Martyrdom*, were to form the first festival. These involved The Fires of London, The Edinburgh Quartet, the St Magnus Cathedral Singers and Kirkwall Grammar School Choir and Chamber Orchestra, amongst others. The first programme had been printed, welcoming visitors to the festival and announcing plans for the following year with a confidence that proved to be well-founded. Even the council had given its blessing - which would become substantial financial support over subsequent years.

There were a few last minute nightmares, of course, but the stage was set, not only for *The Martyrdom of St Magnus*, but for the establishment of Orkney's unique arts festival in the highly appropriate setting of St Magnus Cathedral, where the saint's remains, buried in a sandstone pillar, gave an added resonance to the proceedings. It was the culmination of the tenacious idealism, tempered with hard graft, that had gone into all the plans and negotiations surrounding the first festival. In the event, from high up in the triforium of the cathedral, it was heralded in with a fanfare of trumpets.

"Although the convener, Mr George Marwick, continued to maintain his opposition to giving financial support for the Orkney festival in June, Orkney Islands Council on Tuesday unanimously agreed to underwrite any loss up to £2000 from the oil revenues."
The Orcadian
March 24, 1977

I bumped into Neil Mackie recently in London, not having seen him for more than an age. He has not changed one bit. He still looks angelic - you could stick wings on him and put him on your Christmas tree.

Do not be fooled, he is a little devil. If there was ever a prank pulled, you knew he was behind it. He reminded me that *The Martyrdom* was his first acting job, very early on in his career and I was his first director. He did me proud.
Murray Melvin, director, 'The Martyrdom of St Magnus'

Neil Mackie tenor, 'Magnus', *The Martyrdom of St Magnus*

A surprise telephone call from my agent during the spring of 1976 was to prove to be one of the most important of its kind in my career.

Peter Maxwell Davies (soon to become Max, a much-valued friend and colleague) was looking for a tenor to assume the title role in his new creation, *The Martyrdom of St Magnus*. After a short audition Max smiled and said 'I would like you to be Magnus'. Undoubtedly this marvellous opportunity launched my international career - with Max's celebrated Fires of London I took part in countless well-schooled and cogent performances worldwide. Overnight I had become a member of a very special family!

The initial rehearsals for *Magnus* took place at the BBC studios in London. Soon it was time to leave for the north and after an overnight train journey The Fires assembled at Glasgow airport to await a chartered plane which was to take us on our last leg of the journey to Orkney. The first hour passed and the second and still no plane...my impatient colleagues needed cheering up, I thought.

A line from the opera sprang to mind! In one particular scene where the action was updated, the entire cast, representing reporters, gave news flashes on the worsening situation between the Hakon and Magnus factions in the negotiations on Egilsay. My line was 'Calling Magnus Erlendson'.

Smugly I asked the information desk to page Magnus Erlendson. 'Calling Magnus Erlendson, would Magnus Erlendson please come to the information desk.' My prank raised many smiles amongst my colleagues, including Max. But soon another announcement rang round the airport: 'Would the gentleman who paged Magnus Erlendson please return to the information desk immediately.' With rather an apologetic air, I approached the desk only to find a beaming, six 'footer' plus... Magnus Erlendson from Iceland!

Another new special friend and what an enormous coincidence! To celebrate our extraordinary meeting, Magnus from Iceland plied me with too many whiskies and as a result the following morning I was not in great voice at the first Orkney rehearsal. But all was forgiven. The world premiere was a triumph for us all, not least Max. The St Magnus Festival had truly arrived; so many memories followed, so many glorious times, so many great performances and a string of incredible Orkney Max pieces.

Where love has been, there will always remain the echo of the song that it sang!
Affectionate thanks, Max.

Judy Arnold manager, Sir Peter Maxwell Davies

The plane landed safely in Kirkwall. I remember so well coming down the steps and thinking, 'We have done it - it really is going to happen'. Norman had arranged for a bus to take everyone from the airport to the cathedral. There, we were collected by the people with whom we were staying. I remember a feeling of total panic because I did not know the name or phone number of any of these Orcadian hosts. Meanwhile, Kris and Mark had arrived with the van, and begun the huge task of unloading all the gear into the cathedral, and starting to set up.

We were on our own. And it was freezing. Absolutely freezing. There was no heating on in the cathedral. Although we have had some pretty dreadful weather over subsequent festivals, I think everyone will agree that none of them has matched the coldness of that first festival. And we had no refreshments, so there was no way of warming ourselves artificially. All the musicians were trying to keep their fingers warm so as to be able to actually play their instruments.

Of course, last minute items were needed for the production, as they always are, and I was despatched to purchase them. I had no idea where to find such things. It was all very fraught. These days there is a wonderful removable stage, on which artists can perform in the cathedral. But at that time a special stage had to be constructed, with two ramps on either side, so that the singers could walk on and off. The amount of space that the singers had to perform in was minuscule. Max, as the conductor, was placed on a pedestal behind one of the pillars. He was unseen by the audience, as were the instrumentalists.

I spent the entire time, from Wednesday to Saturday, in the cathedral, supervising and doing whatever needed to be done. I had been billeted in Kirkwall with the Rosie family, who had two teenage daughters. The house was not very far from the cathedral - about seven minutes walk. As always, with Orcadian hospitality, the family were very kind, but I didn't see much of them, leaving early in the morning and returning late at night.

The dress rehearsal was to be on the Friday night, and it was free and open to the public. I suggested to the two Rosie girls that they might like to come along. They replied that they would not. Upon enquiring as to why not, they said that it was to be modern music and that they would hate it. I asked them if they had ever wasted an evening in their lives, and when they agreed that they had, I said that they could waste another one, and come along and see the opera. I left it at that.

The dress rehearsal happened, although lighting was a problem because there should have been some kind of black-out, which wasn't possible in the cathedral. And, of course, it doesn't really get dark at midsummer in Orkney. We had the dress rehearsal at 9pm, as late as possible, which was in line with the time of the actual performance.

There was a lot of clearing up to do after the rehearsal. When I eventually arrived back at the Rosies' house, the two girls were waiting up for me. They said that *The Martyrdom* was the best thing they had ever been to. I was absolutely thrilled. This was why we were here. We had come to

I remember that at the first festival The Fires of London were cold! It was one of those blasting cold Junes, and they were sitting in the cathedral with the wind howling, and they found it quite hard to play. They were all shivering - huddling under overcoats and with gloves on. Eventually the heating was turned on in the cathedral, so it was all right.
Peter Maxwell Davies
(in conversation)

In the early days, things didn't always work - but it almost didn't matter that there was no car to take you from here to there. The best thing about it was the freshness and enthusiasm of the people; they are absolutely wonderful. They really wanted this festival to happen, and the marvellous thing about it was being hands-on and helping to make it all happen. It wasn't just that you were playing the music, but you were part of a festival that could either happen or not happen - it was a make or break situation. I just remember people being very friendly and we all did a certain amount more than we would do if it was just an ordinary series of concerts. We got on with it and we played. We felt that anything we did was making history really.
Philippa Davies, flautist
The Fires of London
(in conversation)

make a festival for the people who lived right here in Orkney, and what Max and The Fires had been able to communicate directly to the two girls was what I saw the whole thing to be about.

Finally, it was Saturday. The monstrous idea which Max had had was about to happen; a festival was going to start. It was all mad and crazy and absurd and out of the question. But here was everyone ready to go, and the press had come up from London to write about it, and Martin Dalby was here with his BBC microphones ready to record the opera, and John Amis was ready to make a *Kaleidoscope* programme, and was going around everywhere with his own microphones. The London press conference had been the vital factor in generating this first great public awareness of the festival, ensuring that the national press were all there in force.

It came towards the evening, and at 7pm Max came to me and said, 'Judy, I can't find my score'. 'Which score?' 'You know, the marked score of *The Martyrdom* from which I am going to conduct.' And so we both proceeded to crawl on our hands and knees, looking under all the chairs in the nave, and everywhere, until we finally located it. It took about half an hour, and was an agonising time.

At 9pm the audience filed in. The cathedral was full. But where was George Mackay Brown? He had said that he hardly went to Kirkwall and he just didn't seem to be there. How could this whole festival, this opera, start without him? I was in a panic. In fact, he had slipped in, at the back, according to his usual custom, and I needn't have worried.

The opera began. Blind Mary is lying on the ground and starts to hum. Gradually the solo guitar joins in. Mary sets the scene. And then, wondrously, from the triforium, comes the sound of the two trumpets. The St Magnus Festival had started. That was the great moment, and I still get goose pimples to this day when I think about it.

At the end of the performance there was total silence as people realised what had happened, and then tumultuous applause. I came out of the cathedral and it was still light. I made a phone call to Michael from the phone box near the cathedral, and said, or rather screamed, 'We have done it!'.

By Monday, the weather suddenly turned and it became boiling hot - typical Orkney weather with constant changes. The press were all extremely favourable, about both *The Martyrdom* and the festival. Arrangements, of course, were not as fluent as they have since become, but everyone had managed anyway. After the festival, Max invited many people over to Rackwick for a celebration party, including players, critics and other friends. The weather was glorious. This set the pattern for all future festivals, as Max always liked to have people come to Rackwick.

Archie Bevan festival vice-president

Midsummer 1977 is bitterly cold. Possibly the coldest in the last fifty years. The north wind blows relentlessly out of a grey sky. Inside the cathedral, where final rehearsals are in progress, the heating system is out of action and the temperature inside the building is even lower than outside. Gloves, scarves and woolly hats are the order of the day.

Meantime, the first festival visitors shiver their way along Broad Street. And out in the country, a distinguished Cambridge professor of archaeology, sampling the wonders of Maeshowe for the first time, fastens the top button of his anorak and assures his wife that, yes, we really must come back in the summer to explore it properly....

It is Saturday the eighteenth of June.

The players are becoming acclimatised to the arctic conditions. There is even some mild euphoria in the wake of a successful dress rehearsal, attended by a large and appreciative audience, and doubtless helped along by the bottle of local malt which has been found by the custodian in the kirk vestry - now empty of course.

The cathedral is packed for the premiere. Many of the audience have only a limited view of the action. But this will not greatly mar their enjoyment of a performance which relies so much on the dramatic power of the word and the music, and the splendid ambience of the great church rather than its makeshift stage.

The voice of Blind Mary (the incomparable Mary Thomas) reaches out to every corner of the nave with thrilling intensity as she weaves the bloody web of war:

The warp is stretched
For warriors' death
The weft in the loom
Drips with blood...

Great brass fanfares ring out from the triforium as battle is joined in the Menai Straits: and the voice of Magnus (Neil Mackie) rises serenely above the strife as he makes his first big pacific gesture.

The Martyrdom achieves its artistic ends with remarkable economy of means. During the hunt for Magnus on Egilsay, the action explodes from the stage out into the dark auditorium, lit only by menacing gleams of torchlight as Hakon's viking henchmen turn into fascist thugs, prowling around the audience in pursuit of their quarry. Meantime, the historical transition from viking Orkney to modern tyranny is accomplished by means of some brilliant musical pastiche, moving swiftly through the centuries from mediaeval plainsong to baroque and romantic and twentieth century foxtrot.

Blind Mary - no longer blind, thanks to the miraculous intervention of the martyred saint - gazes in consternation at an audience of 'blind mouths, crying for sacrifice', and prays to St Magnus to save us all 'from a bedlam

"Text and music fuse in almost unearthly beauty. The audience which had packed the hall seemed to feel the same - that it was an unforgettable experience, and the ancient walls seemed about to fall asunder with the applause."
Morgenavisen, Norway

Mary Thomas as Blind Mary, 1977.

Gunnie Moberg

of sacrifice'. The setting is local and historical, but the message is universal and timeless. The opera ends on a note of quiet serenity as a small choir of monks process with their candles up the aisle of the darkened cathedral, chanting their new litany:

Sancte Magne, ora pro nobis

Switch to Broad Street, where a group of local lads are startled and hugely diverted to see a quartet of monks emerging from the west door of the cathedral. Their catcalls die on the air (briefly of course) as the leading monk extracts a hand from the folds of his habit and offers them a resounding two-fingered salute.

Thus, with a blend of high seriousness and glorious farce, the first St Magnus Festival signals the route it will follow so triumphantly through the next quarter century.

Murray Melvin, director, 1977.

Murray Melvin director, *The Martyrdom of St Magnus*

Prior to the festival I had worked for Max as a performer in the *Missa Super L'Homme Armé* and as director of *Miss Donnithorne's Maggot.* He gave me the libretto of *The Martyrdom of St Magnus* and asked me to direct it. I saw the inscription 'opera' and froze. 'I have never directed an opera,' I said. Max was not fazed and so I took it on. It was the most incredible experience for us all.

We travelled up to Stromness, my first visit, to see the space and meet everyone. We stayed with the Bevans. I remember it all so clearly, even the view from their bedroom window of a calm sea and a flock of swans drifting by.

Enormous decisions were made on that visit, such as the need for a special ramp for the staging of the opera, so that the audience could see the action. There were technical headaches too - where to put the band, in front or behind one of the great pillars. The acoustic. The balance between band and voices in that magnificent cathedral.

I returned home worrying about the huge commitment being made by everyone and the fact that the festival committee was going to build the ramp at great expense to its limited funds. All this on the strength of quick decisions made during a very short visit.

There was such an industry behind the scenes. Everyone worked so hard. We were all aware of the huge responsibility of the commitment.

The piece itself was very exciting and still relevant in today's world. In both the novel and the opera, the action is brought up to date in a most dramatic way, making it far more than just an historical piece.

We all felt the importance of pulling the chestnut out of the bag, because of the festival and the idea of the festival. The knives were out in some quarters I remember. Those original few who had the foresight and courage to hang on to the idea and fight for it, put their heads on the line and at the end of the day won through.

It was all so exciting and terrifying at the same time. The atmosphere the day before the first performance was electric. We were surrounded by the musical critic fraternity. Not the most farsighted lot. I remember coming in for a certain amount of stick from the 'musicos'. Toward the end of the piece I had given the singers movements that were not mentioned in the libretto. They did it so well and enjoyed doing it. I claimed theatrical licence. The musicos were not impressed! When one considers what is done today on the opera stage we can at least claim the badge for being innovative.

My only sadness in recalling those exciting days is that the brilliant and wonderful Mary Thomas, who played Blind Mary so tellingly, is no longer with us to join in this celebration.

It was all the most wonderful special time.

John Wallace trumpet, *The Martyrdom of St Magnus*

When I came to Orkney for the first festival in 1977, I was immediately impressed by the tranquillity and the unselfconscious preservation of a culture which had almost disappeared elsewhere. It struck me as a part of rural lowland Scotland stuck on the top of the Highlands. I liked the people for their openness, generosity, use of language and gregariousness. I liked it very much. We - my fellow trumpeter Norman Archibald, a fellow Scot - and I, stayed at the manse. We didn't get much sleep. We got to know Highland Park and Scapa whisky and Orkney cheese. An insomniac combination. It never seemed to get dark and our biological clocks answered to some long-gone circadian (or was it Orcadian) summer rhythm buried in our genes. I liked Orkney so much I brought my wife and her sister back on holiday later in the summer to Rousay, where again we stayed in a manse, and got to know Jimmy the roadman, and went fishing in the lochs. We watched hen harriers quartering over the overgrown kitchen garden and had a really quiet time.

The performances of *The Martyrdom* were memorable as were the rehearsals. Max was not the mellow creature we have all grown to love. He was a crucible of smouldering fire which ignited at anything which stood in the way of his all-consuming artistic vision. When the performances came they were highly charged and of a searing intensity I had not experienced before. It seemed to matter much more than playing Beethoven's Fifth Symphony again, even with the likes of Karl Böhm. The sandstone cathedral of St Magnus itself was one of the participants in heightening the drama. The sarcophogus of King Hakon, from where we trumpets played on high, reminded me visually of the violence inherent in the history; and some of Max's chosen sounds, such as the wirebrush on the gong, did justice to this violence aurally.

The Martyrdom of St Magnus, St Magnus Cathedral, 1977.

John Wallace

The last time I was in Orkney, with the London Sinfonietta, in 1999, I revisited the 'loft' to play Max's *Litany for a Ruined Chapel Between Sheep and Shore*. The acoustic was just as strange and clear as I remembered it. Quite unique. No other church quite like it. Meanwhile in the intervening twenty-odd years, the population of Orkney seemed to have grown, the car population ten-fold, and I was impressed by how the place had thrived, and attracted many first-generation Orcadians, who had adopted it as a new homeland. I felt like following suit!

Norman Mitchell festival co-founder and co-artistic director, 1977-1979

Successful programming had been essential. The performance of *The Martyrdom of St Magnus*, for which we had all striven, was stunning and there was no one present who could do anything but marvel at the spectacle. This was an occasion of greatness and history was in the making.

There was a Festival Service on Sunday at 11.00am and the Fires gave a concert in the cathedral on the Sunday evening. I distinctly remember the now internationally-famous trumpeter (and principal of the Royal Scottish Academy of Music and Drama) John Wallace, cycling from Orphir with his trumpet on his back to take part in a performance of Vaughan Williams's *Hundredth Psalm* arrangement! In the afternoon there was a joint recital of organ music by Bach played by myself with traditional Scots fiddle music (played by Arthur Robertson from Shetland) and pibroch (played on the Highland bagpipe by a local banker, David Currie).

The Fires hosted the evening concert on the Sunday with more brilliant performances from this ensemble. Works performed included Max's *Dark Angels* (to texts by George Mackay Brown), and his *Scottish Renaissance Dances*. For me, however, the most spellbinding performance came from Gregory Knowles playing Max's *Ave Maris Stella* on the marimba.

On Monday evening the Cathedral Choir sang choral music and the Grammar School Choir and Instrumental Ensemble performed *O Magnum Mysterium*, written by Max in 1960 (whilst he was director of music at Cirencester Grammar School). The Edinburgh Quartet were engaged to play at the final concert on the Tuesday evening. Other musicians, mainly drawn from the Fires, gave afternoon concerts to add further substance to the festival's programme. In addition, a number of local artists led by Gary Gibson had mounted an excellent exhibition in Kirkwall Town Hall. There was a Festival Club at the Kirkwall Hotel and dances arranged to take place at other venues. At the end of five hectic days we were all exhausted. It had worked and it had been a huge success. The gamble had paid off!

This festival emerged from a visit by an 'almost unknown' composer to these shores in the early seventies. A chance meeting with the Bevans, an introduction to George Mackay Brown, the journey to Rackwick, the influence of the St Magnus story, the cathedral in Kirkwall, a meeting with Norman Mitchell, a summer concert series in St Magnus - all these factors fused to create a magical festival of the arts on an island at the northern tip of the Scottish mainland. The survival of this major event is a tribute to those who nurtured it over so many years. Long may it continue to flourish! I am proud to have been its co-founder and first co-artistic director.

Trevor Green former manager, BBC SSO, BBC Philharmonic

Norman Mitchell had lots of energy and vision and was a perfect partner in those early days to fill in the gaps that Max would hate. Being a creative musician, the thought of having to be involved in all the logistical arrangements, such as accommodation and flight schedules, was beyond Max, and he managed to establish a faithful group of disciples who were to be the backbone of the festival. Apart from sharing the artistic responsibilities with Max, Norman also had performances of his own. I was delighted to be invited to play the trumpet with the local orchestra, directed by Norman, in a performance of music by Handel and Peter Maxwell Davies at the 1979 festival. No fee was offered, but an air fare and accommodation with the Mitchells clinched the deal.

My first meeting with Max was in the Festival Club after the cathedral performance. I was quite surprised to meet this 'famous British composer' and observe how shy I thought he was. All around us people were talking and enjoying the post-performance knees-up, but not Max. I loved his quiet authority and the way in which he delegated his festival to the trust of his band of supporters who believed in his infectious personality and thought that the festival was good for the economy and image of these wind-blown islands. Through his commitment to them, by living in, and giving, to the community, these people supported a festival that would eventually become one of the cultural calendar highlights in world music.

I also met Judy Arnold, who had a formidable reputation of being quite tough; a strong and ruthless negotiator and a bit of a 'dragon lady'. Since that first encounter I have spent many wonderful moments in the company of Judy, many of them half-way across the world. She is very special, not only in her commitment to Max, but in her support of 20th century music. She is a fine and very efficient administrator, brimful of energy and always has a smile, even on the darkest days. Max would always have been successful, his music communicates; however, in Judy, he has a great PR lady who totally believes in the man and his music.

Tireless in her support of him, she introduced his music to a world-wide audience, and kept him at the forefront of 20th century music. I don't believe there is another individual who has given so much loving professional care to an artist as Judy with Max. She is quite unique and a wonderful person to be able to call a friend.

George Mackay Brown

"Musicians without instruments and music-lovers arrived from Kirkwall. The Jessie Ellen was crowded as it moved out of the harbour at 8.30am. The huge cloud over Hoy had toppled sideways across the sun. In that shade the air moved cold. We had a serene passage round the east side of Graemsay. There, at the Moaness pier, Jack Rendall and Geoff Clark were waiting with their vehicles. The tide brimmed high and blue over the rocks. Some benign fortune gives us, nearly always, beautiful weather in Hoy. Our car passed the slowly-growing tree plantation and the ancient peat-banks; and there at last Rackwick lay like a green sea-tilted bowl, full of light.

There was no need to hurry. We walked, singly or in small groups, across the perilous side of Moorfea to the high hidden cottage of Bunertoon. Gulls flashed past our faces from the chimney pots of North-house.

To those who suffer, like me, from vertigo, there are anxious moments in the slow climb across that curving hill, Moorfea. The sea, blue and dazzling, lies far below. Above, the serene sweep of sky. Between, this crazy green tilt where we trod hesitantly along ancient sheep paths. One thinks, 'If I stumble, there's nothing to keep me from plunging straight into the Atlantic...!'

I trod, nervously, the last sheer curve, and there were the roofs and chimneys of Bunertoon, with smoke drifting in the lucent air. There is no cottage in the world so dramatically sited.

Through the long day, till 4 pm, we sat around Bunertoon, sun-drenched, talking and eating and drinking good red wine. Groups drifted away towards the Old Man, and drifted back again: as if it was all happening in a blue-and-green-and-gold idyll.

Motionless, as in a dream, rain clouds hung over Caithness, across the Firth, and trailed their slow grey curtains, day-long.
[from 'Under Brinkie's Brae', June 29, 1978]

George Mackay Brown and
Elizabeth Bevan at Bunertoon, 1985.

taking root

The first festival over, and a huge success, the attention of the committee was focused ahead. By 1980, the key features of the St Magnus Festival were in place. Visiting professional musicians; commissions from young composers; celebrity performers; local musical productions, especially featuring children and the Festival Chorus; the Orkney-centred 'A Johnsmas Foy'; the Festival Club; drama, poetry and art - they all had their own niche from which they would develop and grow over the next twenty five years.

Local involvement was even more crucial to the smooth running of the festival, and it attracted this huge commitment, while fielding some serious controversy which erupted locally through the letters page of *The Orcadian*, occasionally spilling further afield to *The Scotsman* and other newspapers. Meanwhile, the roots of the festival proved to be firm, and it emerged and grew on the world stage, attracting great interest and acclaim.

In 1985, the festival received an injection of cash from various sources, significantly the Post Office, which resulted in a bumper tenth anniversary the following year. Also in 1986, present festival director, Glenys Hughes, took up her post along with PMD for a year, Archie Bevan and then Ian Ritchie of the Scottish Chamber Orchestra. Since 1993, Glenys has been sole director.

The first festival had hardly been allowed to lie for more than a fortnight and the organisational process was under way again. More commissions were to be arranged. The Royal Bank of Scotland commissioned Max to write a new theatre work called *Le Jongleur de Notre Dame* which would receive its premiere in Stromness Town Hall. The idea of a 'Stromness day' was born, in order to take the festival to a wider community. Other commissions included *Infinity Contained* for the Cathedral Choir by a new composer, Ian McQueen. In an effort to involve school pupils, Kirkwall Grammar School was to have a new opera, *The Two Fiddlers* (from Max), based upon George Mackay Brown's short story.

*The Two Fiddler*s was to bring even more activity, as later in 1978 it toured in Italy. The British Council arranged for performances in Como, Cremona, Torino, Milan and Rome over ten days. Martin Dalby was commissioned to write a new work for the Fires; *The Dancer Eduardova* had its first performance in 1978.

There was a steady increase in interest from outside Orkney. The festival was now becoming recognised as a quality event in the arts calendar. The BBC had been present at the first festival for their silver jubilee commission. Now, the BBC Scottish Symphony Orchestra was to be invited to perform in the cathedral. A new work, *Source,* was commissioned for the orchestra by the festival committee from Eddie McGuire. This was inspired by Neil Gunn's *The River*. The Fires returned for a further concert and a new piece, *King Harald Sails to Byzantium,* came from the pen of a rising composer Judith Weir.

The Cathedral Choir was also to have a new work. Neil Mackie, the tenor who played the part of Magnus in *The Martyrdom*, was to be the soloist. This idea followed a long discussion between Max and myself, on one evening following the second festival where we, as artistic directors, were seeking new avenues for the next year. The involvement of local people was intrinsic to the continuing success of the festival. It was always to be a joint venture by both professional musicians drawn from an international background and from Orkney residents who were skilled in the arts. *Solstice of Light*, with a text by George Mackay Brown and music by Peter Maxwell Davies, was to be the centrepiece of the 1979 festival. The BBC recorded the performance for Radio 3 and the choristers gave a magnificent performance at the premiere. Richard (Dick) Hughes, the organist at the East Church, was asked to play the accompaniments on the organ and also to perform the highly virtuosic interludes. His playing was exceptional. A number of new works made their debut including *Kirkwall Shopping Songs* - originally called *Kirkwall Messages* - but people south of Scotland would never have heard of this term for groceries, so a modification of the title was required! Many of these new works have been highly successful and have received performances all over the world.

Judy Arnold manager, Sir Peter Maxwell Davies

In the early days, Max was able to create works which were tailor-made for the festival, using the great forces which he knew he had available to him. These forces were: George Mackay Brown, The Fires of London, Norman Mitchell and Dick Hughes - for the chorus and the secondary school children - and Glenys Hughes, until the present day, for the primary school children and as director.

The St Magnus Festival is unlike any other festival because the creative 'doers', from the start, have lived and worked in Orkney. It attracts many visitors, but the festival's main emphasis is for local people. No other festival, for instance, features so many local performers. These have been, in the main, schoolchildren, but there has also been a strong input from the Festival Chorus and other local groups, and from other areas, such as the community drama productions.

The St Magnus Festival also has a composer who lives and works locally, who has written a string of pieces about local places to be performed by local participants. In Max's pieces for children, for instance, the children uniquely bear the weight of the entire production - the singing, playing and the acting. This gives enormous responsibility to the children, who invariably rise to the occasion.

The festival has truly grown out of, and is part of, the Orkney community.

Glenys Hughes festival artistic director, 1986- (in conversation)

Dick and I came to Orkney in 1973, having taught music in London, which is where we met. We both decided that we'd had enough of large comprehensive schools in the inner city and we fancied a change. There happened to be two music teaching jobs going in Orkney that sounded ideal. A house was offered with the job, and Orkney seemed to be an attractive place to go; Dick was intrigued by the fact that on this remote island there was a wonderful mediaeval cathedral with a splendid organ in it. We decided to come and try it for a couple of years and see how things went.

Dick came up for an interview - that was his first visit - but they didn't interview me. He just said that he was about to marry another music teacher and was told to bring me too. It was that casual. So we moved up at about the same time as Max.

We did decide in the mid-eighties to move away, and I got a job in Bristol as an advisory teacher. I headed off for two years, but nothing very attractive ever came up for Dick, so I headed back again. During that time, I spent most of my salary on commuting between Bristol and Orkney. I missed two festivals - 1984 and 1985 - although in 1984 I was so homesick for the

Glenys Hughes

festival that I travelled up on the Friday night and back again on the Sunday, just to be here for the festival Saturday! We never again attempted to move back south, and it was largely the festival that kept us here.

I wasn't involved at all in the first two festivals, but Dick was assistant musical director of *The Two Fiddlers* in 1978, which involved pupils from Kirkwall Grammar School. It was a great success. At that time I was teaching in Papdale Primary School; we had done several quite ambitious musical productions and I thought it would be good if more schools, other than KGS, could take part in the festival. In 1978, there had been a young composer here called Ian McQueen who had been commissioned to write a piece for the Cathedral Choir. While he was here he had led some music workshops in some of the schools, and I wrote to Max suggesting that it would be good to commission Ian to write a piece for Papdale Primary - which he did. It was a very ambitious music theatre piece called *Time Flight*. Looking back, it was a huge undertaking which was challenging for the children and staff, although we did enjoy it.

Time Flight was not quite a whole concert length, so Max suggested writing something for the very young children, as a companion piece for the same concert, and produced the *Kirkwall Shopping Songs*. So that was my first involvement in the festival, in 1979.

Norman Mitchell left Orkney in that same year, and Max invited Dick and I to join the committee. I was asked to be secretary - the previous secretary had been Norman's wife - and I had no secretarial skills at all. I remember asking Max what the job entailed. He said that it was just to be a link between the committee members and himself, so I took it on and it wasn't a hugely onerous task. The number of groups and performers that came was quite small in those days - and there was no orchestra in that year. I remember writing letters by hand; and although I didn't particularly enjoy being the secretary, I enjoyed being involved on the committee. It's been a long time - 1979 until now!

I only stayed as secretary for a short time because I knew it really wasn't my forté. The following year, as a result of the success of the *Shopping Songs*, Max wrote *Cinderella*. That was the area I was particularly interested in - producing music with the children - especially if Max was going to write pieces especially for them. I stayed on the committee and Max wrote a series of great pieces over the next few years for the schools [see *pieces for children*].

For nine years Max had been sole artistic director of the festival, and in 1986 he decided that he wanted a co-artistic director, because he was not always here, and he needed someone to share the artistic responsibility. He asked me if I would take this on, just after I'd returned from my job in Bristol. I was delighted to be asked, but, before I could find my feet, Max stepped down as artistic director. I was wary about taking on full responsibility, so Archie [Bevan], who was chairman during that period, became a co-director in 1987. I remember his saying, 'I'll agree to share the bed of nails'! It was

Time Flight, by Ian McQueen, 1979.

Gunnie Moberg

at the time when there was still local controversy over the festival - with letters to *The Orcadian* - so it was indeed something of a bed of nails, although when Max ceased to be artistic director things did calm down.

The first crisis to be dealt with in 1986 was the withdrawal of the Orkney Orchestra from the festival. We were not happy with one of the pieces which the Orkney Orchestra proposed playing in their festival concert, and so I wrote to the orchestra - I was out of Orkney at the time - asking them to suggest an alternative. It was, I thought, a mildly worded letter, but it provoked a strong reaction. We were accused of dictating what local musicians should play and, despite Archie's and my efforts at conciliation, the orchestra withdrew from the festival, contacting not only the local but the national media. I found myself having to defend the festival's position on Radio Scotland! It was a storm in a teacup really, but it was also a baptism of fire.

Max became honorary president of the festival, and Archie and I were the co-artistic directors until 1988. At that time a third co-director came on board - Ian Ritchie, managing director of the Scottish Chamber Orchestra. It was at the time when the SCO was a pioneering orchestra in terms of their community and education work, and Ian was then very much at the forefront. At that time, too, Max was very involved with the SCO as associate composer, and he was writing his Strathclyde Concertos which had such an innovative education programme attached. So, for all sorts of reasons, it was good to have Ian more closely linked to the festival as an artistic director [see *orchestras and ensembles*].

In 1993 Archie resigned as artistic director, which left Ian and myself, and then Ian moved to Leeds to become managing director of Opera North. This meant that it was no longer feasible for him to be involved with the festival, so I was then left as sole artistic director. That is how it has been ever since. But there was no paid post - everyone was doing it in their own time. I was teaching music, and Archie was deputy rector and head of English at Stromness Academy - so everybody was really busy.

Many people don't realise the number of years the festival continued to be run voluntarily. The only person who did get any payment was Dorothy Rushbrook the administrator, who received a small honorarium - a token really - nothing like the payment she deserved. From about 1995 onwards, everybody on the committee and the board realised that there had to be a paid post, so we started searching for funding and were eventually awarded joint funding from the OIC and the Scottish Arts Council to create a part-time post of festival director. In January 1998 that came into operation. I decided then to give up teaching, and concentrate on the festival.

At first I worked from home, which I didn't enjoy, because by that time Dick had died, and living and working at home didn't really suit me. Now we have the Black Pig, which makes a splendid little office. We are past the point of no return now - we could never go back to working voluntarily - or to people working in their own homes. There were files all over the place,

"The Orkney Orchestra has decided to pull out of this year's St Magnus Festival following a bitter wrangle over the music they should play and allegations of 'dictatorship' by some members of the organising committee....12 players met at the weekend and unanimously agreed to withdraw from the event. Their conductor, Mr Graham Thomson, is sharply critical of the musical direction and various other aspects of the festival. The withdrawal follows a rejection of his choice of music for the orchestra's performance by the co-artistic directors, Mr Peter Maxwell Davies and Mrs Glenys Hughes. Mr Thomson says, 'It is obvious that this festival is becoming more and more a platform for the so-called music specialists who reside in Orkney'."
The Orcadian
April 4, 1986

which was a total inconvenience.

So, that's the history of my involvement. It has been for quite a long time! I still feel the same commitment to the festival, but I do think there has to be a time to give it up and pass it on to someone else - I'm very aware of that. There's always a time for new blood and for someone who will possibly take it in a different direction, so I certainly don't intend to go on forever. It's been a huge part of my life - not only the artistic planning and administration - but the 'hands on' involvement in community projects.

There can't be many music teachers who have had a world-famous composer writing pieces for them to produce with their pupils - and having music composed for particular schools has been very special [see *pieces for children*]. I think it is one of the things that has made the festival remarkable; not just that we have a strong education policy and that we make a point of involving young people, but that those pieces have run like a thread from the second festival and *The Two Fiddlers*, right through. Orkney has always been very strong musically, and the fact that it has a talented team of teachers and instructors working in the schools, and that instrumental tuition is still free, is fantastic. With that bedrock of good teaching, having the festival is the icing on the cake.

"There is probably no other festival in the country which has developed so successfully and so stimulatingly the blend of amateur and professional performance as St Magnus. Native forces have featured prominently in the opening events, all of which have been packed out - who says there is no local interest!"
Michael Tumelty
The Glasgow Herald
June, 1985

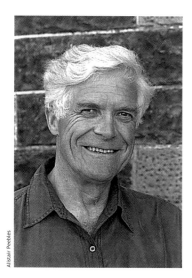

Archie Bevan

Archie Bevan festival vice-president (in conversation)

The festival became fully bedded down in the early eighties, but it was a worrying time when Dick and Glenys decided to move away from Orkney. When Glenys landed a first class job in Bristol, and took it up, Dick didn't get the type of job that he was entitled to look for, and he was stuck here; fortunately for the festival, I have to say. The festival was, at that time, I felt, in a precarious state. Dick had ceased to be organist and choirmaster in the cathedral, and it was all pretty dicey. Glenys eventually came home, which was very good news for the festival. But that was one of the wobbles, and I was very concerned at that time about the future. It was also at a time when the festival was having a bumpy ride PR-wise, and musical politics were looming large then, as they had done at the beginning. Controversy enlivened things, I suppose, and got the festival back into the national news.

There used to be a regular Festivals of Combined Arts conference every year, at which representatives from festivals would exchange news and views and have a dialogue with the Scottish Arts Council. I can remember an agonising debate about how to get decent publicity for events; the joke was that the St Magnus Festival didn't have any difficulty with that - all you needed was a bit of controversy. That was said in fun, but in fact it was true. (Although you can have too much of a good thing that way!)

We came up on the other side of that and were looking towards the 10th anniversary in 1986. That was a great festival year, though in fact it began rather alarmingly with another bout of musical disharmony. But after that, things became much easier.

Ian Barr from the Post Office had first come to the festival in 1984, and the PO injected money into the 1985 festival. They supported one of the music theatre concerts with Max's *Vesalii Icones* and *Eight Songs for a Mad King*. At the end of that festival there was a news conference which announced that the Post Office would be sponsoring some of the anniversary festival concerts in 1986 to the tune of £15,000. It was good timing for us, because we had been looking to the council and to Occidental Oil for funding. The latter had never supported us directly, but we had received a generous amount of money from them through the Arts Society Occidental covenant. For 1986, we badly needed big bucks from the council, which had been financially supporting the festival for some time by then. I remember going to an amicable meeting at which they were really supportive. We had to urge maximum generosity from the council, as Occidental had agreed to match any support the council gave, pound for pound; but it was up to the council to set the amount - which they duly did. It all came through in the end, and the anniversary festival was well-funded.

That year we had an extra long festival - it started on the Wednesday, and lasted for a whole week. It was also the first big orchestral festival experience, which was quite something. I could see that we couldn't retreat from that; the festival had climbed on to a new plateau. It had to be kept up, and it was from there that we went on, although there were still funding problems.

Ultimately, the festival came to be seen as the culmination of a year's worth of artistic activity in the county. It was not an end product, but the big punctuation mark in the year, when people who were otherwise involved in dramatic or choral and instrumental activity felt that they could enhance the quality of the festival by their presence. At that stage, we began to feel really accepted.

Gunnie Moberg

Glenys and Dick Hughes

Conrad Wilson music critic, *The Herald*, formerly of *The Scotsman*

Benjamin Britten, in a famous dictum, declared that a good festival should involve a journey to a special place, preferably not too easy to reach and requiring a certain amount of preparation and effort. Bayreuth, chosen by Wagner partly for its inaccessibility, remains in this respect the classic musical pilgrimage, but Aldeburgh was Britten's ideal. Not only was it his own birthplace but it grew harder and harder to visit once British Rail removed the 'Aldeburgh Flyer', the tiny train that took people on the last exhilarating leg of their journey to the Suffolk coast.

Britten died in 1976, thereby depriving his festival of its great original raison d'être. The founding in 1977 of the St Magnus Festival as a setting for the music of another British genius was thus uncannily timely. Peter Maxwell Davies, then aged 43, was a member of the 'Manchester' school that also included Harrison Birtwistle, Alexander Goehr, and John Ogdon - but he had settled on the dramatic and desolate island of Hoy in the hope of finding the right sort of solitude, silence, and atmosphere in which to compose. Already he was hard at work, attuning himself musically to Orkney's vast seascapes and landscapes as well as to the poetry of George Mackay Brown. With *The Martyrdom of St Magnus* launching the festival in the appropriate surroundings of St Magnus Cathedral, the auguries looked good.

But getting to Kirkwall would prove for many people trickier and more expensive than getting to Aldeburgh. Of the three ways of doing so, all fulfilled Britten's stipulation about a journey to a special place. Flying was the quickest, if the weather did not close in - on one of my visits, some travellers from Iceland to Norway had been stranded in Kirkwall for a week. A train from the south tended to mean an overnight stop in irksome Inverness. Driving supplied the greatest freedom, especially if you wanted to see more of Orkney than the local bus company could rise to.

So, in that first year, I set off from Edinburgh by car, reading *Magnus* in the passenger seat and stopping for lunch in Perth with the publisher John

Calder, whose own indispensable festival, Ledlanet Nights in Kinross-shire, had recently collapsed. Dinner and bed in a country house hotel near Inverness, followed by a dawn start, proved expensive, the proprietor deeply unfriendly. In later years I would prefer to pause in more congenial Dornoch. But the crossing from Scrabster to Stromness, past the Old Man of Hoy and the intimidating cliffs on which Davies established his windswept eyrie, was as tremendous as it was said to be. Back in the car, the first distant glimpse of St Magnus Cathedral from the slopes of the Stromness - Kirkwall road was something which, in subsequent years, would create that sense of arrival which Britten in Aldeburgh had esteemed so highly.

That first festival was an audacious event, smaller than its successors, yet never wholly surpassed by them. The midsummer sun shone constantly, in a way it has seldom done since. Sunset merged with sunrise in skies of indigo blue. Seals basked visibly in a sea of midnight bronze. To savour this, day after day, meant seldom sleeping, but Orkney's festival soon established itself as an event which, like Wexford's, was nothing if not convivial. Those who stayed at the Kirkwall Hotel, on the waterfront, would drink until dawn - but when was dawn? - at the rival hotel, the Royal, in the old town. Those who stayed at the Royal would do the same in reverse. There were meeting points en route where both factions converged. The ebb and flow was reminiscent again of Wexford, where the two main hotels were at opposite ends of town - though in Wexford the food was better, even if full-strength Highland Park seemed a superior tipple to Jameson's.

Orkney established quickly that a good festival is about celebration and conversation as well as about culture - something the Edinburgh Festival took a long time to learn, antagonising many London critics for that reason. But London critics, so long as their papers were prepared to pay them to travel so far, were attracted to Orkney, and 1977 found them in Kirkwall en masse. The austere Peter Heyworth of *The Observer* and the more sociable Desmond Shawe-Taylor of *The Sunday Times*, who had once fallen out over the importance or otherwise of bel canto opera, sat opposite each other at breakfast in the Kirkwall Hotel, each wearing newly-acquired fishermen's jerseys. It had never happened before, and would never happen again. William Mann of *The Times* drove from London with his family tent in which he had camped at festivals all over Europe. There were also agents, publishers, broadcasters, impresarios, and all the usual hangers on. Christie Duncan, music director of the Scottish Arts Council in the days when the music director of the Scottish Arts Council was still a distinguished presence at events, attended everything. *The Martyrdom of St Magnus*, like a harder-edged version of one of Britten's church parables, was a hit, its scariest and most overwhelming moments supplied by the sudden, brief, ferocious updating of St Magnus's martyrdom to the time of Nazi Germany.

With The Fires of London, a very special music troupe who were, more than anyone else, the embodiment of Davies's music at that time, the festival had an already famous team of virtuoso performers as its basis. Its members performed not only Davies but Bach and Beethoven. The adroit, eloquent soloists from the Fires - flautist, clarinettist, hornist, violinist, cellist - were welcome presences around town before and after performances. Their brilliant, idiosyncratic timpanist and percussionist, Greg Knowles, would later inspire Davies to compose a captivating, intricate work for Hungarian cimbalom specially for him. From year to year, the Fires established themselves as vital, radiant figureheads of the festival, sharing their charismatic roles with Davies himself.

By its second year, the mould of the festival had begun to set. In an increasingly crowded programme, requiring audiences to dash from one venue to another at different times of day, there would be a Friday opening performance and a closing concert in the middle of the following week. Sunday became 'Stromness day', with a fine afternoon recital and later a piece of music theatre in the gothic intimacy of the old Academy Hall. Recitalists - Bernard Roberts playing Beethoven, Gennadi Rozhdestvensky and his wife Victoria Postnikova in piano duets - tended to be chosen for intelligent musicality rather than glitter. The Fires revived *Miss Donnithorne's Maggot*, *Revelation and Fall*, *Vesalii Icones*, the *Missa Super l'Homme Armé*, the masterly *Eight Songs for a Mad King*, and other Davies works already established outside Orkney. But, whether in Stromness or Kirkwall, there were also Davies premieres each year. In the exquisite short instrumental opera, *Le Jongleur de Notre Dame*, each player 'voiced' a specific role.

In the witty, melodious, satirical *Cinderella*, Orkney schoolchildren, trained by the resourceful music teacher Glenys Hughes (a pillar of the festival, now its director), replaced the Fires. Davies's modern gloss on the Perrault fairy tale was not the first of his works to fall foul of the local music critic, Clive Strutt, who regarded its cheerful subversiveness as an insult to the armed services. For him, Davies was an intruder who was merely exploiting Orkney and who needed to be curbed. For a while, Davies did indeed seem to

Extracts from letters printed in *The Orcadian* from 1979, voicing Mr Strutt's (Orkney-based composer and music critic) criticisms of the festival.

April 17, 1986

"...the St Magnus Festival is, and always has been, primarily a publicity base for the promotion of Mr Davies's professional career as a composer. Everything else in the festival is incidental to this, however skilfully it may be represented in terms of cultural benefits to the community..."

May 1, 1986

"...In effect, the whole community is robbed in order to indulge a tiny minority of 'new music' enthusiasts..."

Extract representing a series of printed replies to the letters of Mr Strutt.

"The St Magnus Festival exists and is flourishing. It is centred around, but is by no means only concerned with, the work of a locally-based composer who also happens to be a world-class musician willing to put his talents at the service of this community. His status at the top of his profession means that the festival is one of the major events featuring contemporary music in Europe and is an immeasurable boon to its financing and to its attractiveness for visiting artists of the first rank."

Ian McQueen, composer
The Orcadian,
August 19, 1982

soft-pedal his contribution to the festival. But without him the whole event would have lost impetus and have ceased to attract supporters from far afield who now regarded it as an essential date in their calendar.

As a critic from elsewhere, I found the festival essential, too. With a major - often new - work in every concert, there was plenty to write about. One year, it's true, there seemed to be little by Davies himself, other than 'something' on the last night for the late, lamented, wonderfully droll Richard Hughes (Glenys's husband) to play on the cathedral organ, but it turned out to be something on the vast scale of a masterpiece by Messiaen.

The soft-spoken Davies, apart from being a presence at every event, was always happy to be interviewed, though his frank, sharp comments about the oil industry, about uranium and similarly unwelcome developments which he eagerly attacked in *Black Pentecost* and other works, sometimes made his devoted manager, Judy Arnold, afraid to open the next day's paper. And although, before we all used e-mail, it could be difficult phoning hundreds of words to a busy Edinburgh copy-taker (on one occasion I couldn't find a working phone box other than in the Stromness Hotel,

where a rock band was playing), the challenges of one of the world's most northerly festivals were always worth facing.

But in the course of my own fourteen years of uninterrupted attendance, there were inevitably changes, not invariably for the better. On one occasion my paper went on strike and I was ordered to fly home (I didn't). There were years when quality control appeared to falter. The disbanding of the Fires - mainly, so far as I could see, because Davies had moved on to other sorts of music - seemed regrettable, to say the least. A performance by Isaac Stern, with André Previn as conductor, seemed foreign to the spirit of the festival - and Davies's Violin Concerto, which they performed, seems not in retrospect to have been one of his major works. The Phoenix cinema, as a setting for popular concerts, proved squalid and acoustically inadequate, but has at last been replaced.

Yet what had begun as an intimate event, if it was to develop its public, was bound to grow in scale. The good thing has been that, in spite of pressures to broaden its scope, it has inspired so much of importance and so much to remember. No work, for me, sums up Davies's Orkney more profoundly than *The Blind Fiddler*, one of the largest of his settings of George Mackay Brown, an interlacing of seven songs and seven dances, first heard in St Magnus Cathedral at sunset with the adorable Mary Thomas, of the Fires, as singer. Here, in music of the softest subtlety, Davies encapsulated all that Orkney means to him. Whether in conveying the menace of a distant storm, or the peacefulness of a pair of pebbles, or shells, or tiny bells brushing gently against each other, he caught the magic of the place. Walking alone round Kirkwall harbour after the work's premiere, I could hear Davies's music haunting every natural sound.

That, as Britten knew, is what it means to hear music in the surroundings in which it was written. That is what Orkney means to Davies, and what such a festival as the St Magnus should be about. And, we should all be thankful, it is still happening.

the composers

New music has always had a strong platform at The St Magnus Festival, which, from the beginning, has had a committed, on-going policy to commission new work - often from young composers at the beginning of their careers. This has resulted in some exciting pieces of music, and several of the composers have gone on to great acclaim. Some have returned to Orkney to develop their links with the festival and the local community through education projects in schools or other collaborations.

The Summer School for Young Composers, set up by Peter Maxwell Davies on Hoy, in association with the Scottish Chamber Orchestra, was another enriching source of new material for the festival, and incidentally cast an Orkney spell on many of the students who attended the course. Several went on to write festival pieces, or became involved in creative multi-media productions with the local community, such as the ambitious production of *The Beggar's Opera* in 1994.

This robust and innovative aspect of the festival, and the fact that its associated composer, Peter Maxwell Davies, has written a steady stream of new music for festival audiences, entices many contemporary music lovers to the islands, who have become regular festival-goers.

Gunnie Moberg

Ian McQueen, 1979.

I've been involved in the festival since it started twenty-five years ago when, as a member of the Cathedral Choir, I sang a small solo in an Ian McQueen piece. I sang from high up in the gallery of the cathedral and I remember feeling hugely excited. For me, every festival has been the same.
Vivia Leslie
former Cathedral Choir member

Ian McQueen festival composer 1978, 1979, 1986

I was aware of the plans for the first St Magnus Festival while I was studying composition in Denmark with Per Norgård between 1976-77. I remember the grainy grey of the first programme; the tremendous trepidation that went with a new enterprise launched by people unused to such ambitious efforts and proceeding almost as an act of faith.

I remember the tremendous impression made by the first performance of *The Martyrdom of St Magnus*; I really wished I'd been there and was determined to take part in another festival. Little did I know how soon it would be, when Max asked me to write a short choral work for the St Magnus Cathedral Singers for the very next festival in 1978!

I then got my hands dirty - mixing with the extraordinary dynamics created by the small but highly motivated group who had gathered around Archie and Elizabeth Bevan and Norman Mitchell, to realise the more ambitious plans for the second festival.

It seems unbelievable now, when the St Magnus Festival is as much a part of the Orkney scene as the Ring of Brodgar or the Old Man of Hoy - it seems to have always been there! Nevertheless, it aroused controversy and hostility among people who felt very threatened by what seemed to them its audacity and aspiration back then. Ultimately, I don't feel (in retrospect of course: there's a deal of vitriol and indignity in some early post-festival editions of *The Orcadian*!) that this was such a bad thing! There are egos involved in these things by their very nature, and sensitive artists are easily bruised; but latterly peaceful co-existence has re-established itself.

People have come to realise that, beyond the personal opinions and factions to do with style and ideas, the festival has brought a panoply of beautiful and unexpected new artistic riches to the islands, often from beyond the confines of Britain and Scandinavia - Orkney's traditional cultural allies. One thinks of Gennadi Rozhdestvensky's and his wife, Victoria Postnikova's visit from Russia in 1981, or the appearance of Isaac Stern from the US to play Max's Violin Concerto in 1986, to name but three.

When I began work on my poor little number in late 1977 (I was twenty four and it went by the modest name of *Infinity Contained*) I soon learned what highly professional company I was in! The initial draft - replete with all sorts of avant garde trumpery of the time - was soundly rejected, and I was flown up to Kirkwall on a BA flight, hastily arranged by the irrepressible Jack Ridgway, to learn a few lessons in community musical relations which have stood me in good stead ever since!

I suppose the main influence on me among all the gifted and unique talents that have made up the creativity of Orkney during the past twenty five years, has been that of Glenys Hughes and her late and sadly missed husband, Dick. I shan't embarrass Glenys by enumerating all the lessons they taught me regarding musical standards of professionalism and dedication, but anyone

previous page: *Time Flight* rehearsal with Ian McQueen, 1979.

who has attended the festival as performer or audience member must realise their incalculable contribution to the festival's formative years right up to Glenys taking up her present position as festival director.

This was especially felt by me during the preparations for the work I wrote for the third festival at Glenys's specific request - the children's opera *Time Flight*. This was conceived as a piece about the history and ecology of Orkney at a time when it was threatened by uranium exploitation. Some people disapproved of this space-age/stone-age parable, thinking it was 'too adult' for these tender chicks. However, the kids loved it and Glenys was with me all the way! The result was a performance standard which most composers can only dream of, achieved by Glenys and the peripatetic musicians working in the islands along with the completely dedicated and talented children of Papdale Primary School and Stromness Primary Brass Band. I am tremendously grateful to them all, even if the child stars are now grown up with kids of their own!

Judith Weir festival composer, 1979, 1981

After four extended stays at the festival and the Hoy Summer School, Orkney is my top suggestion to intending Scottish tourists. I'll leave the travel writing to someone better qualified, but I have to observe that I've never visited another place which so satisfyingly combines wild cragginess with hypnotic green calm. Does anywhere else have such a perfect selection of ancient stones and mysterious burial grounds, often lying incognito in someone's field? I particularly remember viewing the magical, timeless interior of Maeshowe thanks to the courtesy of its custodian who had just interrupted the washing-up in her nearby kitchen to let me in.

My earliest trips to the festival (I first visited in 1979) started out from Glasgow, and my memory is that it took about three days of non-synchronised buses, trains and boats (including a twenty four hour Sabbath Day halt somewhere in the Highlands) to get there; in those days, taking internal flights within Scotland was still a little recherché. But, having since heard countless such travellers' tales, especially from Hoy Summer School students so strapped for cash that they have, for instance, hitch-hiked and bicycled to their destination, I conclude that the element of pilgrimage is one of the festival's special qualities. For non-Orcadians, to get to the St Magnus Festival, you really have to want to go; and once you arrive, you may as well stay awhile and enjoy yourself.

I relished every mile of the way to my first visits. I had been commissioned to write new works for two of the earliest festivals (*King Harald Sails to Byzantium* in 1979, and *Isti Mirant Stella* in 1981), an honour which I still feel delighted about today. *King Harald Sails* is a tone poem based on an account, found in an Icelandic saga, of a very long-distance viking sea

Part of the magic of my festival visit was the opportunity to escape after my A levels from a grey, grimy Manchester to a place with wide open spaces.

Conducting my own piece in the cathedral was particularly exciting, because my music had never been played to so many people before.

My only uncomfortable experience of the whole trip occurred on a visit to Rousay. I was asked to talk at the local junior school about the piece my friends were about to play. I floundered horribly in my attempts to stimulate the children's interest. In fact, in my fifteen years as a university teacher I have never again faced anything so difficult!
Paul Wingfield
former pupil of Chetham's School of Music, Manchester festival composer, 1980

Judith Weir

Suzanne Jansen

voyage. It was a very experimental piece for me to write, a textural study of water and wave shapes. The instrumental parts can be exhausting to play (evoking that viking sea voyage very closely) and I remember that a lot of the early rehearsal time (under conductor Jan Latham-Koenig) was taken up with The Fires of London heroically navigating their way through some difficult finger-work. From that first performance I have retained an impression of the music being enfolded in the exceptional warmth, visual and sonic, of the interior of St Magnus Cathedral, another of the festival's unique assets.

Isti Mirant Stella is another illustration of viking times, this time an orchestral picture based on a 'frame' from the Bayeux Tapestry which shows an open sky with Halley's Comet appearing in it as a portent of disaster at the time of King Harold of England's coronation in 1066. It is a very still piece, save for a whoosh of energy, the musical equivalent of a comet. Stillness was not characteristic of Jerzy Maksymiuk, the extra-enthusiastic conductor who gave the first performance with the Scottish Chamber Orchestra, and I recall the first performance as being exceptionally fast, though full of vibrant energy; it's worth remembering that, at a world premiere, the music is unfamiliar not only to the audience, but often also to the composer! I still love this piece, which has since been played by many other orchestras and conductors.

At the time I wrote this music, in my mid-twenties, the St Magnus commissions offered me vital encouragement to keep working as a composer, and I know many colleagues have had the same experience. Max's intense understanding of the kind of support young composers need found further expression in his founding the Hoy Summer Schools. It was exciting to assist him teaching at the 1992 and 1993 schools. These fortnight-long courses could well be described as the 'outward bound' school of music. Quite a strenuous effort was required of the eight or so young composers on each course who had to write a complete piece for performance in a concert at the end of the two weeks whilst studying by day at Max's classes in Hoy Kirk and sometimes playing music most of the night in the Hoy Inn.

Composing music can be an annoying and obsessive activity, especially for young people who haven't at all worked out what they are trying to do, and I used to think that one of the course's main achievements was to get the students out of their cramped student rooms at home and into the fresh air, of which there is certainly a lot on Hoy. Max always advises young composers in a courteous and oblique way, and I think by inventing the course as he did, he was pointing out that you can combine hard compositional work (as he has) with a full life in the world, appreciating its beauties.

John Gray festival composer, 1984 and 1985

I remember working on the brass quintet piece, *Splitting the Difference*. I had finished Uni and had recently been on the summer course at Darmstadt and

The relationship between the Scottish Chamber Orchestra and Orkney found a focal point through Max's invitation to realise his plans to run a course for young composers on Hoy. Kathryn [McDowell, development manager of the SCO] took on the management of this, funds were raised and a team of SCO players spent the second week of the course working with Max and the composers in a unique creative environment.
Ian Ritchie, SCO managing director, 1984-1993, festival co-artistic director, 1988-1993

The Summer School for Composers on Hoy was my baby. I did it for eight years, and then you don't want to risk repeating yourself so the time came to stop. I loved it - it was a great thrill. All the preparations with the composers were wonderful. The SCO members came up too, and we always did a concert in the Hoy Kirk.
Peter Maxwell Davies (in conversation)

had returned home completely skint! Max asked to see some of my stuff and as a result he asked me to write a short piece for quintet - six minutes or so would do....

I set off writing six minutes worth at about a minute a month. It may have been all the Darmstadt stuff still ringing in my ears or the fact that I had so much time - whatever it was, the piece ended up a tad demanding, to say the least.

The players were more than patient, even though their comment that the piece almost ended up in the bin I thought a bit harsh at the time. They gave me the enduring advice; never ever give a piece to a brass player that has 'splitting' in the title.

They played splendidly. I was a bit dumbstruck by the whole thing. My grandfather, Captain Gray from Stromness, said it reminded him of seeing icebergs off the coast of South Georgia. The press noted I was a 'man of few words'.

I was asked to do something the following year - a piece for solo trumpet written for my brother, James. This was to be played during a lunchtime concert together with my own performance of *Domaines* by Boulez and a piece for bass guitar and tape written by me for my brother, David. He also prepared the dramatic lighting scheme for the Boulez. I called the trumpet piece *3 for Final* - I had to force myself to settle on something, and I eventually settled on 3 ideas.

James, as always, was very patient with me making him try out ideas at all times of the day. I even dragged him out of bed at one point! He went on to make the piece his own, and performed it at his audition for the Birmingham Conservatoire. Luckily for me he got in, and, I have just been told, was offered a scholarship because he was the first to perform a piece at audition specially written for him.

Gunnie Moberg

James and John Gray, 1985.

"..The sharp and atmospheric play of timbres in Gray's pithy 'Splitting the Difference', a promising work by a former pupil of Stromness Academy, demonstrates the festival's desire to encourage progressive local talents."
Conrad Wilson
The Scotsman, June, 1984.

Glenys Hughes festival director (in conversation)

In 1988 we commissioned James MacMillan to write a piece for the Scottish Chamber Orchestra. This was *Tryst*, which I think was Jimmy's first big orchestral commission and in many ways launched his career. But he was also our first composer in residence and did splendid work leading a composition project called *Upbeat to Tryst*. He took ideas from *Tryst* and encouraged the children to develop the ideas in their own compositions. The presentation of the children's work was a special event. Jimmy linked together what every school had done to make a long piece, and then wrote some short interlude pieces which were performed by players of the Scottish Chamber Orchestra - so there was that professional involvement too. Jimmy introduced the whole thing and it was really splendid. He was involved, too, with Max's Hoy Summer School for Composers, and co-led the course with Max, as did Judith

"The sharing of MacMillan's talents with Kirkwall and Stromness children has generated a series of instrumental inventions and dramatic tableaux attractively stitched together by the children themselves, not without a hint of minimalist and other influences, harnessed by the composer for their use."
Roderic Dunnett
The Times, June, 1989

James MacMillan

"...When they come to write the official biography of James MacMillan they will cite the premiere, in the cinema, of his 'Tryst', the centrepiece of this year's St Magnus Festival, as a turning point..."
The Sunday Times Scotland
June 11, 1989

Simon Holt

Weir, Sally Beamish and Alasdair Nicolson.

The festival did link into the Summer Schools to a certain extent. Composers that Max had felt were particularly outstanding we occasionally commissioned for the festival the following year.

James MacMillan   festival composer, 1989, 1991

I first attended the St Magnus Festival as a student in 1980. I was even then, as a young 19 year-old, fascinated by Maxwell Davies and the idealism behind the St Magnus Festival. I remember camping at the site in Kirkwall and wakening up in a puddle one morning! This did not put me off, however. I returned in 1988 to review the festival for *The Guardian*, and it was clear to me then that none of the idealism had dissipated.

Things began to move very quickly in the next few years, and I began writing prolifically. I was invited to be composer in residence in the run up to the festival in 1989. This involved a lot of visits to the two main secondary schools and some of the primary schools. The festival commissioned *Tryst* for that year, and it was premiered by the SCO. I subsequently assisted Max on the first couple of composers' courses on Hoy.

In 1991 the festival premiered my clarinet quintet *Tuireadh*. This took place at a very moving concert in St Magnus Cathedral, with James Campbell and the Allegri Quartet. The piece had been inspired by the *Piper Alpha* disaster and indeed was a response to a letter written to me by one of the dead men's mothers. This woman, her husband and some other relatives of the dead attended the concert.

Gerard McBurney   festival composer, 1992

In 1992, a small piece of mine, *My Gypsy Life*, was done in the cathedral. It wasn't a big occasion, a lunchtime concert with some odd distractions. But David James sang as though in a trance and I was so delighted to hear the noises that I'd invented swirl round that astonishing space that by then I knew quite well...[see *visitors*]

Simon Holt   festival composer, 1993

Although I have a feeling that my *Minotaur Games* foxed more than a few in the packed Phoenix cinema audience at the opening concert in the summer of 1993, I have only warm and vivid memories of it. Not to mention the huge skies, stone circles, Maeshowe and cullen skink at the Creel Restaurant. I was honoured to be invited.

Glenys Hughes (in conversation)

One big project which was a direct link between the Hoy Summer School for Composers and the festival was the local production of *The Beggar's Opera*, directed by George Rendall in 1994. It was Ian Ritchie's inspired idea to invite six of the most outstanding composers - selected by Max - from recent Hoy Summer Schools to each make their own arrangements of half a dozen songs from the opera and to add pieces of incidental music. The music would then be played by an ensemble from the SCO.

We invited Alasdair Nicolson as music director since he was not only a fine composer but had a wealth of experience in the musical theatre. The whole thing was a nightmare of course - hounding six composers for their scores, getting the instrumental parts copied - then combining cast with the SCO musicians. Some of the composers had written fairly outlandish arrangements of the tunes, so the cast suddenly had to sing the songs against this very challenging accompaniment. To compound the difficulties, the band and conductor were placed at the back of the stage as there was no way of constructing a pit. I remember sitting in the front row with a torch giving essential cues to the singers. It actually turned out to be very successful and a memorable production, but rather frightening to put together! [See *drama*]

Alasdair Nicolson festival composer, 1994, 1996

My first ever visit to Orkney was on a windswept Saturday afternoon to begin work on *The Beggar's Opera* project. I had never travelled in a small propeller plane before and I'm sure that Glenys met a rather white-faced young composer wondering if the plane had landed in the right place. However, I was soon welcomed into the community of the St Magnus Festival and from that moment on have spent many happy times at the festival and with Max on the Hoy composition course. As a west coast islander from Skye I feel a strong affinity with the life on Orkney. I guess every performer has travel stories to do with the festival; it goes with the territory. On subsequent visits I shall never forget getting ten feet above the runway in Kirkwall and then taking off again to return to Inverness, or the flight which was cancelled because someone had seen a mouse on the plane.

The Beggar's Opera was a large-scale community production filling the Phoenix cinema with set, costume, local actors and singers and members of the Scottish Chamber Orchestra. That festival also saw the premiere of my piece *PUNCH!*, commissioned for the Chamber Group of Scotland which has become my most performed work, and has led to several commissions.

In subsequent years I have been back with new works to St Magnus. There were the dance collaborations *Lord of the Mirrors* and *The Stormwatchers*; the first based on a poem and the second on a radio play, both by George

"Six young composers flexed their muscles and produced some dazzling arrangements and incidental music for the St Magnus Players' bawdy and splendidly lit production of 'The Beggar's Opera'. In a riotous extravaganza of styles - every pastiche under the sun from lean Stravinsky to the over-the-top opulence of Richard Strauss - the six composers (Paul Archbold, GP Cribari, Alasdair Edwards, Jennifer Martin, Magnus Robb and Edward Rushton) together with an onstage SCO ensemble under the direction of Alasdair Nicolson, completely enlivened the production and gave an exemplary display of what this craft-learning business is all about."
Michael Tumelty
The Herald, June 20, 1994

Peter Maxwell Davies, Alasdair Nicolson, 1994.

Gunnie Moberg

Mackay Brown [see *drama*]. In the same year my opera *Cat Man's Tale* arrived on its tour, and, as I have done on many occasions, I took great pleasure and almost local pride in showing the company round all the places of interest.

Orkney and the St Magnus Festival have not only offered me opportunities for work but have also acted as inspiration for several of my pieces; *Don't Explain*, *The Isle is Full of Noises*, and *Stone Rituals* have all been written while working there.

Steve King principal viola, Scottish Chamber Orchestra
festival composer, 1995, 1997 (in conversation)

I used to do a great deal of work with the SCO educational unit and the festival often asked me to become involved in educational projects. One time, Glenys and Dick came to stay with me and I took them to Capercaillie. They hadn't heard them live before, and they were amazed. Glenys wondered if she could get them up to the festival the next year [1995] and asked me to write a piece for them. So I wrote *Farewell*, which also involved school pupils as performers - there were 125 kids in a choir, accompanied by a young strings band. The piece lasted about fifteen minutes and was written in a folky style. It was a great hit with Dick [see *the Festival Chorus*].

The best thing of all was that I got to write a piece for the bells of St Magnus. I am nuts about bells - I have my own set of hand bells which I use a great deal in educational and other projects, and I had always wanted to write something for the cathedral bells, and ring it from the bell tower. I asked Glenys if I could ring a bell call for the Festival Service in 1997. I wrote this piece which integrated change ringing systems (which is the English way of ringing bells) with African rhythms and a bit of what they do here (which is a Nordic calling system) - the bell call gets faster and faster and finally you see people running into church! I practised first thing in the morning - waking up Kirkwall - then played it for the Festival Service. It was great.

Then I asked if it would be possible to write and play something for the millennium, and the authorities agreed to that. In England all the bells rang on midday on January the first. I thought it would be a great thing to do up here as well - and so I rang the bells with a millennium piece, just before the New Year's Day ba' game. That was really good fun, and it was something that I will look back on as a personal musical landmark.

Marc Yeats festival composer 1997, 2000

Meeting Max on Hoy at the summer school in 1994 really did change my life. Apart from all the musical spin-offs that occurred after this event, I developed a very fond relationship with Hoy and in particular, Rackwick. I loved Max's

Steve King, 1995.

"Months of hard work had been put in by the local performers and it paid off beautifully as they came together with the members of Capercaillie to really capture the atmosphere of 'Farewell', leaving a few damp eyes in the house at the end."
RL
The Orcadian, June 29, 1995

little house, Bunertoon, and always enjoyed staying there. I was very drawn to the natural drama of Rackwick; the sea and cliffs, the beautiful sandy beach.

I met Archie and Elizabeth Bevan through Max. What lovely people, always so hospitable and kind; you can have a meaningful conversation with them about anything ranging from politics, through religion and on to art. I've stayed with them on many occasions and whenever possible, shared a clandestine roll-up cigarette with Elizabeth in the garden.

1997 was the year of the premiere of my festival commission, *The Anatomy of Air*. The work was very impressionistic, abstract and a little savage. The critics hated it, as did the local rag, but I never was good at being a conservative and polite artist. But after the concert, one elderly concert-goer said to me on her way out - 'Your music reminded me of the weather at the bottom of my garden in winter' - which was a success. It was also what the music was about!

When I visit Max now, it's up to Sanday. The island has a very different atmosphere to Hoy and the new house is spacious and well-equipped. No more outside toilet and tin coffin shower! I have walked around the coast of the island which is quite beautiful and unique in an understated, quiet way.

Marc Yeats, Peter Maxwell Davies.

Sally Beamish festival composer, 1999

I didn't make it up to Orkney myself until 1994, when Max asked me to be his assistant at the Hoy Summer School for Composers. But Orkney had already played a large part in my life; in 1989 my husband Robert Irvine was part of the SCO quartet on the same course, and came home full of enthusiasm for the magic of the place, and the people he had met, including James MacMillan. Both Jimmy and Max were instrumental in persuading us to start a new life in Scotland.

In 1994 the Chamber Group of Scotland, the group that Robert, Jimmy and I had formed in 1991, was invited to play at the St Magnus Festival. Again, to my disappointment, I was unable to go, and again, Robert came home glowing with inspiration. When I finally experienced Orkney for the first time, later that year, the two weeks on Hoy more than fulfilled my anticipation. It was the beginning of an association with Orkney, and with friends there, especially Terry and Jean Thomson, with whom we stayed, who have become close family friends.

When I was commissioned by the festival to write a saxophone concerto for John Harle and the SCO, and discovered that the premiere was to be on the summer solstice, all my experiences of Orkney began to come together - the history, the landscape, the atmosphere and the people. *The Imagined Sound of Sun on Stone* is not only directly inspired by the idea of the light entering Maeshowe on the winter solstice, but is also a celebration of the unique quality of light, and the special spirituality of the islands.

"Beamish's cogently constructed, exotically colourful 20-minute movement, rising to superb climaxes of pagan wildness, though not overlooking the Christian heritage of psalm and chant, received its premiere - with John Harle a soloist of barbarous splendour - on the summer solstice."
The Sunday Times, June, 1999

Stuart MacRae   festival composer, 2001 (in conversation)

I had been wanting to come to Orkney for years, and when I heard my piece, *Portrait II*, was going to be played there in 2001, I jumped at the chance of coming to hear it. I must admit I was rather nervous beforehand; during the performance, however, I just sat back and enjoyed it - and the BBC SSO chamber group played it beautifully. I had a very good view, and it sounded lovely from out there because I could hear all the detail. There are eight sections at the end of the piece with an unfixed order. The conductor can choose to fix them in advance, or, as Martyn Brabbins did, he can improvise as he goes along. He had cards with the numbers of the sections, and held them up to the orchestra before each section so that they would know which one to play next. It was great fun, and adds a sense of drama to a live performance to see something like that. And, of course, the piece is different every time you hear it.

Without doubt, I will be back in Orkney again. I don't know when, but try keeping me away!

Fraser Trainer   festival composer, 1999 and 2001

The Orkney guide book says: 'You will return. It is a sweet compulsion.'

I've made this 'sweet return' to Orkney on a few occasions now and have visited the St Magnus Festival twice to rehearse and perform works I've written for local school children and professional musicians.

In 2001, it was the turn of school children from Kirkwall and Stromness to join forces with London Brass to give the world premiere of *Pulse Fiction*, the third movement of which I called 'Sweet Return'.

Meeting young people is always incredibly refreshing, and in Orkney there is an immediate and warm welcome - you're a special guest, there's a great deal of respect shown and maybe some nerves too, but it's a new experience for everyone. Next there's a time of getting to know each other - it's easy to talk too fast and you can feel you're bringing the noise of the city with you. The children talk quietly and you listen to the sound of that beautifully rounded accent. It's a joy just to hear the sound of voices and names that you know will stick in the memory. Finally we really start to get on. We work hard and have fun.

For me, this festival has a very special feel, mainly because of the character and generosity of the local people. The long-held tradition of local musicians performing in the festival makes you feel very secure as a composer. It means that the artistic work the young people contribute is taken seriously and given centrestage. I hope it continues this radical philosophy and that this area of work is nurtured and developed. After all, that unique musical and human contact is so important. That's why we make that sweet return.

orchestras & ensembles

Seventy musicians jammed into a small venue is an awesome sight in Orkney, and an amazing sound, but the logistics of transporting an orchestra to these relatively remote islands are a nightmare, (not to mention the ever-present fear of fog in an Orkney midsummer). Despite the potential difficulties, however, the orchestras and smaller ensembles keep coming and they are the essential underpinning force in every festival.

Old friends of the festival are the BBC Scottish Symphony Orchestra, the Scottish Chamber Orchestra, the BBC Philharmonic Orchestra and the Royal Philharmonic Orchestra. With the help of an injection of cash from the Post Office, through the late Ian Barr (the Scottish chairman), the RPO was the first full-size orchestra to come to the festival in 1986, taking it into a whole new league, where it has tenaciously remained.

Ian Ritchie, former managing director of the Scottish Chamber Orchestra, cemented the ties between the festival and the SCO by becoming a co-artistic director of the festival in 1988 - a position he held until 1993, when he left the SCO.

Ensembles such as Psappha, London Sinfonietta, the Nash Ensemble, the BT Scottish Ensemble and London Brass, amongst many others, have been welcome visitors, the players often undertaking educational and other collaborative projects with local musicians of all ages, and delighting audiences with their dazzling individual virtuosity.

Trevor Green former manager, BBC SSO, BBC Philharmonic
former head of music, BBC North of England

**BBC Scottish
Symphony Orchestra**
1979, 1984, 1987, 1991, 1998
and 2001

I first arrived in Scotland in 1970 to take up a full time position with the BBC Scottish Symphony Orchestra as a member of the trumpet section. Although I had been a regular visitor to Scotland my travels had not taken me much further than Glasgow and the BBC orchestra. Through various career moves and decisions I found myself the orchestra manager in 1977, and in all this time I had never crossed the Pentland Firth to visit the Orkney Islands.

I was delighted when the invitation came to take the orchestra to the 1979 festival with our chief conductor, Karl Anton Rickenbacher. In those days orchestral 'touring' was limited to odd visits to Edinburgh, Perth, Stirling and other such exotic centres of culture, so a visit 'across the water' to the festival was quite a treat and something we all looked forward to.

I had known of Peter Maxwell Davies since my student days at the Royal College of Music in Manchester. He was a sort of 'prodigal son' in reputation, and had certainly stirred up the very staid and conservative compositional school that had long been established in the 'North'. Together with Sandy Goehr, Harrison Birtwhistle, Elgar Howarth, the pianist John Ogden and David Ellis, he savaged the principles of post-war composition and earned a reputation for having created the 'Manchester School', a maverick group of highly talented musicians who were hungry to explore new frontiers. I remember as a student being told stories of Max living on a remote island in outer-most Scotland without water, electricity, sanitation and sleeping in a coffin surrounded by candles, writing great works of art! Highly exaggerated, but there was still an element of truth, and in those days this was very eccentric behaviour for a 'north country lad' from Salford!

Through this first visit to Orkney and my meeting with the people behind the festival I have held dear the memories of numerous visits and the rich experiences I have observed. This is a very special place, and those fortunate enough to visit and sample the hospitality, enthusiasm and warmth extended to all guests are very privileged; the experience is heart-warming.

Travelling an orchestra can be a logistical nightmare, especially where accommodation is concerned. It is just not possible to provide hotel accommodation for a symphony orchestra in Orkney without involving vast expense and having all the musicians split up over the whole island. So we were to be 'billeted' in private homes around Kirkwall. Persuading my musicians to give up the per-diem facility (a generous daily allowance which can provide sufficient funds to keep an orchestra 'well-oiled' for the duration of a tour) was not an easy task, and some of them were uncomfortable at being in a private dwelling. Eventually they overcame any fears, settled down and made new friends with their host families. Many of these friendships have continued beyond festivals and return visits are not uncommon for holidays and reciprocal exchange.

Peter Maxwell Davies, Trevor Green.

During many of the complex negotiations for the BBC Scottish visit, one individual stands out for me. Jack Ridgway was listed in the early festival programmes as 'publicity', but my memories of him are linked with travel and flights. Even with an orchestra the size of the BBC Scottish, it was not possible to accommodate musicians and the instruments on the same flight. Jack was quite brilliant at arranging all the logistical details for the musical freight to travel by sea (and arrive on time for rehearsals and concerts) and the musicians to fly despite the problems associated with the weather. He was always very pleasant, most affable and good company. As one of the first points of contact for many visiting ensembles he was a superb ambassador for the festival and gave much confidence to those from the south who thought they were at the end of the world.

Hugh Macdonald   director, BBC Scottish Symphony Orchestra

Ask any member of the BBC Scottish Symphony Orchestra to nominate their favourite 'gig' and the St Magnus Festival is bound to be near the top of the list along, perhaps, with the BBC Proms in London or Boston's Symphony Hall. Since its early years the festival has been a recurring pleasure for SSO players who have loved the combination of eager curiosity, sophistication and enthusiasm that is the hallmark of St Magnus audiences. How refreshing to emerge from the cathedral after an SSO performance of Max's monumental and intellectually challenging Second Taverner Fantasy, and overhear a rich Orcadian voice remark 'Well, I'm not sure if I understood it, but I'm glad to have heard it!'. How inspiring to have the chance to play, in smaller groups, to intensely concentrating school pupils in Stronsay or Papa Westray - or later to their parents (taking time off from silage-making) packed into the island church. And how heart-warming to see the audience expand as the late-but-not-entirely-lamented Phoenix has made way for the bigger and acoustically miles better Pickaquoy Centre. And what an object lesson in 'arts management' is this wonderful, exciting, life-enhancing festival that's run in the most caring, professional way by Glenys, her board and their legion of volunteers.

St Magnus Cathedral, 2001.

Martyn Brabbins   conductor, BBC SSO, BBC Philharmonic

The St Magnus Festival has a unique appeal for performers and audience alike. Geographically somewhat remote, logic dictates that once artists have arrived in Kirkwall it is imperative that they remain on the islands for an extended period. This element of 'residency' is so important to visiting musicians, giving them the opportunity to meet outside rehearsal and performance situations. I know just how much the BBC SSO have enjoyed their recent trips to Orkney, able to relax in familiar and friendly surroundings, to feel really valued and appreciated by the fantastic Orkney audiences. No pressure as on a normal 'tour' to travel to the next town on the itinerary, to check in at the next anonymous hotel and this year [2001] to have the privilege of travelling to the smaller islands and share in the music-making of the local community.

My particular passion for Orkney hit me hard on my first trip to the festival in 1998. The fervour and commitment of the Festival Chorus, the power and inspiration of the magnificent cathedral, the festival's creators and generators - Max, Glenys, George - dedicated visionary individuals.

Then the islands themselves. What visitor to Maeshowe has not felt awe-struck at the majesty and ingenuity of this neolithic masterpiece? The exuberance and energy of the beautiful Ring of Brodgar intoxicates. The charming Broch of Gurness is in an unrivalled situation for a 'quiet life'. The magnificence of the western coast from Yesnaby to the Old Man of Hoy has drawn me back on each visit.

The 25th St Magnus Festival epitomised for me what an event of this kind should aspire to. A true celebration of art and culture, firmly seated in and taking its very life blood from its local environment. I will never forget the concert at the Pickaquoy Centre on June 24, 2001. Rarely have I felt so at one with great composers - Richard Strauss, Kodaly and Tchaikovsky - with inspired performers - BBC SSO, Festival Chorus and John Daszak, and with an inspiring audience.

Amanda Shearman   cello, BBC SSO (in conversation)

I first came up to Orkney in 1998, and we were there for midsummer's night, which was incredible - a wonderful experience. In 2001 we did self-catering, which makes it feel more like a holiday than work. At other festivals you sometimes feel that you are dragged in and you play and then go. At the Orkney festival you actually stay two, three or four days and get involved with the whole thing.

Groups from the orchestra went out to the islands; two string groups - one to Stronsay and one to Sanday - and a woodwind group went to Papa Westray. That was amazing. Apparently our principal bassoon player went in to talk to the children and asked them if anyone knew what the bassoon was. A hand went up and the suggestion came that it was a didgeridoo - which was a pretty good guess!

Martyn Brabbins is a very good conductor. He has amazing talent, particularly with contemporary music. He just understands it and never puts a foot wrong when he's conducting; it could be the most complicated rhythm and you just know exactly where to play - he's always right. He is very relaxed at rehearsals - he does what he has to do, but there's no feeling of panic. He's passionate about the orchestra, and that comes across.

Eric Dunlea trumpet, BBC SSO (in conversation)

Our trip to Rousay was wonderful in 2001; the sun shone and the sea was like the Mediterranean - it was so pretty. We were met and went to the primary school, which has twenty four children. They were lovely kids and it was a very easy, relaxed atmosphere. We had lunch with them and the school dinner was stunning - best I've had in years. It was a beef stew with potatoes and vegetables - and for dessert they had local strawberries and shortbread. Fantastic! No wonder the kids look so healthy. And they did seem to enjoy the concert, and were very responsive. One kid kept on conducting, unfortunately not quite in time - but it was a challenge!

After the concert we had great fun - we were met by our hosts and lavishly entertained and I was driven all over the island. At the evening concert there must have been about thirty-five or forty people there. It was a wonderful atmosphere in the school and steaming hot; somebody opened a window to let in a glorious sea breeze. After the concert we went to the local restaurant, which doubles as the pub, and Edwin the landlord played the most divine accordion you've heard in your life - he's so rhythmical and has a very light touch. It was a fantastic delight. We were sitting at the side drinking with our guests and some of the locals, and then Mark got the instruments out of the car and we joined him. He did a solo on the trumpet - a most plaintive and beautiful tune - over the harbour and this lovely scenery. It was just idyllic - a very special night for all of us. We know it was unique and it will never happen again. It's a wonderful atmosphere - a wonderful festival.

The festival is really well put together - and it's all so cosy. We really enjoyed performing in the isles in 2001, and the socialising afterwards. It is amazing how much information you can pick up just sitting in an Orkney cafe!
Gordon Rigby
timpanist, BBC SSO
(in conversation)

Ian Ritchie managing director, Scottish Chamber Orchestra 1984-93; festival co-artistic director, 1988-1993

When I arrived in Edinburgh, in the summer of 1984, to manage the Scottish Chamber Orchestra, it had just celebrated its tenth anniversary. In a relatively short space of time, it had come a long way and, indeed, had travelled considerable distances throughout Europe, across the Atlantic, to the Far East and, most importantly, in the light of subsequent events, to Orkney. International touring, always an important ambassadorial and artistic corollary to the orchestra's work at home, had become increasingly competitive - with chamber orchestras springing up all over the place, including the emerging bands of early music specialists - and decreasingly lucrative. All agreed that it was essential for the orchestra to be distinctive and, in my view, this distinction could not be derived exclusively from the roster of international guest soloists, then as now quite rightly cherished by the orchestra, or within the mainstream classical (and its adjoining baroque and early romantic) repertoire. It was clear that the SCO should not try to be like any other orchestra but instead find and develop its own true voice.

The Scottish Chamber Orchestra
1981, 1983, 1985, 1989, 1990, 1992, 1993, 1995, 1997, 1999

Ian Ritchie

Gunnie Moberg

"The St Magnus Festival can offer an object lesson to those who genuinely want to avoid orchestras becoming musical 'museums'."
John Warnaby
Musical Opinion
September, 1989

When Max started his association with the Scottish Chamber Orchestra and embarked on the Strathclyde Concertos project, the number of Max premieres at the festival dropped dramatically, as all the SCO new works had their premieres in Glasgow. By 1991, Max had further associations with the BBC Philharmonic in Manchester and the Royal Philharmonic in London, and he was writing large numbers of works for them, which were presented either in their own series in London and Manchester, or where there were special invitations to other venues. Thus, the chances of a Max premiere in Orkney during all this later period were much slimmer than before.
Judy Arnold, manager,
Sir Peter Maxwell Davies

I have always held the view that performers need composers at least as much as, and probably more than, composers require performers - and that audiences need both. A large portion of the classical music world and a majority of orchestras had ignored this viewpoint for the best part of 50 years and were failing to equate the shrinking audience with a stagnating and evaporating repertoire. Peter Maxwell Davies had already written for and conducted the SCO, and it was clear, from the shared vision of the quality of the music making, that a special relationship was in the offing. So we invited Max to assume the newly created post of associate composer/conductor in 1985, the first orchestral position of its kind in modern times (although now much imitated), and fortunately he accepted. At around the same time, the SCO appointed its first development manager, by which we meant 'development' in its broadest and deepest senses: a process of growth for the orchestra and all those who might participate in its work as creators, performers and audiences. When Max offered to write ten concertos for the orchestra, with its members as soloists, the SCO entered an era which, in my view (even without the rose-tinted spectacles), stands as the most significant and influential of its short history. The Strathclyde Concertos, as they were soon to be labelled, became a national and international paradigm for the development of music in schools, of composers in the community and of new work for orchestras in the concert hall (simultaneously).

The SCO's development work, and particularly its projects involving school children, found a natural partner in the festival during the late eighties and early nineties. This is hardly surprising given that Archie Bevan and Glenys Hughes, artistic co-directors of the festival during this period, were influential teachers of English and music respectively in their day jobs; and the festival had a long track record of children's performances of works composed by Max especially for them. The efforts of Archie, Glenys and others were in due course rewarded by strong, official and political support of the festival's educational role within the community. Kathryn McDowell had, by now, joined the committee and the official relationship between the SCO and the St Magnus Festival, involving biennial residences, could be fruitful at every level.

Glenys Hughes festival director

Most orchestras and performing organisations now have an education department and are doing some form of outreach and development work, but, at that time, the SCO was really quite outstanding in what it was doing. Ian Ritchie, their managing director, and Kathy McDowell, the development manager of the orchestra, had great vision and imagination. It was a very exciting development for the festival when Ian became a co-artistic director in 1988, and ties between the orchestra and the festival became very close.

There were so many festival projects which involved the SCO: musicians from the orchestra played Max's incidental music for community productions of *Witch* and *The Road to Colonus*, provided string quartet accompaniment for a performance of Britten's *The Little Sweep* and joined some Grammar School instrumentalists in the pit for Richard Rodney Bennett's *All the King's Men*. In 1995 the SCO helped set up our gamelan project *Island to Island* linking the music of Indonesia with Shakespeare's *The Tempest*. And of course the SCO's Steve King has been an inspired leader of some of our most memorable community and schools' events.

Ian Ritchie

The St Magnus Festival was created to be creative, naturally joining together invention, performance and participation into what Benjamin Britten once called the 'sacred triangle' and which reflected the spirit of Peter Maxwell Davies, George Mackay Brown and their fellow Orcadian pioneers.

Throughout history, Orkney has been an international meeting place, where visitors and incomers receive a wonderful welcome. There is no doubt that the tradition and capacity of the local community to absorb new people reflects a depth and richness of Orcadian culture. So we have, in the St Magnus Festival, a natural phenomenon that is at once local and international, traditional and creative, amateur and professional and so on. The Scottish Chamber Orchestra's affinity with the festival goes beyond its important shared relationship with Peter Maxwell Davies, its musical collaborations with James MacMillan and many other composers, a shared commitment to education work and community involvement. Both, in their own ways, are world forces because they are, first of all, local forces. The SCO on tour is of international interest because it carries the fruit of Scottish creativity, and always a little piece of Orkney too, within its veins and within its vice. The best work of the orchestra is characterised by a sense of place, something which is unmistakable to the eyes and ears of everybody who comes into contact with the St Magnus Festival.

Post script: An Orkney Wedding, with Snowfall
When I first visited Orkney in the mid-eighties, I immediately felt at home. By the time I had been invited to become one of the artistic co-directors of the St Magnus Festival in 1988, that sense of belonging naturally deepened but it was only in the following year that I discovered that my great-grandfather had been brought up in Orkney before emigrating to New Zealand while still in his teens. My father spoke of a church, apparently known until quite recently as the Ritchie Kirk, built by my great-great-grandfather during the course of his ministry in Orkney. In 1992, one of my better-informed relatives pointed me in the direction of Rousay and that summer during the festival, Judy Arnold

I see Orkney as a second, spiritual, home. My wife and I come back as much as we possibly can - usually more than once a year - which isn't as much as we would like! I've performed in Orkney on occasions with my string quartet Quartz, which is made up from SCO players. It is special because I feel it is really mine, and my repertoire, and we have done some very rewarding educational work around the schools with that. In 1996, we played on the theatre ship, the *Fitzcarraldo*, when it came to Orkney for the first time. That was great fun.
Steve King, principal viola, SCO (in conversation)

I remember flying above a streaky slate sea on my first visit to Orkney, and as we made slow and bumpy progress some complexions turned green! The last concert I played there included *Helios* by Thea Musgrave, in which Nicholas Daniel was outstanding.

In addition to the consistent warmth and hospitality shown by Orcadians were some (mis)adventures. Running to escape a shower, I slipped on a mossy slab, landing on my new, white and overpriced jacket, turning it bright green before the concert. On another occasion a colleague turned up a quarter of an hour late for a live broadcast, the Orcadian surroundings being so relaxing.

Maurice Checker, 2nd oboe, SCO, 1976-1998

Scottish Chamber Orchestra and Kirkwall Grammar School Girls Choir, 1999.

accompanied me in a bizarre excursion. In the little village of Sourin, we found the church and the mounts which had been built 150 years ago by the Reverend George Ritchie.

The kirk embodied a more sinister story: the local laird known as 'the little general' and for whose family George Ritchie had acted as tutor, cleared the land of its crofters so that he could have uninhibited enjoyment of a sporting estate. The story goes that my ancestor cursed 'the little general' from his pulpit and a few days later the latter collapsed and died in the lavatories of the Athenaeum, his London club!

The 1993 festival was the last in which I was officially involved as an artistic director. In 1996, Kathryn McDowell and I travelled to Orkney for a holiday over the Easter weekend. Somewhere in the Pentland Firth, under the watchful gaze of the Old Man of Hoy, we became engaged: an Orkney wedding beckoned. On April 4 1997, as we all prepared to make our way to St Magnus Cathedral, it started to snow. Ron Ferguson conducted a memorable service. What would the Reverend George Ritchie have made of all of this, 150 years after he led his own congregation to their new church on Rousay? The heaven confetti continued to fall until the service was over and the party began.

Roy McEwan   managing director, SCO

One of the greatest sources of excitement for me in joining the SCO in 1993 was knowing that I would have an opportunity to go to Orkney, be at the St Magnus Festival and get to know Peter Maxwell Davies.

The remarkable combination of a sense of community and artistic adventure makes St Magnus very special. Great memories for me include the premiere of Thea Musgrave's *Oboe Concerto* and Jean-Yves Thibaudet, head to toe in Versace, giving the Stromness recital with Truls Mørk.

Max, Orkney, courage and imagination have gone to make St Magnus memorable and everyone associated with the SCO is privileged to be able to be part of it.

David Nicholson   principal flute, SCO 1974-2001

I have been visiting Orkney with the SCO for as long as the orchestra has been involved with the festival, and for me, as for many of the players, it has always been a highlight of our orchestral year. The combination of good music, wonderful soloists and conductors, with the location, warm hospitality, and supportive but discerning audiences is pretty well unique, in my experience. Then there's the weather..! To be honest, it has not always been great, and for the string players especially, changing in the scout hall, and then making a dash for the old Phoenix cinema, was sometimes a real ordeal. But now of course we have the Picky centre! But there have been times when the light seemed to go on forever, and the colours of land and sea were simply jewel like. To be able to make and share music in such surroundings, with such people was to be privileged indeed. And the wonderful cathedral of St Magnus leaves no one unmoved. It has been the focus of the festival, and I am sure will continue to be so.

For my part, my love for Orkney began long before taking part in the festival: indeed my first visit with the SCO was to play a concerto for two flutes with James Galway, but there have been many memorable visits. The festival's commitment to new music has resulted in premieres such as *Tryst*, by James MacMillan (1989), the Richard Rodney Bennett percussion concerto, with Evelyn Glennie (1990), new pieces by Poul Ruders and Simon Holt, and of course music by Max. A special moment for me was playing the concerto he wrote for me, with Max presiding.

Nicholas Cleobury conductor

I conducted the SCO, The Fires of London and the Britten Sinfonia on my visits, and my abiding memory is of working with Max on his home turf. I have conducted a lot for Max and remember learning a great deal from him always, but one particular time in St Magnus Cathedral he taught me not to be so rigid with tempo. In his *Sinfonia Concertante* with the SCO in 1985, I thought I had all the metronome markings correct (perhaps I had) but he found it inflexible and driven. His words and help at that time I've taken to heart, particularly in contemporary repertoire where there is often little time to get beyond getting the notes right.

I remember too at that same concert doing Beethoven's 1st Symphony in rehearsal, with local children joining the SCO. This was a terrific experience for them and an example of Max's dedication to education. I have certainly done this since in a number of ways and used that rehearsal as a model. The need to integrate amateurs and professionals is so important and Max's contribution to that repertoire is invaluable.

Martin Dalby (former head of music, BBC Scotland) was particularly kind to me on my one free day on one of my visits - what a human, sympathetic and very funny man he is. He gave me the most wonderful tour of the island, with history and backgrounds for everywhere we went, and not least about the American he met who was just off to visit 'scary bra'!

I think it was on that visit too that I got to know Russell Harty, who was doing a documentary on Max. I remember well two late convivial evenings, where we began to hatch plans for a programme together on modern music. I began to follow up our discussions, but, sadly, months later, he died so tragically young. I remember him leaving on the second night in the early

I remember one time, in 1990, when the SCO was playing in the Phoenix cinema. They had reached the interval and moved off the stage when suddenly there was an almighty crack. This piece of glass fell down and landed on the stage - it turned out to be the glass from one of the lamps, which had split in two and fallen. The other half was still up there, and we knew the orchestra couldn't go back on stage while it was there. We all looked up at it and wondered what to do - the stage was full of the orchestra's stuff and we couldn't get a scaffolding on it. Eventually, Bryan [Leslie, former stage manager] found a long pole, which was just the right size. A few of us held a blanket underneath the lamp; Bryan got hold of the pole, lifted off the glass, moved it down then dropped it into the blanket, in front of the whole audience. They gave us a great cheer!
Bob Presland
festival technical crew

hours, hoping amusingly that he wouldn't be raped on the short walk back to his hotel!

But my overall and abiding memory is of the beauty of the place that has imbued so much of itself into Max's music, passing Hoy on the boat from Scotland in particular. I remember conducting Max's *A Mirror of Whitening Light* soon after one of my visits and feeling that I was actually in Orkney, even though the performance was in warm and humid Spain!

Claire Nielson   actor

I remember my husband [Paul Greenwood] and I, both of us in black clothes with whitened faces, standing on shaky chairs, trying to overcome the famous acoustical problems of the Walton/Sitwell *Facade*, which we read with the Scottish Chamber Orchestra in 1989. We juggled with scripts and rather primitive school microphones which it was imperative to shut down while the other person was reading or they caused a terrible buzzing. No wonder Edith Sitwell resorted to the much-criticised megaphone in the original twenties production! Without some sort of amplification readers can't possibly be heard over the orchestra, even though it's a small one. Despite all that it was an amazing experience and a great privilege to work with such an orchestra under the baton of Paul Daniel. Unforgettable.

Archie Bevan   *festival vice-president*

On the face of it, June would seem like the ideal time for a festival such as St Magnus. Daylight lingers far into the evening, and the setting sun is well above the horizon to greet concert-goers emerging from the cathedral or the Pickaquoy Centre.

Alas, there is a down side. The weather which brings blue skies, calm seas and unlimited sunshine to Orkney, also brings great banks of North Sea fog - sometimes lasting an hour or two, sometimes much longer, with consequent disruption to air travel.

Fog loomed large in the minds of the festival organisers of 1986. The event had reached double figures, and the occasion was to be marked by a visit from the seventy-strong Royal Philharmonic Orchestra - the first big professional band to visit Orkney, thanks to the support of the Scottish Post Office and its enlightened chairman, Ian Barr. The logistics were hugely daunting, but by Friday evening the conductor André Previn, and soloist Isaac Stern, had landed safely, together with all the orchestral instruments which had been flown up separately from London. Outside the cathedral, the television van with its satellite dish stood ready to transmit the entire concert live on BBC2.

The weather was warm and settled - ominously so. And the seventy

Ralph Kirshbaum, Nicholas Cleobury, 1985.

Gunnie Moberg

Royal Philharmonic Orchestra
1986, 1996

"[The festival] celebrates its tenth anniversary this year with a crescendo, nothing less than the appearance of the Royal Philharmonic Orchestra in Kirkwall; a transportation with similar difficulties to those which Hannibal faced in the Alps."
Ian MacInnes
The Times Educational Supplement, June 27, 1986

Royal Philharmonic players were still in London.

The sun was shining still brighter on Saturday morning as a small reception party headed east out of Stromness. Max and his driver maintained a tense, tight-lipped silence, until at last they crested the hill beyond Kirkwall and looked down on Grimsetter Airport with its runways gleaming in the sun, no trace of fog, and - glory be! - a large musical Viscount lining up for its final approach.

Max greeted the players individually as they came off the plane. Many of them promptly dropped to their knees and appeared to be kissing the soil of Orkney. It seemed a somewhat extravagant gesture, reminiscent of the Pope in his heyday, until it became clear that their interest was essentially botanical and that Leikas and Kodaks by the dozen were being trained at very close range on Orkney's superabundance of wild flowers.

Presently they were coaxed gently on to the buses, to be transported to the East Kirk car park where a large number of Kirkwall hosts were already assembled, and where Marjorie Linklater and her helpers stood ready to call the roll and distribute the bodies.

Eight hours later, the RPO had been successfully shoehorned into the cathedral crossing, and were delivering a heady mixture of Mendelssohn, Vaughan Williams and Maxwell Davies to a packed house and an overflow in the Arts Theatre. The event was a triumph for all concerned. The festival enjoyed the thrill of its first big band, the BBC had proudly delivered its big culture fix from the far north, and the RPO had revelled in its first colourful encounter with flora Orcadiensis.

Exactly one week later, the fog rolled in over Orkney and stayed there. The airport closed down for the weekend; the *St Ola* was totally invisible as she hooted mournfully out of Stromness. But the late Jack Ridgway - former British Airways manager, founder member of the festival in its early years, and an incurable optimist - seemed quite unshaken by the enormity of what might have happened had the fog arrived a week earlier. He claimed to have a plan for such a contingency.

'Prayer, Jack? - Or parachutes perhaps?'

Jack laughed, but kept his counsel.

Ian Maclay   managing director, Royal Philharmonic Orchestra

I don't think that anything could have prepared us for the extraordinary welcome the Royal Philharmonic received when we first visited Orkney in 1986. Max was at the bottom of the steps of the aircraft and greeted each of the musicians as they arrived. Then the players were introduced to the islanders they were staying with and were whisked off to the houses they would be staying in for the next few days.

When we met up for the rehearsal everyone had a tale to tell of the

"In the 849 years of its history the cathedral has seen many great occasions, but never one quite like this...."
(WH)
The Orcadian
June 26, 1986

I remember taking my sons to the RPO in 1986. I was so proud and thought how lucky they were to have the opportunity to hear them. We couldn't sit together, but at the interval they came up and said, 'Can we go now?'. I could have murdered them! But now they are grown up and they listen to music, and they say that they wouldn't listen to the things they do now, had it not been for that early input. I think it is great that the kids get those opportunities.
Eleanor Laird
festival administrator,
1980-1987

The first time we had the RPO up in Orkney, we had huge problems because the stage was far too small for them. But when I first heard them play at a rehearsal, it was just amazing. Sheer magic.
Bryan Leslie, festival stage
manager, 1982-1994

The Royal Philharmonic Orchestra, 1996.

BBC Philharmonic
1988, 1994, 2000

hospitality they had received. Keys to drinks cabinets had been handed over to the musicians, a very dangerous move, cars and bicycles loaned out so the players could get around the island and everyone had been welcomed into their temporary 'family'.

The parties after the concert and the enthusiasm and goodwill of everyone involved in the trip will always be a very fond memory for me. Although the RPO returned a decade later, it was that first visit that stays in my mind most. It is always a pleasure to work with Max, but to do so in Orkney is an unforgettable experience.

Brian Pidgeon managing director, BBC Philharmonic

The BBC Philharmonic made its first visit to Orkney in 1988 under the baton of Sir Edward Downes. When I arrived with the orchestra from the Royal Liverpool Philharmonic, the constant question was always 'When are we going back?'.

Three months after my arrival in June 1991, Max conducted his first concert with the BBC Philharmonic at the Cheltenham Festival - an occasion recorded live for CD which included performances of his *St Thomas Wake* and a suite from *Caroline Mathilde*. The collaboration worked right from the start. I suggested to Trevor Green, the BBC's head of music in Manchester, that we should see whether Max would be interested in becoming the orchestra's first ever composer/conductor, and the rest is history!

In his ten years as composer/conductor of the orchestra, Max brought the BBC Philharmonic back to Orkney on two occasions, in 1994 and again in 2000, culminating with the premiere of his Symphony No 7. Both visits still live in the memory! 1994 blessed with the most wonderful Orcadian summer evenings, 2000 with constant grey drizzle!

Anecdotes are legion, but perhaps the funniest occurred at the rehearsal in the Phoenix cinema of Max's *Stone Litany*, the work based on the Runic alphabet. The previous evening the work's mezzo soprano, Della Jones, had witnessed a performance by the orchestra of *Cross Lane Fair*, in which Max had written a special cadenza for solo Northumbrian Piper Mark Jordan, in which he juggles with three balls. Not to be outdone, Della, just prior to her extended cadenza in *Stone Litany*, reached into her handbag, removed two oranges, and, whilst singing the cadenza perfectly, juggled with them. Max and the orchestra collapsed!

Mark Jordan BBC Philharmonic

On my first trip to the festival, in 1979, I so fell in love with the place that I soon came back again by myself for a holiday. I was playing in the festival, not with the orchestra but with the English Saxophone Quartet. We played a concert in the cathedral and had a fantastic day when we played for the school on Hoy. Of course we took the boat over in the morning and came back early evening, so we were stuck on the island all day with only an hour-long concert to play. The headmaster of the school volunteered to give us his car for the day so we could look around. We could not imagine anything like this happening anywhere else but such generosity seems commonplace in Orkney...

Neville Duckworth   The English Saxophone Quartet

Mark Jordan, Anthony Houghton, Raymond Scott and I departed from Manchester at 8am, on Thursday, June 14, 1979, all travelling in one car and bound for the St Magnus Festival. Each of us drove about 200 miles, with our Orcadian, Raymond Scott, taking the last leg. We arrived at Thurso to catch the early morning ferry to Stromness. I remember being surprised on the journey up to find dawn breaking at about 3.30am.

    We had two concerts in the cathedral, and then fitted in two schools concerts at North Walls on Hoy and St Andrews School. We brought back many happy memories of exploring this lovely part of the world.

The English Saxophone Quartet, 1979.

Mark Jordan

During my first visit with the BBC Philharmonic in 1988, we played at the Phoenix cinema and were all put up with people in their homes. I remember my host going out to have a game of golf that started at midnight on the longest day of the year.

    The highlight of a later trip was another visit to Hoy, this time to have dinner with Max at Rackwick. Max had gone to a lot of trouble, not only cooking for us but also lugging large quantities of beer and wine up the hilly path to his cottage. It so happened that three out of four on our trip had had a piece written specially for them: Simon Butterworth's saxophone concerto, a piece for piccolo for Stuart McIlwham and *Cross Lane Fair* for me, (which was premiered at the 1988 festival). I play the Northumbrian bagpipes and when Max heard me practising he decided to write the piece, putting the bagpipes with the orchestra. He also included one of my hobbies, juggling, in the performance - which made an unforgettable experience for me and, I hope, for anyone who was at the concert.

    On the last orchestra trip we had the opportunity to take our bicycles again, so a lot of people did more than the usual sightseeing as well as having the pleasure of using the new Picky Centre; a splendid venue with an admirable campsite adjacent. I can hardly wait to return and if the BBC doesn't take me soon I'll have to make my own way.

Mark Brook horn, BBC Philharmonic

In 2000, I was playing cricket in Orkney, can you believe, about thirty minutes before a live broadcast of a concert, including the premiere of Max's 7th Symphony. I had the misfortune to fall awkwardly in my gripless concert shoes. I knew I had probably broken a bone in my right hand, but as there were only two of us horn players around for the first half, I had to do the concert! I struggled through, balancing the horn on my knee. It certainly took the pressure off this world premiere, as I was just attempting to be comfortable! The playing just seemed to happen. Next day I had the hand strapped up, and later put in plaster. As a result, another horn player, Sheila Watson of the BBC SSO, had to fly up from Glasgow!

I have always enjoyed my times on Orkney immensely, especially the convivial times in the Festival Club and the adjoining bar! The endless daylight is always a fascination.

Trevor Green former manager, BBC SSO and BBC Philharmonic

Following a spell in Sydney, Australia, I returned to the UK as head of BBC music in the North of England, being based in Manchester where I was responsible for the wonderful BBC Philharmonic. I arrived in April 1988, and noticed that the orchestra, with its chief conductor, Edward Downes, were scheduled to visit the festival in June - my first visit back to Orkney since 1979.

By this time the festival was in its twelfth year, and had become more professionally focused without losing any of its charm and enthusiasm. Sir Peter (Max) was now the honorary president and a committee had been established with Archie Bevan as chairman, and co-artistic director with Glenys Hughes, and a strong vibrant committee had been established to support the development and growth of the now international music and arts festival. It was a far cry from those early pioneering days when most things were achieved on goodwill and a cheese sandwich!

At this festival we gave a performance of *Black Pentecost*, and over the subsequent years it became a regular repertoire piece for the BBC Philharmonic. It became known as 'Black Pantyhose' - such is the affection for Max's music by the brass section of the Phil.

At the Cheltenham Festival of 1991 the BBC Phil was to perform and record *Foxtrot*. I had been thinking for some time that we should create a position with the BBC Philharmonic of composer in residence, and who better than PMD? The outcome was a collaboration with Max and his music which produced a number of specially-commissioned works featuring the individual members of the orchestra. No greater belief and confidence can be given to an orchestra by a composer than to highlight talented individuals in

[on Black Pentecost] *"...There is an ardent passion evident in every bar of what is essentially a large-scale symphonic structure, and a style of orchestral writing that is sinister, dramatic and superbly evocative. The BBC Philharmonic Orchestra under Edward Downes conveyed this remarkably well, particularly the orchestral opening, a glinting, picturesque, refreshingly abstract impression of an Orkney seascape."*
Kenneth Walton
The Glasgow Herald
June 22, 1988

Gunnie Moberg

Della Jones with
The BBC Philharmonic Orchestra,
Phoenix cinema, 1994.

his compositions.

Our return visit to the 1994 festival included two concerts; one conducted by PMD and a lighter-tone, popular event conducted by Barry Wordsworth. We were to give the world premiere of PMD's *Cross Lane Fair*, a colourful work depicting the Salford fairground of the thirties and featuring one of the Phil's star woodwind players, Mark Jordan, on Northumbrian pipes and dressed as a court jester. Imagine the scene in St Magnus Cathedral: a bearded piper in coloured tights juggling three balls during this exotic work, creating all the atmosphere of a mediaeval fair. For Max it was a trip down memory lane, his childhood days in Salford, but for the audience it was a very different musical experience, visual as well as auditory. It was received with great enthusiasm and we gave it many more performances.

The launch of the 1994 festival was given at the premises of the wonderful Highland Park distillery, and I remember on leaving, after sampling the 'holy water', a nameless colleague managed to bump into the gate posts of the car park, and damaged the rear lights of our hire car. We thought nothing of it at the time, deciding to 'own up and pay the price' on leaving at the end of the festival. However, Barry Wordsworth decided to stay on for a few days and explore the island. With all the excitement of our visit, and we were quite busy, we forgot to tell him about the bump. It was a very embarrassed Barry who tried to explain that to the hire company on departing. I don't think he ever forgave us!

When I leave Orkney I always feel slightly sad. During all the festivals I have attended I have always made new friends, had many new experiences, felt very privileged to have a job that linked music-making with the beauty of nature and the wilderness of those northern islands. I have often wondered what it would be like to live there, especially when I am travelling the world, delayed in airports and surrounded by millions of people. I envy Max with his multi-worlds, but always the knowledge that at some stage he will step off a plane and breathe the fresh air, experience the tranquillity and have the calm of a normal life.

Is that the longing that draws countless people back again and again?

Psappha, 1997, 2000

Phil Lea

Psappha

"The late concert was a gem, one of those rare events where both the atmosphere of the environment and the time of night locked together to present ideal circumstances for the performance - in this case a relatively rare outing for the composer's 'Hymn to St Magnus', a tough, uncompromising piece from the early seventies, delivered with stunning clarity and concentration by Psappha under the expert direction of Belgian conductor Etienne Siebens."
Michael Tumelty
The Herald, June 21, 2000

London Sinfonietta 1998

Judy Arnold manager, Sir Peter Maxwell Davies

Psappha, based in Manchester and formed in 1991, is a new music ensemble very much along the lines of the Fires. They do theatrical works in amongst other new music, and they came to the festival in 2000 with Max's new, commissioned work, *Mr Emmet Takes a Walk*. So far, the theatrical works which Psappha have performed have been exclusively Max's.

Tim Williams artistic director, Psappha

I have been very fortunate in visiting Orkney on three occasions, the first time in 1994 with the BBC Philharmonic and then in 1997 and 2000 with Psappha. For some reason a trip to perform at the St Magnus Festival is like no other festival I have ever visited. The odds are against you from the start... will the ferry sail and get the instruments and set up in time?... will the plane be able to land?... the list goes on. On Psappha's two trips to the festival we were very lucky in that we arrived without any problem but were stuck for an extra night (what a shame!) due to fog.

Psappha premiered *Mr Emmet Takes a Walk* by Max (a co-commission with the St Magnus Festival and Muziektheater Transparant) at the festival in 2000. This is not the most straightforward piece to put on (even for a fully equipped theatre) but somehow Norman Rushbrook and his crew came up with every single item requested by our demanding production team. I stayed with Dorothy and Norman Rushbrook on the *Mr Emmet* trip... there were a number of problems during my stay (to do with late arrivals of planes due to fog, limousines and a diva); Dorothy managed to take the whole thing in her stride with the aid of a box of duty free cigarettes and a large dram of whisky.

Glenys Hughes manages to pull this whole thing together which I find quite amazing, with orchestras and international artists coming in from all over the place. Max as the patron and founder of the festival adds the extra bit of magic, with people travelling from all over the world to spot him wandering around Stromness. I don't know of anyone who wouldn't jump at the chance of a return visit to the festival with its warm welcome and the locals entering into the spirit.

My lasting memories will be the premiere of *Mr Emmet Takes a Walk* at a packed Pickaquoy Centre and performing *Hymn to St Magnus* in St Magnus Cathedral.

Glenys Hughes

In 1998, out of the blue, we were granted a major award by the Britten Pears Foundation in recognition of our commitment to new music. It was to be used to programme performances of contemporary music that might otherwise be beyond the scope of the festival. I decided that we would invite the London Sinfonietta, an ensemble of outstanding players dedicated to the performance of 20th century and contemporary music. Their residency at the 1999 festival was a huge success, including a performance which for some ranks as the most memorable festival concert ever, Messiaen's *Quartet for the End of Time* in the Italian Chapel.

Cathy Graham   managing director, London Sinfonietta

Mark van de Wiel just said to me 'I loved your photos of Orkney'. He saw them on the London Sinfonietta web site along with an article written by John Constable about the remarkable performances of Messiaen's *Quartet for the End of Time* in the Italian Chapel on midsummer's eve 1999. It is 21 October 2001, and we have just left Gatwick on the night flight to Buenos Aires. How strange that he should mention Orkney just this evening, when I had promised myself that I would devote the first part of the flight to recollecting and writing about our visit. How strange also that I suddenly realise that the four musicians from those memorable midsummer's eve concerts - violinist Clio Gould, cellist Anssi Kartunen, clarinettist Mark van der Wiel and pianist John Constable - are all on the flight with me tonight.

The memories I have of our trip to Orkney in June 1999, are many and vivid: the cold, raw chill of the rainiest midsummer I have ever experienced; the wonderful warm welcome of our hosts; the serene calm of the cathedral manse where Anssi and I stayed as privileged guests of Cristine and Ron Ferguson; the slate grey morning, taking the early ferry to Hoy, and the intensity of the performances in Hoy Kirk; the sudden sense of revelation listening to *A Mirror of Whitening Light* in Kirkwall's St Magnus Cathedral; my first oysters with Paul Driver at the Foveran; a rare reminder of childhood security while walking across the playground of Papdale Primary School on the way to a rehearsal of Fraser Trainer's *True to Life*. And now I realise that Fraser's on the flight to Buenos Aires with me too.

In spite of the many wonderful concerts, however, it is the performances in the Italian Chapel on Lamb Holm that return to me most often. Working with and for the musicians of the London Sinfonietta, I often have the privilege of witnessing inspired music-making of the highest quality, but that evening held something extra, something which seems to sum up the heart of my experience on Orkney. There was a real connection between the music and the place, its past and its present; and with the people of Orkney, both those who were there, and those whose spirit only imbued the midsummer night with an even greater magic than usual.

On Orkney I discovered and carried home with me a love for the writing of George Mackay Brown, Judith Glue sweaters and Highland Park.

"It was only after the last extremely soft sounds of the violin and piano had dissolved into a seemingly endless silence that I realised the effect our performance had had on the audience...It was only then that I was aware of the proximity of the listeners, who were in total blackness, and what it must have felt like to be so close to that kind of music.

The music fills you with such exaltation... It was obvious from people's reactions afterwards that something both very deep and personal had been communicated amongst us all. We would always hope to perform with the same intensity, with the same marvellous spirit that exists between Sinfonietta players, but something extra happened – that is the mystery."
John Constable
London Sinfonietta
[Extract from an article first published on the London Sinfonietta web site, 2000.]

Cathy Graham

London Sinfonietta rehearsing in
the Italian Chapel, 1999.

*"Messiaen is gone; Domenico
Chiochetti, the craftsman and
artisan whose construction of
the Italian Chapel unleashed a
stroke of inspirational genius,
died just last month. Both of
their creations from the camps
survive. The bringing together
of these two masterworks from
the war was one of the most
moving experiences of my life."*
Michael Tumelty
The Herald, June, 1999

The Nash Ensemble, 2001

Amelia Freedman, 2001.

Judy Arnold

I also carried home the confirmation of what I had always known to be true: that music and poetry can exist as a natural and vital part of society, an enriching and stimulating force in everyday life.

Ron Ferguson   author and journalist
minister of St Magnus Cathedral 1991-2001

There are so many festival highlights, but perhaps the most unbearably moving was the experience of listening to Messiaen's *Quartet for the End of Time*, played by the London Sinfonietta in the Italian Chapel.

This modernistic work had its premiere in 1941, in Stalag VIIA, where the composer was held captive. It was first performed before 5,000 prisoners, many of whom would never have been to a concert in their lives, yet they were deeply moved by this searing work. So were all of us in the Italian Chapel, one of Orkney's jewels, and itself a living example of how a work of art and worship can be made out of very unpromising materials. The musicians, one of whom stayed with us in the manse, were totally involved in Messiaen's piece. As they played with soul and passion, one could picture in one's mind the prisoners of Stalag VIIA listening intently, and the Italian prisoners of war walking on the horizon from the Churchill Barriers to their Nissen hut accommodation.

Glenys Hughes

A major three-year grant from the Esmée Fairbairn Foundation enabled us in 2000 to co-commission and premiere Max's *Mr Emmet Takes a Walk*. The following year, 2001, we invited the superb Nash Ensemble, who perform a marvellous mixture of standard ensemble repertoire and new music. It was a special privilege that year to see in Orkney their founder and artistic director Amelia Freedman, whose achievements are quite unique in British music.

Amelia Freedman   artistic director, the Nash Ensemble
(in conversation)

When I first arrived in Orkney and walked down the main street in Kirkwall, I was struck by how intimate and friendly it felt. The atmosphere reminded me of the fifties, as did the sweet shop, with the rows of jars in the windows. It took me straight back to my childhood. The people were so kind and helpful - unlike a big city, where everyone is now anonymous and the pace is so fast.

I have many happy memories of my visit. The Kirkwall Hotel provided wonderful breakfasts - I loved the kippers especially. They were less salty than the London variety and tasted so good. And the whisky was wonderful, too!

Orkney is a place of magic, full of spirituality. The Ring of Brodgar is an extraordinary monument, and in Maeshowe I felt touched by the presence of our ancestors. The landscape has a quiet beauty all its own, despite the lack of hills. The sheep and cows were roaming around in freedom, and I was very struck by their apparent quality of life. Having come to Orkney during the foot-and-mouth epidemic, when the fields down south stood bare and empty, it was lovely to see these healthy-looking animals grazing with a dignity and freedom one doesn't see elsewhere. When the sun shone, the mysticism and spirituality of the place really came home to us.

The Nash loved their festival visit. Glenys Hughes is a fantastic artistic director and I was full of admiration for the range and diversity of the programme that she had put together. It was of such high quality, and yet it served the local community thoroughly. She is a very special lady. And it was lovely to meet Max again, in his own surroundings. Each member of the ensemble was touched by the beauty of the islands and the concert venues. In the cathedral, and in the little church in Birsay where Duncan McTier premiered Max's *Lux in Tenebris*, we felt a oneness with the place and the people, who treated us with great kindness. It was a privilege to be asked to the festival, and we certainly hope to be back.

Duncan McTier Nash Ensemble

The logistics of getting me, and my double bass, to Orkney were quite complex, due to the small size of the aircraft flying into Kirkwall. I had to fly from London to Edinburgh, leave my bass flight case at the left luggage desk, and then drive to Scrabster (with the Nash's bassoonist Ursula Levaux) before finally catching the ferry. Nonetheless I was really looking forward to participating in the festival, especially as one of the events would be a cello and bass concert with Paul Watkins, including duos and solo repertoire. When Glenys Hughes told me that she would invite Max to write a solo piece for me to premiere in this concert I was absolutely thrilled! The resulting *Lux in Tenebris* was like a dream come true. Max has an innate way of writing for the bass, exploring a very broad range of sounds and effects - and always very challenging!

I remember the day of the performance very well. Paul and I were given a lift to St Magnus Church, Birsay - what an idyllic spot! I remember the church being very cold when we arrived to rehearse - it was quite difficult to get the fingers to play some of the very fast passages in both the Rossini Duetto and Barrière's *Sonata à Deux*. However that was soon to change. The audience arrived and packed the church to the rafters. This certainly had the effect of warming up the church but the downside for us was that it altered

Orkney is a wonderful setting in which to play chamber music with the Nash Ensemble. I played in Stromness Town Hall and the cathedral, and the concert halls are beautiful. I brought my wife with me and the weather was fantastic. It was very exciting to come to Orkney, and lovely to have a couple of days to look around and enjoy the islands in the warm sunshine. I hope I will be back again some day.
Leon McCawley, guest pianist with the Nash Ensemble, 2001 (in conversation)

"In the little church of St Magnus in Birsay, there [was] a concert to remember, with the most extraordinary and unlikely combination of instruments, cello and double bass, and the peerless masters of these deep musical voices, Paul Watkins and the sensational Duncan McTier, the man who has revolutionised the concept of what the double bass, the old singing wardrobe, can do."
Michael Tumelty
The Herald, June 26, 2001

Paul Watkins, Duncan McTier,
in St Magnus Kirk, Birsay, 2001.

London Brass, 2001

David Purser, 2001.

the humidity dramatically, to the extent that most of our concentration seemed to go on simply trying to maintain contact between the bow and the string! By the end of the concert all the windows of the church were steamed up! Nonetheless the audience was very enthusiastic and there was much positive feedback on *Lux in Tenebris*. It is always a delight to perform with Paul Watkins, but to play in such a splendid setting made it a truly memorable day.

Ursula and I stayed with Tim and Phyllida Wright who couldn't have done more to make us feel welcome and were extremely generous.

David Purser director, London Brass,
trombone, London Sinfonietta

When I touched down at Kirkwall airport with the London Sinfonietta in the midsummer of 1999, I was surprised to find myself surrounded by gentle green rolling countryside, with a calm blue sea beyond. With a typical sassenach's ignorance, I was expecting gaunt grey cliffs, boiling black sea and lashing rain. I didn't know what to expect of the people either, but found them every bit as pleasant and welcoming as the landscape. The three days I spent at the St Magnus Festival were a delight. Festivals today are often largely marketing tools for tourism: and while there were clearly tourists around the islands and at the concerts, it was immediately apparent that this festival was very much owned by the local people. Such was my enjoyment of the London Sinfonietta visit that I contacted Glenys Hughes to see if she would be interested in a project with London Brass. And so it was that we ended up on the stage of the Pickaquoy Centre for the opening concert of the 2001 festival, alongside forty school children, the Kirkwall Town Brass Band and the wind band.

If ever there was a community concert, this was it. We had a newly-commissioned composition, *Pulse Fiction,* from Fraser Trainer, to use with the schools, a jazz concerto by Chris Batchelor to play with the brass band, and Grainger's *Lincolnshire Posy* to share with the wind band: and we started off with a wonderful fanfare by Richard Strauss - London Brass plus twenty Orcadian brass players - a majestic opening to the concert and the festival.

All of which was intensely enjoyable and very gratifying. But it was the day after that opening concert that brought home to me the real flavour of the St Magnus Festival: being stopped in the street and congratulated by a complete stranger; being served fish and chips for lunch by one of the school trumpeters, still glowing with excitement; and then taking the ferry to Hoy and playing to (and later socialising with) an intimate audience of perhaps forty people. This makes for the very special atmosphere of the St Magnus Festival. The itinerant musician's life can take you to many beautiful places and to many lovely festivals. But it is unique in my experience to be treated - as the Orcadians treat you - as one of the community, and as a result to feel that one has played a part in the community. It's a great feeling.

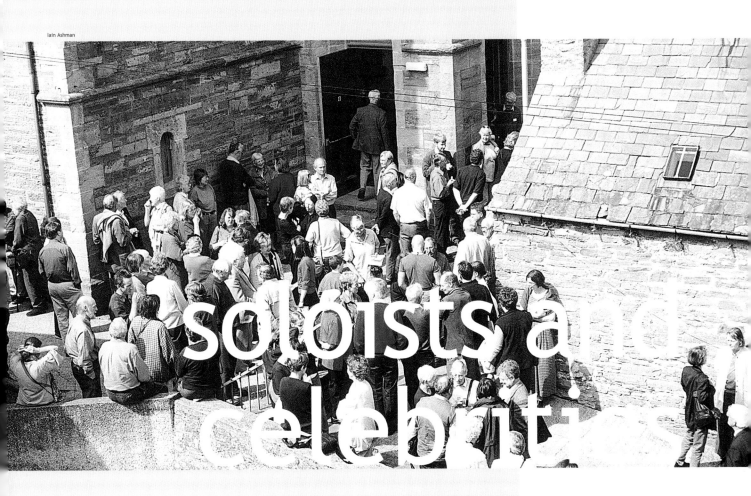

Iain Ashman

soloists and celebrities

The intimacy of the Stromness Town Hall, with its fine acoustic, has made it a special venue for the glittering array of star performers who have played at the festival since Vlado Perlemuter began the tradition in 1978. Whether the performer is a distinguished veteran or a rising star, the celebrity recital is always eagerly anticipated, attracting some of the greatest instrumentalists in the world, including Isaac Stern and Vladimir Ashkenazy. The relative informality of the event is one of its best-loved characteristics. It would be hard to find another festival where an audience member can hail a celebrity in the street, or enjoy a drink with him or her in the Festival Club just a few hours after a recital. (The famous, however, do not always escape Orkney unscathed! See Joanna MacGregor, page 82.)

Not all the stars have been in classical music. The biggest music event ever held in Orkney was the Runrig concert in 1991, which attracted an audience of 5,000. The folk band Capercaillie has also visited, and jazz saxophonists Tommy Smith and Ronnie Scott have both taken Orkney by storm, to name but a few.

The range and quality of the celebrity performances have been a hallmark of the festival. The affection with which many of the recitalists remember their visits, amongst countless performances all over the world, is a testament to the reception they receive in the islands, and the huge appreciation which the festival audiences show.

Vlado Perlemuter

Chamber music sticks in my mind...Vlado Perlemuter playing Ravel and Chopin; Stephen Pruslin introducing Max's new Sonata, with the Rozhdestvensky family leaning over the balcony of the old church in Stromness. Afterwards little Sasha Rozhdestvensky played with me in the garden of the Bevans' house, and I little dreamed that years later I would get to know him in Moscow and he would become one of the tallest violinists that I know. [See *visitors*]
Gerard McBurney
composer and festival visitor

Archie Bevan   festival vice-president

The regular Sunday recital in Stromness Town Hall acquired 'celebrity' status for the first time in the 1983 festival programme. By then it was already six years old and had become one of the most popular events in the festival calendar, its origins dating back to the arrival in Stromness of the Occidental Steinway - that icon of Orkney's oil age. The recital in 1978 was also the very first festival event to be held in Stromness, in its acoustically superior 'Academy Hall' as it was then called, and it began the long-standing festival tradition of 'Sunday in Stromness'.

The first St Magnus celebrity was a venerable French pianist called Vlado Perlemuter. He was over 70, though by how much was unclear, and he had been a pupil of the great Maurice Ravel. He began his first rehearsal by fishing out a huge handkerchief, and giving the ivories and the adjacent woodwork a brisk working over. In the process he was appalled to discover a sweetie wrapper beside the keyboard. He looked decidedly sceptical as we explained how the paper must have drifted down from the gallery to lodge under the lid.

So far, so finicky. But when he laid his hands on the keyboard of the Steinway, all was transformed. Without the least hint of showmanship he conjured golden sounds from the heart of the instrument. He played Debussy and Chopin and of course Ravel, in a performance that was at once marvellously expressive and supremely disciplined - the work of a master craftsman.

He was to be followed in the next 23 years by a glittering procession of hugely talented celebrities. Yet, in his own quiet way, and demonstrating total integrity and musical insight in every note he played, Vlado Perlemuter was perhaps the ideal leader of that select band.

As we left him to a solitary hour of musical communion with his great mentor, a lady chased after us along the street. 'I am Mr Perlemuter's companion,' she said with some urgency, 'and he seems to have mislaid his pyjamas. Can you possibly lend him a pair?' But of course! That, after all, is what committee members are for. And in truth it added an extra frisson to a riveting musical experience.

Stephen Pruslin   pianist and writer

The pioneering festivals had an aura of rough-and-ready surmounting of obstacles. Harpsichords built from self-assembly kits tried valiantly to meet standards for which they were never intended. Generously loaned grand pianos disappeared from their living rooms and were dispersed to different venues. (The arrival of the Steinway constituted a very big step forward.) Moments before going onstage, gloved fingers were crammed between the radiator bars of the St Magnus vestry in the hope of finding a glimmer of warmth. But there were ample compensations. The charisma of Britain's northernmost cathedral suffused every event that took place there. The Stromness Academy Hall had an intimacy that created close contact with the audience. And never mind that you could hardly go offstage in the Phoenix cinema before finding yourself in the street - that was also part of the fun.

Anyone who has attended or participated in the festival has a personal memory bank of images. After performing there throughout the first decade and a half, mine are many and various. Some of the most vivid ones relate to what I experienced as a spectator. On one such occasion, the mellow glow of Mozart's Symphony No 39 pervaded St Magnus during the first appearance in Orkney of a full symphony orchestra. Several other magical moments are described elsewhere in this book. As a pianist, the encounters that undoubtedly meant the most to me were those with Victoria Postnikova and Vlado Perlemuter. When I played PMD's Piano Sonata at the 1982 festival, Postnikova, with the discretion of a true colleague, positioned herself up in the gallery of the Academy Hall so that I couldn't see her, but she had a direct view above the keyboard. She was generosity itself after the performance, but I was very glad that I hadn't known beforehand! At an earlier festival, the dapper and elegant Vlado Perlemuter gave an exquisite afternoon recital of Chopin and Ravel. I was impelled to thank him, and he accepted this with charm and grace. That evening, he attended our Fires concert. To my astonishment, this eminent man, who had no need to make any comment at all, took the trouble to find me afterwards and to say '*Mais vous avez beaucoup à faire*!' (But you have so much to do!). Then again, that is the spirit the festival seems to engender - accustomed to the more usual 'circuit', artists respond to the very rare and genuine atmosphere they discover in Orkney.

**Gennadi Rozhdestvensky
and Victoria Postnikova**

Rosemary Warren-Green (Furniss) formerly violinist with
The Fires of London
(in conversation)

For the most part, I came up to Orkney with The Fires of London in the fairly early days of the festival. In 1983, however, I came up with the group Pagoda, to play in the Festival Club and I was looking forward to a relaxing time. The journey across the Pentland Firth, however, was very rough. I had just discovered that I was expecting my first child, and was horribly sick.

The celebrity recitalist that year was György Pauk. A very short time before his recital was due to begin in the Stromness Town Hall, Judy Arnold appeared, frantic, saying that György Pauk was indisposed, and if I didn't play at the recital it would have to be the sheep! Normally, before a recital, I would practise for weeks - but there was no question of any practice at all in this case. By sheer lucky coincidence, however, I had played several of the recital pieces only the week before and was familiar and comfortable with

Rosemary Furniss

them. So although it was a terrible rush, the recital went well. I just didn't have time to think. The whole thing was done in a lovely spirit, and turned out to be a wonderful experience.

I had also promised to play for György Pauk in his chamber concert later in the week with the SCO. At this, I had to play Mendelssohn's Concerto. Unlike the recital pieces, I had not played this recently; not for many years, in fact. Almost from the moment the recital finished, I went back to my host's, Eleanor Laird's, house, and practised non-stop. I'll never know how Eleanor and her family put up with me - I really did play all the time, trying to perfect the piece before the concert. Also, I didn't have a dress to wear, and Eleanor found one of her own dresses, which she lent to me. In the end, it all went off all right, but it was a rather fraught festival visit!

Ralph Kirshbaum   cellist, 1985

My main memory of the St Magnus Festival is of being in that remote part of the world. I also vividly remember playing in Stromness Academy Hall. At first, when I entered the hall, the surroundings seemed austere, but as the concert progressed it became a warm and even moving occasion.

The concentration of the public, eager to listen, was infectious, and relayed itself to me. That, and the remoteness of the environment, made it such a moving and memorable experience for me.

Neil Price   director, The Mayfield Singers

Peter Maxwell Davies and
Isaac Stern, 1986.

My favourite festival 'chauffering' experience was with Isaac Stern in 1986, when he came to premiere Max's Violin Concerto with the RPO and André Previn, which was being broadcast live from St Magnus Cathedral on BBC2. I met him and his wife at the airport and they exuded all the most charming elements of American Jewishness. They wanted to know everything possible about Orkney and were clearly captivated by the place. The concert was a sell-out and with the heat of the TV lights, our portly celebrity soloist found the whole experience quite a strain. But he coped magnificently and the occasion was nothing but memorable. Immediately after his performance he asked me to take him back to his hotel. During the short drive I tried to speak intelligently about the piece I had just heard for the first time and which he had been studying for months. The slow movement was modelled on a piobreachd (classical Scottish bagpipe music) and, trying to be clever, I said that I particularly liked the piobreachd theme in the middle movement. He looked at me with a tired and sardonic expression and merely said: 'What the hell's that?' The next day, he gave a spellbinding performance of French violin sonatas in Stromness Town Hall with Jean-Bernard Pommier. I will never forget Mrs Stern jumping to her feet at the end of the Franck Sonata in adulation of a great performance. She must have heard her old man play this dozens of times before, but this was still a fresh experience. They could have been anywhere - it didn't matter. Afterwards we drove back towards Kirkwall, aiming for a posh reception at the Foveran Hotel. I said it was a shame that we didn't have time to go up Wideford Hill to see the spectacular view from the top, whereupon Isaac said: 'Oh, what the hell, that lot can wait!' Five minutes later, we were at the summit, with the Sterns being blown around by a stiff Orkney breeze and loving every minute of it. He was a great man who seemed to have sorted out his priorities - a great musician but there was more to life than just music. Another sobering sight later that evening was André Previn alone in deep contemplation, leaning on the harbour wall outside the Ayre Hotel in Kirkwall.

Alastair Hume   The King's Singers, 1986

When I was growing up, Orkney was a place mentioned often by my mother as somewhere connected to our family, but I was foolish enough not to press her into telling me everything about it. So it remained a mysterious place to me, until I became old enough to be aware of my uncle Eric (Linklater) and his wonderful books. These gave Orkney another dimension, one of wild seas and of the sagas and legends of the Norsemen who arrived in their frail open boats across those forbidding seas to settle in Orkney.

By the mid-eighties I was doing a huge amount of travelling with The King's Singers, and by great good fortune the group was invited to the St Magnus Festival in 1986. As is so often the case with some experiences in life, one never quite realises quite how significant they are at the time; and so it was with this my first (as I thought) visit to Orkney. I certainly realised the significance of watching Isaac Stern and André Previn rehearsing in the same festival that I was to appear in! I also realised the significance of having one of the greatest contemporary British composers write a piece for The King's Singers, although this was tempered a little at the time by the rather fundamental necessity of getting it right! Peter Maxwell Davies had chosen to set the poems of George Mackay Brown for his piece *The House of Winter*, and I think I realised at the time that this was a piece that seemed to have got everything absolutely right, unlike, probably, the singers at that first performance! On this occasion, there was certainly an overwhelming sense of rightness about singing George's words set to Max's music in the East Church. I remember it was not too bad for a first performance, and we had a wonderfully warm reception.

I also enjoyed the most marvellous tour with uncle Eric's sister, Elspeth Linklater. She gave me a crash course in Orkney and the Linklaters, and took me round by Skaill House where my grandfather brought his family

"Orkney is a wonderful leveller. Before his celebrity recital in Stromness with pianist Jean Bernard Pommier, Stern felt a twang of nerves and a call of nature. The two men, searching for relief, discovered that they must join the queue at the outside loo which serves the hall. When we recognised our distinguished fellow-sufferers we, of course, gave them priority.

Stern went first. He then held the door open for Pommier, closed it firmly behind him, looked at the queue, grinned and said: 'For once I get to set the tempo,' and scuttled off to the hall."
Michael Tumelty
The Glasgow Herald
July 1, 1986

The King's Singers with
Peter Maxwell Davies, 1986.

in the summer.

I had been sent to stay with the Linklaters when they lived in Ross-shire, and have abiding memories of meals enlivened by Eric giving a passable imitation of a minor volcano. While I was at Cambridge I saw that Eric was giving a talk to a neighbouring college's debating society on 'The old school tie'. He amusingly concluded that its most useful function was to keep his trousers up. I went to him afterwards and reminded him that I was his nephew, but sadly this was not a situation in which he shone, and he just said how nice that was and that he had to rush for a train and Goodbye.

In 1997, I flew up to Orkney for Marjorie's funeral and there was a feeling of things coming full circle. The wake was held in the house that used to belong to Eric and Marjorie, called Merkister, and now an hotel. I learnt that during the war my sister and I were evacuated there, and I met the woman who pushed me along the road in my pram when taking my sister to the local school. Somehow I feel my 1986 festival visit stretches back many years and also forward. I now go back again and again to Eric's books and George's wonderful book on Orkney (*An Orkney Tapestry*) with intense passion and delight, and through the latter's hauntingly beautiful poems I find that Orkney exerts a very real pull on me.

[On House of Winter]
"Here....was Davies doing something he has always done with apparent ease and simple perfection of achievement: writing for unaccompanied voices....Just as he has always done in setting Mackay Brown, Davies honours the text....The work speaks of the deep community of interest between poet and composer...."
Paul Griffiths
The Times, June 15, 1986

Vladimir Ashkenazy pianist, 1987

I vividly remember my visit to Orkney and the recital in 1987. I am very fond of Nordic people - Scots, Scandinavians, Finns (my wife being Icelandic) and I felt very comfortable playing for the festival audience. They were very warm and responsive and I really felt in my element being on a real Nordic island.

Vladimir Ashkenazy

Steven Osborne pianist, 1987, 1988, 1996

My first visit to the festival, aged 16, playing solo and duets with my school friend David Horne, was one of my earliest professional concerts; I can still quote verbatim sections of a review we had! The atmosphere was wholly remarkable: a combination of the unusual, evocative, bleak landscape and the very particular qualities of the locals - great warmth, trust, and, apparently, a complete lack of anxiety on the part of the organisers. These qualities were exemplified in a remark made by our hosts to the effect that any friend coming to visit them, on finding the house empty, would simply let themselves in, make a cup of tea and wait for their return!

I was deeply affected by the landscape, and the remarkable sound of the sea in such treeless surroundings: overwhelmingly powerful, somehow. I will never forget watching the sun set at Skara Brae close to midnight.

I returned in 1996 to commemorate the death of Ian Barr, who used

"After a couple of Schubert's Impromptus, Ashkenazy pounced like a tiger unleashed on the composer's 'Wanderer Fantasy', one of the great seminal works of the nineteenth century. This was piano playing at its most vivid and dramatic, whose glittering brilliance and robust, Beethovenian aggression swept the audience into waves of ecstatic applause."
Michael Tumelty
The Glasgow Herald, June, 1987

his position as head of the Scottish Postal Board to arrange much sponsorship of the arts, including my earlier concert. He was simply a remarkable man: intelligent, extremely knowledgeable where music was concerned, yet profoundly humble. In the friendship that grew out of his initial support, I always knew that despite the difference in age and experience, he treated me as an equal. David Horne wrote a piece that I premiered at this concert, combining intellectual rigour with moments of deep reflection.

Steven Osborne and David Horne

David Horne   pianist and composer, 1987, 1988, 1991, 1996

While my festival visits have been relatively short, I have incredibly warm feelings for both Orkney and its people, who have always been extremely generous and kind. It's worth mentioning how it was that I first came to visit the festival. Steven Osborne and I had been invited up to play, principally by the late and great Ian Barr, then chairman of the Scottish Postal Board. The first couple of days of that trip were a little nerve-wracking for me, as I was still trying to get to grips with Maxwell Davies's fiendishly difficult Piano Sonata. However, there was time to relax, and our friendly hosts showed us around the main island's sights, including, I might add, a somewhat illegal, if thrilling, midnight visit to Skara Brae!

It was entirely fitting that the last time I visited Orkney was to hear Steven perform a new work of mine, *Refrain*, which I'd written for him, in memory of Ian Barr. On that visit, I promised myself that I wouldn't leave it until another festival visit to make it back to the island. Sadly, I haven't fulfilled that promise, but I'm working on it.

Peter Frankl   pianist, 1988

I remember very vividly the experience of performing at the St Magnus Festival in Orkney. Above all, the setting is quite unique and magnificent and reflects Sir Peter Maxwell Davies's taste and personality. I had the great honour to give the world premiere there of András Szöllősy's wonderful piece *Pasaggio Con Morte*, commissioned especially by the festival, which I subsequently performed in many parts of the world.

My very best wishes for the festival on the occasion of its 25th anniversary.

György Pauk   violinist, 1988

Judy Arnold is a very old friend of mine; we have known each other since well before the Max era. It was one of her first professional deeds to get me

"The festival organisers showed a spark of brilliance in inviting back the 18 year-old pianists David Horne and Steven Osborne, who gave one of the most exhilarating performances of Stravinsky's 'Rite of Spring' I have ever heard. Their youth was to their advantage for this work since they captured the almost unbearable exuberance of spring awakening, and unleashed violence of a powerful rhythmic clarity. Of the handful of performances that I will remember for the rest of my life, this will be one of them."
James MacMillan
The Guardian, June, 1988

**Judy Arnold, Peter Frankl, PMD
György Pauk, 1987.**

One day, after a second poetry reading, came a glorious musical experience. In Stromness Town Hall, its windows temporarily blacked out, György Pauk and Peter Frankl - so close you could almost put out a hand and touch them - displayed a joyous rapport. My spirit soared as they brought to life the limpid lyricism and dazzling energy of Beethoven's Spring Sonata.
Stewart Conn,
festival poet, 1988

Evelyn Glennie and Philip Smith, 1989.

"The world premiere of Richard Rodney Bennett's new Percussion Concerto, specially written for the unusual talents of Evelyn Glennie and performed by her with the Scottish Chamber Orchestra, furnished a dazzling climax to this year's festival."
Roderic Dunnett
Music & Musicians, June, 1990

acquainted with Max and his music. This is why I was invited for the first time to the Orkney Festival, which I visited twice, if I remember well.

The place itself was very fascinating for me as it seemed so far away from the mainland, yet it belongs to Great Britain. The journey there is quite an eventful happening, as I am not very fond of flying in small planes. But I got there in one piece!

Musically of course, it is a great experience, having Maxwell Davies at its head. I respect him most sincerely as a wonderful musician, great composer and as a highly intelligent and valuable human being.

I was very pleased indeed when Peter Maxwell Davies asked me to perform his Violin Concerto. I have performed it many times since then, amongst others in London and in Munich, representing Great Britain at the European Music Festival.

My collaboration with Max was also the highlight of my visit to Orkney, where I played the Beethoven concerto at the magnificent cathedral of St Magnus.

Also, on a personal note, it was in Stromness that I tasted the malt whisky, Highland Park, and ever since I became a lover of that wonderful stuff. (Not before a concert!)

Evelyn Glennie percussionist, 1989, 1990 (in conversation)

I have many family members in Orkney from my mother's side; as a youngster I had a couple of holidays there, and visited with the Grampian Schools Percussion Ensemble when I was a young teenager. (This was rather traumatic, as I remember falling down a hole in the cathedral and hurting my knee!)

My recital at the 1989 festival contained many arrangements and transcriptions. I had just left the Academy then and there was just no repertoire to speak of - I knew that I could never survive playing those pieces. Over the years, I have asked composers to write things, but it can take anything up to five years for a piece to be written; that's a long time in a young person's career. It has taken a while just to have this body of work in the repertoire, but I have now commissioned around 120 pieces - mainly concertos and recital pieces - and there is work out there which I am convinced will have a long shelf life. The importance of *Veni Veni Emmanuel* by James MacMillan, for instance, has escalated throughout the world.

With the Richard Rodney Bennett premiere at the festival in 1990, I played with the SCO, and there was just not enough rehearsal time. (This is a problem with British orchestras up and down the country.) The Bennett is a very good concerto and quite complicated. Richard writes so well, but it needs time to really sort out what's going on. Also, the number of instruments required took a large area of the stage, and the platform in the Phoenix was quite squashed. There was no side or back stage, you were just in or out, and

I changed in the back of the truck. It was rather distracting, because you really need to focus when you are giving a premiere. But it was all part of the fun really!

I'm very attracted to festivals, especially when they start from the seed of one person thinking, 'let's have some music' - in this case Sir Peter Maxwell Davies. Living in Orkney, and then 'growing' this festival that has attracted so many people, with the balance between the big names and the younger people, (such as myself at that time), was an important experiment. I just love that sort of thing, which is why I keep going back to Orkney.

The audience makes a huge difference. People in Orkney are eager to listen, to experience and observe; and the people are the festival as well. It isn't just for the performers, it is Orkney's festival, and that includes every person who walks through the doors. That is hugely special. They don't have to leave having enjoyed every single piece - but the point is that they have really listened. (It is the same for musicians dealing with new music - we just happen to have it a little bit longer than the audience.)

At the St Magnus Festival the children are very much part of the attraction. Peter Maxwell Davies really has a sense of community, and to me, this is the absolute key. And he has been hugely encouraging to younger composers. I have many composer friends who have been to Orkney, especially to the Hoy Summer School, and they have all had such a super time.

Living in Orkney would be no problem at all for me! Realistically, it would be more a case of being there part time. If I had a couple of weeks completely clear, I could organise the diary and just totally get away. I would really love that.

Sir Richard Rodney Bennett composer and recitalist, 1990, 1999

I've had wonderful audiences both for my music and for performances I've given at the St Magnus Festival.

I hope it doesn't seem ungrateful to say that best of all I remember the extraordinary beauty of the setting, the landscape and the light. These I will never forget.

Judy Arnold manager, Sir Peter Maxwell Davies

The celebrity concert in Stromness in 1990 was due to be given by the soprano Margaret Marshall, but I received a phone call on the Thursday before the festival to say that the singer was indisposed. In all other circumstances, if such a thing happens, which it does frequently, you phone all the agents in London and get somebody else to do the show. But this does not work for Orkney; it is too far away, and there are not enough planes.

You like to give of your best for the visiting artists, and you do meet a lot of nice people. In the Phoenix, many people in the audience didn't realise that the performers were actually outside when they went off stage and were waiting to come on again. They are very stoical. It was an embarrassment having Evelyn Glennie sitting in the car between curtain calls! It was quite dreadful - but they just seemed to take it all in their stride. You feel whatever welcome you give them is not enough, but hopefully, whatever else we had to offer made up for the discomfort.
Maureen Gray,
former festival board member

**Marion Montgomery and
Sir Richard Rodney Bennett**

Gunnie Moberg

Håkan Hardenberger

Håkan Hardenberger' s recital in Stromness was just phenomenal. He played for an hour and a half - everything from Berio to *Rule Britannia* - and he didn't drop a note all afternoon. He was flawless, and the man next to me was sleeping! A night or two later I was playing with the Orkney Orchestra, and the same guy was there, bright-eyed and bushy-tailed. I remember thinking that he had just slept through one of the very finest musicians in the world, on any instrument, and yet he was wide awake while the Orkney Orchestra was playing - mad!
Brian Jones
brass instructor, Orkney schools

The only solution was to ask Linda Hirst, who was heading to Orkney to perform in the Mozart Requiem, which Max was to conduct with the Scottish Chamber Orchestra. It was likely that Linda was in Thurso, as she was due to cross to Orkney the following day, so I started to phone round hotels there. Eventually I found one with a Linda Hirst, who was dragged out of bed and brought to the phone (it was, by now, quite late). Unfortunately, this was another Linda Hirst and the poor woman was not very pleased to have been woken up!

In the end, I found Linda. She agreed to do the concert, but we needed a pianist. I phoned Stephen Pruslin, who said that he would be prepared to do it. Fabulous. He had to go to Linda's house in London to get the music, before catching the plane to Orkney on Saturday. He went straight to Archie's house to collect the key to Stromness Academy, where Linda and he were to rehearse. The Bevans were out, but Steve knew that the front door would be open. He found the key, and made his way to the rehearsal. It was all brilliant, as was the concert. Real professionals. Bravo.

Håkan Hardenberger trumpeter, 1991

I love Scandinavian music, and when I played Max's trumpet concerto in Orkney in 1991, it felt like I was bringing the concerto home to a Scandinavian type of place. I feel there is a great affinity between Max and Sibelius.

In the cathedral, I was intensely aware of colours, particularly the red stone of the building, while I was playing.

Being Scandinavian-minded, I would not normally accept to come to a midsummer festival, as this is such an important family holiday at home. I agreed, however, and brought my wife and son to Orkney as well. They were worried about missing out on the usual rituals of this holiday, but we looked for Scandinavian things and found herons, and a lovely place with a stone setting that was more intensely Scandinavian than we could have wished for. I also discovered Highland Park whisky. We decided that it had been the best midsummer holiday celebration we had had.

Judy Arnold

Max knew Elgar Howarth and wrote a trumpet sonata for him - in fact, it was Max's opus No1. A few years later, Elgar Howarth phoned me to say that he had heard a young trumpeter called Håkan Hardenberger and Max had to write a concerto for him. We went to listen to him playing, and when he lifted the trumpet to his lips and blew, the roof nearly came off the building. As it turned out, Max did write a trumpet concerto, but for John Wallace, although Håkan Hardenburger has played it several times. I was anxious that he should play it in Orkney, at the festival, and we managed to secure him for 1991.

George Rendall festival chairman, on Runrig, 1991 (in conversation)

I was given the job of organising the Runrig concert because, I think, the committee sensed it would be close to my heart. The idea came from Kate Martin, who was connected with the Highlands and Islands Development Board. She had a deep but eclectic interest in the arts - particularly the Scottish arts - and was seconded by the HIDB to help organise events to mark the passing of the HIDB and the birth of Highlands and Islands Enterprise.

At that time there was a great ground swell of self-confidence in Scotland. It seems to me now, as it did then, that we stopped apologising for being Scots and started being quietly proud of our heritage. Runrig were very much an expression of that feeling. Here was a band, singing in Gaelic much of the time, but drawing massive crowds to rock concerts. It was the time of 'Cool Caledonia'!

Kate infected me with that feeling, but, of course, finding the funding for such an ambitious event was a huge problem. For a start there was no stage big enough. We enlisted the expertise of Pete Irvine and Barry Wright of Regular Music, and they organised the appearance of two pantechnicons all the way from England (ironically). These mammoths folded out, Chinese box style, and in no time you have a lighting rig, a sound rig, a stage and even electricity generators.

Pete and Barry advised us how to create lanes of crush barriers leading up to the venue, and they even advised on the number of toilets we would need. (Our esteemed local authority disagreed and thought we could do with less, which resulted in the men's toilet being overrun by women!) The whole thing was very educative, being on a scale we'd never experienced before. We attracted 5,000 people - although we barely covered costs.

The people who were there still talk about it. The way it happened, with the sun going down over Wideford Hill and the moon rising behind the stage on a glorious cloudless night, was truly memorable. We would have considered ourselves fortunate just to have the rain hold off (it rained throughout the festival except on that day) but to have such a night was beyond dreams. What folly, in hindsight, to put on an open-air concert in Orkney in the middle of June! Fortune on that occasion favoured the foolhardy!

It does disappear in a blur of emotion really. I can remember the moment when the band first struck up; I was on the band-ward side of the crush barriers and I just had to turn and walk away. Tears were threatening - all that effort and it was such a perfect night. The crowd were jostling, jammed up against the barriers, obviously eager to make the most of it. You knew from the first moment that it was a success. What a feeling. And watching Donnie Munro, the lead singer, made me understand why he had become an iconic figure in the Scottish awakening; there was something about his delivery and his demeanour that reminded me of those natural orators who can 'work' crowds.

Runrig, 1991.

The crowd at the Runrig concert.

The refreshment tent.

"Runrig took Orkney by storm...The energy from the crowd was unmatched by anything seen in Orkney before." CP
The Orcadian
June 27, 1991

Donnie Munro,
lead singer with Runrig, 1991.

Afterwards - at three or four in the morning - one of the band went off fishing on Harray Loch. The rest of them stayed on as the crew dismantled the rigs ready to leave later that morning and we had a chance to speak to them. I think the event had been a bit special for them too. Donnie's last words to the crowd had been a heart-felt 'We'll be back!'

The night was a one-off in every way. There was a great splash in the paper and even the councillors who were involved were excited about it. I honestly believe that it was more than just a rock band coming. Scotland was on a roll at that time, and Runrig were on the crest of that wave.

Donnie Munro former lead singer, Runrig, 1991

I remember very distinctly the great excitement which Runrig felt at being invited to perform at the St Magnus Festival in 1991. For a band which had emerged from out of the island communities of the West Coast it was of particular interest to be coming to perform in another island location, especially as part of the St Magnus Festival which had become a major event in the arts calendar.

I remember the wonderful but slightly strange feel of arriving in Orkney and smelling the sweetness carried on the wind - the type you only really experience in the islands - but despite the familiarity, being conscious of an island of a very different nature and physical geography to the one where I myself had grown up. There was a tremendous buzz about the place and a tremendous warmth towards the band that made us feel very much at home.

The setting for the concert itself was utterly unique and I will never forget the special moment, looking out over the crowd as the sun set behind Wideford Hill and the moon rose to light the night sky immediately behind us.

A night of music mingled with the sense of a very special place that will remain forever a special memory.

Tommy Smith, 1991.

Tommy Smith jazz saxophonist, 1991, 2001

The first two things I remember about flying into Orkney in May 1991 are the crystal clear waters that surround the islands and another memory, long forgotten, which suddenly popped back into the present; that this was not my first visit. I had been to Kirkwall and Stromness before with my stepfather when I was ten or eleven. He was working with Pickfords removals and I was earning a few pence for carrying some furniture. Then I recalled the incident with the bed. Nothing obscene, only a painful memory of putting the bed through someone's fine window during an awkward manoeuvre around a tight twisting staircase. Oops.

When you're young and immature things tend to be a blur; I enjoyed both my festival visits tremendously. St Magnus is top rate. From the 1991 visit, I remember vividly that Kenny Munro did an amazing job in motivating children to create massive mobiles inspired by my music that swung and stood on the stage in the old cinema. I still have pictures.

Also in 1991, I saw Norman MacCaig's performance and fell in love with his poetry; met him personally in 1993 and dedicated to him an entire recording called *Misty Morning And No Time,* inspired by 14 of his poems.

In 2001, I saw only the streets and the sunshine. Out of all the 23 solo concerts I performed in 2001, I'll remember St Magnus as the best: the light was beautiful at 6pm as the dying red sun shone on to those old stone cathedral pillars. The sound was wonderful and so were the audience.

I always take a visit to the Ring of Brodgar; it's so inspiring. I visited the site at 7.30am in order to see longer shadows created by a low rising sun; it was spectacular. Alone with the wind and the birds - just like my solo show. In fact, in 1991 I played at the Ring of Brodgar and to my amazement a herd of cows lined up...all forty of them. I have pictures of that too.

Festival memories....changing before the concert in the back of a van with Max....hurtling straight into the side of the cinema through the pouring rain....wonderful atmosphere.... in Stromness Town Hall, people listening intently at all heights all around me, including two girls from Prague whom we had met on the ferry over (through waves of sickness) and who have remained dear friends....a rainy lunchtime concert in the cathedral, love music from the court of Spain, magical. And a fair amount of Highland Park....
Imogen Cooper, pianist, 1992

Tasmin Little   violinist, 1996

I was immediately struck by the tremendously warm and sociable atmosphere of the festival - it was as if a large group of friends had gathered to celebrate the arts in all forms.

Upon arriving in Kirkwall, I was whisked off to Stromness for a wonderful exhibition of art where I met all sorts of interesting people who were either involved in the running of the festival or had been coming to the festival for many years. Although I had not been on the island long, I could instantly see why people return with regularity.

I was also excited to have an opportunity to drive around the island the following day to view all the wonderful and ancient areas of heritage. I had been loaned a car by one of the festival administrators, in order to 'play the tourist' - another example of the immense kindness of the people who run the St Magnus Festival.

It was a tremendous pleasure to play in the St Magnus Cathedral and the audience for my concert with John Lenehan were as attentive and enthusiastic as one could ever hope for - I remember that I gave quite a lengthy programme and was delighted to hear afterwards that my concert was considered 'excellent value for money' by one member of the audience!

In addition to my enjoyment of the concerts, my abiding memory of the St Magnus Festival is of the warmth of all the Orcadians and members of the audience that I met during my stay.

Congratulations on the 25th anniversary of the festival and all best wishes for the next twenty-five!

Tasmin Little

"Tasmin Little effortlessly filled the cathedral, not only with the rich vibrancy of her playing, but also with her infectious enthusiasm. Hearing her perform live, one cannot help but enjoy her music."
Sandy Horsburgh
The Orcadian, June 27, 1996

Joanna MacGregor and
Peter Maxwell Davies, 1996.

Joanna MacGregor   pianist, 1996

Although it was midsummer it poured with rain - but the warmth of the audience at Stromness Town Hall cheered me up. It was a lovely acoustic, I remember - all wood - and while I was rehearsing beforehand an artist was sketching my profile in pastels, all very bright, in red, blue and yellow. When he asked me which portrait I wanted, and I chose, he said 'Damn! Musicians always have an eye for the best picture' - which amused me. I had the drawing framed and it hung in my piano room for ages, before I gave it to my parents - it was quite a spiky, energetic drawing which captured the way I was practising that morning.

The other thing I vividly remember - apart from the standing stones, and visiting the Italian Chapel - was having my right hand bitten by a dog a couple of hours before I was due to play Beethoven's 2nd piano concerto at the Phoenix cinema. There was a terrible commotion over this, and I was bundled off to the local hospital by Judy Arnold (Max's manager) for a tetanus injection. The orchestra (RPO), of course, thought it was hilarious. I remember looking down at my hands during the slow movement and seeing bite marks on my fingers. Such is the life of a concert pianist.

Lucy

Glenys Hughes   festival director

Joanna had been using my piano as a practise instrument, and got on fine with my cocker spaniel, Lucy, who is not always friendly towards strangers. On the Saturday afternoon of the festival I came home to find no Joanna, but Max sitting there looking serious. He explained that Joanna had emerged from the music room and Lucy, waking up suddenly, had gone into guard dog mode and had nicked Joanna's finger. Judy had rushed Joanna to hospital for a tetanus jab. She had a concerto performance that day, so I was very anxious until I saw her appear on the platform of the Phoenix that evening. She was very sweet about the whole thing. I heard that the next time she arrived at an orchestral rehearsal in London, the orchestra greeted her by barking!

Kathryn Stott   pianist, 1997

I gave three concerts during the festival in 1997, the first playing Mozart with the Scottish Chamber Orchestra, conducted by Max. Max and I had met a few years before and he was in the process of writing a piano concerto for me, so it was good to have time to chat and think about the forthcoming premiere. However, in the same concert, Max conducted the premiere of a piece written by Marc Yeats. Unfortunately, I was unable to hear the piece prior to my concerto, as there was no dressing room available in the hall....a cinema I think....and I had to sit outside in the car until time to go on! Marc and I instantly became friends, and three years later I asked the BBC Philharmonic to commission a concerto which we premiered together in the Piano 2000 festival.

Apart from my concert activities, I remember the warmth of the local people...the beautiful open spaces.....the whisky....and trying desperately to look like I knew what I was doing during some rather energetic Scottish dancing back at the club!

Kathryn Stott

David Wilson-Johnson (Jumbo)   baritone, 1997, 1998, 1999

It was possibly the worst hotel I'd ever encountered. The pools of vomit in the street outside should have given it away, but then the absence of ash trays in the downstairs rooms confirmed it...apparently there had been a wedding the day before and as the celebrations hotted up the locals took to hurling these around the room causing injuries to other guests. So was this the St Magnus Festival experience that so many of my friends has spoken of with such enthusiasm? Luckily, No.

Once inside that astonishing cathedral things changed dramatically... In 1997 I remember some Schubert songs I sang in new orchestral arrangements which almost worked in that large resonant space, and the following year there was some glorious oboe playing by the wind players of the Oslo Philharmonic as they rehearsed, especially plangent in the huge space... and a very enthusiastic performance of Max's *The Jacobite Rising* by the Festival Chorus in a terrible dry acoustic, conducted by Martyn Brabbins. I have St Magnus to thank for putting Martyn Brabbins and me together for the first time. We've done many happy concerts together since.

But my deepest and most abiding festival memory is the searing performance of Messiaen's *Quartet for the End of Time* I heard given on one midsummer's evening in the tiny chapel built by prisoners of war [see *orchestras and ensembles*].

That was programming of the utmost inspiration, when the choice of music, performers, venue and date all enhanced each other to lift the spirits... rather than just throw the ashtrays.

Dame Gillian Weir   organist, 1999

Contrasts! - the wonderful, soul-stirring shadows of the ancient cathedral, enfolding one in its warmth and responding with whispers and echoes to the music the organ and I released there to fill its spaces; and on the other hand the light, the intoxicating feeling of space and airiness as I wandered the island. The memories stay with me; thank you, St Magnus!

When Kathy Stott was playing in the festival, we met for the first time in the festival bar, just briefly. Later that evening we all went back to the Bevans, where I was staying. Kathy and I stayed up talking about life, the universe and everything else until it was morning. We eventually fell asleep on the armchairs, covered with blankets. That was the start of a very close relationship which endures to this day. It was also to become a strong artistic partnership, with Kathy giving the premiere of my work for piano and orchestra, *The Round and the Square Art of Memory*, commissioned by the BBC. *Marc Yeats, composer*

[Gillian Weir's] " *consistently breathtaking and almost unbelievable technique left you wondering: how many hands and fingers does this woman possess? The reaction of the large crowd tended to suggest they might well have been thinking the same.*" Michael Tumelty The Herald, June 23, 1999

John Lill and
Peter Maxwell Davies, 2000.

"It's unlikely that anything in this year's St Magnus Festival will rival, in terms of public response, the reception that pianist John Lill received at the end of his celebrity recital in Stromness. The capacity Town Hall audience - I've never seen the place busier - erupted at the end of a typically big-boned, marathon programme from this consummate professional."
Michael Tumelty
The Herald, June 20, 2000

John Lill pianist, 2000

It is a unique and uplifting experience not only to savour the Orkney environment but to marvel at what has been achieved by Max and his festival.

To give concerts in such a peaceful and beautiful area is an inspiring and joyful experience.

May I heartily congratulate all concerned in the outstanding organisation of the St Magnus Festival and the great British composer, whose brain-child it was.

Sir John Eliot Gardiner director, The Monteverdi Choir and Orchestra, 2000

June 17 was the only really hot day of summer, and we spent it - all 50 of us - not, as planned, travelling to Orkney, nor productively rehearsing in a dark studio, but kicking our heels at Stansted airport. The air traffic controllers' central computer had crashed, effectively paralysing all of London's airports. After a six hour wait it seemed as though we might finally be off: we hurried to board our charter plane, buckled up, only to be told that Kirkwall airport had announced that it would close for the night at 7pm - ten minutes before we were due to land! Disconsolately we evacuated the plane and dispersed.

Not only had we lost a vital rehearsal for our concert programme the next day, but gone was any realistic chance for us to get properly acquainted with Orkney. So much hung on this visit: the goodwill of the friendly festival staff, a return on their invitation and investment to get us all the way for the St Magnus Festival; above all the obligation to give a memorable concert as part of our year-long Bach cycle, now approaching its halfway point. To travel to Kirkwall at all we'd had to dig deep into our rapidly vanishing benefactors' fund, and yet here we were, grounded and frustrated at Stansted. It was the first - and only - time in this entire marathon year when the gremlins conspired to undermine our travel plans.

At 7am the next day we reconvened and boarded the charter, an old propeller job known in the trade as a crop-sprayer. Arriving travel-stained at Kirkwall three hours later, we were given a welcome buzz by the bracing air and crystal clear light. The festival administrator, Dorothy Rushbrook, commiserated and drove me directly to St Magnus Cathedral. The pink and ochre sandstone put me in mind of Durham. But its chunky pillars and narrow nave gave the impression of having been carved rather than built. I was relieved to find that for all its beauty and historical importance as a shrine, tourism had not flattened its batteries: it seemed to me a magical, uncluttered place, well suited to meditation and worship - and hopefully, music. There was so much to see and absorb and no time to do it. A few of us made a rushed visit, sandwich in hand, to the henge monuments of Stenness and Brodgar. Even on the briefest of visits, you cannot escape the sense of layered history in Orkney - Neolithic, Pictish and Norse. When you consider that these magic stone circles were there four thousand years before the point-of-sword conversion of the Norse Orcadians, St Magnus Cathedral seems quite a modern building.

We rehearsed there all afternoon. Having lost a whole day at Stansted, we needed to telescope two full rehearsals into one, pull together the strands of all four of the unusually complicated cantatas Bach had composed for Trinity Sunday, adjust to the acoustics, connect with the place and with the Cathedral Choir whom we had invited to join us in the singing of the chorales. A tall order.

So far we seemed to have met our targets reasonably well. We had set out to perform all the surviving church cantatas on the appropriate Sunday in the liturgical calendar which meant that we needed to engage with the set biblical readings and Bach's chosen texts. But then everything in this pilgrimage was a means towards serving the music, putting it first, of finding a modern historic context for it. Most of us were convinced that there is no better music than this, and that gave an urgency to make the most of each first - and probably - last chance of performing it and of conveying our delight in it, even if it meant travelling 2000 miles on the day of a concert to do so!

For all our excitement at visiting the Orkney archipelago, from the moment we arrived 24 hours late and began rehearsing in St Magnus, I think each of us knew that this concert was going to be tough going, even by the exacting standards of this marathon Bach year. On the plus side, this particular group had bonded very well. But we were cramped on the stage, with several of the violins stuck behind pillars and the sound bouncing unevenly off the reflective surface and not travelling easily to the back of the nave.

One wonders how the original listeners responded to hearing the music, a brand new piece each Sunday, week in week out. There is absolutely no documentary testimony: were they delighted, shocked, uplifted or just bemused? With a festive chorale-based cantata like *Gelobet sei der Herr* (BWV 129) with which we concluded our St Magnus programme, one might conjecture that they would have felt if not at home, then at least on familiar territory, the chorales having an icon-like significance to Lutherans in all ages.

For its penultimate movement, Bach came up with one of his most glorious and genial melodies, one that has been a life-long companion ever since I first heard my mother sing it during my childhood. That was a surprising piece of serendipity, since Orkney also has direct family links with me. For many years my aunt Margaret made regular visits to a much loved croft there, and I had eagerly looked forward to visiting the Pier Arts Centre in Stromness, to which she had bequeathed her entire collection of Henry Moore, Barbara Hepworth and other 20th century masters. But it was not to be, at least not on this occasion, thanks to those blessed computers at Stansted. But perhaps another time?

Sir John Eliot Gardiner

The collective feeling that I got is that the performance of the Monteverdi Choir - perhaps due to travelling circumstances - wasn't what people were expecting. Some of the concert was simply outstanding, but the cathedral was jam-packed, and there were maybe too many folk there; it was the right building, but the wrong concert ambience. And you get an entirely different feeling of the sound and spaciousness of the music depending on where you are sitting. One person might be disappointed with a concert while another thinks it's the best sound ever.
David Griffith
woodwind instructor,
Orkney Schools
(in conversation)

"Natalie Clein is a thoughtful and poetic musician, whose tone is never forced."
Kenneth Walton
The Scotsman, June, 2001

Julius Drake and Natalie Clein, 2001.

Sometimes things happen that we can't do anything about - just acts of god. During the Thomas Zehetmair and Ruth Killius concert in the cathedral, for instance, we had several breaks in the recording because of the huge thunderstorm. The 1812 Overture might have been more appropriate music for that! But the cathedral is always a dramatic setting to listen to any sort of music; there is something very special about the building.
David Steele
production coordinator,
BBC Radio Scotland
(in conversation)

Natalie Clein cello, 2001 (in conversation)

Travelling to Orkney was very special. It is a unique place and a unique festival. The audiences are incredibly fresh - totally un-snobbish and open to everything from Webern to Bach and Franck - very responsive. It is a very inspiring feeling to play for people who don't go to recitals every week - they seem to really appreciate the musicians that come to the festival.

I so much enjoyed my recital in the Stromness Town Hall. It has a good acoustic - especially for the audience. Unfortunately, it is nicer for the cello without people in - it's a bit more resonant - but still, as a converted church it has a very special atmosphere. People are sitting very close and it is so intimate; a lovely place for a chamber music recital.

Thomas Zehetmair and **Ruth Killius** violin and viola, 2001
(in conversation)

There was a great thunderstorm while we were playing, and it was exciting to be so surrounded by nature. Sometimes music is about thunderstorms - it's a better noise than trucks or railways! We just concentrated on the music, and hoped the light would stay.

There is some lovely music for the violin and viola, and the Mozart duos come first. They are really jewels of chamber music. Joseph Haydn had had to write six duos for a king or a duke and could only write four. He asked Mozart, through friendship, to write these two duos - and Mozart didn't write his name on them, so they were attributed at first to Haydn.

We very much enjoyed the concert with the BBC Scottish Symphony Orchestra. It was a little worrying because it was a bit squashed on stage. But that's how it is with venues, and I think the atmosphere gave a lot of compensation. Sometimes when one is squeezed together, one has a better feeling with the music.

We have certainly met, as part of the festival, some very genuine, nice people - and we felt a very special atmosphere; a very good feeling. We love the cathedral. It is unbelievable - the acoustic, the atmosphere of this whole building, and the wonderful stained glass window. We could see it when we were playing and it is amazing.

PMD, Ruth Killius, Thomas Zehetmair, 2001.

Roderick Thorne

pieces for children

A generation of children has grown up in Orkney with the festival, and many of them have taken part in a musical production written specially for them by Peter Maxwell Davies. From *The Two Fiddlers* in 1978, there has been a string of innovative pieces written for the children of specific Orkney schools and age-groups, produced by some gifted music and drama teachers who manage to get the best out of both the music and the young performers. By general consent, PMD's children's pieces are universally accessible, and great fun to perform. Unusually, the children sing, act, dance and play the pieces entirely, with no adult presence on the stage; and typically, the children meet the challenges the pieces present, without being stretched beyond their capabilities. The results are hugely rewarding for everyone involved, and it is not unusual to find adults in Orkney who can still sing every word of the PMD children's piece they did in primary school.

Apart from the recognised educational value of the children's pieces, both musically and imaginatively, some of them have taken their place in the essential PMD repertoire, and have been performed all over the world, in many translations.

"A priority for me was writing pieces for the schools straightaway. I remember doing the *Kirkwall Shopping Songs* early on, which Glenys produced wonderfully. I don't think it's for nothing that I taught for three years in a school, from 1959-1962. I was head of music there, which was very useful classroom experience. During those years I really did learn a great deal about writing music for kids."
Peter Maxwell Davies (in conversation)

The *Kirkwall Shopping Songs* was the first thing I performed in at the festival, in 1979, when I was 11. I remember practising as a choir in the infant hall a lot, and I was very nervous when Peter Maxwell Davies came in to hear us and give comments. I certainly understood the whole affair was very important and was in awe of the actual composer coming to hear us!
Glynis Tait (Littlejohn)
Festival Chorus member

Mona Levin   music journalist, Norway

In 1979, a main event was the premiere of Max's *Kirkwall Shopping Songs* - a cycle of songs on what may happen when children go shopping for their mothers. My most happy memory of the festival - aside from meeting Max's personal manager, Judy Arnold, who has ever since been a dear friend, and having coffee and Orkney one hundred per cent proof malt whisky at Max's kitchen table on Hoy - was seeing the composer in blue Norwegian rain clothes, bought the previous year at the International Music Festival in Bergen, walking down the picturesque, fragrant and narrow main street of Kirkwall, totally swamped by happy children, flooding him with love and asking questions: Did you like writing the *Shopping Songs*?; Which one is your favourite?; Do you remember my sister from last year? She was in *The Two Fiddlers*; Do you prefer writing for children or for grown ups?; Do you remember my name?; What will you write for us next?

At that precise moment I knew that all the clichés about having to start with the children to bring forth new music - or classical music at all - are completely true. Max's life in music is one hundred per cent proof of that!

Glenys Hughes   festival director

I suppose it is hardly surprising that throughout his time in Orkney Max has written music for children to perform. After all, back in the late 1950s, as music master at Cirencester Grammar School, he was widely known for his innovative teaching methods and for the music he composed for his pupils. One of those pieces, *O Magnum Mysterium*, was performed by Kirkwall Grammar School at the very first St Magnus Festival, setting the pattern for the annual involvement of Orkney schools which was to become such a uniquely appealing feature of the festival.

After *The Two Fiddlers*, premiered by KGS at the 1978 festival, I wrote to Max - whom I hardly knew at that time - to ask whether there might be a possibility of some primary school involvement in a future festival. Max responded with *Kirkwall Shopping Songs*. Though he had never before written for 7 and 8 year olds, these miniatures were perfectly judged for the age group and they were a joy to teach.

The performance of the *Shopping Songs* went well and Max proposed that, for the 1980 festival, he write an extended work for primary-age children - an opera (or, rather, a pantomime-opera) based on the Cinderella story. The new opera would be performed by Papdale Primary School, with pupils from the Grammar School taking on a few of the roles and providing the string section of the small orchestra.

Max had said that he would write the libretto over Christmas. One evening in December 1979, Dick and I met him in a central London bar, where, to our great surprise, he read out from a large, leather-bound book, the text of the entire opera.

It was evident that there was to be no fairy godmother, but, instead, a magic cat. This version would have three ugly sisters (we had already earmarked three talented boys from the Grammar School) and Cinderella herself - though the local references indicated an Orkney setting - would arrive by train. Knowing that I was eager to involve as many children as wished to take part, Max had included three chorus groups - the train, the magic kittens and the ball guests.

By the middle of January I had Max's hand-written full score of the first act. Propping up the loose manuscript sheets on the piano and playing through, I felt the music looked daunting to say the least. Instead of dialogue, the songs were linked by lengthy passages of recitative; the Cat's music, containing leaps of a diminished fifth, looked particularly awkward for a young singer; the orchestra of recorders, percussion and strings would have to learn and perform a whole hour's continuous music; and though the opera started in the 'easy' key of F major, the music soon strayed into keys less familiar to young players. Still, there were amusing pantomime-style songs for the Ugly Sisters, several touching exchanges between Cinderella and the Cat, and some lively dance numbers for the kittens and the ball guests.

The publisher, Chester Music, had indicated that the printed vocal and instrumental parts would not be ready until April. That was far too late, so Dick and I spent many evenings writing out the parts by hand so that we could make a start.

Sectional rehearsals began and I discovered that the children were able quite naturally to sing those 'difficult' intervals, that they could appreciate the expressive quality of the recitatives (and sing them!) and that the recorders would, with practice, get their fingers through all those flats. By March we were able to tackle a complete run-through of the music. I remember that Max came to that first full music rehearsal, held in the Portacabin which was the primary school music room, and that he seemed pleased with what he heard.

The whole enterprise depended for its success on a committed team of Papdale staff: dances were choreographed, sets designed, Cinderella's coach fashioned by the headteacher out of an old pram, huge train shapes cut out of sheets of polystyrene and acres of fur fabric made into kitten costumes. There were many occasions when we thought it would never all come together; but of course it did and I recall very clearly that first performance at the 1980 festival. The music did not start quite as intended: the arrival on stage of Cinderella's train is heralded by a repeated one-bar figure on the bass xylophone. But the instrument had been knocked off its stand after the final rehearsal and the bars had been replaced by one of the stage crew - in the wrong order. The embarrassed player had to play a very strange sounding little ostinato until she was able, during a few beats' rest, to rearrange the bars.

Otherwise, the performance went remarkably well. Among those in

Cinderella, 1980. Top: Alison Lochhead, Marlene Mainland, Glenys Hughes. Centre: Alison Lochhead and the kittens. Bottom: Simon Chirgwin, Glenys Hughes, Andrew Green, Peter Marshall.

The local children's accents coloured the words and music of Max's *Cinderella* in a way that can only be called Mozartian.
Stephen Pruslin
pianist and writer

Gunnie Moberg

Alistair Peebles

Gunnie Moberg

Alistair Peebles

Gunnie Moberg

Gunnie Moberg

Roderick Thorne

Songs of Hoy, **1982**; *The Spider's Revenge*, **1991**; *Dangerous Errand*, **1990**; *A Selkie Tale*, **1992**; *Six Songs for St Andrews*, **1988**; *Seven Summer Songs*, **1993**; *Jupiter Landing*, **1991**.

the first night audience were the entire Fires of London, John Drummond, head of Radio 3, who leapt out of his seat as soon as the curtain fell to offer congratulations, and Sheila McCrindle from Chester's, who appeared on stage to present the cast with Cinderella's 'wedding cake', as a thank-you gift from the publisher.

Two years later, in 1982, we were invited to revive the production and present *Cinderella* in Bristol at the biennial conference of the International Society for Music Education. Then in 2001, twenty one years after its Orkney premiere, *Cinderella* was performed once again at the festival, with a new generation of Papdale and KGS pupils, some of them children of the original cast. Happily, several of the Papdale staff who had worked on the first production were involved in this new one.

To me, *Cinderella* is a very special piece. Stephen Pruslin has ranked it among the finest of all Max's works, and certainly the composer's fingerprints and the processes which permeate his 'adult' music can be detected on every page of the score.

After *Cinderella*, subsequent festivals saw a stream of songs and music theatre pieces for children - composed for a variety of age groups, often tailored to the needs and resources of a particular school and sometimes, in the case of the smaller schools, involving every pupil: *The Rainbow* for Stromness Primary; *Songs of Hoy* for North Walls; *The Spider's Revenge* for Evie (composed in response to a request for a piece to complement a project on mini-beasts); *The Great Bank Robbery* for Kirkwall Grammar School; *Dangerous Errand* for Papdale Infants; *A Selkie Tale* for Holm Primary; *Six Songs for St Andrews* for St Andrews Primary; and *Seven Summer Songs* for the combined forces of Burray, Holm and Papdale. Sanday School brought *Jupiter Landing* and *Dinosaur at Large* to the festival, and in June 2000, the same school (augmented by some local adult musicians) presented *Songs of Sanday*, composed to celebrate Max's move to the island.

Does *Songs of Sanday* represent the end of the series? Probably - Max has indicated his intention to concentrate on chamber music for the foreseeable future. But we have, in these charming little pieces, a unique legacy of music for children. For almost a quarter of a century they have enriched the festival, enchanting thousands of adults and challenging, inspiring and communicating directly to hundreds of Orcadian children. It has been an extraordinary privilege to have been involved in it all.

Ian Tait 'Storm Kolson', *The Two Fiddlers*, 1978 orchestra, *Cinderella*, 1980 (in conversation)

The pieces Max writes for kids are very successful and I very much enjoyed *The Two Fiddlers*. At the time it was an evolutionary process - my voice hadn't quite broken then and we were having to change parts all the time, just to make it work. It ended up sounding a bit different to the way it was written - especially the bits that were too low. Norman Mitchell was the musical director, and Dick Hughes was involved as well.

I was very glad to have been involved; it's a learning experience. It is not a long piece but it was hard work at the time and it took about a year to learn it all, especially as it had to be smack on for the premiere. Afterwards, that summer, we took it touring to Italy. Jack Ridgway was the stage director. He was very much a character and looked the part in Italy. That was very hard work as we were performing every night for about a week. I remember it being too hot for Orcadians; we weren't used to it and people fainted on stage. We went to Milan, Turin, Verona and Rome, and performed in venues of various sizes. It wasn't La Scala, but we did get some quite large crowds and it was incredibly well-received. We used to have school kids hanging around outside, which was totally bizarre.

I'm not really a stage person as such, but I managed to do it then fairly easily. Mind you, the role didn't demand too much acting ability. Mostly it was singing and playing - not like Shakespeare! It was all pretty good-humoured stuff. I think if I was asked to do it now I'd find it much harder than I did at that age, and the photograph of me in *The Two Fiddlers* makes me cringe!

More recently, I have been singing with the Festival Chorus - for about the past ten years or so - and love taking part in it. It has reached a very high standard for an ensemble that doesn't even hold auditions. We practise for about four months, and often get the chance to sing with guest orchestras, which is great for amateurs.

I always try to go to the festival music events, especially the big ones with the orchestras or ensembles. The standard is so good. Every year you think that it couldn't get better than this, but it does. And it is not purely a music festival, there's a broad spectrum of events that keeps everyone happy. It's local-friendly, and child-friendly too, which is very important. Max has premiered a lot of new pieces here, and it has done us no harm. Some people would argue that it gets more funding than anything else, but if you don't apply for it, you don't get it. In musical circles anyway, I think the festival has put Orkney on the map.

Peter Marshall 'Gavin', *The Two Fiddlers*, 1978
'Hecate', *Cinderella*, 1980, 1982

My involvement with Peter Maxwell Davies's pieces for Kirkwall Grammar School (a fiddler in *The Two Fiddlers*, an Ugly Sister in *Cinderella*) is now two-thirds of a lifetime ago, but many parts of it are still vivid in the memory. Digging the scores out of a box in the attic, I realise I could sing the parts still (hopefully I won't be called on to do so!). In retrospect, I suppose there was

The Two Fiddlers, **1978.**
top: Jack Ridgway with the cast.
centre: Ian Tait, Peter Marshall.
bottom: the cast.

something distinctly unusual about rural Scottish comprehensive school kids performing for the first time substantial works by a leading avant-garde composer. Yet I am quite certain that at thirteen the music did not seem to me alienating, inaccessible, or 'weird'. No doubt it was written with great care so that we would find it manageable and enjoyable. That is not so say that it was not demanding in places (I think it can now be admitted that I never, not once, got my violin part in the opening bars of *The Two Fiddlers* quite right).

A quarter-century on, my overwhelming impression is that it was all hugely enjoyable; the camaraderie and occasional messing around at rehearsals, all the theatrical business with make-up and costumes, the release and relief of the applause at the end of performances.

When we took the production to northern Italy, I remember going with the adults and fellow fiddler Ian Tait to attend a 'press conference' for local music teachers, at which questions were relayed through an interpreter. 'How many hours a day do you practise?' There was much laughter at the ingenuously honest answer: that the violin came out maybe once or twice a week. But that was perhaps the point. We were all ordinary schoolchildren who liked to sing and play instruments, not precociously talented or gifted performers. The fact we were able to do these rather out-of-the-ordinary things was surely the measure of PMD's achievement with that music, though I firmly believe it was possible only in collaboration with some truly inspirational music teachers (Norman Mitchell, Dick and Glenys Hughes) who demanded the best we could give, and made us feel immensely proud of doing it.

Karen Griffith (Moodie) orchestra, *The Two Fiddlers* and *Cinderella* (in conversation)

I took part in *The Two Fiddlers* when I was 13, playing second fiddle in the pit. I did enjoy it but found it quite difficult. The music was challenging for my age and ability, but I do remember enjoying the performance. At the time, of course, you don't think too much about it - you take it for granted.

I was also second fiddle in *Cinderella*, two years later, and enjoyed that very much too. The music was very accessible. Later on at school, and for a couple of years after that, I sang in the chorus, and I still play locally - most recently with Orkney Camerata.

I do remember as a teenager going along to festival performances, especially Peter Maxwell Davies's music theatre pieces. They may sound strange to many fifteen or sixteen year-olds, but I was completely bowled over by them and thought they were wonderful. One of the pieces I remember most is *Vesalii Icones*; it was absolutely amazing. It never occurred to me at the time that it might be seen as different or outlandish. I suppose when you are exposed to new music when you are young, it either puts you off, or you accept it as it is and love it.

On one of my early visits I went to the first performance of *The Two Fiddlers*, with a splendid trolls' mound painted green and made of cardboard. Later, there was *Le Jongleur*, at which I got so excited I jumped out of my seat and a friend rudely slapped me down.

In 1980, my brother Simon and I went to the first performance of *Cinderella* at the Arts Theatre. We laughed so much we nearly had hysterics. And we both still warm to the memory of massed fiddlers on that same stage, our first experience of that strangely delicious sound, like lemon juice inside a sea-urchin.

Gerard McBurney, composer

Simon Chirgwin 'Dragonia', *Cinderella*, 1980, 1982
(in conversation)

I was an ugly sister in the first *Cinderella* in 1980, along with Peter Marshall and Andrew Green. We were about fifteen or sixteen at the time. (In Primary Seven, the three of us had been the Scarecrow, the Tin Man and the Lion in *The Wizard of Oz*, and I assume that is why we were asked to be in *Cinderella* together.) It was great fun to do, and surprisingly easy - although we knew we weren't getting a trip to Italy out of it, like the cast of *The Two Fiddlers*...

A couple of years later, we revived the production for the festival, then took it down to Bristol and Devon. By that time I was eighteen and had just left school, so Bristol was a fun place to go for a week or so! The second production was more enjoyable, partly because we were older and had more input into the performance. And we didn't have to learn anything really, because it all came back very quickly from the first time.

At the time, we didn't think much about the fact that we had been in a new piece by Peter Maxwell Davies. We probably wouldn't have been able to do it if we had realised the significance of it. Looking back on it, however it was marvellous - not something I will ever forget.

Cinderella is a wonderful piece. I stage managed the first production, and even got a piece of music written specially for me! I couldn't do a scene change in time and asked for some more music to fill it in. The next day, the music was there. Later, Max went down south to see a school production, and when he came back he told me that they had this gap in the middle. Afterwards, he asked them about it, and they said they hadn't been able to do the scene change quickly enough! And that was with the new piece of music!
Bryan Leslie
festival stage manager,
1982-1994 (in conversation)

Papdale Primary School

Cinderella, 2001

[Extracts from the children's responses to *Cinderella*]

Alison Graham, ballroom dancer
When I was chosen to be a ballroom dancer I was so excited and a bit frightened. I got on with it and grew to love doing the dances. We had to practise so many times. I had to get used to dancing with a boy. I got better towards the performance. I think the people thought the three ugly sisters were really funny....

Caron Bews, kitten
I had always wanted to be a kitten in the first place. Mrs Adams did some yoga with us first, then we had to move around and show Mrs Adams what we moved like. We had to stay down low quite a lot of times and we had to stretch our paws out wide....

Shaun Tulloch, suitor
I was pleased to be one of the suitors in *Cinderella* because it was the part I wanted. We got a funny style of a walk and we got costumes.....

Katie Walker, the train
In the train I had to practise to the time of the music. The only thing I had to say was 'toot, toot, choo, choo'. It was hard not to roll your eyes around and

"In all the years since I first met him, I don't think I've ever seen Sir Peter Maxwell Davies so genuinely thrilled as he was when he came out of the performance of his opera for children, 'Cinderella'.

Now, 21 years [after the premiere], with hundreds of performances stacked up all over the world, 'Cinderella' celebrated its coming of age by coming home."
Michael Tumelty
The Herald, June 29, 2001

Cinderella, 2001,

I played my violin in the orchestra of the 2001 performance of *Cinderella*. It was a really good experience and very good fun. We had lots of practices after school and nearer the time we got time off school nearly every day to get in some extra practice. I enjoyed playing at the performances because the audience really seemed to like it. There was always a sound or a joke to keep them interested.
Catriona Price
Kirkwall Grammar School

to stay still. Stay like a train. Hecate was very funny. Some bits of the show I thought I missed something because they laughed so much....

Jacqueline Gunn, train and ballroom dancer

Most of the practices were spent by learning dances for the ballroom. For the train we had to keep our arms straight and keep singing while walking across the stage. It was very colourful and people thought it was really good....

Kirsten Grieve, train and ballroom dancer

I didn't really want to be in the train. The movement was forward and back, sliding left and right feet up and down, standing frozen. It was hard but I felt pleased with myself and excited.

Jessica Burton, kitten

Some of the kittens had to move around and on a sofa. I think the people that watched it liked the two cats singing their song with the kittens prancing around them. They laughed at the suitors as well....

Karen Learmonth, train and ballroom dancer

I would rather have been a kitten but I was a lot happier when we found out that we were in the ball. In the rehearsals it was hard but we just had to practise more if we found it difficult....

I am so glad that *Cinderella* was performed again in 2001, because that was one of the first things I remember at the festival. I was in absolute paroxysms of laughter because they were so wonderful - so fresh and fantastic; these were kids who really were coming at it purely from their own imaginations.
Philippa Davies, flautist

Kim Pirie, kitten

Most of our time we had to act like kittens. I think that everyone loved our show and I heard a lot of people say it was very good, they loved it and I wish I could see it again....

The Rainbow, 1981

Peter Maxwell Davies   (in conversation)

When we were doing *The Rainbow* in Stromness, I remember being very worried because I'd never before written anything quite like that for a primary school. I came over from Hoy, and as I walked up from Stevie's boat, on the way to a rehearsal, a kid went by on a bike, whistling. I thought, 'I know that tune'. Then, from behind a wall, I heard somebody else whistling a different tune, and thought, 'Yes, I know that one too!'. It was lovely to hear those tunes coming from the children involved.

The Rainbow, **1981**.

Alison Guthrie (Ritch)   *The Rainbow*, 1981

I was in Primary 7 at the time, and I remember being called into the music room on my own and being asked by Miss Halsall, our music teacher, to sing a piece of music I had never heard before. I was later told that I would be singing a solo part in *The Rainbow*. The part that I was given was a humorous one - Reamy's dog. Pat [the hero] encounters the dog on his quest to find out what the rainbow is, but the dog is more interested in finding a juicy bone than helping.

Although I know that a great deal of hard work and practice went into ensuring that the performances went smoothly, I have only good memories of being involved in *The Rainbow*. As far as I am aware most of the older pupils in the school were involved. Those that didn't have a musical part contributed by making masks and scenery. To this day I can remember the solo songs I sang and those of most of the other characters, which surely goes to show how catchy and memorable both the lyrics and music were.

I suppose at the time none of us really appreciated the importance of this thing we were involved in. On reflection, however, I consider myself lucky to have been involved in it. Peter Maxwell Davies wrote this piece especially for the children of Stromness Primary School to be performed in the St Magnus Festival, which was an honour that most children don't get to experience.

The Rainbow, **1981**.

Graham Garson   'ubiquitous' festival performer

My part in *The Rainbow* was 238 bars of rest before hammering like a maniac on the glockenspiel, if my memory serves me right, and maybe a bit of recorder playing too. As I remember, I was emotionally scarred by not being asked to take part in the televised restaging of the street scene from the show, when *The South Bank Show* did its programme on Max a couple of years later.

Glenys Hughes   festival director

Happy Returns, 1994

In 1994 we wanted to devise a special event to celebrate Max's 60th birthday. Since his vision had always been of a festival which would include the participation of the local community and of young people in particular, it seemed right that the celebration should focus on the music Max had written, over sixteen years, for Orkney children. Many of these songs, music theatre

Happy Returns, 1994.

"It was a unique night. A night when a young community was unleashed in all its power. A night, as someone commented in the post-festival celebrations, of social history in the islands.

From the rejection as an elitist imposition, 18 years ago, of Peter Maxwell Davies's ideas of an island festival, the wheel has turned full circle."
Michael Tumelty
The Herald, June, 1994

I was very moved by the birthday celebration concert. It was lovely - one of those nice things that happen very rarely.
Peter Maxwell Davies
(in conversation)

and instrumental pieces have since become classics in the field of children's music and I felt that to bring them back to Orkney at this time would be a lovely thing to do. Neil Firth of the Pier Arts Centre came up with just the right title - *Happy Returns*.

Music theatre had to be represented of course, so Stromness Primary were invited to revive *The Rainbow* and present it in the Arts Theatre, in a double bill with a more recent children's piece, *Dinosaur at Large*, which Sanday School agreed to produce and bring in to the festival.

But the main event was a huge concert in the Phoenix cinema involving every school on the Orkney mainland plus several island schools - seventeen schools in all. The east mainland schools took the platform for the first half: a choir of 170 primary school children sang *Kirkwall Shopping Songs* with Holm and North Ronaldsay providing instrumental accompaniment and Papdale contributing mime; Shapinsay School danced to music from *The Two Fiddlers*, played by a talented young violinist, Alison Dixon; and Kirkwall Grammar School Girls' Choir sang *Seven Songs Home*. The fun continued after the interval with excerpts from *Cinderella*, with Dick [Hughes], David Griffith (woodwind instructor) and Eric Sinclair (rector of Kirkwall Grammar School) appearing in drag as the Ugly Sisters. Then all the west mainland schools sang *Songs of Hoy*, with mime and dance performed by the children of North Walls, the school on Hoy which had premiered the songs in 1982.

I had thought that the concert should end with something for Max composed by the children, so I asked George Mackay Brown if he would pen a verse which the children could make into a song. So that is how the concert ended; all five hundred children appeared on stage to sing *Birthday Song*, composed by Elizabeth Dearness, a Primary 7 pupil from Holm, and Elizabeth presented Max with a copy of the score at the very end. It was a great event - I thought the applause would never stop - and of course we had to give a repeat performance the following evening for all the people who couldn't get tickets. The real heroes though were the teachers who supervised the vast numbers off-stage in the scout hall across the road.

Songs of Sanday, 1999

Roderick Thorne   librettist, *Songs of Sanday*
former headteacher, Sanday Junior High School

Glenys explained; now that Max had moved to Sanday, he was keen to make a musical gift to the school to mark his arrival. Could I think of some suitable themes or topics, perhaps even try writing words for some songs?

It was great fun, though not always easy. Island life, even day-to-day experience, provides such a rich source of ideas. I wanted to ensure that all of the schoolchildren were involved, and some topics began to order themselves according to their ages.

The youngest would introduce the show with a welcome to Sanday, and each short verse might be about their world - the sea - with creel-boats, cockles, spoots, otters. Later on they'd sing of the land - eyebright, hearts-ease, spring squill, whaups and dunters.

Primary 3-5 boys and girls study the vikings; here was an opportunity for them to celebrate their remarkable heritage - the Scar boat burial and the rune-stone. That summer's North Isles Sports on Sanday was a fiftieth anniversary, so a light-hearted reference seemed appropriate. In contrast, the mass stranding of eleven whales was still a stark memory for older children.

Max was a delightful and encouraging accomplice in what was, after all, his project. He read through the songs, and reflected on possible music; then we spent a few convivial evenings together with Glenys. After one such discussion, we agreed that the commemoration of the island Raft Race should include the appearance, out of the mist, of a ghostly longship crewed by the three vikings who had been buried at Scar a thousand years ago.

The island's children were, of course, stars of the production. It was good, too, to have the participation of the island's music group; and - memorably - Sanday's lighthouse attendant, Andrew Skea, narrated the story of the light to his grand daughter, Hayley, one of the youngest pupils in the school.

Roderick Thorne

Sanday Junior High School, 1999.

Sanday Junior High School

[Extracts from the children's responses to *Songs of Sanday*]

Hayley Skea

I remember doing *Lighthouse* with my grandad Andrew Skea. When me and Grace got told we were doing this, it was so scary. But when it was over and done with I wanted to do it again!

Douglas Drever

The songs were like a story of the past made into a story of sadness or happiness. Our song was about the sperm whales which had been washed up on Backaskail beach. Some people could have heard them crying on the sandy shore but it could have just been selkies on the rocks singing to the moon.

[on Songs of Sanday]
"...*We were treated to a demonstration of how to build a substantial and interesting structure, complete with theatrical elements, from the simplest, essentially basic, material.*"
John Warnaby
Musical Opinion
September, 1999

Michelle Dearness

We had special t-shirts with the Sanday logo on. I'm not sure who put on my make-up but whoever did got it on my t-shirt. I did a solo in the song 'Vikings'. I personally thought it was a really fun experience.

Edrian Skea

I played an old viking rune stone. The costume I had to wear was weird. It had no bottom so I had to hold it down so they couldn't see my boxers. All the teachers were telling us to do our best of course, as we always did. Nobody even doubted us, well maybe except the teachers a little.

Catherine Harvey

I was the Goddess Freya and had to dance around on the stage like some kind of ballet dancer. Personally I hate frilly things, so when I saw my costume I nearly fainted, it was all over frilly. Overall it was good fun.

Thomas Harcus

By the time we were half way through the performance everybody was quite laid back. But then the solos started to come thick and fast and when mine came I went like a clam tight shut and not budging. But it went well and was a lot of fun.

Bryony Newton

We were rehearsing with all our old music teachers, Mrs Dunsmuir, Mrs Hughes and Maggie, so we had three music teachers telling us three different things to do. We grasped some bits straight away and others we hadn't got into our heads. So we did what we thought was right and it turned out fine in the end.

Andrew Skea Start Point lighthouse attendant, Sanday

I was rather nervous to begin with, but after a few rehearsals and a performance in Sanday it was not too bad. I suppose I was more nervous of letting the children down, being the only adult on stage with them, and they seemed so relaxed right through the whole production. I became involved when Rod Thorne, who wrote the script, said he would like me to do it, being the attendant at Start Point lighthouse.

My part in the production was to read to my grand daughter, Hayley, a short history of Start lighthouse from when it was first lit in 1806, up to the present time when it was converted to solar power.

Taking part in a performance at the festival was nerve-wracking and exciting, as well as giving you a feeling of having taken part in something special. I was glad I took part because when it was all over I realised I had really, in the end, enjoyed the whole experience. As for doing it again, I think it was a one-off, and I will retire with my memories.

the Festival Chorus

The Festival Chorus has a long-standing niche at the heart of the festival. From Vivaldi's *Gloria* in 1980 to Kodaly's *Psalmus Hungaricus* in 2001 (sung in Hungarian), the chorus has performed in every festival, without missing a year since it was founded in 1980 by the late Dick Hughes, organist and choirmaster of the cathedral, and head of music at Kirkwall Grammar School. Dick's wife, Glenys Hughes, festival director, took over direction of the chorus in 1996, when Dick died. Over the years, the chorus has grown in stature and confidence, often singing with professional orchestras such as the Scottish Chamber Orchestra and the BBC Scottish Symphony Orchestra, under the baton of conductors including Nicholas Kraemer and Martyn Brabbins. They have also teamed up with the Orkney Orchestra, Orkney Camerata, school orchestras and choirs. For a local chorus, usually around a hundred strong - and for which there are no auditions - it has achieved a remarkable standard. No other locally based performance at the festival annually musters such a large group of committed individuals from the community.

Sir, I am anxious... to bring to the notice of your readers an idea which I would like to see brought to fruition in the 1980 St Magnus Festival....One of the aims of the festival must surely be to encourage as many people as possible to participate in making music together. I say this not purely for musical reasons, but also for social reasons. I believe that music, like religion, can, through misuse, create social barriers; likewise it has the power to break them down.

And so to the idea. I would like to see the formation of a Festival Chorus. Our aim would be to perform Vivaldi's 'Gloria' in the 1980 festival... I would be glad to hear from anyone who would be interested in supporting this venture.

Yours etc,

Richard Hughes

The Orcadian, November 22, 1979

St Magnus Cathedral Choir, 1982.

Glenys Hughes   festival director, Festival Chorus director

Dick succeeded Norman Mitchell as cathedral organist, and, though he was keen to continue the festival involvement of the Cathedral Choir, he felt there was scope for widening the local participation by offering an opportunity for people to sing in a large chorus. The Cathedral Choir members were asked to be the nucleus of the new Festival Chorus for 1980: the plan was that, for a few months leading up to the festival, the first part of the choir rehearsal would be in the cathedral as usual, then everyone would adjourn to the Papdale Infant Hall, where, hopefully, a large number of eager singers would be waiting to join with the Cathedral Choir in rehearsing a work for the festival. There was a huge and enthusiastic response and Vivaldi's *Gloria* was performed that year in the cathedral by a chorus of around eighty singers accompanied by an orchestra of local musicians.

It became clear that there was a strong desire for the Festival Chorus to become an annual event. Over the next few years the chorus performed a variety of works - then, in 1986, the chorus opened the tenth anniversary festival with a memorable performance of Rutter's *Gloria* with the English Brass Ensemble. This was a landmark, since it was the first time the chorus had performed with a professional ensemble. Dick felt that this kind of collaboration should be developed and proposed that, the following year, the chorus should perform with the visiting orchestra. There were concerns among the committee that financially this was too ambitious an undertaking. It did prove financially possible, however, and the chorus gave a splendid performance of the Fauré *Requiem* with the BBC SSO under their principal conductor, Jerzy Maksymiuk.

After that, there was a series of successful collaborations: Purcell's *Dido and Aeneas* with the SCO; opera choruses and folk songs with the

previous page: **Festival Chorus with BBC SSO, 2001.**

Grimethorpe Colliery Band; Mozart's *Requiem* with the SCO. After the performance of the *Requiem* (when space in the cathedral for choir and orchestra had been very cramped) it was clear that future concerts involving chorus and orchestra would have to be held in the Phoenix cinema - even though the acoustic was described by one choir member as 'like singing into a plate glass wall'!

In the early nineties the chorus went from strength to strength. For 1996, a performance of Britten's *St Nicolas* was planned. Dick was very much looking forward to this as he loved Britten's music and *St Nicolas* was a favourite work. Moreover, since the piece was written to be performed by amateur forces, this was to be an entirely local production - for once, he would not have to hand over the baton to the conductor of a visiting orchestra, but would conduct the performance himself. Taking part alongside the chorus would be Orkney Camerata and Dick's Girls' Choir from the Grammar School. It was a cruel blow in 1996 when he died just ten weeks before the performance. At the memorial service, held in the East Church, the chorus sang the final hymn from *St Nicolas* - Britten's setting of 'God moves in a mysterious way'. It felt very appropriate and very moving.

Roger Williams, an old friend and director of music at Aberdeen University, came up to conduct the festival performance and returned the following year to direct Bach's *Magnificat*, again performed with Orkney Camerata.

I have been fortunate to inherit the immense loyalty that the chorus members had for Dick. In 1998 we dipped into contemporary repertoire, performing Max's *The Jacobite Rising* with the BBC SSO; in 1999, for our first concert in the newly-opened Picky Centre, we enjoyed Puccini's *Messa Di Gloria* with the SCO; in 2000 there were two works to be performed with the BBC Philharmonic - Poulenc's *Gloria* and a new work (our first world premiere!) by Max, *Orkney Saga 5*; and in 2001 came a new challenge when we performed Kodaly's *Psalmus Hungaricus* in Hungarian with the BBC SSO.

Over the years the chorus has worked with some wonderful conductors: in the early days Max, then Ivor Bolton, Nicholas Kraemer, Martyn Brabbins (several times) and chorus masters and choir trainers like Christopher Bell. I have certainly learnt a lot from them all.

I feel that the Festival Chorus is one of the real success stories of the festival. It's open to everyone - and it seems remarkable that a place the size of Orkney can muster a four-part choir of eighty to one hundred singers who are quite able to rehearse and perform very creditably with a professional orchestra and conductor. Some members have sung since the very beginning and there are some who have grown up with the festival, taking part as a child in something like the *Kirkwall Shopping Songs*, and later going on to sing in the chorus.

Although we've been going strong for twenty three years, I still feel

Festival Chorus, 1990.

Festival Chorus with the BBC SSO, 1991.

"Sir, - May I express congratulations and sincere thanks to the Festival Chorus? Congratulations for a wonderful concert to end the St Magnus Festival,....and thanks for the warmth of your welcome to me and all the hard work that went into the performance. It has been a great pleasure and privilege to share in your wonderful community music making...You are a unique choir and the contributions you made to the concert were indeed very special."
Dr Roger B Williams
The Orcadian, July 3, 1997

nervous before the first rehearsal of each season. Will anyone turn up? Do they think the chosen piece is too demanding, unattractive, too easy? It's always such a relief on that first evening to see a long queue of people waiting to 'sign on' and collect their scores.

Peter Maxwell Davies (in conversation)

The chorus has worked and worked, and it is growing musically. Dick did a wonderful job as director, and Glenys goes on. Occasionally, I have gone in there to conduct and they have been very well-trained. All I can do is wave my arms about and thoroughly enjoy myself! They have performed such a range of pieces - including Mozart, Haydn, Beethoven, and me - which they did beautifully. I am very impressed and have so enjoyed working with them. It is so lovely to hear in performance all those people. There they are, pitching in and singing some very difficult classical works, or new pieces, and doing them wonderfully well. It is lovely to hear the orchestras that come and play with them say how good they are. It is a great institution.

Glynis Tait (Littlejohn) Festival Chorus soloist

I was always extremely nervous before singing - sweating, shaking and coming out in a nervous rash, but it always seemed to come right when I needed it to. Dick Hughes was very good to me and seemed to have faith in my singing, and I was extremely shocked and delighted to be given the opportunity to perform a solo at the festival in 1985. I was still a teenager and singing with the adults was daunting, but everything on the night went really well.

I had a conflict of interests when performing, as the junior inter county hockey was always happening at that time and I do remember running off the hockey pitch, jumping over the wall to our house - having a quick shower before dashing down the road to the St Magnus Hall to change and go into the cathedral. I think it's called having your cake and eating it, but I certainly wasn't going to miss out.

The festival has been a big part of my younger years, and having the chance to sing with professional orchestras and work with world class conductors, is an opportunity I don't want to miss.

Carolyn Chalmers Festival Chorus soloist

When I first moved to Orkney in the mid-eighties, looking forward to the St Magnus Festival and the start of the chorus rehearsals in February sustained me through the long dark winter months. The dedication and skill of Dick

Alistair Peebles

Peter Maxwell Davies rehearsing the Festival Chorus, 1990.

Alistair Peebles

Festival Chorus with the SCO, conducted by Nicholas Kraemer, 1995.

and Glenys were essential ingredients for honing this 'all comers' choir into one that could perform confidently alongside professional musicians.

In 1989, I was thrilled to be asked to sing as a soloist with the chorus, professional soloists and the Scottish Chamber Orchestra, in a concert performance of *Dido and Aeneas* in the old Phoenix. Kath Hague and I sang the First and Second Witches; Paul Rendall sang First Sailor. Although a little nerve-wracking, it was very exciting and a great honour. Kath and I had been well drilled by Diana Troup, and Dick was always encouraging. The day arrived and the enormity of the occasion hit me when I arrived at the Phoenix for the 'dress rehearsal'. The first thing I noticed was the large van parked outside, with BBC Radio 3 written along the side; this performance was to be recorded! After much adjusting of microphones throughout the afternoon rehearsal, the evening performance seemed to be

flawless; or so I thought until I heard it some months later on the Radio - listening to oneself is always excruciating, but even so, I kept the tape - our Christmas news sounded pretty impressive that year! At the end, the appreciative audience erupted into thunderous applause, and, much to our embarrassment, joined by the orchestra and professional soloists, rose to a crescendo when Kath, Paul and I took our bow - support your local sheriff!

Festival Chorus rehearsal, 1993.

Imagine my disappointment in 1994, when, after all those months of rehearsing, I developed laryngitis a couple of days before our

performance and couldn't sing a note. To add to my frustration, we had Paul Archbold staying with us (one of the brilliant young composers who contributed to the music for *The Beggar's Opera* that year), and conversation was almost impossible; I drove him around the sights of Orkney in near silence! (We did keep in touch for a few years after that, so it couldn't have been all bad.) Fortunately, I managed to acquire a seat (as rare as hens' teeth) to hear the chorus perform Beethoven's Mass in C, with the BBC Philharmonic Orchestra conducted by Sir Peter Maxwell Davies, on the Sunday evening. A very sophisticated lady took the seat next to mine. During the interval we struck up a conversation. 'Have you managed to get to many of the concerts?' she enquired in her soft American drawl. 'One or two' I responded, and shared my disappointment about having to listen rather than sing the Beethoven. 'Have you been to many?' I asked. 'Not yet - but I've played in a few,' she replied. Seeing my quizzical look she introduced herself…. Sylvia Rosenberg - the violinist who had not only performed as soloist with the BBC Philharmonic the previous evening, but had also given that afternoon's celebrity recital in the Stromness Town Hall! We noticed each other at a concert the following day and greeted each other with broad smiles, like old friends - such is the ambience of the St Magnus Festival.

PMD and Sylvia Rosenberg, 1994.

"The Festival Chorus, along with a starry quartet of soloists - Lisa Tyrrell, Margaret McDonald, Neil Mackie and David Wilson-Johnson - outshone itself in a lusty, robust and committed performance (making light of the many technical difficulties they faced) of Peter Maxwell Davies's choral work, 'The Jacobite Rising'."
Michael Tumelty
The Herald, June 25, 1998

Festival Chorus rehearsal

I have been singing with the Festival Chorus since the early eighties, which has been very enjoyable - meeting different people each year, the challenge of different music and working with various conductors in recent times. To me, the most memorable work was Max's *The Jacobite Rising*, in 1998.
Lydia Campbell
festival box office manager

Roy Flett festival board member

The St Magnus Festival Chorus is something very special, if not unique, in the musical world. Participation is open to all, and at festival time every year the chorus provides the centrepiece for a concert involving a professional orchestra and a high calibre conductor. Rehearsals start in the dark days of February and continue more intensively towards midsummer by which time a strong feeling of camaraderie has grown within the chorus.

Visiting artists and conductors often comment on the high quality of the chorus. This is due to the diligence, devotion, and sheer hard work of Dick and Glenys Hughes who founded the chorus and have brought it on so far. Dick's death a few years ago was a devastating blow for everyone, but with Glenys's strength and inspiration the show has gone on - and hopefully it will continue to go on for many happy years to come.

Dorothy Rushbrook festival administrator 1987-2000
(in conversation)

Neil Mackie was coming up to sing Max's *The Jacobite Rising* with the Festival Chorus. I was just about to go to the airport when I got a phone call from Neil to say that he and the soprano, Lisa Tyrrell, had been off-loaded and the flight had taken off without them. This was on the Monday and they were due to rehearse that evening before the concert on the Tuesday. They were to be put up in a hotel and would come up first thing in the morning. What a nightmare! I came storming back into Kirkwall and into the Phoenix (where the rehearsal was to be). The first person I met was Jumbo [David Wilson-Johnson] - the gorgeous baritone - who had been up the previous year as a soloist in the Festival Chorus. 'Oh Jumbo,' I said, 'what am I going to do? - I've got to tell Max they've been off-loaded.' Martyn Brabbins was conducting and I had to tell him, too, that I had lost two of his singers. Fortunately, however, they turned up safe and sound the following morning.

Matilda Tumim artist, Festival Chorus member

Being a member of the large Festival Chorus is racked with both highs and lows over the four month rehearsal period prior to the performance. My own favourite pieces have been Mozart's *Requiem*, Jongen's Mass, Max's *Orkney Saga 5*, Puccini's Messa di Gloria and Britten's *St Nicolas*, before which Dick Hughes, our wonderful choirmaster, died, which gave the performance even more emotion and poignancy.

The main high point is when the piece comes together in the final few rehearsals, especially when the orchestra arrives. There can also be some low moments at this point when we think we are not sounding good and worry that the distinguished orchestra, Glenys and the conductor are all cross with us. However, this is easily compensated for by the tremendous rush of adrenalin just before the concert and the sheer pleasure of being steeped in a piece of music which one has grown to love. The winter rehearsals can be quite hard with a long drive in bad weather and the drudgery of sorting out notes and even new languages when one is too tired or cold-ridden to enjoy it. Equally, there is the euphoria ahead of returning home at night in the midsummer sun after a really good sing, the daffodils glowing as you hum away at your festival tune.

Sandra Ballantine Festival Chorus, 2001

How do I recapture the fear, doubt, nerves, growing confidence and ultimate triumph of being in the Festival Chorus? Remember what it was like learning to drive? Remember trying to manage steering wheel, pedals, gears, mirrors, indicators etc, while keeping your eyes firmly on the road in front? Think back to the confusion you felt then and you will have some idea of what those early rehearsals were like for me - an absolute beginner grappling with notes, rhythms, dynamics - and Hungarian - while trying to keep my head up and my eyes on the conductor. As any learner driver will tell you, the key to success lies in finding a capable and patient instructor, regular practice and a firm familiarity with the Highway Code. In Glenys I found a wonderfully inspiring and sympathetic director who steered me safely through the sometimes tortuous route of Kodaly's *Psalmus Hungaricus* during the regular Monday night rehearsals. (Only the very brave or foolish played hookey!) And a 'Highway Code', provided by Andrew Garden and George Rendall, miraculously made sense of the strange signs and symbols that littered my score.

In a few short months I found myself transformed from a nervous novice into a confident chorus member, ready to benefit from some last minute advice and guidance from Martyn Brabbins who would lead me through the final test - the concert at Picky.

Feeling excited and a little apprehensive (especially about getting that tricky C#), I, with my fellow choristers, faced the Chief Examiner - the Orkney public! After months of hard work and careful preparation it was all over. And the result? I think it's fair to say we passed first time - with flying colours.

...Then came Kodaly's gloriously stirring nationalist anthem, 'Psalmus Hungaricus', with tenor John Daszak in thrilling voice and the St Magnus Festival Chorus, augmented with children's choirs, singing with a quality that was inconceivable a decade ago. Their finest hour - and in Hungarian, too.
Michael Tumelty, The Herald, June 26, 2001

The Festival Chorus has played an important part in my festival involvement, having only missed one year since my voice settled down post-puberty. Under Dick Hughes's directorship to begin with, and Glenys's more recently, we've tackled all kinds of pieces from opera to folk songs, from the baroque to the modern. I'm sure that Dick would have been extremely proud to have heard the chorus sing what must have been one of its biggest challenges, Kodaly's *Psalmus Hungaricus* in 2001, and to see the rave reviews afterwards.
Graham Garson
'ubiquitous' festival performer

In 2001, I had the opportunity to sing, along with many others, with the Festival Chorus for the performance of Kodaly's *Psalmus Hungaricus*. The excitement of performing along with professional musicians is something that is difficult to put into words, and yet is so typical of what can happen in Orkney. This is comparable to what might be available to local singers and musicians in the cities of Aberdeen, Glasgow and Edinburgh when professional musicians visit.
Hugh Smith, headteacher,
North Walls School, Hoy

Dick Hughes -
an appreciation

George Rendall festival chairman,

on Dick Hughes, founder of the Festival Chorus

There were really two Dick Hughes's; one was a stern perfectionist who demanded total commitment from those he worked with, the other was a bawdy, self-mocking comedian who could, on his night, reduce a company to tears of laughter.

When I first met him, the comic aspect was very much to the fore. So funny and so well-told were his stories of former colleagues and acquaintances that to this day we recount many of them even though we never met the people involved.

He had the audacity and honesty to bring people down to size. But if he gave no quarter he expected none either. He could take mockery as well as give it out. He even invited it sometimes, as when he transformed himself into Manuel of *Fawlty Towers*.

Part and parcel with the mimicry was a fascination with language and dialect. His school pupils tell me that he would often get them to say 'Young Fermers' just because he loved to hear the Orkney pronunciation. Then he would refer to the same young fermers as 'adolescent agriculturalists' because he loved the contrast between dialect and standard English.

Dick's ability to amuse is the quality that everyone I have spoken to has mentioned first and foremost; and it is good to remember how much fun he was. However, there was much more to him than that, not all of it pleasant. While he regularly performed acts of kindness and self-sacrifice, he could also wound, because his tongue could be as a sharp as his wit.

I think everyone who knew him was aware that an innocent remark or a thoughtless piece of behaviour might summon up an unexpected storm. The difficulty was that you never quite knew where it was going to strike. But most times his anger would be roused by someone letting him down in some way. And this is where the serious side of Dick came in. He expected pupils, choir members, opera choruses and so on to appreciate the fact that he was putting his musicianship on the line whenever he directed a performance and that turning up for rehearsal was the least they could do.

But when everything was going smoothly Dick was a delight to work with. I was struck when speaking to people just how much enthusiasm he engendered. He somehow managed to entertain as he worked, and music which had seemed difficult often became easy as he picked out with that acute ear of his just where people were having the difficulty.

He never criticised or talked down to anyone whose musical knowledge or ability was not up to his standard - as long as he knew that the person concerned was doing his or her best. But he was also realistic enough to know that at school age (and beyond) the male of the species needs some encouragement to become involved in things musical. Thus the boys whose only desire was to get at the KGS rock band equipment had to 'pay' for the privilege by coming to choir practice first. 'Then,' I was told by one of his pupils (wide-eyed), 'Then he would beam at the tenors and basses and say how great it was to have so many volunteers!'

Brian Jones brass instructor, Orkney Schools (in conversation)

Dick Hughes was a very well-read man - scholarly actually - and he needed to be doing something all the time. He was also a very well-rounded musician. I remember when he played a Handel Organ Concerto with the SCO in the festival; almost immediately afterwards he was playing keyboards with the School Swing Band at the Festival Club.

On my first full day at work in the Grammar School, one of the children said something to which he took exception. He had this lad out in the corridor and just did a Krakatoa, right outside my door. I nearly jumped through the roof! It wasn't for a minute - it was for a lesson! It was only once or twice a year that it happened - he rationed it and got the full effect. He had a booming bass voice; you could imagine Dylan Thomas had written the lines and Richard Burton delivered them.

Steve King principal viola, Scottish Chamber Orchestra

Dick and I got on like a house on fire, and when he died in 1996, it was so sad. In some ways he took a back seat in the festival - he ran the Festival Chorus and did some wonderful work there but he didn't like being too involved in day-to-day festival matters. It was really nice spending time with Dick during the festival because it gave me another side to being in Orkney that wasn't just festival-based. When he died, I felt, like a lot of people, a great loss, and things were never quite the same again.

I managed to get up to Orkney for the day of the funeral, but missed an SCO concert to do that. I think they allowed me to go because the SCO has very strong Orkney associations and they wanted to have a representative at the funeral. I came up on the morning flight with my viola and played before the funeral started - some Bach and Telemann and other things - with Max and other people sitting right in front of me. It was all terribly moving - but it was also a bit like being in an audition. Just before the service started, I wanted to play *Farewell* (which I had written for Capercaillie in 1995), because Dick had liked it. It was just a wee song with a nice little harmonic shift in it, but Dick used to play it and say: 'Steve, that's really great, it gets to your heart doesn't it?' I thought it was a nice way to say goodbye to Dick, and felt so pleased that I managed to get up there and be part of it all.

"A beauty of this festival is the chance to have our own impressive musical resources used to full capacity. It was exciting for those used to being led and taught by Richard Hughes to hear him stretched to his considerable virtuoso ability in Handel's Organ Concerto in F, op. 4 no.5." MAM
The Orcadian, June 22, 1995

Works performed by the Festival Chorus

1980	**Vivaldi** Gloria
1981	**Schubert** Mass in G
1982	**Bernstein** Chichester Psalms **Tippett** Spirituals from A Child of Our Time
1983	**Poulenc** Gloria
1984	**Britten** St Nicolas
1985	**Dvorak** Mass in D
1986	**Rutter** Gloria **Bassano** Praetorius - motets
1987	**Fauré** Requiem, Pavane
1988	**Mascagni, Verdi,** Operatic choruses **Maxwell Davies** Lullaby for Lucy **Robertson, Grainger** folksong arrangements
1989	**Purcell** Dido and Aeneas
1990	**Mozart** Requiem
1991	**Haydn** Maria Theresa Mass
1992	**Haydn** The Creation
1993	**Jongen** Mass **Gabrieli, Bassano** motets
1994	**Beethoven** Mass in C
1995	**Purcell** The Tempest **Handel** The King Shall Rejoice
1996	**Britten** St Nicolas
1997	**Bach** Magnificat, **Vivaldi** Gloria
1998	**Maxwell Davies** The Jacobite Rising
1999	**Puccini** Messa di Gloria
2000	**Maxwell Davies** Orkney Saga V (premiere) **Poulenc** Gloria
2001	**Kodaly** Psalmus Hungaricus

"The cathedral was packed for the last event of the 20th St Magnus Festival which was a choral and instrumental concert dedicated to the memory of Richard V Hughes.

It was an emotional evening for the many people present who had known this mercurial, intensely musical Welshman, chorus master extraordinaire to the Festival Chorus since its inception.

Emotions ran even higher when tenor Neil Mackie paid his personal tribute to Dick when singing a moving unaccompanied arrangement of 'The Lord is My Shepherd' while he walked round the nave... every word crystal clear, and total silence while memories flooded back." JSW

The Orcadian
July 4, 1996

Dick Hughes

local
music

Local involvement in the festival has always been essential, and was possible right from the beginning because of the quality of musicianship that already existed within the community, both classical and traditional. Music has always thrived in the islands, producing some highly skilled players and teachers and attracting a wide variety of professional performers to Orkney through local organisations such as the Orkney Arts Society. Added enticement to visiting players is the quality of some local instruments, including the Steinway piano in Stromness Town Hall, the harpsichord belonging to local chamber ensemble Orkney Camerata, and the fine organ in St Magnus Cathedral.

Over the years, local musicians have made a large contribution to the artistic content of the festival, (although there has been occasional, lively debate about the form this should take). Groups such as the Orkney Orchestra, Orkney Camerata, the Kirkwall Town Band, the Orkney Traditional Music Project, the St Magnus Cathedral Choir and the Festival Chorus, along with several school orchestras, choirs and bands, have performed challenging and varied programmes. There have been collaborations with professional groups and individuals, including a memorable concert featuring Orkney Camerata and the BT Scottish Ensemble in 1998. Successful educational projects, encouraging school pupils to compose and perform music, include the Kirkwall Town Band's concert with London Brass in 2001, and the associated schools work leading up to the concert, with local instructors, members of London Brass and the composer, Fraser Trainer.

Jean Leonard and members of the Orkney Traditional Music Project.

[There was] "a breathtaking display by local young musicians involved in the Orkney Traditional Music Project, which, as an exercise in nurturing and conserving the musical equivalent of the historic oral tradition, has a touch of genius about it."
Michael Tumelty
The Herald
June 25, 2001

Jean Leonard former head of music, Stromness Academy coordinator, Orkney Traditional Music Project

When the St Magnus Festival was proposed, I admit I was one of those who had reservations. I had been trying to teach music, mainly classical, for about ten years prior to the festival with little success. The instrumental pupils were the glorious exceptions, but it was a long haul. As I find modern classical music difficult, I thought other people might also, but thanks to Norman Mitchell at the Orkney end, the festival went ahead.

I have really enjoyed some of the festival performances, especially in Stromness Town Hall. We are fortunate to have such a good piano. The piano recitals alone, like the one given by Vlado Perlemuter when he played Chopin, have been especially spectacular and memorable.

When Dick Hughes died so suddenly in 1996, Glenys asked me to do some rehearsal accompanying for the Festival Chorus. Although I found this tiring, it was exhilarating trying to play along with about 100 voices. My piano technique is on the wane, but I make up for this with confidence and experience.

In 1999, I asked Glenys if she would involve the traditional music pupils in the festival. I am coordinator of the Orkney Traditional Music Project, and always on the look-out for high profile performing opportunities. Glenys came up with the coffee morning concert which has been marvellous for us. In 2000, excerpts were broadcast on Radio 3, and in 2001, we had good feedback from local and national radio and *The Herald*. The project is part of a much broader picture in Orkney; there has always been loads of traditional music in the islands. (There are people like Douglas Montgomery, for instance, who has the wonderful group, Hadhirgaan.) Generally, I feel that the festival could be a bit more cross-cultural, but it has been fantastic for the Traditional Music Project.

I find that now I am retired I can go round the concerts and just really enjoy them. In 2001, the Nash Ensemble were absolutely wonderful. The orchestral concerts have also been a joy, more so since the Pickaquoy venue opened. Although people have been mildly critical of the acoustics I enjoy being close to the players. I also enjoy hearing the gossip from the orchestral musicians - especially what they thought of the conductors and the new compositions!

Graham Garson 'ubiquitous' festival performer

I've been involved in festivals since the early eighties, on and off, more regularly on than off in recent years, in a variety of capacities; musician, actor, singer, director, reader, compiler, audience member, page turner, the list is endless. I even had the dubious honour of being described by Michael Tumelty in a review in *The Herald* as 'ubiquitous'!

My first taste of the St Magnus was in the premiere of Max's *The Rainbow*, composed for the kids at Stromness Primary School in 1981, when I was in about Primary 5. Since then, I haven't looked back, at least not until I was cornered and asked to produce some thoughts on the festival. So that brings me to the question: 'Where do you start?' I suppose my interest in the festival really started with the music, having gone to piano lessons from the age of six, and been dragged to concerts from as early as I could really appreciate them. I have little memory of anything much before secondary school, but since then there have been many memorable events. Probably the most enduring thought I have of a St Magnus Festival concert from that time was a concert of modern compositions for clarinet that a teacher, who will remain nameless, described as 'farting in the bath'! Somewhat irreverent, but very perceptive, nonetheless.

The St Magnus Festival is a great institution. It would be easy to state its importance in bringing tourists to Orkney, but much more importantly it allows Orcadians the opportunity to experience the highest quality of performances in all disciplines first hand, both as audience and participants. It broadens our horizons, and without a doubt, is responsible for the continued growth in interest in the arts throughout the county.

Graham Garson

 **Christina Sargent** founder member, Orkney Camerata, Orkney Ensemble (in conversation)

When I first came to Orkney in 1985, I was completely off performing in concerts, and much more into visual art and organic farming. I had left the SCO and put my oboes away completely. Eventually, I wrote to the education department to see if there was any teaching work going, which is how they discovered that I play the oboe and have a cor anglais.

The Orkney Orchestra was planning a concert for the festival which had a big cor anglais solo, and they wanted to borrow my instrument. In the end, I played it myself at the last minute, because the original player was pregnant and went into early labour. I was still professional enough to just go in and do it, and it was fine.

Things just gradually snowballed. I acquired an oboe pupil, and played in several concerts, and was eventually on the first committee of Orkney Camerata, along with Yvonne Gray, Glenys Hughes, Sandy Dennison and Julia Robinson Dean, amongst others.

A highlight for me on the musical side of things was in 1997, playing Bach's Concerto in D minor for Oboe, Violin and Strings in a concert with the Festival Chorus. It is difficult to keep up a standard on the oboe; it is a very physically strenuous instrument to play. I remember somebody coming and raving about it afterwards, and memories like that are precious. People

The Orkney Orchestra,
St Magnus Cathedral, 1993.

Linda Hamilton

**The Orkney Ensemble,
Balfour Castle, Shapinsay.**

*"Sir Peter Maxwell Davies,
president and founder of the St
Magnus Festival, walked out of
the curtain-raising concert of
this year's festival. He said he
found the sound of the Orkney
Schools' Senior Strings
'unbearable'. Later he explained
that the instruments were out of
tune and it was impossible for
him to listen to any more of the
performance....Sir Peter stressed
that he was casting no reflection
on the children's musical ability.
It had been purely a technical
consideration...*

*The pupils, who are drawn
from the Orkney summer school,
had earlier crossed Junction
Road from the Salvation Army
Hall where they had tuned their
instruments... Sir Peter said that
it was wet weather which had
probably affected the pitch.*

*Sir Peter, an
internationally acclaimed
performer and composer, said
he went off to 'calm down' with
a stiff whisky. There had been
no question of him returning to
the Phoenix."*

The Orcadian, June 28, 1990

have been so sweet through the years. In 1998, I played *Rhapsody for Cor
Anglais and Strings* with Clio Gould and the BT Scottish Ensemble, which
was wonderful too.

One of the criteria for the Camerata was to have a high standard,
which is why we ever became good enough to play with professionals, and
it has worked very well. Funds were raised to pay Julia Robinson Dean as
director of the group. She is extremely musical and very good, and she worked
everybody hard. We did some really good concerts. A smaller, chamber group
called the Orkney Ensemble has since evolved, which has its roots in Camerata,
and there is some crossing over from one to the other.

The Orkney Ensemble has played at the festival several times, and
taken part in two or three excursions to the isles, which were really lovely.
They were always to nearby islands, such as Shapinsay or Flotta. Really, they
were about transporting the festival audience there, rather than the 'festival
on tour' project, which is about taking music to the isles communities.

The festival is all part of the creative and social community in Orkney.
I feel very strongly about putting something back into the community here,
and I would certainly never want to live anywhere else. It would feel very
strange not to be taking part in the festival in some way, whether it's through
music, art, or collaborative community projects. And while it is difficult to
attend everything at the festival, financially and timewise, I have always loved
the fact that it is all going on. People come forward each year that you have
never noticed or known before, and it is very exciting.

Brian Jones brass instructor, Orkney Schools (in conversation)

I had a fiery introduction to the festival! I arrived in 1987, the year after the
Orkney Orchestra had famously withdrawn from the festival, which I had
heard about [see *taking root*]. I remember going to a festival AGM which was
quite acrimonious, and then I was involved in an education project, which
was not a very happy experience, and it culminated in the concert in 1990,
when Peter Maxwell Davies walked out because the children's instruments
were out of tune. That was a hell of a concert! It was a fairly rocky start for
me and it took me a while to recover - but it did get better.

I have been involved with the Orkney Orchestra since the time when
Graham Thomson was conductor. As an instructor, I feel that you have to
give something back to the community. You are taking a living out of the
place, therefore you get yourself involved with anybody who wants you to
be involved - festival or otherwise. These days, the orchestra doesn't rehearse
on anything like a regular basis - they tend to get together for one or two
concerts a year - but they are still flourishing. I've also been playing trumpet
with the Kirkwall Town Band for some time. We used to do concerts in the
festival and then had a Saturday lunchtime slot, which we shared with the

Cathedral Choir in the Town Hall - we had some good times then.

I know some local orchestral players would like to be involved more in the festival, but I'm not sure that the local talent necessarily should be hugely involved. People can sing, and play, but there's a world of difference between top-class players and what people do in their spare time. The festival can give you people who are absolutely on top of their tree professionally, so I wouldn't argue for more local involvement. The Town Band and the Cathedral Choir do a certain amount; the Traditional Music Project have their slot; and other than that there's the Festival Chorus, who are essential, and the children, who will always be involved - and I think that's about right.

It is great to get so close to world-class artists. They take it seriously - they don't come to Orkney and just treat it like a holiday, or put in less effort because it's so far away from London. They really work hard.

Brian Jones, Christina Sargent, 1991.

David Griffith woodwind instructor, Orkney Schools (in conversation)

I first came to Orkney in 1989, and became the conductor of the Orkney Orchestra for a couple of years after Graham Thomson left. One of my fondest memories is a festival concert in 1991, where the orchestra performed Gershwin's *Rhapsody in Blue*, and we also played *Quiet City* by Aaron Copland, with Christina Sargent on cor anglais. It was a very moving performance. Here was a local amateur orchestra performing interesting, challenging works and it was a very smooth, fluid performance.

The other highlight in a later festival was the last performance I did as conductor of the orchestra, when we played Schubert's 'Unfinished' Symphony. We also played a new piece of music by local musician, Sandy Dennison, called *Natural Tones*. We had a whole concert on our own. Towards the end of my time as conductor we shared a festival slot with the Town Band and the Cathedral Choir, which wasn't a format that was really successful.

We did have a pioneering spirit as an orchestra; you're allowed to take a few chances as an amateur group - people are more supportive and forgiving. Musicians are human - it is magical what they can do when the atmosphere is right and everything comes together. And there are some real star players in the Orkney Orchestra; they carried it through, and helped to inspire younger musicians. They sounded professional and it raised the standard. It's still going strong; battling through and trying to recruit new members. It's looking good for the future.

It's interesting to me how the focus on commissioned pieces at the festival seems to have shifted in importance over the years. Sometimes they are a highlight, eagerly awaited, while other years collaborative projects seem to be the main focus. There can be a problem with contemporary classical music, however. If you don't like a piece, the excuse is that you don't understand it unless you listen to it repeatedly, and you are not supposed to comment on

David Griffith in the
Kirkwall Town Band, 2001.

Natural Tones was my personal homage to the music of the American 'minimalists'. I aimed to replicate the sound world of the minimalists by using harmonies associated with their music and a (judicious) amount of repetition, but the resulting piece had a character all of its own. (A number of other influences have been suggested.) On a more anecdotal note, I remember that the principal viola - despite his thorough knowledge of the piece - came in a bar early at a very critical place in the last movement and remained a bar ahead of the rest of the orchestra until nearly the end!
Sandy Dennison
principal viola, Orkney Orchestra, Orkney Camerata

Sandy Dennison with
Orkney Orchestra, 1991.

it immediately. I do feel, however, that one should be able to just listen to a piece of music, and respond.

It is fascinating to see the way the festival has been moulded and shaped over the years, in an almost organic way. I would like to see it become more of a force throughout the year in Orkney, with projects spread out and supported - maybe through visiting professionals or collaborations. That sort of development has a lot of potential. One of the good things about the St Magnus, however, is that, generally speaking, things get better each year and the team work is always there. It has a life of its own, and will always survive because everyone has a stake in it. It is amazing the number of people who have been touched by it all.

Neil Price   director, The Mayfield Singers

My choir, The Mayfield Singers, has appeared in the festival on three occasions. The first was a choral evensong that we sang in St Olaf's Episcopal Church in 1993. I have to say that, for all sorts of reasons, things did not go particularly well. Dick Hughes played for the service in his usual exquisite way, but we were crammed in behind the screen and I had my back to Dick. The first hymn was announced and Dick played through a verse; there followed a seemingly endless silence, finally broken by the rector shouting from the other side of the screen: 'Anything up, Dick?' Our attempts at creating the right atmosphere were well and truly thwarted and it was downhill all the way from there.

The other two occasions were far happier. In 1996, the Århus Sinfonietta were visiting from Denmark with an unusual collection of instruments. When Glenys Hughes said that an extra piece was needed for the programme, I pointed out that their instruments were exactly those required for Max's *Tenebrae super Gesualdo* - the original version for choir and instrumental ensemble - which, it transpired, Max had never heard before. In this piece, the choir sings the late sixteenth century and tortured music of Gesualdo, stopping for interpolations from the ensemble to original music by Max. In the late night atmosphere of St Magnus Cathedral, with the choir and the ensemble throwing sounds at each other from opposite ends of the building as if across the centuries, this was an unforgettable experience. For me, this was what local involvement in the festival should be about; we were taking part in an event, which we could not do in Orkney other than in the festival.

Our last appearance was in 1998 when we opened the second half of a concert in St Magnus Cathedral given by Martyn Brabbins and the BBC Scottish Symphony Orchestra. The orchestra was going to play Max's *Second Taverner Fantasy*; a huge 50-minute work. Max gave an illuminating talk about the piece from the podium before we started. We were then to sing the Benedictus from the Mass *Gloria Tibi Trinitas* by John Taverner on which the piece was based. With a packed cathedral, BBC microphones about and us squeezed into a small space behind the audience at the west end, this was nerve-wracking stuff. All went well, however, and I think our singing helped put Max's piece into context.

Heather Rendall · organist, St Magnus Cathedral

The Festival Service is an opportunity to dedicate all of the activities, whether it be music, drama, art or literature, to God and to thank Him for all the rich talent that has been given to us. I'm glad that within the St Magnus Festival a service is included in the programme and I've been privileged to have been involved in this for the past ten years as organist.

There is always an exciting buzz when you enter the cathedral on festival Sunday, and usually the building is full to capacity - our own congregation, visitors, performers and people of all faiths and traditions joining together praising God. Every service in the beautiful setting of St Magnus is a special event, but there is something extra special about this Sunday. We always enjoy the groups of musicians that play during the service - sometimes a string quartet or a woodwind group, and recently a brass ensemble set the tone for the service.

The St Magnus Cathedral Choir rehearses a larger work for this day, and in 2001 sang a piece which had been commissioned for the St Magnus Day service (April 16) with words by the minister Ron Ferguson and music by Espen Selvik. The piece, entitled *The Spirit and the Song*, very movingly depicts the story of St Magnus and his execution on the island of Egilsay.

Ron Ferguson has been cathedral minister for the past eleven years and his sermons on such a day have been outstanding - usually incorporating writings from our wealth of Orcadian poets.

> *Thou dost the strength to workman's arm impart,*
> *From Thee the skilled musicians mystic art,*
> *The grace of poet's pen or painter's hand*
> *To teach the loveliness of sea and land.*

(Church Hymnary, 3rd Edition. Words by E.E. Dagmore.)

Steve King · principal viola, SCO (in conversation)

All the times I've been up with the SCO as a player have been special - but the orchestra visits many festivals and has played in many beautiful places. The thing that makes me feel great about my involvement in the St Magnus Festival has been all the other projects I have done in Orkney as a music educationalist.

One thing that I enjoyed more than anything was working with the folk from the St Colm's Centre (attended by people with a wide range of

"This was fine singing by all voices...in the correct style with a minimum of vibrato. The cathedral acoustic was meant for this kind of music."
DMMD, The Orcadian
June 25, 1998

Orkney Photographic

Heather Rendall, 2001.

"The St Colm's piece, a gentle rain of hand bells, reflecting Jenny King's sea paintings, had shape and a feeling of joy in its making."
Mary Miller, The Scotsman
June 20, 1994

"This was one of the most interesting concerts of the festival. The combination of two fine musicians, authentic archive material and a speaker who was passionately interested in his subject captured and held the interest of the audience."
DMMD
The Orcadian, July 3, 1997

physical and/or learning disabilities). My first visit there, in 1994, was for an outreach education project, *Sound Pictures*, commissioned by the festival. I get a great kick out of working with a group that doesn't have any specific interest in music; I like to use music as a means of team-building, communication and bonding. They were wonderful to work with, and we actually started off the St Magnus Festival in the Kirkwall Town Hall. We related a music project to some paintings, which were projected on to a screen during the performance. We used various instruments, including hand bells and big plastic drums. It was a very moving thing - they put 110% into their efforts, wanting to do it well. You've got to believe that people have great potential - and then try to release the potential and bring it out. The place was packed, and I remember a lot of people being quite moved by what they heard and saw. Some time after that, I did a project with a group from St Colm's which wasn't part of the festival. We based it around the Earl's Palace in Kirkwall, rehearsing there and then giving a performance of the work. It was a beautiful sunny afternoon; loads of people came and sat on the grass, and, once again, it was a very moving experience.

In 1997 Julia Robinson Dean and I wanted to do a concert in the festival based on the Bartók duos. My idea was not just to play them, but also source some of the original recordings that Bartók made when he went around Hungary, Transylvania and Rumania, recording folk songs. He transcribed them three or four times, to interpret them as exactly as possible. I managed to get hold of some of these recordings. At the concert, we played a duo, and then played material associated with it, and talked about Bartók's life. We filled the Town Hall, and Max was there, and he came up to us afterwards and said, 'Steve, I see you've done your homework well'. That meant a lot. Max has been a great inspiration to me ever since I started with the SCO - he's a great artist, and a great intellectual; I knew that he knew all about Bartók, so his approval meant a great deal.

Julia Robinson Dean violinist, former director, Orkney Camerata

I have had an incredible amount of pleasure from the festival. When I first moved up to Orkney, and didn't even realise what was going on, I was feeling quite a long way from my playing friends. I had to go to Kirkwall for something one day, and suddenly bumped into some ex-colleagues from the BBC Philharmonic, including one player that I had known since Youth Orchestra days. I suddenly didn't feel so far away! In the ensuing years, I have had the opportunity of playing chamber and orchestral music with some wonderful musicians. One year that I especially enjoyed was coaching the Orkney Camerata to a standard that enabled them to join with the BT Scottish Ensemble for a concert. I was incredibly happy that we could produce something so polished.

Orkney Camerata

It goes without saying that meeting Max and playing some of his work, and being involved in new projects is an immense privilege. The festival remains the highlight of my year. Its regularity and predictability means that one can say: 'No, I can't do anything else that week because it's the St Magnus Festival.' I hope that it carries on like that!

Yvonne Gray founder member, Orkney Camerata (in conversation)

It is always stimulating to play with Orkney Camerata, but there is something extra during the festival. Compared to performing at other times of the year there are huge, focused audiences, and an electric atmosphere. It is daunting, but if you can harness the nerves it can bring about a real rapport and you end up playing better than normal.

The very first time I was involved in the festival with Camerata, in 1995, we all felt excited about it. We were a new group, and were raising funds to buy a harpsichord, which would open up new avenues for us. I had been feeling nervous, but not uncontrollably, and I remember going up to the platform at the start of the Albinoni concerto, and panic suddenly descended. I could feel my throat closing up, and I thought I wasn't going to be able to play. It lasted for an instant, but I'll always remember that sensation (perhaps sparked off by seeing such a huge audience).

Everyone has been very supportive of Camerata, and interested in the group. We have been invited to play with other musicians, sometimes locally, but also with professionals who have come up for the festival. In 1996, for instance, we played with the Festival Chorus in Britten's *St Nicolas*, conducted by Roger Williams from Aberdeen. It was refreshing to work with somebody new, and good to have input from somebody very experienced. We also worked with Steve King from the SCO. He is a good example of somebody who has forged all sorts of links with Orkney through the festival.

The festival is not just a showcase for all the international talent that comes to Orkney; there's a real place in it for local people. It is organic in the community, and it brings something into your life that can carry on beyond festival time. Every year schools are involved and a lot of children are benefiting from this. Perhaps the thing that is most wonderful about it is that it is part of the fabric of their existence so that the children hardly see the ramifications themselves, at least until they grow up and look back.

Duncan McLean writer, Lone Star Swing Band
(playing on the theatre ship, *Fitzcarraldo*, in 1997)

It felt slightly strange to be carrying guitars and mic-stands up the gangplank of a moored boat, knowing we weren't sailing away to some music festival

"When the 11-strong BT Scottish Ensemble was joined by roughly the same number of string players from the Orkney Camerata, it was - for the first time - impossible to see the joins.

And the quality of the Camerata can only have been an inspiration to the kids of the Orkney Schools' Strings, who also joined with the professionals in performances of Scott Skinner's reels."
Michael Tumelty
The Herald, June 25, 1998

"Greatly to the credit of the festival organisers over the years has been their insistence on a substantial contribution from local players.

This has rarely been so richly vindicated as in the concert by Orkney Camerata, when a group of our musicians, professional and amateur, gave a short but demanding programme in St Magnus Cathedral...Julia Robinson Dean directed clearly but unobtrusively. She and the group did us proud."
JF, The Orcadian
June 22, 1995

Duncan McLean, 1996.

in exotic Aberdeen or Lerwick. Knowing, in fact, that we weren't sailing anywhere at all, but just sitting in Stromness harbour for the night, moving no more than six inches out from the pier in the gentle midsummer swell. That was the extent of the physical movement, at least. For 90 minutes, Lone Star Stones conjured up a transatlantic journey of the imagination, all the way to the honky-tonks, blue highways and wide-open spaces of Texas.

The evening consisted of music, interspersed with readings from my travel book, *Lone Star Swing: On the Trail of Bob Wills and his Texas Playboys*, which was to be published the following August. The book drew far-fetched parallels between the American South-West and Orkney: the latter an oasis of dry land and civilisation in the middle of the endless ocean, like a dusty cow-town adrift in the rolling undulations of the vast prairie. Making these parallels seem like indisputable common sense, musically at least, were the Smoking Stone Band. The line-up that night was Douglas Montgomery (fiddle), Dick Levens (electric mandolin), Ian Mackay (string bass) and Brian Montgomery (guitar).

For the last set, I joined the band on guitar and vocals, and we did our best to recreate the great sound of Bob Wills' Western Swing - blues mixed with country crashing into jazz mingling with hoedown fiddling. As it happens, I don't think we recreated anything: in fact we created something new. By adding traditional Orkney and Shetland fiddle stylings to the mix, a new good-time, foot-stomping music was born: Northern Swing....

David Purser   manager, London Brass, 2001

A lot of music is learnt in such a short space of time. The sense of a shared task and the excitement of a performance on the opening night of the festival binds and unites us all - gradually the children feel comfortable enough to reveal their true characters - friendly, inquisitive, playful, but above all, committed. It feels a real privilege to be part of all this.
Fraser Trainer, composer on 'Pulse Fiction', 2001
[See also *the composers*]

The composer Fraser Trainer and I had spent a week prior to the festival proper working in three schools, accompanied and discreetly guided wherever we went by Brian Jones, the local peripatetic brass teacher. The students ranged in age from eight to eighteen, and in ability from not much above beginner to conservatoire standard. They learnt to play some of Fraser's music, and - perhaps more importantly - they devised pieces of their own, using elements of his composition. Their devised pieces became part of the concert performance, three interludes between the four movements of Fraser's piece, *Pulse Fiction*. This was a difficult project for the students with many different elements all needing to be memorised. My expectation was that something would go seriously awry at some stage of the performance; but I was quite mistaken. The feeling of concentration from the students was palpable, and they didn't put a foot wrong. A similar sense of concentration accompanied the brass band's performance of Chris Batchelor's *Weasel Words and Winning Ways*. To be frank, several members of the band didn't think very highly of the piece, which was perhaps too modern for their taste. But, by God, they worked hard to get it right....

[See *orchestras and ensembles*.]

Brian Jones

The educational project with London Brass and Fraser Trainer was excellent. They behaved exceptionally well towards the children (and we've seen some prima donnas). The rehearsals went very well; it was short, sharp, and it was well done. I can't speak too highly of them. And the Kirkwall Town Band had a fantastic experience playing with them. I'd forgotten what it was like to play at that high a level - and I wasn't a bad trumpet player! But Andy Crowley was something else - he was absolutely brilliant. We were playing in front of 700 people in the Picky Centre that night; the Town Band rose to it and showed their smiling faces! They were terrific.

Hugh Smith headteacher, North Walls School, Hoy

The Orkney name has always been synonymous with creativity and talent in all areas, and it should come as no surprise to find the St Magnus Festival so firmly established, and other Orkney festivals for folk music, jazz, rhythm and blues and beer, to name but a few.

The visit of London Brass in 2001, and the idea that they would perform with school pupils, the Kirkwall Town Band and other local musicians as part of their programme was exciting. I had recently taken up the conductor's baton of the Kirkwall Town Band and eagerly agreed to conduct the combined ensemble for the opening concert of the festival. For me, this was a dream come true. After many rehearsals, the big night arrived. I polished my baton and purchased a new dinner suit for the occasion.

The Pickaquoy Centre is a large arena in which to perform, and it was going to be a challenge. Waiting off stage, as all the musicians took up their places, was nerve-wracking. This was the moment that everyone had worked hard for. As I made my way to the podium, the audience applauded; I felt an overwhelming sense of pride as school, local and professional musicians sat waiting to perform. (The standard of performance by school pupils and locals in Orkney is very high. Such standards, however, do not happen in a vacuum, and are only due to the quality of people who pass on their skills.)

The following day, London Brass, under the directorship of David Purser, were to give a concert at the school at Lyness and he had suggested that the group come early to do a little sightseeing, and that he would provide a workshop for pupils and other members of the community. In addition, London Brass had agreed to perform two items along with our group as part of their concert programme. The workshop was excellent and the concert a great success. I had a second opportunity to conduct ...and I was in heaven! Orkney hospitality is second to none and was enthused over by our London Brass performers. My last image of the group was saying goodbye to them

Hugh Smith, 2001.

at the Lyness ferry terminal; watching the tuba player serenading the captain and crew on the deck of the *Hoy Head* is something I shall remember for a long time.

I have heard many views about the St Magnus Festival. The most disappointing view is that the festival is out of touch with the people of Orkney and that it is organised by a minority for a minority. I cannot find evidence to support this view, as festival programmes are becoming more diverse and the number of youngsters taking part increasing. Perhaps it is time to acknowledge that all of our festivals, including St Magnus, are part of the culture and magic that we all know is special in Orkney.

Local groups from the early days of the festival.

West Mainland Strathspey and Reel Society, 1981.

Stromness Academy Brass Band, 1981.

Max's festival music

Sir Peter Maxwell Davies and the festival have drawn creative sustenance from each other from the beginning; his music, through the festival, has changed Orkney's cultural landscape, while Orcadian elements have provided inspiration for a huge range of new work. And while Orkney is not the only influence on PMD as a composer, many works have been written to be premiered at the festival, whether by local musicians, the full forces of a visiting orchestra, or a virtuosic ensemble group.

PMD has had many fruitful associations with leading orchestras and ensembles, but The Fires of London, which he founded and directed, was the chief conduit for his creative energy in the early years of the festival. With outstanding musicians, who were not afraid to tackle a bit of drama, the composer had the perfect vehicle for his experimental music theatre pieces. Other essential elements for realising his music in Orkney were the talented instructors and musicians who produced his work with local performers, particularly Norman Mitchell and Dick and Glenys Hughes. And his original inspiration, without whom the Orkney music, and the festival, would be unthinkable, is the gentle, unassuming presence of the great Orcadian writer, George Mackay Brown.

While sustaining his place at the forefront of contemporary music, Peter Maxwell Davies is very much part of the local community and Orcadians are having much less difficulty understanding his musical responses than they did in the days when he was frequently 'outrageous' or 'difficult' as a composer. Like the music, the relationship between PMD and Orkney has matured. The vast majority of local people are quietly proud of his achievements, and proud of the festival - which was, after all, inspired by the composer's intense and lasting response to Orkney and its people.

Gunnie Moberg

Sir Peter Maxwell Davies (in conversation)

The festival has grown so much from when I was artistic director, which is lovely. I'm just amazed at everything that happens, and very pleased that many of my works have been done in Orkney first, including two symphonies, which isn't bad! I've been very careful to steer those pieces towards the festival to be premiered there. At the beginning, the idea of doing a symphony of any kind in Kirkwall was beyond my dreams. To do my own first performances here was marvellous.

After ten years, I was quite happy to step down as artistic director; other people are now doing a far better job, so I am very content. There was a very good team right from the word go, and Glenys [Hughes] and George [Rendall] are both excellent. I do feel that the festival is in very safe hands. I did enjoy certain aspects of directing the festival; it was a big challenge and the results were excellent. But some of the politics involved I found a little bit wearing. It all took time away from writing music.

The festival and my work have always been entwined. With many pieces, I've known while they were being written that they would happen in Orkney in the first instance. That determines a lot about a piece. And in recent festivals, it's been lovely to have the confidence to know that you are going to chuck at the Orkney audience, the festival audience, a piece which is as demanding as anything you will ever write, and that they will be able to take it, criticise it and enjoy it, or not, in a very constructive way. And I do think that, in some instances, if you've lived here, you have a better chance of understanding a piece than someone who hasn't.

Learning to conduct a piece of your own is very strange. You have to detach, although you are still involved; and you have to learn it with beating patterns in mind and not just the sound. No matter how often I do it, I still get nervous about conducting a new piece. I am always very, very pleased if people like it; I can never quite get used to it, having taken so many brickbats. Fewer and fewer people find the 'language' of the pieces difficult, and if they then respond positively, it means a lot to me.

The smaller pieces, such as *Farewell to Stromness*, may not be as serious as some of the others, but I thoroughly enjoy writing them. When I've just completed a huge symphony or concerto, it is very nice to spend a few days doing that kind of thing. A few critics, of course, and some other composers, call me all sorts of things for writing that kind of music. I'm supposed to be still writing the stuff I wrote when I was in my twenties! People are categorised into tiny pigeon-holes all too easily these days; it is almost a sin to write several kinds of music.

This has happened to so many composers. Most of them really developed in their output as they advanced in years; their style or content changed in various ways. Henry Purcell is a good example of that, and Sibelius changed completely - and I think they expected poor Stravinsky to go on

"The range and versatility of his work have no parallel among his English contemporaries: a reputation for making exceptional demands on players and audiences in pieces like 'Eight Songs for a Mad King', 'The Lighthouse' and 'Ave Maris Stella' is tempered by something near genius for re-entering the world of childhood in robust, funny and delectably tuneful fantasies such as 'The Two Fiddlers', 'Cinderella' and 'The Rainbow'."
Michael Ratcliffe
The Sunday Times
June 26, 1983

previous page: **The Fires of London in the Stromness Town Hall.**

writing *The Rite of Spring* to the end, and he was not going to do that! It's all connected, of course, but one changes and should not write the same music.

Coming to Orkney certainly made a huge difference to me; it helped that change so much. It was a very positive thing that I did. I was escaping nothing - just coming to find myself really - and, to some extent, that is how it has worked.

Mona Levin music journalist (Norway)

Even though it is many years ago since I visited the St Magnus Festival, my memories of Orkney, the people I met and the music I heard are still vivid. In 1979, I was, I've been told, the first foreign music journalist to cover the festival. What at that time made it so special, so different from the usual rent-a-festivals around the world, was partly the environment it took place in, partly the old, local culture which is the basis of it, and in great part the initiator of the festival, Max - the vibrant composer Sir Peter Maxwell Davies - without whom there would have been no festival to begin with.

In his quiet way, Max went about his business as a fire of London personified; his ensemble The Fires of London was very much alive and well at the time. He was the festival's artistic and spiritual father with an enormous ability to inspire and ignite his team and every person even only vaguely in touch with it. Not only was he the driving force behind the festival, but he composed much of the music that was performed there, whether by the first rate visiting artists, or by the local amateurs - grown ups and children.

From Hoy, the little island where Max had made his home, and where he was a hospitable host, he took hold of the history of the island kingdom and made it his own, transformed it into music unique, and gave it to the world. The opera *The Martyrdom of St Magnus* put the Orkney past on the musical map of Europe from the moment it was premiered at the first St Magnus Festival in 1977.

Judy Arnold and Mona Levin

"The performance [of The Lighthouse], intensified by everything that makes the Orcadian landscape so atmospheric, was shattering."
Michael Tumelty
The Glasgow Herald
June 27, 1986

The Lighthouse

Paul Driver   music critic, *The Sunday Times*

Like festivals at Aldeburgh and Bayreuth, St Magnus originated in the vision of a composer, Sir Peter Maxwell Davies, and has been sustained by the regular performance of his music, much of it written with the festival in mind. Since *The Martyrdom of St Magnus* in 1977, only the 1985 and 1987 festivals have lacked a new Davies piece. If the new offerings have on occasion been relatively slight - primary and infant school works dominating between 1988 and 1993 - the festival has also seen the launch of another of his operas, *Mr Emmet Takes A Walk*, as well as his Violin Concerto and the sixth and seventh of his symphonies; the eighth, *Antarctic*, had its Scottish premiere at the 2001 festival. Since the first symphony was finished in the same year as *The Martyrdom of St Magnus*, it is the case, significantly or otherwise, that the history of the festival to date coincides with that of Davies's ambitious symphonic cycle, now officially complete.

If these 25 Orkney years define a creative 'period' in Davies's life, they are bound to be a meaningful span, too, to those involved in putting on the festival - one of few international festivals that are community-based at all levels - and to its regular attenders. Many, coming from afar, return each year like migrant birds. Others such as myself are loyal but intermittent. My first visit, largely made possible by Max himself, was in 1979 as a student - and *ad hoc* reviewer for *The Orcadian* - and I have been back half a dozen times as a music critic, most recently in 2000 for the first performances of *Mr Emmet* and the seventh symphony.

One always gains startling impressions of light and space in Orkney - the more intense in proportion as you are inured to cities and noise - and for me, as no doubt for many others, they are inextricably mixed up with, and conveniently dated by, the unveilings of Davies compositions.

The Martyrdom of St Magnus remains the most important of the 46 such premieres so far, standing to St Magnus as *Parsifal* to Bayreuth: a true 'festival drama' (if not unambiguously a 'sacred' one), specially conceived for, and in this case inaugurating, a festival. Not only does it re-enact decisive events in the islands' history, but it was designed for performance in the cathedral devoted to the saint's memory, and its libretto based by the composer on a novel, *Magnus*, by Orkney's preeminent bard, George Mackay Brown, himself one of the festival's founders. It would not be inappropriate if the work were staged each year as a kind of rite from which other festival events might draw an extra meaning. Finances do not of course allow such indulgences, and, indeed, the opera has only been once revisited - in 1987 for the 850th anniversary of the cathedral's founding. But its aura is somehow always there.

The children's opera, *The Two Fiddlers*, that Davies wrote for the 1978 festival is also based on a Brown text, and just as deeply embedded in local history. It is a classic of its kind, one of the most successful school operas since Britten's. School performers were involved, too, in the other new piece that year: *Le Jongleur de Notre Dame*, a masque for mime-juggler, baritone, ensemble and children's band. For the children of Papdale Primary School and their teacher Glenys Hughes (since 1986 the festival's artistic director) Davies devised his charming *Kirkwall Shopping Songs*, premiered at the following festival, whose centrepiece was his cantata for tenor, chorus

I was sitting beside this guy in the Stromness Town Hall, and I'd been assigned to do a particular review, and wasn't looking forward to it at all. Somehow I offered the job to him. I don't know how much he got for it - peanuts, anyway! But that was Paul Driver's first critical assignment in Orkney, for *The Orcadian*!
Archie Bevan
festival vice-president
(in conversation)

and organ, *Solstice of Light* - a setting of nine Brown poems and perhaps the most hauntingly beautiful of all Davies's Orkney evocations.

1980's festival brought another children's opera, the widely performed *Cinderella*, and one of Davies's 'ecological' pieces, *The Yellow Cake Revue*, a protest for singer/reciter (originally Eleanor Bron) and piano against uranium mining on the islands. The pictorial little *Farewell to Stromness* and *Yesnaby Ground* for piano, first presented at this time, have become two of his most popular compositions [see Timothy Walker below].

From 1981 to 1985 Davies reduced the scale of his festival contributions: incidental music to three plays by Brown (that for *The Well*, staged in 1981, reappearing as the cantata *Into the Labyrinth* at the 1983 festival); a music theatre piece, *The Rainbow*, for Stromness Primary School; *Songs of Hoy* for the children of North Walls School on Davies's then home base of Hoy; an expressionistic monodrama, *The Medium*, for solo mezzo-soprano; and a doughty organ sonata. But for the 1986 festival he produced a full-blown Violin Concerto and Isaac Stern premiered it with the Royal Philharmonic Orchestra under André Previn. This proved a rather austere, even distraught work - an essay in complex lyricism that coincided with the death of Davies's mother, and, oddly enough, that of Previn's mother too. Contrastingly light in mood was the overture *Jimmack the Postie*, launched the same year, financed by the Scottish Post Office.

The series of school music theatre pieces introduced at festivals between 1989-92 amazingly included one, *Dangerous Errand*, for performers as young as five. 1994 brought home another 'comedy

Gunnie Moberg

overture' in the vein of *Jimmack the Postie* and Davies's most often played work, *An Orkney Wedding, with Sunrise*, with its bagpipe solo. In *Cross Lane Fair*, performed by the BBC Philharmonic in the now discarded venue of the Phoenix cinema, Northumbrian pipes have the obbligato role, though the work is primarily a conjuring-up of Davies's Salford childhood.

A due solemnity attended the following year's Phoenix premiere: that of the sixth symphony, written in memory of George Mackay Brown and completed on the day of his death. This 50-minute, three-movement score is another of the composer's Orkney seascapes. Wave-forms, buffeting wind sounds, and the spiral architecture of shells variously inform the structure.

Gunnie Moberg

The texturally pared-down Adagio finale embodies an emotional progress from string quartet sounds (prophetic of Davies's current engagement with the medium) at the outset to the hopeful, utterly surprising rattle of rain-sticks in the last two bars.

With two of the four fine works launched at the 2000 festival, Davies sought to close off important areas of his compositional activity. *Mr Emmet Takes a Walk*, staged at the Pickaquoy Centre by the Belgian Musiktheater Transparant and the Manchester-based Psappha Ensemble, was to be his last music theatre piece; the seventh symphony, given in the same place by the BBC Philharmonic, his last proper symphony. (The *Antarctic Symphony* he sees as a sort of tone-poem lying outside the cycle of seven.) Termination is in any case the theme of *Mr Emmet*: the eponymous gentleman is a middle-aged businessman who has decided to walk in front of an oncoming train [see David Pountney p.131]. Conversely, a return to origins distinguishes the symphony. Structured as a sonata movement writ large, the work's fourth and last movement is entitled 'Development' rather than, as might be expected, 'Recapitulation'. Instead of a return to the work's beginning, we have a ringing last chord that declares the strident harmony that opens Davies's first symphony. The cycle is truly complete.

The premiere at the 2000 festival of *Orkney*

Saga V: Westerly Gale in Biscay, Salt in the Bread Broken, performed by the BBC Philharmonic and St Magnus Festival Chorus, broke the mood of millennial stocktaking, for it is part of a continuing project: a series of 14 (mainly) orchestral evocations of sails that were hung in the cathedral in 1993, each depicting a scene from an Orkney crusade to Jerusalem and each supplied with a verse inscription by Brown [see *art*]. The fifth piece enjoyably recreates a storm at sea, bringing in voices to remind us of the Jonah story, pray for sailors, and invoke the saint. The effect was not unlike a Bach cantata.

As for the remaining 2000 premiere, it could only be the most stocktaking event in all Davies's oeuvre. *Grand Oratorio - The Meaning of Life*, a wildly parodic barber-shop quartet to a text of the composer's own, was sung late at night in the Festival Club as a farewell to the festival's long-serving administrator Dorothy Rushbrook [see *the Festival Club*]. This familial and risqué cabaret (not intended for publication) could hardly be further in spirit from the high seriousness of *The Martyrdom of St Magnus*. Yet both works attest the same profound commitment of a composer to his community.

One is reminded again of the sheer breadth of Davies's output, and I haven't mentioned here the countless other works by him, not premieres, that have been heard at the festival, many of them - the wonderful *Hymn to St Magnus*; *A Mirror of Whitening Light*; *Image, Reflection, Shadow* - with vivid Orkney connections. Music by many other contemporary composers - from Judith Weir and Ian McQueen in the early years to Sally Beamish and Stuart MacRae more recently - has of course been played at, and often commissioned by, the festival. It has brought music of all kinds to the islands, in a quantity and of a quality scarcely to be thought of previously. But it is unarguably the access provided to 25 years of sustained musical thinking by Maxwell Davies that is the festival's glory - a luminousness reflecting that of the islands themselves, when the sun is shining in midsummer.

Le Jongleur de Notre Dame, 1979.

Philippa Davies flautist, formerly of The Fires of London
(in conversation)

As flautist with The Fires of London, my first involvement with the festival was in 1979, and I vividly remember the premiere of *Le Jongleur de Notre Dame*, which Max wrote specifically for the festival. It was a difficult piece for all of us, because we had to act; we were monks, and Beverley Davison, the violinist, was the Virgin. Our acting and speaking was through our instruments; we all had cadenzas which were like our soliloquies, and then we had to do all the acting bits - reacting to the juggler, and to the other instruments.

Max writes specifically with the individual instrumentalist in mind; he's very sensitive to the people around him and their instrumental technique. *Le Jongleur* was very much an experimental thing for all of us; Max had a concept and we had to deliver it. It was very exciting.

The pieces we were playing were obviously very influenced by Max, and the audiences were so receptive. It was a new sound, but at the same time his music was so influenced by his life in Orkney. *Ave Maris Stella*, for instance, has a fantastic quality to it, which one appreciates there in that space, where it was written. The last piece we did, *Image, Reflection, Shadow*, is very hard to make work - a different sound altogether. It is a wonderful piece with the Hungarian cimbalom as its core sound.

"Although he stretches instrumental techniques to their utmost, he fully appreciates the limitations, taking care not to overstep the mark, or to inflict difficulty for its own sake."
Kenneth Walton
Classical Music,
August 11, 1984

Maureen Gray Pier Arts Centre, former festival board member

The Fires were wonderful musicians. It was so nice that Philippa Davies (the flautist) came back for the 2001 festival with the Nash Ensemble.

A lot of the music was quite demanding at first, as most of us hadn't heard much contemporary music. We were a bit nervous of it in the early days and people sometimes didn't know how to react. But the first Orkney performance of *Eight Songs for a Mad King*, with Michael Rippon, received a roaring, stamping ovation in Stromness Town Hall. The King took so many curtain calls he was nearly on his knees! Later I read somewhere that the Fires thought it was the best performance they had ever given, and the best reception they had ever had.

Lesley Shrigley-Jones gave a lunchtime cello recital in the cathedral - it was a beautiful day and the sun streamed through a stained glass window on to her hair, making it like a rainbow. She played Bach in a pool of sunlight.

Michael Rippon in
Eight Songs for a Mad King, 1982.

Timothy Walker guitarist, formerly of The Fires of London

Max first performed his *Yellow Cake Revue* in the Stromness Hotel dining room, with the actress Eleanor Bron. I remember that the whole work was a

The first few years I was gob-smacked by The Fires of London because I'd never seen anything like it. They would carry all this outlandish stuff into the pit, typewriters and suchlike - it was just amazing. They came with some weird instruments, but they were a very entertaining group!
Bryan Leslie
festival stage manager,
1982-1994 (in conversation)

Stephen Pruslin and Eleanor Bron, Kirkwall, 1980.

Gunnie Moberg

I remember the experience of *The Yellow Cake Revue* as being a searing debacle in my career, that proved I cannot sing! From that I can salvage the delight of working with Stephen Pruslin and The Fires of London, and eating that delicious, soft Orkney farmhouse cheese in its proper setting.
Eleanor Bron, actor

powerful protest at the proposed uranium mining in the islands and that Max's playing of *Farewell to Stromness* was quite magical. It was so unlike any other work of his I'd heard - in keys one could put a name to and rhythms that didn't make you feel as if dancing on quicksand. It also sounded like it wanted to be played on the guitar.

Steve Pruslin was a most able accomplice in 'borrowing' for me the piano score and I hurriedly (it may even have been at the dead of night!) made a transcription before its disappearance was detected. The reason for all the cloak and daggerishness was because I wanted to surprise Max the following day and play it in a recital I was giving with the lovely, late, great Mary Thomas.

This I did and Max was indeed surprised - to my relief it seemed most agreeably. I, on the other hand, was surprised when he said that he also liked the new harmonisation I'd given the middle section! I went back to the original piano part (quite legally now) and realised that in my white-hot haste to arrange (and practise) the work, I had misread the bass clef of the middle section for the treble, so the harmony was down a third. It still sounded good, so, in fact, the first performance of *Farewell* on the guitar was unintentionally partly a 'variation'!

There are now several versions for different instruments of this hauntingly beautiful work (including for four guitars); I'm delighted to say that it is a popular work in the solo guitar repertoire... and all in the correct key!

Lucy Rendall on *Lullaby for Lucy* (in conversation)

Lullaby for Lucy was written for me when I was only a baby, and I was quite overwhelmed when strangers came up to me over the next few years, asking me what I thought about it. I had only heard it a couple of times, and at that age I was more into nursery rhymes. The piece is quite dramatic and I thought of a lullaby as being something like *Rock-a-Bye Baby*.

I always loved the words, but the piece wasn't my cup of tea then. Now that I am older, I've grown to realise what a privilege it has been for that to have been written for me on my birth, and I'm very proud of it, and listen to it in a different way. When I was wee, I didn't think much about the fact that I was the only child born in Rackwick for such a long time, but now I realise it was a special event.

I live down south now, and I tend not to tell anyone about the piece. My friends looked up a web site, however, and found me on it, and they were amazed. I was quite proud of that then!

The piece is also special because it is an acrostic of my name. I remember George coming over to Rackwick from when I was small, and when we got the piece signed by both Max and George, that was especially exciting. I'll always have that memory of them both when they did that.

A few years ago the one remaining [Rackwick] farmer, Jack Rendall, married and the first child to be born there for half a century opened her eyes on the storied light: Lucy. I wrote a little poem to celebrate her coming, and Max Davies clothed the words in music."
George Mackay Brown on **Lullaby for Lucy**

Let all plants and creatures of the valley now
Unite,
Calling a new
Young one to join the celebration.

Rowan and lamb and waters salt and sweet
Entreat the
New child to the brimming
Dance of the valley,
A pledge and a promise.
Lonely they were long, the creatures of Rackwick, till
Lucy came among them, all brightness and light.

Jack and Lucy Rendall, 1981.

Jack Rendall on *An Orkney Wedding, with Sunrise*
(in conversation)

A few years after Dorothy and I were married Max wrote *An Orkney Wedding, With Sunrise*. We were actually married down south, so the piece was based on the wedding party which we had when we came back. After the party, Max was walking back home at five o'clock in the morning, and the sun was just getting up. He got the piece into his head then, and eventually he sat down and wrote it in 1984.

Friends of ours from Canada, whom we hadn't heard from for years, wrote and said that they had been to Vancouver and heard this great piece there, and they only discovered afterwards that it had been written for us. They had been in Rackwick twenty years before and the piece brought back memories. Because of that, they came across and saw us again in 2000.

It felt very good - to have something written for us by someone as famous as Max. Judy Arnold told me herself that it is the most played piece that he has written.

Ian Maclay managing director, Royal Philharmonic Orchestra

It was a wonderful moment when Isaac Stern played Max's Violin Concerto in the St Magnus Cathedral with André Previn conducting. The RPO had

When we went to the opening of the Scottish Parliament, they played *An Orkney Wedding, with Sunrise*. The lady who introduced the piece asked my Mum and Dad to stand up. There were big TV screens on either side of the stage, and Mum and Dad were suddenly all over the screens. It was amazing, in front of thousands of people. I thought that was really, really special.
Lucy Rendall (in conversation)

Max has been a good friend and neighbour for many years, not only to ourselves, but the whole community; he has enriched all our lives.
Dorothy Rendall

Peter Maxwell Davies and André Previn, 1986.

"The world premiere [of the Violin Concerto] in St Magnus Cathedral... was one of those occasions when the music and the atmosphere of the venue seemed perfectly attuned. Only minutes away from the cathedral you can experience the kind of landscape which has had such an influence on Davies ...expansive, still, somehow timeless."
Geoffrey Norris
The Daily Telegraph
June 23, 1986

I recall the shimmering *Image, Reflection, Shadow* (the first time I'd heard a cimbalom) and the composer's stimulating introductory talk. Awakened too were my memories of Charles Senior, one of whose poems had inspired the sequence.

I still tingle to the eerie majesty of the Ring of Brodgar, that midsummer's night. And as a souvenir I treated myself to a marked-up score of *Eight Songs for a Mad King*, the musical notation on its cover forming a white birdcage on a black background.
Stewart Conn
festival poet, 1988

commissioned the concerto from Max and I was very proud that all the planning and preparation had finally paid off and the performance was actually taking place. We played it in London as well, but it wasn't the same!

Glenys Hughes festival director

Locally, Max's earlier music theatre pieces such as *Eight Songs for a Mad King*, *Vesalii Icones* and *The Medium* were perceived as difficult, both musically and in terms of subject matter. Some people had come to Max's music through the children's pieces and had expected the adult music to be equally approachable and were disappointed when it wasn't! I think the one piece of Max's that really changed the attitude of local people towards his music was *The Lighthouse*, performed in 1986, which is such a stunning piece of music theatre. After that, I felt there was a sea change in people's attitudes.

Rosemary Warren-Green (Furniss) violinist, formerly of The Fires of London (in conversation)

I was always thrilled to be part of The Fires of London. I remember as a young teenager going to hear the group in London and being so excited by them. It was so special coming to Orkney with them a few years later. The Fires were an expression of Max's energy, and when we played in Orkney, where Max had been thinking about and creating his music, it seemed like a distillation of all this intensity and emotion. It was wonderful.

Some time after The Fires of London ceased to be, some of us reformed under a different name - Nouvelles Images. We had realised that nobody was playing Max's intensely difficult, but wonderful, pieces, *Image, Reflection, Shadow* and *Ave Maris Stella*. We got together again really to tour around with those pieces and take them to as wide an audience as possible. When we first played *Image, Reflection, Shadow* in Orkney, it was only the first movement that was ready. It seemed so difficult while we were learning it - it was very intense. Greg Knowles, my ex-husband and percussionist with the Fires, had the added burden of having to learn the cimbalom before he actually learned to play the piece. Subsequently, however, from that first difficult performance in Orkney, we played the piece all over the world.

David Pountney librettist and director, *Mr Emmet Takes a Walk*

When I collaborated with Max on *The Doctor of Myddfai* for Welsh National Opera this was the result of an inspired piece of matchmaking by Matthew Epstein, the director of WNO. I had never met Max before, but knew his work of course. So I was naturally very curious to see how the process of collaboration would be, especially since he had often written his own words in the past.

In the event, the 'process' was mercurial and gnomic in the extreme: I suppose I should take it as a compliment that, by and large, I submitted ideas which Max approved and that was that! At one point I complained that I was never going to make much money out of publishing our acrimonious and emotional correspondence, such as has been known between librettist and composer!

And I was extremely happy with the result, especially as I had then to direct it, which is a position somewhat akin to Gilbert's Lord Chancellor. A director by definition has to adopt a somewhat critical stance to his material: putting something on stage demands a level of analysis and distance. But though I, the director, did not find our work to be too unsatisfactory, I was never entirely sure what he, the composer, thought of it. He gave one of his twinkling smiles and went on his way.

Confirmation only really came when, out of the blue, Max asked me to write another piece with him, a music theatre piece for the Orkney Festival. This was really being invited into the parlour!

Unfortunately, the good news of this commission coincided with some very bad news, the suicide of a dear friend. In a certain sense, I could hardly write about anything else. But these personal details would not of course have any interest for an audience. I had to trust Max absolutely to tell me if I was writing for public or private consumption. Once again, our collaboration went extremely smoothly, to the inevitable impoverishment of my memoirs, but when I finally heard Max's music and saw his emotion at the end of the premiere I was profoundly touched to know that 'my' story had touched him too.

Peter Maxwell Davies's festival premieres (excluding children's pieces)

1977	**The Martyrdom of St Magnus**
1978	**Le Jongleur de Notre Dame**
1979	**Solstice of Light**
1980	**A Welcome to Orkney**
	The Yellow Cake Revue
1981	**Lullaby for Lucy**
	The Medium
	Incidental Music for **The Well** by George Mackay Brown
1982	**Organ Sonata**
	Image Reflection Shadow (first movement)
	Incidental Music for **Bessie Millie's Wind Shop** by George Mackay Brown
1983	**Into the Labyrinth**
	March: **The Pole Star**
	Four Voluntaries by Tallis
	Incidental Music for **Island of the Saints** by George Mackay Brown
1986	**Jimmack the Postie**
	Violin Concerto
	House of Winter
1987	**Guitar Sonata**
1991	Incidental Music for **Witch** and **The Road to Colonus** by George Mackay Brown
1994	**Cross Lane Fair**
1996	**Symphony No 6**
1997	**A Birthday Card for Hans**
1998	**Mrs Linklater's Tune**
1999	**Midhouse Air;** new version **Litany for a Ruined Chapel between Sheep and Shore**
2000	**Mr Emmet Takes a Walk**
	Orkney Saga 5
	Symphony No 7
	Grand Oratorio - The Meaning of Life
2001	**Lux in Tenebris**

John Warnaby music journalist

The collaborations between George Mackay Brown and Peter Maxwell Davies were rarely conventional, and only once did they work jointly on a single project. The usual procedure has involved Max selecting, and adapting, with George's blessing, appropriate texts, and this has continued to the present day. George's reticence - one of his most endearing characteristics - meant that he rarely commented on the results, as he claimed to have an insufficient understanding of music, but it has also meant that his contribution to Max's development, including the many works written for the St Magnus Festival, has been seriously under-valued.

"Part of the alchemy of this Orkney festive occasion is the fusion of Peter Maxwell Davies, the innovator in music, with George Mackay Brown, whose poetry, prose and drama are rooted in tradition."
Marjorie Linklater
The Glasgow Herald
June 21, 1982

It would hardly be an exaggeration to claim that Mackay Brown's poetry helped transform Maxwell Davies from a genuinely avant-garde British composer into the familiar Orcadian symphonist, and this metamorphosis was one of the most significant features of the early years of the St Magnus Festival. Indeed, George's writings, with their unique blend of history, mythology and folklore, engendered a sense of a close community. They encouraged Max to settle in Orkney, and soon gave rise to musical expression. Moreover, George's influence was not confined to settings of specific texts, but pervaded such works as *Hymn to St Magnus*, completed in 1972, the same year as Mackay Brown's novel, based on the life of Orkney's patron saint. The previous year, Max had composed *From Stone to Thorn*, his first setting of a Mackay Brown poem, and the original Fires of London presented both works to the Orcadian public, together with Max's arrangements of music by Buxtehude and Dunstable, on 26 May, 1973. The concert attracted an audience of about 300, and according to the review published in *The Orcadian* of 31 May, they were somewhat bewildered by such a challenging programme. The reviewer described the event as an intellectual exercise, rather than a moving experience, but acknowledged that greater familiarity with the main items would bring its reward. He also wondered what St Magnus's bones, resting in the famous pillar, would have made of Max's treatment of the 12th century hymn, written in his honour. Nevertheless, the concert was adjudged a considerable triumph.

The Fires of London did not return to Orkney for another four years, when the premiere of *The Martyrdom of St Magnus* supported by other events over four days, established the St Magnus Festival.

In 1978, *The Two Fiddlers* was not only the first major community project, but also the first of Max's children's operas, which have appeared regularly at subsequent festivals. *The Blind Fiddler*, drawn from the play, *A Spell for Green Corn*, and also dealing with aspects of the legendary Storm Kolson, was the culmination of a sequence of Mackay Brown-based song-cycles. It was introduced to Orkney by The Fires of London and has since received few performances for such an important score.

The 1979 festival inspired their only joint collaboration, with Mackay Brown supplying a specially-written poem dealing with environmental issues, and outlining

I remember being told that a performance given by the Scottish Chamber Orchestra in St Magnus Cathedral, which included *Dumbarton Oaks* by Stravinsky, was not really music for 'an Orkney audience'. That same informant sang in *Solstice of Light*. I know of no prouder cathedral chorister on that summer evening in 1979!
Norman Mitchell, co-founder and first co-artistic director

the history of the Orkney Islands. The result was *Solstice of Light*, for solo tenor, chorus and organ: another work strongly reflecting the Orkney community in that it was written primarily for the St Magnus Cathedral Singers, who were soon to expand into the St Magnus Festival Chorus.

At the same time, Max adapted a chapter from George's first novel, *Greenvoe*, as the basis of *Black Pentecost*, for mezzo-soprano, baritone and orchestra, which he dedicated to the successful campaign to prevent uranium mining in Orkney. However, the work was not heard in Orkney until the 1988 festival.

In the meantime, 1981 brought the celebrated *Lullaby for Lucy*, for unaccompanied choir; and Max wrote the incidental music for *The Well*: the first of several contributions to productions of George's plays. The music for *The Well* was also significant in that, in conjunction with a text drawn from the play, it formed the basis of the song-cycle, *Into The Labyrinth*, for tenor and chamber orchestra, whose premiere was one of the highlights of the 1983 festival. Thus began Max's association with the Scottish Chamber Orchestra, which soon yielded *Sinfonietta Accademica*, and the ten Strathclyde Concerti, some of which have been heard at subsequent festivals.

Apart from *A House of Winter*, written for The King's Singers in 1986, no other collaborations were directly linked to the festival until Max was inspired by Mackay Brown text for *Orkney Saga V*, for chorus and orchestra, written for the St Magnus Festival Chorus in

Gunnie Moberg

2000. Nevertheless, the work is symptomatic of Max's continuing preoccupation with George's writings, so that many Mackay Brown-inspired scores are available for future festivals. These include the first three orchestral works in the *Orkney Saga* sequence, originally entitled *Sails in St Magnus*, inspired by the captions George wrote for an exhibition of painted sails mounted in St Magnus Cathedral, depicting the role of Orkneymen in the Crusades [see *art*]. The starting point of *A Reel of Seven Fishermen*, for orchestra, was George's celebrated poem, while the structure of *The Beltane Fire*, for orchestra, follows the outline of a typical Mackay Brown short story.

Finally, two works for soloists, chorus and orchestra to Mackay Brown texts should be mentioned. Max incorporated George's poetic text, based on the Christmas story, into his cantata, *The Three Kings* - the first of his recent choral works - while poems from the collection *Winterfold* were used in the *Four Sea Elegies*.

In short, as we celebrate the 25th anniversary of the St Magnus Festival, it is clear that the PMD-GMB collaborations have exerted a major influence. They embody the spirit of Orkney, both past and present, and, in the process, reveal why the St Magnus Festival has been such an outstanding success.

Note: I am indebted to Archie Bevan for his clear recollection of the 1973 concert, and for the research he undertook to locate the review in *The Orcadian*.

"This year the St Magnus Festival kept the best till last. Nothing could have been more redolent of Orkney, or more representative of the romantic side of Peter Maxwell Davies's music personality than the big and beautiful cantata [Into the Labyrinth], to words by George Mackay Brown."
Conrad Wilson, The Scotsman,
June 24, 1983

Janis Susskind director, Composers & Repertoire
Boosey & Hawkes Music Publishers Ltd

To me, Max is one of the composers who represents the sixties and the seventies. He is the 'zeit geist' of the period, although he has always understood the need to evolve creatively and has never been in a time warp. He is on a voyage of permanent self-discovery, which is essential to a composer, always relating his work to what is going on around him. He is not a follower of fashion - his music always emanated from his need to create. Those who try to be very fashionable end up looking very dated. This has not happened to Max.

The St Magnus is a good example of a festival which has grown in a place that is not hide-bound by any particular tradition of classical music. Musically, there was no 'baggage' brought to it, and the people were very open-minded and responsive. This freshness and appreciation has allowed it to grow and evolve healthily.

*Jan Latham-Koenig, conductor
(in conversation)*

My first breath of Orkney air was in March 1977 and in a surprising place. London's Queen Elizabeth Hall was packed for a London Sinfonietta concert of works by Kurt Weill, conducted by my late husband Walter Susskind, and a world premiere by Peter Maxwell Davies led by the composer himself.

It was an evening of firsts: the birth of *A Mirror of Whitening Light* with its alchemical evocation of an Orkney seascape; my own first hearing of Maxwell Davies's music; and a first encounter with Max himself in a brief but electric moment in the Green Room.

Little did I suspect then that, only three years later, I would settle in London, take up gainful employment with Max's publisher, Boosey & Hawkes, and begin an engagement with new music that was to transmute over the years from healthy curiosity to fully-fledged passion. And all the time I was continuing to catch whiffs of that Orkney air and conjure up those extraordinary land and seascapes as each of Max's new works appeared.

I was beginning to feel the compelling need for a visit to Orkney itself - to walk, to touch stones, to see and feel the islands for myself, and of course to experience the St Magnus Festival at first hand. In 1986, having beaten off the opposition (it was a popular trip among B&H executives), I finally managed the transition from 'virtual' to 'real', and it did not disappoint.

Musical memories of that 10th anniversary festival revolve around the sight and sound of Isaac Stern joining André Previn and the Royal Philharmonic Orchestra in St Magnus Cathedral (what a squeeze!) in the premiere of Max's new Violin Concerto.

My return to the festival in 2000 revealed a fully 'grown-up' festival that had lost nothing in charm as it gained in professionalism. The new Pickaquoy Centre had happily supplanted the Phoenix cinema and was busy proving its flexibility in accommodating the world premieres of Max's symphonic works, *Orkney Saga V* and the 7th Symphony, as well as a new music theatre piece, *Mr Emmet Takes a Walk*.

Overlaying the brightness of that return visit was a certain valedictory mood, prompted by Max's revelations in a pre-concert interview with David Pountney. Amidst those world premieres - those 'firsts' - Max spoke repeatedly of 'last' things: his 'last symphony', 'last opera', and 'last music theatre work'. Happily for us all, those self-determined points of closure were soon eclipsed by animated plans for a cycle of string quartets, a Pentecostal Mass, and other projects. A toast to new beginnings!

Alistair Peebles

Peter Maxwell Davies in Bunertoon.

the poets

George Mackay Brown was an essential and unassuming presence at the heart of the festival. He inspired Peter Maxwell Davies from the moment the composer read *An Orkney Tapestry* on his first visit to Orkney, and George became a great supporter of the festival. Until his death in 1996, George chose and invited the distinguished festival poets, many of whom were his friends. The mutual affection and respect between George Mackay Brown and the visiting poet has been captured by the intimate photographs of Gunnie Moberg.

As a precursor to the festival poet 'slot' - officially first filled in 1981 by Norman MacCaig - there had been a literary presence at the festival, at George's instigation. The distinguished Naomi Mitchison (above), already in her eighties, read from her first collection of poetry in 1979; and Ronald Mavor performed a one-man play about his dramatist father, James Bridie, in 1980.

The festival poetry readings are particularly associated with the Pier Arts Centre in Stromness, where the intimacy, the play of reflected light on the walls and the creative environment are very conducive to a poetic atmosphere. Even better when the sound of the sea can be heard lapping, or sometimes lashing, against the sides of the pier during the readings.

The death of George Mackay Brown in 1996 left a permanent gap not only in the festival, but in Orkney and the literary world everywhere. And while the lack of George will always be lamented, the eminent poets continue to come to the festival, building on the grand tradition that George began and sustained.

George Mackay Brown   from *Under Brinkie's Brae*, July 5, 1990

The festival has been fortunate in its choice of poets, a succession of illustrious bards, beginning with the veteran Norman MacCaig.

And we have had the poet laureate, Ted Hughes, and the poet who would certainly be the laureate of the world-wide Irish if there was such an illustrious post, Seamus Heaney. Also Stewart Conn, Richard Murphy, Edwin Morgan, Iain Crichton Smith and Douglas Dunn, amongst others. Some of those poets stayed at Garth, the highest cottage on the mainland, hospitably looked after by Grenville and Elizabeth Gore-Langton (now Earl and Countess Temple of Stowe). Looking out over Hoy Sound and the open Atlantic, those poets must have thought Orkney an unforgettable place indeed.

Seamus Heaney, who may well be Ireland's greatest poet since Yeats, spread good-fellowship wherever he went. Ted Hughes fished the lochs, conducted by a man (Dave Brock) who knows the Orkney lochs and all the subtleties of trout, but alas! they were unlucky.

Are we running out of illustrious poets to invite to our festival? There are verse-makers by the score and by the hundred...There is still a wide field to choose from.

Stewart Conn   on Seamus Heaney, festival poet, 1982 and 1994

The resonance and wisdom of Heaney's poetry mirrored the integrity of the man - no pomposity, no airs and graces, his phrasing clear and rounded, thought and image energising one another. He was solemn one moment, frolicsome the next. We weren't just in the palm of his hand: it was as if he had a divining rod to our innermost feelings.

Afterwards there were conversations among the lupins at the home of Elizabeth Gore-Langton, where Seamus was being put up. For anyone who found it too much there was her husband Grenville's workshop, designated a 'poetry-free zone'.

Seamus Heaney, 1982.

previous page: **Naomi Mitchison and George Mackay Brown, 1979.**

Seamus Heaney is reading to a packed lecture theatre. I find myself sitting next to George Mackay Brown, who appears to know everybody in the room except me. I take out a notebook. So does he. 'I'm doing a write-up for 'The Orcadian'. Maybe we can compare notes afterwards.' I nod weakly. It's one of those terrible moments when you at last meet someone you've admired for decades, and have all these things you want to ask and share, but comment casually on the weather and settle down to listen. In the spellbinding hour that follows, Heaney's warm, Bushmills Malt of a personality infuses some of his most famous work. Next to me GMB gives little grunts of satisfaction at particularly powerful moments. 'That was excellent,' he says afterwards. I nod.

Tom Morton

The Scotsman, June, 1994

"The supreme art of making simple events not only memorable but immortal - Seamus Heaney is a master there, like all the great poets."

GMB

The Orcadian, June 23, 1994

Dave Brock on Ted Hughes, festival poet, 1984

I had been inspired by the writing of George Mackay Brown since he first set my tender young soul on fire with *Three Plays of Orkney*, on TV in 1969. Seeking out his company, we quickly became firm friends. I knew in advance that we shared at least one interest: on the fly-leaf of one of George's books he declared a favourite pastime to be drinking beer in the evening with his friends!

In 1977, I decided to abandon the stultifying materialism of the south and settle on Orkney for good. Fly fishing for wild brown trout had been a passion for many seasons and I'd developed a degree of loch craft. On Swannay, Hundland, Harray, Stenness or Kirbister, I came to know the best drifts, the most beautiful bays. I learned to select and present flies to suit the conditions, and read the face of the water; I could intuit fish.

In 1984, when I was down in Cheshire for a time, George wrote to tell me Ted Hughes was to be the visiting poet and give readings at that year's St Magnus Festival. Ted was a mad-keen fisherman and George had kindly told him there was no one better than me to introduce him to the Orkney lochs. My heart leapt. Ted Hughes was nothing short of a god to me. No man since DH Lawrence had shown such an uncanny insight into nature or could communicate so excitingly well what it might be like to be a bird, a beast, an insect or a plant. It was the chance of a lifetime.

At Kirkwall airport the little reception party waited; George and I, teaching staff and festival officials. But when Ted flew in and approached us - a huge, handsome, really rather magnificent man - it became clear that the most intense and insightful eyes and mind in literature were fully focused on seeking out the man who was to take him fishing....me!

Back at George's, Ted tucked in to the sweet pink flesh of a specimen trout from Swannay Loch I'd caught and cooked the day before. He ate it with relish and declared it, in all sincerity and with genuine astonishment, the

George Mackay Brown, Dave Brock,
Ted Hughes, 1984.

best trout he'd ever tasted. This fuelled Ted's enthusiasm for the next few days which we would spend fishing together.

As we set off each morning, raring to go, it tickled me to note that Ted was wearing Green Flash pumps, identical to mine. There seemed something incongruous here, that he should have something so mundane and commonplace on his feet. But there it was. Ted was my god in Green Flash pumps! (A clue that Ted's celebrity and the legend surrounding his life might make him a target for unwelcome attention came as he carefully covered himself with a baling can when peeing from the boat in case telephoto lenses were being aimed from the shore.)

In Stromness one evening we bumped into Julian Bream fresh from a recital. A meal in the Ferry Inn ensued; George, Ted, Julian Bream and yours truly. George said it was something to tell my grandchildren. Rather disgracefully, I scrounged cigarettes off Julian Bream until he rather firmly suggested I should obtain some of my own.

Ted carried a small note pad and pen which would occasionally appear - then I'd try to erase my presence until the jotting down was done. I'm extremely proud that the masterly, audaciously-ambitious poem Ted wrote for the Queen's 60th birthday, contains a magical reference to the time we spent together on Loch Skaill.

It was courtesy of Elizabeth Gore-Langton that we had two tantalising days on the delicious green waters of the legendary Loch Skaill. Sadly, poaching had seriously depleted her stocks of monstrous fish but there was still a chance of a truly remarkable trout. As luck would have it the fishing conditions had deteriorated with Ted's arrival. All but the rashest juveniles kept their heads well down. We grew more and more determined and tried every trick in the book. Loving every minute of it, the hours and days flew by; there was never enough time.

Only through a monumental effort were we only slightly late for Ted's first reading at the Pier Arts Centre. The audience was ready and waiting. Max met us with a good-natured smile. He considerately smuggled me inside (I hadn't thought to book a ticket) and introduced Ted, who became another person before my eyes. This was the great poet revealing artistically his inner self. With a hint of shyness. But in a superb, deep, strong, honest, surprisingly emotional voice.

When Ted flew out, George and I were late seeing him off from the airport; we could never get anywhere on time to save our lives. I cried my heart out that Ted had gone. I'd met, made friends with and grown to love the greatest writer in English of our age. Some weeks later came the announcement that Ted had been appointed Poet Laureate. He wrote me that

"In Ted Hughes's recital, as in many of the other festival events, we tasted 'the salt mouthful of actual existence,' and the Scottish Arts Council should be interested to know this. For its contribution of £11,000 to the St Magnus Festival, the SAC is getting a bargain."
Michael Tumelty
The Glasgow Herald
June 25, 1984

the best things about the Laureateship were the invitations to fish new waters.

When I look at the framed photo of myself with my arms flung around the shoulders of my two, all-time, favourite poets, making them smile, the memories and the sense of gratitude come flooding back. I'm grateful, too, to Gunnie, for her skill and quickness in capturing that spontaneous moment.

Edwin Morgan   festival poet, 1985 and 1998

I had a wonderful web of weathers, from sunshine to thunderstorm.

I saw the serpents and circles of Alan Davie (now my co-octogenarian) in a web of oils on lucky walls.

I read to audiences seething with interest like bees in a hive.

I carefully paced the Ring of Brodgar in a clockwise direction, feeling something I could not describe.

I watched Andy Howitt's dancers evoke elemental forces.

I was photographed by Gunnie Moberg in a windy courtyard with George Mackay Brown and Peter Maxwell Davies, George and I grinning broadly with our hair everywhere like wild men of the woods (George now gone, but that happy memory is fixed), and Max grinning too, but with his curls held under a natty leather cap - a trio of poetry, storytelling, and music caught by the lens like a tiny icon of festive Orkney.

Edwin Morgan, George Mackay Brown, Peter Maxwell Davies, 1985.

Douglas Dunn   festival poet, 1986

Attending the St Magnus Festival to give poetry readings was a memorable experience. It's the only time I've shared a plane with the Royal Philharmonic and André Previn. Also, having admired George Mackay Brown's poetry and other writing for many years, it was a delight to meet him, as well as an old friend from the 1960s, John Broom. George and I were already occasional correspondents and I always looked forward to his homemade Christmas cards with new and original verses. His company wasn't a disappointment. I was awed by his quiet wisdom, by a presence which was as natural and benevolent as his writing and poetry.

Of course, the premiere of Peter Maxwell Davies's Violin Concerto was the highlight of the festival. It didn't go too well, and the reception afterwards was fraught. I felt glad to be a poet and not a composer, soloist or conductor. After all, a poet's only responsibility at a public reading is to turn up sober. Which I did. Twice. In the second reading, I tried out a new and rather long poem as part of my programme. It went down like a German cruiser in Scapa Flow.

Isaac Stern's chamber recital, with Jean-Bernard Pommier, was unforgettable.

Douglas Dunn, 1986.

Stewart Conn festival poet, 1988
former head of radio drama, BBC Scotland

In the sixties and seventies I visited Orkney a number of times, to make radio programmes or on holiday. There were invigorating cliff-top walks. I sailed to Sanday across a glass-like sea, and flew nervously in a tiny plane past the Old Man of Hoy. I caused havoc by detecting a mouse in the Swannay Farm cheesery, and did my stint of clinging to the lurching rail of the *St Ola*. In 1982 came my first festival.

I was there to discuss with George Mackay Brown the forthcoming adaptation of his play *The Voyage of St Brandon*. An added enticement was Seamus Heaney being that year's guest poet. After toying with the idea of recording his reading, I decided against. There seemed no call, in the Pier Arts Centre, for intrusive microphones: far better preserve, for those fortunate enough to be there, the uniqueness of the occasion [see p.136]. Later, it was off to Kirkwall for a triple bill of George's plays. During the week came concerts by school children for whom, excitingly, music-making seemed as natural as breathing.

As for the script discussions, *St Brandon* duly went out, with Thomas Wilson (who had previously set some of his poems) having in George's words 'woven beautiful music into it'.

My pleasure at being the visiting poet in 1988 was sharpened by an awareness of those who had preceded me, and this being George's bishopric. When the day came he was at the front, for all the world like a benevolent divine in mufti, blue eyes a-glitter, his grey hair like a bow wave. Next to him sat Max, like an eager faun: I felt it would be no surprise if, when the moment came, he were to leap up to conduct me. At the end Max stood waiting as some ladies congregated to discuss my work, and their own. When they showed no sign of flagging, he slipped out. I'll never know what he was going to say. Soon everyone was milling in the courtyard with its sculpture and flower-beds, the tide slapping, Gunnie Moberg's camera unobtrusively clicking.

My poetry reading had included a poem on fishing. Afterwards I was approached by Sandy Orr, then chairman of Scottish Opera, who asked if I fancied a day on the water. Sadly, I said I had no rod. No matter, tackle would be seen to. The following day I met him at the Merkister Hotel, overlooking the Loch of Harray, where he was staying. With flies I'd bought, I made up some casts. When I asked what I ought to give the ghillie he told me to wheesht. Our ghillie turned out to be the hotel owner in person. As our boat put out, those already in the water, recognising him and sniffing fish, upped anchor and came after us in a small flotilla. Half way up the loch he moored, got out for a pee, then returned to the bottom end. None of the others had the nerve to follow. It was a great day. Sandy and I each got a handful of brightly speckled brownies - fighters all. We were told we'd missed dozens more.

My next Orkney visit, though between festivals, was poignantly

George Mackay Brown,
Stewart Conn, 1988.

"Stewart Conn is always coming up against ultimate imponderables and mulling them over with a refreshingly direct style, with no artificiality or affectation....We would gladly have sat listening for much longer."
VL, The Orcadian, June, 1988

interwoven with them. Orkney Arts Society invited me to read, again in the Pier Arts Centre, in the autumn of 1996: five months after George's death. In the presence of some of those closest to him, and among others Yvonne Gray and Pam Beasant of a talented new generation of poets, it seemed he was casting a glow over the occasion. At one point, very movingly, came an unpremeditated moment of shared silence and reflection.

This time I had my rod. Archie Bevan trustingly lent me his car. I stopped near Stenness to study the water, then forgetting I was in a lay-by reversed in slow motion into a soggy ditch. A farmer from down at the main road towed it out with his tractor, with no hint of a smirk and rejecting the note I pressed on him. Luckily, not a scratch. When I confessed to Archie and even before he heard the details, he reacted with the composure and good humour expected of a man who had for years borne much of the burden of the festival on his shoulders.

For 1998 the BBC had commissioned from me a 'distillation' of George's novel *Greenvoe*, to be set to music by Alasdair Nicolson. The premiere, preceded by a talk I called 'Music and Muse', was recorded in Stromness Academy Theatre. The musicians were from the BBC SSO (who were giving three concerts). Under producer Pam Wardell's sensitive guidance James Bryce, Eliza Langland, Vicki Masson and John Shedden, as all the protagonists, straddled the awkwardness of convention between a play and a 'platform' performance. Intimacy with the audience (and listener) was provided by Iain Anderson. Harmoniously and with touches of humour the music evoked the wide-ranging moods of the sea and of the characters, and the passage of time. The one pity was that the composer who was ill couldn't be there to conduct.

Years ago my first experience of divine worship in St Magnus Cathedral, under those funeral banners and with a sermon on the text 'all flesh is grass...', had been a chilling one. Now I saw the light streaming through the radiant stained-glass of the west window, with its images and phrases from George's poetry. The 'rose-red minster' was also the setting for an uplifting orchestral mix ranging from three Scott Skinner reels to DC Heath's violin concerto *The Celtic*, played with captivating purity by Clio Gould, and Elgar's mellow *Serenade for Strings*, the melody swelling, then receding like an ebb tide.

As for the fishing....On Boardhouse, thanks to George's brother Jackie, I had a magical day - despite breaking one of his oars early on, and getting most of my catch while birling in what must have been a watery version of fairy rings. The breakage he gently and smilingly dismissed, saying there must have been a weakness in the wood. On a last outing to Stenness two trout took the dry fly. Then under scudding clouds and intermittent rain so hard it felt like hail, came a little poem about inspiration. The subject seemed fitting, so enrichingly and in so many ways, and for so many people, has Orkney been precisely that.

Stolen Light

*A shiver crosses Loch Stenness
as of thousands of daddy-long-legs
skittering on the surface.
In total stillness
thunderheads close in.*

*Lead-shot from a blunderbuss
the first flurries come.
The elements have their say;
the depths riven
as by some monster.*

*The impulse to run
hell-for-leather
lest this a prelude
to one of the Great Stones
clumping to the water.*

*A friend is writing
a book on poetry
and inspiration.
Brave man - imagine him
in flippers and wet-suit*

*poised on the edge:
a charging of nerve-ends
too rapid to track,
or underwater treasure
you hold your breath and dive for?*

Stewart Conn
From *Stolen Light: Selected Poems*
(Bloodaxe Books 1999)

Paul Greenwood, Archie Bevan,
Claire Nielson; *The Realms of Gold*
1989.

Gunnie Moberg

Next morning the weather closed in. My early flight left. But many of the musicians were stranded, and had to stay on or go by boat. I imagined them gliding out from Stromness, their glissandos lost in the mist, the only response the singing of seals, in a plaintive minor key.

Alasdair Nicolson composer, *Greenvoe*, 1998

In 1998, I was able to encapsulate much of the atmosphere, landscape, community and emotion which I have experienced in my many visits north. I was asked by BBC Scotland to create a piece of music theatre for radio based on the novel *Greenvoe* by George Mackay Brown. The result was broadcast as part of the tribute to George on St Andrew's Night. For this I worked with Stewart Conn who produced the most beautiful distillation of a novel I have ever read. Working with spoken text and underlaying music is always a tricky task, for one wants to add an important layer without being obtrusive. The result was a piece for five actors and the BBC SSO. Unfortunately, although I was to have conducted the premiere, I was struck down by a horrible virus and never made it to Orkney that year. [See also *the composers*]

'The Realms of Gold' 1989

[There was no invited festival poet in 1989. Instead, George Mackay Brown compiled a personal 'voyage' through some of the great poetry in the English language. His commentary was delivered by Archie Bevan, and the poems read by professional actors and festival regulars, Claire Nielson and Paul Greenwood.]

"The poetry reading in the Pier Arts Centre on Saturday morning was no ordinary one. Compiled by George Mackay Brown, it was, in his words, 'a kind of voyage...from the first intoxicating discovery in youth, and on round the many states and kingdoms and western islands "that bards in fealty to Apollo hold".' In the sensitive and professional hands of Claire Nielson and Paul Greenwood, the 60 or so 'passengers' (with water lapping appropriately nearby) were taken on a personal circumnavigation from the first fresh poetic discoveries of Keats, Shelley, Shakespeare, Milton and some of the great poems of the twentieth century, back to Orkney, where literary treasure can be found in abundance. George Mackay Brown's lyrical and moving commentary was read with great sensitivity by Archie Bevan. GMB is to be thanked for new and searching insights into some great and beautiful poems and the nature of poetry itself. Claire Nielson, Paul Greenwood and Archie Bevan are to be congratulated on their clear and thoughtful presentation."
The Orcadian, June, 1989

Simon Hall on Norman MacCaig
(festival poet, 1981 and 1991)

I was seventeen in June 1991, and had recently discovered just how dangerously addictive a drug poetry actually is. Living in Orkney around farms and wild birds, among heather and seascapes, had rendered me particularly susceptible to the lyrics of Norman MacCaig. When I was first shown some of these by my teacher - Frances McKie - I was captivated from the outset. The people, landscapes, birds and beasts of his adopted territory, Assynt in Sutherland, came to life through metaphor which startled me in its freshness, as it still does.

George Mackay Brown, Norman MacCaig 1981.

You can imagine how I felt when my mother told me that Norman MacCaig was to be a guest at our home for the duration of the festival. He arrived on a Friday morning: a tall and still handsome presence in his eighties, with a patrician dignity. We were, I think, all a little nervous about meeting him, but he began at once to charm the entire family, his sense of humour and his warmth setting us more or less instantly at ease.

We had fun and got to know each other a little. I wanted to ask him about his poetry but he was a deeply modest man whose poems had initially only appeared in print because his wife Isabel surreptitiously sent a manuscript to a publisher. He remained exactly the same when he came to Orkney all these years later. I picked up pieces of incidental information, but, whether because of my inability to ask even half-sensible questions or his reluctance to discuss his own work, these conversations didn't go far. What he did instead was reveal the work of Hugh MacDiarmid to me, and for this I will always be grateful. MacCaig wasn't just a great poet - he was also a talented teacher.

Dad brought home a special bottle of Highland Park which Norman enjoyed very much. In a pointless concession (for an octogenarian) which was intended to reduce his tar intake, he was smoking Silk Cut. 'Paying money for fresh air,' he complained, jokingly. As he relaxed in the evenings after his festival readings I listened to the conversation. He told stories about deer stalkers and salmon fishers (poachers all) in Assynt. He spoke also, with profound affection and undiminished grief, of his late friend in Assynt, AK MacLeod, for whom Norman wrote the immensely powerful group of elegies *Poems for Angus*. It was clear that the central tensions of his later poetry, the conflicting urges toward celebration and lament, came from deep within.

Soon he had delighted his audiences in Stromness and Kirkwall and it was time to run him to the airport. We shook hands and that was the last I saw of Norman. Five years later, in January 1996, I was in Glasgow studying for finals in Scottish Literature when I heard he had died. I don't think I would have read much Scottish or any other poetry if it hadn't been for Norman

"He is a wily old performer, Norman MacCaig. A veteran of poetry readings, festivals and ceilidhs - anywhere that words are celebrated - he is most at home teasing and poking fun at his audience - and himself - and he does so with incisive accuracy."
DD
The Orcadian, July 4, 1991

MacCaig, reading him and meeting him. Frances, my former teacher, said that when she heard of his passing she felt the same overwhelming sadness she had experienced on hearing the news of John Lennon's death. Norman didn't touch as many of us as John Lennon, but the impact he made on those who were lucky enough to meet him was, I'm sure, every bit as profound.

Gunnie Moberg

Brian McCabe, 1992.

Brian McCabe   festival poet, 1992

My hosts [in Orkney] were Bob and Pat Hall, who run a hairdressing salon in Kirkwall. One of the nice aspects of the festival is the way that local people volunteer to accommodate all the visiting artists. Pat and Bob had done it for Norman MacCaig the year before, so I knew they wouldn't expect me to be home by midnight for my hot milk. As hosts, Pat and Bob epitomised something about Orkney: Pat was the festival-goer, doing all she could to make it work - while Bob, a committed Philistine, maintained a distrust of all things arty.

George Mackay Brown had donned his best anorak for the festival's launch and was looking distinctly chirpy, with a glint of mischief in his eye. At speech time, Sir Peter had the thankless task of thanking everyone involved in the festival. Simon, Bob and Pat's teenage son, took me to the Phoenix cinema to catch the Ronnie Scott sextet holding down a tight set, as they say. Afterwards, Simon steered me to a pub where some local folk music was going down. It was good stuff, and nobody was paying any attention to it.

Eventually Bob converted me to his form of Philistinism: he took me out on his boat sailing, then brought me home and fed me with the most delicious prawns I have ever eaten.

I am pleased to report I converted him too. As well as taking in the shows, I was doing a few myself. Bob drove me to the first reading... I told him I'd try to make them laugh, make them cry and make them think. The following day, Bob came to hear me. His presence in the audience made me nervous. Afterwards, sailing past the 'Caledonia Star' out into Kirkwall Bay, Bob confessed that he'd had trouble containing his laughter, and that the opening of one story I'd read had brought tears to his eyes. The questions he asked me let me know I'd also made him think, and so all that remained to be done was to take the boat back to harbour, head for the 'Ola' and celebrate our mutual conversion.

(First printed in *Scotland on Sunday*, July, 1992. Extract reprinted by kind permission of the author.)

Knut Ødegård   festival poet, 1993

I am writing from Iceland, but I am a Norwegian. A propos nationality, for me I have this strange feeling of not being abroad at all in Orkney; my forefather left Orkney some hundred years ago and settled down in Bergen, Norway. In my family tree we have a lot of Orcadians, among them Swein Asleifsson the pirate, and also the old earls of Orkney. The family who went to Norway used the family name of Rendall and according to the family tradition, this is one of the oldest family names in Orkney.

My dearest friend in Orkney died some years ago, the poet George Mackay Brown. I visited him twice, and we wrote a lot of letters during some years. When I came first time to Orkney, he wished me 'welcome home' - although it was several hundred years since my family left the islands. The festival was wonderful! I enjoyed myself so much, and I also felt a strong and warm contact with the audience: good listeners, nice and open-hearted people.

Kevin Crossley-Holland   festival poet, 1995

I can see a room in Stromness looking out on to Scapa Flow. Not a gushle or even a gurl of wind! The water is serene and dreaming. But in the room there are tides of talk and laughter. Magnus Linklater stands with his back to the fireplace, chatting with Nicola LeFanu; George Mackay Brown and I stand with Archie and Elizabeth Bevan and several others at the window, reviewing the day's events - yes, and drinking Highland Park; and near the door, my wife Linda is telling Peter Maxwell Davies about the songs of the voyagers who supported the Hudson's Bay company (their last watering-hole before sailing west was, of course, Stromness), and then I hear her beginning to sing.

One of the great joys of the St Magnus Festival is what goes on around the events: talk about the arts, old friendships renewed, new friendships kindled. Another is the way in which the festival brings into contact people working in different disciplines. Shortly after I was invited to serve as festival poet, I received a letter from the artist Elaine Shemilt, whom I had not seen since we worked together at Winchester School of Art in 1984. She said I'd be surprised to hear she was working on a number of prints based on my three poems *Orkney Girls* and would be showing her work in Stromness during the festival. Our Orkney reunion led to further collaboration, and in Orkney too, I first met Mary Newcomb (festival artist in 1995). From time to time, she and I exchange letters and ideas, and at my elbow I have the squinting gull she drew for my sixtieth birthday.

I suppose we all have secret longings. For years, one of mine was to be invited to be the festival poet. Why? Because I love Orkney. Because of the stature-yet-intimacy of the St Magnus Festival, and the high-standing of previous festival poets. Because of my affection for George.

So I was gratified when my chance came in 1995, the year when Nicola LeFanu's and my opera, *The Wildman*, was staged at the festival - and in the event, I believe it was the penultimate time George chose, or helped to choose the poet-in-residence. I can see us sitting side by side on the bench

Knut Ødegård, 1993.

Gunnie Moberg

As Norwegian consul, I have had the privilege of meeting and entertaining many Norwegians at the festival, and the links between the festival and Norway are very positive and strong. The visit of the Norwegian poet, Knut Ødegård, in 1993, was particularly memorable. We spent some time with him and his charming Icelandic girlfriend. Both had a wonderful sense of the ridiculous and were great fun; with the help of a few drams, a hilarious time was had by all!
Bill Spence
Norwegian consul in Orkney

Gunnie Moberg

Nicholas Cleobury, Nicola LeFanu, Kevin Crossley-Holland, 1995.

[The Wildman] "had many powerful forces to tax and work an absorbed audience."
MAM
The Orcadian, June 22, 1995

Gunnie Moberg

Jackie Kay, 2000

"Jackie Kay is not only a poet and an author but a part-time comedienne. The reading was sprinkled with anecdotes concerning her work and experiences and at times the audience barely managed to remain in their seats." LB
The Orcadian, June 29, 2000

outside the Pier Gallery - the most perfect space imaginable in which to show Hepworth, Nicolson, et al. George is shy, smiling, wistful, inward....

It was the last time I saw him. When I came back to Orkney, it was to talk (for radio) to his friends and fellow Orcadians about his undying work.

Jackie Kay festival poet, 2000

I had heard so much about Orkney: the quality of light there, Skara Brae, the history, the lack of trees, how George Mackay Brown hardly left the island, Stromness with the stress not like Inverness, the original birds, the sea, the sea, the sea, the whisky, the people. I already had the island in my head as a cross between the mythical and the real. Orkney didn't disappoint me. It is one of those places that grabs your heart and tugs at your imagination. I can honestly say that I have never had such a good time doing readings as I had in Orkney. The people's response was so wonderfully warm that I felt totally uplifted.

My mum and my son came with me and we arrived at the wee airport. Even the airport is friendly. They had a wonderful time too, driving and walking around the island, meeting people, eating and drinking. There was a fabulous atmosphere there at the festival, both at the events and out in the street. I have never bumped into so many people before who have just been at my reading. It seemed the whole island was there and interested. It seemed that Orkney and books go together, Orkney and literature, Orkney and poetry. Some places have got what it takes.

My son when he was little used to ask me, 'Mum, why are you always going to Poetry?'. He thought poetry was a place, that I boarded a train or a plane and I got off at a place called Poetry. Orkney is that place.

Vikram Seth festival poet, 2001 (in conversation)

I had been asked to come to the festival several times when George Mackay Brown was alive, and I certainly wanted to come and knew that George did not travel. But year followed year, and something or other always happened around that time - my sister got married one year, for instance, and another time I was away in India. I am constitutionally somewhat lazy when it comes to travel, so I put it off.

When George died, I suppose regret, and an irritation at myself as well, crept in, and I became determined to make it to Orkney if they asked. They did ask, and I said yes - and actually it was the only thing I did in 2001, by way of being a writer.

Between books I don't really like doing very much, but if you want a book you have published to live, you must involve yourself a certain amount in the sales drive. One of the disadvantages of this is that you can meet nice people and never see them again, and if you meet people who are not nice, it is not very pleasant. But the thing that really makes it worthwhile is finding the occasional place that you won't forget and you want to come back to.

I think Orkney is such a place. Maybe what gives me that sense is that I was welcomed here not just by the human population, but by the seals as well. My first idea when I came here was not to go to the brass bands, but to actually swim in the sea by the cemetery where George is buried. Strengthened by Highland Park, I swam along the shore and the seals came out and swam very close to me.

It was absolutely startling that evening - almost windless - and it was so clear. There was this ochre rock, and Hoy in the background. When the first seal came near, I thought it was a dog. I thought, 'That dog is as crazy as me to swim'! They are very, very large. I don't know whether they approved of me, but they approved of the activity - that human beings were swimming - at last taking to the water - and certainly they didn't seem to be at all worried by my presence.

I have heard about the porpoises playing around the boats in Orkney waters; sometimes you see them in the bow wave, and sometimes in the wake where the fish have been disturbed. (I wrote an opera libretto once which was based on a Greek myth involving dolphins. In order to research dolphin ways I went to Dingle, on the west coast of Ireland, where there was a dolphin who used to swim with people. I was swimming very early one morning, and there was nothing in the water, at least so I thought. When I came out of the water I asked a bystander if anyone had seen the dolphin anywhere, and was told that it had been behind me all the time - playing with me!)

My main impressions in Orkney have been of the light and space, and there are many places on the islands I would like to visit; the cliffs, the Italian Chapel, the Old Man of Hoy, the prehistoric sites, especially the stone circle - and I would like to see more of the bird and wild life. People may not find trees here, but this Orkney world of changing greens and browns is very appealing. It is hilly, and there is a constantly changing view. One can sit for half an hour and find it transfigured in that short time.

Maureen Gray Pier Arts Centre

The poets all seem to like reading at the Pier. The down side is that sixty is the maximum that can be seated, which in festival terms is not very many - but poets and audiences enjoy the intimate atmosphere. After the readings, if it's a fine day, there is a great gathering on the pier, with no one in a hurry to leave. Marjorie (Linklater) is a great miss on these occasions - she was always there, having her picture taken with the poet, and always in great form.

Norman MacCaig was here twice. The last time, in 1991, Margaret

Vikram Seth, 2001.

The festival poets

1979	Naomi Mitchison
1981	Norman MacCaig
1982	Seamus Heaney
1983	Richard Murphy
1984	Ted Hughes
1985	Edwin Morgan
1986	Douglas Dunn
1987	Iain Crichton Smith
1988	Stewart Conn
1990	Liz Lochhead
1991	Norman MacCaig
1992	Brian McCabe
1993	Knut Ødegård
1994	Seamus Heaney
1995	Kevin Crossley-Holland
1996	Iain Crichton Smith
1997	Kenneth White
1998	Edwin Morgan
1999	John Burnside
2000	Jackie Kay
2001	Vikram Seth

In 2001 we had two players from London Brass staying with us. One sultry afternoon - yes, I kid you not, we did have such a day - a few folk and most of London Brass, all in high spirits after their fantastic lunchtime concert, landed up in our garden. Owen Slade gave an unforgettable rendition of his poem *I'm so in Love with my Tuba*; the two workmen painting our conservatory abandoned brushes and joined us; and Vikram Seth, holding high a glass of Highland Park, toasted with appropriate alliteration 'music makers, poets and painters'.

Vivia Leslie, festival host, former Foy organiser

Gardiner (who founded the Pier Arts Centre) happened to be in Stromness and we went out for lunch (it is the tradition for the Pier to take the poet to lunch). They had met some years previously and they got on famously over a bottle (or two) of red wine. They were great company.

Ted Hughes was standing beside me at his reading. He was an imposing figure, tall and burly, but when he stood up his knees were shaking. The reading had just started and there were cars and motor bikes capering up and down the other pier, blowing their horns. Julian Bream [the guitarist] was in the audience, sitting near the door and he got up, ran down the pier and give them all a piece of his mind. It must have worked, as all was quiet after that!

Seamus Heaney mentioned that it was such an honour to come and read here with George sitting in the audience. George appeared to be in awe of Seamus Heaney too. There was a great mutual respect.

Knut Ødegård's readings weren't as well attended as others, but they were superb. His poem about the drunks in Molde town had a universal theme, resonant of some of George's work and *Under Milk Wood*. Someone asked if he would read in Norwegian - just to hear him read in his own language. It was lovely to listen to, even though most didn't understand the words.

Vikram Seth was a great hit in Orkney - he was asked how long it took to write *A Suitable Boy* - he said it took seven years to write, three years to recover. We took him across the Churchill Barriers and to visit the Italian Chapel. He knew a lot about the history and wanted to know exactly where the U boat had come in to sink the *Royal Oak*. He loved Highland Park - he had never tasted it before, but said he would be forever grateful to Orkney for introducing him to it! He must have bought some as a souvenir, as his bag was making some very bottley sounds.

George Mackay Brown - an appreciation

"In many respects, the St Magnus Festival is the public expression of Mackay Brown's lifelong concern to preserve the traditions of Orkney - always adapting to new ideas, but never forgetting the past."
John Warnaby
Musical Opinion
September, 1989

It is a word, blossoming as legend, poem, story, secret, that holds a community together and gives a meaning to its life. If words become functional ciphers merely, as they are in white papers and business letters, they lose their 'ghosts' - the rich aura that has grown about them from the start, and grows infinitesimally richer every time they are spoken. They lose more; they lose their 'kernel', the sheer sensuous relish of utterance. Poetry is a fine interpretation of ghost and kernel.
(George Mackay Brown, *An Orkney Tapestry*)

Claire Nielson (Isbister)   actor, regular festival participant

I have so many memories of George. Sitting in his living-room among a group of friends being encouraged to finish up the home-brew because he 'needed the bottles empty for the morning'; during performances in the festival his gentle face amongst the audience always making us feel less nervous; and so many times of talk and laughter about so many different things. We never spoke of his work very much, but more about other poets and what we admired or disliked in them. I rather shudder to think that once I asked him what inspired him to write. He just smiled and said, 'a blank piece of paper, Claire'. A good answer to a rather stupid question, but I loved his work so much and longed to know the impossible.

Whenever I read his poems during the festival and he was present, I always hoped I wouldn't let him down, but I needn't have worried because he told me that when he had to read his own poems for an album of his work, he found it harrowing and wasn't sure how to read them! That same album had a picture of him on the cover, standing among the Standing Stones at Brodgar. He laughed at this photo of himself and said 'I look like one of the stones come alive!'.

Archie Bevan   festival vice-president

George made a massive contribution to the festival from its earliest beginnings. His writing provided Max with text and inspiration for many works which have adorned the festival down the years, and several of George's plays were premiered on a festival stage.

The festival poetry reading and the Johnsmas Foy became an established part of the programme early on, and George made a vital contribution to them both. The last poet to accept George's invitation to the festival was his friend Iain Crichton Smith. But of course virtually all those poets who regularly added such lustre to the festival were George's friends, visiting Orkney to see him as much as to entertain us.

Ill health and bad weather increasingly curtailed his attendance at committee meetings. We missed his benign presence, and the witty sotto voce asides that emanated from the corner he shared with Dick Hughes. (Laughter was an essential component of those late-night marathons.)

George was a devoted servant of the festival for nearly twenty years. We can count ourselves fortunate to have been graced by his presence. (First published in *Orkney Arts Review*.)

Peter Maxwell Davies, The Orcadian April 18, 1996
"George and his work effected a magic which informed and transformed my own creations. I have set many of his poems and we collaborated on several projects, perhaps the most ambitious of which was the opera 'The Martyrdom of St Magnus', with which the first St Magnus Festival opened, in the cathedral, in 1977.

"George spoke for Orkney with quiet passion and superb eloquence. He was a master wordsmith, always in supreme control of his medium, with a deceptively simple saga style which invariably carries a large cargo of unspoken meaning and sometimes deep emotion, and which occasionally blossoms into moments of surpassing beauty that brings tears to the eyes.

His celebration of the islands is comprehensive. It embraces the place and the people: their history and rituals and rites of passage: the pageant of the seasons; the 'brutal stations of bread' and 'the drowning wave'.

But it is important for Orcadians to remember that George speaks not only for us and about us, but also to us. Implicitly - and sometimes explicitly - he urges us to maintain our sense of community, and to look to the roots which give us our special identity."
Archie Bevan
The Orcadian April 18, 1996

George was a staunchly supportive friend, and the most modest and unassuming of men, and an exemplary creator, whose work has defined and redefined for me, over a quarter of a century, my perceptions of Orkney, as expressed in my music; he must be the most positive and benign influence ever on my own efforts at creation."

George Mackay Brown, Rackwick, 1985.

Gunnie Moberg

A Landfall
i.m. George Mackay Brown

Far north, in sunlight,
the stone ship ran aground. Larks
sing at the masthead.

Seamus Heaney

(*Dove-Marks on Stone: Poems for George Mackay Brown*; Babel, 1996.
Printed by kind permission of the author.)

A Johnsmas Foy

Marjorie Linklater, (widow of the Orcadian writer, Eric Linklater), was a dynamic member of the festival committee from the beginning. Her passion for Orkney literature led Marjorie to instigate 'A Johnsmas Foy' in 1978, to widen the parameters of the mainly music festival, and give a platform to the exceptionally fine home-grown talent available.

The early structure of the Foy was straightforward. There were readers, often including Elizabeth Bevan, Bessie Grieve and Gregor Lamb, who recited extracts from writers such as George Mackay Brown, Edwin Muir, Eric Linklater and Robert Rendall - usually to a theme - and there was music supplied from the considerable pool of traditional players on the islands. Sometimes there was drama, including premieres of George Mackay Brown plays - and twice there has been film. Younger writers and musicians have also been given a chance to show their skills. Notably, past musical participants have included Jennifer and Hazel Wrigley, the virtuosic fiddlers, and folk/rock singer Ivan Drever, all of whom are pursuing acclaimed professional careers. From its beginning, the Foy made an impact, attracting a local audience along with a steadily increasing number of visitors.

Over the years, the format has changed, as different individuals or groups have compiled the programmes. Essentially, however, it has remained true to its original purpose - providing a selection of local writing, in the appropriate surroundings, involving as many members of the community as possible as participants and audience.

Marjorie Linklater, Sally Linklater, 1995.

Gunnie Moberg

Marjorie was always on the committee, always very bright and she always had pertinent criticisms. Occasionally she went for me quite severely. I had to defend my decisions meticulously, and the things I had said and done. Then she would be quite happy.
*Peter Maxwell Davies
(in conversation)*

Sally Linklater on Marjorie Linklater, founder of A Johnsmas Foy

Marjorie was always full of energy. Whatever was new appealed to her, especially if it was unexpected. When she returned to Orkney after the death of her husband, Eric, she wasn't looking for a walk down memory lane. Finding that Ernest Marwick [historian and writer] felt as angry as she did at the South of Scotland Electricity Board's proposal to the effect that farmers living between Yesnaby and Stromness give up their land so that it might be turned into a base for uranium mining, she joined his anti-nuclear protest and, together with him, organised the march through Kirkwall which finally persuaded the authorities to abandon the scheme.

That march, and the fight against the imposition of an alien plan by a far-away authority, opened Marjorie's eyes to other dangers. The danger, for example, of forgetting our history. People travel from far and wide to enjoy Orkney's unique heritage. But this heritage - the buildings and the prehistoric remains which tell us how past generations lived - is always subject to time and decay. Keenly aware of this, Marjorie became involved in the Orkney Heritage Society which, in conjunction with its architect, aims at preserving our treasures through a combination of local and professional knowledge.

Fresh winds had come blowing, meanwhile, from another direction. From Hoy, where Peter Maxwell Davies had set in motion the idea of the St Magnus Festival. Marjorie helped in the fight to stage *The Martyrdom of St Magnus* in the cathedral [see *setting up*]. She was one of the members of the very first festival committee, and one of the first to stand up and speak. She said she had an important point to make. This festival was very welcome. But it must not be confined to specialists. It should be enjoyed by every single person in Orkney, not simply the professional musicians and the *cognoscenti*. Indeed, what it needed, just like the one in Edinburgh, was a fringe.

The rest of the committee were, I'm told, somewhat alarmed. Here was Marjorie, before the official festival had even been discussed, blethering about a festival fringe - what on earth could she mean?

Marjorie tried to explain. Orkney, she pointed out, possessed a rich heritage in the spoken word. Inspiration for the sagas, it had produced writers, several of whom, during the twentieth century, had become well known south of its islands. She was proud to number her husband among them, and she considered words, as well as music, worthy of celebration.

Committee members sighed with relief. If that was all Marjorie wanted, over to her - she could organise her fringe as she liked. But it had better be good. Also, it had better have a name. Was it George Mackay Brown who suggested calling it A Johnsmas Foy? I don't know, but this became its title; Johnsmas because midsummer, the time chosen to celebrate the festival, was traditionally the time sacred to St John, and Foy because in Old Norse this signifies 'time for enjoyment', or 'fair'. As at a fair, performers would be showing off their wares, all of which would come from Orkney traditions. Marjorie took up the search for such performers with enthusiasm: she discovered a remarkable number of these and every year found herself weaving their stories, poems and songs round a new theme.

The theme might be a reflection of Robert Rendall's quiet observations about '...a pattern of local history reaching back for generations'. Or it might echo Edwin Muir's awe at ploughing horses. Or George Mackay Brown's, when he likened the cliffs of Hoy to: 'A conference of old gods/ their talk more primitive than the Atlantic/ of whales, herrings, ships, fulmars, legends...'

Performed for the first time in the Old Academy Hall, the Foy quickly became part of the official St Magnus Festival. Producing it took time and energy and, as well, there were the problems which faced all the committee; one of the most important, in Marjorie's view, being the question of accommodation. Supply of lodgings for groups of musicians and actors who probably have appointments to keep after visiting Orkney is no easy matter. Orcadians are, of course, renowned for their hospitality, but this doesn't mean they are always well-organised.

But Marjorie was quite good at arranging who should sleep where; indeed, she set about the task in what a friend has called a 'positively military manner'! As well, she offered a hand of friendship to Max: hearing that he needed somewhere to rest during the short period between morning and evening concerts, she invited him along to her house in Kirkwall and let him rest there, undisturbed, in a quiet room.

She remained the Foy's director until she was well into her seventies. The St Magnus Festival was always the focal point of her year, and she always insisted on buying as many tickets as she possibly could. Nevertheless, as time passed, her energy grew less; I remember her saying wistfully, when I had just turned sixty, that she wished she were as young as I was!

Then came the 1997 St Magnus Festival. Certain, as always, that this would be the best one yet, Marjorie had ordered lots of tickets for us all - herself, myself and my sister who had flown over from America. But she was too tired, very often, to leave her armchair, even for a performance she'd been talking about for weeks. All the same, her sense of drama never left her. She managed to attend the festival's first concert and she was determined, come hell or high water, to be at its last. The music, for a start, was to be by three of her favourite composers; Bach, Telemann and Vivaldi and, as well, she was in agreement with Glenys Hughes's observation in the programme book that involvement of the local community was 'central to the ethos of the festival'. The four soloists, of course, would be highly acclaimed professionals. But the music accompanying their performances would be played and sung by Orkney Camerata and the St Magnus Festival Chorus.

Escorting, or rather, propelling Marjorie to the cathedral was no easy matter, but we succeeded in helping her, well wrapped in warm woollens, into a wheelchair. Wheeled down a side aisle, she sat enraptured throughout

Gregor Lamb, Kristin Linklater, Russell Hunter, 1978; the first Foy.

A Johnsmas Foy, 1990;
The Mester Ship.

Gunnie Moberg

the performance and, after the applause had ended, and the audience were streaming out of the great kirk, found herself surrounded by friends with whom she sat blethering for a long time. When, at last, we wheeled her out into the grey midsummer air, I heard a friend express her commiserations.

'I canna get used to this, Marjorie,' she was saying, 'you needing to be pushed in a chair, when it's you generally telling us whar we've to get to next'.

Marjorie nodded.

'But just you wait,' she said. 'In two years' time I'll be ninety. I'll be so strong by that time I'll come striding along to the cathedral!'

She died a month later. Buried in Harray Kirkyard, I'm quite sure that she has gone striding into the Land of the Blest.

Elizabeth Bevan   regular Foy reader (and festival 'godmother')

Looking back to how Marjorie's well-meaning 'fringe' was diverted into the 'Foy' and welcomed into the programme of the second festival, I marvel at its contribution over the years. While the conception of the festival had always included local participation as a 'must', it was that versatile, insistent lady of the winning ways who quickly recognised that the initial musical emphasis should be balanced by something of our own rich literary heritage. So for the past twenty four years the Johnsmas Foy has explored the depth and breadth of the oral and written word of Orcadians over the centuries, further enlivened by local music played on the fiddle, pipe or accordion.

Mostly, performances were anchored to themes, but occasionally free rein was requested and given. Many Orcadians have taken part, from Birsay to Deerness and in between, with school pupils taking their turn. In the eighties we were fortunate and proud to have stiffening from the locally connected and well known actress Claire Nielson (Isbister) [see p.159], who had performed in the GMB stories filmed for television by the BBC in 1970. Mrs Linklater, imaginative and trained in drama, produced the first Foy along with her daughter Kristin, then a teacher of voice in the theatre in New York. Marjorie went on to present five more Foys, but other talented enthusiasts were also persuaded to take a turn. Varying ideas, content and format were introduced. Two films were commissioned, one celebrating the work of George Mackay Brown in 1988, and the moving and successful *Between the Terminals* in 2001, based on a poem by Yvonne Gray. In 1997, the Foy featured *A Place to Keep*, a learned tribute by Professor Ian Campbell of Edinburgh University, honouring George and focusing on his 'unique gift of opening a country and a state of mind to the outside world,' something which I think indeed the whole festival aims to do.

"Elizabeth Bevan reads quite artlessly and beautifully and somehow finds her hearers' feelings with every word."
MAM
The Orcadian, June 26, 1997

The early introduction of 'A Johnsmas Foy' opened new vistas: I remember sitting transfixed as the cadences of Orkney Norn rang out in the sonorous tones of Bessie Grieve.
Stephen Pruslin
pianist and writer

As one of the many readers, I enjoyed participating. Planning and rehearsing was always fun and interesting. The required repetition of familiar or newly discovered poetry or prose, rather than leading to boredom, often further illumined aspects of the work and enhanced our appreciation. We only hoped our enthusiasm would be transferred to the audiences! Maybe indeed it mostly was, as testified by positive feedback from avid Foy followers.

Amateurs on platform can sometimes be cavalier about the preparation and precision necessary for the execution of such events, probably covering up nerves (if you really thought about it you probably wouldn't be able to perform!). So working alongside a brilliant professional like Claire Nielson was a revealing but happy experience. And what a sparkle she brought to rehearsal and performance. I'm sure all performers, as I did, drew from all these sessions life-enhancing richness, whether from the beautiful descriptive or witty prose of Eric Linklater, the visionary poetry of Edwin Muir and George, or the often equally emotive dialect poems of Christina Costie or Robert Rendall, to name some of 'the greats'.

Until the advent of the Foy (and now there are off-shoots like the New Year Foy at the Pier Arts Centre, showcasing entirely new local work) I would say that there had been minimal oral exposure of Orcadian literature since the long ago days of tales told 'around the Orkney peat fires', before radio, television or internet encroached on our leisure time. General awareness of our local culture had probably been somewhat in abeyance - after all, two world wars had intervened. Now there can be few Orcadians who have not been exposed to this treasure in our island heritage, and many are now contributing to its continuity. School education has always done its bit, and now ensures that the local heritage has a special place in the primary and secondary curriculum. Perhaps the Foy, too, can claim some credit for this happy reawakening.

Howie Firth senior producer, BBC Radio Orkney 1977-87

With sheer charm and vitality, Marjorie Linklater always made things happen, and at the radio station I always looked forward to a visit from her and a fresh project to promote. After several superb Foys of Orkney poetry and prose and music, Marjorie wanted to take a break and asked me to look after the event for a time.

It was an opportunity to try out some of the Radio Orkney voices on the stage, and so we had Captain John Gray reading from the poems of Christina Costie, Paul Heppleston with Harry Berry's spellbinding story of *The Driftwood Fiddle*, Gary Gibson with some of the great letters of John D

A Johnsmas Foy, 1996;
Brooms and Cradles and Pots?

Some of the local performers have now become professional and tour the world. We originally saw Jennifer and Hazel Wrigley as young schoolgirls playing for one of the first Johnsmas Foys we ever attended. We now try and hear them whenever they are in London or we are in Edinburgh. Talking about the Foy, we are always slightly amused by the number of local people who come up to us each year concerned that we might not have understood the dialect. Usually we have no problem; after a few days on the islands our ears have become attuned. *Yvonne and Jeremy Clarke annual festival visitors*

Mackay, Edwin Eunson with excerpts from 'Cubbie Roo's' Ba' game reports (prefaced by Willie Marwick from Stromness with a sandwich board to announce the headlines).

We had lovely music from the Holm School; we had visiting participants like Claire Nielson and Paul Greenwood, and Larry and Shirley Peterson with Shetland songs. And we had John Broom reading from the works of William McGonagall.

Now you might think the famous Dundee poet and tragedian to be far removed from Orkney shores, but there is an account of his family spending some years in Orkney, where he is said to have gone to school in South Ronaldsay, and Ernest Marwick noted that the circumstantial evidence around the story did seem to fit reasonably well. Whatever the truth, it seemed a good opportunity to combine the voice of John Broom, in suitably lugubrious mode, with dramatic actions from the rest of the cast, in the tale of the wreck of the steamer *London* while on her way to Australia in the year 1866.

> *Twas all on a sudden the storm did arise,*
> *Which took the captain and passengers all by surprise,*
> *Because they had just sat down to their tea.*
> *When the ship began to roll with the heaving of the sea.*

So the Holm pupils, coached by Claire and Paul, were the passengers, rolling with the ship, and then we needed someone to play the part of 'the famous Shakespearian actor 'Gustavus V Brooke' who unfortunately also went down with the ship but who remained calm to the last. We needed someone who would remain calm while all around them turned into chaos, and I wish I could remember who it was who came up with the perfect solution - Raymie Manson's Labrador dog, Horlicks.

Anyone who had ever seen Raymie driving along with Horlicks by his side, sitting to attention and gazing benignly around, would realise the logic of the choice. And sure enough, the dog was the star. Horlicks stood in centre stage, John declaimed the great man's lyrics, the Holm pupils swayed with the sea, and I remember it with the greatest of happiness.

A Johnsmas Foy, 1984.

Gunnie Moberg

Dave Grieve local actor, set designer, Foy participant
(in conversation)

Various clubs or groups of people have been asked to produce the Foy over the years, and I have been involved in a few along the way. In 1983, David Milsted produced a Foy about wartime and Scapa Flow. It was mainly the Kirkwall Arts Club members who were involved in that, which was appropriate because the club was founded by servicemen who were stationed up here during the war. It was put on in the guide hut in Kirkwall.

In 1987, I took part in a tribute to Edwin Muir, which wasn't strictly a Foy, but was a festival event and very much in the spirit of the Foys, as Edwin Muir was often a featured writer. The tribute was put together by the writer Robert Calder to mark the centenary of Edwin Muir's birth. I remember reading a Hugh MacDiarmid poem, accompanied by a cellist who had set the poem very nicely to music.

Duncan McLean's play *The Horseman's Word* was given its premiere at the Foy in 1995 [see p.160]. I agreed to produce it, and gathered an all-Orcadian cast together because it was written in Orcadian dialect. One of the first things we did was to get Duncan and the cast together, so that they could go through the script and change anything that they felt wasn't authentic dialect. At one point, Bryan Leslie [stage manager] was going to be in it, but he was ill so he didn't manage to do it. It would have been his first role on stage, as opposed to behind the scenes, so that was a missed opportunity!

The film, *Between the Terminals*, in 2001 was a new departure for the Foy [see p.161]. The idea grew out of Tim Fitzpatrick's desire to make an Orkney-based film, and from there it spread out to incorporate new local music too. It was different from the earlier Foys and a very interesting project. I would say that the Foy has really grown since the beginning.

Simon Chirgwin   A Johnsmas Foy, 1988 (in conversation)

The Foy in 1988 was a celebration of George Mackay Brown's work. There were to be readings from George's poetry and prose (by Claire Nielson, Elizabeth Bevan and Dave Grieve), and then the idea emerged to make a film about him to precede the readings, which I was asked to do. The festival only wanted a short film - no more than 15 minutes - which didn't allow for any analysis of the work. I decided in the end to try and produce a picture of the man, working and going about his day-to-day life.

I interviewed George, covering such things as how he felt about Stromness, and writing, and used that as a basis for the structure of the piece. I filmed him at home, going about Stromness, and coming back into the town on the boat from Hoy. We filmed at Warbeth graveyard and then I spent a whole morning filming him while he was writing his weekly column for *The Orcadian*, 'Under Brinkie's Brae'. The film shows him writing, with the light streaming through the kitchen window on to his wonderful, characterful hands. Throughout the whole thing he was wonderfully relaxed, and he talked to me quite naturally, ignoring the camera.

I wished I could have done the whole thing again, with better equipment. There was music on the film, played by Graham Garson and Lawrence Wilson, and balancing the speech against the music on the finished article was difficult. When the film was shown at the Foy, the equipment wasn't right for it, and unless you were sitting in the right place it was difficult to hear the speech above the music.

I am indebted to the festival for introducing me to the wonders of George Mackay Brown's writing. Having gone through the school system in Stromness, I was aware of the existence of George, but there was a definite prejudice against him amongst my peers. The attitude seemed to be that what George wrote about was some non-specific golden age which has never existed, and he really just needed to pull himself together and get back to reality. However, Archie Bevan asked me to provide some musical accompaniment for a Johnsmas Foy he was compiling using only work by GMB in 1988. Well, thank you, Archie. I've been George's greatest fan ever since.

Graham Garson
'ubiquitous' festival performer

The whole thing would have benefited from more time and more money. Basically, however, it is a nice film, and some day I would like to stick all the original tapes in the computer, re-edit them digitally and make something more polished. Now that George is gone, it means more that these images of him exist.

Stewart Conn festival poet, 1988
formerly head of radio drama, BBC Scotland

I was to record for the radio the Johnsmas Foy of 1988. I hadn't anticipated that the tightness of the turn-around and the technicians' schedule would leave no room for rehearsals. I also assumed the sound engineer would be in the hall, or able to monitor visually from his van. Not so.

Nor did our script show when the performers would stand, and when sit. The only hope was to leave all the microphones faded up and the instant someone was located on one, to kill the others - or it would sound as if everyone were in a swimming pool. The show went like clockwork. But each reading started so off-mic as to be virtually inaudible. Mercifully the recording was digital: levels could be boosted, without adding background noise or tape-hiss. An editing wizard did his bit, so that each reader seemed simply to rise and take a couple of steps to the microphone. Or so we persuaded ourselves.

Paul Greenwood actor and regular Foy participant

I first went to Orkney during Stromness Shopping Week with Claire (Nielson), my wife, to do a reading, *Having Words*. We were asked the following year to come back and appear in the St Magnus Festival. Unlike Claire, I have no family connections with Orkney but I have always been made to feel at home there. We were made to feel even more at home by three local ten-year-old boys, during rehearsals for our festival reading - *Inspirations*. They had told us that they would come to our show but we didn't think they would. However, there they were at the first performance in the front row, quietly concentrating. And come the second performance, there they were in the front row, still concentrating but not as quietly.

'Ssh!' said one of our new pals to the audience as we began our recital. Later, just before we began an excerpt from *The Prelude*, he turned to the audience and loudly whispered, 'Listen! This is a good bit.' When we left on the *Ola*, the three of them sat on a huge coil of rope on the end of the pier, waving us off. They shouted and jumped about until out of sight.

Leaving the front door of our friend Phyllis Brown's house and walking just a few hundred yards to hear wonderful music is one of my fondest memories of the festival.

Claire Nielson (Isbister)   actor and regular Foy participant

My memories and impressions of the St Magnus Festival are pervaded by the presence of George Mackay Brown, just as Stromness itself is. This last summer [2001] when I returned after several years, I couldn't believe I wasn't going to see his familiar figure passing along the road between his house and the pier. I first met George in the bar of the Stromness Hotel one evening in September, 1970. We were filming his short story, *A Time to Keep*, as part of *An Orkney Trilogy* for BBC, and the actors and crew had got back from Hoy, wet and windswept and dying for a bath, drink and dinner. He was sitting in the midst of all the talk in the bar, not saying much. He seemed both contained and shy. We all had a few drinks and I happened to mention that my grandfather had been born and brought up in Stromness, and that my real name was Claire Isbister. George was immediately interested and asked me lots of questions. I told him all I knew, including the stories I had been brought up on about my Orcadian background: the harpoon that stood in the corner of the living-room; my great-grandfather, William John Isbister, a ship's carpenter, buried at sea in the Indian Ocean; my great-aunt Elizabeth, a teacher at Stromness Academy, younger than many of the boys she taught; my grandfather, John William, nearly signing up for the Hudson Bay Company but going to Glasgow instead where he became a doctor.

George took delight in little things that people told him. Once, in Rackwick, I cooked sausages over an open fire. The pan I had used was caked solid with burnt stuff, so I devised a brillo-pad out of thick leaves and sand. I told George and he loved this daft story. When I went to Cambridge to do an MA as a mature student in 1985, George was one of my sponsors. He wrote me reassuring, funny letters and encouraged me in every way possible.

It was in the eighties that my husband, Paul Greenwood, who was then playing 'Rosie' in a very popular BBC TV series of that name, was asked to come and open Shopping Week in Stromness, and we were both asked to give some kind of reading at the not-long-opened Pier Arts Centre. We compiled a programme, *Having Words,* and that was how our connection with the St Magnus Festival came about, because the next year we were asked to contribute another reading, *Inspirations*, for that. It was then a great delight to be asked, over the next few years, to help organise and appear in 'A Johnsmas Foy,' in which local people read excerpts from Scottish, and especially Orcadian writings, and which became a regular and well-loved feature of the festival.

Memories of the festival are kaleidoscopic; sea-dappled walls around groups of talking people after Pier Arts Centre shows; looking out of a window in Alfred Street and seeing Ted Hughes walking in the early morning; the delicious shiver of the opening chords of Elgar's *Serenade for Strings* among the massive pillars

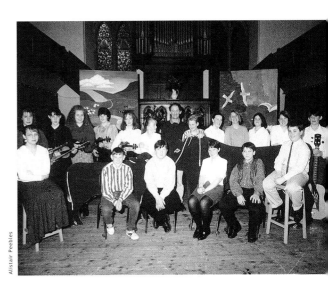

A Johnsmas Foy (Stromness Academy), 1993; 'Man and Beast'.

Alistair Peebles

of St Magnus Cathedral; Peter Maxwell Davies concerts, especially his work with children and his amazing and chilling opera, *The Lighthouse*.

Andro Linklater, Vivia Leslie, 1999.

Eric Linklater

"...Super scenery, catchy music, moving writing and gripping action: what more could one want?"
JC [on 'The Horseman's Word']
The Orcadian, June 22, 1995

Vivia Leslie   festival host, former Foy organiser

Over the past twenty five years the Johnsmas Foy has been toasting and celebrating Orcadian writers. I've compiled and produced a few Johnsmas Foys, all a lot of work and a great deal of fun. Years ago, the then artistic director, Archie Bevan, just said 'choose any theme you like' and I mulled it over for weeks. The Foy 'My, Whit Wather!' in 1992 was the result and probably the Foy I have most enjoyed doing.

In 1999, we devoted the Foy to the work and life of Marjorie Linklater's husband, Eric - 1999 being the centenary of his birth. His sons, Magnus and Andro Linklater, and other members of the family were all in Orkney for the festival, and in particular for the Foy that year. Andro took part in it, delighting audiences with his reminiscences. It's undoubtedly an asset to have a celebrity taking part, but the real backbone of the Foy has always been the local performers who unfailingly give of their time and talents and make the Foy the success it is. I suppose, like me, they just love being a part of the festival.

Duncan McLean   writer, producer 'Horse Island' Foy, 1995

The theme for the Foy was inspired by the old Norse name for the Orkney mainland: Hrossey, 'horse island'. Any doubts that Orkney might have produced sufficient horse-related literature to fill an hour or so was quickly dispelled by my first browse around the library.

Amongst many others, I quickly picked out a dialect tale about the wanderings of the Horse of Copinsay, Edwin Muir's post-apocalyptic *The Horses*, and extracts from the original Statistical Account of Scotland. This last clearly showed that horses in the Orkney of 1800 were far more than just a means of getting from A to B: they were indispensable in all sorts of industry beyond farming, they were treasured and pampered status symbols, the favoured transport of boy racers - as well as essential participants in courting and marriage rituals. The pieces of poetry and prose I came across were equally various in style and substance, and complemented perfectly by Fran Gray's Burray Band.

My own short play, *The Horseman's Word*, was performed for the first time to round off the Foy. Its performance was given extra piquancy by the fact that this very secret - and supposedly long since defunct - association, turned out to be not entirely dead after all. In fact, it was rumoured that one or two members of the play's cast were actually active members! Alas, the fearful oath of secrecy prevents me from saying any more....

Yvonne Gray author, *Between the Terminals,* the poem on which the 2001 Foy film was based

I was really keen to work on a project which would combine poetry and film, excited by the ideas of working collaboratively and of doing something quite new. When Tim Fitzpatrick came up with the idea of using the theme of a journey, I let him see my poem, *Between the Terminals,* written four years earlier and still unfinished. He liked it and proposed to use it as the basis for the film. I was delighted to realise that it did, after all, 'speak', but was still uneasy about certain lines and wanted to make some revisions.

We had a lot of discussion of how *Between the Terminals* could be used in the film and finally the idea emerged of developing a screenplay from the poem. I couldn't imagine writing this, although I was still eager to be involved. It was only when Kevin Coffey, who was already experienced in writing for film, said that he would be willing to work with me on it that I decided I *would* like to try it.

There were meetings then to develop ideas for characters, a conflict, a plot. Gradually the characters got names, homes, histories, idiosyncrasies, achievements, problems, hopes, ideals and so on, and they began to seem very *real*. I was fascinated by Dave Grieve's first storyboards with their tiny sketches of the mourners at the Houton terminal and on the ferry deck, each individualised by some pencil stroke of detail. These were, somehow, another reassuring step on the way to realising the project.

Kevin and I wrote a few scenes each and, satisfyingly, found our characters and dialogue integrated well. From Kevin's concern about over-writing dialogue, I recognised that I did have to check the temptation to explain too much. I found this most with the character of Elizabeth with whom I felt especially involved - I tended to cram her speeches and those of the characters around her with details on her philosophy of life and information about her past. Far more dialogue vanished at a touch of the delete key than was heard in the completed film!

There were other script changes when rehearsals started - and I realised I had to get used to this, to somehow let go and *trust* in the collaborative process. In the end, though, I found I was enjoying this fluidity. And I enjoyed the discussions I had with Tim and with some of the actors about the interpretation of certain lines, the significance of certain words or phrases.

I'd been asked to compile the live part of the Johnsmas Foy as well and I was keen that the material used should integrate well with the film itself. Douglas Montgomery, who had composed the music for the film was now able to perform some of it in full, and singer and songwriter Seona Dunsmuir, who had the main role of Elizabeth in the film, sang her own composition, *Hoy Song,* which had featured in the ceilidh scene.

During the months when *Between the Terminals* was being made I'd been reading the poems of Margaret Tait, the independent Orkney film maker

The film project for the Foy in 2001, *Between the Terminals,* involved a lot of people who had never taken part in such a project before, and it worked very well. It was done by professional film maker Tim Fitzpatrick, and it was the first time he had led a community project, which was quite tough-going for him. It was a bit of a rush, but some of the people involved said they would like to continue to make small films; the interest was sparked off, and the whole thing just gave people confidence. I probably say this every year, but *Between the Terminals* was the best community production I have worked on yet.

Diane Bain, assistant director, 'Between the Terminals' (in conversation)

and was struck by their directness of language and tone, their freshness and lucidity, their insistence of the uniqueness of each experience, and the impossibility of catching truth in a form of words or scientific formula. I decided to read some of her poems at the Foy, delighted to have found this other link between film and poetry: the film maker poet, the poet of film.

Although I knew by heart the poem *Between the Terminals* and much of the screenplay too, and had watched the filming of some of the scenes and seen clips of others at Tim's editing suite at the festival office, I wasn't prepared for its total effect at the Johnsmas Foy screenings. There was Seona's very moving reading of the poem (it came to seem like *her* poem and not mine); the startling juxtaposition of some of the scenes, for example the ceilidh scene and the exterior with the ferry leaving the pier with the hearse alone on the car deck while Elizabeth's song continued; the final exchange of looks between Elizabeth's daughter Rona (played by Louise Campbell) and her mother, Iris (played by Margaret Anderson) and the freeze frame of the two of them leaving the ferry. I was very moved by the film, and overwhelmed by the depth of appreciation of the many people who came up to speak to me at the end of each performance, or at other festival events, or even in the street days later.

Louise Campbell in *Between the Terminals*, 2001.

Alistair Peebles

drama

The first performance of George Mackay Brown's play *The Well* in 1981 set the stage for drama at the festival, which, with some exceptional local community productions and the input of innovative visiting professional companies, developed into one of the richest and most fertile strands of the festival. Under the direction of some inspired and talented local people, an ever more confident pool of local actors, dancers, musicians, designers, stage managers and technicians, (often drawn from groups such as the the Kirkwall Arts Club, Palace Players, Stromness Drama Club and the Kirkwall Amateur Operatic Society), sometimes combined with professional talent, have presented memorable festival productions. The dancer and choreographer Andy Howitt, SCO viola player Steve King, actor and director Eliza Langland and film maker Tim Fitzpatrick have all made a lasting contribution to community productions. In 2000, Alan Plater's adaptation of George Mackay Brown's novel *Greenvoe* was presented to great acclaim in both the St Magnus, and the Edinburgh, Festivals.

Professional theatre companies, including Théatre de Complicité, Tic Toc, TAG, The Phoenix Dance Company, Benchtours and Walk the Plank (on the ship, the *Fitzcarraldo*), have been hugely enjoyed at the festival, as have companies which defy categorisation, such as The Flying Dudes in 2001, who presented their unique aerial ballet show in the main arena at the Pickaquoy Centre.

Morag MacInnes adaptor/director *The Wireless Set*, 1982

Drama in the early eighties depended largely on George Mackay Brown's work. *The Well* was premiered in 1981, and the programme for the sixth festival included 'Three Orkney Plays', featuring that grand old war-horse, *Jock and Blind Mary*, *The Wireless Set* (adapted for the stage by Morag MacInnes), and a little gem of school theatre, *Bessie Millie's Wind Shop*, specially written by George for the occasion. A similar drama event the following year included the premiere of *The Island of the Saints* and *The Battle in the Hills*. In later festivals there would be premieres of *Home is the Sailor* (the story of Gow the Pirate) and *The Road to Colonus* as well as a stage adaptation of *Witch*. A truly remarkable record.
Archie Bevan
festival vice-president

Connie Buchan and Walter Leask;
Jock and Blind Mary, 1982.

previous page: **Witch, 1991.**

George Mackay Brown's short story about the coming of radio to an isolated Orkney valley is a miracle of compression - only seven pages long. It felt presumptuous in the extreme to attempt to adapt it for the stage. But in 1982 that was the task I was given - and at short notice. What's more, it had to be good. Very good. Not just because the festival had barely dipped its artistic toe into the chilly waters of drama in those days, but also because the eminent author would be in the audience. It made no difference that he had dandled me on his knee, told me bedtime stories, written me encouraging letters about my own work. This was the real thing. He gave me free rein and didn't interfere. Indeed, he appeared to have complete faith in me, which was even more worrying.

It's common knowledge, I think, that though George was constantly intrigued by the dramatic form, he was no dramatist. He wrote choral music, settings for voices. Actors were conduits for his poetic vision, not movers and shakers and door slammers. His plays don't really work as plays - but his stories do! All the ingredients are there - tension, incident, characterisation, clear sense of time and place. The only problem for the hapless adaptor is the brutal need for things to happen on stage. A story can leave gaps, suggest nuances, hint at possibility - an audience wants stuff happening.

I got to work, taking liberties with the text I blush to think about - introducing a love interest and a bed-ridden granny. I destroyed the subtle understatement of the story, and replaced the economical description with dialogue - but hope I preserved the central thesis - that life goes on, like the daffodils in the croft house window, despite what science throws at us.

Casting? Luck, again. My father [Ian MacInnes] had acted, years ago. I had seen him and George together telling stories and mimicking local worthies. 'Dad,' I said, 'I want you to play a simple old neighbour who talks to the radio as if it can answer him back.' Since my father regularly talked - indeed ranted - at the radio, it seemed good casting. And Kitty Tait from next door - who brought admirable timing and zest to every part she played - was enlisted, too.

It seemed important not just that the production had a real Orkney feel - I suppose it was a kind of forerunner of the Foy - but that we showed that we could have a native drama with depth, solemnity, a bit of beauty. Our central couple, Hugh and Bessie, were crucial. They had to be capable of comedy and tragedy.

I was lucky again: Willie Muir and Meg Harvey agreed to work with us. Meg was a warm, witty, confident presence on stage, and Willie had just the right intelligent edge. My heartbroken sweetheart was a beautiful young Anne Bevan with a mass of glowing hair; my romantic lead was Donnie Grieve, another seasoned local actor. Jack Rosie supported ably as another neighbour. Finally we needed the Incomer - a missionary who misunderstands the people he's come to save. What luck to have Philip Cooper, a fine actor with exactly the right 'foreign' accent. The only other character was Lord Haw Haw. Our technician, Walter Hancox, another well kent Stromness presence, was an excellent mimic - so he tape recorded himself, complete with authentic whistles and crackles. It was stunning. He was more like William Joyce than William Joyce.

I have praised these actors to the hilt because (I think I'm right) no one had tried to do a tragedy in Orkney dialect till they had a go. They rose to the challenge. And everybody helped with props and costume and set. In those halcyon days, it was a true community production.

The night of the production, in Kirkwall, I paced the back of the Arts Theatre. (I knew exactly where George was sitting.) There is a terrible moment when you're a director. It's when the curtain goes up and you can't stop the process, leap on stage and correct things; you hand the whole thing over. I paced and paced, and don't remember much else, except that folk laughed in the right bits and went quiet in the right bits.

When it was over I said to George, 'Was that all right?' and he said, 'It was just fine.' Which was good enough for me.

The Wireless Set, 1982

Ship Surgeon by Morag MacInnes, 1983.

Alan Cameron director, Orkney Youth Theatre

The festival for the Orkney Youth Theatre was always a welcome moment of public recognition of our work. Most of our activities were focused on particular groups: primary children for our theatre-in-education programmes, a particular community for the community play and the mainly isles audience for our Christmas tour. The shows that we performed at the festival were always the plays that we were touring around schools at that time - they were not specially prepared for the festival. However, they were for us an opportunity to let more people know who we were and the standard to which we aspired.

The venue for our first year of involvement was a hall in Stromness where we drew in a tiny audience. Latterly, we performed to much healthier audiences in the Kirkwall Town Hall. In 1987, there was an article about the Youth Theatre in *The Times Educational Supplement* after our production *Magnus - The Man*. The following year, *The Raven's Nest* was very positively reviewed, and was seen by Catherine Robbins of Eden Court Theatre, who was also complimentary. This professional feedback meant a great deal to us; we wouldn't have had that kind of exposure if it had not been for the festival.

For the company members of the Orkney Youth Theatre the festival also provided a welcome chance to see professional theatre. One year, we had a lovely improvised session with members of Théatre de Complicité in Tankerness House gardens, who demonstrated how to take and give focus between each other. This seems to sum up so much the value of the St Magnus Festival, quite apart from the quality of the performances brought to Orkney.

Orkney Youth Theatre

The [Orkney] *Youth Theatre began life as that much-maligned creature, a Manpower Services Commission scheme. A number of 16 to 23 year-old unemployed islanders are given training and purpose for a year under the expert guidance of director/founder Alan Cameron.*

The Youth Theatre gave us an account of the viking pacifist in Magnus - the Man. They had a less rosy view of him than Max, one of them describing him in a BBC interview as 'courageous but a bit of a pain'.

Neil Munro
The Times Educational
Supplement, June 26, 1987

Orkney Youth Theatre, 1985.

Diane Bain stage manager, community productions (in conversation)

I was in the Orkney Youth Theatre on and off for several years, and my first involvement with the festival was in 1985, in a Youth Theatre play called *How About a Nice Cup of Tea*, which we blithely devised and wrote ourselves. We put it on in the courtyard of Tankerness House Museum, and I remember Russell Harty coming along to the dress rehearsal and leaving after a while saying, 'This is too surreal for me!' But we were really young; we didn't worry about anything and just had a great time.

The Youth Theatre was an amazing set-up. It was Alan Cameron's baby and he was really good. He came from a stage management background and was very good at persuading people to back projects. I worked for the Youth Theatre when I left school, then went to college, did a year of community drama - as a direct result of being in the Youth Theatre - then came back to Orkney and worked for them again. Eventually it became more and more of a struggle for the Youth Theatre to find the cash and Alan Cameron left. It folded soon after that, which is a great shame as it had really put a lot back into the local community.

Penny Aberdein festival drama coordinator (in conversation)

Penny Aberdein, 1994.

I had not long arrived in Orkney, in 1983, and was sitting at home one evening when the phone rang. It was Elizabeth Bevan. 'We're having a festival committee meeting in Hopedale,' she said, 'and wondered if you would you like to join us on the festival committee, for drama and dance?' My absolute passion is theatre, and Elizabeth must have known that I had been involved in drama before I came here, but I was completely taken aback, because the request came out of the blue. I didn't think people knew me at all. I said, 'I don't know what it's going to involve, or how good I would be, or what I could offer - but I'll certainly come along to the next meeting and see how things go'. So, Elizabeth started my whole involvement, nearly twenty years ago, which has stayed with the festival ever since.

The festival wanted a community drama production for 1985, and I chose *The Caucasian Chalk Circle*, because Brecht is easier to tackle with a cast that hasn't had much professional training (although they are very professional in their attitudes, and very responsive, as I've since discovered). I think it was the first time that folk here had worked on anything like this, because with Brecht you use all kinds of devices which are unnatural in the theatre. You take away the tabs and show behind-the-scenes while the play is on - you don't put the audience into darkness. All these were new and exciting things, and people responded to them and the production gathered interest and momentum.

There was one absolutely sublime moment with John Broom, who played the very learned judge, Azdak. He was quite a character this judge, and John was wonderful. At one point, John came on and he had to climb into this throne which looked like a high chair. He came on and said, 'Bring me those books I usually shit on!' I couldn't believe my ears, and, of course, the audience just dissolved!

We collaborated with John Gray for the music in *Chalk Circle*. He has done a tremendous amount of work with us and is a very good person to work with - he really knows how to make music work theatrically. And he also knew the local people. It all worked extremely well.

Some of that original cast are still working with us on productions. There is a core of local people who are very keen on theatre and that is how they want to spend their free time. They come back, so they must enjoy it.

In 1986, we put on *Dr Faustus* for the festival, and then took it to the Edinburgh Festival. I think it was the first time that a production had gone there from Orkney. The cast were quite fired up to do it and we raised the money, partly through the local oil company at that time, Occidental.

John Gray   composer

The music for *The Caucasian Chalk Circle* came about in 1985. Penny had approached me to write something for the show and to be honest I hadn't a clue. What - a play? I don't write stuff for plays.

However, Penny came to see me - I tootled a few tunes on my clarinet and that was the start of that. I got James (my brother) involved on guitar. He was responsible for the chord progressions. Neither of us knew very much about Brechtian theatre - I look back at those progressions and wonder about the instinct involved - one song is based on a Bartókian tritone relationship using the chords of E and Bb major - dialectical opposites, nice and Brechtian!

If we had set out to contrive any of this, I doubt if it would have worked. But it did work and the music has since been used in two productions in Edinburgh. Incidentally, it was the music for the *Circle* that helped secure my present position as lecturer in performing arts at Telford College, Edinburgh.

I also did the music for the 1986 production of *Dr Faustus*, which was a right musical rammy. The ensemble was Peter Pratt on violin, James on trumpet, me on clarinet and David (another brother) on drum-kit - an odd combination - but *The Scotsman* at the Fringe described us as a talented bunch.

Simon Chirgwin   producer (in conversation)

Lady Audley's Secret was utterly unpretentious and made no claim towards being art...and it worked. The festival slot was nine o'clock in the evening,

I just can't resist the roar of the greasepaint and the smell of the crowd, especially when the performances are on the huge scale of St Magnus Festival productions. From new commissions to Greek tragedy, from Shakespeare to Brecht, we've done them all, and always to a standard which surpasses everyone's expectations.
Graham Garson, 'ubiquitous' festival performer

Dr Faustus, 1986.

Lady Audley's Secret, 1987

by which time I reckoned that anyone who had been at concerts all day would be firmly cultured-out; I wanted something which would be a bit of fun, to round off the evening before the Festival Club got going.

The plot of *Lady Audley* is wonderful - it is a pantomime for adults - and it was the right length to fit into the slot, and great fun. I decided to play it very straight, as if we believed it was Shakespeare, which is the only way it would have worked. Because of this, it was a bit of a shock for the cast when the audience found it so funny. They were booing and hissing, clapping and cheering in all the right places and became completely involved in it all.

We had a great set, designed by Leslie Burgher. It is the only time I've ever had set plans that translated exactly into what they were intended to be. The whole thing was stitched together by wonderful silent film music from Robin Cheer, who played the piano. In the end, everybody dies about seven times. It was absolutely preposterous, but very engaging, and the audience loved it.

That year, the theatre company Tic Toc were here from Coventry. They were playing around with farce and were quite interested in the idea of melodrama as a genre. They came to see *Lady Audley* and we chatted about it afterwards. The festival is a good meeting place in that way. Visitors can't just nip off home after a performance, and there is a great opportunity to meet people and chat in a relaxed way.

Crofters, 1988

Roderick Thorne   former headteacher, Sanday School

Sanday's first connection with the festival was instigated by our music teacher. Glenys Hughes had been helping older pupils to write music for our school production of *Crofters* - planned for 1988 to mark the centenary of the visit of Prime Minister Gladstone's Crofters' Commission to the island.

Depute-head James Oliver Alexander used transcripts from that visit as the basis for a school assembly; staff enthusiastically embraced the idea that it could, and should, be developed into an event for the whole island. The Commission of 1888 led to cancellation or reduction of rent arrears, and granted security of tenure to the crofters - it was, according to Ernest Marwick, the historian, 'the crofters' Magna Carta'.

It was one of the great privileges of my time at the school; I knew that if teachers were persuaded of the merits of a project, they would find the energy to ensure its success. So it was with *Crofters*. As the wider island community learned about the plan, so developed the idea of a museum of artefacts - so that as children rehearsed they became surrounded by authentic props from the previous century!

The smallest children learned the games and rhymes of their great-great-grandparents - the sweero stick and Kirsty Kringlick. And there was scope for the imagination in representing the peedie folk, the trows and Ould

Crofters, 1988.

Betso with 'the gift' - of second sight. Against this the main drama was played out; rousing sermons by the minister of the established church, under the laird's patronage, and by the crofters' champion in the free church; and the sheriff conducting hearings and listening to evidence from factors and crofters.

The show was a great success. Glenys reckoned that it would attract an audience in Kirkwall, and two months later the Town Hall staircase queue was thronged. We were a late addition to the festival programme - but once again we had a full house.

Penny Aberdein

We have used the Arts Theatre in Kirkwall for a long time, but we have tried to do different things with it. The tabs were taken away for *The Caucasian Chalk Circle*, for instance, and we put scaffolding up for *Romeo and Juliet* in 1988. The top layer was Juliet's bed chamber, and the lower structure became part of the vault when she was buried. It was where they both died - with their heads towards the audience. They lay absolutely still, and didn't stand up for the curtain call. The audience members were sometimes reluctant to leave because there was still something going on. Credit must go to Alex Rigg and Aimée Leonard, who played Romeo and Juliet, because they didn't flicker an eyelid.

In 1989, we did Stravinsky's *The Soldier's Tale* with the Scottish Chamber Orchestra, which was a great success. By then I felt that we were ready to work with professionals, and to work with other art forms in the theatre, such as music.

Carolyn Bevan | actor, community drama productions (in conversation)

We have had some very good collaborations with professionals over the years. One of the best was *The Soldier's Tale* in 1989, which we did with the Scottish Chamber Orchestra. Before they arrived in Orkney, we had a tape of the music to work with, and the cast ended up calling it 'sing-along-a-Stravinsky' because we knew it so well. I remember that the SCO were very impressed by the time they got here; we could actually move in time to the music, and we had it all ready for them. They thought they were coming to this amateur bunch in Orkney, which we were, but it had all been done really well - so we were chuffed.

It is not just the international stars that make the festival memorable. The performance of Stravinsky's *The Soldier's Tale* at Stromness Academy by local actors and dancers accompanied by an SCO ensemble - this outclassed every professional performance we have seen.
*Yvonne and Jeremy Clarke
annual festival visitors*

Romeo and Juliet, 1988 and *The Soldier's Tale*, 1989

Allistair Peebles

Alex Rigg and Aimée Leonard;
Romeo and Juliet, 1988.

The Soldier's Tale, 1989; Carolyn Bevan (left).

Allistair Peebles

A Midsummer Night's Dream, 1993

A Midsummer Night's Dream, 1993.

Dave Grieve (centre), in
A Midsummer Night's Dream.

Penny Aberdein

In 1993, Steve King from the SCO became involved with the production of
A Midsummer Night's Dream. Steve is a very challenging, focused musician.
He demands complete concentration - you have to be on your toes. The cast
really responded to that. A professional technical team also came in to light
the play, and we had a professional set designed by Anne Bevan - who is very
well known to the festival. So it didn't all fall on local shoulders. This was
a real development in our way of working. It also meant that drama was
acknowledged as an important part of the festival, and we were given a larger
chunk of the budget. It was a big step forward.

Steve King   principal viola, Scottish Chamber Orchestra
              (in conversation)

People who live in Orkney perhaps don't appreciate how well off they are
educationally. Many of the things that happen here don't happen in the rest
of Scotland, or at least to the same degree. The St Magnus Festival, in which
there is always schools involvement, is such a wonderful thing - a catalyst to
great creativity. The projects have far-reaching effects; they are not just for
the festival. Coming up here and working in that situation is a joy; as is
working with people like Penny Aberdein, Ron Ferguson and Andy Howitt.

    In *A Midsummer Night's Dream* we used recycled instruments, such
as big polythene drums and gas pipes. We also used the instruments the KGS
kids played - trumpets, clarinets, guitars and so on. At the dress rehearsal, we
took the drums up to the lighting rig, which is where we were going to play
them. Norman Rushbrook and his crew were there, and when we started the
drumming Norman nearly fell through the roof - he thought the place was
going to fall down! So there was the proof that it was very effective!

Dave Grieve   actor/set designer, community drama productions
               (in conversation)

The community drama is a real strength of the festival. I have been involved
in productions since the first *Cinderella* in 1980, when I designed the set and
costumes, as I was working in Papdale Primary at the time. Other involvements
came mainly via the Kirkwall Arts Club, and through all the clubs getting
together in county productions for the festival. (Often I become involved in
both the acting and the set design - insanity prevails!)

    The set for *The Caucasian Chalk Circle* was made of four or five
long pyramid pieces, which could be moved around so that they became
towers or interiors. The backdrop was painted in a Paul Klee/Breugel style,

and a death's head appeared when the lighting changed. I remember seeing the video much later and being quite impressed by the effect, which I'd forgotten about!

In *A Midsummer Night's Dream*, I was Peter Quince, and Penny left the Mechanicals to their own devices to a certain extent. As a little group we really developed quite a lot of daft things of our own, which added a lot of enjoyment to that particular show. I ended up making a tie, which I wore without a shirt. It was a super production - and the music was impressive too. They hit piping with ping-pong bats to get some of the sounds, and there were some unusual ways of instrumentalising.

Often I open up a box at home, and find something that I've made which has been a prop for some production. It brings back all the memories, which are very happy ones. The community drama has become a very organic thing, and it has forged lasting links between people. We must all get something out of it, or we wouldn't keep coming back for more! It is lovely to think how many children have been involved too. It stretches them and gives them so much. It's great.

George Rendall director

The Beggar's Opera, 1994
[See also *the composers*]

What we strove for in the production of *The Beggar's Opera* was the kind of ragged, fussy appearance that you get in films like *The Fisher King*, *Time Bandits* and *Brazil*, with some of the eccentricity of *The Cook, the Thief, his Wife and her Lover* thrown in. The fact that the production was to take place in Kirkwall's run-down cinema, the Phoenix, gave us a head start, particularly in the smell department. We had no Pickaquoy Centre at that time so the Phoenix was still being used as a cinema. This, coupled with the fact that the Scottish Chamber Orchestra were to perform in the same space as soon as our production was over, meant that we had to get in and out quickly. So a light and minimalist set was required. However, the look we were trying to achieve dictated the exact opposite - heavy, slimy beams with lots of layers and at least two levels (to accommodate the large cast). Not to mention a working hangman's gallows! A self-contained stage, really.

As so often happens, a local hero rose to the challenge. Alan Stout, master mason at St Magnus Cathedral and a sculptor who could turn his hand to anything - even the construction of a fully functional winding staircase - accepted the task. It became a near obsession with him. Layer upon layer of scaffolding and timber appeared under a gentle rain of bird-droppings in the cold, damp bus garage we were using for rehearsals. Even I, not the most prudent of planners, began to have doubts as to whether this behemoth could possibly fit in the Phoenix, let alone be constructed in situ in time. Somehow, through the night before the first Phoenix rehearsal, it happened, though the blood shot eyes of Alan and his assistant the next morning bore witness to

"The local talent who took part in [The Beggar's Opera] must all feel exuberant after being involved in such an exciting, high-quality production...This was truly a triumph for Orkney."
MAM
The Orcadian, June 23, 1994

The Beggar's Opera, 1994.

Alistair Peebles

the feat of endurance involved.

As one who would rather jump into a pit of vipers than act on the stage, I get the most inexplicable thrill out of seeing a production come together. After that you try to be objective but really you're having too much fun. It was just as well that Alasdair Nicolson was involved, he being generous (or desperate?) enough to bring his theatrical experience to bear on the production.

The logistics were complex but the people involved (both volunteer and professional) rose above such mundanities. At the end of the day there was, I think, the kind of camaraderie that you would expect to find in any collection of whores, vagabonds and low-life. And the cast were brilliant as well.

Bob Ross 'Macheath', *The Beggar's Opera*

George Rendall asked me to play the part of Macheath because he said every time he thought about Macheath he thought about me - not much of a compliment really... a womanising thief, murderer and vagabond. I took the view that he meant that I was capable of carrying the part (which satisfied my vanity!).

Over many rehearsals and lessons from Dick and Glenys Hughes, who were so very patient and encouraging, we got to the point where we'd rehearse with the SCO for the first time. Even the best singers were getting nervous. I was on the point of panic.

We needn't have worried. The professionals led by Alasdair Nicolson were friendly and very helpful. The only trouble was that they 'upped the tempo' - suddenly everything was to be sung at double the speed. Glenys came to the rescue again with some well-timed assistance - she conducted me from the front row of the audience and helped me through each performance.

The rehearsals for *The Beggar's Opera* were wonderful - George's laid-back style was a breath of fresh air at that time - I had been used to directors coming into the process with some pretty fixed ideas. George allowed a full exploration of each character, and each scene would be an adventure until everyone was happy with the result. If you have great fun rehearsing you'll show this at the performance. George knew what he wanted, but allowed the actors to feel they had developed the bigger picture or at least had played a major part in it.

I know it worked - because ordinary people told me so - and tourists who managed to fit us in between the busy schedule of the rest of the festival. They had fun because we had fun.

The set, designed by Frances Pelly, was perfect, and Alan Stout made an excellent job of putting it together. And Norman Rushbrook and his lighting team managed to create a wonderfully creepy atmosphere.

What I remember most was the real sense of feeling part of a team. There were no prima donnas - no tantrums - no animosity - only real friendship and support for one another. I just wish I could do it all over again - a magical moment in my life and one I'll remember forever. Thanks, George!

Glenys Hughes festival director

I believe that festivals can and should offer opportunities for artists from different art forms to work together in ways which might not otherwise be possible - and a festival can provide the ideal setting for showcasing new, even experimental, work.

In 1996, we commissioned a dance piece from the talented choreographer, Andy Howitt - previously, festival commissions had been musical ones. Andy collaborated with composer Alasdair Nicolson, who wrote a score for string quartet, solo piano and jazz saxophone. The result was *Lord of the Mirrors*, premiered by four professional dancers plus the Emperor Quartet, pianist Joanna MacGregor and saxophonist Dick Lee. Like *Stormwatchers*, its companion piece *Lord of the Mirrors* took as its starting point a work of George Mackay Brown. Coming so soon after George's death the dance double bill provided not only a spectacular but, sadly, an appropriately moving opening to the festival.

A spin-off from *Lord of the Mirrors* was the splendid work which Andy did with local community dance groups, culminating in *Orkney Dances*. Andy's work was developed over the following two years in *Orkneyinga* [see p.174], and *Sunnifa*.

Andy Howitt dancer and choreographer

It could almost be the plot of some mystical romantic novel where seemingly random events come together as if fated. By chance a young choreographer is given a book of poetry for Christmas. One particular piece - called *Lord of the Mirrors* - takes hold of his imagination. He starts thinking of it as the basis for a new work.

The poem is by an Orcadian, George Mackay Brown. The choreographer finds himself invited to make some work for the music festival which is held in Orkney. He meets the poet and discovers that in the 12th century another choreographer made another piece for some other festival and that was called *Lord of the Mirrors* - a dance Bernard of Ventadour made with masks, lutes and ladies for the investiture of Philip, Count of Norbonne.

Lord of the Mirrors, 1996

"It takes a very special sort of person to take on fifty five unknown recruits aged from five to fifty five and produce an hour-long show of spectacular proportions and exciting colour, rhythm, music and movement. Andy Howitt achieved all this in an amazingly short time." FG
The Orcadian, July 4, 1996

Andy Howitt

The story really begins in Orkney. Alasdair Nicolson the composer and I were at the St Magnus Festival with *Desperate Journey* [TAG Theatre Company] and after the show Max asked us to do some dance there in two years time!

The project *Lord of the Mirrors* had many off-shoots - *Orkney Dances, The Stormwatchers - Lord of the Mirrors.* All three dance works had in my view the same look, which was based on the George Mackay Brown poem.

Orkneyinga, 1997

Steve King, *Orkneyinga,* 1997.

Orkneyinga was the most complicated thing I've ever stage managed! It was horrible weather that year and I was absolutely frozen, even with a jacket on. When we moved in to the cathedral at the end, the crew had walkie-talkies with ear-pieces so that we could communicate without being heard by the audience. I was so cold when I came into the cathedral I couldn't plug in my ear-piece and had to ask a member of the audience to help. You couldn't believe it was summer that year!
Bryan Leslie
festival stage manager,
1982-1994 (in conversation)

Penny Aberdein

With our wonderful history and sites here in Orkney, we came up with the idea of doing a version of the *Orkneyinga Saga*, based in different local sites. At that stage I didn't know exactly where they would be, although I knew that they would be in and around the cathedral. Again, I wanted to collaborate with professional artists and knew that I could work well with both Steve King and Andy Howitt, and that they would provide a powerful creative force. The other person who was heavily involved was Jonothan Campbell, who directed the older school pupils in stilt-walking. We also needed someone to write the piece, and approached Ron Ferguson, (the writer, recently retired as cathedral minister), who is a lovely person to work with. It was a good strong team to lead the whole project. Andy, Steve and I spent a weekend wandering about Kirkwall and deciding where the venues should be. They had to be a fairly close group of buildings, as I wanted the audience to move from site to site. Andy and Steve felt it would be more manageable if each site was art-form specific; one site dedicated to dance, one to music, and the third to drama. They would be connected, however, and would explore the different aspects of the *Orkneyinga Saga* story. Each part would last the same length of time and would play three times, with a five-minute break in between. The audience, split into three parts, would visit each site in turn, moving from one to the next.

There were many times that I thought it would never work, because the timing was so specific. The stage manager, Bryan Leslie, stood at the top of the Moosie Tower in the Bishop's Palace. From there he could see all three sites, and was able to coordinate the start and finish of each section.

The production came together in the cathedral itself. We built some massive puppets of Hakon and Magnus, which were very striking. The part in the cathedral was generally the most difficult to organise - there are no sight lines, and nowhere for the audience to go. They just had to stand between the pillars.

The other person who came in with us is local professional artist, Carol Dunbar, who designed the fabric effects inside the cathedral. She made a white shroud-like hanging, then suspended other fabric pieces and we had a system of pulleys to lower them down. There were ribbons hanging down which the dancers wove together. It was stunning.

The finishing touch was the torches held by torch-bearers who guided the audience from site to site. I made contact with the Up-Helly-Aa torch-makers in Shetland and asked them to make some for the festival. They were sent down on the *St Sunniva*. There were three torch-bearers in *Orkneyinga*, each leading an audience group.

We lit the cathedral and the Earl's Palace, and there was a wonderful atmosphere outside. One of the most amazing images that I link with the show is watching the sun going down and waiting for the cathedral to be lit up. When it happened, it was suddenly luminous. That change in light was really powerful.

Orkneyinga was a collaboration with schools as well and there were kids from schools all over Orkney involved. There were dancers and bell ringers from Papdale, Glaitness and Orphir, and drummers from St Margaret's Hope. The school staff were excellent and very supportive, and I think the children look back on it with fondness. It is amazing how kids can have fun and bounce around, and then give a very disciplined performance - they focus completely.

Orkneyinga, Tankerness House, 1997.

I have used hand bells many times, especially in Orkney. In *Orkneyinga* it was wonderful; I worked with a particularly good Primary 7 group from Papdale. They were stunning actually. Alison Drever was their teacher, and she was fantastic. We worked hard and created this fifteen-minute piece which was performed in the courtyard of Tankerness House. It was incredibly complex what they did, and there wasn't one kid there who was backward in assimilating these ideas. As far as working with primary schools is concerned, I think that is one of the best things I've ever done. *Steve King (in conversation)*

Terry Delaney actor, community drama productions

What's it like to be an actor taking part in a St Magnus Festival production? The word that leaps to mind is painful. When, during the rehearsals for *Orkneyinga*, Penny Aberdein offered her actors the advice, 'Don't worry about the blood!', it came as no surprise to those of us who'd been in previous productions.

Although fear is the predominant emotion during a St Magnus Festival production, it is still true that when the council vetoed Penny's plans for aerial work in St Magnus Cathedral during *Orkneyinga*, most of the cast were openly disappointed. Doing somersaults suspended by wires high above the unforgiving stone floor of the cathedral is precisely the sort of challenge we actors have come to associate with festival productions. One quickly becomes aware that, to achieve the highest standards, one has to suffer for Art's sake.

Of course, if it's not all fun, it is, however, always challenging. Hanging over the battlements of the Earl's Palace to deliver fierce viking orations in the teeth of an Orkney summer gale requires skills in voice projection not normally required on the proscenium arch stage.

I'm particularly fond of one memory. At one point during *Orkneyinga* I had to lead a small band of warriors in a charge against our rivals led, inevitably, by Willie Harper. At the end of the charge I had to freeze in an attitude of what I hoped looked like fierce aggression. At the schools' performance a lad a few yards away in the front rank of the audience remarked in a voice freighted with sarcasm; 'Cor... he's *hard*'.

Orkneyinga, St Magnus Cathedral.

Orkneyinga, Earl's Palace.

Allstair Peebles

"Every year the festival produces one or two things that are remembered for quite a while. Just occasionally, a festival produces one thing that is vividly remembered for ever.

'Orkneyinga' is certainly one of the most exciting events assembled and staged in Orkney in the 21 years of the St Magnus Festival." MAM
The Orcadian, June 26, 1997

The Odyssey, 1999

"The production team of 'The Odyssey' went overboard, creatively throwing everything but the kitchen sink into a production that featured optimum use of the space."
Michael Tumelty
The Herald, June 21, 1999

Walk the Plank,
The Flying Dudes, 2001

Ron Ferguson   minister, St Magnus Cathedral, 1991-2001

The St Magnus Festival has a personal significance for me. I had written a one-man show, *Every Blessed Thing*, about George MacLeod, founder of the Iona Community, and Tom Fleming came to Orkney to premiere the piece in 1993. He played to two packed houses, and electrified the audience with his performance, earning him the first standing ovation in the festival's history. (Incidentally, Tom told me that the St Magnus Festival stage crew is one of the best he has ever worked with.)

In 1996, I was invited by Penny Aberdein to script *Orkneyinga*, which moved from drama at the Bishop's Palace, to music in Tankerness House courtyard, to the front of the cathedral, where the martyrdom of Magnus was enacted in word, dance and action. The cast then moved into the nave of the cathedral behind Magnus, who was borne aloft while a choir sang an eerie requiem from the galleries above. It was extremely moving. *Orkneyinga* was described by Michael Tumelty of *The Herald*, as 'one of the most breath-taking pieces of theatre, in its ambition, its scale and its grand sweep, that I have ever witnessed'. It was a great experience for me to work with Steve King, Andy Howitt, and Jonothan Campbell, as well as with Penny, who produced the show with characteristic brilliance.

Diane Bain   (in conversation)

The Odyssey was a big production to stage manage. It was the first time the festival had done anything in the Picky Centre and it was a huge risk for everyone involved; we all felt the pressure to make it work. The Scottish actress Eliza Langland directed it. She had been up years before with the Scottish Youth Theatre and she had directed community plays in Shapinsay, so she had quite a connection with Orkney already. She was very good and really knew her stuff. That production was technically difficult because of the scale of it. Everybody had to use mics, and we had a few problems with them on the first night which spoiled things a bit. It was a shame because they worked beautifully after that. There were children involved in that production too, and they were superb.

Penny Aberdein

Apart from the community drama, we've had some very good professional companies here too - TAG, Wildcat, Tic Toc, Ridiculusmus. Théatre de Complicité was really wonderful, and Benchtours was very well received as well - and Walk The Plank, on the *Fitzcarraldo*, has really taken a trick, not just with children, but with everybody. The boat was a great venue, and when they did *Moby Dick* in 2001, the natural creaks and groans of the boat in the water made it just perfect.

I do think the festival has opened its doors to other ideas and brought in fresh things. Aklowa - an African drumming group - was brought in and people really responded to them, and the Flying Dudes in 2001 were wonderful too. From their point of view, it was much more exciting to incorporate a story which put their trapeze skills in a different context. I think the audience were a bit taken aback, but it was a brave thing to do.

Théatre de Complicitié
[see Simon McBurney, p.196]

Liz Pugh manager, Walk the Plank Theatre Company, on board the *Fitzcarraldo* (in conversation)

The *Fitzcarraldo*, 1997.

It seems very appropriate to bring a ship to a place like Orkney, where people are used to ferries as part of their daily lives. To turn up on an ex-ferry with a theatre on board, makes sense. The attitude in Orkney is very accommodating and people are always pleased to see us. The harbour masters sort out the berths, and nothing is too much trouble. It is not always like this, and it makes a big difference to us.

There is a real commitment to quality within the festival which is what makes it exciting. It is fantastic to go to a place where the show is sold out in advance. Both times we have visited the festival, in 1997 and 2001, we have put on extra shows, which is great. It was very special going out to Westray in 2001 with the *Moby Dick* show, although the weather was foul and it was a long, bumpy sail - six hours. But to go to a place with a population of 600, and have 125 people come and see the show, was just brilliant. The actors did a workshop in the school too. At the start of the show there, when people were arriving, I turned to one of the kids and said: 'So, do you get many theatre ships in Westray?' - trying to be funny. He looked me straight in the eye and said, 'Yeah, hundreds'. That'll teach me!

Moby Dick, Walk the Plank Theatre Company, 2001.

The Flying Dudes 2001

We had a traumatic journey to Orkney. The plane was cancelled because of fog and we had to take a cab from Inverness to Wick. The ferry agreed to wait and they loaded us on at the last minute.

On the ferry was a group of monks, who live on Papa Stronsay. They offered us a lift, in their van, to Kirkwall. So we ended up arriving at the Picky Centre with a van-load of monks. Half the troupe were already there, because they had come up in the trucks with all the rigging. When they saw us with the monks they thought it was totally surreal. And the monks came in to watch us do our flying. They were fantastic - so nice. They gave a blessing when they left, which was lovely. It's nice to know you have been blessed.

Greenvoe, 2000

Greenvoe, 2000.

I was in the production of *Greenvoe*, and we performed in Kirkwall and Stromness, then took it to the Edinburgh Festival - and we got five stars in *The Scotsman* - the best for any production! It was sold out - and we were all amateur and we got better reviews than the people who got paid to do it.

It was good fun and I enjoyed all the cast in it. It was a bit nerve-wracking on stage and I got a line wrong - 'who put the boy on the ring's finger,' instead of 'who put the ring on the boy's finger'. And my mum [Carolyn Bevan] was my mum in the play as well as out of the play, which was a bit embarrassing. It was quite an experience though.

Stuart Bevan, age 12

Penny Aberdein

As far as community drama is concerned, I think the culmination was *Greenvoe* in 2000. Alan Plater became involved with the adaptation of George Mackay Brown's novel some time ago, and I suggested doing something with it for the millennium year at the festival. He was quite taken with the idea. It was George's work, and Alan felt that it should be produced here, with local voices. The script had to be adapted for our uses by Alan, as it was still written as though for a camera. But with the help of a set designed by Les Burgher, we staged it, and it was the set that held the whole thing together.

It worked because it was so well written, and the cast responded to it and gave it their all. They became very fond of Alan Plater in the process, and he warmed to the cast as well - it was a two-way thing. If professionals had done it they wouldn't have had local voices, which would have been a shame. It worked so well that, for the second time, we decided to take it to the Edinburgh Festival.

To be honest, we weren't expecting it to be the success it was. We wanted an evening slot but were given a slot at 10.15 in the morning. In the event, however, we were surprised beyond belief. It was given a wonderful review - five stars - which was a complete surprise to us. We were completely sold out and had to send people away - even the critic from *The New York Times*!

The children were amazing. They stuck with it, and that type of rehearsal was not easy to sit through, because we had to rehearse small bits at a time because of the structure of the play. There were an awful lot of technical things to remember. Every exit and entrance had to be worked out very accurately and the children had to remember all that too. But they entered into the spirit of it, and I think they really enjoyed the trip to Edinburgh.

There was a high level of trust within the cast and we were very interactive; they all contributed their ideas. It was a great project and a really good team production. We all felt dreadful when it was over.

Alan Plater had been so happy working with us on *Greenvoe* that he felt that he would like to write a piece for us. When he came up to the festival in 2001, he told me about a piece on the Churchill Barriers that he had been mulling over, and asked about the possibility of producing it for 2002. And Max offered to write the music for it. The barriers is a very good subject, so I felt very excited about it.

The drama in the festival has really grown and evolved. The level of skill and confidence has developed enormously, and drama really represents a key part of the festival. People take it seriously, and judge it by high standards.

We have a unique product here. Orkney is a great place for a festival - it is an attractive place, and people want to come and visit. The festival is an amazing achievement, and I think it is in good heart. It hasn't been without its critics but that has made it stronger. People can be quite outspoken about the festival, which shows that the institution itself is strong enough to take it. It is a very strong background from which to take arts in a new direction with amateur productions.

We have had some moments, but the show always goes on. So far! The show has always managed to go on, come rain or shine. We will see where we go from here.

Carolyn Bevan   (in conversation)

When I first started in the drama productions, I didn't know a thing about it. The more productions you are in, however, the more you can see how things work, and you pipe up if you think something is not working. It's good to work with Penny [Aberdein] - she is excellent and has put an awful lot into the festival; hours and hours of work. It's not just turning up for rehearsals, it's all the things you have to do in between as well - working out rehearsal schedules and organising props and all those things.

Greenvoe is the production I have really enjoyed the most so far. It is about a community and we were like a little community ourselves; we could all relate to it so well because it was just like being in Stromness. George [Mackay Brown] had picked up on what folk say on the street so well; walking through town, you found yourself using lines from the play when you were speaking to people, because they were so natural to say. Everybody was brilliant to work with, and Alan Plater took a great interest in the whole production. When we took *Greenvoe* to Edinburgh we were so slick by then; it was just like clockwork because we worked so well together, both on and off the stage.

I'm proud to have been part of it all; it's been such an experience over the years. It's not just doing the performance, but everything else that goes with it. We all work hard, and somehow or other it always comes together.

Diane Bain   (in conversation)

I can never be objective about productions that I've worked in because I loved them all. I just like the whole process; I get to work with the professionals who come up, which is nice - but I am very keen on community theatre and it's good to see everyone involved learning new skills. The whole process - from rehearsals through to the finished thing - gathers more and more momentum. It gets to the point where it seems to go out of control, but then it always comes together and works in the end. That's what I like about it. Every year, people get into a panic about it, and you have to remind them that they felt like that about the last thing at the same stage, and reassure them that it will be all right.

I was very happy to be asked back to write the music for last year's production of *Greenvoe*. Like the *Chalk Circle* in 1985, I began by tootling a few tunes to Penny on one of her visits to Edinburgh. Some of my more outlandish ideas were treated with appropriate disdain but I think we came up with the right tunes for the job. The *Greenvoe* schedule was tight and some of the tunes ended up being written at the last minute in the bar of the Royal Hotel. I am not going to say which ones!
John Gray, composer

"One of Penny Aberdein's great strengths is the commitment and energy she brings out in any cast with which she works. The enthusiasm thus generated gives life to the whole performance."
CJFM
The Orcadian, July 4, 1991

I really appreciate the opportunity to be able to stage manage on a semi-professional scale - and it's good for the CV too! The productions are usually lovely; I always learn something new along the line, and I've made some brilliant contacts. For me, ultimately, it's a job - but most of the others have their own work and they arrange holidays around the productions. I'm amazed at how much commitment people have - it's staggering.

Alan Plater   playwright, adapted *Greenvoe* by George Mackay Brown

John Gray, Alan Plater,
Penny Aberdein, 2000.

Art cannot change the world, but it can and does transform lives. Here are a few morsels of evidence.

A quarter of a century ago I watched a television programme, mainly because it bore the name of John McGrath, a writer and director of high talent and unimpeachable credentials. The programme was a trilogy of short films, set in Orkney, dramatised from short stories from a man called George Mackay Brown, a writer I'd never heard of up to that point. They were bitter-sweet tales, tender and haunting, shot through with a love of place that, as a native of Tyneside, I understood in my bones.

Next day I went to the library in Hull, where I then lived, and ordered everything they had in stock by this man. Within a week or two I had read the lot and I knew that one day I would have to visit these islands.

In the event it wasn't until the early nineties that I first made the trip. What followed was a saga in three acts.

The first was a research trip the length of the British Isles which produced my novel, *Oliver's Travels*, a halfway decent yarn that became a spasmodically embarrassing television series.

The second act - a step towards some sort of redemption - was a television version of George's *Greenvoe* for Channel 4. I wrote the screenplay and we were beginning to grapple with the logistical problems - notably finding actors who could navigate their way through the nuances of the accent - when the man who had commissioned the piece was fired and his successor, keen to demonstrate an independence of spirit, dumped *Greenvoe* along with a desk load of other projects.

As it turned out, Channel 4 did me a favour. The way was now clear for the third act, the community production of *Greenvoe*, initiated and directed by Penny Aberdein at the 2000 St Magnus Festival, and later taken to Edinburgh where it played to packed houses and, famously, the critic from *The New York Times* couldn't get a seat.

The year 2000 was a very good one for me. My play, *Peggy For You*, ran in the West End and was nominated for an Olivier Award. My television film, *The Last of the Blonde Bombshells*, was shown on BBC and in the States and has since won BAFTA and Golden Globe awards. But hand on heart, and without a hint of grovel in my stance, *Greenvoe* was the most exciting experience of the lot.

The reason is simple and straightforward. All of theatre is based on a conspiracy between the performers and the audience. They agree to go together on a journey into an imaginary universe. In *Greenvoe* we all flew together, sometimes dangerously, in a way that simply isn't possible in television or conventional London theatre.

My chief mentor in the writing trade was the late Sid Chaplin, who served his time as a blacksmith in the Durham coalfield before becoming a novelist and short story writer. His relationship with the north-east was similar to that of GMB with Orkney. In the 1960s and 1970s we were lumped together under the heading 'regional writers' - along with people like Keith Waterhouse, Barry Hines, Stan Barstow, Henry Livings and Shelagh Delaney: not a bad bunch to be sharing a lump with.

At one of the conferences that littered those decades, we were asked to define what made a regional writer. Sid's answer was: 'Love of place and love of work.' That was an ex-pitman talking. I knew exactly what he meant. I was born in Jarrow. My father and grandfathers all worked in shipbuilding and steel. They took pride in what they made just as I take pride in the fact that the word 'playwright' (like shipwright or wheelwright) refers to the act of making, rather than writing.

Geordies are, of course, Celts. That being so, I've always responded to the work of writers as diverse as the Welshman, Gwyn Thomas, the funniest novelist of our time (because the jokes are informed by equal parts rage and compassion of a kind absent from Mr Waugh) and the great Lewis Grassic Gibbon; plus too many Irish to count.

All this, in a slightly long-winded way, explains why I fell on GMB's work and - as important - the landscapes that gave him sustenance, with such passion. His characters love their work and the places they live in, but it isn't the sloppy love of romantic fiction and soap opera. It's a love that comes with many qualifications. Fishermen, like miners and shipbuilders, love their work but they know it may kill them. I lived in Hull for thirty years and have seen this phenomenon at close quarters too. One of the leaders of the campaign to find out what really happened to the trawler *Gaul* is a kid I went to primary school with.

George also understood the contradictory nature of small communities: their collective strength and their tendency to stifle. My parents loved Jarrow but couldn't wait to get away. I loved Hull but needed to move to London to breathe more deeply. I've said to young Orcadians, generally after the second Highland Park: 'I bet you can't wait to get the hell off this island,' and had an instant enthusiastic response.

But we all go back because we need the sustenance that only the tap roots can supply.

There's another major paradox. My observation is that Orcadians are not insular. People who live in ports rarely are. Eventually they have to go

Community theatre and dance productions

1981	**The Well** by George Mackay Brown
1982	**The Wireless Set** adapted by Morag MacInnes **Bessie Millie's Wind Shop** by George Mackay Brown **Jock and Blind Mary** by George Mackay Brown
1983	**Ship Surgeon** by Morag MacInnes **Island of the Saints** by George Mackay Brown **The Battle in the Hills** by George Mackay Brown
1984	**Suburb of Babylon** by Hugh Leonard **Home is the Sailor** by George Mackay Brown
1985	**The Caucasian Chalk Circle** by Bertolt Brecht **Me and the Circus** by Orkney Youth Theatre **Lands of Odin** by Lynn O'Brien **How About a Nice Cup of Tea** by Closet Youth Theatre **Orkney Dances** - (Lynn O'Brien Dancers)
1986	**Dr Faustus** by Christopher Marlowe **Peter is a Person and Handicapped** by Alan Cameron **The Crofter of all Seasons** by Lynn O'Brien
1987	**Dance/Sculpture/Instrumental performance** **Street Theatre** (Orcadia Folk Art Studio) **Lady Audley's Secret** by CH Hazlehurst **Magnus - the Man** by Alan Cameron **Seed of Destruction** by Alex Rigg **Edwin Muir and the Labyrinth** by George Mackay Brown
1988	**Romeo and Juliet** by William Shakespeare **The Raven's Nest** (Orkney Youth Theatre) **Crofters** by the people of Sanday
1989	**The Soldier's Tale** by Igor Stravinsky **The Deceivers** (Orkney Youth Theatre) **A Private Ear** by Peter Shaffer **Pirates in the Deep Green Sea** by Eric Linklater
1990	**Towards Spring** (Orkney Youth Theatre) **St Magnus the Cathedral** by Minna Merriman
1991	**Witch** by George Mackay Brown **Road to Colonus** by George Mackay Brown **Five go Green** (Orkney Youth Theatre)
1993	**A Midsummer Night's Dream** by William Shakespeare
1994	**The Beggar's Opera** by John Gay
1995	**The Horseman's Word** by Duncan McLean
1996	**Orkney Dances** (Chor. Andy Howitt)
1997	**Orkneyinga** adapted by Ron Ferguson
1998	**Sunnifa** (Andy Howitt, Anne Bevan and Pete Stollery)
1999	**The Odyssey** Derek Walcott version
2000	**Greenvoe** by GMB, adapted by Alan Plater

aboard one of those ships to explore what's across the water. Indeed, the most insular people I've met are those who live in big cities: the literary or media set in London or New York, the film people in Los Angeles. I know. I've examined them at close quarters.

For example, when I told some of my luvvie chums about the production of *Greenvoe* they responded with great excitement.

'How can we see it?'

'Come to Orkney and buy a ticket.'

That was generally the end of the conversation though one or two of them travelled to Edinburgh and then couldn't get in. That's good. I like poetic justice.

In a way, that anecdote illustrates the unique quality of the St Magnus Festival. In Edinburgh, *Greenvoe* was one of several thousand events of all shapes, sizes and qualities. It's almost impossible in those circumstances to (in the words of an American friend) 'impact on the public perception'. National press coverage tends, in any case, to focus on stand-up comedians, for reasons I can't fathom. I don't remember *The Observer* and *Sunday Times* of my youth giving extensive coverage to Jimmy James and Chic Murray.

Compared with Edinburgh, the St Magnus Festival has a purity, a simplicity and a bedrock relationship with the community. The performers you see in the afternoon frequently turn up in the audience in the evening.

There's no great mystery in this because the two key figures in its history are local men: George and Peter Maxwell Davies. This is a festival bearing their unique and remarkable fingerprints.

art

Orkney has always inspired a creative response from musicians and poets, and, in terms of sheer numbers, perhaps especially from visual artists. The changing light; the elemental, remote beauty of the land and seascapes; the huge skies; the wonderfully preserved and complete historical buildings and sites - they have all been interpreted through visual art for as long as people have lived in the islands. These days, Orkney boasts an astonishing number of working artists and the festival has embraced this talent through some memorable commissions and collaborations.

The focal point for art in Orkney is the Pier Arts Centre in Stromness, soon to be ambitiously extended and refurbished, which houses one of the most important permanent collections of contemporary art in the country. At festival time, the Pier mounts a special exhibition, often featuring an eminent international artist. Other venues around Orkney, such as the Orkney Museum, the Anchor Buildings and the Stromness Library, house additional exhibitions which run concurrently with the festival, showing the recent work of local artists and groups such as the Soulisquoy Printmakers.

There have been some one-off, very special events, such as the gifting to Orkney of panel paintings depicting the martyrdom of St Magnus, which were made and presented to the cathedral by schoolchildren from the Isle of Arran during the 1980 festival. In 2000, a special millennium visual arts project, coordinated by local felt maker and musician, Christina Sargent, involved most of the primary schools in Orkney.

Erlend Brown

"I met Erlend Brown, George's nephew, who had some playful, well-executed prints on show at Stromness Academy. These were semi-abstract things which gained a lot from being emphatically rooted in Orkney. One, 'A New Find', was based on an Orkney ironing-board found the previous autumn. I'm still trying to work out what vikings would want or need to iron, but in any case Erlend's work was impressive."
Brian McCabe
festival poet, 1992
Scotland on Sunday, July, 1992

Pier Arts Centre, 2000.

Erlend Brown curator, The Pier Arts Centre, 1979-1993

Midsummer was always a special time at the Pier Arts Centre. There was not only the magical light, but also the opportunity to show an exhibition that had occupied curator and assistant throughout a long winter. The Pier already had a collection of proven merit, but still we had the need to show quality work at a time when critical eyes were focused on our small island community.

In the eighties, David Hockney was a big name in British art. I was in contact with Kasmin, his dealer in London, to organise an exhibition of Hockney prints. Hockney himself was living in Los Angeles. In February I had to attend a Scottish Arts Council meeting in Edinburgh. From there, I could travel, by bus (always looking for the cheapest option), in snow conditions, overnight to London. This was a mistake, but I was saved by a 9am bath at Margaret Gardiner's Hampstead home, the house which was the first home of the Pier collection, and still full of wonderful works of art. Later Kasmin treated me to a meal in a restaurant near his Cork Street gallery. Here we would meet the man who editioned Hockney prints and posters and could enjoy many of the prints on the restaurant wall. All the business was finished that day and a festival exhibition was launched.

1987 was the centenary of Stanley Cursiter's birth. His last Stromness home was just two piers away - not far to move artworks. But it was not as simple as that. To make a substantial exhibition we had to secure loans from municipal galleries in Edinburgh, Glasgow, Dundee and Aberdeen University. It was well worth the effort since his early 'futurist' works were shown together for the first time. Most of the landscape/seascape works came from homes in Orkney and one major collector of his work. Visitors came in large numbers. Orcadians were honouring one of their favoured sons. The poster image of Shore Street sold out in the first three weeks of a six week exhibition. One even turned up, framed, at an Orkney book auction and sold for £160; not bad for a pound poster!

So many memorable festival exhibitions. I can well remember Captain William Spence, Norwegian consul in Orkney, driving the exhibition *Munch and his Literary Associates* personally, from Edinburgh to Orkney; and un-crating a Henry Moore reclining figure in the street - the crate was too big for the entrance. This brought many quips from the passing Stromnessians. Maybe art has to be out on the street to be fully confronted!

Margaret Gardiner would often visit us at midsummer. At 80-plus she would fall for the visiting poet, but she would also make sure that visitors saw the Pier Gallery collection. Not that they could miss it in such intimate, domestic-scale surroundings. The light was special as it danced on the waves caused by harbour traffic coming and going. The Hepworths, Nicholsons and Wallises sat very happily in this light.

Poetry at the Pier was also special. Readings were part of the annual programme, and at festival time the Pier was bursting at the seams. It was

previous page: *Resound*, 1997, Highland Park distillery.

reassuring to realise that these heavyweights of the literary scene were charming, witty, down-to-earth mortals. It was the tradition to take George and the visiting poet for a meal after the reading. This was always a delight. The cut and thrust of a Norman MacCaig/GMB encounter had us in gales of laughter.

Festival publicity also landed on the Pier desk. We assisted Archie Bevan with flyer and programme. It was often a nightmare to get everything together on time, fully proofed, and delivered from Nevisprint in Fort William. Thank goodness this has speeded up with computer technology and a fully-equipped print works at 'Hell's Half Acre' in Kirkwall.

The exhibition of the Australian painter, Sir Sidney Nolan, in 1989, was a bit of a coup. He had used the saga of Stromnessian, Liza Fraser, in his individual figurative paintings. Her amazing exploits with Australian aborigines and a convict are well-documented in Stromness Museum. The museum had already had contact, but it turned out that he was keen to show a fuller body of his work at the Pier. He would even give a talk. Neil Firth, then gallery technician, and I, installed four large paintings of the Australian outback in the first floor room. One on each wall; north, east, south, west. The horizon line in each was similar in height from the floor. Somehow I had never seen that room look so vast, so open. For the installation of wall works we had a fully notched marking stick. Neil had marked this one 'Australia's greatest living painter'. I was never sure if it was a piece of Neil irony, or was he serious? Whatever, he is now at the helm and must steer the Pier into the 21st century, in expanded premises - no longer the 'small is beautiful' banner - as more is expected from a growing audience, an international audience. But the benchmark will always be the same - to provide a piece of midsummer magic at the festival.

Sir Sidney Nolan,
Pier Art Centre, 1989.

Neil Firth curator, Pier Arts Centre, 1993- (in conversation)

The Pier Arts Centre opened its doors in 1979, which makes it just a little bit younger than the festival. But in 1977, the notion of the Pier would have been firmly established. There was building refurbishment and a long fund-raising campaign before it opened, so the plans would have been firmly in place around the time the festival began.

The festival is firmly rooted in its musical origins, but art has always had an important place. The Pier's influence over the years has at least kept pace with the best intentions of the festival. Coming after the open exhibition for local artists, the festival exhibition is at the centre point of the year, and we have been able to draw some big names in for that, as well as featuring well-known Orcadian artists such as Sylvia Wishart and Gunnie Moberg. There's always this see-saw effect at the Pier between the local visual art community and the visiting solo exhibitions. That, I suppose, echoes the ethos of the festival, too.

Sylvia Wishart, untitled

Alistair Peebles

New Work at the Yards:
Colin Kirkpatrick;
17th Century Low Flying Witch Hunter,
1996.

Apart from the festival artists, we have been involved in setting up 'fringe' events, and have assisted with exhibitions that have been organised through the Pier but haven't been in the Pier building, most of which have featured local artists. The festival organises exhibitions in Stromness Library, but we have always helped in some way - with frames, or helping to hang, or doubling up on the mailing. Fringe exhibitions also take place in venues such as the ferry terminal building, the Anchor Buildings, or Tankerness House in Kirkwall.

There have been some particular collaborations between the festival and the Pier. *Resound*, in 1997, at Highland Park distillery, was a collaboration between local artists, the Scottish Chamber Orchestra and composer, Marc Yeats. Another successful collaboration with the festival was a lovely exhibition, *New Work at the Yards*, featuring local artists whose work was shown in and around the Earl's Palace in Kirkwall.

Visiting artists are always aware that they are part of the festival. The Pier exhibition opens on the Thursday before the festival starts - so it is the visual art centrepiece really. Orkney has usually had some influence on the work of those artists. Mary Newcomb, for instance, fell in love with Orkney and has been back a few times. The place made a big impression on Alan Davie and Jock McFadyen, too. And Julie Roberts, when she went away, said that landscape was an element that hadn't featured in her work, but she was seriously wondering about how it might figure. There must be quite a lot of work out there now with an Orkney edge to it that has filtered through from their visits. It would be lovely to re-show all those artists some day.

Sails in St Magnus: 1993.

Alistair Peebles

Andrew Parkinson Pier Arts Centre (in conversation)

I have been involved in many festival projects over the years, both as an artist and through working at the Pier Arts Centre. There are several personal highlights.

Peter Maxwell Davies had seen some of my work, and decided that he would like to commission some paintings based around Rackwick. I went over to do some drawings of the valley, then made further drawings in the studio. The exhibition, called *Sea Dreams and other pictures*, was held in the Anchor Buildings during the festival in 1992. From the exhibition, Max selected several works. It was a really interesting project and something I enjoyed very much.

For 1993, the big project was *Sails in St Magnus*. The idea was to do something beautiful for the cathedral that would not look out of place. The artists involved - Mary Scott, Dave Jackson, Erlend Brown and myself - thought a great deal about how best to utilise the space. We agreed that the cathedral would be a fantastic place for sails, and through using text by George Mackay Brown it became a very poetic idea.

The whole thing felt fairly magical, and was a very trouble-free process from the beginning.

    A professional sailmaker made the sails and Richardson's boatyard made the strakes and planks, then we painted the sails in the studio. They needed to be bold and vivid in design, and we set to work quite logically, each making three sails at first. It all developed quite organically. The first and the last sail we then made together. The exhibition toured round Scotland, and to the Faroes and Ireland. We made prints from them, but the actual sails belong to the council. They have been brought out and hung again a few times since the original exhibition.

Andrew Parkinson, Maureen Gray, Richard Long, Neil Firth; Pier Art Centre, 1994.

Richard Long   festival artist, 1994

My edited highlight from a warmly remembered visit to Orkney....
A unique memory from my show at the Pier Arts Centre: after making my mud work, I could just cross the quayside, go down the sea-weedy steps, and wash my mud buckets out in the sea. It was the first and only time I have done that. The residue of my work disappeared into the light swell.

It was a very sad Sunday when a group of us, armed with buckets of water and brushes, scrubbed Richard Long's installation off the walls of the Pier Gallery.
Maureen Gray, Pier Arts Centre

Mary Newcomb   festival artist, 1995

One could write for several pages and still not do Orkney justice. It seems to exist in a time warp, with a balance and calm that I've never met elsewhere - it feels like a second home to me.

    My first visit to Orkney was in 1995, to accompany an exhibition of my paintings at the Pier Arts Centre. I had never travelled so far north before so I had only a vague idea of the position of Orkney in relation to the coast of Scotland.

    The journey itself was exciting, travelling by train from flat East Anglia, to the northern tip of Scotland - then on to the ferry - with anticipation. How far away were these islands? On we went, past the spectacular cliffs of Hoy, until, on rounding a corner, we saw what looked like a raft of green islands. Could that little line of buildings along the shore be Stromness?

    The line of buildings became larger, closer, soon a tightly-packed small port within a natural harbour. Suddenly, there we all were, with bags and baggage on the pierhead - people gathering, bunting waving in the stiff breeze - hugs and embraces all round. We were quickly absorbed into such a welcoming community - such hospitality - such very dear people everywhere.

Mary Newcomb, 1995.

I loved every minute of my stay, the mixture of formality and informality of the festival, the diversity of entertainment, the high quality of the performances, the enthusiasm of the residents and the visitors alike.

One of my clearest memories during my stay, is of the interior of St Magnus Cathedral, hung with great sails between the pillars, each boldly decorated with symbols, with quotations of poetry on the arches above - and of the cries of the seagulls outside the windows.

Another memory is of the silence and perfection of the interior of the Italian Chapel - and, of course, many other memories - visiting Skara Brae in wind and rain - hearing the seals singing on the rocks off the shore of Rousay, such a sound I have never heard before - finding my first *Primula Scotica* - the shared concentration of the audience at a poetry reading in the Pier Arts Centre.

Since that first visit I have returned several times, and I hope to come again soon - so please continue to wave in the large colourful ferry with your flags and tea towels, and please keep the bunting flying.

Andrew Parkinson

New Work at the Yards artists
Anne Bevan
Carol Dunbar/Matilda Tumim
John Cumming
Colin Kirkpatrick
Sam MacDonald
Duncan McLean
Malcolm Olva
Glen Onwin
Andrew Parkinson
Frances Pelly/Alistair Peebles
Alan Stout

The *Sails* exhibition led us to explore new possibilities for art spaces in Orkney, and in 1996, *New Work at the Yards* was based in and around the Earl's Palace in Kirkwall. Historic Scotland owns the site, and they were very open and enthusiastic about the idea of exhibiting there. We were able to use the building totally, which meant that we could make work that really looked at the relationship between the art and the building, and get right into the spaces. The visitor numbers for that exhibition were astronomical, and apart from a few complaints from people who said that they would prefer to see the historic sites without modern art all over them, the response was very positive.

Resound, in 1997, was a collaboration between the Pier Arts Centre, the St Magnus Festival and the Scottish Chamber Orchestra. The space - in the malting shed of Highland Park distillery - was challenging and inspiring. The idea was to work with two players from the SCO, and the composer Marc Yeats. The artists were to make work for the space and then the musicians would use the ideas and translate them into music. We were hoping that we could all work directly with the musicians, but as it turned out there was terrible fog that year and they were delayed for hours. It ended up that the collaboration was all done through Marc; he worked directly with the musicians and they recorded the piece. It was a bit frustrating, but it couldn't be helped; overall it was a great project.

Both the festival and the Pier Arts Centre are now mature organisations. They have nurtured a generation of people, and have both involved local artists in a very ambitious international context, which they can deliver because they have been so successful. Hopefully both can continue along that road, and meet up occasionally for collaborations across the artistic disciplines. When the new space at the Pier is fully operational, there is lots of scope for further expansion of projects between the Pier and the festival. The possibilities, based on the success of past projects, are exciting.

Resound: Highland Park distillery, 1997.

Marc Yeats composer and artist

Through my work on the *Resound* project I got to know the folks at the Pier Arts Centre; Neil Firth, Andrew Parkinson and Maureen Gray - all people who care deeply about what they are doing and who are very professional. It's fair to say that we have sunk a fair few bevvies in the pubs and hotels of Stromness over the years and have attempted on more than one occasion to put the world to rights, though apparently with little success! I always warm to people who can talk intensely about art and what they believe in whilst being able to tell the odd rude joke, too!

Resound artists
Anne Bevan
Jenna Hume
John Hunter
Arlene Isbister
Colin Johnstone
Andrew Parkinson
Alistair Peebles
Mary Scott
Judy Spark
Richard Welsby
Marc Yeats

Jock McFadyen festival artist, 1999

My first memories of Orkney are from when I rode my motorbike up from London in an attempt to be the first artist in residence at the Pier. (My wife Susie had persuaded me to apply.) The ride from Edinburgh to Thurso was fabulous except for the very last few miles when the rain was in horizontal sheets. Nothing had prepared me for the dismal spectacle of Thurso on a rainy midweek evening. The chips from the chip shop were not good, the pub was empty and the B&B had a candlewick bedspread.

But it does Stromness no disfavour that Thurso is such a dump. What contrast. After the grandeur of Hoy the first impression of Stromness is that the Feng Shui is all absolutely perfect. After checking in at the Stromness Hotel (perfect proportions) I was straight on my bike round the island and over the Churchill Barriers. I don't want to go on sounding like a tourist brochure but needless to say things got better and better.

My next visit was in 1999 to make some work for my show at the Pier. I had wanted to juxtapose my southern urban landscape with work made on Orkney. It was while painting up the hill at Stromness that news of the Jill Dando murder was newsflashed on Radio 4, a grim reminder of the city of 12 million, which I had left behind.

Will Self wrote a story to accompany my pictures. He is, I think, an urban animal and has been escaping to Orkney for at least 10 years. He had written about my pictures in the past as well as the islands, so it seemed apt to approach him again. He did us proud with *No Reggae in Orkney*. My wife,

Jock McFadyen, *Phoenix Cinema 1999.*

One festival we walked into the Pier Arts Centre to be confronted by Jock McFadyen's picture of Aldgate East Underground Station, notorious to us as the station that Jeremy used to get to work. London returned the favour a few months later when his painting of the Phoenix cinema was hung facing the entrance to Agnew's Gallery in Bond Street.

Yvonne and Jeremy Clarke, regular festival visitors

Anthony Caro and Sheila Girling, 1997.

Callum Innes, 2000.

Susie Honeyman, is a musician with The Mekons and has put the piece to music. She is obsessed with Orkney and wants us to go and live there....

Other memories of Orkney: 'Give Way Otters Crossing' (road sign in Kirkwall).... seals on the beach.... the smell of furniture polish in the Stromness Hotel.... midnight sun.... blockships.... transparent water.... The Italian Chapel.... the light sea-going boats at the ends of the gardens in Stromness.... a Maxwell Davies performance at the Phoenix and hearing Joanna MacGregor there too.... good chips.

Julie Roberts festival artist, 2001

The installation period at the Pier Arts Centre proved to be a very rewarding experience; all of the staff had the perfect balance of professionalism and friendliness. The permanent collection is filled with gems and I felt proud to show my work alongside it. The installation *Dysfunctional Family/Scotland/ Ireland/England/Wales* was made with the space in mind, and I was excited to hear that the response was a positive one.

While on Orkney I collected various research materials. I intend to do a new work as part of my landscape collection. I look forward to seeing the new gallery extension, and hope to be invited back one day.

John Cumming former festival visual arts coordinator

The St Magnus Festival is inclusive. From its outset it has involved the local community in exciting and innovative art. Theatrical events have spilled out of the theatre and on to the streets. Professional artists regularly rub shoulders with locals with never a hint of the patronising or elitist attitudes that bedevil so much art in this country.

This openness has done much to nurture a sense of self-confidence among Orkney artists. In the visual arts it would have been easy to import high profile exhibitions to the Pier Arts Centre and leave it at that, but the festival has consistently commissioned, encouraged and stimulated new activity. This has produced a suite of festival prints and a string of mixed exhibitions reflecting the richness of local culture.

The five-year project to commission an annual print through Peacock Printmakers in Aberdeen was typically bold, when it targeted artists who were weavers, sculptors or painters, rather than printmakers. This produced a varied and exciting suite of screen-prints, etchings and relief prints, encouraging some of the artists involved to extend their work after the commission, as they continued to explore a new medium in greater depth.

Two exhibitions come to mind, both in the tiny library gallery in Stromness. *Play*, a show that featured works that were interactive and child-centred: a show that revealed the child in many of its visitors. I remember, as a curator, watching two weans totally absorbed as they played an invented game involving pebbles and running water, part of a sculpture by John McCallum. I remember the infinite variety of materials, forms and concepts brought to the *Artists' Books* exhibition, which could and should have toured Scotland.

Sound and the visual image came together in an exciting installation at the Highland Park distillery malting shed. These initiatives sought to explore, to irritate, to encourage new ideas, new collaborations, new possibilities. Some efforts missed the mark, but the works were never predictable, formulaic or easy. This sense of art as a joyful adventure is the gift that the festival has given to Orkney. God preserve us from that which is comfortable and genteel.

The Festival Prints, 1997-2001

[In 1997, to celebrate the 21st festival, a fine art print was commissioned, the first in a series of five limited edition prints, each of which was commissioned from a different artist over the next four festivals.]

1997 Mark Scadding

1998 Sylvia Wishart

1999 Frances Pelly, *Roust*

2000 Carol Dunbar, *Midsummer 1906*

2001 Arlene Isbister, *Groovy* (Entoptic Study after Max Knoll)

Special events...

Maureen Farquharson retired art teacher, Arran High School

When the St Magnus Festival was established it seemed to me to be the most exciting event in the country. No one's writing meant more to me than that of George Mackay Brown and the music of Peter Maxwell Davies had long been of real interest to me. That these two artists were working together shaping the festival seemed wonderful. Even in far away Arran one sensed that this event was different, was special, that it was a celebration, that it was about Orkney, its people and their story. It was inspiring.... Could Arran children perhaps do something for it? A painting? They could paint the story of St Magnus.

The Arran children were excited by the story of St Magnus. The background of sea and cliff, as well as the many dramatic elements of the saga, were very real to them. Before starting the panels they had made a short study of Orkney with its wonderful land and seascapes and its dramatic history and were looking forward to the journey north. We took time also to prepare them for the avant garde music which they would hear, assisted in this by a talented local musician who was currently writing film scores and offered them opportunities to make their own improvisations. The results began to

1997

1998

1999

2000

2001

Glenys Hughes

**The panel paintings in
St Magnus Cathedral.**

*"What a splendid gift to Orkney
is the set of panels depicting St
Magnus and the building of the
cathedral in Kirkwall. The artists
are all in their teens, and they
and their art teacher, Mrs
Farquharson, came to Orkney to
hand over the gift in person; and
they came, appropriately, at
midsummer and during the St
Magnus Festival.*

*There is a splendid strength
and energy in the 14 pictures.
Here, out of the imaginations of
these young artists, is much of
the direct strength of the saga
itself. Weaving through all is a
charm and innocence that
belongs to youth; the dew is still
on the grass, the first birds are
still singing.*

*It's marvellous that
children from another quite far-
away island should have been
fired by this Orkney story. It
proves that eight and a half
centuries on it is still valid and
potent, and not just a weave of
mediaeval miracle and fantasy."*
George Mackay Brown
From 'Under Brinkie's Brae'
July 10, 1980

open their minds to new musical ideas.

After all their studies and hard work, when they finally got off the
plane in Kirkwall, they were excited about seeing Orkney, the people and the
events of the festival. Many felt they were already part of it because of their
work on the paintings. Especially important for them was the formal presentation
of the gift of the panels since it focused on the idea of a tribute: the children
understood intuitively that their work was part of something greater. They
were moved by the interior of the cathedral. The story of St Magnus was there
and alive in their minds.

The children attended at least one event each day and some, such as
Pierrot Lunaire, were quite a challenge, although at fourteen they were young
enough to take such things in their stride. After one event in the cathedral
they met up with Peter Maxwell Davies to tell him about their work and
inform him that his portrait appeared in one of the panels. After he failed to
spot it they pointed out the painting of the cathedral showing Bishop William
followed by various Orkney people down the ages - including 'Max', George
and themselves!

If you look carefully at the panels with the Hebridean Hymn you will
see a Jack Russell terrier. On it being suggested to the young artist that this
looked incongruous amongst the mythical beasts he replied: 'Well, that's my
own dog, Patch.' Clearly, Patch was not to be left out and he remains there
to this day. The children hid behind the canvasses little messages about
themselves (not to be removed!).

One morning they travelled to Stromness to meet George Mackay
Brown and found him sitting quietly on a bench by the pierhead chatting to
a fisherman. They gathered around him to talk and listen. Before we left he
asked what they were going to do that day and on hearing that we were off
to see *Cinderella* in the evening he looked slightly wistful. So on the bus back
to Kirkwall we all resolved to send a taxi that night to bring him to the theatre.
He arrived delighted, loved the show and he and the children were invited to
join an impromptu party afterwards to celebrate the last performance.

I do not know whether any of the 'children' have returned to Orkney.
They are all in their thirties now, are scattered round the country and I have
lost touch with them. But I know that the experience of the panels, of the saga
of St Magnus and of their visit to Orkney will always be with them. On Arran
there remains a legacy from that journey: in 1980 our local newspaper quoted
me as saying that the St Magnus Festival was breathing new life into Orkney's
cultural heritage, 'transforming old legends and stories of island life into
striking modern works'. At that time Arran children knew little of their own
cultural heritage and it was evident that something needed to be done. Something
was done and we now have an accumulation of some twenty years of records
of pupils' own research, drawings, photos, tapestries and ceilidhs covering
some of the social history, traditions and folklore of the island here. This
project continues and is now managed jointly by Arran High School and by

a community group. It is hoped that as generations age they will pass on their memories and knowledge to their children and grandchildren.

A book is being published in June, 2002, of the children's collection. We should like Orkney to have a copy of this in recognition of what the St Magnus Festival inspired all those years ago.

Glenys Hughes   festival director

For the 2000 festival we wanted to offer a special project to the schools - something that could involve every school and which would hopefully result in some form of permanent memento of the millennium year. But some schools were already planning their own millennial productions and children from many of the schools would be rehearsing for Orkney's 'Day at the Dome' - so a festival performance project seemed out of the question. Some kind of visual arts project perhaps? But what? Then, by one of those happy coincidences which sometimes occur in the planning of the festival, Christina Sargent came up with the idea of the yurt (a circular tent).

Christina Sargent   felt artist and musician

Years ago, I had been lucky enough to be assisted by our local council to attend the first international felt symposium in Aarhus, Denmark, in 1987, and there, amongst many others, I met Istvan Vidak from Hungary who put me in touch with Stephanie Bunn. Ever since, Steph has been an inspirational friend and has talked to me often about Kyrgyzstan and all her educational projects. When I received Glenys's letter, asking for suggestions for a big visual arts project for 2000, ideas began to form.

I had been muttering to Glenys for ages about cultural links with Central Asia. I had always wanted a yurt but had been too busy and had not had enough energy to make all the felt. But to involve the children of Orkney in such a project, linking two countries through art, architecture, history and folklore seemed obvious and infinitely exciting and valuable. I scribbled my ideas (along with a request for oboe reeds) to those concerned and amazingly, without a formal plan, the idea was accepted happily. Mind you, my insistence on incorporating Kyrgyzstan was viewed with a bit of anxiety, along with the prospect of ruining all the school floors with my messy, wet methods of making felt.

Letters were sent to all 24 of the Orkney primary schools. Twenty classes from seventeen schools - around 350 children - were able to participate. Timetables were drawn up and funds were found. I plucked up the courage to phone the Kyrgyz Embassy and in no time was having long conversations with Rosa Otunbayeva, the ambassador in London, who offered to come to

Christina Sargent

Making felt for the yurt.

The yurt project was a lovely fresh idea - and a huge thing to do; Christina worked so hard. Despite my worries about the amount of water sloshing around the floors of the schools, you couldn't have a more perfect, complete thing made out of lots of parts - it was really very, very good.
Penny Aberdein
festival schools liaison
(in conversation)

Orkney for the festival, meet the children and bring a musician.

I needed to conjure up a theme - to design a good basic framework within which each class and each child could be truly creative and fulfilled. I decided that each class would make one large panel to clothe the inside and the outside of the tent, and the folk tale of how the Orkney Islands came to be formed came to mind - *Assipattle and the Muckle Mester Stoorworm*. It had to look beautiful with a design theme as well as a story - not just a jumble of pictures, so I decided on four colours - blue, red, white and black. (I also decided that each panel would be an arch which could stand on its own after June as a wall panel in each school.)

I started on January 6, 2000. Five months later, on May 30, I worked with my last school - Orphir Primary. I'd been in ferries of all shapes and sizes, in all weathers. The exuberance and delight of the children were a true tonic in moments of utter exhaustion. We worked like crazy ants choosing images, cutting templates, endlessly checking that every child was happy. Black images, blue tears, red flames, nostrils and eyes, blue seas, red fish and crabs, thunder and lightning, great black birds, bats and sea monsters, knights and horses galloping - all became felted in twenty exquisite panels.

Rosa the ambassador did come. We hurtled her to the waiting press and yurt. In a quiet space in the centre of Kirkwall she disappeared into and emerged out of the tent like a beautiful butterfly in national dress.

The project culminated on the last day of the St Magnus Festival in the large concert hall packed with over 1000 people, including the children involved in the yurt project. An extravaganza of singing and dancing in and around the tent followed. There were stories about Orkney and Chinara Sharsenova played her komuz with enormous virtuosity; I stood proudly beside Rosa in her costume. It was an emotional and rousing end to six months of trauma, and, at the end, a few of us were there far into the night, dismantling it all and wrapping up each panel. What one couldn't, or perhaps wouldn't, attempt without friends!

(From an article first published in *Echoes: Journal of International Feltmakers*; Issue 62, 2001)

Rosa Otunbayeva, Kyrgyz ambassador to London,
with the yurt in Tankerness House Gardens, 2000.

Orkney Photographic

Geoffrey Taylor

the visitors

While the festival has been no stranger to a bit of controversy locally, the festival visitors are unanimous: it is wonderful. In many cases, coming to Orkney and the St Magnus Festival is what one does at midsummer, despite travel worries and the uncertainty of the weather on arrival. A large number of people, whether attracted initially by the contemporary music, Max's presence, or curiosity about this far-flung arts event, have become loyal festival supporters; they have made long-lasting friendships in Orkney and have come to enjoy the broad spectrum of events at the festival, becoming as familiar with the local talent in community drama productions or the Johnsmas Foy, as they are with the glittering international soloists and the visiting orchestras and ensembles.

Some of the visitors have also contributed to the festival creatively, and some visit to do other kinds of work: the BBC and other media crews, for instance, who regularly cover the festival events. But even when it is work, there is something about Orkney and the St Magnus Festival to do with the quality of the performances in the often unsuitable, but wonderful, venues - and to do with the light, the history and the people. Together, they cast a spell.

Gerard McBurney with
Elizabeth Bevan, Anne McBurney
and Archie Bevan, 1992.

*For 20 years we have toured the
globe. From Stromness to
Broadway. We came to Orkney
in a yellow post office van. We
drove it from London and took
the ferry to Stromness. It did not
seem far. We breathed deeply and
nervously as we passed the Old
Man of Hoy. As well as the main
theatre we played the streets of
Kirkwall, accosted shoppers, were
invited to stay, and met George.
We were embraced. This altered
the show, and changed us forever.
Because a place is the people who
are there; the Bevans, George and
all the others. And just as memory
itself is not like an image on a
computer, but something created
each time we remember, our time
in Orkney continues to exert its
effect on me 15 years later. It
changes me and gives me hope,
at a time when hope is in short
supply. I am grateful beyond
words and terribly want to return.*
Simon McBurney
Théatre de Complicité

Gerard McBurney composer, festival visitor

How well I remember the excitement of waiting for the first St Magnus
Festival! I was just finishing my English degree at Cambridge and in my
memory it was a hot summer (probably it was raining). Once I daringly went
up to London to go to a rehearsal of *The Martyrdom*. I changed tubes on to
the Bakerloo line to go to BBC Maida Vale, flopped on to a scruffy seat and
stared straight into Max's face opposite me. 'I wonder where you're going
to,' he murmured, without batting an eyelash.

Back in Cambridge my parents announced that they would like to
come to the festival too, (along with Jane Beeson, Fiona Maddocks and my
sister). We all crammed into my father's old Land Rover and hammered up
the A1, the gear box hot enough to roast a joint on.

The highlight of course was *The Martyrdom*. I can still see those
swaying monks singing their way round the dark aisles of the cathedral, and
Max hunched like a hoop over the score. Afterwards I introduced my father
to George. The two men smiled at one another for ages, but said nothing.
Years before, in Cambridge, my father had known EM Forster (known as
Morgan). I remember my father shaking George's hand and walking back to
where I was standing in the south transept. 'That's someone Morgan would
have liked' he declared. There could be no higher praise.

Several of those early festivals almost seem to blur into one in my
mind. I came one year with Mark Beeson, the poet and community thinker
from Dartmoor. He found common cause with Archie and Elizabeth around
their kitchen table, arguing for the local and was most impressed by what
came out of Orkney rather than what had been brought in from outside. I came
with my brother Simon, before he ever played at the festival with his company,
Théatre de Complicité. That must have been in 1980, for we bought four live
lobsters in Stromness and later took them, still alive, to Ross-shire, where we
added champagne and toasted my father who had died six months before.

I must have been to many orchestral concerts. I heard Max conduct
a piece by Judith Weir based on a picture from the Bayeux Tapestry, and,
during a performance of the Britten Serenade the lights went out in the cathedral
but the orchestra carried on regardless and finished to the end in darkness. A
tribute to the unnecessity of the conductor (it wasn't Max!).

Then there's the question of food. Once the wonderful Sheila
McCrindle and I went to lunch in a restaurant in the old mill by Maeshowe.
At the next table were two music critics from the Scottish newspapers, tucking
with loud sucking noises into lobster thermidor and wine on their expense
accounts. All my prejudices about that most doubtful of professions were
confirmed at once (Shostakovich once said to a friend at dinner: 'A musician
is like someone who makes this omelette; a music-lover is the person who
eats the omelette; the music critic is someone who talks about the omelette').
I remember sticky cakes with pink icing in the Pomona café, butteries in

Stromness, the blue smoke of Stephen Pruslin's buccaneering attempt with my brother to make BLTs in the Bevans' kitchen. And most of all I remember the Hoy picnics at Bunertoon. They really did all seem to be sunlit. Once, when Max led the party up the hill at the back for a post-prandial sprint to the Old Man, a fat and tiny music critic (not them again!) collapsed in a drunken heap in the heather. And we left him there to sleep away the afternoon.

George I remember on those occasions, unusually voluble and sociable, sitting on the steps of Bunertoon, gazing with glass and piece in hand at a glittering bay and condemning *The Love-song of J Alfred Prufrock* as 'very camp', a critical judgement of Eliot I'd not heard before. On the way home in Stevie's boat, he produced a bottle and passed it round. By the time it had been twice round the boat there was less left in the bottle. George held it up to the light as we passed the blockship and those Second Symphony stationary waves, shook his head at the little whisky that remained and declared (and it was the whisky he was talking about): 'The tide's going out fast'. Mark Beeson murmured with excitement and admiration: 'That's probably George Mackay Brown's greatest line of poetry'.

Poetry readings I remember too, and the Foys, and plays, and talk....and walking the Ring of Brodgar at midnight midsummer (not widdershins!) with a piper and *The Battle of the Birds*, still one of my favourite pibrochs. Time has become shorter since those early days and, with one exception, it's been many years since I've been able to come to the St Magnus Festival. But when midsummer comes, I still think that that's where I should be. I miss it and I rejoice that it still carries on, changing and developing.

Picnic at Bunertoon, 1994.

Magnus Linklater   former chairman, Scottish Arts Council

I cannot remember a single year when there has not been at least one moment of sheer, unexpected, pleasure in the course of the festival. Particularly memorable was *Orkneyinga* - the 1997 re-creation of the martyrdom of St Magnus in the cathedral, with 16-foot high papier maché models of Hakon and Magnus swaying towards each other down the aisle. The festival has always expanded its boundaries, whether in choosing new locations - the Italian Chapel, for instance, when the London Sinfonietta played Messiaen's *Quartet for the End of Time* in 1999 - or in trying new and adventurous music. Not all of it pleases. My mother Marjorie [original festival committee member, founder of 'A Johnsmas Foy'] used to relish the story of the two Orkney ladies who, after listening to a couple of cellos scraping away at some particularly testing piece of contemporary music, commented: 'At least there's no a smell wi' it'. But the sheer variety and constant experiment of a programme that excites and challenges us every year, is remarkable. The tally of festival premieres over the years must outstrip that of any comparable event anywhere in the world.

Knut Ødegård with Magnus Linklater, 1993.

The magic of the festival is, of course, inseparable from the magic of Orkney itself. The great sweep of its contours, the brilliance of its colours, the scudding clouds in that immense sky - wherever you look there is a grandeur that gives the music and the drama of the festival a backdrop that is without equal, anywhere. The landscape of the islands is an integral part of the festival itself. Add a pint of McEwans in the back bar of the Albert Hotel, and the result is irresistible.

Philip Croft and **David Lipetz**   annual festival visitors

Our first festival was in 1981 and we have been every year since. It was very exciting to anticipate what the festival would be like as we sailed into Stromness following a smooth crossing in deck chairs on the *St Ola*. First impressions, however, were not good. Watching the Kirkwall bus move off while the gangway was being lowered, we wondered how long we would have to wait for the next one. On landing we discovered that tourists were not too well catered for. It was the only bus!

It did not take long, however, to discover that first impressions can be wrong. Where else would you meet a festival director (Max at that time) welcoming members of the audience on the steps of the cathedral? On this first visit we did not appreciate that transport was laid on for the Sunday afternoon recital in Stromness. So, there being no other public transport, we hired bicycles. Orkney can sometimes be quite breezy, and one particular cycle run to Stromness from Kirkwall is memorable in that it took us nearly two and a half hours. Amazingly the wind did not change direction and the return journey was accomplished in only forty-five minutes! The Sunday afternoon recitals have always been special, and, in the early years, Archie Bevan's update on the Town Hall plans and work in progress on the toilets became a fringe event in its own right.

The range and content of events have never failed to surprise and impress. At our first festival we heard *Lullaby for Lucy* and *Kirkwall Shopping Songs* among the musical events. Over the years we have enjoyed a great variety of musical contributions by Max. 2001 included the trendy *Cinderella* after a gap of twenty one years, as well as the slightly more ambitious *Antarctic Symphony*!

In addition, there is the poetry and drama. At one festival we dreaded an Alan Aykbourn play as we hated several of his that we had seen. But we loved it, and the community dramatic productions have gone from strength to strength. *Romeo and Juliet* still stands out as one of the most memorable with the ill-fated lovers remaining 'dead' during the curtain call. Visiting companies have also impressed - the imaginative *Exhibitionists* by Ridiculusmus, to name just one of the more recent performances. It is this talent for spotting the unusual that brings such interest to the programmes.

Philip Croft and David Lipetz.

It is interesting and gratifying that many people come back year after year. Some are attracted by Max's music, by the quality and variety of events and others just by the place - or a combination of all these factors. At the last night of the festival we always announce the dates for the following year, and these regulars put it in their diaries, and it is sacrosanct - that's what they do in June. Their loyalty is immense.
Glenys Hughes
festival director

While not all the venues have been ideal, they do have their own particular charm. There was the hot and steamy Phoenix cinema where, whatever the weather, you needed to be lightly clad inside. The Pier Arts Centre was often crammed to the ceiling to ensure everyone could get in and it felt like being in a sardine tin! But over the years these places acquire their own distinctive atmosphere which makes the modern Picky Centre feel more sanitised with its mod cons. Let's not forget the churches and church halls on the islands. For us 'townies' a bus or ferry trip to hear a concert followed by sandwiches and cakes to fortify us for the return journey is unique. And what sight could be more glorious than the late evening sun on the cathedral?

Over twenty years we have made many friends. We have actually stayed in very few bed and breakfast places, having been thoroughly spoilt for several years by Chrissie Sinclair and previously by the late Mary Dawson, who piled on the food to make sure we were well fed. We soon got to know Lucy (of the *Lullaby*), and her parents, Jack and Dorothy Rendall, and usually stay at their home in Rackwick at the end of the festival, adding to that sense of belonging that makes us feel so at home in Orkney. Local people genuinely want to know what we visitors think of the various events and arrangements. Whenever we meet George Rendall, Glenys Hughes, Archie Bevan or other committee members, there is an immediate and constant desire to have feedback. This adds to the feeling of being very much part of the event and contributes to the eager anticipation of returning again to 'our' festival.

So why have we kept coming back every year? Isn't it obvious - knowing that Glenys and her team will have some surprises up their sleeves, perhaps some new music, possibly some interesting and unusual theatre or other happening? There is now better provision for tourists - more buses, the ro-ro ferries. We have gone soft and retired the bikes, bringing the car across, so we are probably not as fit. But it makes it possible to explore the more distant corners. Above all, it feels that we are spending time with friends.

Yvonne and Jeremy Clarke annual festival visitors

Particular happy memories and highlights are...The 1998 crossing to Hoy for a BT Ensemble concert with glorious sunny weather in both directions - Clio Gould's Stradivarius violin carefully sheltered in the cabin.... Messian's *Quartet for the End of Time* in the Italian Chapel was very moving, resonating with the circumstances of the building of the chapel.... The community theatre pieces, especially in 1997 the promenade *Orkneyinga* in all the historic buildings ending in the cathedral cleared of seats... Leaving the cathedral after a concert when the sunset gives it a deep red glow.

The audience in Orkney must be the most attentive and discerning in the UK, and they mix with the performers throughout the festival in a stimulating and exciting way.

Susan Costello and Robert Clark annual festival visitors

One of the most inspirational aspects of the festival is the discovery of new talent. We have derived enormous satisfaction from being in at the beginning of the careers of Steven Osborne, David Horne and James MacMillan. Indeed, one of the high spots of all our years of festival going was the extraordinary first performance of James MacMillan's *Tuireadh* in the cathedral. It is, in our opinion, one of the finest pieces of chamber music written in the twentieth century.

There have been many wonderful premieres but perhaps the most enjoyable of all was that given by the Nø Boys of Max's piece composed on the occasion of Dorothy's retirement. We remember listening every year to Dorothy Rushbrook's horror stories of artists almost not getting to performances

The Phoenix cinema was a difficult space for an orchestra to perform in; it leaked, smelled and had an air of damp, cold days - the sun never seemed to penetrate. However, at performance times, it was transformed! (I remember once seeing the steam rise off the audience as they dried out during the performance.) We could never play at full string strength at the Phoenix and many a rehearsal was delayed as we tried to squeeze yet another double bass on to the stage. The performances were generally full of pioneering enthusiasm from the orchestra. Max would conduct at times and his wonderful colourful narratives of his works took the audience on journeys from Hoy to Salford through his childhood memories in industrial England to the windswept hills of his spiritual home across Scapa Flow.
Trevor Green
former manager,
BBC SSO, BBC Philharmonic

or getting stuck on the island afterwards. Dorothy always turned these near disasters into howlingly funny stories.

Over the years we have become used to the 'usual festival weather'; on occasions, though, the weather has turned up trumps. We remember coming out of the cathedral one evening and standing with Robert Hardy gazing in awe at the sandstone of the west front glowing in the late evening sun. Perhaps the most notable occasion on which the weather really worked was the outdoor Runrig concert which came to a close as the sun eased its way below the horizon in a completely clear sky. While on the subject, we were much amused by the letter to Radio Orkney beginning, 'It must be festival time again, the farmers are spreading slurry'.

Another memory, from 1990, is the interesting and entirely impromptu talk on the Emperor Concerto that was given by Peter Donohoe sitting on the edge of a table. Later that evening he gave us a wonderful performance of that work in the Phoenix cinema. Richard Rodney Bennett was to have given a talk on his percussion concerto but he was still desperately rehearsing it as the SCO had been delayed by bad weather.

What can we say about the old Phoenix cinema? On many occasions soloists and orchestras rose to the challenge of its appalling acoustic and cramped platform to give us absolutely breathtaking performances. Incidentally the one occasion when the atmosphere inside the cinema did not resemble a Turkish bath was the premiere of the film *Venus Peter* in 1989.

Two last memories are both of the cathedral. We always attend the Festival Service and every year leave with our faith in humanity rekindled. The last is of Neil Mackie's walk around the cathedral in memory of Dick Hughes.

Thomas Schulz   music journalist, Germany

Before I came to Orkney for the first time, I had already read a great deal about the islands, and, above all, about Max, and had always had the same thought: 'Fascinating, but I'm sure I'll never get there as it is so far away and remote'. Then, one day, I met Max - it was in 1992 as a result of a concert of his own works in Dusseldorf, which he was conducting. We spoke, among other things, about the festival. The following year, after I had tossed it around in my mind countless times, I finally made the decision and got myself a ticket to Orkney. Even though I only had a few days to spare, these were enough to infect me with the 'Orkney-bug'. Since then I have been coming every year to the St Magnus Festival.

Now why should someone who comes from a country that is not exactly renowned for its good weather take his holidays in a place where the weather is certainly no better? For one, because I love the islands, with their fresh and ever-changing climate, and because there is a wealth of things to see for an amateur ornithologist like me. Also, because the festival always has something to offer that other festivals don't - Max's works, premieres of young British composers' works, and, above all, theatre and musical drama directed and participated in by the people who live in Orkney.

I believe there are two things which are particularly special about the St Magnus Festival: firstly, that it's equally an event for and of the islands - that it doesn't only belong to the tourists, but primarily to the Orcadians. Secondly, I don't know any other festival where, as part of the audience you automatically become part of the event as a whole. This is, I am certain, due to the fact that the majority of the audience does come to the festival out of an equal love for music and for the islands, and not to show off their latest expensive dresses or suits. I have not only found interesting people but also real friends in the warm and, thank God, unpretentious atmosphere of the St Magnus.

Finally, I would like to wish the festival three things: firstly, that it will never be a mainstream festival. There should always be a lively mix of popular and loved music (such as the beautiful Schubert Octet that was played so wonderfully by the Nash Ensemble in 2001) and unusual things that other festivals don't offer - (perhaps with the help of young and talented 'composers in residence'?). Secondly, that it might somehow be possible to enthuse young people also for the festival. If that doesn't happen, then there will no longer be a festival in a few years, because everyone will be in the cemetery. I know that it's harder than ever now to get young people interested in cultural things, but who knows, perhaps the birth of a new trend will begin in Orkney? Thirdly, that these dreadful seats in the cathedral might finally be removed and replaced with something more comfortable. My (and not only my) tortured back will be very grateful to the powers that be!

Thomas Schulz and
Peter Maxwell Davies.

Nigel Groom and Harvey Pritchard annual festival visitors

We first attended the St Magnus Festival in 1995, shortly after getting to know Max. It was he who suggested that we make the journey to Orkney to experience the festival for ourselves. We had heard something of this most northerly British music festival but knew very little in detail. Who organised it, how did we get there and what were we to expect in such a remote location?

Little then did we imagine that we would be making an annual pilgrimage to Orkney.

Never once have we experienced the magical clear midnight of St John's Eve. On our second visit we had to make emergency purchases of fleece jackets. Our feet are frequently damp, despite the extra application of waterproofing to our walking boots. And our journeys have been disrupted by fog at Kirkwall airport. (This is our summer holiday!)

So why, we ask ourselves, do we keep coming back?

Like the flights of migrating ocean birds congregating on the Noup at Westray, or the seals basking easily in the occasional calm of Rackwick Bay, we come ourselves as summer visitors. We are drawn not only by the music, which is always enlivening and often challenging. We are excited by the interaction of professional artists with the enterprise of local schools and communities. Through the St Magnus we have come to know many Orcadians, whose homes and hearts have been unfailingly welcoming. And here we have made friends both in Orkney and throughout the British Isles, the USA and continental Europe. St Magnus is the only festival we know whose riches annually provide a true occasion of community, friendship and 'festivity'.

David McGuinness producer, BBC Scotland

For some years now, a team from the music department in BBC Scotland has visited the festival to make programmes for Radio Scotland and for Radio 3. The festival's now a regular fixture in Radio 3's calendar, and in many ways it provides the ideal environment for making programmes. There's the rare privilege of parking our humble van in the grounds of the cathedral, as glorious a working environment as you could ever wish for, with Jim Rousay [the custodian] keeping his wise and amused eye on us as we trail in and out with cables, microphones, and an occasionally worried demeanour. And there's the friendliness and co-operation, which spreads from the local people to the visiting artists and makes the whole process very civilised. There's plenty of peace and quiet, so we don't often need to repair to Radio Orkney's soundproof studios, and it's very easy to find contributors or interviewees: they tend to show up in the Festival Club around 11.30pm. Ambush them there, and there's no need to negotiate with their troublesome agents or managers first.

There are many experiences from the last few years that could only have happened at the St Magnus Festival. Here are a few:

....A jam session in the Ring of Brodgar at 4am with members of the Scottish Chamber Orchestra and the band from the Festival Club.

....Vikram Seth passing round his half bottle of Scapa whisky to the crew before reading his poem *The Frog and the Nightingale* outside the Picky Centre. It was 10.30 in the morning.

....Being driven at breakneck speed to Flotta Kirk in the back of a transit van with all our recording gear, after we'd missed the festival boat and taken the passenger ferry instead. We disembarked at the oil terminal with no idea of where we were supposed to be going, and then a voice came from the van parked on the jetty, 'Are you from the BBC?', and we knew everything was going to be fine.

....The passengers on the Hoy ferry all giving our furry microphone boom a friendly pat on the head as they left the boat.

....Jamie MacDougall singing for his supper (it was lunch really) in

Birsay: an aria from Handel's *Samson* in Bertie's sitting room on a Sunday afternoon.

....John Lill explaining to the Stromness Town Hall audience that he couldn't play an encore, as everyone would miss the bus to Kirkwall.

....And of course, the home baking.

The list could go on and on. Thanks to Glenys and her team for all the help they give us, and for always making the St Magnus Festival one of the highlights of our year.

Matt Parkin production controller (classical music)
BBC Radio Scotland (in conversation)

One of the things that makes the St Magnus Festival unusual is the sheer range of events in different types of venues. Since 1997, we have been covering the festival regularly, recording events all over Orkney. In 2000 we went to Hoy and Flotta, and in 2001 we went to Birsay for the Nash Ensemble duo. We also recorded excerpts from *Cinderella*, the Johnsmas Foy and some of the Traditional Music Project. Occasionally the broadcasts are live, but most of the events go out as a week of 'highlights' programmes a few weeks later.

We do have problems sometimes with inclement weather. The thunderstorm during the Thomas Zehetmair and Ruth Killius concert in 2001 affected us quite badly [see *soloists and celebrities*] and we were lucky that it wasn't live; at least with a recording you have some chance to recover. The worst thing was that it was the last day of the festival, so everything was basically finished, including all the presentation links, and we had plotted exactly what was going in each hour and a half's worth of programme. If we had lost any of the three pieces we wanted, we would have been short of twenty minutes of programme, and the links that had been recorded would have been redundant. Linda Ormiston, who presented the programme, had actually left Orkney and was long since on the plane when the concert took place.

Despite the problems, however, we do enjoy our jobs. We love the music and that's why we do it. Coming to the festival there are always real highlights - Natalie Clein and John Lill were two very good concerts, and then there was David Steele (see p.204) crying over Peter Maxwell Davies's *Farewell to Stromness* at the Traditional Music Project in 2000!

There is a good mix of professionalism and informality at the concerts; there's no stuffiness in Orkney about art or music. And the schedule of the festival is very well planned so that the audience can go to just about everything, although it doesn't allow for overlapping of rehearsals so we do need to double up sometimes to cover concerts.

The audiences work very hard and I think we get fewer interruptions in Orkney when we are recording than we do in some places. And the

Some of the BBC Scotland crew;
Linda Ormiston (presenter),
Rhona Morrison (broadcast assistant),
David Steele (production coordinator),
David McGuinness (producer).

atmosphere is great - the way people appreciate the music and the musicians - and the sense of all being involved together. We recorded the Festival Chorus in 2001 along with a children's choir, and were told that one per cent of Orkney's population was singing in the performance. When you think how many more people come to hear the concert, it is just amazing; it all adds to the sense of local ownership and involvement in the festival that visitors always notice.

David Steele   production coordinator, BBC Radio Scotland (in conversation)

In 1987 the BBC were recording a festival concert at the Phoenix cinema. The Friday before the concert I was working in a studio in Glasgow and our manager said, 'I need you to go to Orkney. Now'. I said, 'I'll think about it. OK, I've thought about it - I'll go!' So off I went. There was a pops concert on at the Phoenix with the BBC SSO, and they were short of crew at the last minute. And I was up again later doing *Mr Anderson's Fine Tunes*. We recorded Salsa Celtica - a ten-piece band - from the Radio Orkney studio, which is about the size of a shoe box and built for two people. That was good fun.

I'm often up for the Folk Festival too, and what I admire about the people in Orkney - it doesn't matter whether you like folk music or classical music - is that everybody gets involved and pitches in, and everybody gets something out of it, which you very rarely see in other communities.

For the musicians, the hours they spend wandering about in Orkney are really enjoyable and therapeutic. There's a real benefit to being able to be in one place for a while; it engenders those moments of reflection and soliloquy that are available in a place like this.

As far as the recording is concerned, we've had more than our fair share of technical problems with the equipment we take up with us. In 2001, for instance, we had problems with three out of the five recorders we had. If that happens on day one, it makes the rest of the week a bit of a strain. And the sound effects have to be there too. We literally go out of our way to find sounds that convey the Highlands - and you'd think that would be easy in Orkney, but it's not. It's such a quiet place, and you might have lapping water that is miles away but you can still hear it; or a main road that is nowhere near where we are recording but we pick up the traffic noises. We have one or two places we always go for the wild life, to see what's popped in. The seals at Birsay were very interested in what we were doing; they were very close - no more than twenty feet away. They looked as if they were saying - 'Go away, mad people, where are your houses?'!

Iain Ashman

Birsay

Orkney Photographic

the Festival Club

Usually the final item on each day's programme, the Festival Club is a place to work off the adrenalin built up after a long day's intense culture. It is a meeting place; a dancing, drinking and talking place, where players, audience members - and anybody else who feels the need - can let their hair down. It offers a different, less formal kind of festival music, and can attract people who might otherwise steer clear of festival events.

As a place for music, there is no summing it up. There have been local bands, groups from the visiting orchestras or ensembles and folk and pop bands from all over the UK and beyond. There have been bands from the Orkney schools - and there have even been Peter Maxwell Davies premieres.

One of the club's important functions is as the venue for the farewell speeches; the thanks to all those who have given so much to the festival, and the announcement of the next year's programme - eagerly awaited by regular festival-goers.

"Those with any energy left can repair to the Festival Club for further entertainment and a little refreshment with which to knit together the experiences of the day, and exchange anecdotes."
Michael Tumelty
The Glasgow Herald, June 26, 1991

Jim Park, Debbie Scott and Willie Johnson, 1986.

There were good Festival Clubs in the Kirkwall Town Hall, but they became so popular it was feared that the floor might cave in. When Grand Union were here, everyone was going mad! Normal conversation is impossible at the club, but now in Matchmakers they try to provide somewhere quiet for people who want to have a chat in a convivial atmosphere. It's a lovely place to meet the musicians.
Maureen Gray
former festival board member
(in conversation)

Grand Union, 1988.

previous page: **Zuba, Festival Club, 2001.**

Ian Farquhar Festival Club manager (in conversation)

Helping to run the Festival Club means being on the smallest festival committee - just George Rendall and myself! George is in charge and I suppose I am officially the club manager, but I feel that it basically runs itself. I became involved originally because I work as a DJ in Matchmakers (Albert Hotel), and when the club moved there from the Kirkwall Town Hall, I was needed to help rig up the systems. (Philip Anderson does all the sound for the bands. He does a very good job; in fact, he has the patience of a saint, which is sometimes needed!) From that, I became more involved generally in the festival, and George felt that I should be on the committee. (It can be a dangerous business! I helped to put the sound system together for the trapeze act, The Flying Dudes, when they were in the Picky Centre in 2001, and broke my thumb while we were unloading stuff from the van. I went to hospital, had it x-rayed and strapped up, and I was back working within three quarters of an hour. There was nobody else to take over!) I used to attend the club when it was in the Town Hall. It wasn't such a suitable venue, but there was a good atmosphere - despite the fact that people had to queue up for their drinks, which was a little bit regimental.

George decides on the bands that will come; he works through an agency and they send him tapes of possible acts for the club. We've had some really good bands, but I would say that the club has been a bit quieter over the last few years than it has been in the past. At one time it became a very big part of the festival, and there were lots of children involved - the Orkney Schools' Swing Band played several times, and the club was really busy then.

When Orkney bands are playing, we get a lot more people in who wouldn't necessarily go to other festival events. Three Peace Sweet, for instance, are always an attraction [see p.211]. One year it was all local bands, and it was like a mini folk festival. It changes from one year to the next, and seems to take on a different function, depending on everything else that is going on at the festival. In the past, the club was just seen as a venue for people to relax at the end of the day and chat about the events. Now its role seems to be more a continuation of events, although there are always people who would prefer it to be quieter - who would rather talk than dance to the bands. There is a room at Matchmakers where people can go to talk, if that is what they prefer.

We have advertised the club as a separate item, to get the public in. On the Saturday night particularly, we try to get a band that will suit the night club crowd as well as the festival-goers. It can get very busy, but the festival musicians seem to blend in fine. The more well-known they are, the more they seem to want to be one of the crowd. One year, there was a three day wake for a local man. The people who came to the funeral on the Friday adopted the club, and it was packed out. It was quite an event! But you do need that to a certain extent, and the club has always been open to the public.

The travel arrangements haven't always gone smoothly! One band hired a minibus because they wanted to sight-see in the morning before they left on the *Ola*. They took back the minibus in Kirkwall and we drove through to Stromness, arriving in good time with about an hour to spare. I was just saying goodbye, when they suddenly realised that all their tickets, everything, had been left in the bus. So we tore back through and had to break into the minibus, because it was a Sunday, the hire place was shut, and the band had locked the vehicle and posted the keys through the door. (Fortunately, I know the people at the hire company, so I went back the next day and explained what had happened!) Another time, Charlie McKerron from Big Sky nearly didn't make it to Orkney. He had been delayed and the band, understandably, wouldn't play without him. There was a bit of a panic until I found George and he gave the authorisation to send Tommy Sinclair down in his private plane to pick him up [see p.209].

It's hard to say what will happen to the club in the future; it all depends on what folk want from it. It is more important to some people than others and it's certainly grown from the days when it was just an entertainment at the end of the day. I've really enjoyed it all, and I will certainly keep going - at least until I'm too old to carry loudspeakers and amplifiers!

Dawn Flett manager, the Albert Hotel (in conversation)

The Albert has been the home of the Festival Club for quite a number of years now and it's an important place for everyone to chill out at the end of the day. I'm always there, working - and we do have to keep an eye on who is coming in the door. You can't have anyone rolling in really drunk. But it's good to encourage those who maybe didn't manage to get to the day's events because they were at work or the tickets were sold out. At least it's a chance for them to hear something of the festival.

You do see the same faces year in, year out - both locals and visitors. Local people work so hard for the festival and you can see that some of them are stressed out by the end of the day. We don't always get to know the names of the visitors, but I remember them from what they drink. (One regular reporter is a Guinness and a gin and tonic, and there's a couple who come to the hotel every year - they are a Raven and a Dark Island - both Orkney beers!)

Some of the visitors can be a bit of a handful. They are not just your run-of-the-mill guests. The time scale is so tight at festival time, and somebody always needs something. But for the most part they are very relaxed and down to earth, and we do our best at the hotel to make sure they are all fed and watered in between concerts and performances. The festival is a very busy time for us! It is a great boost at that time of the year.

I would love to go to everything, but there just isn't time. The festival is such a good thing for Orkney - how many places this size have a national

At the club you discover that most artists are just people. They seem to love the informality of it. To be honest, the club doesn't really know what it is - it just rumbles on, which seems to work most of the time, although it is impossible to please everybody; some people want to dance, others would like to talk, while another lot might want a string quartet.

It's a very loosely organised thing which might not work if it were too planned out - and it has on occasion been wonderful.

George Rendall
festival chairman
(in conversation)

Ronnie Scott, 1992.

Gunnie Moberg

orchestra coming to its doorstep? And the club has had some brilliant acts over the years; Zuba, in 2001, were amazing. There were so many different nationalities pulled together in the group and they were just excellent. It would be good if the club could get more local people in; some may not realise that it is open to everyone, and there is such a variety of acts on offer.

Norman Rushbrook festival lighting manager (in conversation)

I don't think there's any other festival that I'm aware of where people can go to the club and meet the folk who have actually performed that night. If it was in Edinburgh or Newcastle, or wherever, the musicians would be driving back home. At the club, you can end up talking to the first trombone, or it could be the conductor or the soloist. But that's why the musicians enjoy coming to Orkney. Normally they move on to the next place after one concert.

Susie Gilbertson Festival Chorus member

At the Festival Club in 1983, John Steer, double bass with the Scottish Chamber Orchestra, rounded up his colleagues. Space was made in the dining room of the Kirkwall Hotel (clubbing in those days did not yet include dancing to music of the 'hot' or 'cool' variety). They sat. They tuned. They played Mendelssohn's Octet. It was midsummer, almost midnight, and the sea was reflecting a rosy sky. Beautiful.

David Steele production coordinator, BBC Radio Scotland (in conversation)

My connection with the St Magnus Festival goes way back and I've been to Orkney many times, with the BBC and other organisations. As a performer I came up first in 1986 with my band, Manray, as we were the light entertainment over the weekend for the club, which was in the Kirkwall Town Hall in those days. It was fantastic because we had all day to ourselves then played from ten in the evening until one in the morning. It gave us a chance to have a look around. It was the year that André Previn conducted the RPO; it was absolutely packed to the gunwales in the cathedral. If I remember rightly, André Previn watched us play at the club. (Not for very long, though - he wandered off after a while.)

It was a very happy time; we were a large, six-piece band, and we all stayed in a big house in Kirkwall. We never saw our host because he was in *Dr Faustus* that year; he would be up at six o'clock in the morning and then off out officiating or performing.

Hom-Bru, 1995.

Gunnie Moberg

"At the 1983 festival there was a 'coupe surprise' - an impromptu performance of Mendelssohn's Octet by members of the Scottish Chamber Orchestra in the Festival Club, which saw the occasion spill over from the bar of the Kirkwall Hotel into the adjoining dining room.

As the eight young string players, at the end of a tiring evening, flung themselves into Mendelssohn's eternally youthful, spirited music, and as through the window one could see the glow of the midnight sun beyond the harbour, one's cup of bliss was full. At such times, Orkney can seem the best and most essential festival in the world."

Conrad Wilson
The Scotsman, June 24, 1983

David Griffith woodwind instructor, Orkney Schools (in conversation)

One event that I particularly enjoyed was when the Orkney Schools' Swing Band played at the Festival Club in 2000. It was one of my proudest moments. The Stromness Hotel sponsored the event and we had a really good turn-out of youngsters; it was absolutely jam-packed and quite a struggle to get them all on stage. There was such a feeling of the audience being with you and having a good time. After all the stress of performance during the day - the high emotion, expectation and concentration, it all gets relaxed and let out during the Festival Club. And it's not just the young ones that let go, which is really nice to see, and doubly satisfying when you are performing. It really feels like a special occasion, not just a group of excellent musicians performing very well.

The way the kids performed brought tears to the eyes; it was really quite superb. They had a great time, gaining professional experience in a very special atmosphere.

"I trundle to the Festival Club, where Boogalusa, one of ten million ersatz Cajun bands currently on the folk circuit, bring viola players and bassoonists and MacLoveys on to the dance floor in their Travoltaesque droves."
Tom Morton
The Scotsman, June, 1994

Charlie McKerron Big Sky/Capercaillie

I play fiddle with the bands Big Sky and Capercaillie, and appeared at the St Magnus Festival Club in 2000 for two nights - but only through the extreme efforts of the Orcadians.

On the day of the first concert, I had to travel from San Moreno (Italy) to Bologna to pick up a flight to Heathrow, only making this due to a flight delay. From Heathrow I just made my flight to Edinburgh to pick up the Inverness/Kirkwall flight. Arriving in Edinburgh I felt a sense of relief and achievement, only to hear that the Kirkwall flight was cancelled. As I was in transit I was entitled to a taxi to Inverness which I shared with two other passengers. Driving at a fair speed we struck up a good rapport. During the journey I was in constant contact with George Rendall on the mobile discussing travel alternatives. The possibility of a boat journey from John O'Groats was considered but rejected due to the time involved. The solution came as a result of phoning one Tommy Sinclair (retired farmer and flying enthusiast).

Tommy flew down to Dalcross, Inverness, to pick me up in his home-made two-seater kit aircraft. A fine machine that he knows like the back of his hand. The journey took 40 minutes travelling at 3,000 ft and reaching land speed of 175 miles per hour. It was a fantastic experience and an amazing view of the north of Scotland on a night with great visibility. Tommy landed the aircraft on a grass strip close to the Italian Chapel. After hand-towing his plane into the hangar he offered me a bottle of beer and a cigarette, which I gratefully accepted. Five minutes later we left for Kirkwall and arrived at the Festival Club venue at 10.30pm. On arrival I gave Tommy two CDs and

"Since its early days as a quiet retreat for the cognoscenti, the Festival Club has changed. Club-goers are now numbered in hundreds rather than tens and throughout the six nights of the festival upwards of 2,000 people will pass through the Albert Hotel's doors."
The Orcadian, June 15, 1995

two packets of duty-free cigarettes, which turned out to be his payment for an incredible gesture. All I could say to him was thank you and that I felt privileged. We did the concerts and had brilliant crack in Orkney.
[From a letter to the festival committee, 2000]

Dorothy Rushbrook festival administrator, 1987-2000
(in conversation)

Dorothy Rushbrook's leaving 'do' in the Festival Club, 2000.

On the final night of my last festival as administrator, I was sitting at home on a total low. I knew that I would have to go to the Festival Club, to hear the speeches and so on - and I was usually given a bunch of flowers, so I though I had better put in an appearance. The stage crew were particularly busy that night and Norman had said that they wouldn't be there until half past one. However, when I went in, there was Norman, which I thought was a bit odd. Then I was given this carrier bag (containing a gift) and I had just got back to the table with it - I think I'd just opened the card - when I was called forward again. Max was there, with a huge grin across his face, and the Nø Boys were standing there, too. Somebody was told to give me a seat and the boys burst into song! The tears ran down my face all the way through it - and Alistair Peebles was clicking away with his camera at the side. It was just absolutely unreal. Something made me decide not to wear mascara on that night. Thank God I didn't - it would have been dripping off my chin by the end of it all! It took me weeks, months, to come back down to earth after all that! I've got the original manuscript, and Michael Tumelty even gave me a mention in the national press!

"*In the Festival Club, an unexpected musical coda protracted the festival in the wee small hours, as PMD produced yet another new piece - an extended barbershop quintet delivered by the local Beach Boys, as a brilliantly witty vote of thanks to a retiring festival administrator.*"
(Michael Tumelty, *The Herald*, June, 2000)

Anyway, that was the fourth world premiere in 2000! And of course, I didn't even have a hankie....

The Nø Boys, 2000.
From left to right: Andy Tait, Mark Rendall, Eddie Nicolson, George Rendall, Ian Tait.

George Rendall The Nø Boys (in conversation)

Dorothy Rushbrook's leaving 'do' at the club in 2000 was very special. I took part as one of The Nø Boys, and it was a big year for us. We opened the concert in the cathedral at ten o'clock with the *Hymn to St Magnus*, which was frightening. Imagine five barber shop singers, who meet on a Thursday night to occasionally slip a few bars of music in between cans of beer, suddenly having to take part in a serious artistic event in a packed cathedral! And then Max had written this piece for Dorothy - the words in one day and the music in another - and brought it in from Sanday about ten days before the performance.

It was eighteen pages of full-size manuscript paper! We were utterly terrified, but Max's ability to gauge the music to fit the forces is second to none. He knew we were a bunch of dafties with maybe a wee bit of music amongst us, and yet he pushed us. It was pitched to stretch us to the limit, but not beyond. It took us all our time to learn it, and half the jokes in it we didn't even get! Glenys, Ian McQueen, Judy (Arnold) and Max were all sitting there listening at the dress rehearsal, and they were laughing at bits which were obviously musical jokes, and we were thinking, 'What's funny about that?'. We just enjoyed it. You don't have to understand it to do that! We performed it for Dorothy in the Festival Club, and her face was a picture. She had no idea anything was going to happen.

Andy Cant Three Peace Sweet

I have played at the St Magnus Festival Club with various local bands over the years (The Ola Band, Hullion, Three Peace Sweet) - all traditional music based. I have also enjoyed listening and dancing to some of the visiting bands - indeed when the festival programme comes out, that's the first bit I look at.

It's an interesting and amusing audience to play for. There is the festival goer 'fae sooth' - far too loud (unlike our music!), wearing white jacket and cravat, wending his way through the crowd, holding a glass of white wine for his wife high above his head whilst getting to know his Highland Park better.... There is the slightly self conscious, kids have left home now, should we go to the Festival Club tonight, local festival-goer.... There are the visiting musicians knackered after counting 107 bars rest in a PMD spectacular - who look longingly at the stage full of musicians enjoying themselves. And there are a few survivors from the front bar of the Ola Hotel, who stand and stare in time to the music.... And then there is George Rendall!

That is at the start of the night. By the end of the night if the user-friendly music has hit the spot they are all merged into one.

Amanda Shearman cellist, BBC Scottish Symphony Orchestra (in conversation)

Everything at the festival is well organised, and the fact that it's so international is fantastic. I've met so many people in Orkney who are from all over the country - whether they're playing in a band or groups from London. The big social whirl after the concerts is great too. At the Festival Club you can let your hair down. It's nice to come out for a couple of hours and have a chat and dance to the band. The SSO jazz group played in 2001, and they are fantastic. This is the first time they've got together as a group of individuals, and it just seemed to run so well - it was so good.

We have been treated to some very memorable ad hoc performances. Two of these are unforgettable. It was a real treat to hear members of the SCO play the Mendelssohn Octet in the Kirkwall Hotel as they picked at plates of fish and chips beside them. More recently, the *Grand Oratorio* written by Max for Dorothy Rushbrook on her retirement as festival administrator and performed by the Nø Boys at the Festival Club was a hilarious and a wonderful tribute to her contribution.
Philip Croft and David Lipetz, annual festival visitors

Three Peace Sweet playing during Orkney's day at the Millennium Dome, 2000.

Jerry Boweh, Zuba, 2001.

John Coletta, Humpff Family.

Tommy Smith (far right) at the
Festival Club, 1991.

Jerry Boweh Zuba, Festival Club, 2001 (in conversation)

Orkney is excellent - fantastic; the people, the music, the singing, the history - it's just down to earth. It's a trustworthy place and the people are so nice and open. I couldn't have had a better time there. We went to see the standing stones and Skara Brae village, and the cathedral - it was all just amazing. In fact, I texted some of my friends from Orkney to tell them they had to come and see it for themselves.

We were very privileged to have been part of the St Magnus Festival, and we really appreciated the invitation. It will go down in our book as a place to remember. We had such an excellent time there - we'll definitely go back.

Magnus Linklater former chairman, the Scottish Arts Council

I have a favourite moment, from the decade and more that I have been going to the St Magnus Festival. It came after a concert at the Phoenix cinema, when the Scottish Chamber Orchestra had, as always, given of its best, and had, as always, repaired to the club at the Albert Hotel to quench its collective thirst. In the back bar, a local group of musicians - a couple of fiddlers, a pianist, and a genius of an accordion player - were playing Scottish country music. Two of the cellists from the SCO had brought their instruments with them (cellists are never parted from their cellos, however bulky and inconvenient), and decided to join in. Tentative at first (it's quite hard to move seamlessly from Tchaikovsky to Kate Dalrymple) they gradually got into the mood and the swing, and before we knew where we were, a full-blown jam session was under way. I don't think I have ever heard music of such energy and dash. There was, of course, a competitive edge to it all, and the whole affair was well lubricated by McEwans 80/-, but if that performance had been on the official programme, it would have gone down in the annals of the festival as a five star act.

It ended sometime in the early hours, and we poured out on to the street where the pearl grey of midnight was giving way to an astonishing coral pink. Some members of the orchestra (not the local band, they were far too sensible) decided to make for the Ring of Brodgar and carry on the celebrations. I cannot comment in any salient detail on what happened then. Suffice it to say that had I been then, as I was later to become, chairman of the Scottish Arts Council, I would have had to consider seriously whether our substantial grant to the SCO was being properly deployed. Naked cellists and half-clad horn-players cavorting amongst the ancient remains of Orkney do not fall within our standard guidelines. I hope that I would, nevertheless, have had the sense to recommend a substantial increase. By the end of a memorable night, only the stones were standing.

Pamela Beasant

behind
the scenes

Some funding bodies outside Orkney have had trouble grasping the fact that, apart from the director and administrator, the St Magnus Festival is run by an astonishingly dedicated army of volunteers. The board members and the various sub-committee members are unpaid, as are the members of the technical crew, the front-of-house and box-office team, the hosts, chauffeurs, celebrity 'minders'.....the list goes on. The festival is hard work, while offering undoubted rewards to those who give so much time and imaginative effort to it every year. For one thing, the people involved have become skilled in their festival jobs, to the degree that visitors do not notice the difference between them and professional crews in city venues (although there have been some comments suggesting that the faces greeting visitors at the festival are overwhelmingly friendly and enthusiastic, which is perhaps not always the case elsewhere). Another reward is the sheer achievement of the festival overall. It inspires people to want to be part of it, and despite exhaustion and anxiety, there is exhilaration and pride at the end of the festival week. To call it a well-oiled machine is true, but mechanical; the people who work behind the scenes build the essential infrastructure of the whole event, which, cumulatively, over twenty five years, has reached a remarkable level of professionalism. It is community effort in the best senses of both words. Without it, quite literally, there would be no festival.

Archie Bevan festival vice-president (in conversation)

The festival administration is a complicated animal. In the early days the decisions were taken collectively for everything except some of the musical items; the Foy, the Festival Chorus and the schools events were all decided by the group, for instance. Now, those things are properly allocated; the central direction is excellent, and we have a web of inter-connecting sub-committees, all with responsibilities, who need to know what's going on elsewhere in the festival as well. We have something like three dozen people who are very actively involved - more than that, if you include all the stage people and the technical crew, who are vital.

Ian Rushbrook and his stage crew have tremendous esprit de corps. They take great pride in what they do, and their ability to be hyper-efficient. Bryan Leslie used to be in charge of technical; Bryan was brilliant too, and he had far fewer, smaller, resources than we have now. I can remember the terrible worry about who was going to replace Bryan, but, of course, Ian was already coming up in the ranks, and the transfer was fairly seamless in the end.

Marion Lochhead was the first secretary, for a year, and then Frances Mitchell took over for the next two years. When Frances and Norman [co-founder and first co-artistic director] moved away, Glenys [Hughes] became secretary for two festivals, and then Eleanor [Laird] came in following the fifth - about a year after I became chairman. Eleanor was there for seven years, and she did a great job; she set the standard of unflappability that Dorothy [Rushbrook] came to personify later. Dorothy had great style - and latterly she became an institution!

Administratively, things are just so much more effective now; there's a fairly small board of directors, chaired with rare efficiency and style by George Rendall, to control the whole show, and they have constant communication with the director, Glenys, which seems to work excellently.

Eleanor Laird festival administrator, 1981-1987 (in conversation)

Glenys stopped me in the street one day and said, 'We're looking for a secretary'. 'I can't do that' I said, 'I know nothing about music'. She told me that it wasn't necessary to know about music, but I did not immediately agree. I went to see a really good friend, and he said, 'Eleanor - it'll broaden your mind'. It certainly did that!

I wasn't that interested in the festival to be honest. It hadn't been going for very long, and I took the job assuming that it would just involve going to meetings, but it turned out to be a hell of a lot more than that! (At that point I didn't have a computer, just an old black typewriter.) I became involved in the whole thing; trying to get sponsorship, arranging transport for

Archie Bevan and Judy Arnold.

"It should be stressed that this is a community festival: definitely not for those commercial operators who value market forces above genuine artistic endeavour."
John Warnaby, Musical Opinion, September, 1989

the artists and helping to allocate accommodation, amongst other things. It was a huge job. I was paid a small honorarium, but the money wasn't the point - I really enjoyed it. It is the best job I have ever had and I met so many really lovely people.

Judy Arnold was never off the phone - she was one of the reasons the festival had to buy me an answering machine! But without her drive and stamina, I don't know where the festival would have been. At night, when I came home, I used to switch on the machine and then sit there writing down all the things I had to do.

There was a lot of stress. Usually by the Friday night, the start of the festival, I was just a wreck. And I never did see any of the events properly, because I was rushing from here to there; I always turned up at the beginning, but quite often there was some reason why I had to leave early.

In 1986, a newspaper journalist asked me to organise Max, a boat and four children with violins, as he wanted to take photographs out in the bay. Both of my sons played the violin, as did two of their pals, so I got Max and the four kids, and off they went. It was quite choppy - I remember standing watching them rather anxiously from the pier. It was The King's Singers concert in the evening, and Max was in between venues. I took him back to the house - but all we were having was ham, chips and peas. I was so embarrassed. And there was no room to sit round the table, because my father was staying. Anyway, Max had to sit down with his plate of ham and chips on his knee, but he didn't seem to mind at all - he's such a lovely person. I gave him lots of malt whisky to wash it down!

I still like to be involved, doing front-of-house and putting people up; and I sang in the Festival Chorus many times. I always preferred to be more in the background of things, but there's no doubt that my involvement with the festival gave me much more confidence. I've had lovely cards from various people who have been up, and the nicest present I received was when I resigned. I didn't go to the meeting, because I knew I would be persuaded to stay, so I wrote a letter, and next thing was that Archie appeared with a whole crate of home brew - which was just lovely. (The committee meetings were such nice, hospitable occasions in Archie's house, with lovely home brew and Elizabeth's delicious sandwiches!) Dorothy took over, and I don't think she realised what she was getting into at first. When I started, I was involved at a time when the festival was growing itself - so I grew with it, and then Dorothy grew with it further.

A committee meeting at the Bevans'; GMB, Dick Hughes, Penny Aberdein, 1990.

It was time to stop, and the job has gradually changed anyway. Now they have the office, and communication is much better with computers and emails. At the end of the day, it is amazing how we got things done; it seemed so casual, but I just loved it.

Dorothy Rushbrook and
Elizabeth Bevan, 1993.

Dorothy Rushbrook festival administrator, 1987-2000
(in conversation)

My husband, Norman, and I have been involved with the festival since 1978.
Norman did the lighting for the first of Max's children's pieces, *The Two
Fiddlers* - but he can't read music, so I was up the lighting rig with him,
cueing him. And from the start I've always had folk to stay. In fact, I ended
up helping Marjorie Linklater with the accommodation, although I didn't go
on to the committee until I was appointed administrator in 1987. And the fact
that Norman and I were both involved led to my son, Ian [see p.220], becoming
involved too.

At the very first committee meeting I ever went to, I was daunted
by the level of knowledge Eleanor [Laird] had when she was trotting out all
this information about the festival. I remember speaking to Judy Arnold one
night at the Festival Club, saying - 'What have I done!'. Basically, the job
was to make sure that everybody was in the right place at the right time, and
that the venues and the hotel rooms had been booked. I also had to oversee
the accommodation, although there is a committee who finds local people to
put up the visiting artists. I had the information about when folk were coming
in or out and had to organise transport for them, buses and so on, and cars to
take soloists to Stromness and back again.

Everybody is supposed to have a 'minder' - somebody that looks
after them while they're here - and it's not easy finding people to do this job,
so you ended up doing it yourself - rushing about like a scalded cat. You could
be sitting at the airport, because there's a plane delayed, thinking, 'I should
be taking someone to a concert in Stromness'. And this was all in the days
before mobile phones. In fact, a pair of roller skates would have been useful!

We've had a few transport nightmares! I remember when the singer,
Della Jones, was coming up on a British Airways sponsorship ticket in 1994.
It was the Friday afternoon and I got this message to say that she had been
lobbed off the plane at Heathrow. I got straight into the car and out to the
airport. It transpired that she was on the flight to Aberdeen, but there was no
way she was going to get from there to Kirkwall. I went absolutely berserk!
I told them to take someone else off - or take off a cello that I knew had a seat
to itself on that plane. (Cellists insist that their cello travels in the cabin - it
has to have a seat, and pays full fare.) Eventually they agreed to off-load
somebody and Della was put on the plane. Della was wonderful; she sang
Max's *Stone Litany* which is all about the runes, and she was thrilled to see
Maeshowe.

There were worse travel problems! In 1998, Pekka Kuusisto - the
Finnish violinist - was coming from Helsinki. He was a young guy, about
twenty one, and he had to get up at 5 o'clock in the morning to catch his plane.
He had managed to get up in time but had fallen asleep at the breakfast table.
Luckily his pianist, Raija Kerppo, phoned him and he managed to make it out

to the airport in time. I happened to be in the British Airways office as the plane was approaching, and I saw that the fog had just suddenly rolled in. The pilot was told to go straight to Wick, as there was no point coming any further. So BA phoned the John O'Groats ferry to ask them to hold it, which they agreed to do, and they also organised buses. (BA staff were such a tower of strength to me all through the job.) In the end, an extra run was put on from John O'Groats, and they arrived at the Albert Hotel at half past eleven at night - absolutely frozen, and without Pekka's luggage. The next morning we dashed up to Sclaters to buy him something to wear for the recital. They were able to produce a smart pair of trousers and a nice shirt. But we were panicking because he didn't have tails to wear for the Sunday concert. Fortunately, however, his luggage arrived in time.

Sometimes you would be standing at the airport waiting for these folk to arrive - knees knocking together - glad when the programme had been published in time so you could look at the photographs and have an idea what they looked like. When the singer Sarah Walker arrived, she said to me, 'I've never met a Dorothy before - I know a song all about a Dorothy'. The song ran: 'Dorothy's a problem, she's got an awful thirst, she eats us out of house and home and always gets here first'. It was on one of Sarah Walker's CDs of cabaret songs (she sent it to me later!), and I was terrified she was going to sing it in Stromness on the Sunday. Thankfully, however, she hadn't brought the music!

There were parts of the job that were less exciting than others! Endlessly sticking labels on brochures and stuffing envelopes, for instance. (Now Angela [Henderson] puts it all on databases, which is much better.) From January onwards, the work gradually increased, and when it came to March or April - gallop! By May there was usually a lull as it was all set up, but you never knew what was round the corner. I was on my own really, although I had a lot of back-up from others. Susan Batty, for instance, was in charge of accommodation for a long time and I left most of that to her.

It's true that a great part of the community has nothing to do with the festival, but I think they enjoy the buzz. It's the same when the Folk Festival is on, or the Science Festival. The whole thing was viewed with an awful lot of suspicion to start with - but it has developed so much, and the Orkney audience is now very sophisticated. One time, when the BBC were up recording a modern piece in the cathedral, I was worried in case people started shifting around in their seats. I was sitting quite far back in the cathedral and was very conscious of the fact that I must not wriggle! Our audience sat as good as gold, and the BBC director and the manager were very impressed.

The first time the Royal Philharmonic Orchestra was here in 1986, the manager stayed with us. Some time later we were down in London and went to the Festival Hall, where the RPO was playing. I was sitting in the audience thinking: 'Here I am, sitting in the Festival Hall, watching the RPO. I can name most of them, and I'll be going back to have a dram with them

Gunnie Moberg

Sarah Walker

It takes such a community effort to get the festival going - I think artists appreciate that and we certainly do, too. The amount of help you get is amazing, and nothing is too much trouble.

The traffic control outside the cathedral during concerts is very impressive. I don't know of any other place which does that. It makes it much easier when we are recording.
Matt Parkin
production controller,
BBC Radio Scotland
(in conversation)

afterwards.' Later I was whooshed backstage and the players greeted me like a long-lost friend. It was wonderful. You make all these friends and that has been one of the great rewards of the job.

Angela Henderson festival administrator

My first experience of the festival was in 1999 when I had been in Orkney for just under a year. I went to a concert with the Festival Chorus and was just walking on air afterwards. They were stunning. By the time I got the job of administrator I had been to two festivals, so I knew much more about it and its reputation and jumped at the opportunity to be involved.

The 2001 festival was my first as administrator, and I thoroughly enjoyed myself. There was a constant stream of tasks to see to, but from the time the festival started, I spent very little time in the office. The work was in the concert halls, with the public, the performers, the orchestra managers, and in the street on my mobile phone. I was in the office on one occasion at midnight, trying to find flight information for one of the orchestra members, whose agent had told him the wrong flight time. I then had to go and seek him out in the Festival Club, which on that night was packed to the gills. There were one or two transport headaches, admirably shouldered by Mary O'Keeffe-Burgher who looks after the accommodation and transport arrangements. In general though, everything went smoothly and everyone I met seemed to be enjoying the festival as much as I was.

Everybody had said what a tall order it would be to administrate the festival, and in some ways they were right - Glenys works far more hours than she is paid for. But now I am into the second year of the job and everything makes so much more sense; there are systems set up, databases designed, processes refined and I am looking forward to the next festival with great expectations. It has periodically struck me as a rather odd thing to be working all year round towards something that lasts only 6 days, but that first festival really brought it home to me what a significant and special event it is on a personal level for so many - for the volunteers, the public and, no doubt, for many of the performers. There was a kind of electricity in the air during that week, and people seemed to have a bond with each other that comes from working so hard on something they believe in. The St Magnus Festival is a passion!

Bryan Leslie festival stage manager, 1982-1994
festival board member (in conversation)

The festival is a wonderful opportunity to work to a professional standard as a stage manager - where else would an amateur get a chance like that? When

the performers turn up they assume that you're experienced - and that's what
we became.

My festival involvement really began in 1980. I was working in the
Arts Theatre and with the opera and the Drama Festival, and Glenys asked
me to help out with the stage management of *Cinderella*, and then other shows
that were in the theatre. I had a couple of years of that, and then I was standing
in Stevenson's newspaper shop one day, and George Rendall was behind me.
'You wouldn't fancy stage managing the St Magnus Festival?' he said. 'It's
a big job that,' I said, 'I'd need to think about it.' And that was taken as a yes!
It was a bit of a shock at first because of all these venues I didn't know.
Suddenly I was doing the cathedral, and it is a wonderful building but it has
so many problems from a stage manager's point of view. Although we did it
many times, it is just not suitable for an orchestra - the audience can't see the
players and the players can't even see the conductor sometimes. But it would
be an awful shame not to put an orchestra there. The Picky Centre is so much
better in that respect, because everybody can see everything.

The Phoenix cinema was not a very nice building. One time we had
sold more tickets than there were seats, and we had to scrabble under the stage
amongst all the mice, trying to find more. We screwed in a couple of extra
rows at the front. I remember because I had a brand new pair of jeans on, and
afterwards I had to throw the jeans out because of the amount of chewing
gum stuck to them from the floor. The building was pretty grotty, but once
the audience was seated, and the lights were on, it looked quite nice. The
council did a lot for us with the Phoenix - they put in a fire exit directly
offstage and installed proper power, which was greatly needed. Then, of
course, the place became obsolete.

The first year I did the whole thing on my own. Of course, we didn't
have so many big events then. It was a good way to learn! After that, I started
building up a stage crew. In the early years, Kris Misselbrook helped with a
lot of shows, although he was really more involved with The Fires of London.
Bob Presland came along early on, too. There was a tremendous amount of
shifting rostra back and forth, and we didn't have McAdie and Reeve [a local
removal firm] in those days, which made things harder. One time I had booked
a van to take rostra from the Town Hall to the Phoenix. It never came and I
was getting desperate. Suddenly, this pick-up truck came round the corner. I
stopped it and said, '£10 if you take this stuff to the Phoenix'. 'I'll do it' said
the driver, but just with that the van turned up. If they had been five minutes
later they'd have been too late - and I would have been ten pounds poorer!

It became much easier once we had a stage crew, but then the shows
got bigger as well. One year I decided to get a bike, thinking it would speed
things up. One of the stage crew, David Hunter, had a red book which he used
for writing notes and drawing plans. He started writing down where I had left
my bike, because we kept losing it; I didn't have the chance to use it half the
time, and kept forgetting where it was! We had a lot of laughs on the crew -

Bob Presland, Catherine Batty,
Bryan Leslie, 1994.

it was great fun.

The festival grew and became more organised, and we kept growing with it. In the early years, I would go to the Festival Club just to find out what was happening the next day, and when rehearsals were starting. In fact, I actually asked to get on to the committee eventually because I needed to know what was going on. Now, of course, the management structure is completely different, but I'm still on the board, and enjoy being involved in the planning side of things.

The festival has its own niche now; it's accepted as part of what happens in June in Orkney. At the beginning there was the feeling amongst Orcadians that it was something imposed on Orkney, which was never the case. Now it's international of course, and very professional, although there is still so much being done by volunteers - the festival wouldn't happen without them.

It's lovely to have all these big stars coming to Orkney, and it's amazing the festival can attract folk like that. Judy and Michael Arnold have always been very involved in getting people to come to Orkney. They have done a lot of negotiating and they have so many contacts. Michael Arnold stays in the background, but he was always a driving force, especially in the early years. And they both still do a great deal for the festival. And Glenys has a knack for organising the right things and bringing up the best people. She just makes the festival. Locally too, she picks a school to do something and it always works - it's always the right school. Without her, the festival wouldn't be half what it is. We are really lucky to have her.

I stage managed the festival for thirteen years, and it was a huge amount of fun. I wouldn't have done it otherwise. By February each year you had to start thinking about it, and it was a huge commitment. Working on the operas for the Kirkwall Amateur Operatic Society, for example, was very relaxed and laid back. The festival wasn't like that. It's deadly serious getting some of those shows to work right; you can't afford to slip up, but there's a huge sense of achievement afterwards.

Ian Rushbrook festival stage manager, 1995- (in conversation)

I was on the lighting bridge with my father during *The Two Fiddlers* in 1978, when I was about twelve. My festival involvement started with that, but I gradually moved away from lighting into stage management.

If there are stage managers for individual events, I work with them and coordinate with front-of-house to make sure that everything is arranged. In the venues where there is no stage we create it with the rostra, and in the Picky Centre we build the acoustic wall as well as the stage. Before the festival, we need to know from the orchestras, or the drama productions or whatever, the area they need for the performance. Glenys and Angela take us through

In the early days, not many of the crew were able to help out during the day because they would be at work. I remember one time I was coming home from work, and passing the Town Hall where there was something on. I worked for the Post Office and was still in my uniform, and Bryan came running out and said, 'Bob, come in - I need you now!' I didn't even have time to go home and change - he had to get something up and running there and then.

It can be hard work being part of the stage crew, but I class it as a hobby. I do for fun, for pleasure.

Bob Presland
festival technical crew

the schedule in advance, and we have a meeting with the orchestra manager. Just before the festival we set up the Picky Centre, which is the most complicated venue to do.

The crew has to be a bit hierarchical to be efficient. Technically, I'm in charge, and Bob Presland is my number two. He's great at recruiting people. All I have to say is, 'Bob, I need a crew,' and he goes and gets one. There is a core of regulars and a committee, but there are different people coming in and out each year. The core is very important - it means you can delegate work and they know what is expected of them.

It can be long hours during the festival. If you don't get things done, however, you run into trouble the next day. Sometimes, there are just three or four of us in the day time and it can take a long time. In the Picky Centre especially, you have to walk much further than in other venues. Walking from one end of the hall to the other is 30 metres every time, and it soon builds up. When you're used to sitting in an office day in, day out, your feet do become sore! But the Picky is a good venue. If we only have half an hour for dinner, the crew can stay together and get something to eat from the café. From our point of view, it is certainly the best venue, even though it involves the most work.

We often have to have items sent up by courier - sometimes at the last minute, because there might be something missing in a delivery, or we haven't been told that something was needed. Local firm McAdie and Reeve have been a big help to us. They have vans, and contacts down south - and they even sponsor us. The black shirts that we wear, so that people can identify us quickly, were bought by the firm.

If we want to hear a concert, or a particular piece, we usually hear it in rehearsal in a comfortable seat - or stand at the back out of the way during the concert, to leave the seats free for the audience. At Picky, we have had seating set out for 600 people, but due to demand managed to set up another 100 seats at the last minute, because folk have been queuing at the door for tickets. Picky can cope with that - not like the other venues such as the Arts Theatre or the cathedral.

I would be very against extending the festival - I'd rather have it as a short sharp shock! I couldn't afford the time if it were longer. But it's good fun stage managing the festival, and very satisfying when things go well. I've never thought of doing stage management professionally, although I was once offered a two month contract by one of the visiting dance companies. Doing it for the festival is quite enough. I enjoy being involved but not being too visible. The crew just want to be in the background, out of the way. That suits us fine.

The festival technical crew 1997.
Back: Sandy Dennison, Colin Watson, Magnus Leslie, Tom King, Norman Rushbrook, Bruce Strouts, David Carruthers.
Front: David Hunter, Bob Presland, Ian Rushbrook, Colin Reeve, Phil Astley, Richard Flett, Jonathan Morson.

Orkney Photographic

McAdie and Reeve are excellent - we couldn't ask for a better removal crew. The first year they helped us out, they moved the Steinway piano to the cathedral. They were setting it up and one of them said, 'why won't the leg go in?' - and then realised that the leg couldn't go in, because they had put the pedal in the leg hole! We've never let them forget it!
Bob Presland
festival technical crew

The stage crew at the festival are hugely experienced. When I asked them if they did other events, they told me that they do anything and everything, as well as the whole of the St Magnus Festival. It is often those people, like busy bees behind the scenes, who hang the whole thing together.
Evelyn Glennie
(in conversation)

"It's often been amusing (to old hands of this cherished festival) to observe the aghast faces of first-time visitors as they watch a symphony or chamber orchestra squeeze itself in, around and behind the great monolithic columns of St Magnus Cathedral, or cramming itself on to the tiny stage in the unrivalled sweatshop of the old Phoenix cinema (or the 'hoenix', as it became universally known after its P fell off).

This year...the gloriously resonant acoustic of the great redstone cathedral will continue to ring with the sounds of orchestral and chamber music. But the rather faded old princess that is the Phoenix has been replaced by the brand-new Pickaquoy Centre in Kirkwall."
Michael Tumelty
The Herald, June 16, 1999

Norman Rushbrook festival lighting manager, 1978 - (in conversation)

I have been doing the lighting in the Arts Theatre for many years, which is how I first became involved in the festival. The lighting was quite basic at first, but it has become much more complicated with all the different venues. Before I retired from my job in the council's department of building services in 1996, I used to take a week's holiday at festival time - it couldn't have been done otherwise.

In the cathedral, the lighting is still fairly basic. We can't touch the fabric of the building, but there are static lanterns set in the triforium. It is all shone down from the crossing, and two bays in the nave from which the stage is lit.

Once it comes to the actual nitty gritty, the time for every show is very short. The actors or musicians have been rehearsing for months, and then we come in at the end. In a drama production we help them to get in and out of the venue, but we have nothing really to do with the design of it. If a production goes out to a venue beyond Kirkwall, or to the isles, we will work with whatever is in the community hall there - which is often just basic lighting and a stage. In the Arts Theatre, everything is there already, but at any other venue it has to be hired in.

It hasn't been all that stressful considering the number of events we cover now. We have our ups and downs and the occasional bit of tension, but things have become progressively more professional. People expect the lighting to be good. In fact, if the audience notices the lighting then it has been rubbish! I think everybody behind the scenes is as professional as they can be; in fact, we have been complimented for being in and out of venues quickly and efficiently. The same people enjoy coming back year after year, so we must be doing something right.

Down south, no audience member would accept sitting behind a pillar in the cathedral, but then again, they are paying twice or three times as much for their ticket down there. But the festival could never earn the money to be able to pay all the people behind the scenes - the venues are too small. They couldn't compensate people for the time they spend, but everybody does it because they enjoy it. Nobody would do it otherwise. It is another unique thing about the festival - there is a real community involvement of a very high standard.

The festival has been accused of elitism, which is exactly what some people in Edinburgh say about the Edinburgh Festival; it's like an inverted snobbery. There has been such a mixture of events over the years. Apart from the classical music, there have been acts like Tommy Smith, Ronnie Scott and Runrig, as well as the late night shows that come to the festival - Richard Rodney Bennett and Eleanor Bron, for instance. And the theatre ship, the *Fitzcarraldo*, has been twice - not to mention all the other theatre productions and the children's concerts, and events like the Johnsmas Foy. Those are shows that the purists wouldn't expect to find in a music festival, but it means there is really something for everyone.

Mary O'Keeffe-Burgher   festival accommodation, 1991-
(in conversation)

The festival is a brilliant thing, and I actually feel honoured to be involved. Being voluntary, at the end of the day, if something goes wrong, I can try my best to sort it out, but I'm not answerable to anyone. I have the best of both worlds - involvement without the headache of being responsible.

I became involved with accommodation in 1991. The SCO was coming up and I remember being very nervous. The bus arrived and then they all had to come to the cathedral and I was supposed to introduce them to their hosts. I didn't even know the hosts, never mind the musicians. In the event, the bus opened its doors and two seconds later the orchestra members were gone! The hosts and musicians all knew each other, as they had been coming back for years and years. They knew which houses they were going to, and if the host wasn't there to meet them, the key was under the mat. After that, I stopped worrying!

We couldn't function without that core of people who are willing to be hosts, which is slightly worrying. Some of those stalwarts are getting older and they feel they've done their stint, and not so many people are coming in. Younger people tend to have smaller houses, and less time, so this is increasingly a problem.

Some of the musicians find the idea of staying in a strange house a daunting prospect if it is their first time. Usually, however, they have a great time, because the hosts are really excellent. We only ask that they give bed and breakfast, as the musicians are given a food allowance from the orchestra, but the hosts usually cook and care for them. People are really fantastic.

It is quite a headache organising it all. We meet just after Christmas, and then write to our potential hosts, and to the orchestra managers to find out about the musicians who are coming. We need to know their age-groups, their dietary requirements and details such as whether or not they are smokers, or suffer from allergies of any kind. Sometimes the orchestras themselves decide where they want to go - it really depends on the manager, and the more efficient they are the better.

Once the festival has started, if you are involved in the organisation you get something called 'festival malaise'. There are black rings round your eyes after the first twenty four hours. You are living on adrenalin for a week, and all kinds of things can happen - you are roped into everything. You are alert the whole time and if people ask you to do something, you just do it. It is exhausting, but brilliant.

The festival is really a centre of excellence. The musicians love it,

Some of the people involved in the festival organisation.
Stuart Burgher, Graham Bevan, Mary O'Keeffe-Burgher, Carolyn Bevan, Paul Turner, Elizabeth Rendall, George Rendall, Lydia Campbell, Angus Campbell, Pam Beasant, Penny Aberdein, Elizabeth Bevan, Duncan Webster.

Archie Bevan

Glenys Hughes

Standing: John Gray, Sheila Cameron, Pat Presland, Bob Presland, Elizabeth Bevan, Denise Thomson, Archie Bevan, Magnus Ritch.
Seated: Vivia Leslie, Maureen Gray, Dorothy Rushbrook, Peter Maxwell Davies.
Kneeling: Drew Thomson, Norman Rushbrook, Bob Moar, Christina Sargent.

too - chatting to people in the streets and going to the club to unwind. (In 2001, London Brass decided to follow in Billy Connelly's footsteps and run naked round the Ring of Brodgar!) It is amazing to me that I have ended up working with professionals through singing with the Festival Chorus and the Mayfield Singers. I don't have an extensive musical background, and yet the opportunity is there to work with fantastic people such as Martyn Brabbins, and Espen Selvik from Norway (who worked with the Mayfield Singers). When Martyn Brabbins conducted the chorus in 2001, he knew the next note and when to turn the page without looking at the score. They are not all like that.

I do worry about the future sometimes. It takes years to get to know the way things work in Orkney, and it would be very difficult for somebody to come in to the set up if they didn't know the Orkney side of things. Glenys's job is a nightmare in itself, and she is only paid part-time. She beavers away finding all the funding, and works very hard with the chorus too. People think the festival is so established, but it could go, just like that. It takes someone like Glenys to keep it all afloat. And, in the end, people come because they want to come. If they didn't want to, they wouldn't - which is one of the great things about it.

Carolyn Bevan   Stromness coordinator, festival board member (in conversation)

When Archie and Elizabeth [Bevan] decided they were going to take more of a back seat in the festival, they asked me if I would help out, which is how I became the Stromness coordinator. It saves them a lot of hassle, although they still come to everything and meet the folk. Archie will introduce players at concerts when I ask him to - I would hate to do that. He is so good at it.

Basically, the job involves meeting people when they come through to Stromness and making sure everything is ready for the venues, seating, transport, front-of-house, etc. Truly a product of community involvement. The Flower Club arranges the flowers for the concerts, so that has to be organised as well. I have a list on the computer, and every year I print it out and start ticking things off when they are done. There is always something that slips your mind, so it is best to have it all written down. Glenys keeps in touch, and tells me the needs of the performers. In 2001, there was a panic when I discovered that Natalie Clein's accompanist, Julius Drake, needed a page turner. At the last moment, Jean Leonard came to the rescue, so it all turned out well.

My 'right hand man' in Stromness is Anne Heddle. She is really good. If you ask her to do something, you know it will be done. She orders the flowers and prepares the drinks and snacks for the performers, which is usually something simple like a cup of tea and a roll; they don't often ask for very much. One year we had to move the flowers because the recitalist was allergic to them, but we have never had anyone who has been difficult or demanding. They have all been very nice people.

I would like to see more Orcadians going to the concerts. People will go if they have members of the family involved, but you don't see so many local faces at the celebrity recital, for instance. With all those visitors, the festival brings an awful lot to the county and to local businesses.

I enjoy being on the festival board as it really gives you an insight into what will be happening, which is exciting. It takes some of the pressure off Glenys and George having the board there - it gives them a back up. (There are only two board members from Stromness at the moment, but it's good to have some Stromness input.)

There is great local support for the festival. We all want it to work and we work hard, because we don't want to let anybody down. And if you really want something to work, it will. Volunteers turn up every year to do front-of-house or whatever, even though they can't go to the events. They are really committed. That's what keeps it going.

Lydia Campbell   festival box office manager, 2001-

I became involved in the festival in the early eighties helping with front-of-house - selling programmes, taking tickets etc - and I have been involved ever since and had lots of fun meeting all the people. My twins, Logan and Catriona, took part in the Glaitness School production of *David and the Giant Philistine*, written by their music teacher, Douglas Watt. This is another exciting aspect of it, seeing young people performing and being part of a much larger festival.

When I took over the box office, it was certainly a new challenge with lots of hard work, but it was worth it when everything came together and finally we were ready for the festival. Some of the duties have involved setting up new booking systems, with the help of Angela [Henderson]; getting all the patron bookings processed and sent out within the deadline, followed by the non-patron bookings. There are also meetings with the tourist office, festival office and all the other people involved to make sure everything is running smoothly. At the events, you have to ensure that tickets, floats and programmes have all arrived. I have the support of a lot of willing helpers, and without them I would not have been able to do so much.

In the early days of the festival, the audiences were mostly incomers, but over the years this has changed, and I would say that it is now fifty per cent local, fifty per cent visitors. There is greater participation by local groups and school children, and, with the festival going out to the islands, this has made it more accessible to a wider audience.

Local people now accept the festival and look forward to it as an annual event on the calendar. As an arts festival, it has put Orkney on the map, and there is always a great buzz in the community during festival time.

Glaitness Primary School pupils, *David and the Giant Philistine*, 1985.

This was especially true in 2001, when we were afraid that the foot and mouth epidemic would keep people away, and visitors said that Orkney seemed to be very vibrant compared to other parts of the country.

Roderick McLeod festival box office manager, 1992-1999

At the Greetin' Meeting [the meeting held to discuss the festival after the event] in 1991, I spoke out about what I saw as the unfairness of the system of distributing tickets. It appeared to me that those who sent in their orders by post got a rough deal compared with those who were able to visit the Kirkwall tourist office in person. I put forward a sensible proposal for an improved system. I should have known better! The committee accepted and invited me to take on the role of box office manager.

For the next seven years I took responsibility for all mail order ticket sales, and liaised with the tourist office for personal sales. The job took nearly all my spare time from April to June each year, including many very late nights. I developed various ingenious computer programs to help me in the task and was ably assisted by, in particular, my daughter, Olivia, and my wife, Emma.

For the most part, things went very smoothly and it gave me a great sense of satisfaction to see every seat in the old Phoenix cinema occupied and to know that most of the tickets had passed through my hands. But it was not always thus. I recall my first year at the Phoenix. I turned up early for an orchestral concert which was sold out. Almost immediately someone came to me and said that they could not find seat A3. A quick check revealed that I had been working from an out of date seating plan. Tickets had been printed and sold for 14 seats which did not exist!

Another problem involved lost tickets. On one occasion a party from England arrived in Orkney, having left their tickets in their car at Scrabster. All was not lost. I had a written record of seats allocated for all mail order sales. I was able to supply them with a letter to take to each performance to allow them to sit in their own seats. They were very impressed.

Not everyone has been happy. Someone complains about seating in the cathedral every year. The prospectus now contains a reminder that whilst it is a wonderful building the cathedral is not a modern concert hall and that many seats provide no view of the performers.

Despite the inevitable complaints, many echoing my original concerns about the fairness of the allocation system, I enjoyed the job immensely. Through it I have met so many interesting people. One person alone would have made all the tedious work and late nights worthwhile. Marie Karioti started making an annual visit from Athens in her late seventies, and eight years later she is still coming. She loves Orkney and its festival with boundless enthusiasm. She walks in from her regular bed and breakfast near the Picky

Centre whatever the weather. When I offered her a lift once she explained that it was far too hot in Athens at midsummer and that she loved the wind and the rain!

Vivia Leslie   festival host, former Foy organiser

For Orcadians, a real bonus of the festival is being able to take part. If we want to sing, play, dance or help behind the scenes - there is always something we can do. I have sung in choirs, written reviews for the local paper, produced the Johnsmas Foy and hosted artists.

I enjoy writing reviews of festival poetry readings and plays for *The Orcadian*. It's difficult to find time to write in the week amidst work, family, the string of concerts and the social whirl. For a fleeting moment I rub shoulders with real critics and live life in proxy. I remember a local production of *A Midsummer Night's Dream*. It was excellent but the fairies were too fat and the lullaby they sang to the fairy queen was more akin to pop rock. I composed laboured euphemisms, but a reviewer for one of the national papers said bluntly: 'Orkney fairies eat porridge and ape Madonna,' and their flimsy tops looked like 'squashed Danish pastries'.

Since we moved into Kirkwall, we keep two musicians every year. Playing host to the musicians makes the festival really special for us. They're practising scales and suddenly our three children have got their instruments out and the place sounds like a conservatoire. The place is buzzing and bulging with people and excitement. I love it.

David and Helen Judson   festival hosts

'As you live near the hall, would you mind offering somewhere for the artists to change?' This proved to be the thin end of a very large wedge! Not that we minded, for we enjoyed looking after the artists, and it all helped to save expense. Entertainment at home was not a cost for the festival to meet. The main problem was that we wanted to go to the concerts as well. This meant that musicians might find a note on the table from their absent hosts; or arriving home late we could not be sure whether the visitors had arrived and were in their beds. We also learnt to try and anticipate their foibles. At times strong nerves were necessary as a performer would still be (to us - very) slowly dressing and drinking coffee five minutes before being due to appear across the road in the Stromness Town Hall. Interval refreshments, as requested, showed wide variations. None was alcoholic! Some musicians had to lie down before a concert, could only eat afterwards, became silent and needed to be alone. Others ate heartily, had no nerves and were talkative. Often, there was a post-performance 'hype' with no prospect of sleep, let alone going to bed!

Stromness Town Hall

The Stromness Town Hall had an antiquated oil heating system with an ancient voracious boiler. Four-inch pipes circled round the skirting boards and a water tank in the roof topped it up. This caused various problems. It took time to learn that heating should be kept on all day; otherwise the auditorium was still cold. A journey had to be made, climbing up to the back of the pews, to tie up the ball cock of the filler tank. If this were not done, during a pregnant silence in the music the gurgling would start. Other odd water noises usually were drowned by the music!

Hospitality is fun. It has involved paddling in the sea at midnight, on the longest day of the year, with two young pianists when an unexpected large wave soaked us all. They left footsteps in the sand inside Skara Brae, for we could not control their enthusiasm. [See David Horne, *soloists and celebrities.*]

There was one family group (recently from Russia) delayed by the weather. They were to be met (because we were at a concert) on the quay by a friend. When we came home there was not a sound and the food provided had not been touched. We decided not to explore in case we wakened them, but equally they might not have made it. Next morning at breakfast a small boy with a black patch over his eye looked round the door and announced that he was a pirate; we knew that they had arrived!

We also had to attend to illness, injuries, and provide missing pieces of clothing, buttons and studs. One large man had forgotten his cummerbund. We managed to borrow one - red silk. It turned out to be a Christmas present, still in its packing and cellophane! Our donor watched from his seat in the audience as this pristine object was showered by saliva as the brass instrument was constantly emptied and shaken. I think we paid for the dry cleaning!

At times it was a strain to fit in our own concert-going with the needs of our visitors. We decided early on that we wanted to share in the festival as well as support it. We were surrounded by an enormous amount of goodwill. Seldom were we confronted as we were once, after our visitors had gone, with coffee stains all over a mattress. (We did sometimes have more heads in the beds than we started with!)

In Orkney you do not change the beds until you are sure that your guests have left the island. The weather can play tricks. We also insisted on having entries to our visitors' book because we needed an address to send those treasures that were so often left behind. Sometimes it was possible to rush down to the boat to return left luggage - on one occasion we managed to throw it on to the boat as it was leaving!

We are still receiving letters and cards years later. Music for us provided not only the listening, but the nurturing - and extended cultural experience. We look back on it with pleasure and gratitude. We watched the festival grow and develop and suck into its listening audience islanders, some of whom had no experience before this of the delights of classical music. It is a tribute to all those who took part, in whatever capacity, that it is now a vintage product (not stored in a barrel). Long may it continue!

Neil Price former festival board member
director, The Mayfield Singers

I first met Max on the old *St Ola*, going south, in December 1979. We were almost the only two passengers on the boat. I introduced myself and we had a long chat. He was travelling down to London by boat and train for an awards ceremony the next day and I offered him a lift down to Lairg. On the way, it transpired that he had the original and only manuscript of *The Lighthouse* sitting in his bag on the back seat of the car. I nearly swerved off the road!

There is absolutely no doubt in my mind that the St Magnus Festival is one of the best things that has happened to Orkney in the 20th century. From an artistic and cultural point of view, it is still regarded locally as a sideline event - what the 'arty-farties' get up to in late June! Sadly cultural inverted snobbery is alive and kicking in Orkney, like it is anywhere else. But certainly, no one objects. There is not a bed to be had in the whole county. The tills flash away in all the shops. The Orkney Islands Council invest a substantial sum in the festival each year and surely they can enjoy no better return on any investment they make.

The festival became known in its early days as an event specialising in new music. This was a misunderstanding based on the involvement of Max, a living and working composer. Neither has it been purely a showcase for his own music. He provided the impetus for its beginning and the invaluable status of figurehead, which attracted the initial outside publicity. Reasonable comparisons were made with Benjamin Britten and the Aldeburgh Festival. But, by the mid eighties, Max was happy to let it go and have its own life, whereas Britten maintained control over Aldeburgh to his dying day. The St Magnus Festival evolved into its unique mix of all arts of all periods, performed or executed by young and old, professional and amateur, local and international or a combination of any of these. I have always felt that its happiest quality is that the visiting artists regard it as a very special treat, almost as a holiday, especially those who are returning after a first taste.

Why is this? Firstly, there can be few other events where the audience is so close to the performers. Everyone seems to be mixed up together. One minute you are listening to a fabulous performance of Rachmaninov's Second Piano Concerto given by John Lill, the next you are propped up at the bar of the Festival Club having a pint with him. Then there is the fact that the festival relies almost entirely on voluntary help and volunteers tend to be pretty informal people. The visitors love this informality and it seems to be a particular attraction of our festival.

I remember transporting Truls Mørk and his £2m cello owned by a Norwegian bank, together with Jean-Yves Thibaudet, over to Stromness on a Sunday morning. Truls suddenly realising that he had left the music for one of his pieces that afternoon in a hotel room in northern Finland spiced the whole thing up. Quick phone calls resulted in the music being faxed to my

Jean-Yves Thibaudet, PMD,
Truls Mørk, 1995.

Gunnie Moberg

office. This also involved the piano part, as Jean-Yves didn't have it with him either. A seemingly flawless performance ensued, but what no audience member or critic realised was that the fax machine had chopped off the bottom of the last page, and Jean-Yves had to busk the left hand for the last few bars - a real pro! He recovered afterwards in the sunshine on the Judsons' lawn, pulling up his bright red socks, eating bere bannocks and home-made cheese and studying the next score on his international itinerary.

Page-turning and music-stand-providing are other activities which hosts/chauffeurs/minders inevitably get caught up in. I really felt I earned my LRAM at page-turning when I turned for Kevin Bowyer in his performance of Max's Organ Sonata. Not only did the pages fly by at terrifying speed, but Kevin also asked me to pull stops at the same time, in the absence of any general pistons on the cathedral organ. Luck was smiling on me that day.

Being a very small part of the St Magnus Festival has been an important part of my life in Orkney. In the depths of winter, there have been times when festival politics have seemingly become a little sordid and I have wondered why I was getting so involved. For instance, it has always been a sadness to me that the festival would not come behind my idea in any way of trying to save the wonderful East Church as an auditorium for Orkney. Instead, we have been consigned to the unsuitable and acoustically questionable surroundings of the Pickaquoy Centre, and the East Church is about to be converted into the inevitable council offices. But at the end of the day, it's the festival that counts and it always turns out to be tremendously enjoyable year after year. We are all so lucky in Orkney to have this internationally renowned event on our doorstep.

Howie Firth   senior producer, BBC Radio Orkney, 1977-87

The first festival in June 1977 came at a good time for Radio Orkney. We had only been on the air for little more than a month, and were looking all the time for material that could demonstrate what local radio could achieve. With a new festival, there were opportunities for previews including some lovely illustrated descriptions by Richard Ingham, who taught music at Stromness Academy; there was a taped interview with Max that I later blended with a script by George Mackay Brown to make the Radio Scotland documentary, 'The Valley by the Sea'; there were up-to-date reports including a superb account by Archie [Bevan] of the premiere of *The Martyrdom of St Magnus*; there was a whole range of fascinating participants who came in to enrich the programme; and whenever there was something we wanted to find, Jack Ridgway would help.

I don't think that I have ever met someone as good at organising as Jack. He was methodical, committed, and had almost boundless energy. Looking back on all that he achieved, in addition to highly efficient management

Howie Firth

of British Airways in Kirkwall and then building up a very successful travel business, I don't know how he managed to find the time, and I wish he were here now to see the outcome of so many projects that he encouraged into fruition.

I knew Norman Mitchell, of course, from having spent a year teaching at Kirkwall Grammar School, where he could always brighten up a day with a story, and his own work in music in Orkney fairly sparkled with developments such as 'Music in St Magnus', and vision and enjoyment and flair. And of course, I knew Archie Bevan as someone with so many talents who was always willing to put them at the disposal of others. He was an inspiring teacher of English, a gifted writer and speaker. If Orkney was to break new ground in creating a world-class festival, the combination of Archie and Norman and Jack was the ideal. Thank you to them, and to so many other people who have worked on the festival over all these years, for bringing so much pleasure and so many opportunities to us all.

Steve King   principal viola, Scottish Chamber Orchestra (in conversation)

The St Magnus is a very highly regarded and respected festival in Europe. Max is the inspiration behind it all, but the way everybody has grouped together to make it happen, is brilliant. The community involvement that has evolved is amazing, as is the calibre of the visiting artists. Judy and Michael Arnold helped all that to happen, especially in the first few years - their contribution must not be underestimated.

Glenys, of course, is wonderful. Down in London, she could have her pick of jobs, and I think she has had one or two offers. She's such an unassuming person - and so clever, and brave in some of the ideas that come out. She has an attitude and a sort of unforced power that make you want to come and work here, collectively as a team, to make all these things happen. If it wasn't for Glenys, none of it would ever happen; it is wonderful to see that somebody can initiate some great ideas, and then let other people get on with it. It's fantastic - it gives you so much empowerment to go and do your own thing in your own way. I have worked all round Scotland and a lot of England, but certainly some of my best work has been up here, because of the people that work with me.

It has been lovely getting to know people like Archie and Elizabeth Bevan - they are both such characters in the cultural heritage of Orkney - and then meeting George Mackay Brown through them. And there are lots of other people, such as the technical crew at the festival. They are amazing - they don't think about it - they just do it. It is fantastic that people give so much, voluntarily, to make this thing happen. I never take this generosity of people's time for granted. These things make it so special; you remember them - some of the big events you don't.

From a community point of view, one of the most important things Radio Orkney can do for the festival is advance publicity; we preview things that are coming up, and speak to kids who are working on productions. But we try not to swamp the programme with the festival, and to a certain extent we have taken the lazy option by wheeling in Michael Tumelty [of *The Herald*] to review the events of the day before. He's very good value, and he always turns it on, even after a late night at the Festival Club (though sometimes it is just as well it's not television!). He is also prepared to say it as he sees it, which doesn't always go down too well! It is a great pity, however, that we have no evening programmes in June - it would be nice to cover the festival in something other than in a pseudo current affairs programme.

Summer in Orkney without the festival would be unthinkable. Along with the social work department, it's probably the thing for which Orkney is best known! Even for people who don't go, there's a great atmosphere about the place over the festival week.
John Fergusson
senior producer,
BBC Radio Orkney
(in conversation)

The festival certainly brings out the best in Orkney. There is so much going on, and a lovely atmosphere abounds. I have always enjoyed the big orchestral concerts in the cathedral, and, for a time, my wife and I used to host a lunchtime reception after the Festival Service, until we found that it gave people too little time to dash through to Stromness for the celebrity recital.

Local opinion was a bit suspicious at first; many Orcadians fought shy of voicing their opinions about certain events and tended to keep their thoughts to themselves. Over the years, however, confidence grew. (I remember one local critic, who had not enjoyed a piece of modern music, likening it to the German planes overhead in wartime!) This increase in confidence is certainly one of the results of the festival, and the event is now very much appreciated by most Orcadians.

The combination of our wonderful cathedral, world-class artists performing and rubbing shoulders with local people, and the summer light, is a heady cocktail. It is also a fine showcase for the best of local talent.

Bill Spence
Norwegian consul in Orkney

Gunnie Moberg photographer and artist

One of the reasons I first came to Orkney was George Mackay Brown. A mutual friend, Kulgin Duval, introduced me to George's writing and we had some correspondence before a friend suggested we went up to Orkney. I jumped at the idea.

We sailed from Leith and arrived in Kirkwall on a cold March day in 1975. It rained, hailed and the wind was blowing at sixty miles per hour the whole three days we were there, but still, you could feel the place was special.

Going to visit George one night, standing in Mayburn Court looking up, we found his house in darkness. A handsome man stopped in the street. 'Are you looking for George? I think I can help you.' This was Archie Bevan and we were taken to Hopedale and welcomed by his wife, Elizabeth. There, by a roaring fire, a mug of home brew in his hand, sat George. It was to be the start of a long friendship with the Bevans and George. I think I must have decided there and then to move to Orkney, but with a husband and four young boys, I had to make doubly sure.

I came back the same autumn with one of my boys, Paul, to do an exhibition in the Kirkwall library, not of photographs, but of batik wall hangings with Celtic and Norse designs. We stayed at Hopedale, and during that fortnight met so many interesting people, both there and at my exhibition; people who were going to make an impact on our lives later. Gerry and Nora Meyer, John Broom, Ian and Jean MacInnes, Arnie and Ola Tait, Andy and Glenys Alsop and Ernest Marwick. No wonder I thought the place interesting!

Archie and Elizabeth's hospitality seemed boundless; it was a wonder there weren't a dozen tramps staying there too!

I also met Max that autumn. I read in my diary: 'September 3, 1975. Maxwell Davies here [Hopedale], with his parents. Max has light.' Reading this now it made me smile. I sound so young but it is a good description of Max all the same. I see we also made two visits to Bunertoon.

I moved up with my family the following year; March 1, 1976. That spring, I met Judy Arnold, Max's manager; the beginning of another long friendship. Although we only meet properly once a year, our Sunday mornings of the festival are set aside for catching up on news and the progress of my garden; a time we cherish together.

Judy has also been a tremendous help with photographing the famous. In the early days, I felt very awkward 'butting in' for pictures. She had the most wonderful way of introducing me. 'This is Gunnie Moberg'; a long pause would follow (as if to say, 'you must know who she is'). 'She would like to take *your* picture,' (in other words - 'you should feel honoured'). Well, that is how it sounded to me and it always boosted my confidence. She also provided me with schedules for rehearsals and told me where I should turn up for a good picture.

I can still remember the excitement of the early days of the festival. What a start it was, with *The Martyrdom of St Magnus*, in the saint's own cathedral. The Fires of London would be up every year and their rehearsals were always very lively! Mary Thomas, for instance, who gave many memorably-staged performances.... one could go on and on.

At Hopedale everyone seemed to congregate; the first festival club! If not staying there, certainly eating, drinking, resting; the telephone in constant use and interviews taking place. After performances, discussions would go on well into the night and there was often a walk out to Breckness as the sun was coming up. Everybody seemed to be on a 'high' all the time.

Apart from enjoying Hopedale, I would go to all the rehearsals photographing, then to the performances - in between cooking for guests and family. Developing films and printing was done at night, ready for the news media the next day (a trip to the airport with urgent pictures was often on the cards). We lived down the road from Archie and Elizabeth, and the 'spill-overs' would come to our garden, for a glass of wine or two; George would often come along, and there were many merry afternoons.

And to end it all, there were Max's parties at Bunertoon (how many sandwiches were made at Hopedale?!). Everyone was in a holiday mood as Stevie's boat took us across to Hoy. At Moaness pier, Jack Rendall was waiting with his car to ferry people across to Rackwick. Many of us would walk through the beautiful valley, then climb up to Max's to be stuffed with food and drink - and the sun always shone! It was a merry bunch who got off the boat in Stromness, some eight hours later, and many farewells were said, 'until next year'.

As the festival grew bigger and bigger I found I couldn't keep up and decided to stop recording events on its 20th anniversary. I still do the odd picture, and always the festival poet for my own collection of writers; one day an interesting exhibition, I hope.

Many picture editors have said to me: 'You must travel a lot to have such a big library of famous artists.' 'No,' I say, 'they all come to me!'

Gunnie Moberg

Crossing to Hoy; Dick Hughes, Neil Price, Gunnie Moberg, George Mackay Brown.

Ron Ferguson author and journalist,
                minister of St Magnus Cathedral, 1991-2001

One of the best bits about being minister of St Magnus Cathedral was involvement with the festival. As someone who, in a previous incarnation, wrote a lot about the Edinburgh International Festival, I found, when I came to Kirkwall, the St Magnus Festival to be a quite astonishing event to be mounted by such a comparatively small island community.

The scale of the St Magnus Festival is much smaller than its Edinburgh counterpart, but the quality is extraordinary. Where it is better than its bigger rival is in its accessibility, especially for children and young people.

Performances in the cathedral were very special, and at night this glorious building played host to visiting ensembles of various sizes. Sight lines of the performers were restricted, so one's thoughts, accompanied by the music, could wander the lofty heights of history and be transported back through time. I will always remember the sandstone pillars with their worn bases, chipped away by the hooves of horses when the worshipping masses brought their livestock into the cathedral, away from the elements battering at the walls.
Trevor Green
former manager, BBC SSO,
BBC Philharmonic

Ron Ferguson

Orkney children are privileged. They live in a community with a rich cultural life. They don't call it culture or maybe even know it's culture - it's simply in the air they breathe.

The St Magnus Festival rightly emphasises the fact that culture is not some separate thing out there, disjoined from the experience of ordinary people. At least it shouldn't be. The arts are about the celebration of life itself, about inspiration, about new ways of seeing. For a child to perform - sometimes with his or her own parents - alongside actors or musicians of the highest calibre, in venues ranging from the street to the cathedral, is a wondrous thing.

Yes, to grow up in a place that de-mystifies the arts for you - and in which it is normal to participate in such ventures with adults from along the street - is to grow up blessed. To have your formative years in such a confidence-building culture, which is artistic without being 'arty', is to grow up rich, even when you are poor.

To grow up in a community with a nearly 900-year-old cathedral in the midst is another privilege. St Magnus Cathedral is a kind of festival itself. It is a building of immense richness, as well as profound simplicity. Its soaring, red sandstone pillars, its stained glass windows, its high arches all speak of artistry of the highest calibre. Its nave, once the chairs have been taken out, transforms itself into a magical viking theatrical space.

The spire of the cathedral points, symbolically, upwards to God. At the heart of the cathedral is its worship, its praise, its preaching, its silence, the soaring sounds of the organ, the red-robed choir singing hymns from many eras, all contribute to the building's special atmosphere. The very stones, having witnessed tears of sorrow and joy over many generations, are impregnated with prayer.

It has always seemed right to me that St Magnus Cathedral should be at the spiritual heart of the St Magnus Festival. There are Christians who believe that churches should be private enclaves entirely separate from the rest of the world - indeed, that they should be refuges from the dangerous snares of drama and music - but I have never agreed with that view.

The mediaeval cathedrals were centres of artistic excellence. Some of the world's greatest music was first heard in churches - indeed, much of it was commissioned by churches. The Mystery Plays - precursors of modern drama - were often performed in the naves and aisles of cathedrals.

Religion has much in common with the arts. Like them, it provides another way of seeing - sometimes a subversive way - especially at a time when the material is deemed to be everything. That's why the Festival Service in the cathedral was so important to me. The very setting spoke of artistic richness. As minister of the cathedral, my desire was to bring together music (both by the cathedral organ and choir and festival musicians), poetry, prayer, silence and preaching in an offering of worship.

I hope that the cathedral will continue to play a central role in the St Magnus Festival. For me, it has been a great privilege.

rounding up, looking ahead

Peter Maxwell Davies's original vision for the festival has stayed true through all its subsequent developments. The essential factor - that it should be locally based and locally run, involving as many members of the community as possible - has, if anything, become even more firmly rooted at the heart of the festival ethos. There are also some promising developments, such as the 'festival on tour' project, which takes the festival to the more remote Orkney communities. In 2001, the success of the BBC SSO visits to some of the smaller Orkney islands set a precedent which, it is hoped, will continue.

Inevitably, there are worries about the future, and at the twenty five year mark there is little complacency about the huge, kaleidoscopic achievement of the festival. But, on the evidence of the contributions to this book, there is a strong faith that the festival will retain its power and its impact, and will find ways of developing and growing from its firm roots. There are no endings to the story, and no lines to be drawn; there is passion and commitment and a strong will to continue. The sheer audacity and vision of that original idea has been not only vindicated, but through the talent, imagination and monumental effort of so many people, it has surpassed itself. An excellent basis from which to celebrate the first twenty five years, and move forward.

Bevan

Glenys Hughes, 2001.

"Possibly more than any other, this Orkney Festival has promoted two things. It has galvanised youth activity, sharpening standards to such a degree that this now enjoys an unusual but deserved reputation nationally. It has also brought to the islands a quality of international performers who might not otherwise have been lured there.

The St Magnus Festival's value is not in doubt. The original vision, a creative marriage of local excellence and imported professionalism, has already long ago been achieved. The future deserves to be bright."

Roderic Dunnett
The Leisure Manager
August, 1990

Glenys Hughes festival director (in conversation)

Anyone taking on the job of director of the St Magnus Festival has to be something of an artistic 'jack-of-all-trades'. A larger festival would have different people responsible for the various areas such as marketing, publicity, fund-raising and education work. But with St Magnus, the director is responsible for all those areas as well as for the planning of the artistic programme.

Festivals are often part of a kind of festival circuit - you see the same soloists, ensembles, orchestras and programmes cropping up again and again at many of the summer arts festivals. It's very important for us to avoid being part of that circuit; after all, if we were putting on events and programmes that people could get to in the central belt of Scotland or in London, why should they come all the way to Orkney? So our concert programmes are, for the most part, put together specially for the festival and are often the result of lengthy discussion and negotiation with performers and agents.

In some ways the festival is very fragile; we rely on a whole army of committed volunteers. Funding is a constant worry and it's a large part of the job all through the winter - making applications to the various funding bodies, sponsors and trusts. And finding major sponsorship is particularly difficult for us. National companies are naturally more attracted towards events which reach huge audiences and offer glitzy venues and opportunities for corporate entertaining. Trusts and foundations are often sympathetic, but they usually make just one-off donations, as they like to spread their funds around. So funding is always something of a gamble - although every year we somehow manage to make ends meet.

To save a substantial amount of money we would have to stop bringing an orchestra, which would be a major loss to the programme and would certainly diminish the festival - it's the one time during the year when local audiences can hear a professional orchestra.

In terms of audience development, taking the festival out beyond Kirkwall and Stromness - especially to the outer isles - is a priority. And thanks to lottery funding we've been able to do that for the past two years. The 'festival on tour' is an initiative which - having raised expectations and created enthusiasm - we must aim to develop over the coming years.

Our other priority, in terms of audience development, should, I feel, be to make a real effort to engage those in their late teens and early twenties - the age group which many arts organisations find it difficult to reach. Last year, in 2001, some events, such as the Flying Dudes and the theatre company Walk the Plank did appeal to this age group. And at the Festival Club, we always aim for a variety of bands that will have a wide appeal.

We do need to think about the musical focus of future festival programmes. Max has now stopped writing music theatre and orchestral works - and I don't think we'll see any more children's pieces; he really does seem to want to concentrate on writing chamber music for the foreseeable future.

But Max's presence will continue to be of great importance to the festival; he is such a charismatic figure that having him there is wonderful. And hopefully the occasional world premiere will still come our way. In the wider musical world the 'Orkney Festival' is still very much associated with his name, which is the way it should be.

I hope and believe that we've retained Max's vision of a festival which would bring first-rate professional performances to Orkney; which would showcase the wealth of talent and creativity that exist here; which would be brave in its championing of new work and which would always seek to have an impact on the lives of an ever-widening circle of people. And of course, Max's own music, and particularly his collaboration with George Mackay Brown, has been an ongoing thread which has made the festival absolutely unique.

Martyn Brabbins and members of the
BBC SSO, St Magnus Cathedral, 2001.

Martyn Brabbins conductor, BBC SSO, BBC Philharmonic

One of my great wishes for the future is to establish a conducting seminar as part of the St Magnus Festival. The precedent set by Max and his composition school on Hoy is the inspiration for this, as yet, fledgling project. I would hope to attract a handful of talented individuals to Orkney for about 10 days - enough time to get to know one another, but not so long as to encourage problems with loose flying egos! A period of intensive individual work using two pianos as a stand-in orchestra prior to the festival would be followed by sessions with the visiting orchestra and ensemble, giving unrivalled opportunity for gifted yet inexperienced conductors. The best lessons a conductor ever has are those given by living, breathing performing groups. I envisage here also a role for local musicians. The Festival Chorus could be involved as a training group for students to work with, and I would give instruction time to aspiring or practising Orcadian conductors.

There is a strong desire, I know, for the Orkney Conductors' Seminar to become more than just an idea in my head, and I believe that this could provide something truly unforgettable for participants.

I hope to see the proposed conductors' school taking off. Martyn Brabbins is excellent - he just gets better and better - and he loves Orkney. If Martyn is involved, I have every faith that it will be wonderful.
Peter Maxwell Davies
(in conversation)

Orkney Photographic

Michael Tumelty   music critic, *The Herald*

If the history of any great festival is charted by landmarks and crossroads in its development, then the St Magnus Festival has reached one, and may be approaching the other.

From its small, modest, and fairly purist beginnings, 25 years ago, it has become a near-unique model of large-scale integration between artist, community and public. There is no other artistic institution or organisation in Scotland, with the possible exception of the Scottish Chamber Orchestra, that has more developed in its short history than the St Magnus Festival.

Almost 20 years ago, when I began covering the festival for *The Glasgow Herald*, as it was then called, the St Magnus Festival was an important event in a music journalist's calendar. Why? Because of the intense focus on new music, particularly that generated by the festival's founder, Peter Maxwell Davies, and played by his specialist group, The Fires of London.

The fact that, in the course of one's residency in Orkney, the visitor was sometimes aware of an atmosphere of suspicion, resentment, and occasional hostility - which annually boiled over on to the letters pages of *The Orcadian* - was something that just had to be tolerated in the course of the job. There were times, when, with the exception of what appeared to be diehard resident supporters of the event, it seemed that the St Magnus Festival was viewed as an imposition by outsiders on a community that was little interested.

Any casual visitor to the festival from those days, returning now after a long absence, would find the St Magnus Festival almost unrecognisable. Sure, the basic concert structure might be similar - a resident orchestra, the traditional celebrity recital in Stromness, chamber groups giving lunchtime recitals. But in every other respect, deep down into its roots, the festival has become a radically different animal, so firmly embedded in the community that, visiting artists apart - who once seemed to be the essence of the festival - the six-day event now appears to flourish from within the soul of the community itself.

In the past, the involvement of island residents, whether schoolchildren, adult players, or amateur singers, was always a worthy, creditable, and laudable method of attempting to integrate the community and the festival. St Magnus has now developed to a point where not only is it unthinkable that these local forces might not be involved, but their actual involvement in the occasion - whether featured in their own right, or integrated within a professional ensemble - is seamless, natural, and authoritative.

To attempt to chart exactly how this process of development has taken place would be a formidable undertaking. It goes way beyond the fact that, for example, consistently over the festival's history, its founder, Sir Peter Maxwell Davies, has provided a rich catalogue of repertoire, from simple songs to complex operas, for children to perform. It goes way beyond the sustained dedication of individuals such as present director Glenys Hughes and her late husband Dick, without whose input the festival would not have its character and stature. And it goes way beyond the multiplying contributions over the years to the infrastructure and administration of the festival by an increasingly large and wide-ranging army of residents from the community. The level of development and sophistication achieved by the festival, in other words, is infinitely more than the sum of its parts.

Look at the evidence in support of this thesis thrown up by the 25th festival. The sheer statistics alone tell a story. A concert given by the London Brass Ensemble featured 40 brass players associated with Kirkwall Town Band, and 42 young brass players from local schools. The St Magnus Festival Chorus fielded 98 singers (all local) to perform with the BBC Scottish Symphony Orchestra, as well as a 55-strong children's choir.

On top of this were the large numbers involved in the community project, *Between the Terminals*, and in the production of Maxwell Davies's children's opera, *Cinderella* - some of these the offspring of parents who themselves had performed in the opera's debut decades before. And then there is the relatively new Orkney Traditional Music Project, which could become an important element in the festival, and which features up to 200 young fiddlers and accordionists who are actively engaged in the rediscovery and propagation of nothing less than the musical equivalent of an oral history tradition.

Then, behind the scenes, there is another Orkney army, and a large one, without which St Magnus, at its current scale, could not happen: the huge community forces involved in every facet of backroom activities - administration, backstage, scenery, lighting, the front of house operation, ticketing, accounting, transport, and the widescale accommodation of artists and musicians from visiting orchestras. The enterprise is phenomenal, and - crucially - it is all voluntary.

But if you don't want to run the numbers, then assess the artistic levels of achievement, and the staggering technical development and expertise of the myriad performers, which has been evolving steadily over the decades and through generations. The standards now attained by the St Magnus Festival Chorus were unthinkable just a decade ago. The cohesion of local and professional brass players in the London Brass concert was seamless. The assured and authoritative delivery of the children, onstage and in the pit, in the performances of the opera *Cinderella*, was as convincing as you would find in any professionally produced version of the work.

Crucial to the understanding of this is the realisation that all of the performers - children and adults - are now operating within a context: there is a tradition; it is the norm. And from that derives the technical and personal authority, self-confidence, and conviction on which any artistic performance, at any level, absolutely depends. And the same applies to the audiences that flock to these events in droves. St Magnus attracts the biggest audiences for any contemporary music performance in Scotland. It fills its venues to capacity, even one as big as the excellent, 700-seat Pickaquoy Centre, as fast as central belt halls empty at the sight of a living composer and the mere 'threat' of new music. It doesn't mean that the Orkney audiences lap it up, or love it. But they're not scared of it. It is the habit. It is the norm. One of the supreme characteristics of the St Magnus music policy over the decades has been its quiet consistency. And that has paid dividends.

Put it all together, the continuum of education, coaching, music, performers, and audiences at St Magnus, and the conclusion is always the same. The St Magnus Festival is a living, working model for any philosophy of how a culture should be intrinsic to society, and not some luxury item grafted on for the handful who can either afford it or are naturally predisposed towards it.

So is that it, then? Is that the end of the story? Well, no it isn't. The landmarks of achievement are well mapped out. But a crossroads looms where decisions taken will profoundly affect the future and the status of the St Magnus Festival. It cannot be taken for granted that the festival will continue to perpetuate itself. Its founder and original artistic director, Sir Peter Maxwell Davies, some years ago handed over the reins of direction to Glenys Hughes, and the festival continued to thrive and develop.

It is an uncomfortable and possibly insensitive question to raise, but what will happen after Glenys Hughes? Is there an assistant or associate director in training? Is there someone in the wings, or coming through the community, who will take on the mantle? And remember that Glenys Hughes is not merely an administrator, not merely a director. She is a musician and teacher. And she is also a long-time and respected member of the community. These roles have been critical to her success in taking over the directorship of the festival. What should be the qualification of a successor? The prospect of a professional administrator being brought in from the outside is, I believe, certainly unimaginable, and possibly unworkable.

And then there is a major issue concerning the actual musical heart of the festival. Through all of its development, the music of Maxwell Davies has been at its core. Within the last two festivals there have been premiere performances of his seventh symphony and his music theatre piece, *Mr Emmet Takes a Walk*, among other works.

But Max has moved on, musically. There will be no more symphonies, no more operas, no more music theatre works, and no more large-scale choral works. The string quartet and chamber music project on which he will embark may well make appearances in Orkney. But what will happen to the festival orchestral programme, in particular the new music core of the programme, without which St Magnus could become a shadow of itself, and without which it would not attract the attention it does from outside the islands? Now that the festival knows there will be no more big Max pieces, it would be a mistake merely to go on churning out performances of extant works. There has to be new blood. Is this being discussed?

In a worst-case scenario, if the St Magnus music programme became routinely mainstream and anodyne, then it would merely replicate what a hundred other organisations are doing throughout the year, elsewhere, and public interest from south of the islands would probably evaporate. Rapidly.

I'm ahead of myself. None of this has happened. Yet. But some of it is around the next corner. The festival needs to ask questions of itself. And it needs to find answers to those questions. There is a very large, hard working community on the festival doorstep with a massive, long-term investment in this event. They will want to hear the answers. All of us who are pundits, observers, and commentators will no doubt have our own views and suggestions. We usually do!

And - to end on a strictly personal note - it's probably fair to keep my own opinions under wraps at the moment, until we see what clues, if any, about its future direction emerge from the administration as the festival embarks on its second quarter century. Suffice to say that the St Magnus Festival has become far too important an entity on Scotland's cultural landscape for it not to be subjected to rigorous scrutiny.

George Rendall festival chairman (in conversation)

About three or four years into the festival, without quite knowing how, I found myself sitting in Hopedale, in Archie and Elizabeth Bevan's front room, wondering what this thing I had got involved in was all about. From there I was pretty quickly roped in as publicity person, then treasurer for a while - and then Archie decided that he wanted to stand down as chairman, and asked me to give it a go.

I'll always remember that first night. The meeting was at Archie and Elizabeth's - as they all were at that time: the home brew meetings with a soupçon of Grouse as well, served on a silver tray. I had never chaired a meeting before, and was painfully aware of Archie's presence, the Godfather of the festival, and of the feeling that I was rattling about in his shoes.

Personally, I am not involved in the festival out of any particular love of the arts, and certainly not out of a love of organising things. It is hard

Alistair Peebles

George Rendall

to pin down the reason, but it is to do with wanting to give something back to the community in which you have been nurtured; it's close to a sense of duty, or even honour, which is due to the place and the event. The festival is not just a serious arts event. It is an occasion - like the County Show is an occasion. It is there; part of the landscape.

When you become involved, the fragility at the heart of it is immediately evident. One of the big problems we have had in trying to establish a modicum of paid time and a permanent office base is that the funding bodies cannot understand that we really are run by volunteers - a fact which is a lot to do with the Orkney community. People become involved because it is a big event. Many take holidays specially. Those who live in less cohesive communities find it all very puzzling: why should people give up so much time and put in so much effort for no financial reward?

But the future is a real concern; in fact it is a burning issue. We are a dedicated bunch of people who have given their all and who have gained a lot of experience along the way, which makes it difficult for others to step in and become closely involved. It seems to the observer that it is all being taken care of, and anyway few people are looking for extra commitments. No one on the committee is getting younger, though, and if mortality doesn't set in, tiredness might!

One approach would be to step back, cut the festival loose and see what happens. But it is difficult to do this; the feeling is that, because it is important, you don't want to let anyone down. It would be nice to see some sort of succession in place.

Max, of course, as the spiritual leader of the festival and the attraction for those 'across the water', is irreplaceable. And equally irreplaceable, in my view, is Glenys. She is a rare mixture of artistic integrity and imagination, tempered with a sense of realism - a 'class act' in every way. Orkney is a long way from the central belt, let alone London, and someone of Glenys's calibre could be running any of the larger festivals. If she decided to move on, the salary for the part-time director's job would not easily attract anybody to Orkney - or not the calibre of person that is needed.

And Glenys's long experience of Orkney is vital - she knows people and understands who does what and how to go about things. Orkney still operates on a 'kent face' system, which is very effective, but takes time to learn. Somebody coming in would inevitably find this very difficult.

Local knowledge is essential because the festival has to remain a community event; it could not happen without the local support. We're not easy on ourselves, either. Any 'quaintness' which the visitor might detect is certainly neither self-conscious nor intentional. We aim to be as professional as possible - for there to be no observable difference between an event at St Magnus and an event at the Queen's Hall!

The reality is, of course, that the place isn't built for big arts events. We just don't have the venues. But we try to make everything run smoothly and professionally. People will always be able to pick holes, but concert-goers of a forgiving nature often relish those little things that happen because the venues aren't entirely suitable or because of the 'part-timeness' of the organisation. Many festival-goers, I believe, see it as something a bit special. Those from 'the sooth', for instance, who are used to looking at artists though opera-glasses, with no hope of ever getting closer than that, are suddenly sitting within two or three feet of them in the Stromness Town Hall - so there are compensations.

I'm not an apologist or a completely blinkered fan of everything that happens at the festival - and I do feel slightly jaundiced about the bureaucratic hoops that we now have to jump through to make it all happen. I shudder to think how many sheets of paper I have written, just to fill somebody's in-tray (at least it seems so in the wee small hours). The festival has had to learn, along with everybody else, that this pain is an inevitable part of the business. You can't survive if you can't find the funding, which is part of the reason we have had to find paid time. In the old days the bureaucracy was less demanding - now there's irony in the fact that you have to find funding in order to pay somebody to find funding.

Whatever happens to the festival in the future, it is certain that it has broadened the horizons of everybody involved - audiences, organisers and participants alike. We Orcadians have made many friends across the water - and we have got rid of the diffidence which at one time would have rendered us incapable of believing that things on such a scale could happen here.

It's always a struggle, but I've yet to attend a St Magnus Festival which didn't seem in the end to have been worth it. I hope that continues to be the experience of those who carry the thing down through the years.

And some last words...

Hugh Macdonald director, BBC Scottish Symphony Orchestra

Are the words 'community' and 'international' a contradiction in terms when applied to an arts festival? Not in Orkney. We love it for its refusal to underestimate its audience, for its admirable ambition to bring the world's finest to a small community. We love it because it reminds us in the most fundamental way how *music* can connect with *people*, and how absolutely essential that is to all of our lives.

Yvonne and Jeremy Clarke regular festival visitors

Over the years we have made many friends. We have fallen in love with beautiful, civilised islands. We have found the two best malt whiskies and excellent Orkney beers. We have been introduced to superb writers, designers, silversmiths and craftspeople. All this in addition to the festival itself; every year we wonder how the next festival can possibly equal, let alone surpass, the previous one. Every year it does. Thank you St Magnus Festival.

Ian McQueen   composer

Peter Maxwell Davies's thirty year love affair with Orkney has proved no case of deracination or 'getting away from it all'. Rather, he has found a true spiritual home among these islands washed by the northern seas and lit with an exquisite light of opaline pearl. In this festival, with its mission to entertain, delight and startle people who live round about and come from far and wide, he has motivated a wonderful mix of local talent from international figures like George Mackay Brown to young schoolboys and girls to give the much-maligned term 'community arts' its true meaning.

The St Magnus Festival seems to me to transport us out of the consumerist culture we're supposed to inhabit into something richer, more vital and more questioning of what we are as human beings through the compassionate and provocative power of the arts at their best.

Alan Plater   playwright

A few years ago we went to the old Phoenix cinema for the premiere of Max's latest symphony. The audience listened, not only with its ears, but with its emotions and, at the risk of sounding arty-farty, its life experience. We later heard the symphony at the Albert Hall Proms and the response, though enthusiastic, was somehow passionless. It reminded me of watching a Yorkshire cricket match as a VIP guest where I sat on the pavilion balcony with a group of businessmen, paying only casual attention to the game, pausing occasionally to say, 'Well played' or 'Good shot' before resuming our conversations.

The St Magnus Festival reminds us that Art isn't a side show but is central to our lives: that, in the long run, the people who matter are the singers of songs and the tellers of tales: and the only questions that matter a damn remain, Where do we come from? How did we get here? What shall we do next? And, as Philip Larkin said, what survives of us is love.

George Mackay Brown

Saint Magnus, keep for us a jar of light
Beyond sun and star.

PMD and GMB, 1992.

St
Magnus
Festival

chronology

1977-2001

note: The chronology is based on the yearly programmes of festival events. Known programme changes or additions are indicated in the text, and every effort has been made to present an accurate picture of the festival over the first twenty five years.

1977

Saturday, 18 June

9pm St Magnus Cathedral
Opera:
The Martyrdom of St Magnus
composer/conductor:
Peter Maxwell Davies
libretto: George Mackay Brown

Murray Melvin: director
Judy Arnold: producer
Sue Plummer: designer
Mark Pritchard: lighting
Kris Misselbrook: stage manager

WORLD PREMIERE

cast:
Neil Mackie: tenor
Michael Rippon: baritone 1
Brian Rayner-Cook: baritone 2
Ian Comboy: bass
Mary Thomas: mezzo soprano

instrumentalists:
Sebastian Bell: flutes
David Campbell: clarinets
John Butterworth: horn
John Wallace: trumpet 1
Norman Archibald: trumpet 2
Gregory Knowles: percussion
Stephen Pruslin: keyboards
Timothy Walker: guitar
Beverley Davison: viola
Lesley Shrigley-Jones: cello

Sunday, 19 June

10.45am St Magnus Cathedral
Festival Service
conducted by Rev William Cant,
minister of St Magnus Cathedral

2pm St Magnus Cathedral
Recital

Norman Mitchell: organ
JS Bach: Fantasia and Fugue in G
minor; Prelude and Fugue in G major

Arthur Robertson: violin
W Marshall:
Air, Chapel Keithack; Slow Strathspey,
Mrs Major Stewart of Java
Glen: March, Captain Campbell
Traditional: Sons of Glencoe
Lowe: Reel, Waverley Bell
ASR: Air, Shorelands;
Hornpipe, Adrian Stuart

David Currie: highland bagpipes
MacCrimmon: Piobaireachd,
Lament for Mary MacLeod

Arthur Robertson: violin
Traditional: Air, Lord Lovat's Lament
Scott Skinner: Slow Strathspey,
The Shakkins of Pocky;
Air, Cradle Song;

Air, The Bonnie Lass of Bon Accord
Duncan: Reel, The Perth Assembly
ASR: Air, Daisybank; Jig, Robbie's
Wedding

8pm St Magnus Cathedral
Concert: The Fires of London

Peter Maxwell Davies: director
Mary Thomas: soprano
Sebastian Bell: flutes
David Campbell: clarinets
Beverley Davison: violin/viola
Lesley Shrigley-Jones: cello
Stephen Pruslin: piano/harpsichord
Gregory Knowles: percussion
Timothy Walker: guitar

William Kinloch/Maxwell Davies:
Kinloche his Fantassie
Maxwell Davies:
Dark Angels
(to texts by George Mackay Brown)
Peter Maxwell Davies:
Renaissance Scottish Dances
Dunstable/Maxwell Davies:
Veni Sancte Spiritus
Maxwell Davies:
Veni Creator Spiritus
Maxwell Davies: Ave Maris Stella

Monday, 20 June

11am St Magnus Cathedral
Recital: The Fires of London

Beverley Davison: violin
Sebastian Bell: flute
Stephen Pruslin: piano/harpsichord
Lesley Shrigley-Jones: cello

Bach: Sonata No1 in G minor for
unaccompanied violin
Debussy: Syrinx, for solo flute
Messiaen: Theme and Variations for
violin and piano
Bach: Sonata in E major for flute
and continuo

8pm St Magnus Cathedral
Concert
The St Magnus Cathedral Singers,
Kirkwall Grammar School Choir and
Chamber Orchestra

director: Norman Mitchell
Richard Hughes: organ

St Magnus Cathedral Singers
12th century: Hymn to St Magnus
Two motets from Music of Scotland:
1500 - 1700
Robert Johnson: Deus misereatur
nostri (Psalm 67)
David Peebles: Quam multi, Domine
(Psalm 3)

Kirkwall Grammar School Choir
and Chamber Orchestra
Maxwell Davies:
O Magnum Mysterium
Bryan Kelly: Tenebrae Nocturnes
Max Reger:
Benedictus, Op 59, No 9
Benjamin Britten:
Rejoice in the Lamb

10pm Kirkwall Town Hall
Orkney Strathspey
and Reel Society

Tuesday, 21 June

2pm St Magnus Cathedral
Recital: The Fires of London

Lesley Shrigley-Jones: cello
David Campbell: clarinet
Stephen Pruslin: piano

Bach: Suite No 3 in C major for
unaccompanied cello
Berg: Four Pieces for clarinet and
piano, Op 5
Stravinsky: Three Pieces for solo
clarinet
Bach: Partita No 4 in D major

8pm St Magnus Cathedral
Recital: The Edinburgh Quartet
Miles Baster: violin
Peter Markham: violin
Michael Beeston: viola
Christopher Gough: cello

Mozart: String Quartet in D minor,
K421
Thomas Wilson: String Quartet No3
Beethoven: String Quartet in F major,
Op 59 No1

10pm The Lynnfield Hotel
Kenny Ritch

Other events

Street shows:
Cheskoo Raree-Show:
Mark Furneaux

The Kirkwall Hotel
Festival Club

Exhibitions

Orkney County Library
Stanley Cursiter

Kirkwall Community Centre
Local Artists

1978

Friday 16 June

7.30pm Orkney Arts Theatre, Kirkwall
Opera: The Two Fiddlers
by Peter Maxwell Davies
performed by the pupils
of Kirkwall Grammar School

producer: Jack Ridgway
musical director: Norman Mitchell
design: Gary Gibson
lighting: Norman Rushbrook,
Nancy Rendall, Mark Ridgway
costumes: Lena Fotheringhame
props: Sandy Firth

cast:
Storm Kolson: Ian Tait
Gavin: Peter Marshall
The Troll King: Andrew Green
The Troll Queen: Ishbel Stanger
chorus of trolls and guests:
Inga Brown: Debbie Chase,
Ingrid Dick: Hilary Donaldson,
Alice Flett, Janice Forsyth,
Ingrid Gibson, Susan Gorn,
Susan Hourston, Jackie Leslie,
Carol Linklater, Susan Lochhead,
Elizabeth Matches, Kim Milligan,
June Mitchell, Mark Rendall,
Denise Rosie, Carol Shearer,
Helen Smith, Christine Taylor,
Donna Taylor, Sara Walker.

orchestra:
1st violins: Susan Johnston (leader),
Joy Taylor,
2nd violins: Catherine Fereday,
Karen Moodie
viola: Louis Newell
cello: David Leslie
bass: Douglas Shearer
flute: Heather Moodie,
Elspeth Bain
oboe: Graham Walker
clarinets: Rosemary Leonard,
Pari Mehrabi, Jane Versteeg
bassoon: Allan Buchan
horn: Maureen Cursiter
trumpets: Alan Rendall,
Neil Robertson
trombone: Helen Thomson
percussion: Joy Anderson,
Susan Cross, Shelagh Fleming,
Florence Gullion, Lesley Herdman,
Sandra Knight, Sharon Ridgway,
Marion Sclater
piano: Richard Hughes
bagpiper: James Stout

10pm Orkney Arts Theatre, Kirkwall
The Northern Echo
Russell Hunter - one man show

Saturday 17 June

Lunchtime Festival Club
A Johnsmas Foy
Presented by Marjorie Linklater
Poems by Edwin Muir, Robert Rendall
and George Mackay Brown, with
Orkney prose by Eric Linklater.

2.30pm St Magnus Cathedral
The Fires of London
Scandinavian Recital

orchestra:
Stephen Pruslin: piano
Timothy Walker: guitar
David Campbell: clarinet
Beverley Davison: violin
Lesley Shrigley-Jones: cello

Grieg: Seven Lyric Pieces
Per Norgård:
Spell, for clarinet, cello and piano
Hans Gefors:
La boite Chinoise, for solo guitar
Grieg: Sonata in C minor for violin
and piano, Op 45

7.30pm Orkney Arts Theatre, Kirkwall
Opera: The Two Fiddlers
(repeat performance)

10pm Orkney Arts Theatre, Kirkwall
The Northern Echo
Russell Hunter (repeat performance)

Sunday 18 June

10.45am St Magnus Cathedral
Festival Service
conducted by Rev William Cant,
minister of St Magnus Cathedral

3pm The Academy Hall, Stromness
Piano Recital: Vlado Perlemuter

Debussy:
Suite pour le piano, 'L'isle Joyeuse'
Ravel:
Valses nobles et sentimentales;
Jeaux d'eau
Chopin: Opus 25 Studies

8pm The Academy Hall, Stromness
Concert: The Fires of London
director: Peter Maxwell Davies
soloists:
Michael Rippon: baritone
Mark Furneaux: mime/juggler

Philippa Davies: flutes
David Campbell: clarinets
Beverley Davison: violin
Lesley Shrigley-Jones: cello
Stephen Pruslin: piano/harpsichord/
celeste
Gregory Knowles: percussion

Stromness Academy Wind Ensemble
directed by Jean Leonard

stage manager/lighting:
Kris Misselbrook

Maxwell Davies:
Le Jongleur de
Notre Dame (staged)

director: Mark Furneaux
designer: Pamela Howard
juggler design/costumes:
Doreen Watkinson
altar: Rory McKenzie

Maxwell Davies:
Eight Songs for a Mad King (staged)

cages made and designed by
John Chapman

12 midnight Ring of Brodgar
Midnight Pibroch
David Currie: highland bagpipe
Piobaireachd: An Cath Gailbeach
(The Desperate Battle)

Monday 19 June

11am The Academy Hall, Stromness
A Johnsmas Foy
(repeat performance)

11am Orkney Arts Theatre, Kirkwall
Festival Film: One Foot in Eden

2.30pm St Magnus Cathedral
Recital: The Fires of London
Mary Thomas: soprano
Philippa Davies: flute
David Campbell: clarinet
Lesley Shrigley-Jones: cello
Stephen Pruslin: piano

Bach: Sonato in E flat major for flute
and keyboard
Hans Werner Henze:
Serenade for violoncello solo
Maxwell Davies:
Hymnos, for clarinet and piano
Schubert and Wolf:
Four Mignon Songs

8pm St Magnus Cathedral
**The St Magnus Cathedral
Singers and Orchestra**
director: Norman Mitchell
organ: Richard Hughes

orchestra:
1st violins: Ruth Ingham (leader),
Libby Kelsall, Ian McKune,
Alan Gifford
2nd violins: Laurel Pegg,
Lesley Bright, Elaine Holder
violas: Louis Newell, Helen Shearer
cellos: David Leslie,
Shelagh Prendergast
double bass: Douglas Shearer
flutes: Heather Moodie, Elspeth Bain
oboes: Ed Holt, Graham Walker
trumpets: Robert Jenner,
Trevor Green, William Buchan
trombones: James Robertson,
Doreen Buchan, Tom Barnes
continuo: Glenys Hughes

chorus:
sopranos: Madge Bertram,
Muriel Donaldson, Rosemary Drever,
Violet Grieve, Margaret Groat,
Thelma Leslie, Vivia Leslie,
Millie Shearer, Jessie Sinclair,
Dorothy Small,
altos: Grace Donaldson,
Molly Hadden, Mary Hancock,
Tina Leslie, Anne Norquay,
Jane Versteeg, Marion Walker
tenors: George Donaldson,
Dennis Eunson,
James Lochhead, Charles Miller,
Michael Pegg, Jack Ridgway
basses: James Couper
Richard Hughes (assistant director),
Ian Deans, David Oddie,
Arnold Rendall
speaker: Ed Holt

Orlando Gibbons:
Hosannah to the Son of David
George Frederic Handel:
Zadok the Priest
Claudio Monteverdi: Beatus Vir
Olivier Messaien:
Two Pieces from L'Ascension
Ian McQueen:
Infinity Contained,
(Festival commission)
JS Bach:
Praise our God who Reigns in Heaven.

10pm Orkney Arts Theatre, Kirkwall
The Sounds of Norway
Eric Bye, Sigbjorn Bernhoft Osa,
Willie Andresen and
The Orkney Strathspey & Reel Society

Tuesday 20 June

11am Kirkwall Grammar School
A Johnsmas Foy (repeat)

11am The Academy Hall, Stromness
Festival Film: One Foot in Eden

Lunchtime, Festival Club
A Johnsmas Foy (repeat)

2.30pm Orkney Arts Theatre, Kirkwall
Opera: The Two Fiddlers (repeat)

8pm St Magnus Cathedral
Concert: The Fires of London
director: Peter Maxwell Davies
Mary Thomas: soprano
Philippa Davies: flutes
David Campbell: clarinets
Beverley Davison: violin/viola
Lesley Shrigley-Jones: cello
Stephen Pruslin: piano/harpsichord
Gregory Knowles: percussion
Timothy Walker: guitar

Kinloch/Maxwell Davies:
Kinloch his Fantassie
Martin Dalby:
The Dancer Eduardova
(Festival commission)
Ian McQueen:
Eighteenth Century Scottish Dances
Maxwell Davies:
The Blind Fiddler

10pm Orkney Arts Theatre, Kirkwall
The Sounds of Norway

Wednesday 21 June

8pm Orkney Arts Theatre, Kirkwall
Festival Film: One Foot in Eden

Exhibitions

Orkney County Library
**Painting and sculpture
by Orkney artists**

Ferry Terminal Building, Stromness
**Batik wallhangings:
Gunnie Moberg**

Street Shows
**Cheskoo Raree-Show:
Mark Furneaux**

1979

8pm St Magnus Cathedral
**BBC Scottish Symphony
Orchestra**
leader: Raymond Ovens
conductor: Karl Anton Rickenbacher

orchestra:
1st violins: Raymond Ovens (leader)
Hugh Bradley (deputy leader)
Michael Dolan (principal)
Robert Bell (sub principal)
Peter Jones, Michael Spencer,
Susan Bromley, Douglas Fraser
2nd violins: John Crossan (principal)
Christopher Latham (asst. principal)
John Scullion, Rae Siddall,
Georgina Mason, Elizabeth McIntosh,
Lucy Thornhill, Jennifer Spencer.
violas: Duff Burns (principal)
Neil Gray (asst. principal)
Alistair Beattie, Patricia Field,
Mysie Ann Pelly, Gillian Beers.
cellos: Anthony Sayer, Anthony
Calverley, Robert Lay, Gerald Gifford
double bass: Peter Moore (principal)
Terry Darke (asst. principal)
flutes: John Wiggins (principal)
George McIllwham.
oboes: Philip Hill (principal)
Rodney Mount.
clarinets: Harry Morrison (principal)
Geoffrey Haydock.
bassoons: Michael Norris (principal)
Andrew Gordon.
horns: David Flack (principal)
Harry Johnstone.
trumpets: Nigel Boddice (principal)
Eric Dunlea.
trombones: Peter Oram (principal)
tuba: Anthony Swainson (principal)
timpani: Gordon Rigby
percussion: Heather Corbett,
Alasdair Malloy
piano: Penelope Smith (principal)
orchestra manager: Trevor J Green
music librarian: Timothy Redman
orchestral attendants:
Andrew Thomson (supervisor),
James McGuire.

Stravinsky: Little Suite No 1
Stravinsky: Dumbarton Oaks

Edward McGuire: Source
(Festival commission)

Stravinsky: Little Suite No. 2
Mozart: Symphony No 39

10pm Orkney Arts Theatre, Kirkwall
**Barry Smith's
Theatre of Puppets**

Pierrot in Five Masks

Act Without Words
Two plays by Samuel Beckett,
A mime for one player

Come and Go
A Dramaticule

The Fair Maguelone

12.30pm St Magnus Festival Club
A Johnsmas Foy
Compiled by George Mackay Brown
Producer: Marjorie Linklater

readers: Inga Adams, Bessie Grieve,
Elizabeth Bevan, Gregor Lamb,
John Broom
musicians: Ingirid Jolly, Hugh Inkster
singer: Johnny Mowat

The works of Edwin Muir,
Eric Linklater, Robert Rendall,
Margaret Tait, George Mackay Brown,
Bessie Grieve

2.30pm Pier Arts Centre, Stromness
Naomi Mitchison
'The Cleansing of the Knife' and
other poems

4pm & 6pm Papdale Primary School
Time Flight and
**Kirkwall Messages
(Shopping Songs)**

Papdale Primary School with
Stromness Primary School Brass
Group

Ian McQueen: **Time Flight**
(Festival commission)

cast:
Computer KGB: Stuart Burgher,
Gordon Deans, Martin Findlay,
Colin Kirkness, Kevin Linklater,
Karl Mooney, David Rendall,
Lawrence Smith, Neil Stevenson,
Gavin Walls, Susan Burgess,
Fiona Dick, Moira Grieve,
Glynis Littlejohn, Karen Mowat,
Barbara Partner, Maureen Norquoy,
Karen Peddie, Dawn Rushbrook,
Diane Sinclair

Chairman and High Priest:
Sean Groundwater

Jakenor: Philip Findlater

Section VII: Dawn Atkinson, Susan
MacLeay, Jack Moodie, Karen Mowat,
Caroline Rendall, Eoin Rendall

dancers: Shirley Johnston,
Tina Leslie, Sandra Shearer,
Rachel Swanney

citizens of Onny and Stoneage
people: Lucy Alsop, Tracy
Bannerman, Paul Bruce,
Caroline Budge, Ingrid Budge,
Heather Campbell, Samantha
Craigie, Susan Dingwall,
Magnus Drever, Angela Easton,
Fiona Gauld, Gina Gibson,
Shona Gibson, Carole Gildea,
Louise Grant, Sheila Hutchison,
Christine Inkster, Karl Johnston,
Paul Kemp, Kelly Leonard, Eric Leslie,
Kenneth Low, Alan MacLeay,
Agnes Miller, Adele Muir, Eileen Reid,
Karen Walker, Astrid Wilson

orchestra:
violins: Ian Dewar, Kathleen Hogarth,
Alison Lochhead, Peter McKinlay,
Maraine Sinclair, Margaret Thomson
cellos: Shelagh Prendergast,
Paul Rendall
recorders: Louise Dennison,
Heather Dunnet, Margaret Innes,
Maureen Innes, Karen McLeod,
Shona Sinclair, Jennifer Young
percussion: Sara Gorn,
Keith Matthews, Ian Sandison,
Shaun Smith, Ola Stuart,
Paul Sutherland

solo wind quartet:
clarinets: Richard Ingham,
Jane Versteeg
oboe: Ed Holt
bassoon: Allan Buchan

piano: Glenys Hughes

Stromness Primary School
Brass Group:
Donna Brown, James Burgon,
Judith Dixon, Keith Garson,
Richard Linklater, Colin Mowat,
Graham Sinclair, Gillian Smith,
Robert Stanger, Jonathon Wood
director: William Buchan

director: Ian McQueen
producer: Barbara Vesco
props: David Grieve
costumes: members of staff

Peter Maxwell Davies:
Kirkwall Messages
(Shopping Songs)

junior choir: Rory Alsop, Colin Begley,
Karen Burgess, Neil Burgess,
Doreen Burton, Ian Croy, Julie Deans,
Janet Donaldson, Alexander Evans,
Susan Fotheringhame, Sarah George,
Norma Hogarth, Gordon Innes,
Fiona Johnston, Leona Kirkness,
Elizabeth Laird, Alison Leonard,
Tracy Linklater, David Marwick,
Paula Marwick, Karen MacFaull,
Rognvald Omand, Elinor Rendall,
Paul Rendall, Katie Robertson,
Maureen Robertson, Helen Ryrie,
Coreen Skea, Susan Stout,
Neil Stockan, Fiona Street,
Fiona Sutherland, Sharon Sutherland,
Catherine Thomson, Lesley Tait,
Paul Watson, Ross Donaldson

recorders: Elizabeth Booth,
Coreen Buchan, Raymond Buchan,
Lynn Campbell, Saffron Eames,
Alice Kelsall, Denise Kirkness,
Angela Wilson

percussion: Richard Flett, Sara Gorn,
Glynis Littlejohn, Beverley Meason,
Dawn Rushbrook, Ola Stuart,
Robert Walker

piano: Allan Buchan

director: Glenys Hughes

8pm Orkney Arts Theatre, Kirkwall
**Barry Smith's
Theatre of Puppets**

10pm St Magnus Cathedral
English Saxophone Quartet
Mark Jordan: soprano
Anthony Houghton: alto
Neville Duckworth: tenor
Raymond Scott: baritone

Stephen Pruslin: piano

Gordon Jacob: Saxophone Quartet
William Byrd: Suite
Jean Francoix: Quartet
Ravel: Sonatine for Piano
Daryl Runswick: Quartet
Raymond Scott: Quartet
Bozza: Nuages

10.45 St Magnus Cathedral
Festival Service
conducted by Rev William Cant
minister of St Magnus Cathedral

3pm The Academy Hall, Stromness
Piano recital: Fou Ts'ong

Mozart: Rondo in A minor, K511
Schubert: Seventeen Landler, D366
Weber: Sonata No 2 in A flat, Op 39
Chou Wen-Chung:
The willows are new
Chopin: Ballade No 1 in G minor,
Op 23;
Four Mazurkas, Op 17;
Two Nocturnes, Op 62, B major,
E major;
Ballade No 4 in F minor, Op 52

6pm The Academy Hall, Stromness
Time Flight and
**Kirkwall Messages
(Shopping Songs)**
(repeat performance)

8.30pm Academy Hall, Stromness
The Fires of London
conductor: Jan Latham-Koenig

soloist: Mary Thomas, soprano
guest artists: Barry Smith's Theatre
of Puppets
Philippa Davies: flutes
David Campbell: clarinets
Beverley Davison: violin
Jennifer Ward Clarke: cello
Stephen Pruslin: piano
Gregory Knowles: percussion

lighting and stage management:
Kris Misselbrook

Peter Maxwell Davies:
Miss Donnithorne's Maggot
(staged)

Ronnie Aim: The Orkney Strathspey
and Reel Society's Silver Jubilee
Salute to Her Majesty The Queen
and The Duke of Edinburgh.
conducted by the composer.

st. magnus
festival

Orkney Islands

Friday 15th – Tuesday 19th June
1979

Programme

Michael Finnissy: Mr Punch
(staged)

Purcell/Maxwell Davies:
Fantasia and Two Pavans

Monday 18 June

Community Centre, North Ronaldsay
**Barry Smith's
Theatre of Puppets**

2.30pm St Magnus Cathedral
Recital: The Fires of London

Philippa Davies: flute
David Campbell: clarinet
Beverley Davison: violin
Jennifer Ward Clarke: cello
Stephen Pruslin: piano

Debussy:
Sonata for Violoncello and Piano
(Jennifer Ward Clarke and
Stephen Pruslin)

Boulez: Sonatine for Flute and Piano
(Philippa Davies and Stephen Pruslin)

Bartók: Contrasts, for violin, clarinet
and piano
(Beverley Davison, David Campbell,
Stephen Pruslin)

8pm St Magnus Cathedral
Concert: The Fires of London
conductor: Jan Latham-Koenig
Philippa Davies: flutes
David Campbell: clarinets
Beverley Davison: violin/viola
Jennifer Ward Clarke: cello
Stephen Pruslin: piano
Gregory Knowles: percussion

Maxwell Davies:
Dances from The Two Fiddlers

Judith Weir:
King Harald sails
to Byzantium
(Festival commission)

Peter Maxwell Davies:
Ave Maris Stella

Sanday School, Sanday
**Barry Smith's
Theatre of Puppets**

10pm Orkney Arts Theatre, Kirkwall
A Norwegian Evening
Aaron Egeland: Hardanger fiddle and
flat fiddle;
Kari Valen: Harpeleik zither
The Orkney Strathspey & Reel Society

Tuesday 19 June

2.30pm St Magnus Cathedral
The English Saxophone Quartet
Mark Jordan: soprano
Neville Duckworth: tenor
Anthony Houghton: alto
Raymond Scott: baritone

Stephen Pruslin: piano

Paul Harvey: Agincourt Song
Dubois: Quatuor
JS Bach: Fugue No 5
John Ellis: Bach Goes to Sea –
satirical suite for several saxophones
Beethoven: Sonata in C minor Op
13 'Pathétique'
Bouvard: Quartet Sinfonia
Frank Cordell: Gestures
Rivier: Quartet

8pm St Magnus Cathedral
**St Magnus Cathedral Singers
and Chamber Orchestra**
director: Norman Mitchell
Kathleen Livingstone: soprano
Neil Mackie: tenor
Richard Hughes: organ

chorus:
sopranos: Doreen Buchan, Muriel
Donaldson, Rosemary Drever,
Violet Grieve, Margaret Groat,
Thelma Leslie, Vivia Leslie,
Millie Shearer, Jessie Sinclair
tenors: George Donaldson,
James Lochhead, Jack Ridgway
altos: Molly Hadden, Mary Hancock,
Tina Leslie, Anna Norquay,
Jane Versteeg, Marion Walker
basses: John Adams, James Couper,
Ian Deans, David Oddie,
Arnold Rendall, Graham Thomson

orchestra:
1st violins: Ian McKune (leader)
Alan Gifford, Libby Kelsall,
Lesley McLeod, Ruth Mathieson,
Elma Marshall
2nd violins: Elaine Grieve,
Susan Johnston, Peter Marshall,
Karen Moodie, Ian Tait
violas: Louis Newell, Helen Shearer
cellos: David Leslie,
Shelagh Prendergast
double bass: Douglas Shearer
flute: Richard Ingham
oboes: Ed Holt, Graham Walker
bassoon: Alan Buchan
trumpets: Trevor Green,
William Buchan
timpani: Sharon Ridgway
continuo: Richard Hughes (organ),
Harry Croft-Jackson (harpsichord)

Handel: Ode for St Cecilia's Day

Peter Maxwell Davies and
George Mackay Brown:
Solstice of Light.
soloists:
Neil Mackie (tenor)
Richard Hughes (organ)

10pm Orkney Arts Theatre, Kirkwall
**Festival finale:
A Norwegian Evening**

Other festival events

Community Centre, North Ronaldsay
Sanday School, Sanday
**Island Puppet Shows:
Barry Smith's Theatre of
Puppets**

Tankerness House, Kirkwall
Art Exhibition

Pier Arts Centre, Stromness
**Twenty Poems
by Hugh MacDiarmid**
with lithographs by William Johnstone

1980

Friday 20 June

<u>2pm Pier Arts Centre, Stromness</u>
Edvard Munch
A talk by Arne Eggum, chief curator,
the Munch Museum, Oslo

<u>8pm St Magnus Cathedral</u>
Concert:
Chetham's School of Music

Maxwell Davies:
Fanfare –
Welcome to Orkney

J Haydn: String Quartet,
Op 76 No 2 in D minor
Jonathan Storer: violin
Caroline Jones: violin
Emma Shewell: viola
Sally Pendlebury: cello

Philip Thorpe:
Horoscope

Shostakovich:
String Quartet No 8 in C minor,
Op 110

Sophie Barber: violin
Richard Milone: violin
Melissa Reeves: viola
Sara Rowbottom: cello

Paul Wingfield:
Concerto for
String Orchestra

Hindemith: Kleine Kammermusik
for Wind Quintet, Op 24 No 2

Jane Speirs: flute
Deborah Jones: oboe
Fay Windsor: clarinet
David Beardmore: bassoon
Huw Fred Williams: horn

Mendelssohn:
Octet for Strings in E flat, Op 20

Sophie Barber: violin
Jonathan Storer: violin
Richard Milone: violin
Caroline Jones: violin
Melissa Reeves: viola
Emma Shewell: viola
Sally Pendlebury: cello
Sara Rowbottom: cello

Saturday 21 June

<u>11am Pier Arts Centre, Stromness</u>
The Bridie Who He?
by Ronald Mavor

<u>2.10pm Festival Club, Kirkwall</u>
A Johnsmas Foy
compiled by Margaret Tait and
George Mackay Brown
producer: Marjorie Linklater
readers: Elizabeth Bevan,
Bessie Grieve, Jan Mackay,
Gregor Lamb, John Broom
players: Ingirid Jolly, Hugh Inkster
singers: Ingirid Jolly, Johnny Mowat

<u>2.30pm St Magnus Cathedral</u>
Recital:
Orkney county music staff
Helen Grace: soprano

Telemann: Sonata in C minor for
treble recorder, oboe and continuo

Jane Versteeg: treble recorder
Robert Coates: harpsichord
Edmund Holt: oboe
Peter Saunders: cello

Robert Coates: Songs of the Nativity
Hugh Black: flute
Josephine Richards: piano

Schumann: Phantasiestücke for
Clarinet and Piano Op 73

Jane Versteeg: clarinet
Janet Halsall: piano

Richard Rodney Bennett: The Aviary

Peter Warlock:
Sleep; Pretty Ring Time
Helen Grace: soprano

Kenneth Leighton: 'Martyrs'
Dialogues on a Scottish Psalm Tune
Op 73
Richard Hughes and Robert Coates
(organ duet)

<u>7.30pm Orkney Arts Theatre, Kirkwall</u>
Opera: Cinderella
by Peter Maxwell Davies
performed by pupils of
Papdale Primary School
and Kirkwall Grammar School

cast:
Cinderella: Alison Lochhead
The Prince: Maureen Norquoy
The Cat: Louise Grant
Widow Grumble: Elspeth Bain
The Three Ugly Sisters:
  Medusa: Andrew Green
  Hecate: Peter Marshall
  Dragonia: Simon Chirgwin
Herald: Heather Dunnet
The Three Commanders-in-Chief of
the Armed Services:
  Field Marshall Sir Wellington
  Bombast-Blimp: Bruce Moar
  Lord Admiral Sir Nelson Drake-
  Victory: Wayne Ward
  Lord Delta Wing Vertical-Takeoff:
  Paul Bruce

The Train:
Susan Bruce, Lynn Campbell,
Sharon Chase, Julie Deans,
Susan Dingwall, Heather Dunnet,
Fiona Fettes, Ray Findlay,
Darren Golding, Kelly Leonard,
Kevin Linklater, Kenneth Low,
Susan McLeay, Melanie Meek,
Kevin Moar, Eric Muir, Eileen Reid

Kittens:
Irene Atkinson, Caroline Budge,
Susan Burgess, Ian Croy,
Magnus Drever, Eileen Drever,

Susan Fotheringhame,
Gina Gibson, Shona Gibson,
Carole Gildea, Kathleen Hogarth,
Fiona Johnston, David Marwick,
William Marwick, Helen Ryrie,
Maraine Sinclair

Guests at the Prince's dance:
Tracy Bannerman,
Heather Campbell, Lynn Craigie,
Donna McCulloch, Samantha Craigie,
Teresa Couper, Debra Foubister,
Lorraine Harcus,
Margaret Innes, Maureen Kent,
Jenny Leslie, Nicola Logan,
Katrina McGinn, Alison Mainland,
Laura Mitchell, Sharon Nixon,
Evan Norquoy, Lorraine Taylor

instrumentalists:
violins: Ian Tait, Karen Moodie
cello: Andrew Walker
double bass: David Leslie
recorders: Louise Dennison,
Maureen Innes, Karin McLeod,
Jennifer Young
percussion: Ross Donaldson,
John Flett, Sara Gorn,
Margaret Marshall, Karen Peddie,
Ola Stuart, Alison Walker
trumpet: Alan Rendall
piano: Allan Buchan

conductor: Glenys Hughes
producer: Marlene Mainland

choreography: Ann McKemmie
design: David Grieve
lighting: Kris Misselbrook,
Rory Mackenzie, Mark Ridgway
costumes and props:
staff and parents
make-up: Marion White, Jack Ridgway
wigs and flats loaned by
Kirkwall Arts Club

<u>10pm Orkney Arts Theatre, Kirkwall</u>
Late Night Cabaret and Jazz
with Eleanor Bron, Peter Maxwell
Davies and The Inversions

Peter Maxwell Davies:
Uranium Songs
(The Yellow Cake Revue)

Sunday 22 June

<u>10.45am St Magnus Cathedral</u>
Festival Service
conducted by Rev William Cant,
minister of St Magnus Cathedral

Introit:
Mendelssohn: Lift thine eyes
Stanford: Te Deum and Jubilate

Anthem:
Parry: I was glad

organ music during the service:
Frank Bridge: Adagio in E

organ music after the service:
William Alcock:
Introduction and Passacaglia

<u>3pm Academy Hall, Stromness</u>
Piano recital: Jeremy Menuhin

Bartók: Sonata
Brahms: 4 Ballades Op 10
Schubert: Sonata in C minor D958

<u>6.30pm Pier Arts Centre, Stromness</u>
Pre concert talk:
Peter Maxwell Davies

<u>8pm Academy Hall, Stromness</u>
Concert: The Fires of London
conductor: Peter Maxwell Davies
Mary Thomas: soprano

Philippa Davies: flutes
David Campbell: clarinets
Beverley Davison: violin/viola
Alexander Baillie: cello
Stephen Pruslin: keyboard
instruments
Gregory Knowles: percussion
Timothy Walker: guitar

Maxwell Davies: Psalm 124

Philip Grange:
Cimmerian Nocturne

Maxwell Davies:
Renaissance Scottish Dances

Maxwell Davies:
Antechrist

Maxwell Davies:
Missa Super L'homme Armé
Mary Thomas: soprano

<u>10.30pm Stromness Hotel</u>
Late Night Cabaret and Jazz
with Eleanor Bron, Peter Maxwell
Davies and The Inversions

Monday 23 June

<u>11am The Academy Hall, Stromness</u>
A Johnsmas Foy

<u>12.30pm Festival Club, Kirkwall</u>
The Bridie Who He?

<u>1pm Academy Hall, Stromness</u>
Lunchtime Jazz:
The Inversions

<u>2.30pm St Magnus Cathedral</u>
Recital: The Fires of London

Philippa Davies: flute
David Campbell: clarinet
Beverley Davison: violin
Alexander Baillie: cello
Stephen Pruslin: piano

Beethoven programme:
Piano Trio in C minor, Op 1 No 3
(Beverley Davison, Alexander Baillie,
Stephen Pruslin)

Andante 'favori' in F major
(piano solo: Stephen Pruslin)

Two folk songs with variations
Austrian Air: A bowl and a saucer are
all my kitchenware, Op 105 No 3

Scottish Air: O Thou art the lad of
my heart, Op 107 No 9
(Philippa Davies and Stephen Pruslin)

Trio in B flat major for piano, clarinet
and cello, Op 11
(Stephen Pruslin, David Campbell,
Alexander Baillie)

6.30pm Papdale Infant School,
Kirkwall
Pre concert talk:
Peter Maxwell Davies

8pm Orkney Arts Theatre, Kirkwall
The Fires of London
Music-Theatre Double-Bill
conductor: Peter Maxwell Davies
Mary Thomas: reciter
William Louther:
choreographer/dancer

Alexander Baillie: cello
Philippa Davies: flutes
David Campbell: clarinets
Beverley Davison: violin/viola
Stephen Pruslin: piano
Gregory Knowles: percussion

Arnold Schoenberg:
Pierrot Lunaire, Op 21 (staged)

Maxwell Davies: Vesalii Icones
(staged)
William Louther:
choreographer/dancer
Alexander Baillie: cello

Tuesday 24 June

11.15am Kirkwall Grammar School
A Johnsmas Foy

11.15am Academy Hall, Stromness
John Amis in Person
a one-man show by the
BBC presenter

2.30pm St Magnus Cathedral
Recital
Mary Thomas: soprano
Timothy Walker: guitar

C Maria von Weber: Group of Songs

Maxwell Davies: Dark Angels
to texts by George Mackay Brown

Benjamin Britten: Nocturnal
(solo guitar)

Roberto Gerhard:
Two Spanish Songs
Three English folksong arrangements

7.30pm Orkney Arts Theatre, Kirkwall
Cinderella

10pm Orkney Arts Theatre, Kirkwall
Spaelimenninir I Hoydølum
The Late Foy
Orkney Strathspey and
Reel Society

Wednesday 25 June

11.15am Kirkwall Grammar School
John Amis in person
(repeat performance)

2.30pm Orkney Arts Theatre, Kirkwall
Cinderella
(repeat performance)

8pm St Magnus Cathedral
St Magnus Cathedral Singers
Festival Chorus and Orchestra
conductor: Richard Hughes

sopranos: Helen Grace, Elspeth Bain,
contralto: Janice Bruce
organ: David Drinkell

St Magnus Cathedral Singers:
sopranos: Meg Groat,
Rosemary Drever, Doreen Buchan,
Muriel Donaldson, Elspeth Bain,
Dorothy Small, Millie Shearer,
Jessie Sinclair, Vivia Leslie,
Janet Halsall, Violet Grieve
altos: Mary Hancock, Tina Leslie,
Grace Donaldson, Anne Norquay,
Jane Versteeg, Marion Walker,
Lillian Miller
tenors: George Donaldson,
Charles Miller, James Lochhead,
Dennis Eunson, Robin Noble,
Robert Coates
basses: John Adams, Ian Deans,
David Oddie, Arnold Rendall,
Graham Thomson.

Bruckner: Christus factus est
Bach: Chorale prelude and motet,
'Jesu Meine Freude'
Alain: Le Jardin Suspendu; Litanies
Mathias: Ave Rex
Vivaldi: Gloria

10pm Ayre Hotel, Kirkwall
Supper and dance

Exhibitions

Pier Arts Centre, Stromness
Edvard Munch and his Literary
Associates
Opened by Arne Eggum, chief curator
of the Munch Museum in Oslo.

County Library, Kirkwall
Photographs: Charles Tait

St Magnus Cathedral
St Magnus Panel Paintings
by school children from Arran

Street Music

The Brass Bands of
Stromness Academy and
Stromness Primary School

1981

8.15pm St Magnus Cathedral
St Magnus Cathedral Singers
Festival Chorus and Orchestra
conductor: Richard Hughes
organ: David Drinkell

St Magnus Cathedral Singers:
sopranos: Doreen Buchan,
Sally Cheer, Irene Donaldson,
Muriel Donaldson, Rosemary Drever,
Violet Grieve, Meg Groat,
Janet Halsall, Vivia Leslie,
Millie Shearer, Jessie Sinclair,
Dorothy Small
altos: Grace Donaldson,
Mary Hancock, Lillian Miller,
Anne Norquoy, Josephine Richards,
Jane Versteeg, Marion Walker
tenors: Robin Cheer,
George Donaldson, Dennis Eunson,
James Lochhead, Charles Millar
basses: John Adams, Ian Deans,
David Oddie, Arnold Rendall,
Graham Thomson
orchestra:
1st violins: Ian McKune (leader),
Alan Gifford, Ruth Ingham,
Libby Kelsall, Peter Marshall.
2nd violins: Leslie McLeod,
Elaine Grieve, Karen Moodie,
Seona Dunsmuir, Ian Tait
violas: Jean Leonard, Louis Newell,
Helen Shearer, Christine Rae
cellos: Peter Saunders, Mark Rendall,
Andrew Walker
double bass: Graham Thomson
trumpets: Lindsay Taylor,
Michael Brands
timpani: Maureen Cursiter
organ: David Drinkell

St Magnus Cathedral Singers:
Bairstow: Let all mortal flesh keep
silence
Stanford: Beati quorum via
Bainton: And I saw a new heaven
Finzi: God is gone up

organ:
Bach: Fantasia and Fugue in G minor

St Magnus Cathedral Singers,
strings and organ:
Purcell: My Beloved Spake

soloists:
alto: Robin Cheer,
tenor: James Lochhead
basses: John Adams,
Graham Thomson

Maxwell Davies:
Three Organ Voluntaries,
Psalm 124 (after David Peebles)
O God Abufe (after John Fethy)
All Sons of Adam

St Magnus Cathedral Singers:
conductor: Peter Maxwell Davies
(not Gennadi Rozhdestvensky, as
programmed)

Maxwell Davies:
Lullaby for Lucy

St Magnus Cathedral Singers:
Britten: Festival Te Deum

Festival Chorus:
Parry: motet – My Soul, there is a
Country

Festival Chorus and Orchestra:
Schubert: Mass in G
Ishbel Stanger: soprano,
Eoin Leslie: tenor
John Flett: bass

11pm Festival Club, Kirkwall
Nascimentos
Larry Frates – Man of Magic

11am Pier Arts Centre
Norman MacCaig poetry reading
for the opening of the exhibition
'Seven Poets'

2.30pm St Magnus Cathedral
St Andrews Renaissance Group

Gregor Aichinger:
Ave Maria (a4); Noel, Noel, Noel (a5)

Juan Navarro:
Regina coeli laetare (a6)

Hans Leo Hassler:
Cantate Domino canticum novum (a5)

Pedro Rimonte:
De profundis clamavi (a7)

Heinrich Isaac:
Virgo prudentissima (a6)

Avery Burton: Hexacord Mass (a6)
Sanctus, Benedictus, Agnus Dei

6pm Papdale Infant Hall, Kirkwall
Concert: Papdale and
Stromness Primary Schools

Kirkwall Shopping Songs
performed by the pupils of
Papdale Primary School, Kirkwall
conductor: Glenys Hughes

singers:
Lesley Adams, Helen Bain,
Colin Begley, Linda Besant,
Karen Burghes, Neil Burgess,
Lynn Campbell, Lynne Craigie,
Samantha Craigie, Rachel Dawson,
Saffron Eames, Fiona Fettes,
Ray Findlay, Diane Flett,
Richard Flett, Susan Fotheringhame,
Sarah George, Mark Gildea,
Katherine Gordon, Mairi Gordon,
Norna Hogarth, Gordon Innes,
Fiona Johnston, Paula Kemp,
Alison Leonard, Tracy Linklater,
Karen MacFaull, Louise MacLennan,
Beverley Meason, Melanie Meek,
Michelle Monkman, Alison Muir,
Tracy Muir, Rognvald Omand,
Paul Rendall, Sandra Ritchie,
Ian Robertson, Leona Robinson,
Diana Rosie, Helen Ryrie,
Coreen Skea, Stewart Stanger,

Fiona Sutherland, Sharon Sutherland,
Lorraine Taylor, Catherine Thomson,
Robert Walker, Paul Watson

recorders: Coreen Buchan,
Raymond Buchan, Dina Burgess,
Janet Donaldson, Eileen Drever,
Gina Gibson, Carole Gildea,
Kelly Leonard, Katie Robertson

percussion: Tracy Bannerman,
Caroline Budge, Ian Croy,
Julie Deans, Ross Donaldson,
Shona Gibson, David Marwick,
Michael Swanney

piano: David Drinkell

The Rainbow
performed by pupils of
Stromness Primary School
producer: Ian MacLeod,
conductor: Janet Halsall

cast:
Pat: Peter Burgon
The Teacher: Tanya Duncan
Mrs Flett: Sheila Robson
Mr Tait: James Leonard
The Dog: Alison Ritch
The Donkey: Ewan Dunsmuir and
Craig Hourston
The Selkie: Audrey Brown

chorus:
Julia Cassidy, Sarah Clubley,
Arlene Croy, Grant Cumming,
Graham Cutker, Lorraine Gilmour,
Jacqueline Gray, Keith Groundwater,
Clifford Gunn, Karen Inkster,
Kenneth Inkster, Hermione Lockley,
Ann-Marie McArthur,
Lachlan McGurk, Glen McLellan,
Debbie-Lee McVean, Vanessa Muir,
Richard Omand, Tracy Peterson,
Keely Pritchett, Sheila Robson,
Ingrid Scott, Martin Steer,
Cameron Stout, Gary Walker,
Dennis Watt, Nicola Wishart

instrumentalists:
Fiona Buchan, Linnet Crichton,
Candace Pratt, Graham Sinclair,
Karen Sinclair, Calum Sutherland

percussion:
Anthony Eggeling, Ingrid Ford,
Graham Garson, Victoria Hare,
Annette Kirkpatrick,
Roderick McGurk, Diane Sinclair,
Frances Troup

pianist: Barbara Mainland
solo violin: Peter Pratt

8.30pm Orkney Arts Theatre
The Well
by George Mackay Brown
incidental music by
Peter Maxwell Davies
producer: Ernie Donaldson

cast:
scene 1:
The Keeper of Water: Linda Tait
Islander: James Miller

Wife: Inga Adams
Son: Sweyn Hunter
Daughter: Samantha McArthur
scene 2:
Woman: Frances Chirgwin
Woman 2: Sylvia Dennison
Woman 3: Betty Robertson
Norseman: Jim Groundwater
scene 3:
Old Woman: Claire Kelday
Girl: Ingrid Donaldson
Monk 1: Mike Turner
Monk 2: Mike Corsie
Monk 3: David Butler
scene 4:
Sigrid: Phyllis Brown
Asa: Allison Dixon
Liv: Lesley Wishart
Ingrid: Samantha McArthur
Islander: Jim Groundwater
Soldier: John Adams
scene 5:
Rachel: Inga Adams
Sonia: Susie Gorn
Sailor: Mike Turner
Factor: David Butler
Farmer 1: Sweyn Hunter
Farmer 2: James Miller
Extra farmers: Jean Hardgreaves,
Alison Scott: Betty Robertson
scene 6:
Girl: Ingrid Donaldson
Farm Wife: Sylvia Dennison
Crofter: John Adams
Old Man: Mike Corsie
scene 7:
Keeper of the Well: Linda Tait
scene 8:
Marilyn: Alison Scott
Rita: Allison Dixon
Paulette: Jean Hardgreaves
Skerry (voice): David Butler
scene 9:
Red: David Butler
Black: John Adams
White: Lesley Wishart
Blue: Phyllis Brown
Islander: Mike Corsie
scene 10:
Voyagers:
Mike Turner, Inga Adams,
James Miller, David Butler,
Frances Chirgwin, Jim Groundwater,
Sweyn Hunter

instrumentalists:
flute: Hugh Black
oboe: Peter Brown
clarinet: Jane Versteeg
bassoon: Graham Thomson
trumpets: Lindsay Taylor,
Michael Brands,
cello: Peter Saunders,
piano: Glenys Hughes
percussion: Robert Coates

conductor: Peter Maxwell Davies

stage management: Bryan Leslie,
Alan Taylor, Brian Watson,
William Windwick
prompt: Alison Fraser
props: Alison Fraser, Maggie Muir,
Pam Byers
costume design: Erlend Brown
costumes: Mrs Middleton, Mrs Crisp,

Dorothy Small, Liz Finch
lighting: Kris Misselbrook,
Norman Rushbrook,
Jack Hargreaves, Stuart Chalmers
make-up: Ola Gorie, Marion Whyte

Sunday 21 June

10.45am St Magnus Cathedral
Festival Service
conducted by Rev William Cant,
minister of St Magnus Cathedral

St Magnus Singers and the
St Andrews Renaissance Group:

Introit:
Hassler: Cantate Domino
Britten: Jubilate
Anthem:
Vaughan Williams:
Lord, Thou hast been our refuge

organ music during the service:
Herbert Howells: Master Tallis's
Testament
organ music after the Service:
Kenneth Leighton: Paean

3pm Academy Hall, Stromness
Piano Recital:
Victoria Postnikova
and Gennadi Rozhdestvensky

Mozart: Sonata in D major, K381
Schubert:
Fantasia in F minor, Op 103
Brahms: Waltzes, Op 39
Rachmaninov: Six Pieces, Op 11

6.30pm Pier Arts Centre, Stromness
Pre concert talk:
Peter Maxwell Davies

8pm Academy Hall, Stromness
Mary Thomas: soprano
Stephen Pruslin: piano

Satie: Sports et Divertissements
Maxwell Davies: Piano Sonata

Maxwell Davies:
The Medium

Monday 22 June

11am Academy Hall, Stromness
A Johnsmas Foy:
Orkney with Love
producer: Marjorie Linklater
readers: Elizabeth Bevan, Bessie
Grieve, Jan Mackay, Gregor Lamb,
John Broom.
players: Ingirid Jolly, Hugh Inkster
singer: Ingirid Jolly

2.30pm Stromness Primary School
Kirkwall Shopping Songs
(repeat performance)

The Rainbow
(repeat performance)

6.30pm Festival Club, Kirkwall
Pre concert talk:
Peter Maxwell Davies

8pm St Magnus Cathedral
Scottish Chamber Orchestra
conductor: Jerzy Maksymiuk
leader: John Tunnell
soloist: Neil Mackie

1st violins: John Tunnell,
Dorothie Bor, Brian Thomas,
Jack Maquire, Beth McKill,
Lorna McLaren, Clive Thomas,
Pamela Marks
2nd violins: Jerre Gibson, Brian Hale,
Susan Rigby, Mary Miller,
Robert Higgs, Catherine Ford
violas: Carolyn Sparey, Julian Shaw,
Brenda Smith, James Swainson
cellos: Haflidi Hallgrimsson,
Winifred Beeston, John Todd,
Helen Hale
basses: John Steer, Adrian Bornet
flutes: David Nicholson,
Sheena Gordon
oboes: Robin Miller, Maurice Checker
clarinets: Lewis Morrison,
Lee Stephenson
bassoons: Melville Jerome,
Peter Moore
horns: Neill Sanders,
Harry Johnstone
trumpets: Barry Collarbone,
Peter Franks
timpani: Caroline Garden

Haydn: Symphony No 48 in C major,
'Maria Theresa'
Britten: Serenade for tenor solo, horn
and strings, Op 31
Mozart: Symphony No 40 in G minor,
K550

10.30pm Orkney Arts Theatre,
Kirkwall
The Game:
Intriplicate Mime Company
Ian Cameron, Mollie Guilfoyle,
Robert Williams

Tuesday 23 June

11am Orkney Arts Theatre, Kirkwall
A Johnsmas Foy
Orkney with Love
(repeat performance)

2.30pm St Magnus Cathedral
Neil Mackie: tenor
Richard Hughes: organ

arr. Kenneth Elliot:
Four Scottish Renaissance Songs
Maxwell Davies: Three Tenor Songs
from 'The Martyrdom of St Magnus'
Reger: Toccata and Fugue in D minor
and major
Kenneth Leighton:
These are thy wonders,
Op 84 (A song of renewal)
Britten: Prayer and Aria from
'St Nicolas'
Messiaen: Two movements from
'La Nativite du Seigneur'

6.30pm Festival Club, Kirkwall
Judith Weir:
Peter Maxwell Davies
A musical discussion

8pm St Magnus Cathedral
Scottish Chamber Orchestra
conductor: Jerzy Maksymiuk
leader: John Tunnell

Britten: Variations on a
Theme of Frank Bridge

Judith Weir:
Isti Mirant Stella

Schubert: Symphony No 3

10.30pm Orkney Arts Theatre,
Kirkwall
A Johnsmas Foy
with West Mainland Strathspey
and Reel Society

leader: George Seator
accordions: Billy Black, Bill Halcro,
John Harvey, Margaret Leask,
Andy Leonard
fiddle: Ian Anderson, Netta Ashburn,
Billy Hancox, Tommy Linklater,
Ruby Manson, Peter Pratt,
George Seator, Stanley Shearer,
Isaac Wilson, Jim Wishart,
Walter Woolley, Jennifer Yates
piano: Jill Leonard

Wednesday 24 June

2.30pm St Magnus Cathedral
Music for Woodwind and Brass
with traditional fiddle music played
by Douglas Lawrence

Kirkwall Grammar School
Wind Group
conductor: Hugh Black

Gabrieli:
arr. G Draper: O Magnum Mysterium
arr. R Miller: Sonata pian'e forte

Lawrie: March, Mrs MacDonald of
Dunach
Trad: Strathspey, Lady Mary Ramsay;
Reel, Sir David Davidson;
Slow Strathspey, The Beauty of the
North;
Reel, Geordie Affleck
Hendry: Slow Air, Robert Cormack
Marshall:
Slow Air, The Marquis of Huntley's
Snuff Mill;
Strathspey, Miss Farquharson of
Invercauld;
Reel, Mrs Charles Stuart
Locke, arr. A Baines:
Music for His Majesty's Sackbuts
and Cornetts
(Hugh Black, Jane Versteeg,
Elsie Black, Graham Thomson)

Alec Templeton: Bach goes to Town
'Prelude and Fugue in Swing'

McDonald/McLennan:
March, The Braes of Castlegrant
Hill: Strathspey, Earl Gray
Lowe: Reel, The Waverley Ball
Gow: Slow Air, Neil Gow's Farewell
to Whisky

McIntosh: Slow Strathspey,
Lady Charlotte Campbell
Marshall:
Slow Air, Mrs Major Stewart of Java
Trad:
Reel, The Marquis of Tulibardine

Stromness Academy Brass Band
conductor: William Buchan
Purcell, arr. F Wright:
Trumpet Tune and Air
Malcolm Arnold:
Little Suite for Brass Op 80

8pm Orkney Arts Theatre, Kirkwall
The Well (repeat performance)

Exhibitions

Pier Arts Centre, Stromness
Seven Poets: Iain Crichton Smith,
Robert Garioch, George Mackay
Brown, Norman MacCaig, Sorley
MacLean, Edwin Morgan, Hugh
MacDiarmid
Alexander Moffat -
paintings and drawings,
Five Orkney Writers: George
Mackay Brown, Edwin Muir, Eric
Linklater, Ernest Marwick, Robert
Rendall

Ferry Terminal, Stromness
Jessie Ann Matthew:
photographs of Seven Poets.

Tankerness House, Kirkwall
Tomb of the Eagles

Stromness Museum
Photographs: William Hourston

Stromness Library Gallery
Orkney Watercolours

Orkney County Library, Kirkwall
Eileen Sclater: photographs

1982

Friday 18 June

6pm Orkney Arts Theatre, Kirkwall
Opera: Cinderella
by Peter Maxwell Davies
performed by pupils of
Papdale Primary School
and Kirkwall Grammar School

cast:
Cinderella: Alison Lochhead
The Prince: Karen Burghes
The Cat: Louise Grant
Window Grumble: Elspeth Bain
The Three Ugly Sisters:
  Medusa: Roy Flett
  Hecate: Peter Marshall
  Dragonia: Simon Chirgwin
Herald: Katie Robertson

The Three Commanders-in-Chief of
the Armed Services:
Field Marshall Sir Wellington
Bombast-Blimp: Robert Walker
Lord Admiral Sir Nelson Drake-
Victory: Paul Rendall
Lord Delta Wing Vertical-Takeoff:
Stewart Stanger

Kittens:
Colin Begley, Coreen Buchan,
Neil Burgess, Morven Cross,
Janet Donaldson, Lynn Edinborough,
Mark Gildea, Lorraine Kelday,
Ingrid Mears, Beverley Meason,
Michelle Monkman, Alison Muir,
Tracy Muir, Leona Rendall,
Stewart Rendall, Dawn Wylie

The Train/Ball Guests:
Lesley Adams, Denise Bruce,
Rachel Dawson, Saffron Eames,
Kevin Farmer, Sarah George,
Paula Kemp, Tracy Linklater,
Karen McFaull, Arlene Peace,
Sandra Ritchie, Diana Rosie,
Beverley Ross, Coreen Skea,
Inga Stewart, Fiona Sutherland,
Catherine Swanney, Paul Watson

instrumentalists:
violins: Ian Tait, Karen Moodie
cello: Peter Saunders
double bass: Graham Thompson
recorders: Raymond Buchan,
Dina Burgess, Alison Leonard,
Catherine Thomson, Elinor Walls
percussion: Richard Flett,
Peter Grant, Robert Leslie,
Margaret Marshall, Rognvald Omand,
Ian Robertson, Alison Walker
trumpet: Kirstin McLeod
piano: Allan Buchan

conductor: Glenys Hughes
producer: Inga Adams
assistant to producer: Ann Torricelli

design: David Grieve
lighting: Kris Misselbrook
costumes: Brenda Dowie
props: Marlene Mainland
stage manager: David Grieve
hair stylist: Pat Hall

8.30pm St Magnus Cathedral
**St Magnus Cathedral Singers
Festival Chorus and Orchestra**
conductor: Richard Hughes
Michael Rippon: baritone
Janet Annand: harp
Gregory Knowles: percussion
David Drinkell: organ

St Magnus Cathedral Choir:
sopranos: Elspeth Bain,
Doreen Buchan, Sally Cheer,
Irene Donaldson, Muriel Donaldson,
Rosemary Drever, Violet Grieve,
Millie Shearer, Jessie Sinclair,
Dorothy Small
altos: Grace Donaldson,
Enid Fleming, Mary Hancock,
Wilma Legget, Marion Walker,
Lillian Miller, Josephine Richards
tenors: George Donaldson,
Dennis Eunson, Sweyn Hunter,
James Lochhead, Charles Miller
basses: John Adams, Robin Cheer,
Ian Deans, David Oddie,
Arnold Rendall

St Magnus Cathedral Choir:
Fauré: Requiem
solo baritone: Michael Rippon

Festival Chorus:
conductor: David Drinkell
Verdi: Ave Maria
Bernstein: Chichester Psalms
soloists:
sopranos: Sally Cheer, Sheena Marr
alto: Marian Walker
tenor: Paul Heppleston
bass: Michael Turner

Saturday 19 June

11am Pier Arts Centre, Stromness
Seamus Heaney poetry reading

3pm St Magnus Cathedral
**Michael Rippon: baritone
Josephine McKinnie: piano**

Dowland: Flow not so fast ye fountains
Purcell: Let the dreadful engines
Handel: Revenge Timotheus cries
Somervell: Selection from Maud
Berkeley: Three Greek Songs
Dalby: 8 Songs from the Chinese

6pm Orkney Arts Theatre, Kirkwall
Opera: Cinderella
(repeat performance)

8.30pm Orkney Arts Theatre, Kirkwall
Three Orkney Plays

The Wireless Set
Morag MacInnes
from a short story by
George Mackay Brown
producer: Morag MacInnes

cast:
Betsy Eunson: Meg Harvey
Hugh Eunson: Willie Muir
Howie Eunson: John Grieve
Samuel Omand: Ian MacInnes
Maria Omand: Anne Bevan

Mr Sinclair, missionary: Philip Cooper
Granny Eunson: Kitty Tait
Postman and Mansie Work:
Jack Rosie
Advertiser: Howie Firth
William Joyce: Walter Hancox

stage managers: David Lennie,
Rupie Merriman, Billy Black
lighting: Norman Rushbrook,
Kris Misselbrook
special effects: Howie Firth
props and set design: Anne Stockan

Bessie Millie's Wind Shop
by George Mackay Brown
producer: Jan Mackay
incidental music
by Peter Maxwell Davies

cast:
Bessie Millie: Tanya Duncan
Fisherman's Mother: Fiona Rendall
Nell: Aimée Leonard
Captain Bendigo: Kevin Garriock
1st Skipper: James Leonard
2nd Skipper: Roddy McGurk
3rd Skipper: Fiona Buchan
4th Skipper: Judith Dixon
5th Skipper: Karen Sinclair
6th Skipper: Martin Gillespie
Crofter: Craig Hourston
Crofter's Wife: Alison Tulloch

instrumentalists:
violin: Barbara Mainland
piano: Jayne Hourston
oboe: Anne Bevan
flute: Duncan Porteous

costumes: Elaine Marshall

Jock and Blind Mary
by George Mackay Brown
producer: Jean Campbell

cast:
Jock: Walter Leask
Mary: Connie Buchan
Old Soldier: Alistair Buchan
Bishop: John Broom
Fisherfolk, Harvesters and Monks:
Ian Anderson, Ian Leask, Paul
Macphail, Tomas Macphail,
Eileen Anderson, Phyllis Brown,
Allison Dixon, Pat Hanley,
Elma MacLeod, Mary Hutchinson
Mans: Ian Leask
Hild: Mary Hutchison

Sunday 20 June

10.45pm St Magnus Cathedral
Festival Service
conducted by the Rev William Cant
minister of St Magnus Cathedral

introit:
Walford Davies: God be in my head
anthems:
Weelkes: Gloria
Patrick Hadley: My beloved spake
organ music during the service:
Jean Langlais: Ave Maris Stella
organ music after the service:
Flor Peeters: Ave Maris Stella

3pm Academy Hall, Stromness
Parikian Fleming Roberts Trio
Manoug Parikian: violin
Amaryllis Fleming: cello
Bernard Roberts: piano

Mozart: Trio in B flat, K502
Beethoven: Trio in D Op 70, No 1
'Ghost'
Shostakovich: Trio Op 67

6.30pm Pier Arts Centre, Stromness
**Pre concert talk:
Peter Maxwell Davies**

8pm Academy Hall, Stromness
The Fires of London
conductor: John Carewe
baritone: Michael Rippon
cimbalom: Gregory Knowles
juggler: Johnny James

Stromness Academy Wind Group
conductor: Jean Leonard

JS Bach/Maxwell Davies:
Prelude and Fugue in C Sharp major
Prelude and Fugue in C Sharp minor

Maxwell Davies:
Image Reflection Shadow
(1st movement)

Maxwell Davies:
Le Jongleur de Notre Dame

Monday 21 June

11am Orkney Arts Theatre, Kirkwall
**A Johnsmas Foy
Heart of Orkney**
readers: Elizabeth Bevan,
Jan Mackay, Bessie Grieve,
Michael Corsie
music: Hugh Inkster, Ingirid Jolly,
Johnny Mowat
compere: Howie Firth
compiled and produced
by Marjorie Linklater

2.30pm Academy Hall, Stromness
Schools Concert
North Walls School, Hoy
conductor: Glenys Hughes
director: John Eccles

Maxwell Davies:
Songs of Hoy

Stromness Academy Strings:
conductor: Jean Leonard
Elgar:
Serenade for Strings in E minor,
Op 20;
Traditional Tunes and Airs

Kirkwall Grammar School Girls' Choir:
conductor: Josephine Richards
Nicholas Maw:
Calico Pie and
other Nonsense Rhymes

6pm Papdale Infant School, Kirkwall
Schools Concert
(repeat performance)

8.30pm Orkney Arts Theatre, Kirkwall
The Fires of London
conductor: John Carewe
baritone: Michael Rippon

Maxwell Davies: The Bairns of Bruch
Anthony Payne:
A Day in the Life of a Mayfly
Anonymous/Davies:
Sixteenth Century
Scottish Dances
Maxwell Davies:
Eight Songs for a Mad King

Tuesday 22 June

11am St Magnus Cathedral
Philippa Davies: flute
Stephen Pruslin: piano

Haydn: Sonata in C major, ob XVI:48
Ravel: Menuet sur le nom de Haydn
Debussy: Hommage a Haydn

Mhairi MacInnes:
Gniew
(Festival commission)

JS Bach: Partita in A minor
Debussy: Syrinx
Mhairi MacInnes:
Gniew
(second performance)

2pm Primary School Hall, Stromness
Wildcat Theatre Company:
1982
by David MacLennan
and David Anderson

director: Ian Wooldridge

2.30pm St Magnus Cathedral
Grampian Percussion Ensemble
conductor: Ron Forbes

Ron Forbes: Autun Carillon
Barrozo: Baia
Trad: My love she's but a lassie yet
Ron Forbes: Circles
Marvin Hamlisch: The way we were
Richard Carpenter:
Carpenters Medley
Ron Forbes: Polymers
Margaret McKinnon: Little Dancer
Ron Forbes: Erlangen Polka
JS Bach: Aria
Ron Forbes: Drumtime
Ron Forbes: Dance Suite for Insects

7.30pm Orkney Arts Theatre, Kirkwall
Three Orkney Plays
(repeat performance)

10pm Orkney Arts Theatre, Kirkwall
A Johnsmas Foy
and Whassigoes
A late night performance of Orkney
prose, poetry, music and song

Wednesday 23 June

11am Academy Hall, Stromness
A Johnsmas Foy
(repeat performance)

2.30pm Academy Hall, Stromness
Grampian Percussion Ensemble
(repeat performance)

7pm St Magnus Cathedral
Richard Hughes: organ
Scottish Early Music Consort

Maxwell Davies:
Organ Sonata

Le Roman de Fauvel:
The story of Humbug the Tawny Ass

Linda Ormiston: mezzo soprano
Fiona Milne: mezzo soprano
Paul Hindmarsh: tenor, nakers
Jennifer Hill: recorders, douçaine
Daphne Godson: rebec,
medieval fiddle
Warwick Edwards: harp, shawm
Jane Cakshott: speaker

9.30pm Orkney Arts Theatre
Wildcat Theatre Company:
1982
(repeat performance)

Exhibitions

Pier Arts Centre, Stromness
David Hockney: drawings and prints

Tankerness House Museum
Birsay: portrait of an Orkney Parish

Corrigall Farm Museum
Beremeal and Burstin:
the history of threshing and milling
grain in Orkney

Stromness Museum
Days of Cord and Canvas:
a century of sail trading in Orkney

Stromness Library
Erlend Brown/John Cumming

Friday 17 June

8pm St Magnus Cathedral
Music in the Cathedral
St Magnus Cathedral Choir
conductor: David Drinkell
organ: Robin Cheer
Festival Chorus
conductor: Richard Hughes
organ: David Drinkell
Orkney Youth Brass
conductor: John V Jones

Orkney Youth Brass:
Handel:
Music for the Royal Fireworks

St Magnus Cathedral Choir:
Claudio Monteverdi: Beatus Vir
Geoffrey King:
Then Jacob Awoke -
(festival commission)

Orkney Youth Brass:
Tallis, arr. Maxwell Davies
Four Voluntaries:
Veni Redempto 1;
Ex More Docti Mistico;
Ecce Tempus;
Veni Redemptor 2
Gesualdo, arr. Maxwell Davies:
Two motets:
Peccatem me quotidie;
O vos Omnes

Festival Chorus
Tippett: Three spirituals from
'A Child of Our Time':
Steal Away; Nobody Knows;
Go down, Moses

Poulenc: Gloria
solo soprano: Sally Cheer

Saturday 18 June

11am Pier Arts Centre, Stromness
Richard Murphy poetry reading

4pm St Magnus Cathedral
Noye's Fludde
Benjamin Britten
producer: Ingirid Cosby
conductor: David Drinkell

chorus of animals and orchestra:
Stenness, Orphir, Stromness and
Papdale Primary Schools;
Kirkwall Grammar School,
Stromness Academy

cast:
The Voice of God: Michael Turner
Noye: Dr William Watson
Mrs Noye: Anne Scott
Sem: Louise Grant
Ham: Stewart Stanger
Jaffett: Sweyn Hunter
Mrs Sem: Diane Sinclair
Mrs Ham: Glynis Littlejohn
Mrs Jaffett: Elizabeth Hume
The Raven: Petrina Thomson
The Dove: Phoebe Bewley
Mrs Noye's Gossips: Jacqueline Byers,
Alison Lochhead, Barbara Matches,
Anne Mowatt, Alison Walker.

6pm St Magnus Cathedral
Noye's Fludde
(repeat performance)

8pm Orkney Arts Theatre
Three Orkney Plays

Ship Surgeon
Morag MacInnes
producer: Philip Cooper

cast:
Singer: Doreen McLellan
Landlord: John Broom
Ella: Anne Stockan
David Murison: Alex Rigg
John Drew: Dennis Bullen
Robert Dow: Charlie Fraser
Mrs Aitchison: Allison Dixon
Capt Aitchison: Walter Leask
Mrs Spence: Alice King
Betty Spence: Anne Bevan
Samuel Spence: James Gray
Mr Grahame: Ian MacInnes

lighting: Mark Ridgway

The Island of the Saints
by George Mackay Brown
producer: Andy Eyre
incidental music by
Peter Maxwell Davies

cast:
Glum: Willie Muir
Sib: Meg Harvey
Willie: Donnie Grieve
Factor: Brian Flett
Nell: Jean Work

instrumentalists:
Hugh Black: flute
Anne Bevan: oboe
Gillian Tullock: clarinet
John V Jones: horn
Peter Saunders: cello
Josephine Richards: piano

The Battle in the Hills
by George Mackay Brown
producers: Jean Campbell and
Connie Buchan

Gunchild: Morag Black
Solveig: Pat Hanley
Thora: Phyllis Brown
Ragna: Megan Eggeling
Anna: Allison Dixon
Ingerd: Connie Buchan
Voice of the Herald: Walter Leask

stage managers: David Lennie and
Billy Black

lighting: Mark Ridgway

10pm Kirkwall Hotel
Festival Club Jazz: Pagoda
Mark Glentworth
Isobel Ward
Christopher Gregory
Malcolm Morton
Erica Harold
Greg Knowles

Sunday 19 June

10.45am St Magnus Cathedral
Festival Service
conducted by the Rev RS Whiteford,
associate minister of St Magnus
Cathedral

introit:
Tye: Laudate Nomen Domini
Nielsen: Jeg Ser Deg, O Guds Lam

anthem:
Parry:
I was glad when they said unto me

organ music: for the offertory:
Hindemith: Sonata II (1st movement)
Harwood: Postlude:
Sonata in C minor (1st movement)

3pm Academy Hall, Stromness
Celebrity Recital
Rosemary Furniss: violin
Emiko Tadenuma: piano
Günther Bauer-Schenk: piano

Beethoven: Sonata in F major Op.
24 (Spring Sonata)
Debussy: Sonata in G minor
Schubert: two military marches
Mozart: Sonata (piano duet)

(note: György Pauk, the programmed
recitalist, was indisposed at very
short notice. Rosemary Furniss
stepped in, along with Günther Bauer-
Schenk, who played duets with the
programmed accompanist, Emiko
Tadenuma.
     The original programme was
slightly altered, but Ms Furniss played
two of the intended pieces. The
Schubert marches and the Mozart
sonata were additions to the original
programme.)

8pm Academy Hall, Stromness
Fana Church Choir
Plaine Musicke Duo

Fana Church Choir:
Edvard Grieg: Ave Maris Stella Varen
LM Lindeman: Knut liten og Sylvelin
Halfdan Kjerulf: Brudeferden
Alfred Paulsen: Når fjordene blåner

Ingunn Skage: soprano
Edvard Grieg: Jeg elsker deg
           En svane
           Solveigs sang
           (from 'Peer Gynt')

Fana Church Choir:
Folk song, arr. Eivind Alnaes:
Å vesle Kari vår
Sparre Olsen:
Gud signe Noregs land
Henrik Lyssand: Trolldans, Bukkevise
Geirr Tveitt: Fløytelåt
Folk song: Kjerringa med staven,
Pål sine høner

Monday 20 June

11am Academy Hall, Stromness
A Johnsmas Foy:
Orkney At War
producer: David Milsted
performed by members and friends
of Kirkwall Arts Club

1pm Academy Hall, Stromness
Lunchtime Jazz: Pagoda

2.30pm St Magnus Cathedral
Fana Church Choir
conductor: Sigmund Skage
vice-conductor: Håkon Helland
organist: Sigmund Skage

organ:
Gottfred Pedersen:
Improvisata over Hellig Olav

Fana Church Choir:
Lars Heggen:
Salige er de som hører Guds ord
Ludvig Nielsen:
Jeg ser deg o Guds lam
Egil Hovland: Og ordet ble kjød
Edvard Grieg: I Himmelen
(soprano soloist: Ingunn Skage)
Knut Nystedt: Salme 100

Ingunn Skage: soprano
Norwegian folk tune:
Den storehvite flokk
Norwegian folk tune:
Se solens skjønne lys og prakt
Dvorak: God is my shepherd
Handel: With thee th'unshelter'd
moor I'd tread

Fana Church Choir:
GA Homilius: Deo dicamus gratias
Christopher Tye:
Laudate nomen Domini
Johann Rosenmüller:
Nu farvel du verdens rike
Anton Bruckner: Locus iste
Hugh S Roberton:
All in the April Evening
Mozart: Laudate Dominum
(soprano soloist: Ingunn Skage)

organ
Egil Hovland: Orgeltoccata over 'Nu
takker alle Gud'

6pm Papdale Infant Hall, Kirkwall
Choral and Instrumental
Concert
Kirkwall Grammar School Girls' Choir
conductor: Richard Hughes
Stromness Academy Brass Band
conductor: John V Jones

Vaughan Williams arr. Frank Wright:
Folk Song Suite:
Seventeen Come Sunday;
My Bonny Boy;
Folk Songs from Somerset

Kodaly:
Three Part Songs:
Fiddle-Dee;
'Mid the Oak Trees;
Hippity-Hoppity

Maxwell Davies:
The Pole Star

Maxwell Davies:
Seven Songs Home

Phillip Malbon:
Bollin Hill Suite

8pm Orkney Arts Theatre, Kirkwall
Aklowa
African Drummers and Dancers

Tokoe: a puberty dance
Kpanlogo: a captivating social dance
Adzogbo: a warriors' preparation
dance
Damba Takai: a ceremonial dance
of the Dagombas
Sekyi: a social dance of the Ashantis
Gazo: warriors' preparation dance
Akan: ceremonial dance
Adowa: Ashanti ceremonial dance
Sohu: a cult dance
Nandom: a festival dance
Kpatsa: a social lovers' dance
Muaga: a ceremonial manhood
dance

10pm Kirkwall Hotel
Festival Club Jazz: Pagoda

Tuesday 21 June

11am St Magnus Cathedral
Plaine Musicke Duo
Jolande van der Klis, Espen Saetre

programme including:
The Division Flute (1706) and works
by Turloch O'Carolan (1670-1738)

1.05pm St Magnus Cathedral
The St Magnus Trio
Neil Mackie: tenor
Richard Watkins: horn
Günther Bauer-Schenk: piano

Britten:
Canticle No 3 Op 55
Still falls the rain
(Edith Sitwell 1887-1964)

Purcell, realised by Britten:
Three Songs:
I'll sail upon the dog-star
If music be the food of love
Man is for the woman made

Maxwell Davies:
Sea Eagle for solo horn

Two Unaccompanied Prayers
Britten: St Nicolas
Maxwell Davies: St Magnus

Three Old English Songs
arr. Frank Spedding
The Miller of Dee
The Oak and the Ash
The Lass of Richmond Hill

2.30pm Stromness community centre
Aklowa
(repeat performance)

8pm St Magnus Cathedral
Scottish Chamber Orchestra
conductor: James Conlon
violin: Rosemary Furniss
(not György Pauk as programmed)

Stravinsky: Concerto in D for Strings
Mendelssohn: Violin Concerto in E
minor, Op 64
Mozart: Symphony No 38 in D major
'Prague'

1st Violins: John Tunnell,
Brian Thomas, Paul Manley,
Julie Taylor, Gregory Squire, Lorna
McLaren, James Clark, Dorothie Bor
2nd violins: Jerre Gibson,
Rosemary Ellison, Susan Rigby,
Mary Miller, Niamh Lyons, Brian Hale
violas: Paul Silverthorne,
James Sleigh, Mary Breatnach,
Stephen Shakeshaft
cellos: William Conway,
Simon Morris, Maureen Morrison,
Rhydian Shaxson
basses: John Steer, Adrian Bornet
flutes: David Nicholson,
Ewen Robertson
oboes: Robin Miller, Maurice Checker
clarinets: Lewis Morrison, Lorna Cook
bassoons: Melville Jerome,
Peter Moore
horns: Hugh Jenkins,
Harry Johnstone, Chris Griffiths,
Stewart Benzie
trumpets: Barry Collarbone,
Peter Franks
timpani: Caroline Garden

Wednesday 22 June

12am Guide Hall, Kirkwall
A Johnsmas Foy
(repeat performance)

2.30pm Kirkwall Grammar School
Aklowa:
African Dance Workshop

2.30pm Academy Hall, Stromness
Choral and Instrumental
Concert
(repeat performance)

8pm St Magnus Cathedral
Scottish Chamber Orchestra
conductor: James Conlon
tenor: Neil Mackie

Mozart:
Symphony No 25 in G minor, K183

Maxwell Davies:
Into the Labyrinth.
(commissioned by the
Scottish Chamber
Orchestra)

Schubert:
Symphony No 4 in C minor, D417
'Tragic'

Exhibitions

Tankerness House Museum, Kirkwall
The Great Orkney Kelp Boom

Corrigall Farm Museum, Harray
Horse-drawn farm machinery

Stromness Museum, Stromness
The Sunken Fleet

Graemeshall, Holm
The Norwood collection
of antiques

Pier Arts Centre, Stromness
Ferry Terminal, Stromness
Stromness Library
Vestlandsutstillingen:
art from West Norway

1984

Friday 15 June

8pm St Magnus Cathedral
Music in the Cathedral

St Magnus Cathedral Choir
Tudor Anthems
master of the music: David Drinkell
assistant organist: Robin Cheer
Festival Chorus
Britten: St Nicolas
conductor: Richard Hughes
organ: Robin Cheer
tenor: Malcolm Aitken

St Magnus Cathedral Choir:
Thomas Tallis:
O Nata Lux de Lumine;
'Iam solus ortus sidere'
organ: Robin Cheer
attrib. John Mudd:
Let thy merciful ears, O Lord
Weelkes: Gloria in Excelsis Deo;
Hosanna to the Son of God
Jehan Alain: Deux Chorals; Variations
sur un Theme de Clement Jannequin
organ: David Drinkell
Gibbons: This is the Record of John
alto solo: Robin Cheer
organ: Richard Hughes

Festival Chorus and Orchestra:
conductor: Richard Hughes
soloist: Malcolm Aitken
treble soloist: Raymond Buchan

Benjamin Britten: St Nicolas

'Three Pickled Boys':
Jill Donaldson, Karen Oddie,
Justine Jamieson
organ: Robin Cheer
piano: Allan Buchan, Rachel Hart
with Kirkwall Grammar School
Girls' Choir
conductor: Sean Hart

Festival Orchestra:
violins: Rosemary Furniss,
Ian McKune, Libby Kelsall,
Elaine Grieve, Elaine Gordon,
Lesley McLeod, Alan Gifford,
Peter Pratt, Barbara Mainland,
Alice Kelsall, Susan Stout
violas: Louis Newell, Helen Shearer;
Jean Leonard
cellos: Emma McLeod,
Peter Saunders
Percussion: Gregory Knowles,
Josephine Jones, Douglas Watt,
Hugh Black

10pm Orkney Arts Theatre
Kirkwall Arts Club:
Suburb of Babylon
by Hugh Leonard

part one:
A Time of Wolves and Tigers
Jumbo Beamish: David Milsted
Radio Newscaster: Dick Campbell
director: Jan Holt
Nothing Personal
Pat Nagle: Richard Welch
Philip Agnew: Dave Grieve
Betty Hand: Laura Chirgwin

director: Dave Grieve
part two:
The Last of the Last of the Mohicans
Dominick Studley: Aly Bruce
Finbar Reidy: Tommy Wylie
Grace Lamb: Cathy Lyner
Ita Studley: Morag Blance
Seamus Lamb: Andy Eyre
Radio Newscaster: Dick Campbell
Director: Andy Eyre

set designer: Dave Grieve
lighting: Norman Rushbrook

Saturday 16 June

11am Pier Arts Centre, Stromness
Ted Hughes poetry reading

3pm Papdale Infant Hall
Schools Concert
Kirkwall Grammar School Wind Band
Papdale Primary School
Glaitness Primary School
Festival Youth Orchestra

Kirkwall Grammar School
Wind Band:
conductor: Hugh Black
flutes: Coreen Buchan, Gina Gibson,
Louise Grant, Donna Sim,
Catherine Thomson
alto clarinet: David Marwick
bass clarinet: Gillian Tullock
clarinets: Elizabeth Booth,
Doreen Burton, Ruth Lea,
Christine Inkster, Glynis Littlejohn,
Elinor Rendall, Ailsa Ritchie,
Shona Ritchie, Lesley Tait,
Angela Wilson
oboes: Helen Kemp, Katie Robertson
cornets and trumpets:
Richard Gregory, Marian Rendall,
Sandy Rendall, Ian Robertson.
baritones: Dawn Hourston,
Stewart Stanger
saxophones: Elinor Walls,
Dougie Shearer
euphonium: Sean Hart
french horns: Paul Dixon,
John V Jones
trombones: Christopher Shearer,
Inga Stewart
percussion: Shereen Hasham,
Yvonne Harcus, Kirsten McLeod,
Paula Marwick, Robert Leslie

Clare Grundman: Little Suite
for Band
Stephen Sondeim, arr. Cofield:
Send in the Clowns
Harry Stone: The Time is Now

Papdale Primary School:
The Demon of Adachigahara
libretto: Ted Hughes
music: Gordon Crosse

Glaitness Primary School:
Zacchaeus the Taxman
lyrics: Fiona Menzies
performed by Primary 4 and 5

cast:
Zacchaeus: Graham Sinclair
Jesus: Damien Barnett

crowd: Logan Campbell,
Malcolm Dowell, Erik Drever,
Paul Drever, Mark Holmes,
Brian Markey, Ian Rendall, Alan Scott,
John Scott, David Taylor,
Jacqueline Anderson, Nicola Ashley,
Catriona Campbell, Anne Clouston,
Caroline Hume, Fiona Kirkness,
Louise Kleboe, Lynn Mackay,
Theresa Moar, Sheryl Norquoy,
Theresa Scott, Diane Seator,
Audrey Mackay, Nerys Thomas,
Lenore Learmonth,
Gwen Heppleston

choir: Garry Eunson, Trevor Kinghorn,
Greg Learmonth, James Livitt,
Gareth Pratt, Mark Poresland,
Sweyn Robinson, Justin Reid,
Clarke Ross, David Rendall,
Peter Shearer, Nicholas Swanney,
Matthew Wright, Sarah Collinson,
Susan Eccles, Katie Hancock,
Hazel Kent, Jane Rodger, Ola Scott,
Inga Falconer, Susan Firth.

musical director: Douglas Watt
piano: Douglas Watt
bass guitar: Sean Hart
percussion: Neil Stevenson
production: F Menzies
scenery: D Grieve, W Allan
costumes: V Steele and P6 pupils

Festival Youth Orchestra:
conductor: Richard Hughes

Maxwell Davies: Five Klee Pictures

violins: (Stromness Academy):
Barbara Mainland, Peter Pratt,
Kathleen Mainland, Polly Cheer,
Alison Ritch, Calum Sutherland,
Jane Baikie, Karen Sinclair,
Karen Inkster, Susan Corrigall,
Avril Mathers, Isabel Garson,
Jacqueline Gray, Graham Garson,
Sarah Scarth, Annette Kirkpatrick,
Catriona Wood, Dawn Johnston,
Hermione Bewley, Judith King
(Kirkwall Grammar School):
Mairi Gordon, Kathleen Hogarth,
Arlene Peace, Erika Jolly, Helga Jolly,
Angela Shearer, Beverley Meason,
Susan Sinclair, Tracey Muir,
Alice Kelsall, Susan Stout,
Heidi Zighart, Fiona Cromarty,
Ingrid Donaldson, Monica Reid,
Amy Robertson
violas: Grant Cumming, Louis Newell,
Helen Shearer, Jean Leonard
cellos: Cameron Stout, Paul Rendall,
Robert Walker, David Rendall,
Peter Saunders
double basses: Victoria McEwan,
Dougie Shearer
flutes: Stefan Birch, Coreen Buchan
oboes: Aimée Leonard, Helen Kemp
clarinets: Christine Inkster,
Gillian Tullock
bassoons: Hugh Black, Allan Buchan
horns: Paul Dixon, John V Jones,
Michael Riches
trumpets: James Gray, Ian Robertson
trombones: Craig Hourston,
Anna Winters

8pm Orkney Arts Theatre
Festival Drama and Foy

Home is the Sailor
by George Mackay Brown
producer: Fraser Dixon

cast:
Captain Scarth: John Broom
Mistress Richan: Phyllis Brown
Bessie Millie: Allison Dixon
Gow: Dennis Bullen
Thora: Anne Robertson
Sander Walls: Alex Rigg
Bella Jean Walls: Doreen McLennan
Willa: Ingirid Morrison
Sailor: Brian Flett
Sailor: Eddie Cummins

stage manager: Dennis Bullen

A Johnsmas Foy
compiled and produced by
Howie Firth, with Claire Nielson and
local artists

Between Mouthfuls
by Alan Ayckbourn
producer: Bob Ross
performed by Palace Players

cast:
Donald Pearce: Ken Martin
Emma Pearce: Liz Finch
Martin: Chris Matthews
Polly: Maggie Muir
Walter: Willie Harper
backstage: Jean Hargreaves,
Inga Adams

10pm Kirkwall Hotel
Club Jazz: Pagoda

Sunday 17 June

10.45am St Magnus Cathedral
Festival Service
conducted by Rev W Cant

3pm Academy Hall, Stromness
Julian Bream

JS Bach: Sonata No 1 in A minor,
BWV 1001
Fernando Sor: Variations on a theme
of Mozart, Op 9
Peter Maxwell Davies: Hill Runes;
Farewell to Stromness
Frederico Mompou: Suite
Compostelana,
Manuel de Falla: Homenage pour
le tombeau de Claude Debussy;
Miller's Dance (Tricorne)
Enrique Granados: Valses Poeticos

7pm Pier Arts Centre
Pre concert talk:
Peter Maxwell Davies

8pm Academy Hall
Albany Brass Ensemble
trumpets: Paul Archibald,
Graham Ashton
horn: James Hardy
trombone: David Whitson
tuba: James Gourlay

Witold Lutoslawski: Mini Overture
Maxwell Davies: Brass Quintet
JS Bach: Toccata and Fugue in
D minor
Victor Ewald: Quintet No 3
Malcolm Arnold: Quintet for Brass

10pm Stromness Hotel
Festival Club Jazz: Pagoda

Monday 18 June

11am Academy Hall
A Johnsmas Foy
(repeat performance)

11am Kirkwall Grammar School
**Albany Brass Ensemble:
Workshop**

6pm St Magnus Cathedral
Albany Brass Ensemble
trumpets: Paul Archibald,
Graham Ashton
horn: James Hardy
trombone: David Whitson
tuba: James Gourlay

Michael Praetorius:
Dances from Terpsichore
Eugene Bozza: Sonatine
Dominico Scarlatti: Tri Essercizi

John Gray:
Splitting the Difference
(Festival commission)

Gesualdo, arr. Maxwell Davies:
Peccatem me Quotide O vos omnes
Leonard Salzedo: Capriccio

8pm Orkney Arts Theatre
Bankhead Youth Theatre: Coda
a rock opera performed by the pupils
of Bankhead Academy, Aberdeen

cast:
Thomas: Mark Cheyne
Pilate: Alan Hunter
Jesus: Alan Reid
Judas: Stewart Prockter
Roman Soldiers: Darren Coutts,
Paul Manson
Mary Magdalene: Rona Milne
Mary: Sandra Morrison
Angel: Fiona McCabe
Gardener: Gerrard Rattray

disciples/crowd: Arlene Allan,
Heather Lawrence, Sara Prockter,
Alison McConnell, Marie Yule,
Julie Pratt, Jacqueline Sutherland,
Julie Hampton

stage manager: Diane Paterson
lighting: Malcolm Hart,
James Johnson
costume: Ruth Lough
set design: WJ Ward
musical director: Jim Addison
director: David Ward

band:
flute: Iona Lawrence
oboe: Audrey Mutch
clarinet: James Addison Jnr.

saxophone: Alison Christie
lead guitar: Martin Innes
bass guitar: Richard Farnan
percussion: David Brown
drums: Evan McEwen
keyboards: Jim Addison

10pm Kirkwall Hotel
Club Jazz: Pagoda
Greg Knowles, Rosemary Furniss,
Malcolm Morton, Christopher
Gregory, Isobel Ward, Mark
Glentworth, Beverley Davison

Tuesday 19 June

11am Guide Hall, Kirkwall
A Johnsmas Foy
(repeat performance)

11am Academy Hall, Stromness
**Albany Brass Ensemble
Workshop**

2pm Orkney Arts Theatre
Bankhead Youth Theatre: Coda
(repeat performance)

8pm St Magnus Cathedral
**BBC Scottish Symphony
Orchestra**
principal conductor: Jerzy Maksymiuk

1st violins: Geoffrey Trabichoff
(leader), Ben Buurman (assistant
leader), Bernard Docherty,
Peter Jones, Caroline Ellis,
Deborah Preece, Gerard Doherty,
Peter Isaacs, Annamaria McCool
2nd violins: Philip Burrin (principal),
Christopher Latham (assistant
principal), Diane James,
Georgina Mason, John Hounam,
Elizabeth Wallace, Alistair Sorley,
John Scullion
violas: Carolyn Sparey-Gillies
(principal), Joy Watson (assistant
principal), Elizabeth Maskey (sub-
principal), Patricia Field,
Alistair Beattie, Charles Ketteringham,
Mysie Ann Pelly
cellos: Anthony Sayer (principal),
Katrin Eickhorst (assistant principal),
Anthony Claverley (sub-principal),
Myra Chahin
double basses: Donald Walker
(principal), Terrence Darke (assistant
principal), Alan Ferguson
flutes: Rosemary Eliot (principal),
George McIllwham
piccolo: George McIllwham
oboes: Philip Hill (principal),
Barbara Rhodes
clarinets: Geoffrey Haydock
(principal), Duncan Nairn
Eb clarinet: Geoffrey Haydock
bass clarinet: Duncan Nairn
bassoons: Michael Norris (principal),
Andrew Gordon
horns: David Flack (principal),
Shelagh Watson, Kenneth Blackwood
trumpets: Nigel Boddice (principal)
Eric Dunlea
trombones: Peter Oram (principal)
timpani: Gordon Rigby (principal)

Martin Dalby:
Nozze di Primavera
(Festival commission)

WORLD PREMIERE

Mozart: Sinfonia Concertante;
Symphony No 36 in C (Linz)

10pm Orkney Arts Theatre
**Théatre De Complicité:
A Minute too Late**
Simon McBurney, Joseph Houben,
Marcello Magni

Wednesday 20 June

11am Phoenix cinema
**BBC Scottish Symphony
Orchestra**
schools concert
conductor: Jerzy Maksymiuk
presented by Peter Maxwell Davies

2.30pm Academy Hall, Stromness
Schools Concert
Kirkwall Grammar School Wind Band
Papdale Primary School
Glaitness Primary School
Festival Youth Orchestra
(repeat performance)

8pm St Magnus Cathedral
**BBC Scottish Symphony
Orchestra**
conductor: Jerzy Maksymiuk

Stravinsky: Pulcinella Suite
Maxwell Davies: Sinfonietta
Accademica
Mendelssohn: Symphony No 4
'Italian'

10pm Orkney Arts Theatre
**Kirkwall Arts Club:
Suburb of Babylon**
(repeat performance)

10.30pm Kirkwall Hotel
BBC Wind Ensemble

Exhibitions

Pier Arts Centre, Stromness
Land Art – a response to Orkney
Brian Blanchflower,
Andrew Drummond, Glen Onwin;
Sculptures for a Pier
Arthur Watson, Frank Pottinger,
Doug Cocker, Fred Bushe

Ferry Terminal, Stromness
Soulisquoy Printshop

Kirkwall Library
**Glaitness Primary:
Orkney - A Centre of Interest**

Stromness Museum
Shipwreck

Corrigall farm Museum
The Orkney Farmhouse

Tankerness House Museum
Secrets of the Howe -
treasures from an ancient
Orkney mound

1985

8pm Pier Arts Centre, Stromness
Charles Harrison/Erlend Brown
a lecture related to the Ben Nicholson
exhibition in the Pier Arts Centre

Friday 21 June

7pm community centre, Stromness
**Orkney Youth Theatre:
Me and the Circus**

8pm St Magnus Cathedral
Music in the Cathedral

St Magnus Cathedral Choir
master of the music: David Drinkell
assistant organist: Robin Cheer

Orkney Amateur Orchestra
conductor: Graham Thomson

Festival Chorus
conductor: David Drinkell
organ: Robin Cheer

St Magnus Cathedral Choir:
Martin Dalby:
Two Liturgical Canticles
soprano soloist: Muriel Learmonth

Britten:
Rejoice in the Lamb
soprano: Muriel Learmonth
alto: Irene Donaldson
tenor: Jim Lochhead
bass: David Oddie

Orkney Amateur Orchestra:
conductor: Graham Thomson
leader: Ian McKune
Handel: Water Music

1st violins: Alan Gifford,
Graeme Walker, Ian Tait,
Libby Kelsall, Elaine Gordon,
Lesley MacLeod, Douglas MacArthur
2nd violins: Elaine Grieve,
Colin Rendall, Polly Cheer,
Alison Dixon, Susan Stout,
Alice Kelsall, Beverley Meason,
Morven Meason
violas: Louis Newell, Helen Shearer,
Douglas Shearer, Nicola Gray,
Erica Jolly
cellos: Peter Saunders, Mark Rendall,
Linda Hamilton, Paul Rendall
double bass: Nick Pollock,
Susan Penny
flutes: Heather Rendall, Elspeth Bain
oboes: Ed Holt, Katie Robertson
clarinets: Robin Cheer,
Glynis Littlejohn
bassoons: Gwen Exton, Francis Eccles
horns: Harold Exton, Margaret Butlet,
Paul Dixon, Brian Davidson
trumpets: James Gray, Ian Robertson
timpani: Michael Riches

Festival Chorus:
Dvorak: Mass in D Op 86
soprano: Glynis Littlejohn
tenor: Eion Leslie
alto: Irene Donaldson
bass: Richard Hughes

10pm Ayre Hotel
**Festival Club Jazz/Rock:
X-Ray**
Eric Anderson: drums
Stewart Cordiner: guitar/vocals
Al Hyland: sax/vocals
Bruce Johnson: guitar/vocals
William Kay: keyboards
Dave Keay: bass

Saturday 22 June

11am Pier Arts Centre, Stromness
Edwin Morgan poetry reading

1pm St Magnus Cathedral
Marjorie Bruce: organ

Durufle: Prelude
Franck: Cantabile
Tournemire: Te Deum
Langlais: Scherzo Cats; Evocation;
La Nativité
Messiaen: Les Anges;
Les Enfants de Dieu
Dupre: La Fileuse
Dupré: Finale

2.30pm Papdale Infant Hall
Schools Concert
Papdale Primary School
Glaitness Primary School
Kirkwall Grammar School

Papdale Primary School:
Michael Hurd: Little Billy

soloists:
First Mate: Richard Gorn
Gorging Jack: Morven Meason
Guzzling Jim: Nicola Burghes
Little Billy: Mark Skea
chorus of sailors and girls:
The Senior Choir of Papdale
Primary School
producer: Linda Tait
musical director: David Drinkell

Glaitness Primary School
Douglas Watt:
David and
the Giant Philistine
(Festival commission)

musical director: Douglas Watt
lyrics: Fiona Menzies
stage production: Inga Adams
scenery: Dave Grieve and pupils of
P1,2&3
costumes: staff of Glaitness School

David: Graham Sinclair
Goliath: Robin Freeth
King Saul: Damien Barnett
Jesse: Ian Rendall

Kirkwall Grammar School:
Paul Patterson: Rebecca
conductor: Richard Hughes,
speaker: Alice Kelsall

4.30pm Tankerness House courtyard
Orkney Dances
performed by
the Lynn O'Brien Dancers

6pm St Magnus Cathedral
**Käraste Bröder and
Scholae Collegium**

8pm Orkney Arts Theatre
The Caucasian Chalk Circle
By Bertolt Brecht
producer: Penny Aberdein
music: John and James Gray

cast:
Georgi Abashwili: Andy Eyre
Natella: Isobel Eyre
Michael: Finn Aberdein
Shalva: Aly Bruce
Arsen Kazbeki: Alan McFarlane
Bizergan Kazbek: Chris Matthews
Nurse: Alison Leonard
Niko Mikadze: Gerry Taylor
Mika Loladze: Chris Matthews
Architects:
Gerry Taylor, Chris Matthews
Natella's maidservants:
Carolyn Bevan, Aimée Leonard
Corporal: Andy Eyre
Private: Alex Rigg
Peasant: Aly Bruce
Peasant's wife: Alice King
Merchants: Megan Eggeling,
Raymond Lamb
Lavrenti Vashnadze: Gerry Taylor
Aniko: Allison Dixon
Peasant woman: Megan Eggeling
Jussup: Aly Bruce
Monk: Raymond Lamb
Azdak: John Broom
Shauwa: Aly Bruce
Grand Duke: Andy Eyre
Ludovica: Allison Dixon
Innkeeper: Raymond Lamb
Stableboy: Alex Rigg
Peasant woman: Marilyn Davey
Irakli: Alex Rigg
Three wealthy farmers:
Alan McFarlane, Chris Matthews,
Gerry Taylor
Illo Shuboladze: Chris Matthews
Sandro Obaladze: Gerry Taylor
Old married couple: Marilyn Davey,
Alan McFarlane
Cook: Alice King
Ironshirts: Tristan Kennedy,
Anthony Eggeling, Graham Garson
Dancers: Fiona Birch,
Phoebe Bewley, Hermione Bewley,
Kirsten Slater, Penny Black
Peasant women: Dina Burgess,
Caitrian Baikie

narrator: David Grieve
singer: Aimée Leonard
musicians: John Gray, James Gray
prompt: Doreen McLennan

set designer: David Grieve
stage manager: Andy Eyre,
Maureen Heddle
photographer: Fraser Dixon
lighting: Norman Rushbrook
costumes: Sue Bewley, Isobel Eyre
props: Chris Matthews
make-up: Pat Hanley

10pm Ayre Hotel, Kirkwall
**Festival Club Jazz/Rock:
X-Ray**

Sunday 23 June

10.45 St Magnus Cathedral
Festival Service
conducted by Rev William Cant
minister of St Magnus Cathedral
master of the music: David Drinkell
assistant organist: Robin Cheer
music by Viadana, Charles Wood
and Handel

1pm Pier Arts Centre Courtyard
Orkney Dances
(repeat performance)

3pm Academy Hall, Stromness
**Celebrity Recital
Ralph Kirshbaum: cello
Ian Brown: piano**
Beethoven: C major Sonata
Bach: Suite No 2 in D minor
Shostakovich: Sonata
De Falla: five pieces from
Suite Populaire Espagnol

5.30pm Pier Arts Centre
Edwin Morgan poetry reading
(repeat performance)

7pm Pier Arts Centre
**Pre concert talk:
Peter Maxwell Davies**

8pm Academy Hall
The Fires of London
Philippa Davies: flute
David Campbell: clarinet
Rosemary Furniss: violin
Jonathan Williams: cello
Michael Finnissy: piano
Gregory Knowles: percussion

Maxwell Davies:
Dances from The Two Fiddlers
Schoenberg, arr. Webern:
Kammersymphonie
Maxwell Davies:
Image Reflection Shadow
cimbalom: Gregory Knowles

10pm Stromness Hotel
**Festival Club Jazz/Rock:
X-Ray**

Monday 24 June

10.30am Academy Hall, Stromness
A Johnsmas Foy
compiled and produced by
Howie Firth
with Claire Nielson and local artists

11am Kirkwall Grammar School Hall
**Classic films from the
Post Office**
introduced by Martin Cummins

1pm Academy Hall, Stromness
Lunchtime Concert
John Gray: clarinet
James Gray: trumpet, guitar
David Gray: bass guitar

Gray: Circle Dance
Maxwell Davies:
Sonatina for solo trumpet

Gray: Three for Final
(Festival commission)

WORLD PREMIERE

Gray: Fundamental-E
Boulez: Domaines

6pm Orkney Arts Theatre
Lands of Odin
a Folk Art production by Lynn O'Brien

cast: Gillian Cuthbert, Linda Muir,
Melanie Lee, Sheila Robson,
Lynn O'Brien, Sharon Aitken,
Susannah Wake, Inga Lamb,
Ruth Frame, W Andrew Walker,
John Eccles, Dinah Wake, Liz Aitkin,
Liz Lamb, Sylvia Eccles, Deirdre Hill,
Laura Johnston, Catriona Campbell,
Kate Irving-Lewis, Elizabeth Wake,
Jan Eccles, Kes Eccles, Ross O'Brien,
Kriss O'Brien, Gregor Lamb

instrumentalists:
fiddle: John Ayre, Graham Garson
Tristan Cooper
recorder: Melanie Lee
recorder/mandolin: John Eccles
recorder/whistle: W Andrew Walker

producer/director/choreographer:
Lynn O'Brien
scenic/publicity designer:
Mike McGovern
lighting design: Len O'Brien
composer: Seona Dunsmuir
musical director/arrangement:
W Andrew Walker
costumes: Rita Cuthbert,
Sylvia Eccles, Liz Aitkin, Liz Lamb
props: Liz Aitkin, Nicola Thompson
stage managers: Ruth Frame,
W Andrew Walker
stage crew: Ben Geddes,
Graham Aitkin
front-of-house: Sue Irving-Lewis,
Doreen Wake

8.15pm St Magnus Cathedral
Scottish Chamber Orchestra
conductor: Nicholas Cleobury

Holst: St Paul's Suite
Delius: On Hearing the First Cuckoo
in Spring
Maxwell Davies: Sinfonia Concertante

Edward Harper:
Fantasia V for
Chamber Orchestra
Passacaglia on EH3 7DC
(Festival commission)

WORLD PREMIERE

Elgar: Introduction and Allegro

1st violins: John Tunnell,
Brian Thomas, Anders Fog-Nielsen,
Julie Taylor, Gregory Squire,
Brian Hale, Jurgen Hess,
Dorothie Bor
2nd violins: Jerre Gibson,
Rosemary Ellison, Susan Rigby,
Niamh Lyons, Fiona Higham,
Robert Simans
violas: Paul Siverthorne,
James Sleigh, Mary Breatnach,
Stephen King

cellos: William Conway, Frank Dodge,
Winifred Collarbone,
Maureen Morrison
basses: John Steer, Adrian Bornet
flutes: David Nicholson, June Scott
oboes: Robin Miller, Maurice Checker
clarinets: Lewis Morrison,
Christopher Craker
bassoons: Barth Newman,
Peter Morgan
horns: Robert Cook, Harry Johnstone
trumpets: Peter Franks,
Barry Collarbone
timpani: Caroline Garden

10.15pm Orkney Arts Theatre
Théatre de Complicité:
More Bigger Snacks Now
Directed by Neil Bartlett
Tim Barlow, Jos Houben,
Marcello Magni, Simon McBurney

Tuesday 25 June

11am Guide Centre, Kirkwall
A Johnsmas Foy
(repeat performance)

11am Academy Hall, Stromness
Classic Films from the
Post Office
(repeat performance)

11am Dounby Primary School
Théatre de Complicité:
Workshop

1pm St Magnus Cathedral
Lunchtime Recital
The Fires of London Trio
Madeleine Mitchell: violin
Jonathan Williams: cello
Michael Finnissy: piano

Beethoven: Sonata in D major Op 70
No2 'Ghost'
Brahms: Sonata in C major

6pm Orkney Arts Theatre
The Caucasian Chalk Circle
(repeat performance)

6.15pm Royal Hotel, Kirkwall
Classic Films from the Post
Office
(repeat performance)

8.15pm St Magnus Cathedral
Scottish Chamber Orchestra
conductor: Nicholas Cleobury
cello: Ralph Kirshbaum

Beethoven: Symphony No 1
Tchaikovsky: Variations on a Rococo
Theme for cello and orchestra Op 33
Haydn: Symphony No 103 in E flat
major 'Drum Roll'

10.15pm Orkney Arts Theatre
A Johnsmas Foy
(repeat performance)

in addition:
The Yellow Cake Revue by
Peter Maxwell Davies
singer and player: Mary Thomas

Wednesday 26 June

11am Community Centre, Stromness
Théatre de Complicité:
Workshop

1pm St Magnus Cathedral
Lunchtime Recital
David Drinkell: organ
Mhairi MacInnes: flute
Michael Finnissy: piano

Paul Hindemith: Sonata No2
Frank Martin:
Ballade for flute and piano
Carl Reinecke:
Sonata 'Undine' Op 167 for flute and
piano
Jean Adam Guilain: Suite sur le
deuxieme tune
Henri Mulet: Carillon-Sortie

2.30pm Papdale Primary School
Théatre de Complicité:
Workshop

2.30pm Tankerness House Gardens
The Closet Youth Theatre:
How about a nice cup of tea?
by Mandie Smith & Jacqueline Baikie
cast: Mandie Smith, Jacqueline
Baikie, Diane Bain

8pm Academy Hall, Stromness
Lands of Odin
(repeat performance)

8pm Orkney Arts Theatre
The Fires of London
Nicholas Cleobury: conductor
Mary Thomas: soprano
Tom Yang: dancer
Philippa Davies: flute
David Campbell: clarinet
Madeleine Mitchell: violin
Jonathan Williams: cello
Michael Finnissy: piano
Gregory Knowles: percussion

Maxwell Davies: Miss Donnithorne's
Maggot; Vesalii Icones

Exhibitions

Tankerness House Museum
Fortress Orkney

Corrigall Farm Museum
Tom Kent - photographs

Stromness Museum
The Sinking of the Royal Oak

Kirkwall Library
Ian MacInnes - paintings

Ferry Terminal Building, Stromness
Soulisquoy Printmakers

Kirkwall Community Centre
Sea and Land

Pier Arts Centre, Stromness
Ben Nicholson

Stromness Library
Camera Club

1986

Wednesday 18 June

11.15am Academy Hall, Stromness
The English Brass Ensemble
concert for schools

3.10pm Kirkwall Grammar School
The English Brass Ensemble
concert for schools

6pm Tankerness House Gardens
Orcadia Folk Art Studio
street theatre

musicians: W Andrew Walker,
Tracy Laurenson, Graham Garson,
Wet Peat and the Red Hot Gumboots,
Karen and Lynn Tait, Tanya Davidson,
Ross and Kris O'Brien, Sharon Aitken,
Freya Cooper, Susannah Wake,
Allan Drever, Stephanie and
Teresa Omand
children: Nicola Watson, Inga Lamb,
Lynn and Karen Tait, Tanya Davidson,
Ross and Kris O'Brien, Sharon Aitken,
Freya Cooper, Dinah and Susannah
Wake, Stephanie and Teresa Omand.
adults: Peter Drever, Lynn O'Brien,
Liz Lamb, Mina and Arnie Flett

director/choreographer:
Lynn O'Brien

musical director: W Andrew Walker
costumes: Rita Cuthbert
poster design: Mary Flett
stage crew: Len O'Brien,
Martin Dowell, Karl Robinson,
Mary Flett, Keith Swift,
Nicola Thomson

8pm St Magnus Cathedral
Music in the Cathedral
St Magnus Cathedral Choir
master of the music: David Drinkell
organ: Robin Cheer

Festival Chorus:
conductor: Richard Hughes

The English Brass Ensemble:
Paul Archibald: trumpet
Richard Martin: trumpet
James Handy: horn
Christopher Mowat: trombone
James Gourlay: tuba
with Alan Friel, John Philip: trumpet
John Vernon Jones: horn
David Drinkell: organ
Aileen Laird: timpani
Ian Robertson,
Raymond Kelday: percussion

Britten: Fanfare for St Edmundsbury
for three trumpets

St Magnus Cathedral Choir:
Vaughan Williams: The Hundredth
Psalm
Thomas Weelkes: Hosanna to the
Son of David

English Brass Ensemble:
Samuel Scheidt: The Battle Suite

St Magnus Cathedral Choir:
Viadana: Exsultate justi
Haydn: Insanae et vanae curae

Festival Chorus and Brass:
Pachelbel: Nun Danket alle Gott
Bassano: Dic Nobis Maria
Praetorius: In Dulci Jubilo

English Brass Ensemble:
Paul Patterson: Mean Time

Festival Chorus, brass, percussion
and organ:
John Rutter: Gloria

10pm Town Hall, Kirkwall
Festival Club:
Gerbil

Thursday, 19 June

11.15am Academy Hall, Stromness
A Johnsmas Foy
compiled by Howie Firth
and Claire Nielson

1pm St Magnus Cathedral
The English Brass Ensemble
Paul Archibald: trumpet
Richard Martin: trumpet
James Handy: horn
Christopher Mowat: trombone
James Gourlay: tuba

Moszkowski: Spanish Dances Op 12
Poulenc: Trio
Shostakovich: Quartet No 7 Op 108
Penderecki: Capriccio for Tuba
Previn: Four Outings for Brass

6pm Town Hall, Kirkwall
Ruth Rosen
a tribute to the Scottish poet
WS Graham

8pm Orkney Arts Theatre, Kirkwall
Wildcat: Heather up your Kilt
by David Anderson and the company

10pm Town Hall, Kirkwall
Festival Club:
Login's Well Folk Club
Charlie Saksena, Gudrun Südmersen,
W Andrew Walker, Arnie Flett,
Kitty Halcrow, Bill Halcrow.

Friday, 20 June

1pm Academy Hall, Stromness
Lunchtime Concert
John Gray: clarinet
Glenys Hughes: piano
Peter Pratt: traditional fiddle

Harrison Birtwistle: Verses; Linoi
Sven Weber:
Stronsay Remembered
(Festival commission)

Traditional Fiddle:
Ian S Robertson: Slow Air;
The Bees' Wing Hornpipe;
guitar accompaniment: Stefan Birch
James Dillon: Crossing Over
Chris Fox: or just after…

Traditional fiddle:
Reels: The Tusker; Mill Brae;
The Lament to the death of the
Rev Archie Beaton
Hornpipe: Crossing the Minsch;
The Banjo Breakdown

3pm Academy Hall, Stromness
Orkney: Three Films
BBC video of a trilogy of plays by
George Mackay Brown

6pm St Magnus Cathedral
Richard Hughes: organ

JS Bach: Prelude and 'St Anne' Fugue
in E flat; Two Chorale Preludes from
the 'Orgelbuchlein'
Messiaen: L'Ascension
Vierne: Impromptu
Karg-Elert: Symphonic Chorale No 3

8pm Orkney Arts Theatre, Kirkwall
Doctor Faustus
by Christopher Marlowe
Producer: Penny Aberdein
Music composed by John Gray
(Festival commission)

Doctor John Faustus: Andy Eyre
Mistress Wagner: Megan Eggeling
Valdes: Alan McFarlane
Cornelius: Chris Matthews
Pope Adrian: Raymond Lamb
Raymond: Alan McFarlane
Bruno: Mark Hull
Cardinal of France: Alex Rigg
Cardinal of Padua: Chris Matthews
Archbishop of Rheims:
Anthony Eggeling
Charles V: Alan McFarlane
Martino: Alex Rigg
Fredericko: Cara Grieve
Benvolio: Chris Matthews
Benedick: Mark Hull
Duke of Vanholt: Alex Rigg
Duchess of Vanholt: Megan Eggeling
Robin: Alex Rigg
Dick: Alan McFarlane
A Vintner: Alice King
A Vintner's boy: Mark Hull
Horse Courser's boy: Tristan Cooper
The boy's friends: Mark Eggeling,
Peter Eggeling, Robert Eyre
Good Angel: Marilyn Davey
Bad Angel: Cara Grieve
Mephistophilis: Aly Bruce
Lucifer: Isobel Eyre
Beelzebub: Raymond Lamb
Pride: Alan McFarlane
Covetousness: Sheena Marr
Envy: Jacqueline Cromarty
Wrath: Alice King
Gluttony: Anthony Eggeling
Sloth: Chris Matthews
Lechery: Carolyn Bevan
Alexander the Great: Alex Rigg
His Paramour: Marilyn Davey
Darius: Anthony Eggleing
Helen: Carolyn Bevan
An old woman: Alice King
Solo Chorus: Sheena Marr
musicians: Peter Pratt: violin
Ian Robertson: trumpet
John Gray: clarinet
David Gray: percussion

fight designer: Graham Morris
make up: Pat Hanley
stage manager: Dennis Bullen
scenic designer: Alex Rigg
wardrobe mistress: Isobel Eyre
lighting: Norman Rushbrook

10pm Town Hall, Kirkwall
Festival Club:
Manray
Eric Anderson: drums
Stewart Cordiner: guitar/vocals
Al Hyland: sax/vocals
Bruce Johnson: guitar/vocals
William Kay: keyboards
Dave Steele: bass

Saturday, 21 June

11.15am Pier Arts Centre, Stromness
Douglas Dunn poetry reading

1pm Tankerness House Gardens
Orcadia Folk Art Studio
street theatre

2.30pm Orkney Arts Theatre
Doctor Faustus
(repeat performance)

6pm Papdale Infant Hall, Kirkwall
Schools Concert

Kirkwall Grammar School
Brass Ensemble:
director: John Vernon Jones
Ian Robertson: trumpet and cornet
Amanda Jackson: trumpet and cornet
Marian Rendall: trumpet
Paul Dixon: horn and tenor horn
Raymond Kelday: horn
John Vernon Jones: horn, trombone
Stewart Stanger: tuba, euphonium

Scott Joplin, arr. Alan Gout:
Combination March
G Burgon: Divertimento for Brass
Quartet
L Kesztler: Three Trios for Horns
Mozart, arr. Friedrick Gabler:
Two Trios for Horns
Bartók, arr. Stratton: For Children
K Grange: Rag Burlesque

Orkney's Young Musicians 1985:
Peter Pratt: violin
Halcyon Weber: clarinet
Stefan Birch: flute
Jean Leonard and Sven Weber:
accompanists
James Gray: cello continuo

Ibert: Two Interludes
Spohr: Slow movement from the
Clarinet Concerto
attrib. Handel: Trio Sonata in G Minor
Traditional fiddle music

Junior Choir and Senior Recorder
Ensemble: Papdale Primary School:
A Pride of Lions
music: Phyllis Tate
libretto: Ian Servaillier

producer: Elaine Grieve
conductor: David Drinkell.

St Magnus Festival
programme • Wed 18th - Tues 24th June 1986

8pm St Magnus Cathedral
Royal Philharmonic Orchestra
conductor: André Previn
Isaac Stern: violin
Barry Griffiths: leader

Mendelssohn: Hebrides Overture
Maxwell Davies:
Violin Concerto
(RPO commission)

Vaughan Williams: Fantasia on a
Theme of Thomas Tallis
Mendelssohn: Incidental Music to
'A Midsummer Night's Dream'

10pm Town Hall, Kirkwall
Festival Club: Manray

Sunday, 22 June

10.45am St Magnus Cathedral
Festival Service
conducted by Rev W Cant with the
choirs of St Magnus Cathedral and
Borgundkirke, Alesund
music by Berthier, Monteverdi and
Karlsen

1pm Pier Arts Centre, Stromness
Orcadia Folk Art Studio
street theatre

3pm Academy Hall, Stromness
Celebrity Recital
Isaac Stern: violin
Jean-Bernard Pommier: piano

Mozart: Sonata in C major K403
Fauré: Sonata in A major Op 13
Debussy: Sonata
Frank: Sonata in A major

6pm Academy Hall, Stromness
Douglas Dunn poetry reading
(repeat performance)

8pm Phoenix cinema, Kirkwall
Royal Philharmonic Orchestra
leader: Barry Griffiths
conductor: Peter Maxwell Davies
Lorraine McAslan: violin

Maxwell Davies: Overture
Jimmack the Postie
Bruch: Scottish Fantasia for
violin and orchestra, Op 46
Beethoven: Symphony No 7

10pm Town Hall, Kirkwall
Festival Club: Manray

Monday, 23 June

11.15am Academy Hall, Stromness
Hjellestad School Band

1pm St Magnus Cathedral
Choirs of Borgundkirke

Norwegian Religious Folk-Tunes
Vierne: Organ Music: Final, from
Symphony No 1 in D, Op 14

Church Music from Norway
and Britain

3pm Town Hall, Kirkwall
Orkney Youth Theatre:
Peter is a Person
(and handicapped)
by Alan Cameron
director: Alan Watters

cast:
Jean: Brenda Gunn
Peter: Angus Leslie
Sarah: Fionna Stewart
Evelyn: Aimée Leonard
Bill: Roy Scott
Doctor, Raymond & Shopkeeper:
Andy Wishart
Nurse, Mrs Donaldson, Mrs Petrie &
Mae: Rosemary Sutherland

administrator: Catherine McDonald
set design: Fionna Stewart
set construction: Jane Leonard and
Alan Cameron

6pm Tankerness House Gardens
Orcadia Folk Art Studio
street theatre

7.30pm East Church, Kirkwall
The King's Singers
Jeremy Jackman, Alastair Hume,
Bob Chilcott, Antony Holt,
Simon Carrington, Colin Mason

Watching the White Wheat:
Folk Songs of the British Isles
arr. Richards: The Padstow
May Song
arr. Jackman: Early one morning
arr. Ives: Migildi, Magildi
arr. Runswick: She moved through
the Fair
arr. Langford: There's nae luck about
the House

A Madrigal History Tour:
anon: La tricotea Samartin
Senfl: Ach Elslein
Lassus: Bonjour, bonjour
Tompkins: Too much I once
lamented
Striggio: Il gioco di primiera

Maxwell Davies:
House of Winter

Richard Mannes: Five songs on
poems of Robert Frost

9.30pm Town Hall, Kirkwall
A Johnsmas Foy
(repeat performance)

Town Hall, Kirkwall
Festival Club:
Debbie Scott: fiddle
Willie Johnson: guitar
Jim Park: bass guitar

Tuesday, 24 June

10am Papdale Primary School
Hjellestad School Band

1pm St Magnus Cathedral
Lunchtime Recital
Hjellestad School Band

Purcell, arr. Henderson: Trumpet
Voluntary
Braein: Towards the Ocean
Scarlatti, arr. Johnson: Aria and
Minuet
arr. Ployhar: A Mighty Fortress is
Our God
Grieg, arr. Flisnes: Spring
Lindberg, arr. Johannesen: Old
'Fabods' - hymn
Mendelssohn, arr. Nilsen: Nocturne
Palestrina, arr. Leckrone: Chorale
and Hosanna
Tchaikovsky, arr. Nilsen: Chanson
Triste
Sullivan, arr. Ployhar: Onward,
Christian Soldiers

3pm Orkney Arts Theatre
Orkney: Three Films
(repeat performance)

6pm Town Hall, Kirkwall
Paul Galbraith: classical guitar

Dowland, arr. Galbraith: Sir John
Langton's Pavin
Anon. arr. Duarte/Poulton: Three
Voltes
Dowland, arr. Galbraith: Farewell
Schoenberg, arr. Behrend: Six Kleine
Klavierstücke Op 19
Haydn, arr. Galbraith: Sonata for
Piano No 34
Weiss: Passacaglia
Bach, arr. Galbraith: Partita No 2 in
D minor for violin

7.30pm Town Hall, Kirkwall
Pre concert talk:
Peter Maxwell Davies

8.30pm Phoenix cinema, Kirkwall
The Lighthouse
(opera in a prologue and one act)
by Peter Maxwell Davies
Neil Mackie: tenor
Henry Herford: baritone
Raimund Herincx: bass
conductor: Günter Bauer-Schenk
director: David William

The Fires of London:
Madeleine Mitchell: violin
Rebecca Hirsh: viola
Jonathan Williams: cello
Peter Buckoke: double bass
Helen Keen: flute
David Campbell: clarinet
Richard Watkins: horn
Simon Wills: trombone
Robert Farley: trumpet
Timothy Walker: guitar
Mark Glentworth: percussion
Stephen Pruslin: percussion

cast:
Sandy, Officer One: Neil Mackie
Blazes, Officer Two: Henry Herford
Arthur, Officer Three, the Voice of
the Cards: Raimund Herincx
designer: Ray O'Neil
uniforms: Michael Kennedy
technical team: Timothy Anger,
Kris Misselbrook, Ace McCarron
wardrobe: Katie Birrel

9pm Pier Arts Centre, Stromness
The Crofter of all Seasons:
Orcadia Folk Art Studio
producer: Lynn O'Brien
musical director: W Andrew Walker

cast:
Child: Sharon Aitken
Young woman: Gillian Cuthbert
Mature woman: Lynn O'Brien
Young man: Michael McBurney
Old fisherman: Peter Drever
Piper: Arnie Flett
Bride's Parents: Mina and Arnie Flett
Groom's Parents: Liz Lamb and
W Andrew Walker
Minister: Gregor Lamb
Best Man: Graham Garson
Best Maid: Tracy Laurenson
guests/children: Susannah and
Dinah Wake, Teresa and Stephanie
Omand, Lynn and Karen Tait,
Tanya Davidson, Freya Cooper,
Ross and Kris O'Brien; Nicola Watson

10pm Town Hall, Kirkwall
Festival Finale: Gerbil

Exhibitions

Corrigall Farm Museum
Cubbies, Huvies and Luppies

Tankerness House Museum
Ane Full Burgh Royal

Kirkwall Library
Camera Club

Ferry Terminal, Stromness
Soulisquoy Printmakers

Town Hall, Kirkwall
**St Magnus Festival Tenth
Anniversary Exhibition**

St Magnus Hall, Kirkwall
**St Magnus Festival
Craft Exhibition**

Pier Arts Centre, Stromness
**British Printmakers
1960–1985**

Stromness Museum
Eliza Frazer, Castaway

1987

9pm Arts Theatre, Kirkwall
Edwin Muir - A Tribute
compiled and presented
by Robert Calder
with Janet Adam Smith,
Elizabeth Bevan and Dave Grieve
fiddlers: Len Wilson,
Johnny Morrison.
arranged by Orkney Heritage Society

9pm St Magnus Cathedral
The Martyrdom of St Magnus
by Peter Maxwell Davies
after the novel 'Magnus' by
George Mackay Brown

Günther Bauer-Schenk: conductor
Mary Thomas: mezzo soprano
Neil Mackie: tenor
Christopher Keyte: baritone 1
Brian Rayner Cook: baritone 2
Conor Biggs: bass

instrumentalists:
Judith Hall: flute
David Campbell: clarinet
Peter Francomb: horn
Robert Farley: trumpet 1
Anthony Cross: trumpet 2
Madeleine Mitchell: viola
Jonathan Williams: cello
Robin McGee: double bass
Mark Glentworth: percussion
Stephen Pruslin: keyboards
Timothy Walker: guitar

production manager:
Kris Misselbrook
lighting: Ace McCarron
costumes: Claire Mitchell
production: David William
rehearsed by: Michael McCarthy
The Fires of London productions
manager: Judy Arnold

Neil Mackie: Earl Magnus, Prisoner,
Reporter I, Monk
Christopher Keyte: Norse Herald,
King of Norway, The Tempter,
Herald of Earl Magnus, Reporter II,
Lifolf the Butcher, Monk
Brian Rayner Cook: Welsh Herald,
Keeper of the Loom, Herald of Earl
Hakon, Reporter III, Monk
Conor Biggs: Earl Hakon,
Military Officer, Reporter IV,
Bishop of Orkney, Monk
Mary Thomas: Blind Mary, Mary
O'Connell, The Girl Ingerth

11am Pier Arts Centre, Stromness
Iain Crichton Smith poetry reading

1pm Town Hall, Kirkwall
Mary Thomas: mezzo soprano
Timothy Walker: guitar

Weber: Lass mich schlummern;
Die Zeit; Wiegenlied; Bettlerlied
French songs (arr. Matyas Seiber):
Hélas que je suis desolée; Je suis
trop jeunette; Ne l'oserais-je dire

Peter Maxwell Davies:
Guitar Sonata

Spanish songs
for voice and guitar,
arr. Roberto Gerhard:
La Indita; El Toro; La Ausencia;
Sor, arr. Roberto Gerhard:
Las Quejas de Muraja
Yarrow, arr. Walker: Autumn to May
Trad, arr. Walker: All my trials;
Dance to your daddy

2.30pm Tankerness House Gardens,
Kirkwall
Orcadia Folk Art Studio
street theatre
artistic director: Carl Robinson
artistic coordinator: Lynn O'Brien
technical and musical director:
W Andrew Walker

3.30pm Arts Theatre, Kirkwall
Edwin Muir and The Labyrinth
A one-man play
by George Mackay Brown
Edwin Muir: John Broom
director: Fraser Dixon
stage manager: Dennis Bullen

6pm Arts Theatre, Kirkwall
Festival Video
Peter Maxwell Davies: An Orkney
Wedding, with Sunrise; Songs of Hoy
video projection: George McEwan

7.30pm Phoenix cinema, Kirkwall
BBC Scottish Symphony
Orchestra: Pops Concert
conductor: Günther Bauer-Schenk
leader: Geoffrey Trabichoff
piper: George McIlwham
Bruce Hubbard: baritone
La Verne Williams: mezzo soprano

John Williams: Star Wars;
Olympic Hymn
Gershwin, arr. Richard Rodney
Bennett: Songs from Porgy and Bess
Peter Maxwell Davies: Suite from
'The Boy Friend'
Strauss: Die Fledermaus; Emperor
Waltz; Thunder and Lightning Polka
Peter Maxwell Davies: An Orkney
Wedding, with Sunrise

9.30pm Arts Theatre, Kirkwall
St Magnus Players:
Lady Audley's Secret
by CH Hazlerust
producer: Simon Chirgwin
set designer: Leslie Burgher

Sir Michael Audley: Willie Harper
Robert Audley: Sean Cormack
George Tallboys: Christopher
Matthews
Luke Marks: Damon Thompson
Lady Audley: Gillian Blackmore
Alicia Audley: Cathy Lyner
Phoebe Marks: Jo Sparkes

10pm Town Hall, Kirkwall
Festival Club:
Artist Decided – Norwegian Jazz
Rymsakse – Norwegian Folk Music

9.30am St Magnus Cathedral
Festival Service
conducted by the Rev W Cant
with the choirs of St Magnus
Cathedral and Stord, Norway
master of the music: David Drinkell
assistant organist: Robin Cheer

William Mathias:
Thus saith God the Lord
(An Orkney Anthem)
(Festival commission)

1.00pm Pier Arts Centre, Stromness
Orcadia Folk Art Studio
street theatre

2.30pm Academy Hall, Stromness
Iain Crichton Smith poetry reading
(repeat performance)

4.45pm Academy Hall, Stromness
Celebrity Recital:
Vladimir Ashkenazy: piano

Schubert: Impromptus D946 No 1
and 2; Wanderer Fantasy
Schumann: Novelettes Op 21
Nos 1 and 2; Sonata in F sharp
minor Op 11

8pm St Magnus Cathedral
Festival Chorus
Kirkwall Grammar School, Glaitness,
Papdale and St Andrews Primary
Schools,
BBC Symphony Orchestra
conducted by Jerzy Maksymiuk and
Richard Hughes
Brian Rayner Cook: baritone
Kathleen Hague: soprano

Wagner: Siegfried Idyll
Fauré: Pavane
Maxwell Davies: First Ferry to Hoy
Fauré: Requiem

10pm Town Hall, Kirkwall
Festival Club:
Gerbil and **Isosceles**

1pm St Magnus Cathedral
Stord Choir
conductor: Roald Sangolt
John Magnuson: baritone
Tor Grøn: organ
Anne Karie Tøien: flute

Kjell Habbestad: Accipite from
Mostrasuite
Ludwig Nielson: Intrada gotica; Coral
Cantata over 'Kling no Klokka'
Norwegian religious folk tunes:
arr. Skage: Jeg ser dig O Guds lam
arr. Nystedt: A saeilast stund
arr. Sommerro: Som den gylkdne
sol frembryter
arr. Grieg: Hvad est du dog skøn;
I himmelen
Oscar Hansen: Variations on a
Norwegian Folk Tune 'Eg veit i
himmerik ei borg'

Music for organ:
Knut Nystedt: Three motets:
Velsignet vaere han; Peace unto you;
I will praise thee O lord

Kjell Habbestad:
And I, John

Karlsen:
Psalm 98 - Deilig er jorden

3pm Academy Hall, Stromness
Dance/Sculpture and
Instrumental Concert

Orkney Young Musicians
of the Year:
Alison Ritch: violin
Handel: Sonata no 4 in D
Larghetto; Allegro

Raymond Kelday: horn
Handel: I see a Huntsman

Polly Cheer: traditional fiddle
Louis' Waltz; Mason's Apron;
Whistle o'er the Lave o't

Aline Cross: clarinet
Bauermann: Adagio

Alison Dixon: violin
Tchaikovsky: Canzonetta from Violin
Concerto

Kathleen Mainland: piano
Debussy: Arabesque No 2

Dance/sculpture:
sculptor: John Cumming
music: David Gray
photography: Cara Grieve,
Sandy Matthews, Jon Trevor
stage manager: Graham Morris
lighting: George McEwan
dancers: Penny Aberdein,
Carolyn Bevan, Alison Bowman,
Wendy Bullen, Cara Grieve,
Cathy Lyner, Sandy Matthews

6pm St Magnus Cathedral
David Drinkell: organ

Mendelssohn: Sonata in F minor
Buxtehude: Gigue Fugue in C major;
Prelude and Fugue in G minor
Murschhauser: Variationes super
cantilenam 'Last uns das Kindelein
Wiegen' per imitationem Cuculi
Alan Ridout: Dance Suite
Tippett: Preludio al Vespro di
Monteverdi
Wagner, arr. Edwin Lemare: The
Ride of the Valkyries

7.30pm Phoenix cinema, Kirkwall
BBC Scottish Symphony
Orchestra
conducted by Jerzy Maksymiuk and
William Sweeney
leader: Geoffrey Trabichoff
David Campbell: clarinet

William Sweeney:
Cumha
(Festival commission)

Mozart: Clarinet Concerto in A, K622
Sibelius: Symphony No 1

9.30pm Arts Theatre, Kirkwall
A Johnsmas Foy
compiled and produced
by Gregor Lamb

Karl Cooper, Betty Garson,
Ralph Groat, Knowe o' Deil,
John Linklater, Gregor Lamb,
Sid Nicolson, Sarah Scarth,
Kathy Sclater, Stenness Peedie Folk

10pm Town Hall, Kirkwall
Festival Club: Artist Decided
Norwegian Jazz
Per Jørgensen, Rolf Prestø,
Magne Birkenes

Tuesday 23 June

10.45am Academy Hall, Stromness
Saltire Piano Recital:
David Horne and **Steven Osborne**
introduced by
Sir Peter Maxwell Davies

Beethoven: Sonata in C major Op 53,
'Waldstein'
Maxwell Davies: Piano Sonata
Stravinsky: Petrushka, reduction for
piano duet

1pm Tankerness House Gardens
Lunchtime Jazz: Artist Decided

2pm Stromness Academy, Garson
Theatre Workshop: Tic Toc

2.30pm Academy Hall, Stromness
Stord Choir
conductor: Roald Sangolt
flute: Anne Kari Tøien
piano: Anota Thorvaldsen

Norwegian folksongs:
Sommerfeldt: Springar Frå Bergen;
Egge: Den dag kjem aldri;
Hildre: Å vesle-Kari vår;
Søderland: Folkevise
Rveitt: Sumarnatta
Grieg: Våren
flute and piano:
Sparre Olsen: Intermezzo from
Serenade
FJ Gossec: Tambourin
Three madrigals: Pavane; Tourdion;
Pastime
Sommerfeldt: Three Spring Tunes
Choral music: Hei knut; Eg å du;
Bilongo; Ha, da!; Auld lang syne;
Oh, what a day

5pm Town Hall, Kirkwall
Orkney Youth Theatre:
Magnus - the Man
by Alan Cameron
director: Jon Trevor

Beverly Alcock, Jane Baikie, Lousie
Grant, Jerry Hope, Clare Milner,
Marion Reid, Malcolm Wishart
administration: Rosie Sutherland
costumes: Jane Leonard
stage manager: Aileen Waugh

7pm St Magnus Cathedral
Consort of Musicke
director: Anthony Rooley
Emma Kirkby: soprano
Andrew King: tenor
Evelyn Tubb: soprano
Rufus Müller: tenor
Mary Nichols: alto
Alan Ewing: bass

Schütz: Sleve beate; Alma afflitta;
Dunque addio; Ride la primavera;
Feritevie, ferite
Monteverdi: O come gentile; Vorrei
baciarti; O sia tranquillo il mare
Ward: No object dearer; Down in a
dale; Cruel unkind; If heaven's just
wrath; If the deep sighs
Lawes: This mossy bank; I laid me
down; Amintor's welladay; Awake,
fair Floramell; When death shall
snatch us

8.30pm Tankerness House Gardens
Stord Choir

9.30pm Arts Theatre, Kirkwall
St Magnus Players:
Seed of Destruction
writer/director: Alex Rigg
music by David Gray

Spirit of grief: Megan Eggeling
Seed of destruction: Raymond Lamb
people: Carolyn Bevan,
Wendy Bullen, Sandra Craigie,
Allison Dixon, Alice King, Judith King,
Christine Meek, Ana Winters
lighting: Norman Rushbrook
stage management: Graham Morris
wardrobe: Carol Peebles (et al)
video footage: Alex Rigg, David Gray,
Alan McFarlane
technical assistance: George McEwan

10pm Town Hall, Kirkwall
Festival Club
Jim Robertson: saxophone
Adrian Stuart: keyboards
Ronnie Marwick: drums

Wednesday 24 June

11.15am Academy Hall, Stromness
A Johnsmas Foy
(repeat performance)

1pm St Magnus Cathedral
The Edinburgh Quartet
Miles Baster: violin
Peter Markham: violin
Michael Beeston: viola
Mark Bailey: cello

Haydn: Quartet in D minor, Op 42
Edward Harper: String Quartet No 2
Beethoven: Op 74 in E flat

2pm Academy Hall, Stromness
Orkney Youth Theatre
Magnus - the Man
(repeat performance)

2.30pm Papdale Infant Hall, Kirkwall
Theatre Workshop by Tic Toc

7pm St Magnus Cathedral
St Magnus Cathedral Choir
master of the music: David Drinkell
assistant organist: Robin Cheer
Orkney Orchestra
conductor: Graham Thomson

Anon: Hymn to St Magnus
Egil Hovland: Improvisata, Hymnus
in Honorem Sancti Magni, Comitis
Orcadiae
arr. Bjarne Sløgedal: For Guds folk
er hvilen tilbake
William Mathias:
Thus saith God the Lord
'An Orkney Anthem'
Orlando Gibbons, arr. Ledger:
Drop, drop slow tears
Thomas Weelkes: Alleluia! I heard
a voice
Basil Harwood: O how glorious is
the Kingdom
Britten: Hymn to the Virgin
Handel: Zadok the Priest
William Alwyn: Suite of Scottish
Dances
arr. Britten: Soirées Musicales -
Suite of movements from Rossini

8.30pm Arts Theatre, Kirkwall
Tic Toc Theatre:
Hooligans
written and directed by Jon Gaunt

Dave Findlay, Paul Nolan,
Robert Wilkinson
designer: Lisa Roberts
lighting: John Laidlaw
administrator: Caroline Butcher

10pm Town Hall, Kirkwall
Festival Club:
Gerbil

Exhibitions

Pier Arts Centre, Stromness
Stanley Cursiter:
centenary exhibition

Town Hall, Kirkwall
Edwin Muir:
centenary exhibition

Ferry Terminal, Stromness
The Saint Magnus Tapestry

St Magnus: Kirkwall Library
Soulisquoy Printmakers

New Stromness Academy, Garson
Stromness Revisited

Stromness Library
**Erlend Brown, John Cumming,
Colin Johnstone**

Town Hall, Kirkwall
**Scottish Music
Information Centre**

Anchor Buildings, Kirkwall
Crafts Exhibition

Highland Park distillery
Frances Pelly, artist in industry

Tankerness House Museum, Kirkwall
The Norse Connection
cultural and religious contacts,
Orkney-Norway 800-1200

Stromness Museum
The Ice-Bound Whalers:
Orkney and the arctic whaling

1988

Friday 17 June

7pm St Magnus Cathedral
St Magnus Cathedral Choir
conductors: David Drinkell
and Robin Cheer

Thompson: Alleluia
Byrd: Ave Verum; Sacerdotes Domini;
arr. Jacob: Brother James' Air
Darke: Meditation on Brother
James' Air
Croft-Jackson: Paradise Woods
Rutter: Christ the Lord is risen again;
Duet on an Easter Hymn
Britten: Jubilate Deo

8.15pm Arts Theatre, Kirkwall
St Magnus Players:
Romeo and Juliet
producer: Penny Aberdein

music by John Gray
(Festival commission)

Escalus: Alice King
Capulet: Raymond Lamb
Lady Capulet: Margaret Hay
Second Capulet: Alice King
Juliet: Aimée Leonard
Nurse: Megan Eggeling
Tybalt: Carl Jeffries
Petruchio: Sarah Clubley
Sampson and Hilary: Cameron Stout,
Sarah Clubley
Peter: Peter Eggeling
Anthony and Potpan :
Ewan Bowman, Fraser Bowman
Paris: Graham Garson
Page to Paris: Fraser Bowman
Page to Tybalt: Ewan Bowman
Montague: Tommy Wylie
Lady Montague: Juliet Kepl
Romeo: Alex Rigg
Benvolio: Cathy Lyner
Mercutio: Graham Morris
Balthasar: Finn Aberdein
Servant to the Montagues:
Kim Garson
An Apothecary: Sarah Clubley
Friar Lawrence: Alasdair MacEwen
Friar John: Cameron Stout
Chorus: Sarah Clubley

fight designer: Drew Kennedy
prompt: Dina Burgess
costume: Carol Peebles
set: Alex Rigg
make up: Stromness Academy pupils
masks: designed by Alex Rigg and
made with the help of Brenda
Johnstone and pupils from
Stromness Academy
lighting: Norman Rushbrook,
Stewart Chalmers
photography: Alistair Peebles
stage managers: Donella Kirkland,
Carol Budge, Alison Blacklock,
Carolyn Bevan

musicians:
Leslie Child: violin
Angela Child: cello
Brian Jones: trumpet
Graham Thomson: bassoon
Glenys Hughes: harpsichord

Saturday 18 June

10.30am Pier Arts Centre
Stewart Conn poetry reading

12.30pm Town Hall, Stromness
Festival Lecture: Beethoven
by Sir Peter Maxwell Davies

1.30pm Town Hall, Stromness
Celebrity Recital
Peter Frankl: piano

Schubert: Three Klavierstücke
Beethoven: Sonata No 15 in D Op 28
Liszt: Nauges gris; Schlaflos; Toccata
Andräs Szöllösy:
Passagio con morte
(festival commission)
Kodaly: Meditation
sur un motif de Debussy
Bartók: 15 Hungarian Peasant Songs

2.30pm Albert Street, Kirkwall
Grand Union Street Band

4pm Arts Theatre, Kirkwall
Romeo and Juliet
(repeat performance)

7pm Papdale Infant Hall, Kirkwall
Schools Concert
Kirkwall Grammar School Wind Band
and Girls' Choir
Pupils of St Andrews and
Holm Primary Schools

Kirkwall Grammar School Wind Band
conducted by Graham Thomson
Alford: March - Colonel Bogey
Sondheim, arr. Cofield:
Send in the Clowns
arr. Desmond Walker:
Lowdown on the Hoedown

St Andrews Primary School
Peter Maxwell Davies:
Six Songs for
St Andrews

Holm School Fiddlers
selection of fiddle and folk music

Kirkwall Grammar School Girls' Choir
conducted by Richard Hughes
Lloyd Webber: Memory;
I don't know how to love Him
Rossini: Duet for two Cats
soloists: Beverley Meason,
Lesley Tait
Bach, arr. Bennett Williams:
Bourrée for Bach

8.30pm Phoenix cinema, Kirkwall
Grand Union Orchestra:
A Book of Numbers

musicians:
Dave Adams, Chris Biscoe,
David Clarke, Josefina Cupido,
Ros Davies, Claude Deppa,
Louise Elliott, Carolos Fuentes,
Andy Grappy, Tony Haynes,
Dave Hassell
Clare Hirst, Gerry Hunt, Ken Johnson,
Robin Jones, Sarah Laryea,

Joan McKay, Avelia Moisey,
Keith Morris, Kevin Robinson,
Barbara Snow, Balu Srivastav,
Rick Taylor, Vladimir Vega

10pm Town Hall, Kirkwall
Festival Club:
Gerbil and **Isosceles**

Sunday 19 June

11.15am St Magnus Cathedral
Festival Service
conducted by Rev W Cant
master of the music: David Drinkell
assistant organist: Robin Cheer
Music by Batten, Vaughan Williams
and JS Bach

1pm Pier Arts Centre, Stromness
Stewart Conn poetry reading
(repeat performance)

2.30pm Town Hall, Stromness
Celebrity Recital
György Pauk: violin
Peter Frankl: piano

Mozart: Sonata in B flat K454
Bartók: Sonata no 2
Maxwell Davies: Dances from 'The
Two Fiddlers'
Beethoven: Sonata in F major Op 24

5pm Town Hall, Stromness
A Johnsmas Foy
compiled by Archie Bevan
producer: Marjorie Linklater
A celebration of the work of
George Mackay Brown
read by: Claire Nielson, Elizabeth
Bevan, Dave Grieve, with a film by
Simon Chirgwin (Festival commission)
Graham Garson: fiddle
Lawrence Wilson: tin whistle

7pm Phoenix cinema, Kirkwall
The Orkney Orchestra
conductor: Graham Thomson
Brian Jones: trumpet

Berlioz: Hungarian March
Haydn:
Trumpet Concerto in Eb major
Bizet: Farandole (L'Arlesienne)
Mozart, arr. Thomson:
Theme from 'Elvira Madigan'
(from Piano Concerto No 21)
Kaempfert, arr. Thomson:
Bye Bye Blues
Dvorak, arr. Stone: Slavonic Dance
Herold, arr. Lauchbery: Clog Dance
Berlioz, arr. Carter: March to the
Scaffold

8.30pm Arts Theatre, Kirkwall
Bristol Express Theatre Co:
Between the Lines
by Alan Cubitt

cast:
Sergeant Hogg: Vernon Thompson
Lieut Stephen: Graham Christopher
Biles: Adam Warren
Hogg: Max Jacobson-Gonzalez
Kedge: Joe Hutton

Todd: Adrian Hardwicke
Liz Todd: Niki Hollinshead,
Anna Tymoshenko
Richards: Kevin Williamson
Nurse Marshall: Deirdre Osborne
Staff Nurse Thomas: Camilla Gibbs
Nurse Hall: Kate Goodson
Nurse Peters: Katerina Tana
Mane: Ross Kenworthy
Mason: Collin Johnson
Doris: Lucy Capito
Nance: Petina Hapgood
Quilt: Ben Foster
Photographer: Graham Christopher
Mavis: Katerina Tana

director: Andy Jordan
designer: Michael Vale
lighting: Martin Haylewood
music: Alan Lawrence

10pm Town Hall, Kirkwall
Festival Club:
Grand Union Cabaret Band

Monday 20 June

11am Stromness Town Hall
Bristol Express Theatre Co
(repeat performance)

3pm Town Hall, Kirkwall
Orkney Youth Theatre
The Raven's Nest
directed by Alan Cameron
cast:
Louise Grant, Jerry Hope,
Antony Robertson, Simon Robinson,
Leslie Truman, David Wenzel,
Dominique White

1pm St Magnus Cathedral
Os Kammerkor
conductors: Henrik Lyssand,
Jan Ove Petersen

Magnus Hymn: Nobilis Humilis
Poulenc: Magnum Mysterium
Anderssen: Kyrie Elieson
Mozart: Ave Verum Corpus
Folk Tunes: Eg veit i himmerik ei
borg (arr. Nielson); Som den gyldne
sol (arr. Sommerro); Jeg rade vil
alle (arr. Sommerro)
from Gospel by Robert Ray:
Agnus Dei; Sanctus
Tallis/Bonar/Lyngar:
Jeg horte Jesu stemme si
Hovland: Og ordet ble kjød
Öhrwall: Fabod Psalm

Sigmund Skage: organ
Sløgedal: Variations on the Norwegian
folk tune - Aa hvor salig det skal blive

6pm Arts Theatre, Kirkwall
The Two Fiddlers
by Peter Maxwell Davies
Hutchesons' Grammar School,
conductor: Norman Mitchell
producer: John McKie

cast:
Storm Kolson: David McKie
Gavin: Christopher Elwell-Sutton
Troll King: Jonathan Quin

Troll Queen: Lucy Manson
chorus of trolls and party guests:
Ayman Axmy, Elaine Burton, Athol
Haas, Judith Higson, Lisa Hill, Dawn
Houston, Duncan Ireland, Fraser
Lees, Polly McKie, Hilary McLeod,
Sarah Marr, Carolyn Matheson,
Hayley Miller, Jane Proudfoot, Lesley
Ross, Candice Sammeroff, Rebecca
Smith, Myra Stevenson, Campbell
Williams, Helen Wilson

instrumentalists:
violins: Gie Ming Kuo (leader),
Adrienne Quin, Susie Shenkin,
Seong Sin Han
viola: Catriona Taylor
cello: Laura Finlayson
double bass: Robbie Fraser
flutes: Gillian Morton, Jennifer Irons
oboe: Ruth Watkins
clarinets: Alasdair McGhie,
Shirley Cohen
bassoon: Sam Wilkins
trumpets: Ian Jenkins, Harry Smith
horn: Ishbel McGhie
trombone: Scott Dunbar
timpani: Karen Sherman
percussion: Jill Armit, Richard Bell,
Euan Lees, Marion McLaren, Murray
Macpherson, David Pomphrey
piano: Kenneth Walton
bagpiper: Margaret Marr

7.30pm Phoenix cinema, Kirkwall
BBC Philharmonic Orchestra
conductor: Edward Downes
leader: Dennis Simons
La Verne Williams: soprano
Alan Oke: baritone

Maxwell Davies: Black Pentecost
Tchaikovsky: Symphony No 6

9.45pm Arts Theatre, Kirkwall
A Johnsmas Foy
(repeat performance)

10pm Town Hall, Kirkwall
Festival Club:
Adrian Stuart and **Jim Robertson**

Tuesday 21 June

11am Arts Theatre, Kirkwall
The Two Fiddlers
(repeat performance)

1pm Stromness Town Hall
David Horne & Steven Osborne

Schubert: Fantasia in F minor
Ravel: Introduction and Allegro
Debussy: Six Epigraphes Antiques
Stravinsky: The Rite of Spring

3.30pm Stromness Town Hall
Os Kammerkor
conductors: Henrik Lyssand,
Jan Ove Petersen

MacFarlane, arr. Lyssand: Kirkwall
Norwegian folk songs:
arr. Alnaes: Knut Liten aa Sylvelin
arr. Groven: Jeg lagde mig så silde

arr. Skauge: Bukkevise
arr. Nystedt: Kjerringa med staven
arr. Dagsvik: Pål sine høner
Øhrwall: Ae tjaente så laenge
Nyhus/Øvredal, arr. Lyssand:
Brudmarsh från Jämtland
Mossafin, arr. Lyssand: Bergrosa
Gibbons: Ein golo gut
Altaingnant: The Silver Swan
Dowland: Tourdion;
Fine Knacks for Ladies
Grieg/Vinje arr. Lyssand: Vaaren
Grieg Arr. Lyssand: Vals
Lyssand/Lygre: God natt
Lyssand/Sande: Fabel
Sigurjo'nsson: Sofðu ungo Ástin min
Højgaard/Djurhuus:
Ta' ið Teir so' u landið
arr. Lyssand: Tuku Tuku Lampaitani
folk song: I Skovens Dype Stille Ro
Bellman: Two songs
Maxwell Davies: Lullaby for Lucy
Møller/Bang: Århus Tappenstreg

Sigmund Skage: piano
Grieg: I hjemmet
Såverud: Kjempevises låtten

5pm St Magnus Cathedral
Norman Mitchell: organ

JS Bach:
Prelude and Fugue in C Major S545
Festing: Largo, Allegro Aria and Two
Variations
Purcell/Vaughan Williams/Hurford:
Chorale Preludes
Rheinberger: Scherzoso
Hindemith: Sonata II
Howells: Rhapsody in Db
Yon: Toccatina for the Flutes
Mulet: Carillon-Sortie

5.45pm Kirk Green, Cathedral
Grimethorpe Colliery Band
outdoor performance
conductor: Howard Snell

Barraclough: March - Simoraine
Rossini, arr. Hawkins:
Overture - William Tell
Lear: Lear's Carnival
Rose, arr. Farr: Holiday for Strings
Gliere, arr. Todd:
Russian Sailors' Dance

6.45pm Town Hall, Kirkwall
Pre-Concert Talk:
Philip Grange

7.30pm Phoenix cinema, Kirkwall
BBC Philharmonic Orchestra
conductor: Sir Peter Maxwell Davies
leader: Dennis Simons
violin: György Pauk
piper: George McIlwham

Beethoven: Egmont Overture
Philip Grange:
Concerto for Orchestra
(festival commission)

Beethoven:
Violin Concerto in D
Maxwell Davies:
An Orkney Wedding, with Sunrise

WORLD PREMIERE

9.45pm Arts Theatre, Kirkwall
Joint Action: Interiors
dancer: Rosina Bonsu
actor: Mary McCluskey
musician: Karen McIver

Telephone Song
choreographer: Tamara McLorg

Black Babies
choreographer: Heather Munson
script: Paula McGhee

The Room at Arles
choreographer: Cheryl Strong
script: Anne-Marie Di Mambro

director: Maggie Kinloch
designer: Minty Donald
composer: Karen McIver
lighting/stage manager: Susie Caird

10pm Town Hall, Kirkwall
Festival Club: Gerbil
Club Cabaret at 11.15pm
with Aimée and Damon

Wednesday 22 June

11am Phoenix cinema, Kirkwall
Grimethorpe Colliery Band
concert for schools

Sousa: March: Stars and Stripes
Williams, arr. Farr: Superman
Bizet, arr. Rimmer: Farandole
Lear: Hogarth's Hoedown
James arr. Howarth:
Concerto for Trumpet
cornet soloist: Alan Morrison

1pm St Magnus Cathedral
La Verne Williams: soprano
Mary Nash: piano

Schubert: Three Songs
Mahler, orch. Berio:
Fünf Frühe Lieder
Massenet: Aria from Herodiad
Copland: Early American songs
Work/Adams/Perkinson: Three
songs by Black American composers
Three Spirituals

2.15pm Stromness Academy, Garson
Orkney Youth Theatre:
The Raven's Nest
(repeat performance)

3.30pm Town Hall, Kirkwall
Crofters by JO Alexander
performed by Sanday School

producer: Sue McArthur
musical director: Glenys Hughes

stage manager/costumes:
Sylvia Thorne

5pm Tankerness House Gardens
Os Kammerkor
(repeat performance)

6.15pm Arts Theatre, Kirkwall
Joint Action: Interiors
(repeat performance)

8pm Phoenix Cinema, Kirkwall
Grimethorpe Colliery Band
conductor: Howard Snell
Festival Chorus
conductor: Richard Hughes

Elgar: A Severn Suite
Henze: Ragtimes and Habaneras
Mascagni:
Intermezzo from Cavalleria Rusticana
soloist: Peter Roberts, soprano
cornet;
Easter Hymn from Cavelleria
Rusticana
soprano soloist Pat Burton

Verdi: Speed Your Journey from
'Nabucco'
Mussorgsky: Pictures at an Exhibition
Holst: A Moorside Suite
Walton: The First Shoot
Sparke: Pantomime
Trad./Maxwell Davies:
Two settings for unaccompanied
chorus: Flow gently sweet Afton,
Lullaby for Lucy.
Grainger:
I'm Seventeen Come Sunday
Stravinsky, arr. Farr: Two movements
from 'The Firebird Suite'

10pm Town Hall, Kirkwall
Festival Club:
Adrian Stuart and **Jim Robertson**

Exhibitions

Pier Arts Centre, Stromness
The Pier Gallery:
The First Ten Years

Stromness Library
Five Years On -
The Soulisquoy Printmakers

Ferry Terminal, Stromness
59°N/3.2°W
Neil Firth, Colin Kirkpatrick,
Teresa Swanney

Town Hall, Kirkwall
Crofters

Tankerness House Museum, Kirkwall
All in a Lifetime

Stromness Museum
Frozen in Time -
The Franklin Expedition

1989

Friday 16 June

2-3pm Congregational Church Hall, Kirkwall
The Orkney Youth Theatre: Slide Workshop
Glaitness School Special Education Unit and Primary 5
slide sessions: Mary Walters and Julie Bills
sculpture sessions: Rhona McNicol, Sheila Cameron and Christina Smith
music director: Leslie Truman

6pm Arts Theatre, Kirkwall
Schools Concert
Pupils from
Kirkwall Grammar School, Stromness and St Andrews Primary Schools
Orkney Young Musicians

James MacMillan:
The Cumnock Orcadian
(Festival commission)
group 1:
oboe: Claire Beaton
clarinets: Aline Cross, Gina Beaton
trumpet: Alistair Harvey
trombone: Adam Beaton
violins: Alison Dixon, Sarah Russell
group 2:
clarinets: Rebecca Welsh, Jackie Anderson
trumpet: Tristan Cooper
violins: Jennifer Wrigley, Louise Sinclair, Kelda Dinsdale
cello: Rohan Casey
piano: Lisa Newton
conductor: James MacMillan

Ritual
a creative music project by pupils of Stromness and St Andrews Primary Schools developed with James MacMillan

The Great Bank Robbery
by Peter Maxwell Davies
cast:
Father: Raymond Hutchison
Mother: Annelie Ross
Peter: Rognvald Gourlay
Pat: Suzanne Johnston
Bank Robbers: James Freeman, Jodi Swan
Security Guards: John Drever, James Duncan, Erik Firth, Malcolm Rosie
Policemen: Roy Davidson, Christopher Gee, James Livitt, Mark Williams
TV Receptionist: Helen Batty
Film Director: Craig Spence
Blonde Actress: Kelda Dinsdale
Actor: John Laughton
TV Personality: Ann-Marie Martin
Newsreader: Christine Work
Reporter: Judith Mair

bank clerks, townsfolk and film crew:
Monica Bews, Wendy Bews, Fiona Burns, Emma Burt, Ann Campbell, Karen Craigie, Lynn Craigie, Anna Davidson, Claire Drew, Morag Findlay, Lynn Foubister, Fraser Gilmour,

Kathryn Gray, Richard Hampton, Katie Hancock, Linda Harcus, Dianne Hume, Karoline Jolly, Emma Laughton, Susan Leslie, Julie McCairn, Lesley MacDonald, Katrina McGregor, Mairi McIver, Judith Mair, Jill Malcolm, Linette Meason, Katherine Moylan, Stuart Muir, Nicola Neish, Erika Partner, Shona Paterson, Jennifer Reid, Donna Robertson, Jane Rodger, Ingrid Rorie, Kirsten Ross, Lynnda Schofield, Catriona Shaw, Gillian Simmons, Rosalind Smyth, Jacqueline Stevenson, Janine Stevenson, Barry Sutherland, Karyn Tait, Vanda Taylor, Ingrid Ward, Anna Whittles, Sonja Wishart, Christine Work, Kirsty Weatherill

Instrumentalists:
violins: Alison Dixon, Sarah Russell, Jennifer Wrigley, Louise Sinclair
cellos: Olivia McLeod, Rohan Casey
double bass: Mark Skea
flutes: Gwen Heppleston, Carol Lennie, Catherine Batty
clarinets: Jackie Anderson, Theresa Moar, Aline Cross
trumpet: Alasdair Harvey
trombone: Stephanie Stanger
percussion: Anne Clouston, Lenore Learmonth, Lynn Mackay, Anna Mainland, Ingrid Omand, Robert Tulloch
piano: Melville Wallace
conductor: Glenys Hughes
choreography: Maggie MacGregor
scenery/props: Sam MacDonald, Arthur Pottinger
costumes: Katy Holmes, Joanna Kendall

8pm St Magnus Cathedral, Kirkwall
The Scottish Chamber Orchestra
conductor: Paul Daniel
leader: John Doig
trumpet: John Wallace

Haydn: Symphony No 60 in C
Harrison Birtwistle: Endless Parade
Beethoven: Symphony No 2 in D major

10pm Town Hall, Kirkwall
**Festival Club:
SCO Dance Band**
director: Alan Gout
Gerbil

Saturday 17 June

11am – 4pm Congregational Church Hall, Kirkwall
Slide Workshop
(repeat performance)

10.30am Pier Arts Centre, Stromness
The Realms of Gold: poetry reading
Claire Nielson, Paul Greenwood and Archie Bevan
a personal anthology of poems with a commentary by George Mackay Brown (read by Archie Bevan)

1pm St Magnus Cathedral, Kirkwall
**John Wallace: trumpet
Simon Wright: organ**

Cabezon, Heredia, Vazquez, Flecha:
music from the golden age of the Spanish Renaissance
Cimarosa: Concerto in C
Gomez: Air Andaluces
Jimenez: Battaglia
Purcell: Overture to 'The Indian Queen'
Handel: Suite in G
Bizet: Serenade Espagnol
Clark: Suite - Prince of Denmark

3pm Albert Street, Kirkwall
Grand Union Street Band

4pm Arts Theatre, Kirkwall
Hoy Dances
London Contemporary Dance School
director: Royston Maldoom
dancers: Cheryl McChesney, Dennis Vincent, Chick Eldridge; Pupils of North Walls Junior Secondary School

6.30pm KGS Games Hall, Kirkwall
Upbeat to Tryst
with James MacMillan, pupils from Kirkwall Grammar School and Stromness Academy and members of the Scottish Chamber Orchestra

8pm Phoenix cinema, Kirkwall
**The Scottish Chamber Orchestra:
St Magnus Festival Chorus**
conductors: Paul Daniel and Sir Peter Maxwell Davies
chorus master: Richard Hughes
Christine Cairns: mezzo soprano, Charles Johnston: baritone, Lorna Anderson: soprano, Catherine Denley: contralto, Roger Hamilton: harpsichord, Kevin MacCrae: cello

Purcell: Fantasias Nos 4 and 13
James MacMillan:
Tryst
(Festival commission)

Purcell: Dido and Aeneas
Dido: Christine Cairns
Aeneas: Charles Johnston
Belinda: Lorna Anderson
Sorceress/Spirit: Catherine Denley
First Witch: Kathleen Hague
Second Witch/Second Woman: Carolyn Chalmers
First Sailor: Paul Rendall
chorus of courtiers, witches and sailors

10pm Town Hall, Kirkwall
**Festival Club
Grand Union Cabaret Band**

Sunday 18 June

11.15am St Magnus Cathedral
Festival Service
conducted by the Rev W Cant
organist and master: Robin Cheer
music by Wood, Stanford, Langlais and Gigout

1pm Pier Arts Centre, Stromness
The Realms of Gold (repeat)

2.30pm Stromness Town Hall
**Celebrity Recital
Evelyn Glennie: percussion
Philip Smith: piano**

Chopin, arr. Glennie:
Etude Op 10 No 4 in C Sharp minor
Tanaka: Two movements for Marimba
arr. Glennie: Hornpipe Selection
Price: Solo for Snare Drum No 1
Glennie: Light in Darkness
DePonte: Concertino for Marimba
Abe: Michi
Liszt: Impromptu in F Sharp; Etude, La Campanella
Smadbeck: Rhythm Song
Creston: Concertino for Marimba

5.30pm Stromness Town Hall
A Johnsmas Foy
produced by Marjorie Linklater and Alistair Peebles
readers: Elizabeth Bevan, Pam Beasant, Susan Corrigall, Jocky Wood, Gregor Lamb, John Aberdein
musicians: Ingirid Jolly, Ivan Drever, Tommy Mainland, Dick Clarke
paintings: Fiona MacInnes

7.30 Stromness Academy Hall
The Scottish Chamber Orchestra Ensemble
conductor: Paul Daniel
reciters: Claire Nielson and Paul Greenwood
The St Magnus Players

John Doig: violin
Kevin MacCrae: cello
John Steer: double bass
Lewis Morrison: clarinet
David Nicholson: flute
Ursula Levaux: bassoon
Peter Franks: trumpet
Lance Green: trombone
Lawrence Gill: saxophone
Caroline Garden: percussion

Walton: Facade
Stravinsky: The Soldier's Tale

Narrator: Megan Eggeling
Soldier: Alasdair MacEwen
Devil: Graham Morris
Princess: Cathy Lyner
Soldier's Sweetheart: Carolyn Bevan
Soldier's Mother: Alison Blacklock
Mme Chapuis: Wendy Bullen
Children: Kate Bullen, Emma Bullen, Heather Aberdein
Devil's Attendants: Finn Aberdein, Martin Brown
Queen: Sarah Clubley
dancers/chorus: Carolyn Bevan, Alison Blacklock, Wendy Bullen
stage management: Carol Budge, Graham Garson
costumes: Jane Leonard
prompt: Dina Burgess
lighting: Norman Rushbrook
art: John Cumming, Frances Pelly
producer: Penny Aberdein

10pm Stromness Hotel
Festival Club: SCO Dance Band
director: Alan Gout

Monday 19 June

11am Phoenix cinema
Grand Union Cabaret Band
schools concert
Gerry Hunt, Ros Davies,
Sarah Laryea, Claude Deppa,
Tony Haynes, Vladimir Vega,
Ken Johnson, Josefina Cupido

12 noon Stromness Town Hall
Festival Lecture:
Sir Peter Maxwell Davies
Beethoven and the works to be
performed by Bernard Roberts

1pm Stromness Town Hall
Beethoven Recital:
Bernard Roberts: piano

Sonata No 30 in E major Op 109
Sonata No 31 in A flat major Op 110
Sonata No 32 in C minor Op 111

1.30pm
Grand Union: schools' workshops

6.30pm St Magnus Cathedral
The Scottish Early Music
Consort
director: Warwick Edwards
Fiona Milne: mezzo soprano
Harry Nicoll: tenor
Alan Watt: baritone
Jennifer Hill: recorders
Crolyn Sparey-Gillies: rebec
Marjorie Rycroft: viella
Warwick Edwards: harp

Including the music of:
Anon, L'Escurel, Muset, de Meaux,
le Vinier
Judith Weir: Scenes from 13th
Century Parisian Life

8.30pm Arts Theatre, Kirkwall
Tic Toc Theatre Company:
School's Out by Jon Gaunt

Janet Hughes: Kathy/Cookie
Paul Nolan: Micky
Robert Wilkinson: Rich/Greggy
directors: Gerard Purfield & Jon Gaunt
designer: Lisa Roberts
sound/lighting: John Laidlaw
administrator: Caroline Butcher

10pm Town Hall, Kirkwall
Festival Club:
Grand Union Cabaret Band

Tuesday 20 June

11am Arts Theatre, Kirkwall
Tic Toc Theatre Co:
School's Out (repeat performance)

1pm St Magnus Cathedral
The Scottish Early Music
Consort
directed by Warwick Edwards
baritone: Charles Johnston

Chanterai por mon coraige -
medieval songs of love and war:
Songs of the Crusades
Songs of Scotland
Oswald von Wolkenstein

2pm Stromness Academy Hall
A Johnsmas Foy (repeat)

3.30pm Town Hall, Kirkwall
Orkney Youth Theatre:
The Deceivers

cast:
Dina Burgess, Charlotte Frederick,
Emma Harris, Kirstie Kinney,
Leslie Truman, Krishna Paine,
Sarah Parsons

devised by the Orkney Youth Theatre
script/director: Alan Cameron
musical director: Tom Johnston
set design: Marian Ashburn
stage manager: Krishna Paine
administrator: Tim Dowan

6.30pm Phoenix cinema, Kirkwall
The Orkney Orchestra
leader: Ian McKune
conductor: Graham Thomson
guest conductor: Edgar Williams

Ed Holt: oboe
Paul Dixon: horn
Gina Beaton: clarinet
Graham Thomson: bassoon

Offenbach: Overture - Orpheus in
the Underworld
Mozart: Sinfonia Concertante
Maxwell Davies, arr. Thomson:
Farewell to Stromness
Vaughan Williams: English Folk Suite

8pm St Magnus Cathedral
The Endellion String Quartet

Andrew Watkinson: violin
Ralph de Souza: violin
Garfield Jackson: viola
David Waterman: cello
with David Campbell: clarinet

Haydn: Quartet Op 64 No 5
'The Lark'
Bartók: String Quartet No 4
Brahms: Clarinet Quintet Op 115 in
B minor

10.15pm, Arts Theatre, Kirkwall
Kirkwall Arts Club:
A Private Ear by Peter Shaffer

Ted: Leif Hunter
Bob: Iain Dunkley
Doreen: Katie Robertson
producer: Laura Grieve
prompt: Karen Presland
props: Abigail Foulis
sound effects: Simon Chirgwin
scenery/stage crew: Dave Grieve,
John Fiddler, Richard Neish,
Leif Hunter

10pm Town Hall, Kirkwall
Festival Club:
The Alex Sutherland Band

Steven proctor: guitar
Bill Kemp: drums
Alex Sutherland: keyboards
Gwen Brechin: vocalist

Wednesday 21 June

10am KGS Hostel
Master Class for Young
Clarinettists: David Campbell
Aline Cross and Rebecca Welsh
(Pupils of Kirkwall Grammar School
and Stromness Academy)

Stromness and Kirkwall
Tic Toc Theatre Co
Workshops in schools

1pm St Magnus Cathedral
The Endellion String Quartet

Beethoven: Quartet No 1 in F Op 59
Mozart: Quartet in F K590

3.30pm Stenness Community Centre
Pirates in the Deep Green Sea
by Eric Linklater
pupils of Stenness Primary School

Hew: Katrina Naughton
Timothy: William Sutherland
Sam: Sally Kirkland
Gunner Boles: Ellen Baikie
Cully: Inga Cromarty
Horatio Spens: Calum Carlyle
Mrs Matches: Carley Mackay
Davy Jones: Yvonne Seator
Aaron Spens: Debbie Ross
Dan Scumbril: Holly Crow
Inky Poops: Carol Leslie
fish: Lydia Crow, Arlene Garriock,
Gillian Learmonth,
Graham Sutherland, Daisy Giles,
Jenny Ireland, Dawn Johnston,
Emma Robinson, Wayne Johnston,
William Ancell
Davy Jones's Army: Susan Irvine,
Alex Crow, Ruth Drever,
Fiona Johnston, Stuart Flett,
John Sutherland, Alistair Mitchell,
Rosslyn Carlyle, Jenny Kirkland,
Mandy Ross, Barbara Scollay
pirates: Diane Garriock,
Caroline Naughton, Andy Irvine,
Graham Sclater, Keith Seator,
Karen Sutherland, Robbie Ireland,
Inga Naughton

script: Gregor Lamb
(from the book by Eric Linklater)
music: Thora Linklater
production: Donella Kirkland
stage hands: Robert Scott,
Adam Johnston
costumes: Ann Giles and parents
scenery: Laura May
accompaniment: Moira Summers
lighting: George McEwan,
Dave Robinson

6.45pm St Magnus Cathedral
St Magnus Cathedral Choir
directed by Robin Cheer

SCO Brass
Peter Franks: trumpet
Shaun Harrold: trumpet
Harry Johnstone: horn
Peter Harrap: trombone
Francis Magee: tuba

Fanfare
Byrd: Ave Verum
JC Bach: Magnificat
Pachelbel, arr. Frackenpohl: Canon
Handel, arr. Franks: Suite from the
Water Music
Vittoria: O quam gloriosum
Pezel: 3 pieces for 5-part brass music
JS Bach, arr. Caens:
Fugue in F minor
Frescobaldi, trans. Franks: Toccata
Purcell: Music for Queen Mary II

8.30pm Phoenix cinema, Kirkwall
Film Premiere: Venus Peter
from 'A Twelvemonth and a Day' by
Christopher Rush (adaptor: Ian Sellar)
director: Ian Sellar
producer: Christopher Young

actors:
Ray McAnally, David Hayman,
Sinead Cusack, Gordon Strachan,
Caroline Patterson, Peter Caffrey

10.45pm Phoenix cinema, Kirkwall
Venus Peter (repeat performance)

10pm Town Hall, Kirkwall
Festival Club: Gerbil; SCO Brass

Exhibitions

Pier Arts Centre, Stromness
Sidney Nolan

Ballroom Gallery, Kirkwall
Soulisquoy Printmakers

Town Hall, Kirkwall
Scottish Music Information Centre

Highland Park distillery:
Love and Diagrams (Anti Body)
Colin Johnstone

Highland Park Distillery:
Frances Pelly – New Sculpture

Ferry Terminal Building, Stromness:
Up By Degrees:
Neil Firth, Colin Johnstone, Colin
Kirkpatrick, Teresa Swanney

Stromness Library:
The Decade 1960 Brian Thorogood

Stromness Museum
Midshipman on the Bounty

Tankerness House Museum
A Haven for Vikings

1990

6.45pm Kirkwall Grammar School
**Pre-concert
workshop/performance**
With Richard McNicol and pupils of
North Ronaldsay Primary School,
Sanday Junior Secondary School and
Kirkwall Grammar School

8pm Phoenix cinema, Kirkwall
**Royal Bank Family Concert
The Scottish Chamber Orchestra**
conductor/presenter: Richard McNicol
Linda Hirst: mezzo soprano

Orkney Schools' Senior Strings
and Wind Band
conductors: Clive Thomas and
Edgar Williams
backdrop: Carole Harvey and
Carol Peebles; primary school pupils

Orkney Schools' Senior Strings:
Vivaldi: Concerto Grosso in D minor
soloists: Sarah Russell,
Douglas Montgomery

Orkney Schools' Senior Wind Band:
John McLeod:
A Dramatic Landscape
soloist: Gillian Orr

The Scottish Chamber Orchestra:
Berio: Folksongs
Stravinsky: Four Norwegian Moods
Trad: Drunken Sailor
Grieg: Holberg Suite
Grainger: Scotch Strathspey

The SCO, Orkney Senior Strings
and Wind Band:
Gershwin/Gout: They All Danced

10pm Kirkwall Town Hall
**Festival Club:
Ness River Rhythm Kings**
Pat Strachan:leader, trombone, vocals
Tommy Taylor: cornet, clarinet, vocals
Mike Mackenzie:clarinet, saxophone,
washboard
John Manson: tuba
Tom Jamieson: banjo, guitar

10.30am Pier Arts Centre, Stromness
Liz Lochhead poetry reading

11.45am Stromness Pierhead
The Lone School Band
Director: Espen Selvik

1pm St Magnus Cathedral, Kirkwall
Ernst Kovacic: violin
Ysäye: Solo Sonata Op 27 No 1
Bach: Chaconne from Partita in D
minor
Stravinsky: Elegy
Bartók: Solo Sonata

2pm Tankerness House Gardens
**St Magnus Cathedral Choir
and Kirkwall Town Band**

director: Robin Cheer

3.30pm Albert Street, Kirkwall
Inner Sense Street Band

4pm Hoy Kirk
Music Theatre Wales Ensemble

violins: Madeleine Mitchell,
Cecilia Romero
viola: John Rayson
cello: Sharon McKinley
flute: Sue Buckland
clarinet: Dov Goldberg
horn: David Cox

Lynda Cochrane:
String Quartet
Gordon McPherson:
String Quartet:
Civil Disobedience
on the Northern Front
Powers: Sea/Air for Solo Clarinet
Richard Rodney Bennett:
Sonata No 2 for solo violin
Peter Maxwell Davies:
Sea Eagle for Solo Horn
Martin Davies: Lagrime d'amante
al sepulcro de amata
Mozart: Flute Quartet No 1
in C major

6.30pm Broad Street, Kirkwall
The Lone School Band
director: Espen Selvik

7pm Kirkwall Town Hall
Ian Ritchie: a talk on the SCO

7.30pm Broad Street, Kirkwall
Kirkwall City Pipe Band

8pm St Magnus Cathedral
**The Scottish Chamber
Orchestra
St Magnus Festival Chorus**
conductor: Sir Peter Maxwell Davies
chorus master: Richard Hughes

William Conway: cello
Julia Gooding: soprano
Jamie MacDougall: tenor
Linda Hirst: mezzo soprano
Jonathan Best: bass

Mozart: Overture, 'The Magic Flute'
Maxwell Davies: Strathclyde
Concerto No 2 for Cello and
Orchestra
Mozart: Requiem in D minor K626

10pm Kirkwall Town Hall
Festival Club: Inner Sense

11.15am St Magnus Cathedral
Festival Service
conducted by Rev W Cant
master of the music: Robin Cheer

Jackson: Music from the Sky
Stanford: Justorum animae
Buxtehude: Praludium, Fuga und
Ciacona

1pm Pier Arts Centre
Liz Lochhead reading

2.30pm Stromness Town Hall
**Celebrity Recital:
Linda Hirst: mezzo soprano
Stephen Pruslin: piano**
(not Margaret Marshall, Semyon
Rozin and Lewis Morrison as
programmed)

5.30pm Stromness Town Hall
**A Johnsmas Foy:
The Mester Ship**
compiled and produced by
Alistair Peebles

readers: John Aberdein,
Pam Beasant, John Broom,
Edward Cummins, Bessie Grieve,
Alison Skene, Capt Robbie Sutherland

musicians: Maureen Cursiter,
Jennifer and Hazel Wrigley
set design: Carole Harvey and
Carol Peebles, based on art works
produced by primary school pupils

8pm Stromness Academy Theatre
**Music Theatre Wales:
The Fall of the House of Usher**
A chamber opera by Philip Glass

conductor: Michael Rafferty
director: Michael McCarthy

William: Richard Stuart
Roderick Usher: Julian Pike
Madeline Usher: Mary Seers
Servant: Nigel Fair
Physician: Tom Marandola

violins: Madeleine Mitchell,
Cecilia Romero
viola: John Rayson
cello: Sharon McKinley
bass: Alun Williams
flute: Susan Buckland
clarinet: Dov Goldberg
bassoon: David Buckland
horn: David Cox
guitar: John McHugh
percussion: Philip Girling
keyboards: David Fisk

designer: Richard Aylwin
lighting: John Bishop
lighting designer: Ace McCarron
repetiteur: David Fisk
production manager: Juliet Marsh
stage manager: Liz Cowling
sound: John Whiting

10pm Stromness Hotel
Festival Club: Bootfare

11am Kirkwall Town Hall
Liz Lochhead poetry reading

1pm St Magnus Cathedral
Music Theatre Wales Ensemble

instrumentalists:
Madeleine Mitchell, Cecilia Romero,
John Rayson, Sharon McKinley,
Susan Buckland, Dov Goldberg,
David Buckland, David Cox

Gordon McPherson: String Quartet:
Civil Disobedience on the
Northern Front
Lynda Cochrane: Quartet
Schubert: Octet in F major D803

2pm Stromness Academy Theatre
Inner Sense

2pm Papdale Infant Hall, Kirkwall
Primary Schools Concert
Open Dress Rehearsal

5.45pm Papdale Infant Hall, Kirkwall
Primary Schools Concert
with pupils from Dounby, Holm
and Papdale Primary Schools

St Magnus the Cathedral
by Minna Merriman
performed by Dounby School

cast:
Rachel: Rachel Scarth
Inga: Leona Benston
Erlend: Erland Johnston
Thora: Judith Sinclair
St Magnus: Erlend Grieve
1st Boy: Emma Robertson
2nd Boy: Suzanne Craigie
Sweyn: Jamie Irvine
Ronald: Lindsay Irvine
Hakon: Katherine Johnston
Ingarth: Katrina Johnston
Hakon's Follower: Cherie Newlands
Lifolf: Paul Todd
Magnus's Follower: Lorraine Flett
Magnus's Follower: Vicky Peppit
Woman 1: Ginette Spence
Woman 2: Sandra Whitelaw
Woman and Child: Gina Copland and
Emma Robertson
Kol: Derryn Hazlehurst
1st Mason: Kylie Tullock
2nd Mason: Lisa Norquoy
3rd Mason: Ariane Newlands
4th Mason: Shauna Spence
Frenchman: Hanna Phillips
Boatman 1: Nicola McGowan
Boatman 2: Susie Spence
Town Crier: Maxine Garson

producers: Margaret Irvine,
Chris Holmes
music: Hilary Morrell, Janet Richards
stage manager: Liz Johnston

costumes: Karen Johnston,
Beth Spence
scenery, props and costumes made
by the school; scenery painted by
Jennifer Davies and Helen Johnston

Dangerous Errand
by Sir Peter Maxwell Davies

Pat: Elaine Hutchison
Mother: Laura Barnett
Father: Gareth Thomson
Bully Boy: Nicki Monkman
Dog: Natalie McAdie
Sparrow: Ian Hutchison
Cat: Emma Stephen
Mrs Stickleback: Colette Allen
Shopkeeper: Dean MacPherson

cats, dogs, sparrows:
Peter Gauld, Steven Miller,
Laura Petter, Angela Loutitt,
Mandy Byers, Marie-Louise Donald,
Tracy Dennison, Gary Kemp,
Stewart Cursiter, Gemma Welsh,
Shereen Linklater, Inga Wallace,
Nicole Norquoy, Alice Mowatt,
Louise Bevan, Keith Harcus,
Kerry Scott, Elizabeth Grant

recorders: Laura Foulis, Sarah Glue,
Anna Laughton, Donna Rendall,
Kelda Dearness
tuned percussion: Adam Stanger,
Steven Groat, Steven Gray,
Ross Lawson, Ross Watt,
Suzanne Gray, Gary Johnston,
Mark Norquoy
untuned percussion: Arlene Miller,
Patrick Highley, Lynn Douglas,
Ingrid Austin

Along Came Man
words and music by Linda Marsh
performed by Holm Primary School

Spirit of the Earth:
Catherine MacDonald, Andrea Seatter
the Jungle: Karen Aim,
Katherine Ashcroft, Amy Cromarty,
Matthew Finn, Spencer Gaudie
the Sea: Alasdair Laughton,
Craig McInnes, Graham Moar,
Oliver Mowat, Craig Wright
the Desert: Sarah Hague, Gilly Irving-
Lewis, Joanne-Marie Leslie,
Lorraine Thomson
Man: Clare Budge, Vickie Copland,
Neil Cormack, Marie Cromarty,
Peter James Gaudie,
Graham Laughton, Peter Logie,
Selina McHarg, Clare McInnes,
Shona Marwick, Andrew Russell

7.30pm Phoenix cinema, Kirkwall
Phoenix Dance Company
Director: Neville Campbell

dancers:
Stephen Derrick, Chantal Donaldson,
Dawn Donaldson, Donald Edwards,
Ricky Holgate, Pamela Johnson,
Booker T Louis, Edward Lynch,
Seline Thomas, Douglas Thorpe
technical manager: Mark Smith

Rights:
choreographer/designer:
Michael Clark
music: Big Hard Excellent Fish

One Love:
choreographer: Gary Lambert
music (tape): Linton Kwesi Johnson
speaker: Clinton Blake

Haunted Passages:
choreographer: Philip Taylor
music: Britten, 'Lachrymae'
designer; Heidi de Raad

Human Scandals:
director: Neville Campbell
music (tape): Shaun Campbell,
Paul Cantillon

9.45pm Arts Theatre, Kirkwall
A Johnsmas Foy
(repeat performance)

10pm Kirkwall Town Hall
Festival Club: Inner Sense

Tuesday 26 June

11am Phoenix cinema, Kirkwall
Phoenix Dance Company
(repeat performance)

1pm Stromness Town Hall
Festival Lecture
Sir Peter Maxwell Davies
(the ever-changing sonata principle)

2.30pm Stromness Town Hall
Peter Donohoe: piano

Beethoven: Sonata in E flat Op 31
No 3
Alban Berg: Sonata Op 1
Bartók: Sonata
Liszt: Sonata B minor

5pm Kirkwall Town Hall
**Orkney Youth Theatre:
Towards Spring**

Jonathan Livingston Seagull:
Stuart Crisp
Roy/Fletcher Seagull: Tim Dowan
Sue/Ma Wright: Caroline Docherty
Eddie/Pa Wright: Craig Muir
Jo/Ingrid Seagull: Charlotte Frederick
Terrence Seagull: Edward Mitchell
Dot: Jo Winters

director: Alan Watters
devised by Andrew Neil

6.45pm Phoenix cinema, Kirkwall
The Orkney Orchestra
conductor: Graham Thomson
leader: Ian McKune

Shostakovich: Festive Overture
Mozart: Concerto No 1 in D major
for Horn and Orchestra
(soloist Paul Dixon)
Lennon and McCartney, arr. Calvin
Custer: The Best of the Beatles
Lloyd Webber, arr. Calvin Custer:
Selections: The Phantom of the Opera

8.30pm Arts Theatre, Kirkwall
Fascinatin' Rhythm
Richard Rodney Bennett and
Marion Montgomery

10.15pm Kirkwall Town Hall
Festival Club: Bootfare

Wednesday 27 June

10am Stromness Academy Theatre
A Johnsmas Foy
(repeat performance)

1pm St Magnus Cathedral
Jennifer Bate: organ

Bach: Fantasia in G
Mendelssohn: Sonata No 6 in D minor

Franck: Grande Pièce Symphonique
Mathias: Fenestra
Jennifer Bate: Cantilena; Toccata
on a Theme of Martin Shaw

3pm Arts Theatre, Kirkwall
All The King's Men open rehearsal

5.30pm Kirkwall Town Hall
Peter Donohoe: a talk
(not RR Bennett as programmed)

6.30pm Arts Theatre, Kirkwall
All The King's Men
by Richard Rodney Bennett
pupils from Kirkwall Grammar School

cast:
King Charles I: Christopher
Fotheringham
Queen Henrietta Maria: Abigail Foulis
Dr Chillingworth: Jodi Swan
King's Herald: Michael Halleran
Drummer Boy: Suzanne Johnston
King's Generals: James Livitt,
Olivia MacLeod, Jamie Russell,
Stephanie Stanger
King's Soldiers: Carol Clanachan,
Laura Crabtree, Angela Craigie,
Julie Drever, Christopher Gee,
Lianne McDonald, Isla MacIntosh,
Susan Pirie, Sarah Reid,
Mary Ann Robertson, Leona Rosie,
Elena Scott, Emma Scott,
Shona Sutherland, Sacha Wright
Queen's Ladies: Alison Drever,
Katrina McGregor, Karen Presland,
Sarah Simmons, Sallyann Smales,
Lucy Thompson
Colonel Massey: Mark Skea
Messenger: Claire Ross
Colonel Massey's Soldiers:
Gillian Anderson, Rachel Cromarty,
Emma Deans, Michelle Drew,
Carol McEwan, Laura McIver,
Neil Moir, Julie Marr, Nicola Neish,
Shona Paterson, Hannah Pirie,
Daniel Sargent, Janine Stevenson,
Claire Sutherland, Gillian Swanney,
Leesa Thomson, Ben Whittles
Women and Children of Gloucester:
Fiona Burns, Ann Campbell,
Sally Hall, Judith Mair,
Katherine Moyland, Kirsten Ross,
Debra Scott, Catriona Shaw,
Rosalind Smyth, Ingrid Ward,
Christina Work

1st violins: Sarah Russell,
Douglas Montogmery
2nd violins: Fiona McArthus,
Anna Whittles
3rd violins: Caroline Rosie,
Louise Sinclair
flutes: Catherine Barry,
Gwen Heppleston
oboe: Christine Kemp
clarinets: Aline Cross,
Jackie Anderson
horn: Paul Dixon
trumpet: Alasdair Harvey,
Tristan Cooper
tuned percussion: Anna Mainland,
Annelie Ross
unpitched percussion: Ann Clouston,
Katie Hancock, Robert Tullock

piano duet: Lynda Cochrane,
Glenys Hughes

String Quintet (members of the SCO)
violins: James Clark, Pauline Doig
viola: Catherine Marwood
cello: William Conway
bass: John Steer

conductor: Richard Hughes
director: Penny Aberdein

set design: Alan Watson
set construction: Tom King with third
year pupils
costumes: Katy Homes, Vi Rorie,
Carol Taylor and parents
make up: Alison Blacklock,
Richard Neish
props: Margaret Sutherland,
Catriona Nelson

8pm Phoenix cinema, Kirkwall
**The Scottish Chamber
Orchestra**
conductor: Ernst Kovacic
Evelyn Glennie: percussion
Peter Donohoe: piano

Elgar: Serenade for Strings in
E minor Op 20
Richard Rodney Bennett:
Concerto for Percussion
and Orchestra
(Festival commission)
Beethoven: Piano concerto No 5 in
E flat 'Emperor'

WORLD PREMIERE

8pm Kirkwall Town Hall
**Festival Club: Bootfare
Orkney Schools' Swing Band**

Exhibitions

Pier Arts Centre, Stromness
5000 Years of Orkney Art

Ferry Terminal Building, Stromness
**Orkney – An Illustrated
Architectural Guide**

Alliance & Leicester Building Society
**Exhibition of Mini Prints:
Soulisquoy Printmakers**

Stromness Library
**Making Molehills Out of
Mountains: Andrew Parkinson**

Town Hall, Kirkwall
**Scottish Music Information
Centre**

Tankerness House Museum
The Broch People

Stromness Museum
To the Nor'Wast
Orkney's links with Hudson Bay

1991

Friday 21 June

3.30pm Arts Theatre, Kirkwall
Witch and **Road to Colonus**
by George Mackay Brown
open dress rehearsal

7.30pm Arts Theatre, Kirkwall
St Magnus Players:
Witch
incidental music by Sir Peter Maxwell
Davies played by a Scottish Chamber
Orchestra Ensemble

Neil Gillies: flute
Lorna Maclaren: violin
Lawrence Gill: clarinet
Stephen King: viola
Kevin MacCrae: cello

cast:
Marian Isbister: Allison Dixon
Laird's Wife: Megan Eggeling
Stephen Buttquoy: Harris Playfair
Andrew Monteith: Walter Leask
Janet Bourtree: Ingirid Morrison
Master Peter Atholl: Ian Johnstone
Farm Girls: Carolyn Bevan,
Alison Blacklock, Wendy Bullen
Jailer: Juliet Kepl
Prison Warden: Wendy Bullen
Sheriff Malachi Lorimer:
Graham Morris
Sheriff's Page: Allan Chalmers
Jean Scollit: Juliet Kepl
Maud Sinclair: Carolyn Bevan
Margaret Gray: Alison Blacklock
Simon Leslie: Magnus Dixon
John St Clair: Jim Groundwater
William St Clair: Walter Leask
Clerk of the Court: Ian Johnstone
Piers (executioner): Raymond Lamb
Children: Heather Aberdein, Kate
Bullen, Emma Bullen

costumes: Jane Leonard
set: Teresa Swanney
make up: Gillian Johnstone,
Josephine Playfair
stage management: Neil Firth,
Christine Eccleston
props: Pat Presland, Margaret
Sutherland, Lorraine Harcus
producer: Penny Aberdein
conductor: Richard Hughes

The Road To Colonus
Old Man: Alan Watters
Girl: Cathy Johnson
Soldier: Ken Martin
Innkeeper: Richard Welch
Masquer: Leif Hunter
Ferryman: Jim Ramsay

producer: George Rendall
conductor: Glenys Hughes
set: Alan Watson, Sam MacDonald

10pm Broad Street, Kirkwall
Firefest :
procession and fireworks
music: Grand Union
10pm Broad Street
11.15pm Peedie Sea - bonfire lighting
12.10 -1am Ayre hotel
(midnight: fireworks display)

Saturday 22 June

10.30am Pier Arts Centre, Stromness
Norman MacCaig poetry reading

1pm Stromness Town Hall
David Horne: piano
with **SCO String Trio**
Lorna Maclaren: violin
Stephen King: viola
Kevin MacCrae: cello

Scarlatti: Two Sonatas; D minor
K141; G major K 146
Mozart: Sonata in B K333
Judith Weir: Serbian Cabaret
Ravel: Gaspard de la Nuit
Liszt: Six Paganini Études

3.30pm Tankerness House Gardens
A Musical Interlude:
St Magnus Cathedral Choir and
Kirkwall Town Band
conductor: Robin Cheer

5pm Kirkwall Town Hall
Faroese Ensemble
Ernst Dalsgaro: flute, voice
Anna Klett: clarinet
Jogvan Zachariassen: bassoon
Kari Baek: oboe
Pall Solstein: French horn
Laila Neilsen: viola
Jesper Kosk: piano, harpsichord

Atli Petersen: Woodwind Quintet
Sunleif Rasmussen: Fantasi yvir Tivils
Dotur
Kristian Blak: Trio
Wm Heinesen: Variationer over Vagn
op of sla på dine Strenge
Pauli i Sandagerøi: Songs
Atli Petersen: Kvaeoio fyri
pinnabrenni
Sunleif Rasmussen: Vetrarmyndir
(Winter Pictures)

7pm Kirkwall Town Hall
Sir Peter Maxwell Davies
talk: Beethoven's Symphony No 5

8pm St Magnus Cathedral, Kirkwall
BBC Scottish Symphony
Orchestra
leader: Geoffrey Trabichoff
conductor: Sir Peter Maxwell Davies
trumpet: Håkan Hardenberger

Beethoven: Overture 'Coriolan'
Peter Maxwell Davies: Trumpet
Concerto
Beethoven: Symphony No 5 in C
minor Op 67

10pm Albert Hotel, Kirkwall
Festival Club
Grand Union Cabaret Band

Sunday 23 June

11.15am St Magnus Cathedral
Festival Service
conducted by the Rev Ron Ferguson
master of the music: Robin Cheer
music by Harris, Parry, JS Bach,
Karg-Elert

1pm Pier Arts Centre, Stromness
Norman MacCaig poetry reading

2.3pm Stromness Town Hall
Celebrity recital:
Håkan Hardenberger: trumpet
John Constable: piano

Maxwell Davies: Sonata for trumpet
in C and piano
Clergue: Sarabande et Gigue
Ibert: Impromptu
Antheil: Sonata
Berio: Sequenza X
Satie: Sonatine Bureaucratique
Thomson: At the Beach
Hartmann: Fantasia brillante on the
air 'Rule Britannia'

5pm Stromness Town Hall
A Johnsmas Foy:
Sifting the Grain
producer: Vivia Leslie

readers:
Linda budge, Barbara Foulkes,
Jocky Wood, Harvey Johnston
musicians: Hazel & Jennifer Wrigley
singers: Barbara Grieve, Freddie Tait

7pm Kirkwall Town Hall
Pre-concert talk:
Lyell Cresswell

8pm Phoenix cinema, Kirkwall
BBC Scottish Symphony
Orchestra
St Magnus Festival Chorus
conductors: Takuo Yuasa and
Sir Peter Maxwell Davies
chorus master: Richard Hughes

Patrizia Kwella: soprano
Neil Mackie: tenor
Elizabeth McCormack: mezzo
Alan Watt: bass

Elgar: Introduction and Allegro
for String Op 47
Lyell Cresswell: Ylur
(Festival commission)

Haydn: 'Maria Theresa' Mass

9pm Stromness Hotel
Grand Union Cabaret Band

10pm Albert Hotel, Kirkwall
Festival Club:
Gerbil
Orkney Schools' Swing Band
conductor: David Griffith

Monday 24 June

11am Kirkwall Town Hall
Norman MacCaig poetry reading

1pm St Magnus Cathedral
Owen Murray: accordion

Messiaen: Jésus Accepte la
Souffrance des Anges
Holmboe: Sonata for Accordion Op
143a
Dempster: Modern Athenians

Mozart: Andante fur eine Walze in
eine kleine Orgel (K616)

John McLeod:
The Passage of
the Divine Bird
JS Bach: Prelude, Fugue
and Allegro in Eb major BWV998
Schmidt: Toccata No 1

6pm St Magnus Cathedral
The Allegri String Quartet
Peter Carter: violin
David Roth: violin
Roger Tapping: viola
Brun Schrecker: cello

Mozart: String Quartet No 15 in
D minor K421
Ravel: String Quartet in F major

8pm Phoenix cinema, Kirkwall
BBC Scottish Symphony
Orchestra: 'pops' concert

leader: Geoffrey Trabichoff
conductor: Takuo Yuasa
David Horne: piano
Tommy Smith: saxophone

Bizet: Carmen Suite no1
Delius: On Hearing the First Cuckoo
in Spring; Summer Night on the River
Ravel: Piano Concerto in G major
Barber: Adagio for strings
Sweeney: An Rathad Ùr
Bernstein: On the Town
(Three Dance Episodes)

8pm Pickaquoy Park, Kirkwall
Runrig
Donnie Munro: lead vocals
Malcolm Jones: guitars, accordion,
mandolin
Peter Wishart: keyboards
Rory Macdonald: bass, harmonies,
vocals
Iain Bayne: drums, percussion
Calum Macdonald: percussion

supporting band: **Rock the Tribe**

10pm Albert Hotel, Kirkwall
Festival Club

Tuesday 25 June

11am Stromness Academy Theatre
Owen Murray: accordion
Chris Brannick: percussion

Dempster: Modern Athenians
Zolotarev: Children's Suite No 1
John McLeod: The Passage of the
Divine Bird
Sheila Nolan: Nocturne
(for accordion and percussion)
David Osbon: Brain Salad
Torbjorn Lundquist: Duell

1pm St Magnus Cathedral
The Allegri String Quartet
James Campbell: clarinet

Mozart: Clarinet Quintet in A major
K581

James MacMillan:
Tuireadh

2pm Papdale Primary School
Owen Murray: Accordion
workshop for schools

6pm Arts Theatre, Kirkwall
Schools Concert

Jupiter Landing
by Peter Maxwell Davies
performed by Sanday School

Pat: Selina Cobley
Mum: Barbara Drever
Space Captain: Edward Kendall
Chief Space Engineer: Alistair Thorne

toys
Teddy Bear: Christina Wenham
Policeman: Danny Fisher
Tin Soldier: Robert Ward
Woolly Rabbit: Shona Grieve
Puppet Clown: Lorna Muir
Piggy Bank: Rachel Jacobs
space people: Catherine Buchan,
Josh Butcher, Clare Gibson,
Elizabeth Lennie, Victoria Lennie,
Verity Luke, Andrew Moore,
Kerry Muir, Greig Munro,
Tanya Sichel, Jacqueline Tulloch,
Leona Tulloch, Monica Tulloch,
James White
space monsters: Barry Allan,
Christopher Bain, Gary Brown,
George Brown, Raymond Brown,
Graham Clarke, Leander Cobley,
Malcolm Lennie, Jamie Lewington,
Anthony Mills, Christopher Monahan,
Alan Muir, James Muir, Adam Towrie
constellation: Kevin Clarke,
Katie-Anne Drever, Angus Fisher,
Charlotte Gibson, Emma Grieve,
Zara Grieve, Christopher A'Hara,
Andrew Linton, Karl Muir,
Michael Muir, Amy Peace,
David Peace, Bella Sichel,
Emma Tulloch

orchestra
recorders: Beinn Muir, Kaye Bain,
Tammy Lewington
violins: Tristan Thorne,
Matthew McArthur
glockenspiels: Barbara Drever,
Helen Towrie, Clare Walsh
chime Bars: Lynn Peace,
Pamela Wilson
xylophones: Jennifer Muir,
Linda Towrie
bass xylophone/keyboard:
Rachel Drury
percussion: David Buchan,
Victoria Wenham, Joanne White

costumes: Sylvia Thorne, with
Jean Sword, parents and friends
monster masks and star costumes
designed by secondary pupils
scenery: Sylvia Thorne
stage crew: Adrian Clarke,
Lance Gibson, Graham Munro
musical director: Glenys Hughes
production: Sue McArthur, with
primary class teachers

The Spider's Revenge
by Peter Maxwell Davies
performed by
Evie Primary School

children: Nathan Brown,
Fiona Nicolson
spiders: Kirsty Balfour,
Victoria Batchelor, Selena Harrison,
Robert Learmonth, Ruth Ludgate,
Christopher Welsby, Nicola Wills
caterpillars and butterflies:
Michelle Beharie, Simon Brown,
Herbie Hughes, Jessica Rastall,
Laura Stevenson, Madeleine Brown,
Graham Firth, Ronan McSkimmin,
Carol Sinclair, Lisa Ward
snails: Darren Heddle,
Dwayne Irvine, Luke McSkimmin,
Gary Skea, Adam Twatt
birds: Christopher Brennan,
Darren Irvine, Garth Thomas,
Daniel Twatt
ladybirds: Leah Balfour,
Jennifer Beharie, Vicky Brown,
Ellen Casey, Dee Harrison,
Hero McCallum, Kirstin Mainland,
Ellie Naylor, Rebecca Stevenson,
Nicky Ward
pond creatures: Heather Batchelor,
Margaret Coward, Gemma Cursiter,
Joanna Fergus, Amy Harrington,
Vicky Beharie
dragonflies: Vicky Harrington,
Rachael Ludgate, Annette Miller,
Victoria Seyd, Sarah Stevenson
bees: Nicolas Balfour, Robbie Balfour,
Alice Chalmers, Ben Coward,
Gillian Firth, Rachael Jenkins,
Melissa Spence
Queen Bee: Kate Reynolds

orchestra:
recorders: Simone Chalmers,
Stephanie Seatter
guitars: Sandra Mainland,
Susan Stevenson
cello: Rohan Casey
tuned percussion: Hayley Harrington,
Ruth Miller
unpitched percussion:
Nicola Learmonth, Miranda Seyd

musical director: Moira Summers
artwork: Teresa Swanney,
Claire Welsby
costumes: L Harrington, K Neil,
V Reynolds, G Thomas, B Vesco,
C Welsby
production: Barbara Vesco and staff

7.30pm St Magnus Cathedral
Nouvelles Images
Philippa Davies: flutes
Rosemary Furniss: violin/viola
Stephen Pruslin: piano
David Campbell: clarinet
Jonathan Williams: cello
Gregory Knowles: cimbalom

Peter Maxwell Davies: Three
Renaissance Realisations
Schoenberg/Webern:
Kammersymphonie Op 9
Peter Maxwell Davies:
Image Reflection Shadow

7.45pm Arts Theatre, Kirkwall
Schools Concert
(repeat performance)

9.30pm Phoenix cinema, Kirkwall
The Tommy Smith Group

Tommy Smith: saxophone
Mick Hutton: bass
Mike Walker: guitar
Ian Thomas: drums

Sculptures by Kenny Munro and
pupils of Stromness Academy and
Kirkwall Grammar School

10pm Albert Hotel, Kirkwall
Festival Club: Liam and Co.

Wednesday 26 June

11am Stromness Academy Theatre
A Johnsmas Foy
(repeat performance)

1pm St Magnus Cathedral
Nouvelles Images

Mozart: Adagio and Rondo K617
Beethoven: Variations for cello and
piano on 'Bei Mannern' from
Mozart's 'The Magic Flute'
David Horne:
Contraries and
Progressions
(Festival commission)
Mozart: Trio in E flat K498
(Kegelstatt) for clarinet, viola

5pm Kirkwall Town Hall
Orkney Youth Theatre:
Five Go Green

Equal: Fiona B Watt
Baz: Anthony Donaldson
Charles: Elliott Carroll
Juliet: Fleur Bartlett
Mandy: Rose Strang
devised by Orkney Youth Theatre
director: Alan Watters
dance tutor: Brigid McCarthy

Just A Word
devised by Surprised Halibut
director: Cara Grieve

6.30pm Papdale Infant Hall, Kirkwall
The Orkney Orchestra
leader: Ian McKune
conductor: David Griffith
trumpet: Brian Jones
cor anglais: Christina Sargent
piano: Harris Playfair

Bizet: Danse Bohème from Carmen
Respighi: The Ancient Airs and Dance
Suite 1
Copland: Quiet City
Gershwin: Rhapsody in Blue

8pm St Magnus Cathedral
The Scottish Chamber
Orchestra Singers
conducted by Stephen Clarke
Neil Mackie: tenor
Richard Hughes: organ

Bach: motet 'Singet dem Herrn'
Maxwell Davies: Three Arias from
the Martyrdom of St Magnus
Howells: Take him, earth, for
cherishing
Maxwell Davies: Solstice of Light

10pm Albert Hotel, Kirkwall
Festival Club:
The Tommy Smith Group

Exhibitions

Pier Arts Centre, Stromness
Føroykst List - Faroese Art

St Magnus Hall, Kirkwall
The Slockit Light: Mary Scott
and Dave Jackson

Black Pig Gallery, Kirkwall
Erlend Brown: Recent Work

Stromness Library
John and Gloria Wallington:
paintings and collages

Town Hall Foyer, Kirkwall
Maurizio Bottarelli:
pastels on sandpaper

Ferry Terminal, Stromness
Soulisquoy Printmakers

Tankerness House Museum
Grave Matter
Orkney's Bronze Age Burials

Strynd Playgroup, Kirkwall
Alan Watson and Frank Donnan
drawings and paintings

1992

Friday 19 June

2pm Kirkwall Town Hall
Steps Out
The education unit of Scottish Ballet

Les Marionettes:
North Walls Junior Secondary School,
Flotta Primary School
music: Gabriel Grovlez
musician: David Munro
animateur: Eric Tessier-Lavigne

Trismos:
Glaitness Primary School
music: Steve King (SCO)
musicians: Pupils from Papdale
Primary School and SCO Quartz

Wildlife 1:
Glaitness Aurrida School
animateur: Winnie Armitage
choreographer: Neville Campbell

7pm Orkney Arts Theatre, Kirkwall
A Selkie Tale
The Little Sweep

A Selkie Tale
by Peter Maxwell Davies
performed by Holm pupils

Mansie: Oliver Mowat
Selkie-wife: Gilly Irving-Lewis
Miss Trowie-Tattibogle: Jo-Jo Leslie
Minister: Lorraine Thomson
Mansie's Bairns: Alan Aim,
Fiona Aim, John Dearness,
Liam Finn, Lucy Hague, Steven Moar,
Sharmi Norris, Steven Paterson,
David Tait
crew of fishing boat: Amy Cromarty,
Matthew Finn, Spencer Gaudie,
Graham Moar, Lorraine Thomson
selkies: Karen Aim,
Katherine Ascroft, Kate Askew,
Lisa Cursiter, Sherine Deakin,
Elizabeth Dearness, Rosalind
Eunson, Sarah Hague, Victoria Logie,
Inez Moss, Victoria Rushton,
Rachel Stacey, Gina Tait
waves and wedding guests:
Robert Ascroft, Gary Berston,
Andrew Firth, Brendan Fletcher,
Craig Home, Paul Sneesby

solo violin: Sarah Russell
flute: Magnus McKie
clarinets: Theresa Leslie,
Katrina Smith
tuned percussion: Claire Budge,
Marie Cromarty, Catherine
MacDonald, Selina McHarg,
Shona Marwick, Andrea Seatter,
Jenna Tait
unpitched percussion: Ann Campbell,
Judith Mair, Stephanie Stanger
trumpet: Alasdair Harvey
cello: Cathy Johnson
musical director: Glenys Hughes
production: Rosey Whittles
choreography: Avril Cromarty
costumes: Alison Aitken and
Holm parents
scenery: Sheila Cameron, Brian Aim
make-up: Sue Irving-Lewis

The Little Sweep
by Benjamin Britten

Black Bob: David Hall
Clem: Graham Bruce
Sam: Adam Stanger
Miss Baggott: Colette Ruddy
Juliet Brook: Ishbel Fraser
Gay Brook: Thomas Moylan
Sophie Brook: Debbie Ross
Rowan: Kathleen Hague
Jonny Crome: Sach Wright
Hughie Crome: Jo Hill
Tina Crome: Shereen Linklater
Tom: David Hall
Alfred: Graham Bruce
singers from Kirkwall Grammar
School

SCO Quartz
Bernard Docherty: violin
Lorna McLaren: violin
Stephen King: viola
Kevin MacCrae: cello

Kirk Richardson: percussion
piano duet: Glenys Hughes,
Harris Playfair

conductor: Richard Hughes
director: George Rendall
set design: Alan Watson
set construction: Jim Ramsay,
Tom King
costumes: Katie Holmes
props: Pat Presland
hair stylist: Rachel Swanney

9.15pm Phoenix cinema
Ronnie Scott Sextet

Ronnie Scott: tenor sax
Martin Drew: drums
John Critchinson: piano
Mornington Lockett: tenor sax
Andy Cleyndert: bass
Dick Pearce: trumpet

10pm Albert Hotel, Kirkwall
Festival Club: The Ola Band

Mickey Austin: banjo
Ian Chisholm: vocals/guitar
Diarmaid Flemming: accordion
Colin Pirie: fiddle
Alan Reid: guitar
with Seona Dunsmuir, Billy Peace
and The Wrigley Sisters

Saturday 20 June

10.30am Pier Arts Centre, Stromness
Brian McCabe poetry reading

12.30pm Stromness Town Hall
Michala Petri: recorder
Hanne Petri: harpsichord

Vivaldi: Sonata in C major
JS Bach: Sonata in C minor
Christiansen: Serenade Op 25
Krähmer: Introduction, theme and
variations
Buck: Hymel
Maros: Impromptu
Albinoni: Sonata in G major

2pm Kirkwall Town Hall
St Magnus Cathedral Choir
Kirkwall Town Band
directors: Heather Rendall and
Brian Jones

2.30pm Pier Arts Centre, Stromness
Rebecca Hossack
an illustrated talk on the work of
aboriginal artists

5.30pm Arts Theatre, Kirkwall
A Selkie Tale
The Little Sweep
(repeat performance)

8pm Phoenix cinema, Kirkwall
St Magnus Festival Chorus
Haydn: The Creation
chorus master: Richard Hughes
Scottish Chamber Orchestra
conductor: Ivor Bolton

Fiona Cameron: soprano
John Michael Mulroy: tenor
Gerald Finley: bass

10pm Albert Hotel, Kirkwall
Festival Club:
Ronnie Scott Sextet

Sunday 21 June

11.15am St Magnus Cathedral
Festival Service
conducted by Rev Ron Ferguson
director of music: Heather Rendall
St Magnus Cathedral Choir
SCO String Quartet: Quartz

Mozart: Divertimento in D major;
Divertimento in F major
Posegate: Holy, Lord of Hosts
Stanford: Te Deum Laudamus
Pachelbel: Canon
Grayston Ives: Organ Intrada

1pm Pier Arts Centre, Stromness
Brian McCabe poetry reading
(repeat performance)

2.30pm Stromness Town Hall
Celebrity recital:
Imogen Cooper: piano

Schoenberg: 6 Kleine Klavierstücke
Op 19
Schubert: Sonata in G major D894
Schubert: 16 German Dances D783
Janácek: Sonata
Smetana: Polkas

5pm Stromness Town Hall
A Johnsmas Foy:
'My, Whit Wather'
producer: Vivia Leslie

readers: Linda Budge,
Barbara Foulkes, Harvey Johnston,
Jocky Wood
musicians: Douglas Montgomery,
Robin Nicholson

7.15pm Kirkwall Town Hall
Pre-concert talk:
Poul Ruders

8pm St Magnus Cathedral
Scottish Chamber Orchestra
Ivor Bolton: conductor
Michala Petri: recorder

Telemann: Suite in A minor for
recorder and strings

Poul Ruders:
The Second Nightshade
(Festival commission)

Asger Lund Christiansen:
Dance Suite Op 29

Haydn: Symphony No 101
in D major, 'The Clock'

10pm Albert Hotel, Kirkwall
Festival Club:
Ronnie Scott Sextet

Monday 22 June

11am Stromness Academy Theatre
A Johnsmas Foy
(repeat performance)

11am Kirkwall Town Hall
Brian McCabe poetry reading
(repeat performance)

1pm St Magnus Cathedral
Music from Norway

Knut Hamre: Hardanger fiddle
Reidum Horvel: soprano
Geir Botnen: piano

Folk Tunes, arr. Geirr Tveitt:
Welcome, with honour
Toloen
The mountaineer's daughter
The most beautiful song on earth
The boasters' ballad
The lad with silver buttons
The call of the shepherd's horn
The hasty wedding
What beer!
Fjellstev
Consecration of the new beer
Home brew

Folk Tunes and Dances,
arr. Edvard Grieg:
Wedding march of the goblins
Calling the flock
Folkdance from Os
A small grey man
In Ola-valley, in Ola-lake
cradle song
Rotnams-Knut from Hallengdal
Small was the fellow
Tomorrow you'll marry her
Knut Lurasen's Halling 1

2.30pm Papdale Infant Hall
Edinburgh Puppet Company:
The Girl From The Sea
by George Mackay Brown

director: Wojcieh Wieczorkiewicz

performers: Alan Craig,
Heather Fraser, Judith Aitken

6.30pm St Magnus Cathedral
Hilliard Ensemble:
Sound Patterns

David James: alto
Rogers Covey-Crump: tenor
John Potter: tenor
Gordon Jones: bass

Anon, 14th century: Tu Civium
primas; Alma polis religio; Verburn
bonum et suave; Musicalis sciencia;
Thomas Gemma de Cantuariae
Anon, 12th century: Reginarum
dominarum
Pärt: Summa
Bryars: Glorious Hill
Moody: Three songs from the 'Song
of Songs'
Morley: Fire and Lightening
Desprez: Tu solus qui facis mirabilia
Cage: Litany for the Whale
Morley: In nets of golden wires
Purcell: Joy, mirth, triumphs
Machaut: Gloria 'La messe de notre
dame'

8.30pm Arts Theatre, Kirkwall
The Medieval Players
Shakespeare's Hamlet
director: Ben Benison

cast:
Michelle Butt, Nicholas Collett, Mark
Knight, Patrick Knox, Will Lawrence,
Susannah Rickards, Roy Weskin

producer: Dick McCaw
designers: Emma Ryott,
Rachael Gorton
stage managers: Victoria Horne,
Tuddi Cobbin
casting: Richard Evans
music: Roy Weskin
assistant directors: Nicholas Collett,
Dick McCaw

10pm Albert Hotel, Kirkwall
Festival Club:
Orkney Schools' Swing Band
director: David Griffith

Tuesday 23 June

11am Kirkwall Town Hall
Gerard McBurney: a talk

1pm St Magnus Cathedral
Hilliard Ensemble

Music from the Chapels of Ferdinand
and Isabella

Mondéjar: Ave rex noster
Peñalosa: Inter vestibulum;
Ne reminiscaris; Sancta mater;
Magnificat
de Rivaflecha: Vox dilecti mei
Escobar: Clamabat autem mulier
Anon: Di, por que mueres en cruz
Josquin des prez: In te Domine
speravi; Ecce tu pulcra es
de la Rue: Ave Regina; O alutaris
hostia
Ockeghem: Salve Regina

2pm Stromness Academy Theatre
Might and Main:
The Visitation

performers: Sue Pendlebury,
Katherine Ratcliffe, Gail Fhialaine
Sixsmith, Miltos Yerolemou

6pm Papdale Infant Hall
Orkney Orchestra
conductor: David Griffith

Sadie Koninsky: Phoebe Thomson's
Cake Walk
Bizet: L'Arlesienne – Suite No 1
Praetorius: Dance Suite from
'Terpsichore'
Britten: Five Courtly Dances from
'Gloriana'
Copland: Variations on a Shaker
Melody

7.30pm St Magnus Cathedral
Chameleon

Gustav Clarkson: violin
Elizabeth Perry: violin
Simon Rowland-Jones: viola
Angela Malsbury: clarinet
Elizabeth Wilson: cello
Andrew Ball: piano

Prokoviev:
Overture on Jewish Themes
Elena Firsova:
Misterioso for String Quartet

Dmitri Smirnov: Abel

Messiaen:
Quartet for the End of Time

9.30pm Arts Theatre, Kirkwall
The Scottish Ballet 2

That Certain Feeling
choreography: André Prokovsky
music: Gershwin: The Song Book;
The Cuban Overture
design: The Scottish Ballet
dancers: Julia Barbone,
Claire Mahon, Leesa Sparkes,
Victoria Willard, Mikhail Botting,
Michael Crookes, Fabrice Maufrais

Macbeth
Macbeth: Michael Crookes
Lady Macbeth: Julia Barbone
choreography: André Prokovsky
music: David Earl
lighting: Robin Don
piano: Karen MacIver
artistic director: Ken Burke

10pm Albert Hotel, Kirkwall
Festival Club:
Melanie O'Reilly and Her Trio
Brian Kellock: piano
Fred T Baker: bass guitar
John Rae: drums

Wednesday 24 June

11am St Magnus Cathedral
Chameleon

Gustav Clarkson: violin
Elizabeth Perry: violin
Simon Rowland-Jones: viola
Angela Malsbury: clarinet
Elizabeth Wilson: cello
Andrew Ball: piano
with David James: alto

Poul Ruders: Vox in Rama

Gerard McBurney:
My Gypsy Life

Arvo Pärt:
Es sang vor langen Jahren
Shostakovich:
Piano Quintet Op 57

2pm Orkney Arts Theatre, Kirkwall
The Scottish Ballet 2
(repeat performance)

6pm Kirkwall Town Hall
Might and Main
(repeat performance)

8pm Phoenix cinema, Kirkwall
Scottish Chamber Orchestra
conductor: Sir Peter Maxwell Davies

Imogen Cooper: piano
George McIlwham: bagpipes

Maxwell Davies: Ojai Festival Overture
Mozart: Piano Concerto in Bb K456

Maxwell Davies: Concert Suite –
Caroline Mathilde
Maxwell Davies: An Orkney Wedding,
with Sunrise

10pm Albert Hotel, Kirkwall
Festival Club:
Melanie O'Reilly and Her Trio

Exhibitions

Pier Arts Centre, Stromness
Songlines: aboriginal art

Black Pig Gallery, Kirkwall
Peter Davis

Just About Anything, Kirkwall
Sea Dreams and other pictures:
Andrew Parkinson

Ferry Terminal, Stromness
Orkney Prints 1992:
Soulisquoy Printmakers

Woodwick House, Evie
Gunnie Moberg

Woodwick House, Evie
The Garden of Earthly Delights

Stromness Academy Foyer
Imprints
Erlend Brown and Bryan Thurston

Stromness Library
Book Tokens, Books and
Objects: Colin Johnstone and
Tam Macphail

Woodwick House, Evie
The Garden of Earthly Delights
Richard Welsby

The Bu Gallery, Stromness
Ian MacInnes

Tankerness House, Kirkwall
The Air Defence of Scapa Flow

Stromness Museum
St Ola Centenary Exhibition

Corrigall Farm Museum
Staigs and Staigymen

1993

Friday 18 June

6pm Papdale Infant Hall
Gemini Family Concert
Mary Wiegold: soprano
Ian Mitchell: clarinet
Jo Cole: cello

with Orkney school pupils

Firth pupils:
Alayne Dickey, Vicky Stevenson, Dylan Sinclair, Scott Sutherland, Steven Young, Stephen Wake, Rosemary Whalley, Sandy Cadger, Siobhan Cooke, Mary Sparrow, Mark Aim, Ruth Fraser, Keith Shearer, Gemma Russell, Helen Gordon, Lorna Flett, Ellen Moar
Stenness pupils:
Karen Sutherland, Marian Long, Robbie Ireland, Rosslyn Carlyle, Mark Francis, Cate Finlayson, Jenny Kirkland, Gillian Learmonth, Arlene Garriock, Graham Sutherland, Inga Naughton, Zebua Hemmings, Lydia Crow, Martin Alexander, Barbara Scollay, Stephanie Long, Catriona Kennedy, Jennifer Ireland, Dawn Johnston, Emma Robinson, Keith Shearer, Wayne Johnston

Seven Summer Songs
by Peter Maxwell Davies

Burray pupils:
Danielle Corsie, John Dewar, Paul Hewison, Gemma Miller, Michelle Shearer, Gavin Sutherland, Mary Anne Bews, Alex Dewar, Rosemary Donaldson, Lorraine Simpson, Jenna Smith, David Kirkpatrick, Sadie Bews, Lesley Craigie, Tracey Drever, Alan Miller, Garry Sutherland, Lindsay Whitehead
Holm pupils:
Alan Aim, Fiona Aim, John Dearness, Liam Finn, Lucy Hague, Steven Moar, Sharmi Norris, Steven Paterson, David Tait, Kate Askew, Sherine Deakin, Inez Moss, Victoria Rushton, Robert Ashcroft, Brendan Fletcher, Paul Sneesby, Liam Swanney, Graham Horne, Erin Askew, Aimee Dennison, Helga moss, Laura Sneesby
Papdale pupils:
Jenna Bews, Louise Campbell, Ruth Drever, Jenna Flett, Kirsty Gilbert, Holly Laing, Tracy Linklater, Emma Mulraine, Lee Sinclair, Rachel Glue, Gemma Burger, Catherine Matches, Becky Manson, Michael Sinclair, Sonia Rosie, Jamie Donaldson, Euan MacAskill, David Austin, Ritchie Laughton, Michael Twatt, Michael Walsh, Natalie Nezhati, Hannah Robertson, Amy Thomson, Keith Hartmann, Christopher Logie, Robbie Martin, Donna Borwick, Kerrie Craigie, Lisa johnston, Gemma Pirie, Krystle Sutherland, Malcolm Flett, Scott Martin, Paul Norquoy, Jenna Drever, Shelagh Graham, Alison Mackay, Carmen Taylor

instrumentalists:
violins and recorders: Elizabeth Dearness, Victoria Logie, Karen Aim, Sarah Hague, Gilly Irving-Lewis
xylophones: Deborah Marwick, Fiona Laird, Julie Munro, Carly Simpson, Shereen Linklater, Elaine Hutchison, Kelda Dearness
glockenspiels: Mandy Ross, Lucy Manson, Emma Drever
metallophone: James Baster
untuned percussion: Calum MacAskill, Stephen Kemp, Ben Hogan, Shirley Watson, Sharon Stephen
piano: Glenys Hughes
conductor: Frances Gray
percussionists trained by Joan Jones

7.15pm Kirkwall Town Hall
Simon Holt: Pre-concert talk

8pm Phoenix cinema, Kirkwall
Scottish Chamber Orchestra
Sir Peter Maxwell Davies: conductor
Sarah Walker: mezzo soprano

Simon Holt:
Minotaur Games
(Festival commission)
Berlioz: Les Nuits d'Été
Beethoven: Symphony no 4 in Bb

10pm Albert Hotel, Kirkwall
Festival Club: Brasshoppers

Saturday 19 June

10.30am Pier Arts Centre, Stromness
Knut Ødegård poetry reading

11.30am Pierhead, Stromness
Brasshoppers:
street performance

1pm St Magnus Cathedral
Nicolas Kynaston - Organ

Buxtehude: Toccata in D minor
Bach: Allein Gott, in der Hoh sei Ehr' BWV676;
Prelude and Fugue in Eb BWV552
Saint-Saëns: Fantasie No 2 in Db
Franck: Choral No 3 in A minor
Jongen: Sonata Eroica

2.30pm Orkney Arts Theatre
A Midsummer Night's Dream
by William Shakespeare
St Magnus Players
producer: Penny Aberdein
music: Steve King with KGS pupils
set: Anne Bevan with Stromness Academy pupils and John Hunter
lighting: Rob Norman, Voirrey Watterson, with pupils of Stromness Academy

Theseus: Eric Sinclair
Hippolyta: Jacqueline Purdy
Egeus: David Murdoch
Hermia: Margaret Hay
Lysander: Willie Harper
Demetrius: Terry Delaney
Helena: Chris Meek

Philostrate: Liz Robertson
Oberon: Graham Morris
Titania: Cynthia Chaddock
Lady in Waiting: Anne Rae
Puck: Martin Brown
Robin Good Fellow: Finn Aberdein
Peaseblossom: Kes Eccles
Cobweb: Lesley Johnston
Moth: Aimée Bevan
Mustardseed: Heather Aberdein
Changeling Boy:
John Somhairle MacLeod
Peter Quince: Dave Grieve
Nick Bottom: George Swan
Francis Flute: Graham Garson
Snug: Keith Wright
Snout: Megan Eggeling
Robin Starveling: Jeroen Vanhaecht
fairy band: Kath Hague (soloist), Carolyn Bevan, Wendy Bullen, Phyllis Brown, Rachel Sinclair, Sarah Hague, Lucy Hague
musicians:
Sacha Wright: flute
Thomas Moylan: clarinet
Katrina Smith: clarinet
Freya Butcher: trumpet
Magnus Dearness: trombone
Leesa Thomson: violin
Gillian Anderson: viola
Eric Grieve: guitar
Gordon Connell: guitar
Alison Lamont: percussion
Ann Campbell: keyboard
Mary-Ann Robertson: keyboard
Finn MacLeod: keyboard
Jodi Swan: director
Mechanicals' music:
Jocelyn Hamilton: recorder
Tanya Wright: violin
Katie Bichan: violin
Shona Ritch: glockenspiel
Steven Donald: bass xylophone
Charlotte Learmonth: tambourine
slide production:
Louise Barrington, Fiona Brown, Angela Cursiter, Naomi Dixon, Kes Eccles, Hilary Goggin, Diane Grieve, Eilidh Harcus, Rebecca Wood, Cherie Newlands, Katrina Naughton, Theresa Omand, Elaine Richardson, Laura Sclater, Lynn Sutherland, Joanna Walker, Nina Wolstenholme

lighting: Nicola Marlow, Hilary Goggin, Karen O'Connor
costumes: Janice Hunter, Katie Holmes, Anne MacLeod
make-up: Gillian Johnstone
stage manager: Alan Taylor
set building: Magnus Dixon, Sally Meek
props: Pat Presland, Margaret Sutherland, Denise Wright
prompt: Margaret Sutherland

3pm Albert Street, Kirkwall
Brasshoppers:
Street Performance

6pm St Magnus cathedral
The Tallis Scholars

director: Peter Phillips
sopranos: Deborah Roberts,

Tessa Bonner, Ruth Holton, Sally Dunkley
altos: Caroline Trevor, Robert Harre-Jones
tenor: Philip Cave, Robert Johnston
bass: Donald Greig, Francis Steele

Byrd: Sacred Masterpieces
Laudate Pueri; Quomodo Cantabimus; Haec Dies; Turn our captivity; Sing Joyfully; Vide Domine; O Lux Beata Trinitas; Christe Qui Lux; Ad Dominum cum tribularer

8pm Orkney Arts Theatre
A Midsummer Night's Dream
(repeat performance)

10pm Albert Hotel, Kirkwall
Festival Club: Brasshoppers

Sunday 20 June

11.15am St Magnus Cathedral
Festival Service
conducted by Rev Ron Ferguson
preacher: Tom Fleming
director of music: Heather Rendall
assistant organist: Tim Geddes

St Magnus Cathedral Choir
Members of Gemini
Anon: motet
Skempton: Lullaby
Dunstable: Hymn, Salve Regina
Stanford: Justorem Animae
Parry: I was glad when they said unto me
Roe: Salve Regina (Edington Monody No 1)
Karg-Elert: Nun danket alle Gott

1pm Pier Arts Centre, Stromness
Knut Ødegård poetry reading

2.30pm Stromness Town Hall
Celebrity recital:
Sarah Walker: mezzo soprano
Malcolm Martineau: piano

Enesco: Sept Chansons de Clément Marot, Op 15
Debussy: Trois Chansons de Bilitis; Deux Chansons de France
Honegger: Saluste du Bartas
Fauré, Debussy, Hahn: Settings of four Verlaine poems

5pm Stromness Town Hall
A Johnsmas Foy: Man and Beast
pupils of Stromness Academy
producer: Jocky Wood

readers/performers:
Emma Grieve, Simon Henderson, Jamie Irvine, Shauna Spence, Marcus Tait, Rachael Scarth, Steven Sinclair, Emma Robertson, Rachael Scott, Allan Chalmers, Alistair Flett, Rachel Ludgate, Erica McLennan, Kenneth Ross

musicians: Sally Kirkland, Jacqueline Nicolson, Lyndsey Grant, Shona Harvey, Keri Seator, Michelle Garson

ST MAGNUS Festival
FRIDAY 18 JUNE '93
PROGRAMME £1

ST MAGNUS Festival
SATURDAY 19 JUNE '93
PROGRAMME £1

ST MAGNUS Festival
SUNDAY 20 JUNE '93
PROGRAMME £1

ST MAGNUS Festival
MONDAY 21 JUNE '93

ST MAGNUS Festival
TUESDAY 22 JUNE '93
PROGRAMME £1

ST MAGNUS Festival
WEDNESDAY 23 JUNE '93
PROGRAMME £1

8pm St Magnus Cathedral
Music for Voices and Brass:
St Magnus Festival Chorus
conductor: Richard Hughes
The Tallis Scholars
director: Peter Phillips
The Wallace Collection
director: John Wallace
Nicolas Kynaston: organ

Giovanni Gabrieli: Canzon Duodecimi
Tuoni a 10; La Spiritata
Andrea Gabreli: Deus, qui beatum
Marcum; Egredimini et videte; Maria
Magdalena et altera Maria; Jubilate
Deo; Ricercar del Duodecimi Tuoni
Adriano Banchieri: Canzon in Echo
Giovanni Gabrieli: Dic nobis Maria;
Hodie Christus natus est
Giovanni Gabrieli: in Ecclesiis
Josquin: Ave Maria
Lassus: Alma redemptoris Mater à
8; Ave Regina caelorum à 6, Tui sunt
caeli à 8
Jongen: Mass Op 130
soloists: Ruth Holden, Caroline Trevor,
Robert Johnston, Francis Steel

10pm Albert Hotel, Kirkwall
Streetwise
Phil Anderson: lead guitar, vocals
Billy Peace: keyboards, vocals
Ian Mackay: bass, vocals
Jim Marwick: drums
Joanna Kendall: vocals

Monday 21 June

10am Orkney Arts Theatre
A Midsummer Night's Dream
Performance for schools

1pm St Magnus Cathedral
The Wallace Collection
director: John Wallace
trumpets: John Wallace, John Miller,
Roy Bilham
french horns: Michael Thompson,
Richard Watkins, Phillip Eastop,
Peter Blake
trombones: Susan Addison,
James Casey
bass trombone: Phillip Brown
tuba: David Powell
percussion: Kevin Hathway

Dukas: Fanfare pour Précéder la Péri
Ravel: Fanfare pour l'Eventail de
Jeanne
Roussel: Fanfare pour on Sacre Païen
Schmitt: Le Camp de Pompée
Couperin, arr. Wallace: Les
Bacchanales
Poulenc: Sonata for Horn, Trumpet
and Trombone
Tippett: Sonata for Four Horns
Britten: Fanfare for St Edmundsbury;
Russian Funeral; Theme, Percussion
Variation and Finale from 'The Young
Person's Guide to the Orchestra'

6pm St Magnus Cathedral
Orkney Orchestra
conductor: David Griffith
Kirkwall Town Band
conductor: Brian Jones

St Magnus Cathedral Choir
director: Heather Rendall

Erik Satie, arr. Clive Strutt:
Concert Waltz: 'Je te veux'
Sandy Dennison:
Natural Tones
Schubert: Symphony
No 8 in B minor 'Unfinished'
Rimmer: March, Slaidburn
arr Langford: My love is like a red
red rose. (solo Graham Sutherland)
Lloyd: View me Lord a work of Thine
Myers: Cavatina
Mozart: Alleluia (solo Alasdair Harvey)
Robertson: Flow Gently Sweet Afton
Somerset Folk Song: O Waly Waly
Maxwell Davies: Lullaby for Lucy
Dacre: Jamie's Patrol
Purcell: Rondeau
Indrehus: A Poem for Shelter (GMB)
John Rutter: A Gaelic Blessing

WORLD PREMIERE

8.15pm Orkney Arts Theatre
Tom Fleming in
Every Blessed Thing
An Evening with George MacLeod
written/compiled by Ronald Ferguson

FIRST PERFORMANCE

10pm Albert Hotel, Kirkwall
Festival Club:
Scottish Syncopators
Mike Hart, John McGuff, Dave Strutt,
Donald Corbett, Jack Duff, Murray
Smith, Roy Percy, Wendy Weatherby

Tuesday 22 June

11am Kirkwall Town Hall
Knut Ødegård poetry reading

12 noon Pier Arts Centre
Riss Dansekompani
Resten – an open air performance

1pm Stromness Town Hall
Barry Douglas: piano

Beethoven: Sonata in Eb Op 27 No1
Rachmaninov: Moments Musicaux
Tchaikovsky: pieces from The Seasons
Chopin: Sonata No 3 in B minor Op16

3.30pm Pier Arts Centre
A5 Theatre Group:
Exploring Holberg
Riv Bergesen, Finn Lunker,
Kai Johnson with dancers from the
Riss Dansekompani

5pm St Olaf's Church, Kirkwall
Choral Evensong: sung by
The Mayfield Singers
director: Neil Price
Weelkes: Gloria in Excelsis Deo;
Evening Service for Trebles; O Lord
Arise into Thy Resting Place
(4.40pm: renaissance organ music
played by Richard Hughes)

6.15pm Kirkwall Town Hall
Deborah Randall: poetry reading

7pm St Magnus Cathedral
Gemini
Mary Wiegold: soprano

Ian Mitchell: clarinet
Joanne Cole: cello
Will Sleath: flute
Yuko Inoue: viola
Andrew Ball: piano

Grainger: 'Handel in the Strand'
Messiaen: Le Merle Noire
Britten: Lachrymae
Edward McGuire:
Soundweft
Ravel: Chansons Madécasses
Simon Holt: Tauromanquia
Scelsi: Suite
Josephine Wilson:
Tomato Songs

UK PREMIERE
WORLD PREMIERE

9pm Orkney Arts Theatre
Every Blessed Thing (repeat)

9pm Phoenix cinema
Mouth Music
James Mackintosh, Quee MacArthur,
Andy Thorburn, Jeremy Black, Martin
Swan, Michaela Rowan, Jackie Joyce:

10pm Albert Hotel, Kirkwall
Festival Club:
Scottish Syncopators

Wednesday 23 June

10.30am Orkney Arts Theatre
A Johnsmas Foy (repeat)

music: 'A Midsummer Night's Dream'
created and performed by KGS pupils
under the direction of Steve King:
Sacha Wright, Thomas Moylan,
Katrina Smith, Freya Butcher,
Magnus Dearness, Leesa Thomson,
Gillian Anderson, Eric Grieve,
Gordon Connell, Alison Lamont,
Ann Campbell, Mary-Ann Robertson
Finn MacLeod, Jodi Swan

12 noon Kirk Green
A5 Theatre Group:
Exploring Holberg (repeat)

1pm St Magnus Cathedral
Gemini
William Sweeney: Trio
Villa-Lobos: Jet Whistle
Robert Godman:
Lemmings
Judith Weir:
King Harald's Saga
Rebecca Clarke: Prelude, Allegro
and Pastorale
William Campbell:
The Struggle of Will
arr. Mitchell: Medieval Sequence

WORLD PREMIERE
WORLD PREMIERE

2pm Stromness Academy
A Johnsmas Foy (repeat)

3.30pm Kirk Green
Riss Dansekompani Resten –
an open air performance

6pm St Magnus Cathedral
Grieg Anniversary Concert
The Grieg Ensemble
Atle Sponberg: violin
Anne Nitter Sandvik: piano

Magnhild Mo: cello
Linda Øvrebø: voice
Berit Opheim: voice
Wenche Gausdal: voice/synthesiser
Dag Arnesen: keyboard
Olav Dale: saxophone
Frank Jacobsen: percussion
Einar Mjolsnes: Hardanger fiddle
Leif Rygg: Hardanger fiddle
Geir Østensjø: sound engineer
Kjell Olav Heggstad: producer

Folketone e. Kaja Gjendine Slalien:
Gjendines bådnlåt
Edvard Grieg: Gjendines bådnlåt Op
66 No 19; Fra Holbergs tid Op 40;
Verk 137 Andante con moto;
Fiolinsonate No 3 c-moll Op 45; Jeg
elsker dip Op 5 No 3; Solveigs sang
Op 52 No 4; En drøm Op 48 No 6;
(etter Knut Dale), Knut Luråsens
halling 1 Op 72; (halling etter Knut
Dale) Haugelåt, moderne rytmisk
musikk
Grieginspierert rytmisk musikk:
Gangar;
Solveigs sang
Slåtteavdeling: etter Sjur Helgeland:
Dei tre budeiene på Vikafjell
etter Ola Mosafinn: Kjepphesten
Kenneth Sivertsen: På veg til
Hardanger
Dag Arnesen: Rusler rundt 152

8pm Phoenix cinema
Scottish Chamber Orchestra
Sir Peter Maxwell Davies: conductor
Barry Douglas: piano
David Nicholson: flute

Ravel: Le Tombeau de Couperin
Maxwell Davies:
Strathclyde Concerto No 6 for Flute
Beethoven: Piano Concerto No4 in G

10pm Albert Hotel, Kirkwall
Mouth Music

Exhibitions

St Magnus Cathedral
Sails in St Magnus

Stromness Library
Movements
new work by Mary Scott

Black Pig Gallery, Kirkwall
Ocean Heath Shore
John Cumming

Bu Gallery Stromness
Marian Ashburn - new work

St Olaf's Church Hall, Kirkwall
Benedicite

Tankerness House Museum
No Ordinary Journey John Rae

Stromness Museum
An Orcadian In The Arctic
photographs by James W Sinclair

Pier Arts Centre, Stromness
North - sculpture by Jake Harvey

1994

Friday 17 June

10am Phoenix cinema, Kirkwall
The Beggar's Opera
performance for schools

3.30pm Ayre Hotel, Kirkwall
Mr Anderson's Fine Tunes

5.45pm Kirkwall Town Hall
Sound Pictures
Steve King, with adults from
St Colm's Centre, Kirkwall
paintings: Jenny King

Alasdair Nicolson, with pupils from
Kirkwall Grammar School

6.45pm St Magnus Cathedral
Draumkvedet (Dream Song)
Halvor Håkanes: voice
Monica Jangaard: organ

8pm Phoenix cinema, Kirkwall
The Beggar's Opera by John Gay

St Magnus Players
Scottish Chamber Orchestra
Ensemble

director: George Rendall
music director: Alasdair Nicolson
music (devised from the original airs):
Paul Archbold, GP Cribari,
Alasdair Edwards, Jennifer Martin,
Magnus Robb, Edward Rushton
Alasdair Nicolson.
cast:
The Beggar: Aly Bruce
The Player: Bob Ross
Peachum: George Swan
Mrs Peachum: Kathleen Hague
Polly Peachum: Kathy Johnson
Filch: Ann Campbell
Captain Macheath: Bob Ross
Lockit: Dennis Gowland
Lucy Lockit: Louise Grant
Jemmy Twitcher: Aly Bruce
Crook-fingered Jack: Eric Sinclair
Wat Dreary: Fred Soutar
Robin of Bagshot: Michael Thorpe
Nimming Ned: Jim Groundwater
Harry Padington: Geoff Noble
Matt of the Mint: Chris Matthews
Ben Budge: Keith Wright
Mrs Coaxer: Margaret Green
Dolly Trull: Jacquelyn Purdy
Mrs Vixen: Megan Eggeling
Betty Doxy: Eleanor Laird
Jenny Diver: Phoebe Thorpe
Mrs Slammekin: Cynthia Chaddock
Suky Tawdry: Jan Stockan
Molly Brazen: Kelly Leonard
women of the town: Lydia Campbell,
Lesley Cheer, Margaret Hinkley,
Joyce Howard, Sue Whitworth
musicians:
clarinets: Janet Tortoiseshell
trombone: Nigel Cox
violin: Lorna McLaren
viola: Steve King
cello: Kevin MacCrae
double bass: John Steer
percussion: Ian Coulter
keyboards: Edward Rushton
conductor: Alasdair Nicolson

musical coordinator: Glenys Hughes
set design: Frances Pelly, Alan Stout
costumes: Morag Tweedie,
Lynne Campion
props: Pat Presland, Denise Wright
hair/make-up: Rachel Swanney
production assistant: Alison Fraser
stage manager: Bryan Leslie

10pm Albert Hotel, Kirkwall
The Festival Club:
Orkney Schools' Swing Band
director: David Griffith

Saturday 18 June

10.30am Stromness Academy
Seamus Heaney poetry reading

12.30pm Stromness Town Hall
Della Jones: mezzo soprano
Malcolm Martineau: piano

Schubert: Five Italian Songs
Rossini: Three French Songs;
Giovanna d'Arco
Poulenc: Banalités
Satie: Trois Melodies; Three Welsh
Songs
Weill: Songs from 'The Threepenny
Opera'

3pm Kirkwall Town Hall
St Magnus Cathedral Choir
director: Sandy Horsburgh
Kirkwall Town Band
conductor: Brian Jones

3.30pm Phoenix cinema, Kirkwall
Meet Susan Sharpe
of BBC Radio 3 and make a request
for Midweek Choice.

4.30pm Phoenix cinema, Kirkwall
The Beggar's Opera
Repeat performance

7pm Kirkwall Town Hall
Meet Susan Sharpe

7pm Broad Street, Kirkwall
Lone School Band
director: Espen Selvik

8pm Phoenix cinema
BBC Philharmonic Orchestra
conductor: Sir Peter Maxwell Davies
Sylvia Rosenberg: violin
Mark Jordan: Northumbrian pipes

Maxwell Davies:
Cross Lane Fair
(Festival/BBC
Philharmonic commission)
Prokoviev:
Violin Concerto No 2 in G minor
Mendelssohn:
Symphony no 3 in A minor 'Scottish'

10pm Albert Hotel, Kirkwall
Festival Club: Bongshang
JJ Jamieson: banjo, vocals
Leonard Scollay: fiddle
Bryan Peterson: bass
Neil Preshaw: guitars
Christopher Anderson: drums

Sunday 19 June

10am St Magnus Cathedral
Festival Service
conducted by Rev Ron Ferguson
St Magnus Cathedral Choir
director: Sandy Horsburgh
organist: Heather Rendall
SCO Ensemble

Tallis: O Nata Lux
Fauré: Cantique de Jean Racine
Guilmant: Grande Choeur

1pm Stromness Academy Theatre
Seamus Heaney poetry reading
(repeat performance)

2.30pm Stromness Town Hall
Celebrity recital:
Sylvia Rosenberg: violin
David Owen Norris: piano

Stravinsky: Suite Italienne
Bartók: Sonata for Solo Violin
Maxwell Davies:
Five Little Pieces for Piano
Beethoven: Sonata for Violin and
Piano Op 30 No 2 in C minor

5pm Stromness Town Hall
A Johnsmas Foy:
Witches, Trows and Fairy Folk
presented by pupils of
Stromness Academy
producer: Jocky Wood

readers/performers:
Alistair Flett, Jamie Irvine,
Marcus Tait, Steven Sinclair,
Kenny Ross, Allan Chalmers,
Shauna Spence, Rachel Scott,
Emma Robertson, Emma Grieve,
Sally Kirkland, Michelle Garson,
Lindsey Grant, Keri Seator,
Jacqueline Nicolson, Shona Harvey

6.45pm St Magnus Cathedral
Draumkvedet
(repeat performance)

8pm Phoenix cinema, Kirkwall
BBC Philharmonic Orchestra
St Magnus Festival Chorus

chorus master: Richard Hughes
conductor: Sir Peter Maxwell Davies

Della Jones: mezzo soprano
Christine Bunning: soprano
Mark Curtis: tenor
Ian Caddy: bass

Mendelssohn: Overture, The
Hebrides
Maxwell Davies: Stone Litany
Beethoven: Mass in C Op 86

10pm Albert Hotel, Kirkwall
Festival Club: Boogalusa
David Oundney: accordions, vocals
Bill Higgins: guitar, vocals, bass guitar
RG McGlone: drums, bodhran
Alan Wilson: rub board, percussion
Kevin Findlay: fiddle
Hugh Kelly: bass guitar

Monday 20 June

11am Kirkwall Town Hall
Seamus Heaney poetry reading
(repeat performance)

1pm St Magnus Cathedral
Folk Song Recital
Christine Bunning: soprano
Mark Curtis: tenor
Ian Caddy: bass
Malcolm Martineau: piano
Clare Dixon: violin
Peter Dixon: cello
Simon Butterworth: clarinet

Haydn: Four Scottish Folk Songs
John McCabe: Three Folk Songs for
clarinet, soprano and piano
Brahms: Six Folk Songs
Britten: Four Folk Songs
Beethoven: Three Folk Songs

4pm and 6pm Orkney Arts Theatre
The Rainbow
by Sir Peter Maxwell Davies
performed by pupils of Stromness
Primary School

Pat: Barry Park
Teacher: Emma Poke
Mrs Flett: Helen Chalmers
Mr Tait: Stuart Thomson
Reamy's dogs: Nicola Stanger,
Morag Bryden
Donkey: Heather Aberdein,
Aimée Bevan
Selkie: Sean Holland

children/selkies:
Jacqui Marwick, Kim MacIver, Marie
Flett, Aimee Flett, Gemma Herdman,
Fiona Isbister, Karl Scott, Joseph
Robertson, Zoe Morrison
dogs/fishermen:
Nicola Stanger, Kerra Park,
Vanessa Laidlow, Candy Adamson,
Gemma Dorricott, James Groat,
Brian Wilson, Richard Towers,
Morag Bryden, Daniel Gunn
traffic/Brinkie's Brae:
Sean Chalmers, Peter Hayes,
Christopher Colquhoun, Erland Ritch,
Steven Reid, Barrie Moar,
Andrew Sclater
musicians:
Jo Richards, Jennifer Tait, Shona
Harvey, Keri Seatter, Michelle Garson,
Pauline Heddle, Lindsey Grant, Sadie
Merriman, Lyndsey Rae, Roy Temple
musical director: Tim Geddes
producer: Ingrid Morrison
costumes: Jeannie Blagg
dance sequences: Penny Aberdein

Dinosaur at Large
performed by pupils of
Sanday Junior Secondary School

Pat: Christina Wenham
Teacher: Adam Towrie
Brachiosaurus: Clare gibson, Rachel
Jacobs, Lorna Muir, Leona Tulloch
Museum Attendant: George Brown
Elizabeth 1: Jacqueline Tulloch
Walter Raleigh: Magnus Thorne

Roman General: Robert Ward
Budicca: Shona Grieve
children/Budicca's warriors:
Fay Boswell, Emma Grieve, Kelly
Harcus, Shane MacDonnell, Michael
Muir, Amy Peace, David Peace, Bella
Sichel, Wayne Sinclair, Emma Tulloch,
Alex Wilson, Fiona Wilson
Budicca's porters: Graham Clarke,
Alistair Thorne
Roman soldiers: Caroline Boswell,
Robert Boswell, George Brown, Jeffrey
Chapman, Paul Greves, Sean Greves,
Jamie Lewington, Verity Luke, Emily
MacLeod, Monica Tulloch, Adam
Towrie
Elizabeth's courtiers: Gary Brown,
Katie-Anne Drever, Charlotte Gibson,
Zara Grieve, Elizabeth Lennie, Victoria
Lennie, Andrew Linton, Ben Lynch,
Karl Muir, Kerry Muir, Martha
Schofield, Tanya Sichel, Nicola Stuart
dinosaurs: Gary Brown, Paul Greves,
Andrew Linton, Ben Lynch, Elizabeth
Lennie, Victoria Lennie, Emily
MacLeod, Karl Muir, Kerry Muir,
Martha Schofield, Tanya Sichel
baby dinosaurs: Vikki Brown, Louisa
Drever, David Findler, Thomas
Harcus, Mark Linton, Jacob Lynch,
Bryony Newton, Clare-Jane Peace,
Owen Rudge, Katrina Skea, Vanessa
Skea, Richard Thomson, Donna
Trudghill, Donna Tulloch, Carrie Walls
tyrannosaurus rex: Christopher
A'Hara, Graham Clarke, Alistair Thorne
instrumentalists:
recorders: Beinn Muir,
Thomas Moylan
tuned percussion: Jennifer Muir,
Linda Towrie, Helen Towrie,
Clare Walsh, Pamela Wilson
unpitched percussion: Selina Cobley,
Sarah Crabtree, Lynne Peace
trumpet: Linda Laird
cello: Helen Newman

musical director: Glenys Hughes
production: Sue McArthur,
Myra Stockton, May Allen
drama consultant: Penny Aberdein
scenery/props: Sylvia Thorne, David
Kemp, Bill McArthur, Dean Chaplin,
Jean McLaughlan, Maurice Soord
costumes: Sylvia Thorne, Carol Dean,
Jean Soord, Marian Robertson,
Iris Golding, parents and friends
dinosaur heads: P6/7 pupils
tyrannosaurus rex: Christopher Bain
time machine: Jamie Lewington,
Tristan Thorne

8pm Phoenix cinema, Kirkwall
BBC Philharmonic Orchestra
conductor: Barry Wordsworth
David Owen Norris: piano
Della Jones: mezzo soprano

Weber: Overture, Der Freishutz
Mozart: Piano Concerto in A K488
J Strauss II: Overture, 'The Gipsy
Baron', Pizzicato Polka
O Strauss: Je t'aime from 'Les Trois
Valses'
Zeller: Roses from Tyrol, from 'The
Bird Seller'

Lehar: Vilja, from 'The Merry Widow'
E Strauss: Bahm Frei (Train Galop)
J Strauss II: Egyptian March
Josef Strauss: Polka: Ohne Sorgen
J Strauss II: Waltz, The Blue Danube

10pm Albert Hotel, Kirkwall
**Festival Club: Orleysa
Jazz from Norway**

Tuesday 21 June

11am Stromness Academy Theatre
A Johnsmas Foy
repeat performance

1pm St Magnus Cathedral
Orleysa

Jan Magne Førde: trumpet/flugel horn
Arve Furset: keyboards
Rolf Prestø: bass
Terje Isungset: drums/percussion
Berit Opheim: voice

1.30pm Orkney Arts Theatre
**Desperate Journey:
TAG Theatre Company**
performance for schools

2.30pm Stromness Town Hall
David Owen Norris: piano

Purcell: A New Scotch Tune
Berkeley, Mathias, MacMillan,
Victory: Variations on a theme of
Henry Purcell in homage to
President Kennedy
Schubert: 12 Ecossaises
MacMillan: Piano Sonata

5.15pm Phoenix cinema, Kirkwall
In Tune
presenter: Geoffrey Baskerville
live Radio 3 music programme

6.30pm St Magnus Cathedral
**The Chamber Group of Scotland:
Music for Theatre**
John Grant: flute
Lawrence Gill: clarinet
Ruth Crouch: violin
Robert Irvine: cello
Ian Coulter: percussion
Graeme McNaught: piano

Harrison Birtwistle:
Four Interstices from 'Monodrama'
Sally Beamish: Commedia
Oliver Knussen: Masks
Alasdair Nicolson: Punch!
(Festival commission)
Debussy: Cello Sonata,
'Pierrot angry with the moon'
Edward McGuire: Euphoria

8.30pm Orkney Arts Theatre
**Desperate Journey:
TAG Theatre Company**
director: Andy Howitt
composer: Alasdair Nicolson
designer: Kate Borthwick

cast:
Aled Evans, Jane Howie, Andy Howitt,

Jenny McLachlan, Karen Murdoch,
Christine Primrose
musicians:
Karen Murdoch: clarinet
Colin Young: percussion

10pm Albert Hotel, Kirkwall
**Festival Club:
Khartoum Heroes**

Atholl Fraser, Andy Robinson,
Een Anderson, Kenny Anderson,
Jason Brass, Dougi McMillan

Wednesday 22 June

1pm St Magnus Cathedral
**The Chamber Group of Scotland:
Music for Dance**

Maxwell Davies:
Renaissance Scottish Dances
Stravinsky: Dances from The Firebird
Lutoslawski: Dance Preludes
Martin Dalby: The Dancer Eduardova
Maxwell Davies: Dances from
'The Two Fiddlers'

6pm St Magnus Cathedral
Lone School Band
director: Espen Selvik
Orkney Orchestra
conductor: David Griffiths
St Magnus Cathedral Choir
conductor: Sandy Horsburgh

Ingunn Skage: soprano
Heather Rendall: organ

Haydn: Little Organ Mass
Espen Selvik: Introduction
Telemann: Andante-Allegro
Clive Strutt: Osmanie Imperial March
Debussy: Marche Ecossaise
Andrew Lloyd Webber: Pie Jesu
Espen Selvik:
Echo from the Norsemen
Sullivan: Overture 'The Gondoliers'

7.30pm Phoenix cinema, Kirkwall
Happy Returns: a birthday
retrospective of Sir Peter Maxwell
Davies's Orkney music for children

Kirkwall Shopping Songs:
singers: Burray, Holm, Hope,
Glaitness, North Ronaldsay, Papa
Westray and St Andrews Primaries
Orkney fiddle music:
Kirkwall Grammar School Traditional
Music Group
Stewart Sinclair reads 'The Old
Fiddle' by Bessie Skea
Dances from The Two Fiddlers:
solo violin: Alison Dixon
dancers from Shapinsay Primary
Seven Songs Home:
Kirkwall Grammar School Girls' Choir
Max Cats!:
Papdale Max Cats: Ingrid Austin,
Laura Barnett, Louise Bevan, Donna
Borwick, Shelagh Graham, Elizabeth
Grant, Suzanne Gray, Steven Groat,
Jennifer Heddle, Alice Mowatt,
Gemma Pirie, Donna Rendall, Krystle
Sutherland, Carmen Taylor

Cinderella: Elaine Hutchison
solo cat: Shereen Linklater
Ugly Sisters: Dick Hughes,
David Griffith, Eric Sinclair
Songs of Hoy
singers: Dounby, Evie, Firth, Orphir
and Stenness Primary Schools
instrumentalists: Kirkwall Grammar
School
cast:
Widow Grumble: Sarah Gillespie
Cat: Adam Clark
Dr Trickett: Alaster Groat
children: Elspeth Groat, Ewan Groat,
Patrick Hardcastle, Coleen Leslie,
Heather Leslie, Aaron Spence
lone child: Jason Kirkpatrick
neighbours: Daisy Bateman, Helen
Budge, Amanda Melbourne

Birthday Song
(unprogrammed)
by Elizabeth Dearness
words by George Mackay Brown

10pm Albert Hotel, Kirkwall
**Festival Club:
Khartoum Heroes**

Thursday 23 June

7pm Phoenix cinema, Kirkwall
Happy Returns
(repeat performance)

Exhibitions

Pier Arts Centre
Richard Long

St Magnus Cathedral
Draumkvedet

Stromness Library
**Soulisquoy Printmakers:
Source**

The Bu Gallery, Stromness
Sandy Budden, Sheila Cameron
pottery and prints

The Black Pig Gallery, Kirkwall
Matilda Tumim - Sand and Blood

St Olaf's Church, Kirkwall
Giulio Brajuha - Revelation

Tankerness House Museum
Scar
An Orkney Viking Boat Burial

Stromness Museum
75 Years On
archive photographs of the German
High Seas Fleet in Scapa Flow

The Hoy Gallery
Studies from Berriedale
Richard Welsby

1995

Friday 16 June

6pm King Street Hall, Kirkwall
Island to Island
a piece of music theatre exploring
themes from Shakespeare's
'The Tempest'

Gamelan overture and storm
sequence devised by children from
Eday, Egilsay, Papa Westray and
North Ronaldsay Primary Schools

artists-in-residence: John Pawson,
Liz Haddon, Tim Ward Jones

8pm St Magnus Cathedral
Scottish Chamber Orchestra
conductor: Nicholas Kraemer

Truls Mørk: cello
James Clark: violin
Richard Hughes: organ

Locke: The Tempest
Handel: Organ Concerto in F Op 4
No 5
Thea Musgrave: The Seasons
Haydn: Cello Concerto in C
Vivaldi: Spring and Summer from
'The Four Seasons'

10.15pm Orkney Arts Theatre
A Johnsmas Foy:
Horse Island
compiled by Duncan McLean
producers: Dave Grieve,
Sandra Ballantine

readers: Naismi Flett, Inga Gilmour,
Spencer Rosie, Eric Sinclair
musicians:
The Burray Band: Fran Gray,
Billy Dass, John Tullock, Pete Webb

The Horseman' Word
by Duncan McLean

cast:
Thomas Swanney: Michael Corsie
Kirsten Scott: Linda Tait
Peggy Muir: Joey Tait
Billy Scott: Mike Drever
John Muir: Jim Groundwater
George Halcrow: Derek Tait
Peter Knight: Richard Flett

10pm Albert Hotel, Kirkwall
Festival Club:

Orkney Schools' Swing Band
director: David Griffith
The Ola Band
Micky Austin: banjo, mandolin
Andy Cant: fiddle
Iain Cooper: bass
Billy Peace: keyboards, accordion
Colin Pirie: fiddle
Alan Reid: guitar
Alan Tullock: drums

Saturday 17 June

10.30am Pier Arts Centre, Stromness
Kevin Crossley-Holland
poetry reading

10.30am King Street Hall, Kirkwall
Gamelan For All
with John Pawson, Liz Haddon and
Tim Ward Jones

11.45am Stromness
Horse and Bamboo:
Street Procession

12.30pm Stromness Town Hall
Jean-Yves Thibaudet: piano

Debussy: Préludes Book 2
Debussy: Three Etudes
Liszt: Jeux d'eau à la Villa d'Este;
Ballade No 2
Wagner/Liszt:
Liebestod from 'Tristan and Isolde'
Liszt: Mephisto Waltz No 1

2.30pm Kirkwall Town Hall
St Magnus Cathedral Choir
conductors: Sandy Horsburgh,
Heather Rendall
Kirkwall Town Band
conductor: Brian Jones

3.30pm Stromness Academy Theatre
Horse and Bamboo Theatre:
Dance of White Darkness

Liam Carroll: horse handler
Nicky Fearn: performer
Gerald Hebburn: musician/lighting
Vicky Jassey: musician
Laurence Kaye: musical director
Frances King: performer
Jo King: tour director
Elaine Kingston: performer
Chrissie Ruckley: performer

director/writer/designer: Bob Frith
choreographer: TC Howard

6pm King Street Hall, Kirkwall
Island to Island
(repeat performance)

7.15pm Kirkwall Town Hall
pre-concert talk:
Thea Musgrave

8pm Phoenix cinema, Kirkwall
Scottish Chamber Orchestra
leader: James Clark
St Magnus Festival Chorus
chorus master: Richard Hughes

conductor: Nicholas Kraemer
Nicholas Daniel: oboe

Purcell: The Tempest
Libby Crabtree: Amphitrite
Teresa Shaw: Ariel
Harry Nicoll: Aeolus
Richard Jackson: Neptune/First Devil
Stephen Richardson: Second Devil

Handel: The King Shall Rejoice
Thea Musgrave:
Oboe Concerto 'Helios'
(Festival commission)

10pm Albert Hotel, Kirkwall
Festival Club:
Hom-Bru

Sunday 18 June

11.15am St Magnus Cathedral
Festival Service
conducted by the Rev Ron Ferguson

St Magnus Cathedral Choir
director: Sandy Horsburgh
organist: Heather Rendall

Nicholas Daniel and
The Britten Sinfonia

Mozart: Oboe Quartet (finale)
Fenton: Sacris Solemniis
Handel: Zadok the Priest
Mozart: Oboe Quartet (slow
movement)
Fenton: Veni Sancte Spiritus

1pm Pier Arts Centre, Stromness
Kevin Crossley-Holland
poetry reading (repeat performance)

2.30pm Stromness Town Hall
Celebrity recital:
Truls Mørk: cello
Jean-Yves Thibaudet: piano

Schumann: Adagio and Allegro
Op 70
Prokoviev: Sonata in C Op 119
Sibelius: Malinconia Op 20
Grieg: Sonata in A minor Op 36

5.15pm Stromness Academy Theatre
A Johnsmas Foy
Repeat performance

8pm Orkney Arts Theatre
The Wildman
music: Nicola LeFanu
libretto: Kevin Crossley-Holland
conductor: Nicholas Cleobury
director: Graham Devlin
orchestra: The Britten Sinfonia

cast:
Gwion Thomas, Richard Jackson,
Virginia Kerr, Richard Edgar-Wilson,
Emma Silversides, Stephen
Richardson, Harry Nicoll,
Teresa Shaw

orchestra:
violin: Pauline Lowbury (leader)
viola: Rachel Bolt
cellos: Martin Loveday, Ben Chappell
double bass: Paul Sherman
flute/piccolo/alto flute: Kate Hill
oboe/cor anglais: Richard Simpson
clarinets: Joy Farrall
horn: Stephen Bell
trumpet: Tony Cross
percussion: David Hockings,
Martin Allen

10pm Albert Hotel, Kirkwall
Festival Club:
Hom-Bru
Gary Peterson: banjo
Davy Henry: banjo, mandolin, guitar,
vocals
Peter Miller: bass guitar, guitar, vocals
Andrew Tulloch: guitar, vocals
John R Deyel: fiddle

Monday 19 June

11am Kirkwall Town Hall
Kevin Crossley-Holland
poetry reading
(repeat performance)

1pm St Magnus Cathedral
Nicholas Daniel: oboe
Julius Drake: piano

Schumann arr. Ferguson:
Three Duos
Bach: Sonata in A BWV 1032
Hindemith: Oboe Sonata
Maxwell Davies: First Grace of Light

David Knotts:
and fall and rise
and fall and rise
again

Bach:
Sinfonia from the Easter Oratorio
Schumann: Adagio and Allegro

6.30pm St Magnus Cathedral
Orkney Camerata

Purcell: Trumpet Overture from
'The Indian Queen'
Albinoni: Concerto a cinque Op 9
No 9 in C
Pachelbel: Canon and Gigue
Grieg: Two Elegiac Melodies
Bach: Brandenburg Concerto
No 2 in F

Orkney Camerata:
1st violins: Julia Robinson Dean
(leader), Ian McKune, Rhona Casey
2nd violins: Julian Cann,
Lesley McLeod, Karen Griffith,
Sally Kirkland
viola: Cathy Johnson,
Sandy Dennison
cellos: Linda Hamilton,
Joanna Richards, Sarah Thomson
flute: David Wood
oboes: Christina Sargent,
Yvonne Gray
trumpet: Kenny Jones, Brian Jones
harpsichord: Glenys Hughes

8pm Orkney Arts Theatre
The Wildman
(repeat performance)

10pm Albert Hotel, Kirkwall
Festival Club:
The Humpff Family

John Coletta: lead vocals, mandolin,
harmonica
Malky Stevenson: vocals, bass
Stevie Gillies: vocals, guitar
Davy Taylor: slide guitar
Bill Hamilton: drums
Jamie Wilson: fiddle

Tuesday 20 June

11am Stromness Academy Theatre
A Johnsmas Foy
(repeat performance)

6.30pm St Magnus Cathedral
The Britten Sinfonia
conductor: Nicholas Cleobury
Teresa Shaw: mezzo soprano

violin: Pauline Lowbury (leader),
Miranda Dale
viola: Rachel Bolt
cello: Martin Loveday
double bass: Paul Sherman
flute: Kate Hill
oboe: Richard Simpson
clarinet: Joy Farrall, Andrew Webster
bassoon: Julie Andrews
horn: Stephen Bell
trumpet: Tony Cross
trombone: Jim Casey
percussion: David Hockings
harp: Hugh Webb

Maxwell Davies: Serenade
Carolisima
Nicola LeFanu: Deva
(solo cello Martin Loveday)
Magnus Robb: Lios Mor
Bridge, arr. Britten: There is a Willow

Mahler, arr. D Matthews:
Four Ruckert Songs

Britten: Sinfonietta

8.30pm Phoenix cinema, Kirkwall
Horse and Bamboo Theatre:
Dance of White Darkness
(repeat performance)

10pm Albert Hotel, Kirkwall
Festival Club:
The Humpff Family

Wednesday 21 June

1pm Stromness Town Hall
Young-Choon Park: piano

Mozart: Sonata in A K331
Beethoven: Sonata in D minor
Op 32 No 2 'Tempest'
Bartók: Suite Op 14
Chopin: Scherzo in B flat minor
Op 31

6pm Orkney Arts Theatre, Kirkwall
Tag Theatre Company:
The Magic Islands
by Liz Lochhead

cast
Drinculo: John Kazek
Prospero: Dougal Lee
Ariel: Alby Manley
Antonio: Raymond Short
Fernandelle: Judi Stewart
Caliban: Andy Williams
Miranda: Julie Wilson Nimmo
director: Lesley Finlay
designer: Suzanne Field
musical director:
Andrew Cruickshank

8pm Phoenix cinema, Kirkwall
Capercaillie

Karen Matheson: vocals
Fred Morrison: small pipes, whistles
Manus Lunny:
bouzouki, guitar, vocals
Charlie McKerron: fiddle
John Saich: bass, guitar, vocals
Donald Shaw: accordion, keyboards
Iain Murray: drums
Wilf Taylor: percussion

Steve King: Farewell
(Festival commission)

singers:
Evie Primary School: Jack Aylward,
Nicolas Balfour, Robbie Balfour,
Ben Coward, Paul Norquay,
Geoffrey Purnell, Claire Cadman-
Hope, Alice Chalmers, Gillian Firth,
Rachael Jenkins, Fiona Nicolson,
Melissa Spence, Caroline Vincent,
Stuart Baker, Adam Twatt,
Darren Heddle, Ian Purnell,
Robert Hinkley, Leah Balfour,
Ellie Naylor, Ellen Casey,
Kirsten Mainland.

Holm Primary School:
Alan Aim, Fiona Aim, John Dearness,
Liam Finn, Lucy Hague, Steven Moar,
Steven Paterson, David Tait,
Robert Ascroft, Kate Askey,
Sherine Deakin, Brendan Fletcher,
Inez Moss, Victoria Rushton,
Paul Sneesby, Liam Swannay

St Andrews Primary School:
Laura Aitken, David Drylie,
Caroline Eunson, Laura Eunson,
Rosalind Eunson, Sarah Fegan,
David Foubister, Lianne Foubister,
Kimberley Gill, Edward Gilmour,
Amy Goodill, Lucy Holt, Eric Hornby,
Michael Kemp, Fraser Laird,
Neil Manson, Brendan Moyland,
Julie Munro, Bruce Omand,
Alan Peach, Samantha Robertson,
Tracey Ross, Sarah Rowe,
Jay Spooner, Joanna Stephenson,
Gary Ward

Kirkwall Grammar School:
Ben Adams, Catherine Adams,
Karen Aim, Ingrid Austin,
Elizabeth Brookman, Tracy Dennison,
Marie Louise Donald,
Theresa Findlay, Ruth Goodwyn,
Elizabeth Grant, Sarah Hague,
Britt Harcus, Sally Harrison,
Jennifer Higgins, Elaine Hutchison,
Shereen Linklater, Grant McKenzie,
Lauren McKie, Nicole Norquoy,
Victoria Olsen, Emma Rosie,
Steven Roy, Gareth Scott,
Kerri Shearer, Isla Rae Shortland,
Gillian Skea, Elizabeth Squires,
Emma Stephen, Kirsteen Stewart,
Laura Swannie, Melanie Thompson,
Lee-Ann Wylie

Stromness Academy:
Lorna Flett, Ruth Fraser,
Claire Sinclair, Helen Gordon,

Elizabeth Peebles, Charlotte Peppitt,
Suzanne Steer, Ashleigh Venables,
Rebecca Work, Katie Fergusson, Zoe
Eccles, Amy Liptrot, Trudi Newton,
Kristen Heddle, Cate Finlayson,
Karen Hinkley, Inga Naughton,
Lisa Ward, Selena Morrison.

strings:
violins: Kenneth Ritch, Selina Cobley,
Keri Seator, Jaqueline Nicholson,
Shona Ritch, Ruth Hutchison, Alistair
Thorne, Tristan Thorne, Fiona Drever,
Michelle Garson, Marie Sinclair,
Gemma Laughton, Victoria Logie,
Elizabeth Dearness, Ian Hutchison,
Susan Anderson, Julie Foxcroft
violas: Susan Bichan, Gillian
Anderson, Pauline Heddle
cellos: Joanna Richards, Sarah
Thomson, Anita Hall, Jenny Kirkland,
Kelda Dearness.

10pm Albert Hotel, Kirkwall
Festival Club:
The Smoking Stone Band

Douglas Montgomery: fiddle
Dick Levens: mandolin
Jim Hall: five-string banjo
John Adams: fretless bass

Thursday 22 June

7.30pm Phoenix cinema, Kirkwall
Capercaillie

7.30pm St Margaret's Hope School
Horse and Bamboo Theatre
(repeat performance)

Horse and Bamboo
street processions:
Stromness: Saturday June 17
St Margaret's Hope:
Thursday June 22

music: Ken Slaven/Dave Jackson

Exhibitions

Pier Arts Centre, Stromness
Mary Newcomb

Stromness Library
Sample Book - a series of small
tapestries and prints by Carol Dunbar

Ferry Terminal, Stromness
Repossessed - prints by Elaine
Shemilt in collaboration with Kevin
Crossley-Holland

The Bu Gallery, Stromness
Small Sculptures
work by Orkney artists

Kirkwall Town Hall Foyer
Roger Warhurst - photographs

St Olaf's Church, Kirkwall
Moods:
Margaret Smailes: free machine
embroidery; Ken McKay: landscape
paintings; John Morson: silver spoons

The Hoy Gallery
Mike Cairncross
paintings and sculpture

Soli Deo Gallery
Northern Shore
paintings by Doug Muir

Woodwick House, Evie
Beauty and the Beast
Helen Denerley: collaborations

Kirkwall Library
Bibliotheck - old Orkney books

Tankerness House Museum
Building the Churchill Barriers

Stromness Museum
Fortress Orkney

1996

Friday 21 June

5.15 - 7.30pm St Magnus Cathedral
In Tune Linda Ormiston presents
Radio 3's music programme.

7.30pm Phoenix cinema, Kirkwall
Lord of the Mirrors
choreographer:
Andrew Howitt
composer:
Alasdair Nicolson
lighting designer: George Tarbuck
costumes: Tait and Style

dancers:
Paul Joseph, Jenny McLachlan,
Pauline Smith, Tom Ward and
performers from the festival
community dance project.
musicians:
The Emperor String Quartet
Joanna MacGregor: piano
Dick Lee: saxophone
Swing '96

dances:
Orcadian Swing
The Stormwatchers (inspired by
George Mackay Brown's play)
Lord of the Mirrors (inspired by
George Mackay Brown's poem)

9.45pm Orkney Arts Theatre, Kirkwall
A Johnsmas Foy:
'Brooms and cradles and pots?'
compiled and produced by:
Greer Norquoy, Karen Essen and
Margaret Irvine

cast:
Issy Grieve, Linda Ross,
Kristen Wylie, Margaret Irvine,
Bobby Bews, Rachel Scarth,
Lindsay Irvine, Kylie Tullock,
Leona Coghill, Lisa Norquoy,
Lesley Scarth, Anna Spence,
Jenny Johnson, Steven Wylie,
Jamie Irvine, Kenneth Ross,
Joanna Grieve, Emma Grieve,
Jon Ross
musicians: Minna Merriman,
Tommy Mainland

10pm Albert Hotel, Kirkwall
Festival Club:
Orkney Schools' Swing Band
director: David Griffith
Dick Lee and Swing '96

Saturday 22 June

10.30am Pier Arts Centre, Stromness
Iain Crichton Smith poetry reading

10.30am Kirkwall Town Hall
St Magnus Cathedral Choir
conductors: Sandy Horsburgh,
Heather Rendall
Kirkwall Town Band
conductor: Brian Jones

12 noon Broad Street, Kirkwall
Dancebite
A 'taster' of the
Festival community dance project

1pm St Magnus Cathedral, Kirkwall
Tasmin Little: violin
John Lenehan: piano

Brahms: Sonatensatz FAE
Bach: Partita No 2 in D minor
Poulenc: Sonata
Szymanowski: Fountains of Arethusa
Ravel: Tzigane

3.30pm Dounby School Hall
Tam O'Shanter's Bairns:
Baldy Bane Theatre Company

cast: Garry Stewart, Hugh Larkin,
Sharon Millar, Diane Sobolewska
writer and director: Garry Stewart
costume and set: Alison Couston

3.30pm Woodwick House, Evie
Jouissances des Dames

Lucy Ballard: voice
Rebecca Prosser:
recorders/renaissance flute
Jessica Gordon:
lutes/renaissance guitar

6pm King Street Hall, Kirkwall
Orkney Dances

Orcadian Swing:
dancers: EJ Budge, Moira Carlyle,
Stacey Flett, Lorna Hirst,
Maggie Gorn, Laura Harcus,
Janine Hughes, Emma McLeod,
Becky Manson, Laureen Miller,
Sharyon Mooney, Nicola Stewart,
Susan Warren, Tanya Wood,
Caroline Wylie
music:
Django Reinhart: Place de Brouckete;
Moppin' the Bride
Dick Lee: G and A Blues

Orcadian Rap:
dancers: Kate Birkett,
Elizabeth Dearness, Ruth Goodwyn,
Laura Laughton, Victoria Logie,
Carmen McEwan, Lucy Rendall,
Raksha Revis, Lorien Roberts,
Jay Spooner, Simon Varley,
Lee-Anne Wylie
music: Talitha Mackenzie: Seinn O

Orcadian Fiddle:
dancers: Heather Aberdein,
Candy Adamson, Aimée Bevan,
Jude Barnes, Carolyn Bevan,
Wendy Bullen, Ellen Casey,
Margaret Coward,
Christine Eccleston, Katie Fergusson,
Catriona Headley, Clover Giles,
Emily Gordon, Karen Hinckley,
Kelly Hounslow, Linda Johnston,
Amy Liptrot, Rachel McKinlay,
Zoe Morrison, Elizabeth Peebles,
Clare Sinclair, Barbara Smith,
Ashleigh Venables, Rebecca Welsh,
Rebecca Work

fiddle: Graham Garson

Music: Stronsay Waltz; The Stones
of Stenness
Rock Salt and Nails: Life

Orkney Anthem:
dancers: the company
music: Ivan Drever: Orkney Anthem

7pm Kirkwall Town Hall
Pre-concert talk:
Sir Peter Maxwell Davies

8pm Phoenix cinema, Kirkwall
Royal Philharmonic Orchestra
conductor: Sir Peter Maxwell Davies
Joanna MacGregor: piano
Jonathan Carney: violin

Maxwell Davies:
A Spell for Green Corn
Beethoven:
Piano Concerto No 2 in B flat
Maxwell Davies: Symphony No 6
(commissioned by the
RPO; dedicated to
George Mackay Brown)

10pm Albert Hotel, Kirkwall
Festival Club: The Ola Band
Mickey Austin: banjo, mandolin
Andy Cant: fiddle
Iain Cooper: bass
Billy Peace: keyboards, accordion
Colin Pirie: fiddle
Alan Reid: guitar
Alan Tullock: drums

Sunday 23 June

11.15am St Magnus Cathedral
Festival Service
conducted by Rev Ron Ferguson

St Magnus Cathedral Choir
director: Sandy Horsburgh
organist: Heather Rendall

Members of the
Royal Philharmonic Orchestra

Stanford: Justorum Animae
Monteverdi: Beatus Vir
Handel: Minuet from 'Music for the
Royal Fireworks'

12.20pm Graham Place, Stromness
Dancebite

1pm Pier Arts Centre, Stromness
Iain Crichton Smith poetry reading
(repeat performance)

2.30pm Stromness Town Hall
Celebrity recital:
Joanna MacGregor: piano

Bach: French Suite in G BWV 816
Ravel: Miroirs
Schumann: Kinderszenen Op 15
Corea: Children's Songs
Bartók: Sonata

5.15pm Stromness Academy Theatre
A Johnsmas Foy
(repeat performance)

8pm Phoenix cinema, Kirkwall
Royal Philharmonic Orchestra
conductor: Sir Peter Maxwell Davies
Tasmin Little: violin

Maxwell Davies: Time and the Raven
Sibelius: Violin Concerto
Tchaikovsky: Symphony No 4
in F minor

10pm Albert Hotel, Kirkwall
Festival Club:
Dick Lee and Swing '96
Dick Lee:
clarinets, saxophones, recorders
Phil Adams: electric solo guitar
John Russell: acoustic rhythm guitar
Roy Percy: double bass

Monday 24 June

11am Kirkwall Town Hall
Iain Crichton Smith poetry reading
(repeat performance)

1pm St Magnus Cathedral
RPO Wind Quintet

Stewart McIlwham: flute
Christopher Cowie: oboe
Douglas Mitchell: clarinet
David Chatterton: bassoon
Paul Gardham: horn

Farkas: Ancient Hungarian Dances
Barber: Summer Music
Arnold: Three Sea Shanties
Patterson: Comedy for Five Winds

6pm King Street Hall, Kirkwall
Orkney Dances
(repeat performance)

8pm St Magnus Cathedral
The House and Gate of Heaven:
A Requiem for 500 Years
The Orlando Consort
Robert Harre-Jones: alto
Charles Daniels: tenor
Angus Smith: tenor
Donald Greig: baritone
Robert Hardy: speaker

including:
Elizabeth Liddle:
Limekilns and
the Carpenter

10pm Albert Hotel, Kirkwall
Festival Club: The Ola Band

Tuesday 25 June

11.30am St Olaf's Church, Kirkwall
BBC Invitation Concert:
The Orlando Consort

1pm St Magnus Cathedral
Embedsmandsduoen
Neils-Ole Johanson: trombone
Ulrich Spang-Hanssen: organ

Holst: Duo Concertante
Hartman: Fantasia in A for organ
Erland von Koch: Trombonia
Kim Borg: Church Music

Niels Marthinson: Toccato

Áskell Másson:
Kadenza for solo trombone

Egil Hovland: Cantus V for trombone and organ
Rossini arr. Liszt: Cuius Animam

6pm Orkney Arts Theatre, Kirkwall
Tam O'Shanter's Bairns
(repeat performance)

8pm St Magnus Cathedral
Århus Sinfonietta

Søren K Hansen: conductor
Neils Chr. Øllgard: violin

The Mayfield Singers
Neil Price: director

Ravel, arr. Marthinson: Sonatina
Kaija Saariaho: Lichtbogen

Karl Aage Rasmussen:
Violin Concerto
Maxwell Davies:
Tenebrae super Gesualdo

flute: Charlotte Norholt
oboe: Henrik Husum
clarinet: Vibeke Kørsgaard Lembcke
bassoon: Jacob Dam
horn: Mark Hughes
trumpet: Martin Schuster
trombone: Niels Ole Bo Johansen
violins: Signe Madsen, Jens Astrup, Ina Tagmose
viola: Brigitte Barentzen-Pihl
cello: Jens Lund Madsen
bass: Peter Prehn
harp: Mette Nielsen
piano: David Strong
percussion: Mads Bendsen, Helen Poulsen

10pm Albert Hotel, Kirkwall
Festival Club: Gammar

Björn Thoroddsen: guitar
Stefán Stefánsson: saxophones
Thórir Baldursson: keyboards
Bjarni Sveinbjörnsson: bass
Halldór Hauksson: drums

11am Stromness Academy Theatre
A Johnsmas Foy
(repeat performance)

1pm St Magnus Cathedral
Århus Sinfonietta

Søren K Hansen: conductor
Lars Thygesen: flute

Maxwell Davies: Seven In Nomine
Arne Nordheim:
Tractatus for flute and ensemble
Stravinsky: Suite - The Soldier's Tale

3pm Stromness Town Hall
Steven Osborne: piano
A tribute to Ian Barr (1931-1995)

Bach: Partita No 1 in Bb BWV 825
Beethoven: Sonata in D Op 10 No 3

David Horne: Refrain

Schubert: Impromptu in Bb D935
Liszt: Bénédiction de Dieu dans la Solitude

6pm Orkney Arts Theatre, Kirkwall
Haroun and the Sea of Stories
by Salman Rushdie
devised and performed by **Benchtours**

Peter Clarke, Clark Crystie,
Stewart Ennis, Catherine Gillard,
Peter Livingstone, Rebecca Robinson

director: John Cobb
designer: Karen Tennent
composer/musician:
Peter Livingstone
lighting design/stage management:
Camilla O'Neil

8pm St Magnus Cathedral
Choral and Instrumental Concert
conductor: Roger Williams
Neil Mackie: tenor

Orkney Camerata:
leader: Julia Robinson Dean
St Magnus Festival Chorus
pupils of Kirkwall Grammar School
and Stromness Academy
director: Louise McLean
members of the Århus Sinfonietta

Hebden:
Concerto for Strings No 2 in C
Handel:
Trio Sonata in Bb for oboes and continuo
Britten: Now sleeps the crimson petal
Boyce: Symphony No 1 in B flat
Britten: St Nicolas (dedicated to the memory of Richard Hughes)

Orkney Camerata:
1st violins: Julia Robinson Dean,
Ian McKune, Douglas Montgomery,
Ian Tait
2nd violins: Lesley McLeod,
Karen Griffith, Rhona Casey,
Sally Kirkland
violas: Cathy Johnson,
Sandy Dennison
cellos: Linda Hamilton, Nigel Pendrey,
Stephen Cameron, Sarah Thomson
bass: Alan Seaton
flutes: David Griffith, David Wood
oboes: Christina Sargent,
Yvonne Gray
horn: Louise MacLean
harpsichord: Glenys Hughes
*piano duet: Fran Gray,
Glenys Hughes
*percussion: David Griffith,
Ruth Harvey, George McKinlay
*organ: Heather Rendall

Members of the Århus Sinfonietta
*violin: Signe Madsen, Ina Tagmose
*viola: Brigitte Barentzen-Pihl
*bass: Peter Prehn
*percussion: Helen Poulsen

* St Nicolas only

St Magnus Festival Chorus

sopranos: Glenys Alsop,
Lydia Becker, Lorraine Bichan,
Lydia Campbell, Frances Donald,
Millie Duncan, Vicky Duncan,
Chris Fawcett, Avril Featherby,
Rhoda Featherstone, Joyce Howard,
Margaret Inkster, Kathleen Ireland,
Muriel Learmonth, Nina Leitch,
Glynis Littlejohn, Chris Meek,
Elsie Norquoy, Margaret Porteous,
Jenny Prior, Maureen Purvis,
Grace Tait, Matilda Tumim,
Susan Warren, Diana Wrightson.

altos: Sheila Beaven,
Christine Courtney, Avril Cromarty,
Victoria Fairnie, Margaret Green,
Lesley Gordon, Carol Hartmann,
Susan Hill, Margaret Hinkley,
Aileen Laird, Pat Leslie,
Emma McLeod, Isabel Meil,
Judy O'Connor, Marguerite Reardon,
Marian Rendall, Lynne Scott,
Lorna Scott, Sandra Shearer,
Sue Simpson, Margaret Sutherland,
Carole Sunter, Lakey Teasdale,
May Walker.

tenors: Russell Aitken, Mim Baster,
Avril Clark, Jeff Clark,
Megan Eggeling, Bernadette Garriock,
Graham Garson, Sweyn Hunter,
Eoin Leslie, Gifford Leslie,
Stephen Lovick, Nila McCallum,
Majorie MacLean.

basses: James Curran,
Sandy Horsburgh, Roderick McLeod,
Eddie Nicolson, Mike Palmer,
Neil Price, George Rendall,
Eric Ritchie, Jim Purvis, Fred Souter,
Cameron Stout, Ian Watson,
Duncan Webster.

**Pupils of Kirkwall Grammar School
and Stromness Academy**
sopranos: Laura Aitken,
Laura Barnett, Geira Bews,
Elizabeth Dearness, Kelda Dearness,
Laura Early, Lianne Foubister,
Lucy Holt, Hannah Laird,
Victoria Logie, Sarah Moar,
Deirdre Towrie, Emma Quimby,
Jane Wishart.

altos: Victoria Batchelor,
Katie Fergusson, Ruth Goodwyn,
Jocelyn Hamilton, Karen Hinkley,
Angela Louttit, Trudi Newton,
Elizabeth Peebles, Charlotte Peppitt,
Emma Rosie, Gillian Skea,
Jay Spooner, Suzanne Steer,
Christina Wenham, Tanya Wright.

treble soloists: Jo Early,
Keith Hartmann, Magnus Thorne

10pm Albert Hotel, Kirkwall
Festival Club: Gammar

Festival on Tour

8pm Stronsay Community Hall
Tam O'Shanter's Bairns
(repeat performance)

8pm Sanday School Hall
Haroun and the Sea of Stories
(repeat performance)

Earl's Palace, Kirkwall
New Work at the Yards
A collaborative partnership
between St Magnus Festival,
The Pier Arts Centre
and Historic Scotland

Pier Arts Centre, Stromness
Gunnie Moberg photographs

Soli Deo Gallery, Kirkwall
A Woman's Place......
Patty Boonstra, Sharyn Crossley,
Lesley Murdoch, Tracey Hall,
Elli Pearson, Louise Scott, Leila
Thomson, Morag Tweedie

Woodwick House, Evie
Richard Welsby selected works

Anchor Buildings, Kirkwall
Nothing
Neil Firth, Colin Kirkpatrick,
Andrew Parkinson, Mary Scott

Stromness Library
Soulisquoy Printmakers
contemporary prints

Stromness Museum
Ship Ashore!
Three centuries of Orkney Shipwrecks

Tankerness House Museum
The Merchant Lairds
Orkney in the 18th century

1997

1.30pm Highland Park distillery
Resound:
The Whispering Gallery Project

SCO Players:
Su-a Lee: cello, Alison Waller: clarinet

artists: Anne Bevan, Jenna Hume,
John Hunter, Arlene Isbister,
Colin Johnstone, Andrew Parkinson,
Alistair Peebles, Mary Scott,
Judy Spark, Richard Welsby,
Marc Yeats.

St Andrews Primary School:
Graeme Aitken, Erin Askew,
Mark Caswell, Leonard Craigie,
Emily Earley, Sebastian Eunson,
Elizabeth Foubister, Derro Gilmour,
Heather Hornby, Graeme Horne,
Helga Moss, Laura Pahnke,
Isla Purdy, Laura Sneesby,
Jared Tylman, Helen Wallace.

Kirkwall Grammar School:
Laura Aitken, Kate Askew,
David Austin, Ingrid Austin,
Katherine Beaven, Alan Bruce,
Ryan Craigie, Elizabeth Dearness,
John Dearness, Matthew Drever,
Laura Eunson, Kate Smee Giles,
Kimberley Gill, Suzann Gray,
Lucy Holt, Ian Hutchison, Craig Moar,
Inez Moss, Bruce Omand,
Nathan Prestwood, Lorien Roberts,
Sean Smith, Jay Spooner.

7.30pm Phoenix cinema, Kirkwall
Scottish Chamber Orchestra
conductor: Sir Peter Maxwell Davies
Kathryn Stott: piano

Marc Yeats:
The Anatomy of Air
(Festival commission)

Mozart: Piano Concerto in Bb K595
Beethoven:
Symphony No 6 in F 'Pastoral'

10pm Around St Magnus Cathedral
Orkneyinga
director: Penny Aberdein
writer: Ron Ferguson
musical director: Steve King
choreographer: Andy Howitt
stilts choreographer:
Jonothan Campbell

community performers:
actors:
Ben Chaddock, Cynthia Chaddock,
Terry Delaney, Graham Garson,
Willie Harper, Sweyn Hunter,
George McKissock, Emma McLeod,
Jim Scott, Eric Sinclair, George Swan,
Tommy Wylie

musicians: Kate Beale,
Sheila Beaven, Katherine Beaven,
Cristine Ferguson, Ishbel Fraser,
Ann Gosman, India Harcus,
Marguerite Rearden, Karen Rendall,
Sue Whitworth

dancers:
Michael Alexander, Carolyn Bevan,
Moira Carlyle, Christine Copland,
Jenny Deans, Kate Deans,
Christine Eccleston, Calum Finlayson,
Cate Finlayson, Clover Giles,
Daisy Giles, Oscar Giles,
Fiona Gilmour, Inga Gilmour,
Karen Hinckley, Catherine Johnston,
Linda Johnston, Shona Johnston,
Victoria Logie, Carmen McEwan,
Ann Mackie, Rachael McKinlay,
Carol Shearer, Kevin Smith,
Lee-Anne Wylie

stilt walkers:
Heather Aberdein, Aimée Bevan,
Rosslyn Carlyle, Zoe Eccles,
Erlend Gilmour, Amy Liptrot,
Elizabeth Peebles, Scott Tulloch,
Rachal Thomson, Ashleigh Venables

torch bearers:
Sinclair Dunnet, Antoine Pietri,
Alan Richards
ushers: Kim Foden, Maggie MacGregor
Gunnhilda Iversen

participating schools
Glaitness Primary School
dancers: Hannah Beaven,
Jenna Barnett, Erin Burns,
Simon Byers, Maxine Cooper,
Helen Craigie, Susan Cruickshank,
Kevin Drever, Adrian Dunnett,
John Kemp, Heather Leisk,
Rachel Rosie, Eilidh Ross,
DeeDee Scott, Jamie Shek,
Richard Thomson
Alan Bichan: class teacher
Val Steele: head teacher

Orphir Primary School
dancers: Louise Bichan,
David Clouston, Ewan Kennedy,
Lisa MacKenzie, Eric Macleod,
Kirsten MacLeod, Russell Mainland,
Lynsey Moir, James Paterson,
Darren Prestwood, Owen Robinson,
Rhys Robinson, Jenni Ross,
Clare-Lousie Savage, Leanne Savage,
Eric Sclater, Rachel Sclater,
Kazia Tait, Raina Tait, Sean Young
Liz Baxter: head teacher

Papdale Primary School
dancers: Candace Adam,
Cally Amos, Cheryl Campbell,
Susan Campbell, Rachel Casey,
Abbey Edwards, Kevin Firth,
Caroline Foulis, Sweyn Kirkness,
Mark Liddle, Steven Marwick,
Sharyon Mooney, Hayley Reid,
Steven Rendall, Jonathan Richards,
Stewart Ross, Paul Shearer,
Alistair Tait, John Wade,
Michael Walker, Sharlene Walls
Inga Adam: class teacher

Karis Christie, Christopher Craigie,
Gemma Croy, Craig Gall,
Erlend Gilmour, Amy Graham,
Robert Harcus, Nicola Hartmann,
Janine Hughes, Daniel Johnston,
Charlene Leisk, Sean MacDonald,
Craig Mackay, Sam McLeod,

Dylan Manson, Gary Manson,
James Matches, Carrie Norquoy,
Naomi Pirie, Adele Reid, Neil Rosie,
Kevin Smith, Kristin Soames,
Kirsten Stephen
Barbara Johnston: class teacher

handbell ringers: Naomi Baster,
Eric Bruce, Sam Craig, Stewart
Featherby, Magnus Flett, Stacey Flett,
Steven Johnston, William Leonard,
James Linklater, Sara MacIntosh,
Laura Miller, Rachael Moffat,
Mark Munro, Kyle Norquay,
Chandra Rendall, Andrew Scollie,
Katie Stevenson, Nicola Stewart,
Patricia Watson, Jayne White,
Dawn Wood
Alison Drever: class teacher
Peter Diamond: head teacher

St Margaret's Hope Primary School
drummers: Robert Banks,
Mandy Cromarty, Shaun Gutcher,
Kirsten Phillips, Jodie Scott,
Megan Scott, Nicola Stevenson,
Jamie Taylor, Johnny Taylor,
James Thomson
Ralph Robinson: class teacher
Hilary MacIntosh: head teacher

set design: Dave Grieve, Carol Peebles
costume design: Liz Coward
stage manager: Bryan Leslie
site managers:
Earl's Palace - Ian Ballantine
Tankerness House – Diane Bain
Cathedral Steps – Pat Presland,
Margaret Sutherland
production assistant:
Norman Rushbrook
bell ringer: Stuart Burgher

10pm Albert Hotel, Kirkwall
Festival Club: Sola

Jeremy Black, Craig Gaskin,
Marion Kenny, Neil MacArthur,
Quee MacArthur, James MacKintosh,
Kaela Rowan

10.30pm The Fitzcarraldo,
Stromness Harbour
Lone Star Stones
The Smoking Stone Band
with Duncan McLean

10.30am The Fitzcarraldo, Stromness
Kenneth White poetry reading

10.30am Kirkwall Town Hall
St Magnus Cathedral Choir
Kirkwall Town Band

1pm Stromness Town Hall
Kathryn Stott: piano

Grieg: Lyric Pieces Op 43
Chopin: Sonata no 3 in B minor
Op 58
Maxwell Davies: Five Pieces for
Piano Op 2
Rachmaninov: Variations on a
Theme of Corelli

Glinka, arr. Balakirev: L'Alouette
Lyapunov: Lezghinka

3.30pm The Fitzcarraldo,
Stromness Harbour
Gulliver's Travels:
Walk the Plank Theatre Co

adaptor and director: Andy Farrell
designers: Julian Crouch,
Graeme Gilmour
music: Olly Fox
lighting: Paul Colley
cast: Tony Cairns, Gregory Gudgeon,
Ros Philips

5.30pm Woodwick House, Evie
Sarajevo Circle

Erivin Baucic: performer
Jelena Radan: performer
Julija Zlopasa: female vocalist
Vladimir Nothig: male vocalist
Edin Dino Zonic: composer
Royston Maldoom: choreographer
Bariz Zonic: stage manager

7.30pm St Magnus Cathedral,
Scottish Chamber Orchestra

conductor: Matthias Bamert
David Wilson-Johnson: baritone

Mozart: Cassation K63 in G
MacMillan: Tryst

Schubert, orch. Harper:
Three Songs

Schubert: Symphony No 8
in B minor 'Unfinished'

10.30pm The Fitzcarraldo,
Stromness Harbour
On Board with Quartz

Lorna McLaren: violin
Fiona Alexander: violin
Steve King: viola
Kevin MacCrae: cello

10pm Albert Hotel, Kirkwall
Festival Club: Sola

11.15am St Magnus Cathedral
Festival Service
conducted by Rev Ron Ferguson

St Magnus Cathedral Choir
conductor: Ed Holt
organist: Heather Rendall
Papdale Primary School
handbell ringers
director: Steve King

festival bell call:
composed and played on
the cathedral bells by Steve King

Batten: Lord, we beseech thee
Wesley: Wash me throughly
Meditation (performed by Papdale
hand bell ringers)
Karg-Elert: Nun danket alle Got

1pm Pier Arts Centre, Stromness
Kenneth White poetry reading
(repeat performance)

2.30pm Stromness Town Hall
Yggdrasil Quartet of Aberdeen
Kathryn Stott: piano

Henrik Peterson: violin
Per Oman: violin
Robert Westlund: viola
Per Nystrom: cello

Beethoven: String Quartet Op 18
No 3
Carlstedt: String Quartet No 5
Dvorak: Piano Quintet Op 81

5.30pm Stromness Town Hall
A Johnsmas Foy: A Place to Keep
readers: Archie Bevan,
Elizabeth Bevan, Harvey Johnston
music: Lesley Mcleod

8pm Stromness Academy Theatre
Music Theatre Double Bill:
Psappha Contemporary Music
Ensemble

Maxwell Davies: Vesailii Icones
Maxwell Davies: Miss Donnithorne's
Maggot (performance dedicated to
Mary Thomas, who died on April 17
1997)

Paul MacAlindin: conductor
Emma Turnbull: mezzo soprano
Tom Yang: dancer
Jennifer Langridge: solo cello
Benjamin Twist: director
Matt Johnson: designer
(Miss Donnithorne)
Ian Spink: original choreography
(Vesalii Icones)
Ace McCarron: lighting design
Sam Fraser: stage manager

Psappha:
David Routledge: violin
Heather Wallington: viola
Jennifer Langridge: cello
Claire O'Neill: flute
Dov Goldberg: clarinet
Richard Casey: piano
Tim Williams: percussion

10pm Stromness Hotel
Festival Club: Green
Clare Lindle: fiddle, viola and vocals
John Mitchell: guitar and vocals

Monday 23 June

11am Kirkwall Town Hall
Kenneth White poetry reading
(repeat performance)

1pm St Magnus Cathedral, Kirkwall
Psappha Contemporary Music
Ensemble
Paul MacAlindin: conductor
Emma Turnbull: soprano
Tim Williams: percussion

Maxwell Davies:
A Birthday Card for Hans

McPherson: Moses
Weir: King Harald sails to Byzantium
Hellawell: Truth or Consequences
Grange: Des fins sont des
commencements

**5.15 - 11.30pm East Church and
Ayre Hotel, Kirkwall**
Orkney Sunset: BBC Radio 3
a celebration of 21 years of the
festival with an evening of music,
poetry and discussion, broadcast live
from Kirkwall

5.30pm Kirkwall Town Hall
**Yggdrasil String Quartet of
Aberdeen**

Brahms: String Quartet Op 51 No 1
Shostakovitch: String Quartet No 8

7pm The Fitzcarraldo, Kirkwall Pier
Gulliver's Travels
(repeat performance)

**7pm and 9.30pm
St Magnus Cathedral, Kirkwall**
Orkneyinga
(repeat performance)

10pm Albert Hotel, Kirkwall
Festival Club: Green

Tuesday 24 June

11am Kirkwall Town Hall
Duo Recital
Julia Robinson Dean: violin
Steve King: viola

Maxwell Davies: Midhouse Air
Seiber: Four Duos
Bartók: Duos
Mozart: Duo in G (1st movement)
Trad. Scottish: Duo Medley

1pm St Magnus Cathedral, Kirkwall
Music for Voices and Lute
Mhairi Lawson: soprano
Catherine King: mezzo soprano
Jacob Heringman: lute

Jones: Sweet Kate;
Farewell fond youth
Straloch manuscript: Lute solos
Scottish 16th century:
In a garden so green;
Remember me, my dear;
What mightie motion;
Woe worth thee tyme;
O lusty May
Morely: Canzonets
Ballard: Entrée et Courante
Boesset: Une jour Amarille et Tirsis
Anon: Je ne puis bien
Moulinié: Je suis ravi
Boesset: N'espérez plus mes yeux
Ballard: Branles de Village
Coprario: In darkness
Dowland: Weepe you no more
Danyel: What delight

6pm The Fitzcarraldo, Kirkwall Pier
Gulliver's Travels
(repeat performance)

8pm St Magnus Cathedral, Kirkwall
**Royal College of Music
Chamber Choir**
director: Paul Spicer

Brahms: Three Motets Op 109
Frank Martin: Mass
Howells: Even such is time
Maxwell Davies: Corpus Christi with
Cat and Mouse
Tippett:
Two Songs from the British isles
Wood: Hail Gladdening Light

10pm Albert Hotel, Kirkwall
Festival Club:
The Humpff Family
John Coletta: mandolin and vocals
Mike Goodwin: drums
Willy McCann: guitar and vocals
Lorna Thomas: bass

Wednesday 25 June

**1.30pm & 3.30pm
Balfour Castle, Shapinsay**
Royal College of Music students
sopranos: Natalie Clifton-Griffith,
Thessy Wincent
altos: Alexandra Gibson, Helen Foster
tenors: Andrew Nicholson,
Richard Barrowclough
basses: Nigel Brookes,
Jonathan Gunthorpe

Vaughan Williams: The dark-eyed
sailor; The lover's ghost; As the tide
was flowing
Gibbons: The Silver Swan
Bennet: Weep O mine eyes
Morley: April is in my mistress' face
Tompkins: Too much I once
lamented
Anon: Sumer is icumen in
Maxwell Davies: Lullaby for Lucy
Morley: Sing we and chaunt it;
I love, alas, I love thee
Farmer: Fair Phyllis
Morley: No, no, no, no Nigella

8pm St Magnus Cathedral, Kirkwall
**Choral and Instrumental
Concert**

Roger Williams: conductor
Mhairi Lawson: soprano
Catherine King: mezzo soprano
Christina Sargent: oboe
Julia Robinson Dean: violin
Steve King: viola
Meinir Wyn Thomas: soprano*
Joanne Lunn: soprano*
Rachel Lindop: alto*
Stephen Brown: tenor*
Damien Thantry: bass*

Orkney Camerata
St Magnus Festival Chorus

* members of the RCM Chamber
Choir

Vivaldi: Ostro Picta
(introduction to the Gloria); Gloria
Bach: Concerto in D minor for oboe
and violin

Telemann: Viola Concerto in G
Bach: Magnificat

Orkney Camerata
1st violins: Julia Robinson Dean
(leader), Ian McKune,
Douglas Montgomery, Sally Kirkland,
Brian Batey
2nd violins: Lesley McLeod, Ian Tait,
Karen Griffith, Fran Gray,
Jean Leonard
violas: Sandy Dennison, Steve King,
Cathy Johnson
cellos: Linda Hamilton, Nigel
Pendrey, Sarah Thomson
bass: Stephen Cameron
flutes: David Griffith, David Nicholson
oboe/oboe d'amore:
Christina Sargent, Yvonne Gray
bassoon: Alison Bargett
trumpets: Kenneth Jones,
Brian Jones, Charles Dearness
harpsichord: Glenys Hughes
organ: Heather Rendall
timpani: Ruth Johnston

10pm Albert Hotel, Kirkwall
Festival Club: The Humpff Family

11pm Kirkwall Harbour
Festival Finale:
S.S. Pandemonium!

Exhibitions

Pier Arts Centre, Stromness
The Caros
Anthony Caro: sculpture
Sheila Girling: watercolours

Highland Park distillery, Kirkwall
Resound
Anne Bevan, Jenna Hume,
John Hunter, Arlene Isbister,
Colin Johnstone, Andrew Parkinson,
Alistair Peebles, Mary Scott,
Judy Spark, Richard Welsby,
Marc Yeats
Resound is presented jointly by
St Magnus Festival, the Scottish
Chamber Orchestra, Highland Park
distillery and the Pier Arts Centre

Stromness Library
Graphik - Neil Firth, Marian Ashburn,
Colin Kirkpatrick, Erlend Brown,
Peter McLaren, Malcolm Olva,
Mark Scadding, Sylvia Wishart

Ferry Terminal, Stromness
White World: Kenneth White

Anchor Buildings, Kirkwall
Saga Prints
Soulisquoy Printmakers

Tankerness House Museum
The Skaill Hoard

Stromness Museum
**Explorers and Adventurers
with Orkney connections**

1998

Friday 19 June

1.30pm Orkney Auction Mart
Sunnifa
A collaboration in dance, music and sculpture between Orkney and Aberdeen.
choreographer: Andy Howitt
sculptor: Anne Bevan
composer: Pete Stollery

Orkney dancers:
Heather Aberdein, Penny Aberdein, Carolyn Bevan, Moira Carlyle, Liz Cormack, Christine Eccleston, Clover Giles, Catherine Johnson, Amy Liptrot, Ashleigh Venables.
Aberdeen dancers:
Bruce Duncan, Lorna Malcolm, Louise Marshall, Emma Morrison, Faye Panchal, Sailesh Panchal, Dave Thomas, Mandy Watson.
musicians:
Yvonne Gray: oboe
Christina Sargent: oboe/cor anglais
drawing:
John Cumming, Jack Chaddock, Lisa Ward, Donald Morrison
photography:
Alistair Peebles, Cate Finlayson, Lena Maurer, Sharon Miller
sculpture:
S1 and S2 art pupils of Stromness Academy

costume: Bruce Duncan
stage management: Diane Bain, Aimée Bevan, Colin Keldie

7.30pm St Magnus Cathedral
BT Scottish Ensemble
Clio Gould: artistic director

Aly Bain: fiddle

Grieg: Holberg Suite
Hellawell: Sound Carvings from the Water's Edge
Shostakovitch:
Two Pieces for String Octet
Sommero: Follow the Moonstone

10pm Kirkwall Town Hall
The Exhibitionists:
Ridiculusmus Theatre Company

10pm Albert Hotel, Kirkwall
Festival Club: Drop The Box

James L Henry: guitar, vocals
Inge Thomson: accordion, vocals, percussion
Fraser Mouat: bass guitar
Kevin Henderson: fiddle
Aky Gilliland: drums

Saturday 20 June

10.30am Pier Arts Centre, Stromness
Edwin Morgan poetry reading

10.30am Kirkwall Town Hall
Kirkwall Town Band
An informal programme of music

Brian Jones: conductor

12.30pm Stromness Town Hall
Pekka Kuusisto: violin
Raija Kerppo: piano

Bartók: Romanian Folk Dances
Brahms: Sonata in G major Op 78
Ravel: Sonata
Prokoviev: Sonata in D major Op 94

2pm and 4pm Hoy Kirk
Musical Excursions

Two informal concerts given by a string quartet from the BT Scottish Ensemble

Clio Gould: violin
Andrew Storey: violin
Gillianne Haddow: viola
Alison Lawrance: cello

Purcell: Chaconne
Puccini: Crisantemi
Tchaikovsky: Andante Cantabile
Shostkavoitch: String Quartet No 8

5.30pm Orkney Auction Mart
Sunnifa
(repeat performance)

7.30pm Sanday School
BT Scottish Ensemble Quintet

BTSE Quintet:
Cheryl Crockett: violin
Roderick Long: violin
Rebecca Low: viola
Rebecca Gilliver: cello
Diane Clark: bass

Sanday Fiddle Club:
Vikki Brown, Douglas Drever, Katie Anne Drever, Louisa Drever, Emma Grieve, Zara Grieve, Victoria Gibson, Kelly Harcus, Thomas Harcus, Claire Hardwick, Ken Hardwick, Mary Harris, Bethan Newman, Carys Newman, Megan Newman, Amy Peace, John Redmonds, Louise Redmonds, Vanessa Skea, Ian Simpson, Richard Thomson, Magnus Thorne, Donna Tulloch, Emma Tulloch, Carrie Walls, Fiona Wilson, Vivienne Wilson

Mozart: Divertimento in D K136
Tchaikovsky: Andante Cantabile
Mike Newman: Two Pieces
Holst: Brook Green Suite
Trad: Scottish Tunes
Shostakovitch: String Quartet No 8

7.30pm St Magnus Cathedral
BBC Scottish Symphony Orchestra

conductor: Martyn Brabbins
Paul Meyer: clarinet

Britten: Four Sea Interludes from 'Peter Grimes'
MacMillan: Tuireadh
Mackenzie: Benediction
Elgar: 'Enigma' Variations

10.15pm Stromness Hotel
All About H. Hatterr:
Ridiculusmus Theatre Company
followed by
The Smoking Stone Band
Dick Levens: mandolin
Jim Hall: banjo
Dougie Montgomery: fiddle
Brian Cromarty: guitar
Ian Mackay: bass
Duncan McLean: vocals

10pm Albert Hotel, Kirkwall
Festival Club: Drop The Box

Sunday 21 June

11.15am St Magnus Cathedral
Festival Service
conducted by Rev Ron Ferguson with St Magnus Cathedral Choir and members of the BT Scottish Ensemble
director of music: Edmund Holt
organist: Heather Rendall

Purcell: Chaconne
Shostakovich: Quartet No 8 (5th mvt)
Puccini: Cristantemi
Batten: O Praise the Lord
SS Wesley: The Wilderness
Elgar: Imperial Melody

1pm Stromness Academy Theatre
Edwin Morgan poetry reading
(repeat performance)

2.30pm Stromness Town Hall
Celebrity recital:
Paul Meyer: clarinet
Eric Le Sage: piano

Brahms: Sonata in Eb major Op 120
Schumann: Phantasiestücke
Arnold: Sonatina
Copland: Sonata
Stravinsky: 3 pieces for solo clarinet
Bernstein: Sonata

5pm Stromness Academy Theatre
A Johnsmas Foy:
For Those in Peril ....
producer: Graham Garson
performed by members of Stromness and Birsay drama clubs and friends

7.30pm St Magnus Cathedral
BBC Scottish Symphony Orchestra
conductor: Martyn Brabbins
Pekka Kuusisto: violin
The Mayfield Singers

Dukas: Fanfare from 'La Péri'
Sibelius: The Swan of Tuonela, from Four Legends Op 22
Bruch: Violin Concerto No 1 in G minor
Taverner: In Nomine from 'Missa Gloria Tibi Trinitas'
Maxwell Davies: Second Fantasia on an In Nomine of John Taverner

10pm Albert Hotel, Kirkwall
Festival Club:
All About H Hatterr
(repeat performance)

followed by
Three Peace Sweet
Raymie Peace: highland bagpipe
Duncan Peace: percussion
Alan Peace: bass guitar, vocals
Davie Miller: highland bagpipe
Andy Cant: fiddle, highland bagpipe
Stewart Shearer: guitar, vocals
Philip Anderson: keyboards, guitar, vocals

Monday 22 June

11am Kirkwall Town Hall
Edwin Morgan poetry reading
(repeat performance)

1.30pm Phoenix cinema, Kirkwall
BBC Scottish Symphony Orchestra schools' concert
conductor: Martyn Brabbins
Paul Meyer: clarinet

2.30pm Stromness Town Hall
Eric Le Sage: piano

Poulenc: Humoresque, Two Novelettes, Three Intermezzi
Schumann: Humoresque
Poulenc: Promenades
Schumann: Sonata No 1 in F# minor

5.45pm Stromness Academy Theatre
George Mackay Brown's
Greenvoe:
BBC Invitation Concert with an ensemble from BBC SSO

adaptor: Stewart Conn
music: Alasdair Nicolson
cast:
James Bryce, Eliza Langland, Vicki Masson, John Shedden
narrator: Iain Anderson

producer/director: Pam Wardell

8pm St Magnus Cathedral, Kirkwall
Serenade for Strings
BT Scottish Ensemble
Orkney Camerata
Orkney Schools' Strings

Clio Gould: artistic director/solo violin
Christina Sargent: cor anglais

Scott Skinner: Three Reels
Pachelbel: Canon in D
Dag Wiren: Serenade
Heath: Violin Concerto 'The Celtic'
Elgar: Serenade for Strings
Jacob: Rhapsody for Cor Anglais and Strings
Vaughan Williams: Fantasia on a Theme of Thomas Tallis

BT Scottish Ensemble:
violins: Clio Gould, Edmund Coxon, Cheryl Crockett, Andrew Storey, Jonathan Morton, Roderick Long.
violas: Gillianne Gaddow, Rebecca Low
cellos: Alison Lawrance, Rebecca Gilliver
bass: Diane Clark

Orkney Camerata:
violins: Julia Robinson Dean,
Douglas Montgomery, Ian McKune,
Ian Tait, Andrew Garden,
Lesley McLeod, Karen Griffith,
Brian Batey
violas: Sandy Dennison,
Rhona Casey
cellos: Linda Hamilton, Nigel Pendrey
bass: Stephen Cameron

Pupils of Kirkwall Grammar School
and Stromness Academy:
violins: Laura Aitken, Kate Askew,
Angus Ballantine, Eric Baster,
Chris Baxter, Katherine Beaven,
Morag Bryden, Selina Cobley,
Kerry Croy, Elizabeth Dearness,
Laura Eunson, Paul Greves,
James Groat, Brit Harcus,
Ian Hutchison, Ruth Hutchison,
Gemma Laughton, Victoria Logie,
Rachel McKinley, Inez Moss,
Martha Schofield, Ingrid Seatter,
Lisa Smith, Gina Tait, Alice Thomson,
Judith Thomson, Fraser Tulloch,
Jackie Tullock
viola: Elizabeth Peebles
cellos: Ellen Casey, Nicola Hartmann,
Lucy Holt, Jenny Kirkland,
Clare Omand, Islay Roberts

10pm Albert Hotel, Kirkwall
Festival Club: Hullion

Andy Cant: fiddle, mandolin,
highland bagpipe
Micky Austin: banjo, mandolin
Billy Jolly: vocals, mouth organ,
bodhran
Owen Tierney: guitar, mandolin,
vocals
Ingirid Jolly: guitar, vocals

Tuesday 23 June

11am Stromness Academy Theatre
A Johnsmas Foy:
For Those in Peril....
(repeat performance)

1pm St Magnus Cathedral
Kevin Bowyer: organ

Bach: Prelude and Fugue in D
BWV 532
Bach: Trio Sonata in G
BWV 1039/1027a
Maxwell Davies: Organ Sonata;
Reliqui Domum Meum
Alain: Premiere Fantasie;
Postlude pour l'office de Compline
Franck: Choral in A minor

5.30pm St Magnus Cathedral
Oslo Philharmonic Wind Soloists

flute: Tom Ottar Andreassen
oboes: Erik Niord Larsen,
Simon Emes,
clarinets: Leif Arne Tangen Pedersen,
Fredrik Fors,
bassoons: Per Hannisdal,
Eirik Birkeland
horns: Inger Besserudhagen,
Kjell Erik Arnesen

Mozart: Overture 'Don Giovanni'
Nielsen: Wind Quintet Op 43
Kvandal: Octet
Mozart: Serenade in Eb K375

8pm Phoenix cinema, Kirkwall
BBC Scottish Symphony
Orchestra
conductor: Martyn Brabbins

Paul Meyer: clarinet
Lisa Tyrrell: soprano
Margaret McDonald: mezzo soprano
Neil Mackie: tenor
David Wilson-Johnson: baritone
St Magnus Festival Chorus

MacCunn:
Land of the Mountain and the Flood
Weber:
Clarinet Concerto No 2 in F minor
Maxwell Davies: The Jacobite Rising

St Magnus Festival Chorus
sopranos: Glenys Alsop,
Sylvia Barnett, Dorothy Beynon,
Lindsay Blair, Lydia Campbell,
Carole Coghill, Irene Donaldson,
Avril Featherby, Lillian Hutchison,
Margaret Inkster, Margaret Learmonth,
Muriel Learmonth, Nina Leitch,
Glynis Littlejohn, Lorraine Littlejohn,
Chris Meek, Elsie Norquay,
Mary O'Keeffe Burgher,
Charlotte Peppitt, Margaret Porteous,
Andrea Price, Marilyn Richards,
Jean Robertson, Inga Scholes,
Isobel Scholes, Dorothy Swanney,
Grace Tait, Alison Traumschek,
Matilda Tumim, Sue Whitworth,
Diana Wrightson, Doreen Wake
altos: Sheila Beaven, Avril Cromarty,
Angela Drummond, Victoria Fairnie,
Doreen Faulds, Margaret Green,
Carol Hartmann, Carol Hoey,
Eve Isaac, Pat Leslie,
Margaret Linklater, Anne McLean,
Emma McLeod, Isabel Meil,
Judy O'Connor, Julia Robinson Dean,
Margaret Sutherland, Lakey Teasdale,
May Walker, Gloria Wallington,
Rosey Whittles
tenors: Miriam Baster, Chris Boulton,
Stephen Cameron, Ruth Forbes,
Bernadette Garriock, Graham Garson,
Nigel Groom, John Hoey,
Sweyn Hunter, Joan Jones,
Eoin Leslie, Stephen Lovick,
George McKinlay, Stewart Walker,
Allan Whitely
basses: John Devine, John Flett,
Roy Flett, David Fidler,
Paul MacAlindin, David Griffith,
Allan McCafferty, Eddie Nicolson,
Neil Price, George Rendall, Ian Rolfe,
Andy Tait, Ian Tait.

10pm Albert Hotel, Kirkwall
Festival Club: Salsa Celtica
Steve Kettley: saxophone
Barney Barnett: saxophone
Toby Shippey: trumpet
Dougie Hudson: congas
'Chimp': bongos
Guy Nicholson: timbale

Paul Harrison: piano
Dave Donnelly: bass guitar
Jenny Gardner: fiddle
Galo Caron Carrasco: guitar

Wednesday 24 June

1pm St Magnus Cathedral, Kirkwall
Oslo Philharmonic Wind Soloists

Mozart: Overture 'The Magic Flute'
MacMillan: Untold
Gounod: Petite Symphonie
Seiber: Serenade
Hummel: Partita

5pm Kirkwall Town Hall
Artists' Question Time:
BBC Radio 3
chaired by James Naughtie
guests including:
Sir Peter Maxwell Davies,
Martyn Brabbins, Nicholas McGegan

6pm King Street Hall, Kirkwall
Opera Circus:
workshop performance

Peta Lily: director
Susan Bisatt: singer
Thangam Debbonaire: cello
Louise Tischler: stage manager
Tina Ellen Lee: artistic director

workshop participants:
Westray Junior Secondary School:
Alice Brown, Vicki Costie,
Daren Drever, Leanne Harcus,
Neil Harcus, Louise McCracken,
Kerry Michie, Karriz Rendall,
Trevor Rendall, Erika Rosie,
Alan Stout, Gary Stove
Kirkwall Grammar School:
Laura Aitken, David Austin,
Laura Barnett, Henry Bateman,
Louise Bevan, Corrine Corse,
Charles Dearness, Clare Drylie,
Ian Hutchinson, Laura Early,
Kimberley Gill, Natasha Groundwater,
Tony Leask, Chris Logie,
Rachael Mackay, Bruce Omand,
Barry Park, Tom Pickles,
Gemma Pirie, Thomas Pirie,
Islay Roberts, Dawn Simison,
Jay Spooner

8.30pm Orkney Arts Theatre, Kirkwall
Cat Man's Tale:
Opera Circus
composer: Alasdair Nicolson
writer: David Harrower

singers: Susan Bisatt, Carole Irvine,
Bruce Evans, Richard Morris
musicians:
Thangham Debbonaire: cello
Neyire Ashworth: clarinet
Andy Martin: percussion

director: Peta Lily
musical director: Jonathan Cooper
design: Jamie Vartan
lighting design: Ian Scott

10pm Albert Hotel, Kirkwall
Festival Club: Salsa Celtica

Exhibitions

Pier Arts Centre, Stromness
Alan Davie

Stromness Library Gallery
Play

Kirkwall Town Hall
Sunnifa: pupils of Stromness
Academy

Tankerness House Museum, Kirkwall
A Fairy Palace on the Edge of
the Northern Seas
Melsetter House centenary exhibition

St Magnus Cathedral, Kirkwall
A Journey of Threads
Ragnhild Monsen

Anchor Buildings, Kirkwall
Soulisquoy Printmakers

Stromness Museum
Voices from the Great War
Orkney and Orcadians
in World War One

St Magnus Cathedral, Kirkwall
George Mackay Brown
1921-1996

1999

Friday 18 June

7.30pm The Pickaquoy Centre,
**The Odyssey:
a stage version by Derek Walcott**
director: Eliza Langland
photography/visuals designer:
Tim Fitzpatrick
music/audio effects: David Goodall

cast:
Blind Billy Blue: Graham Garson with
David Fidler and Laura Early
Odysseus: George McKissock,
Willie Harper
Telemachus: Jim Scott
Penelope: Jenny Deans, Phyllis Brown
Eurycleia: Inga Gilmour
Eumacus: David Fidler
Antinous: George Swan
Melantho: Matilda Webb
Nausicaa: Ruth Forbes
Anemone: Laura Barnet, Laura Earley
Chloe: Clover Giles, Louise Drever
Alcinous: Martin Earley
Philosopher: Tommy Wylie
Circe and entourage:
Donella Kirkland, Cally Bevan,
Matilda Webb
Anticleia: Naismi Flett
Cyclops and Athena:
Cynthia Chaddock

chorus other company members:
Katy Chalmers, Sandra Craigie,
Kate Deans, Ann Earley, Emily Earley,
Martin Earley, Cate Finlayson,
Fiona Gilmour, Yvonne Gray,
Ross Harnden, Fergus Harnden,
Finlay Harnden, Catherine Johnson,
Amy Liptrot, Jane Liptrot,
Carlyn MacDonald, Chris MacRae,
Marguerite Reardon, Afra Skene
solo violin: Julia Robinson Dean

Dounby Primary School
(movement sequence):
Kayleigh Archibald, Caroline Breck,
Deryck Brown, Gary Chalmers,
Charles Copland, Catherine Dabbs,
Megan Davidson, Joannah Fergusson,
Gary Hamilton, Magnus Harrold,
Claire Harvey, Kristan Harvey,
Megan Hourston, Natalie Hourston,
Belle Keenan-Smith, Ingrid Kirkness,
Karen McIver, Nicola Morgan,
Bryony Muir, Lorraine Nicolson,
Helen Norquoy, Cassie Paterson,
Colin Paterson, Dawn Sinclair,
David Sinclair, Jenny Skene,
Craig Slater, Cally Stanger,
Shona Stanger, Nathan Williams

Evie Primary School - singers:
Zoe Baker, Graeme Flaws,
Caroline Firth, Nicholas Firth,
Colin Flett, Craig Gillon,
Johnny Gillon, Daniel Hellewell,
Kate Jenkins, Susan Linklater,
Amanda Mainland, Graeme Mainland,
Garry Montgomery, Ian Nelson,
Kelly Nicolson, Christopher Purnell,
Kim Robertson, Esme Robinson,
Merry Robinson, Hannah Side,
Jessica Side, Douglas Spence,
Theresa Spence, Calum Stevenson,

Carrie Stevenson, Emma Stevenson,
Katie Stevenson, James Stevenson,
Jamie Stevenson, Andrea Wilson,
Kelly Wilson

Glaitness Primary School - singers:
Alison Ballantine, Kimberley Burns,
Calvin Cooper, Craig Corse,
Ross Foubister, Lydia Foulis,
Rowan Hodgson, Andrew Lanni,
Jeana Leslie, Inga Loughran-
Dalrymple, Candy Ho, Kristin Leslie,
Catriona McCulloch, Laura Peace,
Scott Paterson, Charlotte Rendall,
Claire Sabiston, Natasha Shek,
Lianna Spence, Christopher Sulat,
Ross Sutherland, Eden Thom.

The Mayfield Singers:
sopranos:
Glenys Alsop, Marie Fotheringhame,
Irene Monge, Mary O'Keeffe-Burgher,
Andrea Price, Marilyn Richards,
Doreen Wake
altos: Mary Doyle, Tina Smith, Jill Strutt
tenors: Tim Barthorpe, Colin Borland
basses: Simon Gordon, Mike Palmer,
Neil Price

Orkney Camerata:
pre-recorded instrumental music:
Julia Robinson Dean: violin
Ian McKune: violin
Sandy Dennison: viola
Nigel Pendrey: cello
Steven Cameron: bass
Tom Pickles: flute
Yvonne Gray: oboe
Charles Dearness: trumpet

assistant director: Dave Grieve
musical director: Glenys Hughes
lighting design: Norman Rushbrook
stills/video assistants: Ginny Shroder,
Bert Baikie, James Baster
design co-ordination: Les Burgher
sound/studio support: Owen Tierney
stage manager: Bryan Leslie
deputy stage manager: Diane Bain
costumes: Morag Tweedie,
Sue Beverton
props: Pat Presland,
Margaret Sutherland

10pm Albert Hotel, Kirkwall
Festival Club: Tartan Amoebas
Fraser McNaughton, Julie Fowlis,
Tom Dalzell, Paddy Devlin, Scott
Moncrieff, Jason Wotherspoon,
Gavin Rutledge: drums

Saturday 19 June

11am Pier Arts Centre, Stromness
John Burnside poetry reading

12.30pm Stromness Town Hall
**John Harle: saxophone
Richard Rodney Bennett: piano**

Poulenc: Oboe Sonata
(arranged for saxophone)
Corea: Three Children's Songs
Schulhoff: Sonata
Bennett: Sonata, Three Piece Suite
Sondheim, arr. Bennett: Three Waltzes

3.30pm Pickaquoy Centre, Kirkwall
The Odyssey (repeat performance)

4pm Hoy Kirk
London Sinfonietta
Clio Gould: violin
Mark van de Wiel: clarinet
Anssi Karttunen: cello
John Constable: harpsichord

Stravinsky: Three pieces for solo
clarinet
John Tavener: My Gaze is ever
upon You
(new version
for violin and cello)

17th Century:
Pieces from Parthenia In-Violata
for solo harpsichord
Maxwell Davies: Midhouse Air
(new version for
violin, cello, clarinet
and harpsichord)

7.30pm St Magnus Cathedral
Scottish Chamber Orchestra
conductor: Joseph Swensen
Steven Isserlis: cello

Mozart: Symphony No 31 'Paris'
Dvorak: Cello Concerto in A major
Strauss: Metamorphosen

10.15pm Orkney Arts Theatre
**Nobody Else But Me:
Richard Rodney Bennett:**

10pm Albert Hotel, Kirkwall
Festival Club: Tartan Amoebas

Sunday 20 June

11.15am St Magnus Cathedral
Festival Service
conducted by Rev Ron Ferguson
with St Magnus Cathedral Choir and
members of Orkney Camerata

Batten: Haste Thee, O God
Purcell: Jehova quam multi sunt
hostes
Bach: Prelude and Fugue in B flat

1pm Pier Arts Centre, Stromness
John Burnside poetry reading
(repeat performance)

2.30pm Stromness Academy Theatre
**A Johnsmas Foy: A celebration
of Orkney writer Eric Linklater**
compiled by Vivia Leslie, John Flett
readers:
Linda Bonner, Naismi Flett, Simon
Hall, Spencer Rosie, Andro Linklater

4pm Stromness Town Hall
Steven Isserlis: cello

Bach: Suite No 5 in C minor;
Suite No 6 in D major
Britten: Suite No 3
Carl Vine: Inner World (cello and tape)

7.30pm Pickaquoy Centre, Kirkwall
Scottish Chamber Orchestra

conductor: Christopher Bell
Toby Spence: tenor
David Wilson-Johnson: baritone
St Magnus Festival Chorus
Kirkwall Grammar School Girls' Choir

Beethoven: Overture –
'The Consecration of the House'
Mendelssohn: Incidental music to
'A Midsummer Night's Dream'
Puccini: Messa di Gloria

St Magnus Festival Chorus
sopranos: Glenys Alsop, Helen Ball
Sylvia Barnett, Katherine Beaven,
Dorothy Beynon, Lindsay Blair,
Val Cameron, Lydia Campbell,
Carolyn Chalmers, Carole Coghill,
Sheila Drever, Vicky Duncan,
Rhoda Featherstone,
Marilyn Gowland, Kath Hague,
Lucy Holt, Joyce Howard,
Lillian Hutchison, Margaret Inkster,
Muriel Learmonth, Nina Leitch,
Christine Liddell, Loraine Littlejohn,
Chris Meek, Irene Monge Hernandez,
Elsie Norquay, Mary O'Keeffe-Burgher,
Charlotte Peppitt, Maureen Purvis,
Marilyn Richards, Inga Scholes,
Isobel Scholes, Dorothy Swanney,
Grace Tait, Alison Tramschek,
Matilda Tumim, Marjolein van Schyk,
Sue Whitworth, Diane Wrightson
altos: Sheila Beaven, Clare Burgher,
Avril Cromarty, Jill Dean,
Angela Drummond, Victoria Fairnie,
Cristine Ferguson, Isla Flett,
Lesley Gordon, Lucy Hague,
Carol Hartmann, Margaret Hinckley,
Thelma Holt, Cathleen Hourie,
Kathleen Hunter, Kathleen Ireland,
Eve Isaac, Aileen Laird,
Margaret Linklater, Janice Mackie,
Emma McLeod, Judy O'Connor,
Marguerite Reardon, Lynn Rendall,
Marian Rendall, Barbara Robertson,
Lorna Scott, Sandra Shearer,
Carole Sunter, Margaret Sutherland,
Carol Taylor, Lakey Teasdale,
Karen Walker, May Walker,
Rosey Whittles
tenors: Miriam Baster, Pat Begley,
Stephen Cameron, Jennifer Devine,
Pam Farmer, Ruth Forbes,
Bernadette Garriock,
Graham Garson, Nigel Groom,
Ruth Jepson, Rachael King,
Eoin Leslie, Stephen Lovick,
Nila McCallum, Mark Rendall,
Alan Scott, Andy Tait, Stewart Walker
basses: John Devine, David Fidler,
Arthur Flett, John Flett, Roy Flett,
Andrew Garden, Edmund Holt,
Chris Macrae, Allan McCafferty,
Eddie Nicolson, Mike Palmer,
Neil Price, Jim Purvis,
George Rendall, Fred Soutar,
Ian Tait, Andy Walker

Kirkwall Grammar School Girls'
Choir: Laura Aitken, Kate Askew,
Laura Barnett, Katherine Beaven,
Rhona Bertram, Vicky Brown,
Corrine Corse, Sherine Deakin,
Elizabeth Dearness, Jenna Drever,
Louise Drever, Ruth Drever,

Laura Earley, Laura Eunson,
Sarah Firth, Kimberley Gill,
Lucy Hague, Britt Harcus, Lucy Holt,
Laura Laughton, Shereen Linklater,
Victoria Logie, Catherine Matches,
Inez Moss, Alice Mowat, Laura Pettet,
Islay Roberts, Victoria Rushton,
Fiona Sutherland, Inga Wallace,
Lee-Anne Wylie

10.15pm & 11.30pm Italian Chapel
**Messiaen's Quartet for the End
of Time: London Sinfonietta**
Clio Gould: violin
Mark van de Wiel: clarinet
Anssi Karttunen: cello
John Constable: piano

10pm Albert Hotel, Kirkwall
Festival Club: Blue Mother
Leah Johnston, Ian Cooper,
Ian Farquhar, Keith Berg

Monday 21 June

10am Stromness Town Hall
**Elf Consortium Masterclass:
Steven Isserlis**

11am Kirkwall Town Hall
John Burnside poetry reading
(repeat performance)

1pm St Magnus Cathedral
London Sinfonietta

Turnage: Cortège for Chris
Janácek: Violin Sonata
Lutoslawski: Dance Preludes
Lindberg: Steamboat Bill Jr
Bartók: Contrasts

6pm Orkney Arts Theatre
The Odyssey and
Songs of Sanday

The Odyssey: junior version,
performed by pupils of St Margaret's
Hope Primary School

cast:
Odysseus: Alexandra Logie
Polites: Kathryn Banks
Eurylochus: John McKay
Zeus, God of Gods: David Mackenzie
Poseidon: Thomas Levens
Athene: Jennifer Rheubottom
Hermes: Clarissa Linnitt
Greek chorus: Charlene Nicol,
Sarah Dawson, Ross MacLeod
Polyphemus: Gary Omand
Circe: Johan Thomson
Tiresias: Gary Omand
Scylla: Charlene Nicol,
Sarah Dawson, Ross MacLeod
Penelope: Clarissa Linnitt
Telemachus: John Thomson
Polybus: John McKay
Alexander: Kathryn Banks

Songs of Sanday
by Sir Peter Maxwell Davies
words: Roderick Thorne
performed by the pupils
of Sanday School
Overture: Sanday Fiddle Club

fiddles: Katie-Anne Drever,
Louisa Drever, Haley Harvey,
Bethan Newman, Fiona Wilson
recorders: Thomas Harcus,
Bryony Newton, Kirsty Redmonds,
Donna Tulloch
percussion: Katie-Anne Drever,
Aaron Poole, Louise Redmonds,
Magnus Thorne, Emma Tulloch,
Fiona Wilson
singers: primary 1, 2 & 3:
Calder Grieve, Benedict Wood,
Ashleigh Masson, Alistair Dearness,
Jonathan Evans, Shaun Thomson,
Glynn Walls, Susan Boyd,
Kirsty Drever, Grace Peace,
Hayley Skea, Heather Harvey,
Carys Newman, Megan Newman,
Jennifer Rae, Sarah Sinclair,
Claire Wilson
Primary 4 & 5:
Douglas Drever, Thomas Newton,
Michelle Dearness, Cassie Enticknap,
Anwen Evans, Kirsten Masson,
Arlene Walls, Christopher Masters,
Daniel Meek, Michael Moodie,
Tom Rudge, Edrian Skea, Andrew
Walls, Wesley Walls, Catherine Harvey,
Bethan Newman, Clare-Jayne Peace
Primary 6 & 7:
Thomas Harcus, Bryony Newton,
Kirsty Redmonds, Donna Tulloch,
Mark Linton, Owen Rudge,
Richard Thomson, Vikki Brown,
Louisa Drever, Samantha Howley,
Katrina Skea, Vanessa Skea,
Carrie Walls
Secondary 1 & 2:
Aaron Poole, Wayne Sinclair, Magnus
Thorne, Kelly Harcus, Fiona Wilson,
David Peace, Katie-Anne Drever,
Victoria Gibson, Amy Peace,
Louise Redmonds, Bella Sichel,
Emma Tulloch
solo violin: Mike Newman
lighthouse keeper: Andrew Skea

8pm Pickaquoy Centre, Kirkwall
Scottish Chamber Orchestra
conductor: Joseph Swensen
John Harle: saxophone

Maxwell Davies: Serenade Carolisima
Sally Beamish:
The Imagined Sound
of Sun on Stone
(Festival co-commission)
Beethoven: Symphony No 3 'Eroica'

10pm Albert Hotel, Kirkwall
Festival Club: Blue Mother

Tuesday 22 June

11am Orkney Arts Theatre
A Johnsmas Foy (repeat)

1pm St Magnus Cathedral
Dame Gillian Weir: organ
Jongen: Sonata Eroica
Schnitzer: Sonata in C major
Bach: Toccata and Fugue in F major
Franck: Choral No 2 in B minor
Françaix: Suite Carmelite
Hampton: from 5 Dances for Organ
Jongen: Toccata in D flat major

2.30pm St Magnus Cathedral
Printmaker's Talk: Jurek Putter

3pm Flotta Island
Flotta excursion: Orkney Ensemble
Christina Sargent: oboe
Julia Robinson Dean: violin
Mike Newman: viola
Linda Hamilton: cello

Mozart: Duo for violin and viola
Suk: Trio in C
Maxwell Davies: Midhouse Air
(original version for violin and viola)
Mozart: Oboe Quartet in F

7.30pm Pickaquoy Centre, Kirkwall
London Sinfonietta
conductor: Nicholas Kok
Pupils of Firth, Papdale and
St Andrews Schools

Birtwistle: Ritual Fragment
Trainer: True to Life
MacMillan: ....as others see us....
Adès: Living Toys

Firth percussion group: Keith Aim,
Alyson Bain, Jordan Balfour, Helen
Cooke, Andrew Cowan, Carley Drever,
Richard Duncan, Ryan Farley, Anna
Huggard, Aaron Kennedy, Matthew
Lynch, Christopher Hopkins, Becky
Huggard, Jennifer McKinlay, Rebecca
McKinlay, Robert Miller, Tom Miller,
Lizzie Pendrey, Helga Pire, Inga Pirie,
Emma Pottinger, David Pottinger,
Ewan Ross, Graham Tulloch, Michelle
Tulloch
Papdale vocal group: Clare Anderson,
Jackie Buchan, Michelle Budge,
Jennifer Carroll, Dana Copland, Jane
Cuddihy, Michelle Firth, Karin Flett,
Erin Foulis, Fiona Gilmour, Sarah
Gall, Laura Gray, Sarah Harcus, Jodi
Heggie, Pamela Hutcheon, Hannah
Johnstone, Erica Learmonth, Cheryl
Leask, James Leonard, Kevin
Johnston, Karlyn Macleod, Rachel
Mainland, Karen Merriman, Danielle
Mosdie, Connor Quinlan, Susan
Rorie, Joanna Shearer, Aileen Strutt,
Carla Thomson, Rachel Thomson,
Lindsay Walker, Dale Watt
St Andrews percussion group:
Stephanie Davies, Katharine Deans,
Leila Dearness, Inga Donaldson, Sam
Douglas, Lauren Henning, Diane
Joyce, Robert Lennie, Charles Moore,
Dawn Norquoy, Vicky Paterson, Sarah
Quimby, Rebekah Ruddick, Hannah
Rushton, Caroline Shearer, Richard
Stevenson, Vicky Tait, Clare Wallace,
Inez Ward, Amanda Wood
London Sinfonietta:
Helen Keen, Gareth Hulse, Mark van
de Wiel, John Orford, Michael
Thompson, John Wallace, David
Purser, David Alberman, Joan
Atherton, Levine Andrade, Anssi
Karttunen, Adrian Bradbury, Mary
Scully, John Constable, Simon Haram,
David Hockings, Christopher Hinde

10pm Albert Hotel, Kirkwall
Festival Club: Zubop

Wednesday 23 June

1pm St Magnus Cathedral, Kirkwall
London Sinfonietta
Nichols Kok: conductor
John Wallace: trumpet
Pupils of Kirkwall Grammar School
Festival Chamber Choir

Maxwell Davies:
Litany - for a ruined
chapel between sheep and shore;
First Ferry to Hoy;
A Mirror of Whitening Light

recorders and percussion:
Jennifer Alexander, Cally Amos, Chris
Amos, Hannah Beaven, Naomi
Baster, Vicky Bown, Katy Chalmers,
Charles Dearness, John Dearness,
Emily Earley, Hazel Eunson, Sebastian
Eunson, Elizabeth Foubister, Bridget
Gordon, Edward Gilmour, Nicola
Hartmann, Susannah Holt, Hollie
Laing, Erik Laughton, Catherine
Matches, Sarah Olsen, Jenna
Omand, Sheree Peace, Sheetal Revis,
Jonathan Richards, Roxanne van
Schayk, Dee-Dee Scott, Ingrid Seatter,
Victoria Sinclair, Anna Tait, Helen
Wallace, Dawn Wood
Festival Chamber Choir:
sopranos: Glenys Alsop, Katherine
Beaven, Lindsay Blair, Kath Hague,
Lucy Holt, Lorraine Littlejohn,
Charlotte Peppitt, Julia Robinson Dean
altos: Sheila Beaven, Victoria Fairnie,
Lesley Gordon, Carol Hartmann, Lucy
Hague, Margaret Sutherland
Tenors: Stephen Cameron, Graham
Garson, Eoin Leslie, Stephen Lovick,
Mark Rendall, Andy Tait
basses: David Fidler, Roy Flett, Eddie
Nicolson, Mike Palmer, George
Rendall, Ian Tait

3pm Kirkwall Town Hall
Orkney Rhythm and Rhyme
Janet MacInnes with Orkney pupils

6.30pm, 9pm St Magnus Cathedral
The Mystery Plays
adaptor/director: Richard Williams
music: Joanna MacGregor
cast: Beejaye, Jo Castieton,
Kwei-Lin Hsu, Martin Nelson, Joseph
Noble, Rachel Pittman, Paul Ryan,
Jonathan Savage, Amanda Symonds
percussion: Chris Brannick
musical director: Stephen McNeff
designer: David Collis

10pm Albert Hotel, Kirkwall
Festival Club: Zubop

Exhibitions

Pier Arts Centre, Stromness
Jock McFadyen

Stromness Library
John McCallum

The Orkney Museum
Eric Linklater 1899-1974

Sites throughout Orkney
Poetry in Place

2000

Friday 16 June

6.30pm Pickaquoy Centre, Kirkwall
Pre-performance discussion
with David Pountney and
Sir Peter Maxwell Davies
chaired by Paul Driver

7.30pm Pickaquoy Centre, Kirkwall
Music-theatre Double Bill:
Psappha
Musiektheater Transparant

Maxwell Davies:
Eight Songs for a Mad King
Maxwell Davies:
Mr Emmet takes a walk
(commissioned jointly
by Psappha,
Musiektheater Transparant
and St Magnus Festival)

WORLD PREMIERE

Eight Songs for a Mad King
Kelvin Thomas: bass-baritone
Tim Carroll: director
Sioutr Gilmour: designer
Simon Opie: lighting designer
(Psappha's production, unconducted)

Mr Emmet takes a walk
conductor: Etienne Siebens
Rebecca Caine: soprano
Adrian Clarke: baritone
Jonathan Best: bass-baritone
David Pountney: librettist and director
Robert Innes Hopkins: designer
Davy Cunningham: lighting designer
(A co-production between Psappha
and Musiektheater Transparant)

musicians:
Claire O'Neill: flute
Dov Goldberg: clarinet/saxophone
Tracey Redfern: trumpet
Mark Paine: french horn
Richard Casey: piano
Tim Williams: percussion
David Routledge: violin
David Adams: viola
Jennifer Langridge: cello
Jeffrey Box: double bass

10pm Albert Hotel, Kirkwall
Festival Club:
Orkney Schools' Swing Band

Saturday 17 June

10.30am Pier Arts Centre, Stromness
Jackie Kay poetry reading

10.30am Kirkwall Town Hall
Morning Coffee Concert
Orkney Traditional Music Project
coordinator: Jean Leonard

Tankerness House Gardens, Kirkwall
Readings in the
Festival Storytelling Tent (yurt)

11am Marita Lück - 'The hero's
journey from Orkney to Mongolia'
2.30pm Jackie Kay - poetry for
children
3.30pm Marita Lück

12.30pm St Magnus Cathedral
Priya Mitchell: violin
Robert Kulek: piano

Mendelssohn: Sonata in F major
Schnittke: Sonata No 1
Saint-Saëns: Sonata in D minor Op75

3.30pm Stromness Town Hall
Greenvoe
by George Mackay Brown, adapted
by Alan Plater

cast:
Bert Kerston: Willie Harper
Samuel Whaness: Eric Spence
Rachel Whaness: Phyllis Brown
Skarf: Dave Grieve
Bella Budge: Doreen McLellan
Ben Budge: Walter Leask
Ivan Westray: Graham Garson
Olive Evie: Maggie Hay
Joseph Evie: Jim Chalmers
Alice Voar: Carolyn Bevan
Margaret Inverary: Carol Taylor
Timmy Folster: Tommy Wylie
Agatha Fortin Bell: Cynthia Chaddock
Colonel Fortin Bell: Chris Macrae
Inga Fortin Bell: Sandra Craigie
Elizabeth McKee: Allison Dixon
Prosecutor: Terry Delaney
Ellen Kerston: Kristen Wylie
Scorradale: David Fidler
Mansie Anderson: Jim Chalmers
Tammag Brown: Terry Delaney
Leonard Isbister: Tommy Wylie
Dod Corrigall: Chris MacRae
Andrew Hoy: David Fidler
Sandy Manson: Willie Harper
Hector Anderson: Magnus Dixon
Simon McKee: Sweyn Hunter
Dewas Singh: Alex Hearn
McIntosh: Terry Delaney
Aloysius: Alex Hearn
Matron: Cynthia Chaddock
Controller: Maggie Hay
Ernie Kerston: Finlay Harnden
John Corrigall: Ross Harnden
Tom Kerston: Ben Chaddock
Sophie Voar: Niamh Delaney
Sander Voar: Stuart Bevan
Shirley Voar: Louise Leask
Sam Voar: Ciaran Delaney

director: Penny Aberdein
assistant director: Graham Garson
composer: John Gray
stage management: Pete Folan,
Jude Barnes, Barbara Smith
set design: Les Burgher,
Marian Ashburn
costumes: Laura Grieve
props: Pat Presland,
Margaret Sutherland
musicians: Julia Robinson Dean,
Yvonne Gray, Nigel Pendrey, Tim
Geddes

4pm Hoy Kirk
Psappha String Trio
David Routledge: violin
David Adams: viola
Jennifer Langridge: cello

David Matthews: String Trio Op 48
Beethoven: String Trio Op 3 in Eb

4pm Birsay Church
Music in St Magnus Church
Psappha Ensemble

Claire O'Neill: flute
Dov Goldberg: clarinet
Richard Casey: harpsichord

JS Bach: Sonata in G minor for flute
and harpsichord
Villa-Lobos: Choros No 2
JS Bach: French Suite in G major
Jolivet: Sonate for flute and clarinet
Devienne: First Sonata for clarinet
and keyboard

6pm Pier Arts Centre, Stromness
The Constant Moment
An illustrated lecture on Scottish
sculpture: Andrew Patrizio
(launching Orkney's millennium art
project)

8pm Pickaquoy Centre, Kirkwall
BBC Philharmonic
conductor: Martyn Brabbins
conductor: Sir Peter Maxwell Davies*
Janice Watson: soprano
St Magnus Festival Chorus

Bridge: Suite: The Sea
Britten: Les Illuminations
Maxwell Davies:
Orkney Saga 5*
(BBC commission)

WORLD PREMIERE

Poulenc: Gloria

St Magnus Festival Chorus:
sopranos: Glenys Alsop, Helen Ball,
Dorothy Beynon, Claire Cadman-
Hope, Val Cameron, Lydia Campbell,
Carolyn Chalmers, Carole Coghill,
Sheila Drever, Vicky Duncan,
Marilyn Gowland, Kath Hague,
Joyce Howard, Lillian Hutchison,
Margaret Inkster, Helen Johnston,
Loraine Littlejohn, Elsie Norquay,
Andrea Price, Marilyn Richards,
Eileen Russell, Inga Scholes,
Isobel Scholes, Glynis Tait,
Grace Tait, Alison Tramschek,
Matilda Tumim, Marjolem Van
Schayk, Sue Whitworth,
Emma Wrigley
altos: Avril Cromarty, Jill Dean,
Elsa Devis, Angela Drummond,
Victoria Fairnie, Cristine Ferguson,
Di Grieve, Lucy Hague,
Carol Hartmann, Margaret Hinckley,
Cathleen Hourie, Kathleen Hunter,
Kathleen Ireland, Aileen Laird,
Greta Laird, Margaret Linklater,
Janice Mackie, Isabel Meil,
Judy O'Connor, Marguerite Rearden,
Julia Robinson Dean, Lorna Scott,
Maggie Scott, Margaret Sutherland,
Carol Taylor, Anna Whelan
tenors: Mim Baster,
Stephen Cameron, Jennie Devine,
Bernadette Garriock, Graham Garson,
Nigel Groom, Joan Jones,
Archie Knox, Eoin Leslie,
Stephen Lovick, Caitriana McCallum,
Nila McCallum, George McKinlay,
Oliver Mowatt, Andy Tait,

Karen Walker
basses: Steve Callaghan,
John Devine, David Fidler,
Arthur Flett, John Flett,
Andrew Garden, Edmund Holt,
Chris Macrae, Alan McCafferty,
John MacLeod, Mike Palmer,
Neil Price, George Rendall, Ian Rolfe,
Jim Sunter, Ian Tait, Andy Walker

chorus director: Glenys Hughes
rehearsal pianist: Jean Leonard

10pm Albert Hotel, Kirkwall
Festival Club
Bongshang and **Loyko**

Bongshang:
'JJ' Jamieson: banjo, vocals
Gordon Tulloch: guitar, vocals
Christopher Anderson: drums,
percussion
Leonard Scollay: fiddle
David Hourie: bass
Loyko:
Sergei Erdenko, Oleg Ponomarev,
Vadim Koulitskii

Sunday 18 June

11.15am St Magnus Cathedral
Festival Service
conducted by Rev Ron Ferguson
with St Magnus Cathedral Choir and
Orkney Camerata

Manuel Cardoso: Asperges Me
Walford Davies: Psalm 121
Guilmant: Grand Choeur

1pm Pier Arts Centre, Stromness
Jackie Kay poetry reading
(repeat performance)

2.30pm Stromness Town Hall
Celebrity recital:
John Lill: piano

Haydn: Sonata in Eb major
Hob XV1/52
Brahms: Variations and Fugue on a
Theme of Handel Op 24
Shostakovitch: Three Preludes and
Fugues Op 87
Beethoven: Sonata in F minor
Op 57 'Appassionata'

5pm Stromness Academy Theatre
A Johnsmas Foy:
Selkies, Trolls and other tall tales
producer: Vivia Leslie
readers: Linda Bonner, Jenny Deans,
John Flett, Naismi Flett, Billy Jolly

8pm St Magnus Cathedral
The Bach Cantata Pilgrimage:
The Monteverdi Choir and
English Baroque Soloists

conductor: Sir John Eliot Gardiner
Ruth Holton: soprano
Paul Agnew: tenor
Claudia Schubert: alto
Peter Harvey: bass

The St Magnus Cathedral Choir

Four Cantatas for Trinity Sunday

Cantata BWV 165:
O heil'ges Geist - und Wasserbad
Cantata BWV 194:
Höchsterwünschtes Freudenfest
Cantata BWV 176:
Es ist ein trotzig und verzagt Ding
Cantata BWV 129:
Gelobet sei der Herr, mein Gott

10pm Albert Hotel, Kirkwall
Festival Club: Loyko

Monday 19 June

11.30am Kirkwall Town Hall
Jackie Kay poetry reading
(repeat performance)

1.30pm St Magnus Cathedral
**Bach and the
Court of Frederick the Great:
English Baroque Soloists**

Alison Bury: violin
Rachel Beckett: flute
Melanie Meek: cello
Howard Moody: harpsichord

Quantz: Trio Sonata in Eb for flute, violin and continuo
Benda: Sonata in C minor for violin and continuo
CPE Bach: Sonata in A minor for solo flute Wq 132
JS Bach: Six Part Ricercar from 'The Musical Offering';
Trio Sonata from 'The Musical Offering'

6pm Orkney Arts Theatre
**Wonderful Beast:
Tatterhood**

musical director: Alison Blunt
designer: Naejin Kim
Norwegian folk song coach:
Anne Kleivset
movement adviser: Graham Allum
cast:
Anne Aass, Sam Scudder, Jane Barber

8pm Pickaquoy Centre, Kirkwall
BBC Philharmonic
Martyn Brabbins: conductor
Sir Peter Maxwell Davies: conductor*
Priya Mitchell: violin

Mendelssohn: Overture: Calm Sea and Prosperous Voyage
Mendelssohn: Violin Concerto Op 64 in E minor
Maxwell Davies: Symphony No 7*
(BBC commission)

10.30pm St Magnus Cathedral
Psappha
conductor: Etienne Siebens
Tamsin Dives: soprano
Claire O'Neill: flute
Dov Goldberg: clarinet
Tim Williams: percussion
David Adams: viola
Jennifer Langridge: cello

Sir Peter Maxwell Davies:
Hymn to St Magnus

Preceded by a performance of the original 12th century hymn by
The Nø Boys: Eddie Nicolson, George Rendall, Mark Rendall, Andy Tait, Ian Tait

10pm Albert Hotel, Kirkwall
**Festival Club:
Out of Hours –
BBC Philharmonic Jazz Group**

Julian Gregory: electric violin
Martin Winter: trumpet
Francis Hannah: vocals/electric violin
Matthew Compton: piano
Paul Turner: drums
Peter Wilmott: bass guitar

Tuesday 20 June

11am Orkney Arts Theatre, Kirkwall
A Johnsmas Foy:
(repeat performance)

1pm St Magnus Cathedral
Psappha

Claire O'Neill: flute
Dov Goldberg: clarinet
David Routledge: violin/viola
Jennifer Langridge: cello
Richard Casey: piano
Tim Williams: percussion

Bach/Maxwell Davies:
Prelude and Fugue in C# minor,
Prelude and Fugue in C# major
Yeats:
A Waiting Ghost in the Blue Sky
Turnage: Sleep On
Powles: Quartet
Maxwell Davies:
Dances from The Two Fiddlers

2.45pm Flotta
**Flotta Island Excursion:
Orkney Ensemble**
Christina Sargent: oboe
Julia Robinson Dean: violin
Seona Dunsmuir: violin
Mike Newman: viola
Linda Hamilton: cello

Arnold: Oboe Quartet Op 61
Dvorak: String Quartet in 'The American'
(1st, 4th movements)
Haydn: Sonata No1 for violin and viola
Halvorsen: Passacaglia for violin and viola
Mike Newman: Quinary
Kramár-Krommer: Oboe Quartet No1

8pm Pickaquoy Centre, Kirkwall
BBC Philharmonic
Martyn Brabbins: conductor
John Lill: piano

Dvorak: Carnival
Rachmaninov: Piano Concerto No 2 in C minor
Rimsky-Korsakov: Scheherazade

10pm Albert Hotel, Kirkwall
Festival Club: Big Sky
Charlie McKerron, John Saich, Laura McKerron, James Gash
Brian McAlpine

Wednesday 21 June

1pm St Magnus Cathedral
**Music for Piano and Wind:
BBC Wind Ensemble**

Richard Davies: flute
Jennifer Galloway: oboe
John Bradbury: clarinet
David Chatwin: bassoon
Jonathan Goddall: French horn
with Richard Casey: piano

Poulenc: Sextet for piano and wind
Mozart: Quintet in Eb K452 for piano and wind

5.30pm Pickaquoy Centre, Kirkwall
Stories and Songs

On April 14, 2000, pupils from 16 Orkney schools travelled to London's Millennium Dome to present their own 'Story of Orkney', told through music, dance and drama. At this festival concert they re-created their Dome performance, joined by a massed choir of 250 children from all parts of Orkney.
   Two schools - Firth and St Margaret's Hope - presented extracts from their own millennial productions; the small isles schools performed a specially devised dance piece; and all the children presented the result of a major, five-month festival project led by Christina Sargent - the Storytelling Tent (yurt).

Additional music from the central Asian country of Kyrghyzstan was played on the komuz by Chinara Sharshenova.

Participating schools:
Dounby, Eday, Evie, Firth, Flotta, Glaitness, Hope, Kirkwall Grammar School, North Ronaldsay, North Walls, Orphir, Papdale, Papa Westray, Pierowall, St Andrews, Sanday, Stenness, Stromness Primary, Stromness Academy, Stronsay

8pm King Street Hall, Kirkwall
Greenvoe (repeat performance)

10pm Albert Hotel, Kirkwall
Festival Club: Big Sky

The Nø Boys
Eddie Nicolson, George Rendall, Mark Rendall, Andy Tait, Ian Tait

Sir Peter Maxwell Davies:
Grand Oratorio -
The Meaning of Life
(unprogrammed -
a surprise performance
for Dorothy Rushbrook -
retiring festival administrator)

Exhibitions

Pier Arts Centre, Stromness
Callum Innes

Stromness Library
Artists' Books

Tankerness House Gardens, Kirkwall
The Storytelling Tent

The Orkney Museum
How did we do it?
5,000 years of Orkney skills
The Airmail Trail
Ted Fresson and the first airmail service to Orkney

Stromness Museum
Orkney Pirates and Privateers

2001

7.30pm Pickaquoy Centre, Kirkwall
London Brass

trumpets: Andrew Crowley, John
Barclay, Tony Cross, Martin Hurrell
horn: Richard Bissill
trombones: Bryon Fulcher,
Richard Edwards, David Purser,
Stephen Saunders
tuba: Owen Slade
with Kirkwall Town Band and friends,
Pupils of Kirkwall Grammar School,
Stromness Academy, Dounby,
Papdale, St Andrews and Stromness
Primary Schools

Richard Strauss: Feierlicher Einzug

Fraser Trainer:
Pulse Fiction
(Festival
commission)

Percy Grainger: A Lincolnshire Posy
Chris Batchelor: Weasel Words and
Winning Ways
Tony Hymas: Blow Blue Bugle Mama
Blow Blue
Stan Kenton: Big Band selection

Kirkwall Town Band and friends:
cornets: Ken Jones, Charles
Dearness, Graham Sutherland,
Brian Jones, Edward Gilmour,
Kristin Leslie, Kevin Barton,
Tina Wood, Heather Aberdein,
James Isbister
horns: Joan Jones, Jim Stanger, Eoin
Leslie, Lorraine Stanger
trombones: Jim Robertson, Magnus
Dearness, Jim Scott
baritones: Keith Hartmann,
David Griffith
euphoniums: Matthew Butcher,
Jeff Thomson
Eb Bass: Chris Logie
Bb Bass: Andrew Stanger
flutes: Tom Pickles, Heather Rendall,
Charlotte Rendall, Fiona Isbister,
Alison Ballantine
clarinets: David Griffith, Ingrid Leslie,
Amy Kirkness, Corine Corse
oboes: Christina Sargent,
Susannah Holt
saxophones: Heather Bichan, Afra
Skene, Mike Killeen, Peter Kovaciah,
Gareth Thomson
drums: Eric Spence

Pupils of Orkney Schools:
Dounby Primary:
Jon Ross
Papdale Primary:
Fraser Allan, Michael Amos, Rhona
Carse, Heather Coultherd, Andrew
Cuddihy, Shauni Findlater, Caleb
Fraser, Helga Garrioch, Mary Grieve,
Marcus Price, Laura Sinclair
St Andrews Primary:
Amy Walker, Magnus Walker
Stromness Primary:
Caron Oag, Finlay Harnden, Ross
Harnden, Holly Sonnabend,
Katherine Stockan

Kirkwall Grammar School:
Matthew Butcher, Charles Dearness,
Hazel Eunson, Charis Fraser, Edward
Gilmour, Keith Hartmann, Natasha
Kilean, Kristin Leslie, Steven Logie,
Hayley Reid, Scott Spence, Kayleigh
Stanger, Clare Wallace, Tina Wood
Stromness Academy:
Heather Aberdein, Alexandra
Ashman, Ben Chaddock, Joshua
Fraser, James Isbister, David Leisk,
Bobby Oag, Lizzie Pendrey, Anna
Saleh, Jim Scott, Kirsty Stevenson,
David Stockan

10pm St Magnus Centre, Kirkwall
A Johnsmas Foy:
Between the Terminals - a film

director/editor: Tim Fitzpatrick
screenplay: Kevin Coffey, Yvonne
Gray, Tim Fitzpatrick
music: Douglas Montgomery
'Hoy Song': Seona Dunsmuir

cast:
Rona: Louise Campbell
Elizabeth: Seona Dunsmuir
Fraser: Bob Ross
Raymie: Terry Delaney
Willick: Walter Leask
Iris: Margaret Anderson
James: Jim Chalmers
Anna: Inga Gilmour
Jackie: Dave Grieve
Undertaker: John Corse
Hearse driver: George Moncrieff
mourners: Andy cant, Jenny Devine,
Ann Earley, Martyn Earley, Emily
Gordon, Ann Gossman, Yvonne Gray,
Bill Hamilton, Billy Jolly, George
McKissock, George Swan
ceilidh band a.k.a. ShaggaRinkle:
Jim Hall, Colin Keldie, Dick Levens,
Douglas Montgomery, Michael Smith,
Magnus Spence, Spiv

art director: Dave Grieve
assistant director: Diane Bain
2nd assistant director: Islay Roberts
3rd assistant director: Graham
Garson
production assistants: Jenny Deans,
Malcolm Hamilton, Jennifer Irvine
camera operators: Lucy Alsop,
Christian Marwick
second unit camera: Laurie Mitchell
(assistant) Mags Mitchell
sound operator: Graham Worrall
sound assistants: Malcolm Hamilton,
Aaron MacGregor
lighting: Ian Ballantine
lighting assistants: Malcolm
Hamilton, Richard Wishart
costume: Julie Marwick, Clover Giles
make-up: Liz Coward

musicians: Douglas Montgomery,
Ingrid Seatter, Dick Levens

10.30pm Albert Hotel, Kirkwall
Festival Club:
Three Peace Sweet
Phil Anderson: keyboards, guitar,
vocals
Andy Cant: fiddle, bagpipes

Kenneth Harcus: drums
Davie Miller: bagpipes, guitar
Alan Peace: bass guitar, vocals
Raymond Peace: bagpipes,
percussion
Stewart Shearer: guitars, vocals

10.30am Pier Arts Centre, Stromness
Vikram Seth poetry reading

10.30am St Magnus Centre, Kirkwall
Morning Coffee Concert
Orkney Traditional Music Project
coordinator: Jean Leonard

12.30pm Stromness Town Hall
The Nash Ensemble

Philippa Davies: flute
Gareth Hulse: oboe
Richard Hosford: clarinet
Ursula Levaux: bassoon
Richard Watkins: horn
with Leon McCawley: piano

Beethoven: Piano Quintet in Eb Op16
Judith Weir: Airs from Another Planet
Jean Françaix: Quartet for flute,
oboe, clarinet and bassoon
Maxwell Davies: The Kestrel paced
around the sun (for solo flute)
Poulenc: Trio for oboe, bassoon and
piano

1pm The New Phoenix, Kirkwall
Scott of the Antarctic - film

3pm The Fitzcarraldo, Stromness
Harbour
Walk the Plank: Moby Dick

cast:
John Langford, Max Rubin,
Nicholas Chee Ping Wellington,
Madelaine Bowyer

adaptor: Jim Burke
director: Lee Beagley
producer: Liz Pugh
designer; Kate Borthwick
music: Andy Frizzell
lighting: Geoff Farmer, Patrick Collins
video design: Adrian Challis
costume: Nicky Ranson

3.30pm St Magnus Church, Birsay
Members of
The Nash Ensemble
Paul Watkins: cello
Duncan McTier: double bass

Barrière: Sonata à deux
Britten: Second Suite for cello Op 80
Maxwell Davies:
Lux in Tenebris for
solo double bass
Oliver Knussen:
Eccentric Melody for solo cello
Rossini: Duetto for cello and bass

7.30pm The Fitzcarraldo, Stromness
Harbour
Walk the Plank: Moby Dick
(repeat performance)

6.30pm The New Phoenix, Kirkwall
Antarctica – The British Antarctic
Survey today

8pm Pickaquoy Centre, Kirkwall
BBC Scottish Symphony
Orchestra
conductor: Sir Peter Maxwell Davies
conductor: Martyn Brabbins*
Natalie Clein: cello

Sibelius: Finlandia

Maxwell Davies:
Antarctic Symphony

Dvorak: Cello Concerto in B minor
Op 104*

6pm & 10.30pm St Magnus Cathedral
Tommy Smith: Alone at Last
solo jazz performance

10.30pm Albert Hotel, Kirkwall
Festival Club: Drop the Box
James Henry: guitar and vocals
Inge Thomson: accordion, fiddle,
vocals
Eilidh Shaw: fiddle
Robbie Thomson: drums
Jonathan Ritch: keyboard, bass

11.15am St Magnus Cathedral
Festival Service
Conducted by Rev Ron Ferguson with
St Magnus Cathedral Choir and
London Brass
music:
JS Bach, Espen Selvik, Karg-Elert

1pm Stromness Academy Theatre
Vikram Seth poetry reading
(repeat performance)

2.30pm Stromness Town Hall
Celebrity recital:
Natalie Clein: cello
Julius Drake: piano

Bach: Suite No 2 in D minor BWV
1008
Webern: Three Little Pieces
Debussy: Sonata
Franck: Sonata

5pm Stromness Academy Theatre
A Johnsmas Foy: (repeat)

6pm The New Phoenix, Kirkwall
Scott of the Antarctic - film

8pm Pickaquoy Centre, Kirkwall
BBC Scottish Symphony
Orchestra
conductor: Martyn Brabbins
John Daszak: tenor
St Magnus Festival Chorus,
Firth and St Andrews Primary
Schools, Kirkwall Grammar School

Strauss: Don Juan
Kodály: Psalmus Hungaricus
Tchaikovsky: Symphony No 6 in B
minor Op 74 'Pathétique'

St Magnus Festival Chorus:
sopranos: Helen Ball, Katherine Beaven, Sylvia Barnett, Mary Bess, Dorothy Beynon, Lydia Campbell, Carolyn Chalmers, Carole Coghill, Sheila Drever, Vicky Duncan, Marilyn Gowland, Lillian Hutchison, Margaret Inkster, Helen Johnston, Muriel Learmonth, Loraine Littlejohn, Elsie Norquay, Mary O'Keeffe-Burgher, Margaret Porteous, Andrea Price, Marilyn Richards, Julia Robinson Dean, Inga Scholes, Isobel Scholes, Grace Tait, Alison Tramschek, Matilda Tumim, Diana Wrightson
altos: Sandra Ballantine, Sheila Beaven, Ishbel Borland, Clare Burgher, Polly Cheer, Avril Cromarty, Angela Drummond, Cristine Ferguson, Lesley Gordon, Carol Hartmann, Jayne Haydn, Margaret Hinckley, Thelma Holt, Kathleen Hunter, Margaret Linklater, Isabel Meil, Kathy Pickles, Lesley Poulton, Marian Rendall, Val Cameron, Angela Henderson, Geraldine Loughran, Lorna Scott, Louise Scott, Maggie Scott, Alison Skene, Helen Smith, Rosemary Smyth, Margaret Sutherland, Carol Taylor, Lakey Teasdale, Anna Whelan
tenors: Mim Baster, Colin Borland, Steve Cameron, Jennie Devine, Pam Farmer, Bernadette Garriock, Graham Garson, Nigel Groom, Keith Hartmann, Joan Jones, Archie Knox, Eoin Leslie, Stephen Lovick, Catriona McCallum, Nila McCallum, Peter Power, Allan Scott, Hugh Smith, Karen Walker
basses: Bill Bess, John Devine, David Fidler, Arthur Flett, John Flett, Andrew Garden, Dennis Gowland, Kieran Henderson, Victor Hernandez, Edmund Holt, David Hunter, Allan McCafferty, Mike Palmer, Neil Price, George Rendall, Ian Tait, Leslie Tait, Magnus Thorne, Andrew Walker

chorus director: Glenys Hughes
rehearsal pianist: Jean Leonard

children's choir:
Firth Primary School:
Karoline Bain, William Clouston, Donald Cowan, Jenny Drever, Maggie Gordon, Katie Green, Rosie Hart, Hollie Hutchison, Jennifer McKinlay, Kenneth McKinlay, John Morrison, Esther Nicolson, Alex Pendrey, Emma Pottinger, Katrina Pottinger, Inga Pirie, Terri Reid, Charlotte Slater, Kerri Thomson, John Wallace
St Andrews Primary School:
Robert Alexander, Erika Budge, Hayley Budge, Carly Caswell, William Caswell, Danny Cormack, Ashleigh Dale, Scott Drever, Emma Eunson, Johanna Firth, David Hayne, Inga Kemp, Allan Lennie, Ewan Loudon, Ailsa Moar, Josh Palmer, Stuart Paterson, Rebecca Peace, Joanne Pottinger, Thorfinn Tait, Magnus Walker, Julie Wilson
Kirkwall Grammar School:
Jennifer Alexander, Leila Dearness,

Hazel Eunson, Rowan Hodgson, Jeana Leslie, Dawn Norquoy, Catriona Price, Charlotte Rendall, Joanne Shearer, Vicky Tait, Clare Wallace, Dawn Wood

10.30pm St Magnus Cathedral
The Nash Ensemble
Richard Hosford: clarinet
Ursula Levaux: bassoon
Richard Watkins: horn
Marianne Thorsen: violin
Elizabeth Wexler: violin
Lawrence Power: viola
Paul Watkins: cello
Duncan McTier: double bass

Schubert: Octet in F major D803

10.30pm Albert Hotel, Kirkwall
Festival Club: Drop the Box

Monday 25 June

11am The New Phoenix, Kirkwall
Vikram Seth poetry reading

11am St Magnus Centre, Kirkwall
The Nash Ensemble: with
Leon McCawley: piano
John Mark Ainsley: tenor

Concert for Schools:
Martinu: Nonet
Bartók: Rumanian Dances
Schubert: Song: Die Forelle 'The Trout'
Schubert: movements from Piano Quintet in A 'The Trout'

1pm St Magnus Cathedral
London Brass

trumpets: Andrew Crowley, John Barclay, Tony Cross, Martin Hurrell
horn: Richard Bissill
trombones: Byron Fulcher, Richard Edwards, David Purser, Stephen Saunders
tuba: Owen Slade

Dowland, arr. Harvey: Airs and Dances
G Gabrieli: Canzon Primi Toni a 8; Canzon Septimi Toni a 8
Banchieri: Fantasia 'In Echo'
Gordon Crosse: Peace for Brass
Bach, arr. Mowat: Suite for Brass
Gibbons: In Nomine

11.30am and 2.30pm
Shapinsay Excursion:
Orkney Ensemble
Christina Sargent: oboe
Julia Robinson Dean: violin
Mike Newman: viola
Linda Hamilton: cello

Stamitz: Flute Quartet in Eb major
Mozart: Adagio K580a (arr. for cor anglais and string trio by J W Brown)
Mathias: Divertimento for violin and viola Op 1
Britten: Phantasy Quartet for oboe, violin, viola and cello
Molter: Sonata a 4 in F

7.30pm St Magnus Cathedral
The Nash Ensemble
Philippa Davies: flute
Gareth Hulse: oboe
Richard Hosford: clarinet
Ursula Leveaux: bassoon
Richard Watkins: horn
Marianne Thorsen: violin
Elizabeth Wexler: violin
Paul Watkins: cello
Duncan McTier: double bass
with John Mark Ainsley: tenor
Leon McCawley: piano

Britten: Sinfonietta
Ravel: Le Tombeau de Couperin for wind quintet
Vaughan Williams: On Wenlock Edge for tenor, string quartet and piano
Vaughan Williams: songs from Ten Blake Songs for tenor and oboe
Schumann: Piano Quintet in Eb Op 44

10pm The Fitzcarraldo, Kirkwall Harbour
Walk the Plank: Moby Dick
(repeat performance)

10.30pm Albert Hotel, Kirkwall
Festival Club:
Stephen Duffy/Duncan Nairn Trio

Tuesday 26 June

11am St Magnus Centre, Kirkwall
Pomona Pomona
a celebration of Orkney by KGS and Stromness Academy pupils

1pm St Magnus Cathedral, Kirkwall
The Nash Ensemble
Philippa Davies: flute
Gareth Hulse: oboe
Marianne Thorsen: violin
Elizabeth Wexler: violin
Lawrence Power: viola
Paul Watkins: cello
with John Mark Ainsley: tenor

Mozart: Flute Quartet in D K285
Delius: Interlude from 'Fennimore and Gerda' for flute, oboe and string quartet
Warlock: The Curlew for tenor and ensemble
Bax: Oboe Quintet

5.30pm The Fitzcarraldo, Kirkwall Harbour
Walk the Plank: Moby Dick
(repeat performance)

6pm Orkney Arts Theatre, Kirkwall
Cinderella
by Sir Peter Maxwell Davies

cast:
Cinderella: Leanne Harcus
The Prince: Hayley Scadding
The Cat: Cassie Henning, Gemma Rendall
Widow Grumble: Lucy Holt
Ugly Sisters:
  Medusa: Edward Gilmour
  Hecate: John Dearness

Dragonia: Joe Earley
The Herald: Julia Price
Field Marshall Sir Wellington Bombast-Blimp: Christopher Norquoy
Lord Admiral Sir Nelson Drake-Victory: Eric Kemp
Lord Delta Wing Vertical-Takeoff: Shaun Tulloch

the train/ball guests: Jennifer Austin, Natalia Bain, Alan Brown, Julie Campbell, Lisa Collingwood, Shari Cramb, Tara Croy, Annie Glue, Alison Graham, Kirsten Grieve, Jacqueline Gunn, Karen Learmonth, Rachel Leask, Stacey Mackie, Fiona Miller, Ingrid Moffat, Laura Morris, Nicola Muir, Charlotte Platt, Jamie Ross, Laura Sinclair, Michaela Sinclair, Cara Stephen, Abigail Suttie, William Thomson, Katie Walker, Sarah Work

Kittens: Lindsay Anderson, Caron Bews, Steven Bruce, Jessica Burton, Lauren Christie, Danielle Cooper, Erika Leslie, Gordon Mowat, Kim Pirie, Laura Ryrie, Beth Seatter, Daisy Wood

orchestra:
violins: Catriona Price, Inga Donaldson
viola: Rachael Butler
cello: Fiona Wilson
double bass: Leila Dearness
recorders: Rowan Hodgson, Kathryn Banks, Roxanne Van Schayk
percussion: Katrina Seatter, Samantha Nicol, Charlotte Rendall, Tina Wood, Diane Joyce, Vicky Tait
trumpet: Charles Dearness
piano: Ingrid Seatter

directors: Alison Drever, Marlene Mainland
coordinator: Penny Aberdein
musical director: Glenys Hughes
costumes: Gillian Dearness
props: Jane Bruce
lighting: Norman Rushbrook
set: Dave Grieve, Peter Diamond
set construction: Edric Clouston

8pm St Magnus Cathedral, Kirkwall
BBC Scottish Symphony Orchestra
conductor: Martyn Brabbins
Thomas Zehetmair: violin
Ruth Killius: viola

Elgar: Introduction and Allegro Op 47
Mozart: Sinfonia Concertante in EB K364
Stuart MacRae: Portrait II
Beethoven: Symphony No 4 in Bb Op 60

10.30pm Albert Hotel, Kirkwall
Festival Club: Zuba
Jerry Boweh: vocals/guitar
Nerea Bello: vocals
Robin Miller: lead and acoustic guitar
Andrew Wood: bass
Dave McGrath: drums/ percussion
Anne Marie Murray: percussion
Hubert Hove: keyboards

continued

Wednesday 27 June

11am St Magnus Centre, Kirkwall
A Johnsmas Foy
(repeat performance)

1pm St Magnus Cathedral
Thomas Zehetmair: violin
Ruth Killius: viola

Mozart: Duo for violin and viola in
G major KV423
Martinu: Madrigale Nos 1-3 for violin
and viola
Mozart: Duo for violin and viola in
B major KV424

4pm and 6pm Orkney Arts Theatre
Cinderella
A pantomime-opera
by Peter Maxwell Davies
(repeat performance)

8pm Pickaquoy Centre, Kirkwall
The Flying Dudes:
Beings of Light
an aerial ballet inspired by the ballad
of Nuncio and Nunita

10.30pm Albert Hotel, Kirkwall
Festival Club: Zuba

11pm Kirkwall Harbour
Festival Finale: Walk the Plank's
maritime son et lumière

Festival on Tour

Wednesday 20 June

7.30pm Gill Pier, Westray
Walk the Plank: Moby Dick

Saturday 23June

7.30pm North Walls School
London Brass

Monday 25 June

7.30pm Sanday School
BBC SSO String Ensemble

7.30pm Stronsay School
BBC SSO String Ensemble

7.30pm Rousay School
BBC SSO Brass Quintet

7.30pm Beltane House,
Papa Westray
BBC SSO Wind Quintet

Tuesday 26 June

7.30pm Sanday School
Antarctica - talk

Exhibitions

Pier Arts Centre, Stromness
Town and Country: Julie Roberts
paintings and drawings

Kirkwall Town Hall
Antarctica: photographs

Custom House, Kirkwall
Art and Architecture:
Marian Ashburn, Sharyn Crossley,
Carol Dunbar, Isobel Gardner, Colin
Johnstone, Doug Muir, Malcolm Olva,
Andrew Parkinson, Alistair Peebles,
Frances Pelly, Hazel Ritch, Mark
Scadding,

Pickaquoy Centre, Kirkwall
Hearts and Minds:
Matilda Tumim

Stromness Library
Musing on Myths:
Christina Sargent

The Orkney Museum, Kirkwall
The Unknown Cathedral
lesser known aspects of St Magnus
Cathedral

Stromness Museum
The Model Show
A collection of ship models from local
collectors

contributors' index